Working-Class New York

ALSO BY JOSHUA B. FREEMAN

In Transit: The Transport Workers Union in New York City, 1933–1966

*Who Built America? Working People and the Nation's Economy, Politics,
Culture, and Society* (co-author)

*Audacious Democracy: Labor, Intellectuals, and the Social
Reconstruction of America* (co-editor)

WORKING-CLASS NEW YORK

Life and Labor Since World War II

JOSHUA B. FREEMAN

THE NEW PRESS   NEW YORK

Published in the United States by The New Press, New York, 2000
Paperback edition, 2001
Distributed by Perseus Distribution

The publisher is grateful to reproduce the following copyrighted material:

Excerpt from *Bloodbrothers* by Richard Price. Copyright © 1976 by Richard Price. Reprinted by permission of Houghton Mifflin Company. All rights reserved.

Excerpt from *Death of a Salesman* by Arthur Miller. Copyright © 1949, renewed © 1977 by Arthur Miller. Used by permission of Viking Penguin, a division of Penguin Putnam Inc.

Excerpt from *The Hawsepipe*, the Newsletter of the Marine Workers Historical Association. Copyright © 1984 by the MWHA. Used by permission.

Excerpt from "The House I Live In," words by Lewis Allen, music by Earl Robinson. Copyright © 1942, renewed by Music Sales Corporation (ASCAP) and Chappell and Company. International copyright secured, all rights reserved. Reprinted by permission of Music Sales Corporation.

LIBRARY OF CONGRESS CATALOGING-IN-PUBLICATION DATA

Freeman, Joshua Benjamin.
    Working-class New York: life and labor since World War II/Joshua B. Freeman
    p. cm.
    Includes bibliographical references and index.
    ISBN 978-1-56584-575-6 (hc.)
    ISBN 978-1-56584-712-5 (pbk.)
    1. Working class — New York (City) — New York — History — 20th century. 2. Labor unions — New York (City) — New York — History — 20th century. 3. New York (City) — New York — Social conditions — 20th century. I. Title.
    HD8085.N5 F74 2000
    305.5'62'09747109045 —dc21 99–087940

The New Press was established in 1990 as a not-for-profit alternative to the large, commercial publishing houses currently dominating the book publishing industry. The New Press operates in the public interest rather than for private gain, and is committed to publishing, in innovative ways, works of educational, cultural and community value that are often deemed insufficiently profitable.

www.thenewpress.com

Printed in the United States of America

4 6 8 10 9 7 5

For Harold and Beatrice Freeman
Beth Freeman Prince
Deborah Ellen Bell
Julia Freeman Bell
and Lena Freeman Bell

CONTENTS

List of Illustrations   ix

Chronology   xi

Introduction: What Made New York Great   xiii

Part One. Proletarian City

1. A Non-Fordist City in the Age of Ford   3

2. Working-Class New York   23

3. Labor Days   40

4. The Rise of a Social Democratic Polity   55

5. The Cold War in New York   72

Part Two. Labor's City

6. Big Labor   99

7. "A Decent Home"   105

8. "Adequate Medical Care"   125

9. "A Useful and Remunerative Job"   143

10. Goodbye Molly Goldberg   167

Part Three. Strike City

11. Freedom Now   179

12. Municipal Unionism   201

vii

13. "A Man by the Name of Albert Shanker"   215

14. Longhairs and Hardhats   228

15. The Fiscal Crisis   256

Part Four. Trump City

16. Global Dreams and Neighborhood Realities   291

17. Hanging On   306

18. The Ghost of Class   326

Conclusion: New York and the Nation   334

Acknowledgments   338

Notes   340

Index   397

LIST OF ILLUSTRATIONS

Following page 190

1. Striking longshoremen under police watch on the Manhattan waterfront in 1951. Within a generation their jobs would disappear from the Manhattan scene.

2. The huge, union-sponsored Penn South Housing Cooperative in the heart of Manhattan, opened officially by President John F. Kennedy, Jr. in 1962.

3. An aircraft carrier being built at the Brooklyn Navy Yard. Once the largest industrial facility in New York, the yard was closed in 1966.

4. The changing image of working-class New York on television: *The Goldbergs, The Honeymooners,* and *All in the Family.*

5. Michael J. Quill, the most charismatic of New York's postwar labor leaders, asking transit workers to vote on a job action in 1950.

6. Nelson A. Rockefeller campaigning for governor at a baseball game in 1958. Despite his background and wealth, he worked closely with many leading New York unionists.

7. Harry Van Arsdale, leader of the International Brotherhood of Electrical Workers and long a force in the New York labor movement, at his home in Queens in 1957.

8. Robert Moses, who single-handedly changed daily life in New York for half a century, in his office in 1963.

9. In the mid- to late 1960s, massive labor unrest—such as the transit strike in 1966 and the Ocean Hill/Brownsville teacher conflict in 1968—threatened to rend the fabric of New York.

10. UFT President Albert Shanker's in-your-face style was emblematic of the New York labor movement in the late 1960s.

11. Mayor Abraham Beame holding the famous "Ford to City: Drop Dead" issue of the *New York Daily News*, October 1975. Just after the photograph was taken Beame ripped up the paper.

12. By the late 1970s, arson and widespread abandonment of housing had left large swaths of New York—like the South Bronx—in rubble.

13. In the late 1990s, working-class militancy continues on: tens of thousands of construction workers shut down Madison Avenue in 1998 to protest use of non-union labor.

CHRONOLOGY

JANUARY 1944	President Franklin D. Roosevelt calls for an Economic Bill of Rights
SEPTEMBER 1945	World War II ends
SEPTEMBER 1945	Elevator operators' strike ties up Manhattan
NOVEMBER 1945	William O'Dwyer elected mayor
FEBRUARY 1946	Tugboat strike cuts off fuel supplies
JUNE 1947	Congress passes Taft-Hartley Act
MARCH 1948	Clerks strike the New York Stock Exchange
NOVEMBER 1948	The Congress of Industrial Organizations revokes charter of the Greater New York Industrial Council
MAY 1950	New York State institutes rent control
JUNE 1950	Korean War begins
SEPTEMBER 1950	Vincent Impellitteri becomes mayor when O'Dwyer resigns
NOVEMBER 1953	Robert F. Wagner, Jr. elected mayor
OCTOBER 1954	Sitdown strike fails to stop American Safety Razor from moving to Virginia
NOVEMBER 1955	Two thousand Parks Department workers hold one-day strike
DECEMBER 1955	The American Federation of Labor and the Congress of Industrial Organizations merge to form the AFL-CIO
APRIL 1956	Commercial containership operation begins in port
MARCH 1958	Mayor Wagner establishes collective bargaining procedures for city employees
APRIL 1958	The Brooklyn Dodgers move to Los Angeles, the New York Giants to San Francisco
NOVEMBER 1958	Nelson Rockefeller elected governor
FEBRUARY 1959	New York City AFL and CIO Councils merge
MAY 1959	Local 1199 strikes voluntary hospitals
DECEMBER 1962	114-day newspaper strike begins
FEBRUARY 1964	Public-school boycott demands racial integration

JULY 1964	Rioting in Harlem and Bedford-Stuyvesant
OCTOBER 1965	Congress passes immigration reform act
NOVEMBER 1965	John V. Lindsay elected mayor
JANUARY 1966	Transit workers hold a twelve-day strike
JUNE 1966	Brooklyn Navy Yard closes
NOVEMBER 1966	Voters reject a police civilian review board
SEPTEMBER 1967	Teachers strike for higher pay
MAY TO NOVEMBER 1968	Teachers strike four times in Ocean Hill–Brownsville community control controversy
DECEMBER 1968	Co-op City opens
MAY 1969	CUNY student protests lead to open admissions
JUNE 1969	Stonewall Inn patrons fight police raiders
MARCH 1970	Postal workers strike
MAY 1970	Construction workers attack antiwar protesters in lower Manhattan
NOVEMBER 1973	Abraham Beame elected mayor
SPRING 1975	New York City fiscal crisis begins
OCTOBER 1975	"FORD TO CITY: DROP DEAD"
JULY 1977	Widespread looting during citywide blackout
NOVEMBER 1977	Edward I. Koch elected mayor
APRIL 1980	Transit workers strike for eleven days
SEPTEMBER 1981	Two hundred thousand march in revived Labor Day Parade
DECEMBER 1983	First residents move into Charlotte Gardens in the South Bronx
OCTOBER 1987	Stock market plunges
NOVEMBER 1989	David Dinkins elected mayor
OCTOBER 1990	147-day strike at *Daily News* begins
NOVEMBER 1993	Rudolph Giuliani elected mayor
OCTOBER 1995	John Sweeney elected president of AFL-CIO
SEPTEMBER 1996	Labor Day Parade moved to weekend after Labor Day
JUNE 1998	Protesting construction workers paralyze midtown Manhattan

INTRODUCTION:
WHAT MADE NEW YORK GREAT

A visitor wandering the streets of mid-twentieth-century New York would have had no trouble discerning the social centrality of its working class. It was palpable in the bustling port and manufacturing districts in the heart of the city, in the sprawling residential neighborhoods of Brooklyn, the Bronx, and Manhattan, in the strikes that periodically crippled the region, in the mass following of the American Labor and Liberal parties, in musical and comedic styles that became internationally renowned, and in the argot with which local denizens communicated. Working-class New Yorkers, through political groups, tenant and neighborhood associations, fraternal and ethnic societies, and above all unions, played a pervasive role in shaping the city's social, economic, and political structure. Their culture, style, and worldview, elements of which were appropriated and disseminated by intellectuals, artists, entertainers, and merchants, helped pattern the moral and aesthetic fabric of the city and the nation.

The cosmopolitanism, energy, and sophistication of New York's working population was a major factor in the city's post–World War II success in projecting itself as the global center of power, innovation, and modernity. Over time, though, workers and their institutions proved unable to check a series of developments that led to their marginalization. By the 1990s, the tenor and trajectory of New York increasingly derived from its position as a global city connected to markets and tastemakers throughout the world, while its own toiling majority receded into the background.

The story of working-class New York is one of triumph and confinement. It is a saga of growing power and declining influence, of institutions that served their constituents well but stopped being seen as central to the future. It is a story of massive movements of population and industry, tenacious struggles for rights and equality, and ongoing discrimination and inequity.

Yet the remarkable history of New York workers and their families since World War II remains almost wholly unknown outside the ranks of those who lived through it. The vast literature celebrating postwar New York—by E. B. White, V. S. Pritchett, Jan Morris, Truman Capote, Willie Morris, and others—generally ignores the very existence of workers, an astonishing blindness since, during what is usually hailed as its heyday, New York was a

working-class city, demographically, economically, politically, and socially.
When workers do appear in these accounts, they usually do so as picaresque
ethnics, providing colorful background for more illustrious protagonists.[1]
Too often, chroniclers of New York see their own kind—writers, artists,
businessmen, and politicians—as *the* creators of the city and its ethos, ignoring the millions of workers and husbands and wives and children of workers
who populated it, kept its economy going, and gave it cultural greatness.
Scholars have not done much better; given the economic, political, and cultural importance of New York City, they have written remarkably little about
the history of its working class during the last half century.[2]

Without taking into account the impact of labor, no rendering of New
York's past can explain why the city's political, social, economic, and even
physical development so deviated from national norms. By the same token,
looking at New York forces a rethinking of the history of American labor. New
York workers and their organizations did not fit the picture usually found in
histories of post–World War II labor, which emphasize mass production industry and heavily male industrial unions affiliated with the Congress of Industrial Organizations (CIO).[3] In New York, small firms and craft or
conglomerate unions, with a large number of female members—most often
affiliated with the American Federation of Labor (AFL)—dominated. Yet
unionism in New York proved more resilient than elsewhere; in most of the
country the percentage of the workforce belonging to unions dropped
sharply between World War II and the late 1980s, but in New York it remained steady (so that in the 1990s it more than doubled the national figure).[4]
Furthermore, while organized labor usually is portrayed as having had its
greatest political influence during the 1930s and 1940s, the power of the New
York labor movement peaked between the early 1950s and the mid-1970s.
Understanding why New York remained a union town while labor waned nationally helps explain the character of the modern labor movement and its
place in the political economy.

The title of this book knowingly goes against academic and political fashion. In contemporary discourse, the very term "working class" is jarring. For
a century it was a common part of the lexicon of industrialism. Usually it simply referred collectively to those people in nonmanagerial positions who
worked for wages. That is how I use it in this book, encompassing both blue-
and white-collar workers and their immediate family members. These days,
when Americans speak of class at all, they usually define it not by the type of
work people do but by their level of income or wealth. Occasionally, I use

such categorizations, too, for example the terms middle-class or low-income. But a central thesis of this book is that New York workers, at many times and in many circumstances, thought and acted in ways that stemmed, at least in part, from their structural position in the economy, with important consequences for themselves and their city.[5]

Unless otherwise noted, I use the term New York to refer to New York City proper. Many studies of postwar New York stress the importance of looking at the metropolitan region as a whole to understand any of its parts.[6] This study stresses the importance of city institutions and city politics in shaping the everyday lives of city residents.

I spent most of my childhood and nearly all my adult life in New York City during the period this book covers. Though in no way a memoir, occasionally I have drawn on my experiences or those of my family for illustration. Like most New Yorkers, I have deeply conflicted feelings about the city. Endlessly frustrated by its difficulties and brutalities, try as I may I find it difficult to imagine living elsewhere. What keeps me in New York is neither the high culture of museums and concert halls nor the unrivaled opportunities for working, eating, and spending that New Yorkers revel in. Rather it is a sensibility that is distinctly working-class—generous; open-minded but skeptical; idealistic but deflating of pretension; bursting with energy and a commitment to doing. This was the sensibility of my grandparents, who after hard days of work spent evenings and weekends at union meetings, fraternal affairs, lectures, and amusement parks. Poor people, they lived full lives raising children, caring for parents, trekking off to the country, and, in modest but self-conscious ways, seeking to revolutionize society in the name of justice and equality. I still glimpse this sensibility in the subways and on the streets and in the public schools.

As its working class has lost influence, New York has become a less civilized, more alienated community. I for one neither want to nor believe it possible to return to a putative golden past. Fifty years ago the Dodgers may have played in Brooklyn, but for most New Yorkers life meant grueling work, little security, and much prejudice. But I do hope that this book illuminates the possibilities for ordinary people to play a greater role in shaping their city and nation than they do today. So much of what made New York great came from their labor, their struggles, their jokes, and their songs. Forgetting that impoverishes us all.

Working-Class New York

PART ONE
Proletarian City

Without our brain and muscle not a single wheel can turn.

—"Solidarity Forever"

CHAPTER 1.

A Non-Fordist City
in the Age of Ford

On September 24, 1945, barely three weeks after the end of World War II, the main business districts of New York City ground to a halt. For a week over a million-and-a-half workers milled around the streets or stayed home. Mail and railway express delivery halted, and federal tax collections fell by eight million dollars a day. This estimated one hundred million dollar loss to the economy stemmed from a strike by fifteen thousand elevator operators, doormen, porters, firemen, and maintenance workers employed in commercial buildings.

In an era when automated elevators were a rarity, elevator operators played an indispensable role in high-rise cities. Their strike, after a prolonged dispute over whether or not building owners would accept contract recommendations made by a War Labor Board panel, revealed the power of New York labor as the postwar epoch began. "The normal routine of thousands of professional, financial and manufacturing establishments," the *New York Herald Tribune* reported, "was at a near standstill in the world's financial and business capital." Hundreds of thousands of blue-collar workers, executives, clerical workers, mailmen, deliverymen, and tax collectors could not or would not walk up dozens of flights of steps to reach their shops or offices. The garment district completely shut down as a quarter of a million members of the International Ladies Garment Workers Union (ILGWU), the Amalgamated Clothing Workers (ACW), the Hatters, Cap and Millinery Workers, and the Fur and Leather Workers stayed out of work, following "an unwritten law" to respect picket lines. The militance of the strikers made wholesale use of strikebreakers impractical. When the owners of one insurance company building tried it, twenty-year-old Evelyn Wensel, a striking elevator operator from the Bronx, slapped and punched her replacement, leading to the walkout's first arrest. After five days of mounting economic damage, Governor Thomas E. Dewey pressured both sides to declare a truce and accept his appointment of an arbitrator, who ultimately dictated settlement terms favorable to the strikers.[1]

The building workers' walkout commenced a yearlong series of strikes that touched the lives of virtually all New Yorkers, part of the greatest strike wave in United States history. Nationally, in 1945, 3.5 million workers struck, topped the next year by 4.6 million, over 10 percent of the work force.[2] In New York, the breadth and complexity of the labor movement gave it access to multiple pressure points capable of crippling the city.

New York strikes during the year after the war included a weeklong walkout by ten thousand painters; a four-week strike by seven thousand members of the American Communications Association that disrupted telegraph communication into and out of the city; a 114-day strike against the Brooklyn-based Mergenthaler Co., the largest maker of linotype equipment in the country; and a series of trucking strikes culminating in a September 1946 walkout by twelve thousand Teamsters that led to empty grocery store shelves and factory closings.[3] Sprinkled among these clashes were a myriad of smaller confrontations: a strike of Times Square motion picture projectionists, a lockout of thirty Newspaper Guild members at *Billboard* magazine, a walkout by eight hundred Brooklyn and Manhattan bakers.[4]

Some of the largest clashes took place on the waterfront. On October 1, 1945, almost immediately after the building workers' strike, stevedores at six Chelsea docks walked off their jobs to protest a proposed contract their union president, Joseph P. Ryan, had negotiated with the New York Shipping Association. Their wildcat strike quickly spread to thirty-five thousand members of the International Longshoremen's Association (ILA) throughout the port.[5] Ryan's proposed agreement failed to address many worker demands, including modifications in the shape-up system for hiring and a weight limit on sling loads, which had increased greatly during the war. Equally important, workers wanted more say in their union. Many ILA locals rarely met, Ryan recently had been designated union president for life, and corruption and thuggery was widespread.[6]

At first the strikers had no organization, no spokespeople, not even formal demands. But with the help of the Communists—a dockside presence, particularly in Brooklyn—they soon formulated demands and selected a leadership. Realizing that the contract he negotiated had become irrelevant, Ryan pressed the employers to grant new concessions while urging the longshoremen to return to work.

After two weeks, the dockworkers began to drift back to their jobs. With the strike effectively broken, negotiations between the ILA and the shipping association resumed. Eventually an arbitrator granted the workers a larger wage hike and better conditions than in the contract Ryan had negotiated, but not a limit on sling loads, the issue that helped set off the walkout.[7]

Just four months later, labor turmoil in the port resumed when 3,500 tugboat workers walked off their jobs. Like elevator operators, tugboat men held a strategic place in the life of New York: in addition to docking large vessels, they moved freight back and forth across the harbor, including barges that delivered 65 percent of the city's coal and 95 percent of its fuel oil. With fuel supplies already low, their midwinter strike raised the specter of buildings without heat, closed industrial facilities, and a grinding halt of the transportation system. Newly-inaugurated Mayor William O'Dwyer declared it "the worst threat ever made to the city."[8]

The tugboat workers' strike raised a question affecting labor relations throughout the country: what would be the postwar relationship between wages, prices, and profits? During the fight against the Axis, the federal government had controlled wages and prices. Through most of 1946 it kept some price controls in place to check anticipated inflation. The tugboat owners, like many employers, wanted assurances that they would be allowed to raise their prices to cover increased labor costs before they granted substantial wage increases. By contrast, the labor movement and federal government argued that most employers could raise wages without raising prices and still make a healthy profit.[9]

With bargaining at a standstill, on February 6, 1946, the third day of the strike, President Harry S Truman seized control of the struck tugboats. The strikers, unimpressed, voted two-to-one to remain off their jobs. With fuel shortages looming, O'Dwyer took drastic action. First, he ordered that outside advertising lights be turned off, temperatures in most buildings be lowered to sixty degrees, heat be shut off on subway and trolley cars, and that no fuel be delivered to schools or amusement places.[10] On February 11 he went further, ordering all schools, stores, libraries, museums, theaters, restaurants, and "business and industrial establishments" closed. Policemen, dispatched to subway stops, railway stations, and ferry terminals, urged the public not to enter midtown or downtown Manhattan. The next day, according to the *New York Times*, saw "the most drastic disruption in the city's life since the Civil War draft riots." In imagery seemingly taken from a film noir, a *World-Telegram* reporter wrote that "tugstruck New York's millions . . . struggled to do all their accustomed little things while a dreadful, unnamed power held them in its grasp. An air of unreality hung over the city. Incidents took on a staccato, dream quality; sharply etched, touched with hysteria, cockeyed." The next day the tugboat strike ended when both sides agreed to the mayor's proposal that they submit their differences to a board of arbitration.[11]

In late 1945 and 1946, as local labor conflicts buffeted New York, massive national strikes captured headlines throughout the country and sparked fierce debate in Washington over whether or not unions had accumulated too much power. Most struck national corporations operating large-scale facilities, a type of plant uncommon in the city. Of the 750,000 steelworkers who walked off their jobs on January 21, 1946, only 12,500 worked in the New York area and fewer than 2,000 in the city itself.[12] But a national strike of copper workers did have a strong presence in New York. The bulk of the 6,000 strikers who worked in New York–area copper plants lived in the city. Furthermore, most of the copper companies had their headquarters in Manhattan.

The fight against Phelps Dodge was especially rough. In an effort to keep operating its plant in Elizabeth, New Jersey—just across the harbor from New York—the company brought in scabs by boat from Brooklyn. Anthony Anastasia, brother of mob leader Albert Anastasia and the power behind several Brooklyn ILA locals, supervised the operation. New York City police boats escorted strikebreakers to the plant and shipments of wire from it. The strikers had boats, too, leading to fierce fighting in the harbor. In the course of the eight-month strike, Mario Russo, a veteran and father of four, was killed on an Elizabeth picket line, and numerous others were injured. In a final calamity, while folksinger Woody Guthrie sang to an Elizabeth rally marking the end of the strike, a fire in his Brooklyn apartment killed his four-year-old daughter.[13]

And so it went. In early 1946 a three-week strike against the "Big 4" meatpacking companies idled over two thousand workers in the city and forced many retail butcher shops to close.[14] A nationwide railway strike in May halted New York's extensive commuter rail system.[15] Then, in the fall, New York harbor was again shut down by a seventeen-day national shipping strike. Less than two weeks later came yet another shipping strike, this time by licensed engineers and deck officers.[16] In 1946 alone nearly a quarter of a million New York workers took part in walkouts, with 9 percent of the nation's strikes taking place in the city. Only during the strike wave that followed World War I did more New York workers walk off their jobs.[17]

At the end of World War II, New York was a working-class city. In 1946, of the 3.3 million employed New Yorkers, less than 700,000 were proprietors, managers, officials, professionals, or semiprofessionals. The other 2.6 million men and women neither owned the businesses for which they worked nor had substantial authority over their operations.[18] They were, to use an old-fashioned term, proletarians. By themselves they made up one-third of the city's population of nearly eight million. Along with their husbands, wives, and children they were a clear majority.

The size, strategic importance, and demonstrated power of the working class allowed it to play a major role in determining what kind of city New York would become in the postwar era. When the war ended, the city stood on a cusp of history. "All the signs," Jan Morris later wrote, "were that it would be the supreme city of the Western world, or even the world as a whole." Seeming miracles of technical and social modernity abounded, from the television industry, then just getting started, to the United Nations.[19] Yet as obvious as the future was the past. In a city where the largest, most advanced warships and passenger liners in the world regularly docked, fish still got delivered to the Fulton Fish Market in sail-powered boats. Horse-drawn wagons remained a common sight, delivering or selling coal, laundry, milk, vegetables, and fruit. In a city where sophisticated defense electronics got designed and built, St. Patrick's Cathedral and Bellevue Hospital still operated on DC current. One police precinct had gas lights. In a city where preliminary work for atomic fission had been done, potbellied stoves were being sold for home heating, and ice blocks were delivered for home refrigeration.[20]

Culturally, socially, and politically, blue-collar workers loomed larger at the end of World War II than at any time before or since. During the war they had been courted and celebrated as key to the Allied victory. Everywhere Americans looked—in newspapers and magazines, on billboards, and at the movies—blue-collar workers were heroically portrayed. The sense that they finally had come into their own was not just the product of official and unofficial opinion makers; as the war ended, manual workers had tremendous élan, a self-confidence growing out of the successful unionization campaigns before the war and their strategic position, steady work, and rising income during it.[21]

At the end of World War II, roughly half of New York's wage workers made, moved, or maintained physical objects for a living, everything from corsets to skyscrapers to aircraft carriers. In 1946, 41 percent of the employed labor force consisted of craftsmen, operatives, laborers, foremen, and kindred workers, the occupational groupings usually considered blue collar. Another 12 percent were service workers, many of whom performed manual labor: domestic servants, firemen, janitors, elevator operators, and the like.[22]

Manual workers could be found in many settings — driving trucks, constructing buildings, cleaning hospitals, unloading ships — but the largest number by far worked in manufacturing. As John Gunther wrote in his 1947 best-seller, *Inside U.S.A.*, New York City was "incomparably the greatest manufacturing town on earth." In 1947 over thirty-seven thousand city establishments were engaged in manufacturing, employing nearly three-quarters of a million production and 200,000 non-production workers.[23]

The centrality of manufacturing to the New York economy undoubtedly surprised many readers of Gunther's book (as it surprises many now), for the common image of New York was just the opposite. As a wartime Regional Plan Association (RPA) study noted, "A visitor to Manhattan seeing the tall office buildings dwarfing all other structures, and passing no huge steel mills with blast furnaces belching fire and smoke as in Chicago or Pittsburgh, or giant automobile factories as in Detroit, or long cotton mills as in New England or the South, might easily conclude that New York was mainly a region of white-collar workers supported by wholesale trade and banking." But the RPA study found manufacturing "the chief support of the New York Metropolitan Region."[24]

New York had been a major manufacturing center since the earliest days of the republic. In 1950, 28 percent of the city's employed workers were in manufacturing, two points above the national figure. The *percentage* of the city workforce employed in manufacturing had been declining since 1910, when it had peaked at just over 40 percent. However, except during the 1930s, the actual *number* of manufacturing workers in the city had risen each decade of the century. When World War II ended, New York manufacturing was at an all-time high.[25]

In 1950 seven of the nation's ten largest cities had a higher percentage of their workforces engaged in manufacturing than New York did. Nonetheless, in *absolute* terms New York City had a goods-producing economy unprecedented in size, output, and complexity. In 1947, New York had more manufacturing jobs than Philadelphia, Detroit, Los Angeles, and Boston put together.[26]

The sheer size of the New York metropolitan area — in 1950 more than one out of every twelve Americans lived there — accounted for some of the distinctive characteristics of the city's goods-producing sector. The New York market for capital and consumer goods was so large that manufacturing strictly to supply local needs was a huge enterprise. Four of the largest manufacturing establishments in New York City were local newspapers, while more than twenty-two thousand New Yorkers made bakery products, largely for local consumption.[27] Even in the case of New Yorkers producing goods that sold nationally, a substantial part of their output was consumed in the region.[28]

The large local market gave a competitive advantage to New York firms in many industries, from hatmaking to linotype equipment, and contributed to the extraordinary heterogeneity of local manufacturing. A 1959 RPA study by Edgar M. Hoover and Raymond Vernon reported that "the pervasive impression of the Region's manufacturing economy is one of diversity — diversity of product, of process, and of environmental needs," a characterization seconded by many observers. In the immediate postwar years, Brooklyn alone had pencil and chewing gum factories, sugar and oil refineries, a naval shipyard, several large pharmaceutical plants, many machinery making companies, a kosher winery, and the world's largest producer of leis. Hoover and Vernon reported that firms in 420 of the 450 industrial categories used by the Bureau of the Census could be found in the region.[29]

For all its diversity, New York did not simply mirror the national economic structure. Far from it. The region dominated many small manufacturing industries, from umbrellas to scientific instruments, but of the seventeen largest manufacturing industries in the country (measured by employment), New York was heavily represented in only one, apparel.[30]

In 1950, 70 percent of New York City manufacturing workers made nondurable goods (generally consumer items meant to last three years or less). By contrast, nationally only 46 percent of manufacturing workers made nondurables. 340,700 men and women — over a third of the city's manufacturing workers and a tenth of its total work force — made apparel or related products. Another 119,200 were in printing and publishing, and 98,300 produced food or beverages. These three groups — apparel, printing and publishing, and food — together accounted for over half of the manufacturing employment in the city and 16 percent of all jobs.[31] Other manufacturing industries each employed only a small fraction of the city's blue-collar workers, but some, by any standard other than New York's, were themselves large: electrical equipment and supplies (52,600 employees in 1950), nonelectrical machinery (31,800 employees), chemicals and allied products (42,300 employees), and leather and leather products (37,400 employees).[32]

Across this spectrum of manufacturing were some common characteristics that distinguished New York City from other centers of goods production. One was the small size of the typical establishment. In 1947 manufacturing establishments in the city employed an average of twenty-five workers, less than half the national average of fifty-nine. Counting only production workers, city manufacturing shops averaged twenty workers.[33]

This low average reflected the rarity of large factories. One 1947 survey located only 348 plants with 500 or more workers in the entire New York–northeastern New Jersey metropolitan area, with most outside the city proper. It also reflected the presence of a vast number of tiny enterprises. Half the metropolitan-area manufacturing establishments had fewer than ten employees. In the city proper, 11,773 had fewer than four employees, including a quarter of all the garment shops and a third of all printing and publishing establishments.[34]

The smallness of New York manufacturing enterprises was not simply a matter of industrial mix. The industries most heavily represented in New York tended toward small-scale operation, but even within given industries New York shops generally were smaller than their counterparts elsewhere. The average New York garment shop, for example, had only twenty employees (including seventeen production workers), in contrast to the national industry average of thirty-five. Nonelectrical machinery shops employed an average of eighty-six workers nationally, but only twenty-eight in New York. Household furniture makers averaged forty-seven workers nationally, eighteen in New York. Printing and publishing was something of an exception: the average New York establishment was considerably larger than those elsewhere. But this was because New York was a major center for white-collar publishing jobs; if only production workers are compared, the difference becomes negligible.[35]

The scarcity of land, its high cost, and zoning regulations limited New York City factory size.[36] But more basic was the concentration of New York firms on custom or "small batch" production. Most New Yorkers who manufactured things either made one-of-a-kind products, such as fine jewelry or specialized machinery, or items such as blouses or stock certificates that were produced in only modest quantities in any particular style, size, or version. Although custom or small batch manufacturing was not necessarily small-scale — shipbuilding, for example, except in wartime, was a made-to-order business — in general establishments that made nonstandard goods were smaller than mass production facilities.[37]

The New York region had some mass production plants, mostly outside the city. Typically these utilized a very detailed division of labor, a high degree of mechanization, many special purpose machines, the mechanical transfer of goods along a sequential path of assembly, work pacing through assembly line timing or other technical means, and a high ratio of semiskilled operatives to skilled workers. Right across the Hudson River from Manhattan, for example, in Edgewater, N.J., sat an assembly plant of the Ford Motor Company, the firm that had virtually invented mass production (originally known as "Fordism"). Its rival, General Motors, had assembly plants in nearby Tarrytown, N.Y., and Linden, N.J. Westinghouse and General Electric employed over thirteen thousand workers in the New York area, mostly in northern New Jersey, many in mass production processes. Even in Manhattan there was some mass production. Emerson Electric Company made radios and televisions on the West Side until 1950, when it moved its operation to Jersey City. Benson and Hedges had a cigarette factory on Water Street. But such plants were the exception, not the rule, together employing only a small minority of New York's manufacturing workers.[38]

Firms doing custom or small-batch production—more typical of New York manufacturing—generally had a less developed division of labor, used less specialized equipment, and employed more highly skilled and versatile workers than mass production companies. They also tended to use nontechnical means to set the pace of work, such as piecework (which was widespread in the garment industry). However, there were wide variations among such firms, even when making similar products. After World War II, for example, a growing number of garment shops abandoned traditional "tailor work" for "section work," which entailed a more extensive division of labor and required a less-skilled workforce. Still, in 1950 there were almost as many skilled blue-collar workers in New York City as there were semiskilled manufacturing workers, while in Flint, Michigan, the center of General Motors' mass production empire, there were only about half as many.[39]

Versatility—as much or more than low unit price—was a key to success in New York manufacturing. In some cases versatility was a trait of individual businesses. In other cases it was a trait of constellations of firms, each of which in itself might be quite specialized. For example, the apparel industry was not really one industry but many: women's dresses, women's blouses, men's and boys' suits and coats, children's dresses, millinery, fur, corsets, knitted outerwear, men's neckwear, and so on. Within each of these sectors were jobbers, who designed and sold apparel and sometimes cut the needed material; contractors, who made apparel from material and specifications given them by others; and manufacturers, who performed both functions.

Contracting was more prevalent in New York than in smaller apparel centers, where manufacturers were more prominent. Its great advantage was the flexibility it provided in a seasonal, boom-bust industry dependent on the vagaries of fashion. Rather than having to maintain manufacturing facilities and a workforce sufficient to meet peak needs, jobbers made samples and then, based on orders actually received, contracted for most or all of the production. Contractors, in turn, tried to ensure steady business by developing relationships with many jobbers.[40]

Contracting allowed even small companies to produce a vast array of styles of apparel by dealing with highly specialized firms that marbled the industry. If embroidered blouses became fashionable one season, for example, jobbers and manufacturers, who might not know how or be able to afford to set up their own embroidery operations, could send work out to specialized embroidery firms, which at other times might work on bedspreads or skirts.

Many types of firms supplied, serviced, and profited off of the apparel industry. There were button companies; sewing machine dealers; factors and bankers; truckers; textile, thread, and box suppliers; and fashion models and salespeople (since New York was the industry's sales as well as manufacturing center). These ancillary industries made it possible for apparel makers to start up with minimal capital and avoid large investments in equipment, space, or supplies.[41]

For manufacturers to be able to make use of what economists call "external economies"—wholesalers, subcontractors, and service firms performing functions that otherwise would have to be done in-house—they needed to be close together to allow the cheap, rapid transfer of material and frequent face-to-face communication to deal with the problems that inevitably arise when new products are made.[42] This was why New York manufacturers tended to congregate in compact industrial districts. An astounding half million manufacturing jobs were clustered in Manhattan south of Central Park. These constituted over half the manufacturing jobs in New York City and well over a quarter of those in the twenty-two-county metropolitan region. Manhattan had more manufacturing jobs than any other county in the country, with the exception of Cook County, which contains Chicago and its suburbs.[43]

Some sections of Manhattan housed manufacturing of all kinds, for example the area known as the Valley before being dubbed SoHo. But more typically, particular industries clustered in particular neighborhoods. The garment district—the center of women's and children's clothing design, sales, and manufacture—occupied eighteen blocks of loft buildings bounded by 34th and 40th Streets and Sixth and Ninth Avenues. The fur district was nearby. So was the millinery industry, which was so concentrated that 15 percent of the country's entire millinery output came from a single building at 65 West 39th Street. Men's clothing was made between 14th and 26th Streets, while undergarment manufacturing took place downtown, along lower Broadway.[44]

Commercial printing operations clustered in several Manhattan districts. Those that specialized in financial and legal printing congregated near City Hall; those that served the retail trade and bulk mailers settled in the West 30s, near the main post office; and those that serviced the advertising industry and corporate headquarters positioned themselves on the East Side above 42nd Street. Generally these shops were small and did work requiring close consultation with customers, short production runs, or fast delivery. They subcontracted out much of their typesetting, photoengraving, and binding, and depended on nearby type, ink, and paper houses to enable them to create products of almost every conceivable design and color without having to maintain large stores of supplies. Some large printing companies had plants in Long Island City, the Bronx, or Newark, where land was cheaper than in Manhattan but still near enough to allow customer contact.[45]

The Queens and Brooklyn shores of the East River and the Inner Harbor lodged a whole series of industrial neighborhoods—Long Island City, Williamsburg, Greenpoint, and Bush Terminal. Along Newtown Creek, on the Brooklyn-Queens border, were Maspeth and Woodside. Many establishments in these areas required water access or large sites or engaged in noxious activities, for example, shipyards, chemical processing plants, and sugar, oil, and copper refineries. But there were numerous food processing, machine building, box making, furniture, paint, and electronics plants in these areas as well. Meat processing plants sat on the West Side of Manhattan, while slaughterhouses and tanneries bunched in Turtle Bay on the East Side until the United Nations displaced them.[46]

Of course, not only manufacturing firms clustered in specialized districts. There was an insurance district, a diamond center, a wholesale flower district, several wholesale food districts, a leather district, and booksellers' row (the center of the used book trade). Wall Street was synonymous with finance; Madison Avenue with advertising.[47]

The industrial geography of New York, divided as it was into specialized economic zones, imparted a particular character to the city's economic life, labor relations, and even its culture. Areas like the garment district or the diamond district were chock-full of restaurants, cafeterias, bars, clubs, employment agencies, and union halls where employers and workers exchanged information, sought work or workers, socialized, organized, and developed shared ideas about life, work, and politics. Managers and workers—even owners—often identified more with their trade than with a particular company. The constant exchange of ideas, techniques, and personnel within industrial districts helped generate, attract, and retain firms that survived through flexibility. Any thing, person, or idea that a company might need to make a particular product usually could be found nearby. But while the industrial districts provided economic advantages for custom and small-batch producers, they had disadvantages for bulk producers.[48]

It was almost a rule of New York manufacturing that as soon as a product became standardized and began to be sold in large quantities, its production was moved out of the city, and often out of the region entirely. Companies engaged in predictable, high-volume production of standard goods did not need the external economies that industrial districts provided: they could afford to have specialized in-house services, maintenance operations, and extensive inventories of supplies. Also, as production became routinized, they no longer needed access to a large pool of skilled workers. For firms that competed on the basis of price rather than the uniqueness of their products, speed of delivery, or quality of workmanship, the high unionization rate and high costs of labor, land, rent, taxes, energy, and shipping in New York became significant locational disadvantages.[49]

Take electronics. Since the days of Thomas Edison, New York was a pioneer in the development and manufacture of electric and electronic components and equipment. In their early stages of development, making these products required the close collaboration of scientists, engineers, and highly skilled workers, all of whom could be found in large numbers in New York. But with standardization, jobs moved away. The city had been an early center of electronic tube manufacture. However, once tubes were no longer made in small batches by skilled craft workers (usually men) but on assembly lines by less-skilled workers (usually women), companies moved their operations to New Jersey and beyond, where they could find cheaper space, better rail connections, and lower-cost labor. Similarly, until the mid-1920s, New York was a major center of radio manufacturing, generally by small firms, but as radios became standardized, larger firms with larger factories became dominant, and the industry began moving elsewhere.[50]

The disadvantages of the New York area—especially the city proper—

for mass production meant that the region was significantly underrepresented in the industries that grew most rapidly during the first four decades of the twentieth century, including the automobile, petroleum, and rubber industries. New York was largely a bystander as a giant complex of industries developed to manufacture, fuel, and otherwise accommodate motor vehicles, a complex which at its height employed one out of every six American workers. In short, New York was a non-Fordist city during the age of Ford. This was true on the level of consumption as well as production: in 1950 there was one car in New York City for every 6.9 residents, in contrast to one for every 3.8 people nationally.[51]

New York's manufacturing sector of 1945 in some respects looked more like its manufacturing sector of 1845 than contemporaneous centers of mass production like Pittsburgh or Detroit. The concentration on consumer nondurables; the crowded industrial districts, with their loft buildings and tiny workshops; the webs of contractors and subcontractors; and the persistence, at least in some trades, of highly skilled craftsmen working alongside less skilled and more poorly paid operatives—all of which characterized blue-collar New York at the end of World War II—bear an uncanny resemblance to industrial New York a century earlier.[52] But the New York manufacturing economy of 1945 was not simply atavistic; while it contained many archaic elements, it also had some strikingly advanced ones.

Electronics components again furnish a good example. While it was true that by 1954 *standardized* tube production had largely left the region, non-standard tube production had not. In fact, more area workers than ever before—some twelve thousand—were making tubes, generally specialized, highly sophisticated devices. A similar situation prevailed in electronic end-products. After World War II, New York was not a major center for mass market consumer electronics, but it was for scientific, industrial, and military electronics, which tended to be the cutting edge of the industry. Some of this work was done in New York City proper—during the 1940s, for example, several companies made radar devices in the city—but increasingly it was concentrated on Long Island, which also was a major center for military aircraft production.[53]

The manufacture of diverse products in short production runs using versatile equipment and personnel—what some economists call "flexible specialization"—was neither less modern than mass production nor inevitably doomed by it. Rather, it was an alternative system that, depending on the product involved and the particular economic, social, and political circumstances, might be more or less efficient and more or less profitable than mass production. For workers, it had both advantages and disadvantages.[54]

Many workers found flexible production jobs more rewarding than Fordist production. Machinists making complex equipment, for example, faced an ever-varying series of challenges that called for skill, experience, and ingenuity. Cutters in the apparel industry had to mobilize dexterity, strength, and know-how to maximize the number of garments that could be made from a given stock of material. But diversity of product did not necessarily mean challenging work. A lathe operator in a furniture factory might help produce small batches of furniture in varied sizes and styles, but if a separate setup man prepared the lathe for each new run, as was often the case, the lathe operator experienced little difference between making numerous identical parts (Fordism) or small batches of different parts (flexible specialization). Likewise, while blouse or skirt styles might radically change from year to year, the tasks of a sewing machine operator under the section work system remained essentially the same, day after day, year after year.[55]

Many small New York manufacturers were technically primitive. The typical New York dress or blouse company during the mid-1950s was capitalized at only about twenty-five thousand dollars. Few could afford to buy advanced equipment or experiment with new methods. Many small manufacturers survived only by squeezing labor as hard as possible. The small firm size, continual search for credit, intense competition, rocky labor relations, and need for timely deliveries characteristic of so much New York manufacturing opened the door for organized crime, which played a major role in clothing, paper box, leather goods, and a number of other industries.[56]

Short lead times and small production runs often meant seasonal employment. Production of fur garments and women's clothing, for instance, was keyed to annual selling seasons. In 1950, operators in the women's coat and suit industry averaged only thirty-eight weeks of work in Manhattan and thirty-five in Brooklyn. The toy and cosmetics industries sold a large percentage of their annual output during the Christmas season; after holiday production came slack periods with extensive layoffs. Some workers, particularly women who were second breadwinners in their families, liked annual layoffs, when unemployment insurance, which in effect subsidized seasonal industries, gave them continuing if reduced income. But for many workers seasonal layoffs meant sojourns working out-of-town or in other industries, such as taxi-driving or longshoring, or severe economic hardship.[57]

Which workers experienced the positive side of flexible specialization and which the negative depended in part on gender and ethnicity. Apparel cutters, for example, were almost exclusively men and, except in poorly paid, nonunion "cut-up shops," almost exclusively white: Jews and Italians in clothing, Jews and Greeks in fur. Section work, by contrast, was largely done by women, in the postwar decades mainly Jews, Italians, and Puerto Ricans.[58]

In 1947 women made up 38 percent of the manufacturing production workers in New York City (compared to 26 percent nationally), including 56 percent of those in the apparel industry. Among men there were two skilled blue-collar workers (in 1950) for every semi-skilled manufacturing operative, but among women there were *nineteen* operatives for every worker in a skilled blue-collar job. Although government skill classifications do not always correspond to actual job content, clearly there were radically different occupational structures for men and women. This contributed to a huge disparity in remuneration: in 1947 male manufacturing production workers in New York City earned a weekly average of $67.58, women an average of $42.92.[59]

The tendency for flexible production and inequitable labor market segmentation to go hand in hand was even more evident in construction than manufacturing. Like the apparel industry, the construction industry maintained a high degree of flexibility through the extensive use of subcontracting. Its workers produced custom or semi-custom products, which continually presented new problems that could be solved only by drawing on training, past experience, and a creative cast of mind. Of the 144,000 New Yorkers who worked in the construction industry in 1950 (including in office jobs), fewer than 4 percent were women. Furthermore, the industry was overwhelmingly white (in a city that was over 9 percent African-American), with nonwhite workers largely restricted to positions as laborers or hod carriers. Many trades had literally no journeymen who were not white men.[60]

In postwar New York, then, the world of the versatile, all-around, highly-skilled industrial worker still flourished, largely as a result of a concentration on flexible production. But it did so, essentially, just for white men. Most female and nonwhite workers, and many white men as well, inhabited a world of subdivided, semiskilled labor. For them, the difference between batch and bulk production mattered little in their daily tasks.

Manufacturing was just one part—though the largest—of the goods production and distribution complex at the heart of the city's economy. In the early nineteenth century, New York rose to national dominance not as a manufacturing center but as a commercial hub. New York's superb natural harbor and its links westward via the Erie Canal and, later, several trunk railroads made it an ideal entry and egress point for goods and people. Much of the city's manufacturing sector arose as an adjunct to trade: building ships and barrels for transporting goods, providing luxury items to the merchant elite, and processing trade commodities, such as raw sugar.

By the mid-twentieth century, manufacturing had come to dwarf trade as a source of employment. But New York's port—by far the largest and most important in the nation—still was vital to the city's economy. In the late 1940s, one-fifth by weight and one-third by value of the country's maritime imports and exports went through New York.

The Port of New York was vast; within a twenty-five mile radius from the Statue of Liberty nestled more than 750 miles of developed shoreline. During the immediate postwar years, the New Jersey side of the Hudson housed cargo handling facilities in Port Newark, Jersey City, and Hoboken, but most of the port's cargo—75 percent as late as 1960—was handled in New York City. The West Side of Manhattan had the greatest concentration of deep-water general cargo piers in the world. It also housed most of the port's passenger ship facilities. In Brooklyn, miles of docks, warehouses, and shipyards lined the shore. Staten Island had more of the same, on a more modest scale. Extensive lighterage and carfloat operations crisscrossed the harbor and the rivers that flowed into it, compensating for the poor rail connections between various parts of the port, particularly between New York City and the Jersey railheads.[61]

Local officials estimated that in the late 1940s and early 1950s, 400,000 workers were dependent on port activities. About a quarter were directly involved in marine transportation, including 14,000 sailors and deckhands and 36,000 longshoremen. Another 40,000 worked in port-related trucking, railroad, and warehouse operations, and over 30,000 in ship construction and repair. The rest worked for import-export firms, in foreign banking, marine insurance, or admiralty law, or in material handling, refining, and manufacturing operations closely tied to the port.[62]

The flow of goods, people, and ideas through the port gave working-class New York an unusual worldliness. Sailors returned from sea with first-hand accounts of the rise and fall of fascism, the devastation of World War II, the turmoil in the colonial world, the spread of Communism, the outbreak of the Cold War. Mere proximity to the waterfront brought whiffs of exotica.

From his days in Brooklyn Heights, Truman Capote remembered seeing "Crane-carried tractors and cotton bales and unhappy cattle sway above ships bound for Bahia, for Bremen, for ports spelling their names in Oriental calligraphy." Foreign sailors drank and talked with the longshoremen, truckers, and native seamen who frequented the bars and flophouses on the perimeter of the port. The port made New York the country's great immigrant city, a city of unparalleled human diversity. An entrepôt from its founding, mid-twentieth-century New York had strands running through its port connecting it to places, people, and ideas truly foreign to most of America.[63]

Distributive activities, of course, were not restricted to the harbor. In 1948, New York City had over 35,000 wholesale establishments, employing 315,000 workers. One-fifth of the wholesale trade of the entire country took place in New York, and in many product lines the majority of all sales took place there.

As one would expect, there was great variety within this vast landscape of buying and selling, which included everything from Manhattan's famed Fulton Fish Market to national sales offices of giant manufacturers. Mostly, though, the field consisted of highly competitive small shops. Over half the wholesale establishments in the city had three or fewer employees; fewer than five hundred had one hundred employees or more. In part because most shops were small, there was unusually close contact between white- and blue-collar workers. A typical wholesaler might have buyers, salesmen, clerical workers, warehouse employees, and processing workers all in the same location. Women, who held most of the clerical positions, made up a quarter of the wholesale workforce.[64]

Wholesale trade had a culture of fast talk and sharp deals. Top salesmen could earn a very good living. But for most workers, wholesaling was the "measly manner of existence" that Biff Loman described in Arthur Miller's *Death of a Salesman* (1949). "To get on that subway on the hot mornings in summer. To devote your whole life to keeping stock, or making phone calls, or selling or buying. To suffer fifty weeks of the year for the sake of a two-week vacation, when all you really desire is to be outdoors, with your shirt off. And always to have to get ahead of the next fella."[65]

Retail trade could be worse. In 1948, New York City had an astounding 104,000 retail establishments, one for every seventy-six residents. Over a half million New Yorkers worked in retail trade. Roughly 10 percent were employed by department stores, which housed some of the largest congregations of workers in the city. In 1947 twenty-one department stores and fifty-one other retail establishments employed at least five hundred workers. At the other extreme were the tens of thousands of neighborhood groceries, butcher shops, vegetable stands, pharmacies, and candy stores, many tiny family operations. The nearly one hundred thousand "active proprietors of unincorporated businesses" in the retail sector included numerous members of what C. Wright Mills called "the lumpen-bourgeoisie," earning at best a modest income by working physically exhausting and emotionally deadening hours and exploiting their own family members. (Bernard Malamud captured the cramped agony of this life in his novel *The Assistant*.) Also in retail trade were 134,000 New Yorkers who worked in the city's more than 18,000 "eating and drinking places."[66]

As important as goods production and distribution was to New York (in 1950 it accounted for three out of five jobs), it was in *relative* decline during the postwar years. Another economy, which operated alongside it, though smaller when World War II ended, grew over the following decades. It consisted of the finance, government, and service industries. Rather than dealing in tangible goods like ships, cookies, or corsets, this world centered around intangible forms of property, such as insurance and stock; on the creation of rules; and on the provision of services.[67]

The centrality of administrative and service industries to the local economy stemmed, in part, from the city's world position. By 1945, New York was, as historian Thomas McCormick put it, the "central metropolis" of the capitalist world system, the "dominant city that acts as the coordinating point and clearing house of international capital."[68] As the center of international finance and headquarters of 140 of the nation's 500 largest industrial corporations, New York was the site of unprecedented economic power.[69] The leading local businessmen were the most important economic decision-makers in the world. What they decided, and what happened on local financial and commodity markets, affected the lives of billions of people.

In 1950, 242,000 New Yorkers—7.4 percent of the employed workforce—worked in finance, insurance, and real estate. What most people meant when they said Wall Street—securities firms, commodity brokers, investment companies, and the stock and commodity exchanges—employed surprisingly few workers, under 30,000. Banks had twice and real estate firms over three times that number on payroll. The insurance industry employed 76,000 New Yorkers, the majority women. In the late 1950s, Metropolitan Life alone had 15,000 workers at its home office on Madison Square, dwarf-

ing any local manufacturing enterprise. Such massing of white-collar workers, most doing routinized work, was not unusual. The images of the
emergence of mass society in New York—for example, in King Vidor's brilliant 1928 movie *The Crowd*—were not of workers on an assembly line but of
rows and rows of clerical workers engaged in seemingly mindless, inter-
changeable, soul-deadening labor.[70]

Over 580,000 New Yorkers worked in service industries, a catchall category for enterprises that did not primarily make things. They ranged from
teachers and hospital workers to employees of advertising agencies, automobile repair shops, and corporate law firms. Women constituted the majority
of professional and personal service workers; men dominated entertainment,
business, and repair services. Because New York was a culture capital, it had
an unusually large number of men and women who provided "entertainment
and related services," 50,000 according to the 1950 census. Nearly a quarter
of a million people provided "personal services." They included 75,000
women and 4,000 men who reported their occupation as private household
worker, a quarter of whom lived with their employer. A much larger number
of New Yorkers—1.7 million, 99.7 percent of whom were women—reported
their occupation as "keeping house." However, because they were keeping
their *own* houses, and not receiving wages for doing so, statisticians did not
consider them part of the labor force.[71]

Finally, in 1950, 87,000 New Yorkers worked for the federal government
(just over half were postal workers), 9,000 for the state government, and over
220,000 for the municipal government, which was, by far, the city's largest
single employer.[72]

The sheer size of New York, and the complexity of twentieth-century life,
meant that at the end of World War II the great metropolis's economy was
extraordinary in scope and diversity. Yet compared to a half-century later,
the degree to which its diverse parts were physically and socially integrated
is striking. Take a look at the wonderful photographs by Andreas Feininger
of New York during the 1940s.[73] Over and over again his images include
both soaring office towers, where power and paper were manipulated, and
gritty work sites where blue-collar labor took place. In the 1940s it was almost
impossible to look out of a skyscraper window and not see men engaged in
physical labor, be it pushing racks of clothes in the garment district, floating
railroad cars across the harbor, or maneuvering trucks full of printed material,
toys, or machine tools through the congested streets of Manhattan. When

financiers and lawyers and marketing men left their offices they rubbed shoulders in the streets and subways with the secretaries and clerks and elevator operators with whom they shared their buildings and the furriers and typographers and waitresses and warehousemen who worked nearby.

At the midpoint of the twentieth century, to a far greater extent than at its end, producing, distributing, selling, and financing goods and services were, in New York, geographically proximate processes. Clothes were often designed, modeled, sold, financed, made, and distributed all from the same building. In the early days of television not only were the network's financial and administrative offices located in New York City, most of their shows were produced there as well. New York–area television stations and advertising agencies employed thousands of performers, authors, directors, producers, and scenic workers. Nearby, over 6,000 workers made television sets or their components, 10,500 workers sold them, and 5,000 mechanics serviced them.[74]

The long-run history of capitalism entails the abstraction of value out of and away from the labor process, separating mental labor from manual labor and the circulation of money from the distribution of things. Central to the story of postwar New York were the different fates of goods production and symbol manipulation. In 1945 a bifurcation of the economy already was evident. Still, just blocks from Wall Street, where paper symbols of property—securities, bonds, and commodity futures—were traded, there were wholesale markets for butter, eggs, cheese, tea, coffee, and spices where not just the ownership of those goods but the goods themselves were exchanged. As the postwar era dawned, the sounds of tugboats and the smell of freshly-roasted coffee beans still penetrated the corridors where bankers and businessmen accumulated money and power on a scale unsurpassed anywhere in the world.[75]

CHAPTER 2.

Working-Class New York

From the 1920s through the 1970s, in literature, scholarship, and reportage about work and industrial relations, automobile workers often were held forth as the archetypical proletarians. Most worked in the giant factories and on the assembly lines that artists, academics, and journalists associated with modernity. For many Americans, the United Automobile Workers (UAW), which helped set the national pattern for wages and benefits, epitomized the labor movement.[1] But in the realm of workers' culture and home life— workers away from work—the national media were more likely to portray a New Yorker, and typically not a factory worker, than an auto worker from Detroit or Cleveland.

Probably the best-known working-class families of the 1950s were the fictional Kramdens and Nortons of Bensonhurst, Brooklyn, whose domestic doings and comic misadventures kept *The Honeymooners* near the top of the television ratings for eight years. Jackie Gleason's Ralph Kramden drove a bus on Madison Avenue, while Art Carney's Ed Norton was a sewer worker, occupations that had little to do with the heroic image of the proletarian so popular among leftists and liberals.[2]

The Kramdens and Nortons were everymen, whose struggle for dignity and to keep their heads above water (in Ed's case literally) had universal meaning. Because New York was an entertainment and literary center, it was natural that New York workers were used as representatives of the common man. Yet in some respects the Kramdens and Nortons were distinctly New Yorkers. Where else did neighbors visit one another via the fire escape?

In the metaphorical device used to project the pluralist vision of the nation which came to the fore during the 1940s, the small group of diverse characters forced to work together for their mutual survival (the platoon or the survivors of a shipwreck), the working-class New Yorker (usually a Brooklynite) was one of the stock characters, along with the Appalachian, the upper-class WASP, and the Midwestern farm boy. Who could forget William Bendix dying in *Lifeboat* (1944), with his last, delirious thoughts of the Brooklyn Dodgers and dancing at Roseland? In images of mid-century America, working-class New Yorkers were portrayed as their own ethnic group, full of idiosyncrasies that set them off from the rest of America.[3]

New York's peculiar economy, demography, and social geography, and its status as a national and world center, gave its working class a distinctive character. In the years after World War II, that distinctiveness led and enabled working-class New Yorkers to push their city along a path of development unlike that of the most of the country.

To speak thus of a working class, of course, is to assume that workers and their families had enough in common with one another to make them a recognizable social entity. In postwar New York that was indeed the case. As a result of the kinds of jobs they had, workers lived in particular places and in particular ways, shared common experiences and similar constraints, and developed like ways of understanding the world. Economic class alone did not define their sense of self, or that of their families. Ethnic, racial, and religious identifications were powerful. Divisions along lines of occupation, politics, and sensibility arose, too. But at least episodically, a sense of class became unmistakenly evident among New York workers and their families.

Never was that more so than during the post–World War II strike wave, which was notable not only for its scale but for the spirit of solidarity that accompanied it. The widespread refusal of workers to cross picket lines exemplified this. So did the participation of nonstriking workers in picket lines and protests supporting strikers. Mario Russo, killed in the Phelps Dodge strike, belonged to a union local that itself was not party to the conflict. When during the May 1946 railroad strike President Truman called for a law allowing him to draft strikers, thousands of New York workers rallied on twenty-four hours notice to protest the measure. And in October 1946, after *New York Times* columnist Hanson W. Baldwin accused unions of undermining the merchant marine and denigrated the wartime service of merchant seamen, three thousand workers picketed the newspaper, leading it to all but repudiate Baldwin and run a lengthy statement by the protesters.[4]

Workers made considerable financial sacrifices on one another's behalf. Some unions, like the United Electrical Workers (UE), did not have strike funds, leaving them dependent on contributions from their members, other unions, and the public to provide relief for strikers. During the 1946 electrical industry strike, UE Local 475, based in Brooklyn, and Local 453, in Yonkers, together "adopted" a local of workers on strike at a Westinghouse elevator plant in Jersey City, sending over caravans loaded with food as well as contributing cash.[5] In late 1945, local unions affiliated with the Congress of Industrial Organizations (CIO) established a Joint CIO Strike Support

Committee. Under its auspices, four thousand unionists contributed three tons of food and toys for striking General Motors workers.[6]

The size of the postwar strikes, their near or actual simultaneity, and acts of solidarity among workers gave the strike wave the look of a class movement. In reality, it was not a coordinated, class-wide movement. A spirit of camaraderie and class solidarity was widespread, but most strikes were discrete struggles by particular groups for specific contractual arrangements. Sometimes workers fought one another. During the Phelps Dodge strike, some of the scabs at the Elizabeth plant belonged to the AFL's International Brotherhood of Electrical Workers (IBEW), which was battling with UE—the CIO union which represented the strikers—to organize New York's small and midsized electrical manufacturing shops.[7]

New York workers could be remarkably combative during the mid and late 1940s. They tended to be most militant when on the defensive, when companies like Phelps Dodge seemed determined to break their unions or roll back prior gains. Unions rarely sought radical departures from established patterns of industrial or social relations. But when faced with racalcitrant bosses, time after time workers stood up for one another.[8]

Tension between solidarity and division, militance and accommodation, and parochialism and cosmopolitanism structured working-class New York. These oppositions were not unique to the city. But as a result of New York's peculiarities, they played out differently there than elsewhere.

Part of what was distinctive about New York's working class was its foreignness. When World War II ended, New York was a city of immigrants and their children. In 1950 foreign-stock (first and second generation) whites made up a majority of the city population and nearly two-thirds of those of prime working age (twenty to sixty-four). As late as the mid-1950s, John Mollenkopf and Manuel Castells have noted, "blue collar white ethnics were the single largest social stratum" in New York City.[9]

The size of New York's foreign-stock population and its composition—primarily Italians, Eastern European Jews, Germans, and Irish—gave the city a unique religious profile. A 1952 survey found that nearly half of all New Yorkers were Catholic and over a quarter Jewish. Among whites, Protestants made up just 16 percent of the population. Rare have been the times and places in United States history when Protestants have ranked so low among religious groups.

The huge size of the Catholic and Jewish populations—New York housed the largest concentration of Jews ever to assemble, at any place, in any era—gave the city much of its cultural particularity and contributed to the widely shared sense, among both New Yorkers and non-New Yorkers, that New York was in the United States but not of it. Norman Podhoretz recalled that growing up in working-class Brownsville, he never "thought of myself as an American. I came from Brooklyn, and in Brooklyn there were no Americans; there were Jews and Negroes and Italians and Poles and Irishmen. Americans lived in New England, in the South, in the Midwest: alien people in alien places."[10] The sense of not being part of America often had a contemptuous edge, from the *New Yorker* advertising slogan of the 1920s, "not for the old lady in Dubuque," to Woody Allen's joke about California in *Annie Hall*, that he could not live in a place whose main contribution to culture was the right turn on red. In Thomas McGrath's novel about the 1945 longshoremen's strike, *This Coffin Has No Handles*, a midwestern soldier disembarking in the city says to his buddy, "I don't like New York. It's just another foreign country." His friend, from the West Side of Manhattan, replies, "Maybe it is a foreign country. I always figured Hoboken was the West Coast, myself," a sentiment that brought fame to Saul Steinberg, whose satirical drawing, "New Yorker's View of the World," became a classic.[11]

The foreign-born were not the only newcomers to the city. In 1940 there were 641,000 whites born somewhere in the continental United States other than New York State living in the city. Their number declined to 492,000 in 1960. By contrast, there was a net in-migration of 221,000 African-Americans during the 1940s and 154,000 during the 1950s.[12] Those same years also saw a massive movement of people from Puerto Rico to New York. During each year in the 1950s an average of 41,000 more Puerto Ricans moved to the mainland than returned to the island, with most settling in New York. By 1960, 613,000 New Yorkers—almost 8 percent of the population—either had been born in Puerto Rico or had a parent born there.[13]

Many observers contended that what made New York special was that so many of its residents had made a conscious choice to move there. E. B. White, in his 1949 celebration *Here Is New York*, wrote that there were "roughly three New Yorks. . . . the New York of the man or woman who was born here. . . . the New York of the commuter. . . . [and] the New York of the person who was born somewhere else and came to New York in quest of something." White believed that each contributed to the character of the metropolis, but it was the "settlers" who made the city great, who gave it "passion," its "high-strung disposition, its poetical deportment, its dedication to the arts, and its incomparable achievements."[14]

White was in a long tradition of hailing New York as a city of newcomers, a self-selected congregation of the fearless and energetic, arriving from all over the world to make their fortunes. The demographic reality was more complex. In 1950, 4.8 million of New York's 7.9 million residents had been born in the city. To the extent that New York was a magnet, its polarity reversed during the 1940s. That decade roughly one-tenth of the municipal population chose to leave. For the first time in modern history more people moved out of New York than moved in, a trend that accelerated during the 1950s. Only natural increase kept the population stable.[15]

Among the foreign-stock population, immigrants were a minority, outnumbered by their children. Furthermore, they were an aging group: while in 1950 foreign-born whites made up 23 percent of the city's population, they constituted only 2 percent of those under age twenty and 61 percent of those sixty-five and over.[16]

Immigrants still wielded great influence. New York's first two postwar mayors, William O'Dwyer and Vincent Impellitteri, had been born abroad. Into the 1950s an extensive web of immigrant-built institutions remained largely intact, from the "national" Catholic parishes, such as the Irish, Italian, Polish, and Croatian churches on Manhattan's West Side, to the nearly two thousand *landsmanshaftn* (fraternal societies of Jewish immigrants from the same hometown). When in 1948 the Board of Transportation raised subway and bus fares, it advertised the changes in English, Italian, Russian, Greek, Yiddish, Spanish, German, Polish, and Hungarian language newspapers.[17]

In the postwar era, however, it was the children of immigrants, more than immigrants themselves, who set the cultural tone of the city and established its image for the rest of the country, be it television comedians like Jackie Gleason (whose parents were Irish-born) and Sid Caesar (son of a Polish-born father and Russian-born mother) or "New York intellectuals," like Alfred Kazin, Irving Howe, and Norman Podhoretz (all children of working-class, Eastern European Jews). Such children of immigrants were of two worlds. On the one hand, they usually were at least familiar with the language, culture, and values their parents brought with them from their native lands. On the other hand, the United States—and more particularly New York—was their home; its streets, jobs, games, language, and values were assumed norms. The drive, uncertainty, and pain of this transitional generation have been central themes of modern American literature. More than anywhere else, New York was the arena in which this story of two generations and two cultures played itself out.[18]

Joining the children of immigrants as a growing presence in the city were blacks and Puerto Ricans. Their arrival was linked to the success of second-generation immigrants in escaping the working class, or at least moving into skilled positions within it, creating a labor shortage in low-wage manufacturing and service jobs. Most African-Americans who moved to New York came from the South, particularly the Carolinas, Virginia, and Georgia, seeking jobs and escape from limited economic opportunity, severe discrimination, and the threat of racial violence.[19] Similarly, Puerto Ricans most frequently cited their desire to get a job in New York or to join a family member who had one as their reason for moving there. Employment per se was not the motive; most migrants who had wanted a job already had had one in Puerto Rico, where, occupation by occupation, unemployment was generally lower than in New York during the years of peak movement. But new arrivals typically doubled their island income as soon as they found a job in New York. By 1959, the median family income of Puerto Ricans in New York was three times what it was in Puerto Rico.[20]

The wartime and postwar increase in the Puerto Rican and African-American population of New York, historian Oscar Handlin noted, was "comparable in scale to that of the Irish and Germans between 1840 and 1860 and of the Jews and Italians, 1890-1915."[21] Unlike earlier immigration, however, the influx of African-Americans and Puerto Ricans did not swell the total population of the city, because of a simultaneous, massive outmigration of whites. Between 1940 and 1970, the non–Puerto Rican white population of New York fell from roughly seven million to five million, largely due to suburbanization.

In the postwar years, the suburban counties surrounding New York boomed. Workers formed a significant element of the outward flow. Even before the end of World War II, New York newspapers were carrying ads for modestly-priced homes in Nassau County requiring no down payments for veterans. Starting in the 1960s, in addition to the exodus to nearby suburbs, a growing number of New Yorkers (including many retirees) headed to other parts of the country.[22]

Postwar working-class New York was not stable. Neighborhoods, unions, political parties, governmental agencies, and cultural institutions faced major, sometimes rapid, shifts in their makeup or constituencies. How they dealt with the process of population change helped determine how the city developed during the decades after World War II.

With so many New Yorkers born elsewhere or raised by parents who were, ethnicity loomed large in the life of the city. In the 1940s and 1950s, most working-class New Yorkers lived in neighborhoods that had a distinctly ethnic flavor: Brooklyn's Sunset Park, for example, with its heavy concentration of Scandinavians, or Brownsville, Williamsburg, and Borough Park, Jewish neighborhoods in the same borough, or Harlem, with its African-American, Puerto Rican, and Italian enclaves, or Chinatown, then emerging as the largest concentration of Asians in the Western hemisphere. Greenpoint, Brooklyn was Polish; Yorkville, on Manhattan's Upper East Side, German, Irish, and Hungarian. Such clustering was to some extent voluntary. But it also resulted from discrimination. New York State did not outlaw discrimination in public housing until 1955, and in private, multi-unit dwellings until two years later. (Federal law did not ban housing discrimination until 1968.) African-Americans had little choice as to where they could live because realtors and building owners in most parts of the city would not sell or rent to them. Puerto Ricans, Jews, and Chinese faced similar, if less pervasive discrimination.

Ethnic neighborhoods had their own retail and entertainment districts, and some housed substantial industrial employment. Pitkin Avenue, the central commercial street of Brownsville, Alfred Kazin recalled, had "Banks, Woolworth's, classy shops, loan companies, Loew's Pitkin, the Yiddish Theater, the Little Oriental restaurant—except for Brownsville's ancestral stress in the food, the Yiddish Theater, the left wing–right wing arguments around the tables in Hoffman's Cafeteria, the Zionist appeals along the route, it might be Main Street in any moderately large town."[23]

But of course what made Brownsville Brownsville were precisely the "ancestral stress in the food, the Yiddish Theater, the left wing–right wing arguments . . . the Zionist appeals." The concentration of people who shared the same language, history, and traditions reinforced ethnic identity on a daily basis. So did ethnically-based religious institutions: national Catholic churches, or the Pentecostal Puerto Rican churches in East Harlem and "El Bronx," or the storefront shuls that dotted poor Jewish neighborhoods, or the African-American churches, small or grand. And ethnic identity was reinforced by specialized neighborhood services, from kosher butchers to botanicas to storefront Italian social clubs.[24]

In the memories and memoirs of working-class New Yorkers, the neigh-

borhood looms large. Many thought of themselves not as citizens of the nation or the city but of a particular neighborhood or block. "Each street was a
village," recalled advertising executive Jerry Della Femina, son of a *New York
Times* pressman, about Gravesend, the Italian neighborhood in South
Brooklyn where he grew up during the 1940s.[25]

The intensity of neighborhood attachment had a material basis. In New
York, working people were far less likely to own their homes than elsewhere
in the country, and far more likely to live in large rental apartment buildings.
In 1950 only 8 percent of the dwelling units in the city were detached, single-
family homes, compared to 17 percent in Chicago, 48 percent in Detroit, and
54 percent in Los Angeles. Fewer than 20 percent of New York residential
buildings were owner-occupied. Nearly 40 percent had twenty or more units.

The fact that the New York working class did not own real property had
important political implications. It meant, among other things, that New York
workers had less interest in keeping down real estate taxes than workers elsewhere, and that homeowners associations were not a major political force
within the working class. But the New York housing pattern had cultural and
emotional implications as well. Dense population, small stuffy apartments,
and shared hallways and stoops meant that life was exposed and often communal. Living on Harlem's 116th Street, thought Lutie Johnson, a character
in Ann Petry's 1946 novel *The Street*, was "like living in a tent with everything
that goes on inside it open to the world because the flap won't close."
"Crowded, contiguous ethnic neighborhoods," one historian of the Bronx
noted, "allowed for the nurturing of community feeling and an intense street
life—memories of which account for much nostalgia and idealization."[26]

The thick ethnic air of working-class neighborhoods did not mean that
they were homogeneous. Quite the opposite was true. Most "Jewish" neighborhoods, for example, had substantial non-Jewish populations. In some—
like Williamsburg—Jews were actually a minority. Even in the most heavily
Jewish neighborhoods, like Brownsville or Brighton Beach, a fifth to a third
of the residents were Gentile. A similar situation prevailed in El Barrio—
Spanish Harlem; Dan Wakefield, who lived in the neighborhood in the late
1950s, reported that "there is hardly a block . . . that does not have at least
several families left from the older settlements of Jews, Irish or Italians." In
Brooklyn, in 1950 only 35 percent of the black population lived in census
tracts with over 80 percent black residents.

Neighborhood heterogeneity could be a transitory moment in the ragged
process of ethnic succession: for example the transformation of Bushwick

and Ridgewood from predominantly German to predominantly Italian, or East New York from a largely white area to an African-American and Puerto Rican one. But sometimes there was long-lasting ethnic mixing, such as the generally peaceful cohabitation of Bensonhurst by Jews and Italians. Occasionally heterogeneity was a conscious choice. According to Deborah Dash Moore, many second-generation Jews liked having large numbers of non-Jews living amongst them or nearby because it allowed ethnic camaraderie without the sense of living in a ghetto.[27]

Growing up in a neighborhood with a particular ethnic character, then, did not preclude ongoing, even intimate contact with those from different backgrounds. If anything, such contact was the norm. In *Family Installments*, for example, Edward Rivera recalls having Italian classmates and non-Hispanic teachers in his parochial school in Spanish Harlem. (Because of a severe shortage of Puerto Rican priests and a decision by Francis Cardinal Spellman not to establish national churches for Puerto Ricans, Puerto Rican Catholics were mainly served by non-Hispanic clergy.) Very often schools, especially junior high and high schools, which drew from large catchment areas, were sites for ethnic mixing.[28]

Youth gangs demonstrated the complexities of ethnic loyalty. In the 1940s and 1950s such gangs were widespread and a source of considerable concern to public authorities. Almost invariably they were territorial. Often gangs were made up exclusively of members of a particular ethnic group, and some gang clashes had a distinct ethnic dimension. No New York gangs were more famous than the fictional Jets and Sharks of *West Side Story*, warring tribes of Italians and Puerto Ricans whose portrayal was based on actual conditions on the rapidly changing West Side of Manhattan. But gangs were not always ethnically constituted. The Enchanters, one of the most powerful East Harlem gangs of the early 1950s, with branches throughout the region, was largely Puerto Rican but had African-American and a few Italian members as well. Other East Harlem gangs also evolved from being strictly Italian or Puerto Rican to being multiethnic. "Racial and ethnic backgrounds," one official study concluded, "are not at the heart of gang strife."[29]

Intricate patterns of ethnic segregation and mixing at work and at home reinforced one another. Workers in some industries tended to reside close to their jobs in neighborhoods that mirrored the ethnic composition of the industry workforce. Italian longshoremen, who dominated the Brooklyn docks, tended to live in Redhook and other harborside Brooklyn neighborhoods, the world Arthur Miller captured in *A View from the Bridge* (1955).

Many Scandinavian maritime workers lived in nearby Sunset Park. In Manhattan, many Irish longshoremen lived in Chelsea and worked in all-Irish gangs on nearby Hudson River piers. But other longshoremen working in the area were Italian or black and did not dwell nearby.[30] Some light manufacturing companies located their plants near poor neighborhoods to take advantage of a ready pool of women eager for work. They offered short work days and flexibility about absences to meet family obligations, but paid very low wages.[31]

Sometimes workers in a particular industry lived together but distant from their jobs. Jewish needle trades workers heavily populated neighborhoods such as Crotona, Kingsbridge, and Pelham Parkway in the Bronx and Williamsburg, Brownsville, and Brighton Beach in Brooklyn, areas that had good subway connections to the garment and fur districts. Unskilled black and Puerto Rican laborers with jobs in New Jersey or Long Island City tended to settle in upper Manhattan, not because of its convenience but because they were shut out of other areas by price or discrimination. Skilled, white, blue-collar workers preferred outer borough neighborhoods or suburbs that had affordable single-family housing. In 1940 they had a higher suburbanization rate than even professionals.[32]

Such residential bunching by occupation deepened solidarities among workers and their families, contributing to class consciousness and the strength of the labor movement. Attitudes and identities formed at work spilled over into neighborhood life, and vice versa. The Brownsville Boys Club is an instructive example. The club was formed in 1940 when the Board of Education closed after-school recreation facilities to boys fourteen and over. Its founders were members of a Brownsville basketball team who organized a protest petition to the board. The leader of the group, sixteen-year-old Jacob Baroff, later remembered that "We were insulted, shocked. . . . We were angry about being shut out. We were innocent. We believed in democracy and rights."

The Brownsville Boys Club was a neighborhood group of youth who had little if any work experience, yet its existence was intimately linked to the experiences workers had as workers. As the club's historian, Gerald Sorin, wrote, "The fact that these second-generation Jewish boys were raised by immigrants who were often active in mutual-aid societies, unions, and progressive social and political organizations helps explain their emphasis on 'rights' and their proclivity for collective peer-group initiative and the organizational mode." Alfred Kazin, the son of a housepainter and a dressmaker, recalled that he grew up in Brownsville with an "instinctive belief in class struggle." It was this belief in class and class struggle, learned from working-class parents, that led Brownsville boys to see a battle for basketball courts as a struggle for rights. It prompted them to organize collectively and strive to transcend ethnic boundaries by recruiting African-Americans for their club.[33]

The complex demography of neighborhoods and occupations spurred working-class New Yorkers to both embrace and transcend ethnic, racial, and religious loyalties. In many ways, New Yorkers were a remarkably parochial lot. Take Vito Marcantonio, the seven-term congressman from East Harlem. The son of a native-born Italian-American carpenter, Marcantonio grew up in an English-speaking household in Italian East Harlem, where he lived his entire life. In one spectacular way Marcantonio violated community norms: he married a Protestant New Englander. But in every other respect he embraced conventional Italian-American life: He became fluent in Italian, wore religious medals (though he rarely went to mass), and stayed close to home, never learning to drive a car nor venturing outside the United States. He was, in his own words, "the most provincial so-and-so in the world." Yet many of Marcantonio's deepest passions dealt with national and international issues, be it ending Jim Crow, reversing United States foreign policy during the Cold War, or winning independence for Puerto Rico.[34]

Many working-class Italian neighborhoods had a palpably closed air, their residents traveling elsewhere only when absolutely necessary and exhibiting deep hostility to outsiders. The intense familialism that southern Italians brought with them gave their communities greater stability than other ethnic neighborhoods, and greater insularity. Literary critic Marianna De Marco Torgovnick described Bensonhurst, where she grew up during the 1950s, as "dedicated to believing that its values are the only values." Yet she emerged from her youth thoroughly cosmopolitan, with the covert support of a father who superficially seemed utterly parochial.[35]

World War II enlarged working-class New York's cosmopolitan strain. The political, economic, and social demands of the war undercut ethnic and racial insularity and accelerated the fight for racial justice. Although the armed services were racially segregated, they brought soldiers into contact with a far wider range of men than most had dealt with before. Men who had rarely if ever left New York found themselves sharing the most intimate experiences with men from profoundly different backgrounds, opening their eyes to the particularity of their own ideas and way of life. One Brooklyn infantryman wrote from Luxembourg to his wife that "more than half of my platoon is

from the South. Almost all of them are farmers—many of them are genuine
hillbillies, with all that implies. One thing I know is that we don't know the
U.S. New York . . . [is] out of this world."[36]

Total war broadened the vistas of even workers who did not serve in the
armed services. War industries tended to have heterogenous work forces
since they needed to rapidly recruit workers in a tight labor market. At the
Brewster Aeronautical factory in Long Island City, which built fighter planes,
the ten thousand workers—Italians and Irish with a sprinkling of Jews,
African-Americans, and German-Americans—formed friendships along ethnic lines but overcame interethnic tensions to build a powerful union, crossing ethnic boundaries when voting for leaders.[37]

The democratic ideology used to build support for the war amplified its
structural impact. The pluralist redefinition of national identity and greatness, promoted by the Popular Front and elements of the New Deal during
the 1930s, reached fruition during 1940s. Nothing better symbolized its broad
acceptance than the playing at the 1940 *Republican* national convention of
Earl Robinson's "Ballad for Americans," which defined America as the sum
of all the races, religions, nationalities, and occupations to be found within it.
A 1945 Academy Award–winning short film of Frank Sinatra singing another
Popular Front pluralist paean, "The House I Live In," carried the same message: "The people that I work with/The workers at my side . . . The right
to speak my mind out/That's America to me." The idea that the country's
strength lay in its diversity and in tolerance became official ideology, saturat-
ing political rhetoric and the mass media.[38]

Nothing better symbolized the cosmopolitan, pluralist spirit that infused
New York in the wake of World War II than the Brooklyn Dodgers, the Jackie
Robinson Dodgers. The roster of the 1949 team reads like a line from "Ballad
for Americans," with its three African-Americans, one Jew, one Hispanic,
two Poles, a Slovak, two Italians, two Scandinavians, and an Italian Hungarian. Most white Dodger fans did not root for the team because it was the first
in the major leagues to be racially integrated (though that breakthrough did
reflect New York's racial liberalism). Integration brought tension to the
stands at Ebbets Field, which were no longer homogeneously filled by
working-class white men. Yet the Dodger faithful, perhaps begrudgingly, accepted and were even proud of the team's role in breaking down racial exclu-
sion. When in 1957 the team threatened to move, one fan wrote to Mayor
Robert Wagner: "I cannot impress upon you too much how important it is to
keep the Dodgers in Brooklyn. . . . The Dodgers, being composed of

Negroes, Spanish, and Whites, are a good example of how good you can get if everyone works together regardless of race or color."[39]

New York provided extraordinary opportunities to escape parochial bounds. Its incomparable subway system, with its low fare—a nickel until 1948 and only fifteen cents as late as 1966—made the whole city in all its richness accessible to almost everyone: museums, libraries, jazz clubs, concert halls, street festivals, parks, demonstrations, debates, theater, and the city colleges, which until 1976 had no tuition. In Shirley Clarke's movie *The Cool World* (1963), a subway trip to Coney Island by a Harlem teenager who has never seen the ocean is an occasion of joyous, liberating discovery (though ending in a tired, sad trip back to a life whose confinements were clearer than ever). Generations of young New Yorkers would ride the subway to arbitrarily-picked stops, just to see what was there.[40]

The proximity of so many ethnic and racial groups made the city an arena for the creation of cultural hybrids whose innovations recast local, national, and even world culture. Active efforts at cultural crossbreeding—driven in part by ideological concerns—helped catalyze the process. Nowhere was the postwar explosion of cosmopolitan creativity more evident than in the world of music.

Cuban and African-American sounds, for example, were brought together in the 1940s at dance halls like the Palladium by such seminal figures as trumpeters Mario Bauza (who was classically trained in Cuba) and Dizzy Gillespie, laying the roots for what later developed into salsa and introducing new rhythmic structures to jazz, rhythm and blues, and later rock and roll. The audience for the new music was not just Hispanic. "The 1949 recordings of Machito's 'Asia Minor,' 'Noro Morales' '110th Street & 5th Avenue' and Tito Puente's 'Abaniquito,'" wrote Latin-music expert Max Salazar, "created a bond between . . . New York City's ethnic groups. Jewish, Italian, Greek, Irish and Afro-Americans danced side by side with Cubans and Puerto Ricans." One of the first Latin music radio shows in the city was broadcast over WEVD, which was owned by the Yiddish, socialist newspaper, the *Daily Forward*.[41]

Dion DiMucci, growing up in the working-class Italian neighborhood along Belmont Avenue in the Bronx (from which his group took its name), achieved stardom adopting a cappella and doo-wop styles from black teenagers. He wrote his hit song "The Wanderer" as an attempt to imitate the rhythm and blues songs he learned from the African-American superintendent of an apartment building near his home. Unlike some white musicians who blandly covered black hits, Dion produced a sound with what one black disc jockey called "street attitude. . . . Dion, he had a New York swagger, a New York walk, a New York way of talking, that New York style."[42]

That New York style. For all the differences among ethnic groups, something of a transethnic working-class persona could be found in post–World War II New York. The most obvious shared cultural trait of working-class New Yorkers was that they were contentious, referential, ironic talkers. Ordinary New Yorkers had something to say about everything, whether in Spanish, Yiddish, Italian, or English, and did so at such a rapid clip that outsiders often could not understand them. Ideas, insults, and commentary spewed forth in argots that deeply enriched the national language.[43]

New York talk had a wise-guy quality to it. Wherever you looked, there was a know-it-all, a smart aleck, somebody looking for an angle. This side of the New York persona could be rollickingly funny, for example in the hands of comedians Phil Silvers and Sid Caesar. But many outsiders found unattractive its city slickers' presumption that everyone else was a rube.[44]

In a shrewd essay published in 1961, Daniel Bell attributed this side of New York culture to the city's economic structure. It was the world of highly competitive, small-scale manufacturing and services, "in which survival depends upon ingenuity, 'shmearing,' cutting a corner, trimming a margin, finding some other way to make a fast buck in the swift race," argued Bell, that gave New York "its particular beat and distinctive character."[45]

For Bell it was the Jewish petite bourgeoisie, immersed in the garment and wholesale trades, that set the cultural tone of the city. Through their disproportionately large role as both producers and consumers of entertainment and culture, Jews had a huge influence on the texture of the city. Yet the fast-talking New Yorker with an explanation for everything was as likely to be an Italian baker or an Irish transit worker as a Jewish garment shop owner.

The very harshness of life in the city—"its hazards and its deficiencies," as E. B. White put it—contributed to the sharp, wisecracking, improvisational culture of its working class. Nowhere was this clearer than in the play of children, who turned obstacles into opportunities and created games like stoopball, boxball, punchball, stickball, Chinese handball, skelly, and potsie that took advantage of the peculiarities of the dense, urban environment.[46]

The fast-talking New Yorker was not simply a *handler*. Interwoven with the search for a deal was a democratic ethos, a willingness to listen to one and all. Some commentators and memoirists, like Irving Howe, saw this as specifically a Jewish trait as well. But a lack of deference toward elites, a willingness to hear out others, and a skepticism often edging into cynicism could be found among working-class New Yorkers from other backgrounds, too.[47]

While there was a certain amount of swagger in the New York working-class persona, and more than a little of what later came to be called attitude, there was a tentativeness as well, stemming from the outsider's uncertainty, the sense of marginality that many felt as a result of their status as immigrants or children of immigrants, nonwhites, nonnative English speakers, or simply workers. Brewster Aeronautical unionist Al Nash recalled "how articulate the workers were in the men's room, while it seemed so hard for so many of them to speak up and express themselves at union meetings or before a supervisor." Yet sometimes stolid workers took the lead. One former worker at a New York warehouse recalled that "the primary leader . . . was George, a huge, mean-looking but soft-spoken African-American who was painfully inarticulate. When he had to explain something from scratch, . . . he rambled all over the place telling fractured, incomprehensible stories and attempting to link them to equally incomprehensible principles." Yet George, not the official union representative, got the workers to understand the key issues in their confrontation with management.[48]

The marginality that many working-class New Yorkers felt, which often manifested itself as timidity and social awkwardness, could be converted through a kind of cultural jujitsu into coolness. This was a trait often associated with African-Americans, but at least to some extent it could be found among working-class New Yorkers of all sorts. Once, Jerry Della Femina recalled, several members of the St. Louis Cardinals baseball team made an appearance at Coney Island. "The whole neighborhood showed up, but even then we were *very* cool, we just watched. There wasn't any loose talk about this guy's trading card, or that one's autograph."[49]

Sports were enormously popular with working-class New Yorkers, especially men, but tastes ran eclectic. In New York working- and middle-class culture of the 1940s, sports, jazz, classical music, serious literature, and modernist art inhabited the same universe, all consumed by the same individuals or at least the same communities. Even if they were sometimes intimidated by the guardians of high culture, New York workers embraced the arts with enthusiasm. Opera had a legion of followers who might not be able to afford performances at the Metropolitan Opera but who listened avidly to its weekly radio broadcasts and to the Enrico Caruso records they invariably owned. Symphonic music could be heard for fifty cents at the outdoor concerts at City College's Lewisohn Stadium, a favorite summer outing.[50]

Alongside this enthusiasm for the arts lay a facet of working-class life that historians have downplayed, its brutality. New York working-class life was tough, and toughness was common and respected. Gangsters and petty criminals were a daily presence in working-class life. They could be found at work, selling jobs and protection, stealing goods, taking bets, making loans, running racketeer unions, and acting as management goons. In neighborhoods they ran numbers, made book, and dealt drugs. Most illegal activity did not require violence, but when need be, mobsters and crooks were capable of stunning brutality.

Many workers abhorred mobsters, and some fought heroically against them. But others accepted their presence and even admired them. In Brownsville, home base of "Murder Inc."—a notorious racketeering outfit—many teenagers looked up to the gangsters, hanging around pool halls and candy stores hoping to attract their attention. The seeming ability of mobsters to command their own fates led black transit worker Robert Fulton to want to be one before he eventually settled on unionism as an alternative path to mobility and power.[51]

It was not just the crooks who were tough, and who admired toughness. Consider the following obituary of one Barney Brostoff that appeared in *The Hawsepipe*, the newsletter of the Marine Workers Historical Association, a group of retired maritime workers, largely left-wingers:

> Our dear Brother Barney died April 11, 1984. Barney fought in the ring as a flyweight and was a contender. He fought the shopowners' goons as a rank and filer of the N.M.U. [National Maritime Union] and he fought the fascists in Spain as a member of the Abraham Lincoln Brigade. Barney was awarded the Distinguished Service Medal during WWII. He leaves his wife of 34 years, Marilyn and his daughter, Ivy. He was a loving Husband, devoted Father and a loyal Union Man. We will miss him.[52]

Notable are both how tough Brostoff must have been and how it was his penchant for and prowess in combat that his colleagues chose to emphasize in memorializing him. In a world where raw power was repeatedly experienced from the receiving end, those who could dish it out, who could play hard ball, held an allure. Both gangsters and working-class leftists reveled in watching boxing, with its ritualized reproduction of the brutality that was so often the stuff of their daily lives.[53]

Both *A View from the Bridge* and *On the Waterfront*, the movie by Arthur

Miller's erstwhile collaborator, Elia Kazan, captured the infiltration of the rough, corrupt ways of the waterfront into the most intimate relations of their longshoremen protagonists. Miller and Kazan had a tendency—typical of artists who came of age during the 1930s—to see heroism in physical labor. Hubert Selby Jr.'s extraordinary, sad, sprawling 1964 waterfront novel *Last Exit to Brooklyn* spurned that saving grace, painting a picture of routine brutality in the lower depths of working-class New York: neglected children, alcoholism, sexual frustration and assault, prostitution, violence, drugs, and poverty.[54]

High culture and rough culture, provincialism and cosmopolitanism, the smart aleck and the cool coexisted in working-class neighborhoods, families, and individuals. It was this rich, complex stew—the product of a particular history, occupational structure, population mix, and social geography—that made the New York working class so vibrant.

The sensibility of New York workers—savvy, opinionated, democratic—helped set the tone of the nation in the postwar years. It got broadcast by labor leaders like Transport Workers' Union president Michael J. Quill and ILGWU president David Dubinsky. It spread through comics and singers like Jackie Gleason and Frank Sinatra. It percolated up through intellectuals, writers, filmmakers, record producers, and academics who grew up in New York working-class homes and moved on to more exalted circles without completely leaving behind the worldview and manner that surrounded them as youths.[55]

Locally, the sensibility of New York workers had more direct impact. The vast New York labor movement was shaped by the complexities and contradictions of the culture of its members. Like the men and women who built it, it was a movement that was vibrant, inventive, powerful, tough, and sometimes self-defeating. Through it New York workers played a major role in shaping the politics and future of the region.

CHAPTER 3.

Labor Days

From the era of the American Revolution through the end of the twentieth century, organizations of workers—called variously benevolent societies, trade associations, brotherhoods, trade unions, and labor unions—strived to advance the interests of working men and women in a society dominated by those with greater economic and social resources. Unions and groups closely allied with them—known collectively as "organized labor" or "the labor movement"—spearheaded efforts to improve workers' wages and employment conditions. Unions helped democratize America by serving as the most important channel, other than the ballot box, for workers to influence society.[1]

No country has a more epic labor history than the United States. Places like Lowell, Homestead, Pullman, Coeur d'Alene, Ludlow, Lawrence, Gastonia, and Flint—sites of now largely-forgotten battles—testify to the ferocity of the struggle organized labor had to wage to establish itself in the face of unremitting employer resistance and harsh legal restrictions. At incandescent moments, organized labor surged forward, in the process reinventing itself, only to be thrown back by economic downturns, harsh repression, and its own mistakes.

When World War II ended, labor's most dramatic moments lay behind it, the violent clashes that left piles of bodies on history's stage. The relative routinization of post–World War II labor relations reflected organized labor's strength, not its weakness. During the 1930s, the Congress of Industrial Organizations (CIO), which split from the American Federation of Labor (AFL) in 1935, finally cracked such corporate bastions of antiunionism as General Motors and U. S. Steel, helping to spark a general expansion and invigoration of labor. By the time World War II ended, the labor movement had achieved a size, robustness, legal standing, and degree of influence previously outside its grasp. Nowhere was that more true than in New York.

To fight their postwar battles, New York workers mobilized a sprawling set of institutions that had been erected over the course of nearly a century. In 1947, New York City's labor movement, vast and complex even compared to that in union strongholds like Chicago, Pittsburgh, and Detroit, included an extraordinary 1,107 private-sector union locals, ranging from obscure groups like the Russian Bath Rubbers and the Wholesale Paint Salesmen to the 35,000-member Transport Workers Union Local 100, notorious for repeatedly threatening to shut down the city's mass transit system, and Musicians Local 802, whose 25,000 members included the New York Philharmonic Symphony and top solo artists. New York housed the national headquarters of three dozen unions, including all the major apparel unions, the United Electrical Workers (UE), the Retail, Wholesale and Department Store Union (RWDSU), several transportation and maritime unions, and organizations of entertainment, newspaper, and communications workers.[2]

Although no accurate union membership figures exist for individual American cities, in the early 1950s at least one million New York City workers paid union dues, and quite possibly more, constituting over 6 percent of all the nation's unionists and between a quarter and a third of the city workforce.[3] A roster of New York unions has a Whitmanesque quality to it, evoking the extraordinary range of productive activity and human experience in the nation's greatest city: there were four locals of Airline Dispatchers; eleven of Barbers and Beauty Culturists; eleven of Boilermakers; forty-two of Carpenters; one of Commercial Artists and three of Coopers; one each of Dental Technicians, Diamond Workers, Firemen, Foremen, and Funeral Chauffeurs; thirty-eight of Hodcarriers, Building and Common Laborers (including the House Wreckers and the Curb Setters); twenty-five of Machinists; fifty-three of Railway and Steamship Clerks; one each of Screen Publicists, Seltzer Water Workers, Sightseeing Guides, and Theater Ushers; six of Upholsterers; and one of Vending Machine Service Workers.[4]

Not all types of New York workers were equally likely to belong to a union. As the postwar strike wave made clear, transportation, communications, and some types of service workers were unusually well-organized. Unionized construction workers at least matched them in number, making up a fifth to a quarter of the local labor movement. And they in turn were outnumbered by unionized manufacturing workers.[5]

The structure of the labor movement mirrored and reinforced working-class tendencies toward both cosmopolitanism and parochialism. Virtually every type of union organization that existed in the country could be found in New York, from pure industrial unions, like the Marine and Shipbuilding Workers, who built and repaired ships at yards scattered around the port, to pure craft unions, like Ironworkers Local 40, the men who assembled steel frames for New York skyscrapers. But most New York unions fell someplace in between.

Craft unions represented workers who engaged in a particular activity—
for example, carpenters—no matter where employed. Generally their members had specialized skills, developed through a formal or informal
apprenticeship prerequisite to full union membership. In addition to bargaining with employers, craft unions helped their members get jobs. In New
York, in the late 1940s and early 1950s, union-run hiring halls were the exclusive or a main way workers found employment in the maritime, construction,
building service, hotel and restaurant, commercial printing, brewery, and retail industries. While forging membership loyalty, hiring halls provided a service to employers in industries with jobs of short duration and employment
needs in constant flux. To get a plumber or a welder or a typographer, all you
had to do was call the union hall. By training workers, supplying them to employers, and enforcing minimum levels of competency, unions helped sustain
the small-scale, flexible production so central to the New York economy.

Controlling the labor supply allowed unionists to push up wages and
preserve jobs for their kin, conationalists, or political colleagues. Until the
1947 Taft-Hartley Act made them illegal, unions used closed shop
contracts—which required employers to hire only their members—to exert
labor market control. In New York such agreements were extremely common
in the printing and construction industries and spreading elsewhere. In late
1946, for example, more than a quarter of the members of UE Local 475, a
large Brooklyn-based union that represented workers in machine shops and
metalworking factories, were covered by such contracts. After Taft-Hartley,
unions continued to run hiring halls, though in theory nonmembers now
could use them, and sign union shop agreements, which required all employees, once hired, to join a particular union. Union-run apprenticeships, such
as the six-year program of Typographers Local 6, further reinforced control
over the job market. At the major newspapers, senior Local 6 members—
"situation holders"—in effect owned their jobs, with the right to be temporarily replaced by "substitutes" when they chose not to work.

Controlling the gates to employment reinforced the craft identification
and fraternalism that kept unions of skilled workers tight-knit. Some, like the
construction electricians, largely restricted membership to sons or other
close relatives of members, ensuring them well-paying jobs and giving these
organizations unusually strong cohesion since they were literally family affairs. But labor market control also enabled unions to engage in discriminatory practices that fragmented the working class and bred ethnic, racial, and
gender resentment.[6]

Industrial unions represented all the workers in a particular industry or at a particular work site, regardless of what function they performed or how skilled they were. Generally these unions had less control over hiring than craft groups, if any at all. Confronting an employer-selected workforce pushed industrial unions toward inclusive membership policies and even social egalitarianism. Mutual dependence rather than craft identity served as their basis of solidarity. To attract members, retain their loyalty, and further bonds across employer, craft, ethnic, and racial lines, some industrial unions sponsored extensive social activities. Local 65 of the RWDSU, which represented blue- and white-collar workers in wholesale shops, had sports teams, theater parties, a photography club, educational classes, "socials," more elaborate "affairs," and a union-run nightclub that during the 1950s featured prominent blacklisted entertainers.[7]

Though labor groups sometimes presented craft and industrial unionism as opposites, most New York unions incorporated elements of both. The needle trade unions, to which about a quarter of the unionists in New York belonged, provided a model. Emerging out of much-celebrated Progressive Era struggles, these unions reached their peak membership only after World War II. Even as they grew, they remained ideologically and culturally rooted in radical immigrant subcultures. Idiosyncratic in some ways, they nonetheless exemplified much of what made New York labor distinctive.

With over half its national membership in New York, the International Ladies Garment Workers Union (ILGWU) was by far the city's largest union. At the end of World War II it had some 150,000 New York members. By the early 1950s its area membership had grown to nearly 200,000, and it remained close to 180,000 into the early 1960s. The ILGWU's huge size gave it extraordinary financial and political power. In 1950 its assets included sixteen medical clinics, a resort in the Poconos, and four radio stations (one of which, WFDR, broadcast from New York). That year, the union put on a lavish celebration of its golden jubilee that featured Vice President Alben Barkley, congressmen, ambassadors, opera stars, and a union-produced movie.[8]

The ILGWU represented virtually everyone producing women's and children's clothing, including some ancillary workers like truckers who carried goods between jobbers and contractors. However, unlike a true industrial union, the ILGWU divided its members among over two dozen locals according to their craft (for example, cutters) or the branch of the industry in which they worked (for example, corset and brassiere workers). Further complicating its structure, separate locals represented Italian-American cloak-makers and dressmakers. (Jews dominated many non-Italian locals, some of which conducted business in Yiddish.)[9] The Hatters, Cap and Millinery Workers (with 22,000 New York members), the Fur and Leather Workers (14,000 New York members), and the Amalgamated Clothing Workers (75,000 New York members) had similar setups.[10]

To coordinate bargaining and other activities, apparel locals belonged to "joint boards." These were the centers of union power. The ILGWU Joint Board of Cloak, Suit, Skirt, and Reefer Makers' Unions, for example, bargained for 40,000 workers in eight locals, enforced contracts, organized non-union shops, administered member benefits, and supervised the work of business agents appointed by its constituent units.[11]

Many New York unions used variants of this structure. The Painters, Decorators and Paperhangers, for instance, had locals defined variously by craft, location, type of work, and nationality, with a District Council bargaining for ten Manhattan and Bronx affiliates. The Hotel Trades Council, a permanent group with its own staff, bargained and administered a master industry contract that covered 35,000 members of seven different unions. Joint boards, district councils, and similar forms of organization suited well the many New York industries that had a large number of small employers, a great variety of skills and skill levels, enclaves of craft tradition, and ethnically diverse workers. They allowed even small groups of workers to bargain through entities that dwarfed most employers in size and which could afford large, sophisticated staffs with specialized skills in areas such as research, education, and political action.[12]

In part to counter the power unions gained through agglomeration, employers joined associations of their own. In New York, only a small minority of contract negotiations involved a single union and a single employer. One study found that at least three-quarters of New Yorkers employed under union contracts were covered by an agreement with either an employers' association or an informal employers' group. By contrast, nationally only about a quarter of unionized manufacturing workers and a third of other union members were covered by contracts negotiated with employers' associations.[13]

Joint boards and district councils, even as they promoted the professionalization of labor relations, industrial solidarity, and economies of scale, allowed the continued existence of ethnic and craft collectivities with distinctive values, traditions, internal politics, and relationships to the community.

This was not, however, a pluralist idyll. Locals based on nationality, for example, created myriad possibilities for discrimination, particularly the reservation of superior jobs for members of a particular group. The 1945 New York State Anti-Discrimination Act (the Quinn-Ives law) in theory made it illegal for unions to exclude members on the basis of race or national origin.[14] Nonetheless, two years after its passage, unions reporting nationality or foreign-language locals included the Actors and Artistes of America, Meatcutters, Typographers, ILGWU, and Furriers.[15]

The durability of nationality locals testified to the continued salience of ethnicity in working-class New York and the reluctance of union leaders to disrupt important power bases. ILGWU Local 89, for example, the Italian Dressmakers, in the early 1950s had nearly 30,000 members, five branch offices, and a weekly radio show. Its longtime general secretary, Luigi Antonini, used it as a foundation from which to wield power in the Italian-American community, local electoral politics, and even Italy itself, organizing a series of Italian-American labor coalitions that were extremely active before World War II in the anti-fascist struggle and after the war in blocking the formation of any Italian government that included Communists.[16]

The problems associated with nationality locals became particularly severe when the makeup of the workforce shifted, as happened in New York during the two decades after World War II. By then, the once sharp tensions between Jews and Italians in the needle trades had become largely a thing of the past as a result of decades of shared experience, mutual acculturation, and union propaganda. But as Puerto Ricans and African-Americans began entering the industry in large numbers, interethnic tensions again became common amid charges of union discrimination against the newcomers. Similar problems developed in unions without nationality locals, but the existence of such units legitimized the primacy of ethnicity and bred resentment among incoming groups not granted their own locals.

The ILGWU was particularly egregious in its refusal to recognize the changing ethnic makeup of its membership. By 1952, 13 percent of the union's New York membership was Puerto Rican and 10 percent African-American; by 1962, 24 percent was "Spanish" and 16 percent African-American. But the leadership acted as if the union were still the Jewish-Italian organization it had been decades earlier. Jews and Italians dominated the union hierarchy and the best-paying jobs, while the union loaned or gave millions of dollars to favored Jewish and Italian causes. ILGWU officials refused requests to set up Spanish-language locals, failed to translate membership material, and, when under pressure to add Spanish-speaking organizers, exhibited their visceral distrust of Puerto Ricans by hiring Sephardic Jews.[17]

Craft units within or parallel to broader union structures also bred parochialism. In many unions, one or more craft locals opted out of joint bargaining arrangements believing that they could cut better deals on their own. In the mass transit industry, a series of craft and occupational groups sprung up in the 1950s, some seeking to displace TWU Local 100 as the bargaining agent for their members. The form that dissatisfaction with the TWU took reflected the way the union's own structure—dozens of "sections" corresponding to particular crafts, job titles, and work sites—reinforced craft identities and parochial concerns.[18]

Joint boards and district councils provided little opportunity for workers from different crafts or ethnic groups to interact with one another. Typically these delegate bodies, with officials selected by and responsible to either a coterie of leaders of affiliated locals or the international officers above them, distanced rank-and-file workers from both members of other locals and top union leaders.[19] They contributed, too, to the paucity of female leaders exercising real power.

The New York labor movement had an unusually high percentage of female members, reflecting the nature of the city's economy. Women formed a majority of the membership of the Amalgamated Clothing Workers (ACW) and the ILGWU and a substantial proportion of unionists in some other types of manufacturing (like electrical equipment production), hotels and restaurants, retail trade (more heavily-unionized in New York than elsewhere), communications, and government service. Yet in spite of this strong representation, very few women unionists achieved prominence.[20] The many obstacles they faced included greater domestic responsibilities than men, less confidence about taking part in public activities, and open hostility from male compatriots.[21] Since, by rule or custom, advancement in unions was generally a gradual, step-by-step affair, the interrupted work careers that women typically had put them at a disadvantage. Nationally, for example, between 1956 and 1958 the ILGWU, with a membership the latter year of 442,000, enrolled 185,000 members while losing 187,000. This high turnover, one expert wrote, largely reflected "women, who leave the shop because of marriage or pregnancy, often to return when their children are older." In part for this reason, the ILGWU middle and upper-level leadership was overwhelmingly male. Every added hierarchal level made it more difficult for women to achieve policy-making positions. During the postwar years, Local 6 of the Hotel and Restaurant Employees, which was one-third female, generally had only two women on its executive board of about fifteen members, while the joint board to which it was attached generally had only one woman out of thirty to fifty members.[22]

By joining together diverse groups of workers, the hybrid craft-industrial structure, that played so large a role in the New York labor movement, facilitated the massive displays of worker power evident in the postwar years. However, having the prime arenas of union activity defined by craft, product, or nationality simultaneously tended to limit workers' horizons and leave the direction of the union movement in the hands of a self-perpetuating leadership. A structure that gave workers strength harbored within a potential for weakness.

New York unionists took seriously the injunction—central to the union gospel but often honored in the breach—to organize the unorganized. For some, this reflected a commitment to unionism as a social crusade, an end in itself or a step on the road toward broad societal transformation. For others, it stemmed from a desire to preserve or extend organizational and personal power.

Organizing blue-collar workers generally entailed less hardship and a greater likelihood of success during the quarter-century following World War II than later on. Many workers associated unionism with a better life, while often employers seemed resigned to its inevitability. Organizing sometimes involved little more than distributing literature and membership applications outside a work site, making a few home visits, and winning a government-run election.[23]

Unions leveraged strength in one field to organize others. Starting in the mid-1920s, for instance, electricians in International Brotherhood of Electrical Workers (IBEW) Local 3 refused to use or install electrical equipment unless it had been made by members of the local. This proved to be a highly effective means of unionizing electrical equipment shops, though it pushed up the cost of local electrical work and bred considerable resentment among IBEW locals in the rest of the country.[24]

Some unions had to constantly organize simply to maintain their existing bargaining power, as the small scale, low capital requirements, and razor-thin margins typical of New York industry brought high business turnover. Nonunion apparel shops, for example, kept popping up even in the heart of the garment district, and unionized jobbers tried to avoid union wages by shipping goods out-of-town to non-union contractors. In May 1949, ILGWU organizer William Lurye, a forty-year old presser on leave from his shop, was killed in the lobby of a midtown building housing several struck nonunion firms. Lurye's murder was apparently the work of mobsters with ties to nonunion manufacturers, garment trucking firms, and some shady AFL locals. By keeping the garment district under continual surveillance, launching periodic organizing drives, hiring strongarm men (from the Seafarer's International Union), holding mass demonstrations, and calling selective strikes, the ILGWU contained nonunion production but never eliminated it.[25]

Organizing white-collar workers proved more difficult than signing up blue-collar workers. Many labor leaders spurned office workers, dismissing them as lacking bargaining power or as insufficiently proletarian. But they were key to labor movement growth. Postal, railway, and retail clerks—mostly men—long had been unionized, in part because they worked in proximity to blue-collar unionists. A significant number of entertainment and communications workers belonged to unions, too. But otherwise white-collar workers were almost entirely unorganized; nationally, in 1946 union contracts covered fewer than 20 percent of clerical, retail and wholesale, and professional workers, compared to over 80 percent of railroad, construction, and trucking workers, and 69 percent of manufacturing employees. This differential became critically important as rapid postwar growth of service, office, and professional activities led white-collar workers to outnumber those engaged in manual labor by 1956.[26]

A few New York unions did make concerted efforts to organize white-collar workers. They generally had the most success at companies where unions already represented the blue-collar workforce. The ILGWU and the ACW organized garment industry office and sales employees, while UE won the right to represent a thousand Sperry Gyroscope clerical and technical employees in Brooklyn and Long Island. The American Newspaper Guild bargained for newspaper reporters, sales, and clerical employees, and the CIO's United Office and Professional Workers of America (UOPWA) and its AFL rival, the Office Employees International Union (OEIU), represented clerical workers at a variety of manufacturers and food companies.[27]

For white-collar unionization to become solidly established, though, labor needed to organize "paperwork 'factories'," establishments where white-collar work was the core function, not ancillary to blue-collar activity. The most aggressive efforts to do that were launched by the left-wing UOPWA. In

New York, where it was headquartered, the UOPWA organized credit clearinghouses, direct mail firms, and book publishers. It also made strides among workers at nonprofit social service agencies. Its most important targets, however, were the insurance and finance industries.[28]

UOPWA had surprising success among insurance firms. A wartime organizing drive resulted in contracts with a dozen regional companies and three national giants, Prudential, John Hancock, and Metropolitan Life. These agreements generally covered only insurance agents. But Prudential alone had 14,500 agents, 1,850 of whom were in New York City, while Metropolitan Life had over 2,000 in the New York area.[29]

Finance proved to be a harder nut to crack. A pre–World War II UOPWA drive went nowhere. A second effort during the war, when inflation eroded already-low white-collar salaries, yielded modest gains at Republic National Bank, Bankers Trust Company, and New York title companies.[30] Soon after the war, UOPWA made inroads at several other banks. According to one historian, by early 1947 about 10 percent of the financial employees in the city belonged to the union.[31]

With a union breakthrough threatening, employers stiffened their resistance. For the UOPWA, the key test came in mid-1947. The union had been focusing on the Brooklyn Trust Company, one of the nation's largest banks. However, as soon as Congress passed the Taft-Hartley Act, which placed new restrictions on unions, the bank fired three activists, transferred others, and threatened mass dismissals. In response, the union went on strike, apparently the first walkout ever at a major United States bank.[32]

From the start, the strike was a rough affair. Perhaps because the president of Brooklyn Trust was a former Police Commissioner, the police seemed to go out of their way to aid the bank, using clubs to break up a large picket line and repeatedly arresting picketers. The union fought hard, too, picketing the homes of nonstrikers and mobilizing hundreds of demonstrators from other unions. In one incident, the police arrested two members of the National Maritime Union for assaulting a bank teller on his way to work.

The union claimed that 200 of the bank's 750 workers were on strike, but the bank said only eighty employees walked out. Able to maintain most of its operations, the bank refused to negotiate with the union and spurned State Labor Board efforts at mediation, saying that it would only deal with the union if it was a government-certified bargaining agent, knowing that the UOPWA would not seek a recognition election because, like many labor groups, it refused to comply with a Taft-Hartley provision that required

union officials to take a non-Communist oath in order to use the services of
the National Labor Relations Board. As the strike dragged on, the number of
picketers dwindled. Unprotected by federal labor law and unable to mobilize
a majority of the bank's employees, the union could not find a way to pressure
it into a settlement. Finally, after a month, the strikers voted to return to work
without having even discussed their demands with the bank. UOPWA continued to represent workers at other banks and kept up its organizing efforts,
but the Brooklyn Trust debacle marked the beginning of its decline.

As UOPWA's fortunes began to fade, momentum passed to the United
Financial Employees (UFE). Organized in 1942 as an independent union of
Wall Street workers, the UFE signed a contract with the New York Stock Exchange (NYSE) a year later. In 1946 it affiliated with OEIU as Local 205, and
within a year had contracts covering employees of the NYSE, the Cotton Exchange, the Curb Exchange (predecessor of the American Stock Exchange),
A. M. Kidder & Co., and bond clerks at twenty brokerage firms.[33]

Less than a year after the UOPWA lost its Brooklyn Trust strike, the
UFE tested its strength in a dramatic Wall Street showdown. The immediate
issue was its desire to add a union shop clause to its contracts with the three
exchanges. Perhaps more important, it hoped that a show of force would en-
ergize its stalled organizing campaign at the brokerages.[34] As long as the UFE
remained weak and largely restricted to the exchanges, the brokerage houses
that ran the trading centers tolerated it. But when the union began trying to
organize the brokerages themselves, forbearance ended. The issue was ideological as well as financial. According to sociologist Joseph Fitzpatrick, the
brokers had "the tendency to picture their own advance as a result of their
own initiative and ability, and they look[ed] upon . . . union activity as the
refuge of the careless and lazy who try to get by pressure what they have failed
to get by work or brains."[35]

After working for nearly a month without a contract, on March 29, 1948
over a thousand employees from the Stock and Curb Exchanges—mostly
men—walked off their jobs. The UFE drew support from the AFL and
Catholic social activists. More importantly, the Sailor's Union of the Pacific
and the Seafarer's International Union strongly backed the stock exchange
workers. The Seafarer's offices, located near Wall Street, served as the
strike's headquarters, a reminder of the historic links between New York's
maritime trade and its financial industry.[36]

At the strike's outset, five hundred sailors joined the financial workers on
picket lines outside the struck exchanges. The second morning all hell broke

loose. In an effort to keep the NYSE from opening, pickets from the UFE and the seamen's unions blockaded its entrance by lying down on the sidewalk. The police responded by charging the pickets with, the *New York Times* reported, "a flurry of club swinging, so furious that at least one policeman broke his nightstick." Within ten minutes twelve people had been injured and forty-five arrested. It was a morning of incongruous sights: a woman in a fur coat lying on the sidewalk, daring the police to attack her; burly, white-capped sailors battling policemen before an audience of hundreds; police wagons inching their way forward through crowds of financial workers trying to get to work. The next day, newspapers at home and abroad prominently displayed photographs of the "Battle of Wall Street."[37]

At first the UFE maintained the loyalty of the majority of workers at both exchanges, repeatedly throwing up picket lines of a thousand people or more. However the exchanges, having prepared carefully for the strike, sustained near normal business using supervisory and brokerage house personnel. After thirteen days, as strikers at the Curb Exchange drifted back to work, the union signed a contract there providing for a 10 percent pay increase but no union shop. The UFE held out for two more weeks at the NYSE, but management did not budge. Ultimately the union accepted essentially the same contract terms offered before the walkout. Hundreds of NYSE workers dropped out of the union.[38]

Although not quite the disaster that the Brooklyn Trust strike had been, the Wall Street strike was a major setback. By taking a hard, antiunion line, using managerial personnel to maintain operations, and mobilizing police support, the financial industry effectively checked postwar unionization efforts. In the short run this had slight impact on labor's power, but in the long run it proved terribly important, stymieing expansion of the union movement's white-collar beachhead and ensuring that one of the city's most important and fastest-growing industries would remain largely nonunion.

The size of the New York labor movement, the militancy it displayed during the postwar strike wave, and its extensive political activities forced a broad range of local institutions to recognize it as a major social actor. This reinforced a local predilection for business and government to join together with labor to resolve disputes and promote social harmony. This corporatist approach prevailed both within particular industries and, to a limited degree, across them.

At the end of World War II, New York already had a long history of labor-management cooperation, going back most famously to the Protocols of Peace proposed by Louis Brandeis to end the 1910 cloakmakers strike. The garment industry abandoned this elaborate system of industrial governance within six years, but the emphasis it placed on collaboration, order, and productivity, and its positioning of industrial relations as a public rather than private matter, helped shape the views of a generation of trade unionists, businessmen, and politicians.[39]

After the collapse of the Protocols, the garment industry adopted a system of grievance arbitration that forbid strikes and lockouts during the life of a contract and gave ultimate power to resolve disputes to an impartial chairman. Widely copied, by the late 1940s the New York metropolitan area had more than thirty permanent industry arbitrators or impartial chairmen with jurisdiction over fifty branches of industry, 22,000 employers, and 397,000 workers.[40] Some industries had substantial labor-management structures. In the electrical contracting industry, for example, labor-management cooperation under the New Deal's National Industrial Recovery Act led to the formation of a Joint Conference Board to resolve disputes. Joint employment and pension bodies followed. In 1943 these were all folded into a Joint Industry Board which, financed by a 1 percent assessment on wages, ran a hiring hall, supervised apprenticeship training, and administered contracts, pensions, and vacations.[41]

Business-labor interaction across industry lines occurred on a more ad hoc basis. The organizational fragmentation of New York business made the construction of permanent corporatist structures difficult. Labor had effective peak organizations in the AFL Central Trades and Labor Council and CIO Central Labor Council. By contrast, the major groups joining businesses together across industrial lines, like the Commerce and Industry Association and the Chamber of Commerce, tended, as Alice Cook and Lois Gray noted, "to be dominated . . . by national corporations with New York headquarters and by the city's largest financial houses" which had "national rather than local orientation." These associations took stands on labor issues, for example supporting the Taft-Hartley Act, but given the diversity of their membership, which included union and nonunion firms, and the national orientation of their leadership, they kept aloof from local industrial relations.[42]

It usually took the initiative of the city government to bring labor and business leaders together to resolve conflicts outside of their own industries.

New York mayors had a history of injecting themselves into labor-management contests to maintain order, end economic disruption, and curry favor with various constituencies. As soon as he took office in January 1946, William O'Dwyer found himself swamped by the strike wave, then at its height. In October, recognizing that "stop-gap emergency measures . . . would not suffice," he established a Division of Labor Relations. It intervened in disputes by first pressuring the parties to negotiate, coordinating its efforts with state and federal agencies. If that failed, O'Dwyer typically appointed a tripartite committee, consisting of a "public" member (often a judge or retired judge) and labor and business representatives to attempt to settle the dispute.

In its first three years, the Division of Labor Relations intervened in over 150 disputes.[43] Perhaps its most impressive achievement was brokering a "stabilization agreement" between nearly three dozen unions and the Building Trades Employers' Association in response to a slump in construction growing out of a fear of inflation and unpredictable labor costs. The pact they adopted after months of negotiations keyed wages to the cost of living, pre-dating by several months the better known adoption of a cost-of-living-adjustment by General Motors and the United Automobile Workers (UAW).[44]

The city brought labor and capital together for other purposes as well. In 1947, for example, in reestablishing a Department of Commerce to encourage local economic development, O'Dwyer included in its structure both "Business Executive" and "Labor" advisory committees. When three years later the mayor appointed a committee to study "the cause of decline in water-borne commerce," he chose a tripartite group consisting of government officials, labor officials, and representatives of affected businesses.[45]

Some advisory groups merely served as window dressing. Nelson Rockefeller resigned as provisional chairman of one business advisory group (that also had labor members) because O'Dwyer proved so lax in following up on its recommendations.[46] Nonetheless, at least on the level of symbol and etiquette, by the late 1940s New York political leaders accepted labor as a leading institutional force, deserving consultation on a broad range of matters, and useful in maintaining social harmony.

Not only government recognized labor. By giving nearly six million dollars to various charities and social service agencies between 1943 and 1946, "CIO stature in New York and the relationship between labor and the community was immeasurably enhanced," as one unionist put it. NYC CIO

Council secretary Saul Mills noted in late 1945 that "No major community health or welfare agency serving our city is without CIO representation."[47]

By the late 1940s, organized labor had solidly established its presence in the City of New York. Though not always welcomed into the inner circles of power, it generally had at least a seat at the table when its interests were at stake. What labor would do with the impressive measure of power, or at least potential power, it had achieved was not at all clear. That was a question of politics and ideology, matters about which New York workers were by no means in complete accord.

CHAPTER 4.

The Rise of a
Social Democratic Polity

During the years after World War II, New York's working-class neighborhoods, its loft districts, even its City Hall, crackled with the political energy of a mobilized working class. Building on the foundations of wartime antifascism, the New York labor movement led the city toward a social democratic polity unique in the country in its ambition and achievements. New York became a laboratory for a social urbanism committed to an expansive welfare state, racial equality, and popular access to culture and education. Ultimately, most Americans—including many working-class New Yorkers—rejected this vision, preferring suburban-style, single-family home living, racially exclusive neighborhoods, and low taxes. But in its exceptionality, working-class New York blazed an alternative path of postwar social development, nurturing cultural and political leaders who transmitted some of its values to the country at large.

A passion for politics and public issues permeated working-class New York. Most workers did not actively engage in politics, but a large minority did, arguing issues, attending meetings, working in election campaigns, and participating in periodic mass mobilizations. Broadcaster Larry King recalled that in the Brooklyn of his youth even children were devoted newspaper readers, preferring the tabloids but sampling all the papers, including the Communist *Daily Worker*.[1]

Mass political engagement of a degree almost unimaginable later on could be witnessed at Madison Square Garden. The arena—which could hold over twenty thousand people—served as a major sports venue in the 1940s, just as it did later, but it also hosted numerous political rallies, many sponsored or cosponsored by the labor movement. Garden events in 1945 included a CIO-backed rally demanding that the United States break diplomatic relations with fascist Spain, a "World Unity Rally," also backed by the CIO, a "Negro Freedom Rally," a celebration of the 26th anniversary of the Communist party, and a rally to kick off Jonah J. Goldstein's Liberal-Republican-Fusion mayoralty campaign. The next year the Garden housed a rally supporting the Fair Employment Practices Committee, another calling for "Big Three Unity for Colonial Freedom," a meeting protesting racial violence, another to back striking maritime workers, two Communist party rallies, and a rally cosponsored by the CIO for gubernatorial and Senate candidates it endorsed.[2]

The roster of Garden rallies testifies to a remarkable aspect of postwar New York—its large, vibrant political left. The forty thousand people who came out on May 1, 1946, to watch the first May Day parade since before Pearl Harbor, saw many of its elements on display. The two largest contingents came from the Communist party (CP) and the International Workers Order (IWO), a Communist-led fraternal group. Union delegations included two thousand sailors from the National Maritime Union (NMU), large groups from the Furriers and Local 65 of the Retail, Wholesale, and Department Store Union (RWDSU), and smaller contingents from the Office Workers, Shoe Workers, Furniture Workers, Painters, Bakers, Jewelry Workers, and United Electrical Workers (UE). Unofficial contingents included some two thousand dressmakers and cloakmakers.

It took the marchers—newspaper estimates of their number ranged from 18,000 to 100,000—four hours to enter Union Square. There they heard speeches by Communist leader William Z. Foster and three members of the New York City Council. Though small stuff by European standards, the parade was an impressive display by American ones.[3]

The wartime struggle against fascism gave the left unprecedented legitimacy. Working-class New Yorkers had made huge sacrifices. Transport Workers Union (TWU) Local 100 suffered seventy-six deaths among its 5,380 member-servicemen. IBEW Local 3 had 3,081 members in the armed services, thirty-eight of whom were killed. Under the banner of antifascism, a resolve that such human expenditure not be in vain animated leftists and liberals.[4]

Electoral politics provided a measure of left-wing strength. In the 1945 city council elections the top vote-getter in the city was TWU president Michael J. Quill, a candidate in the Bronx of the left-liberal American Labor Party (ALP). Quill received the first-choice vote of nearly one out of five Bronx voters in the complex proportional representation system New York used to choose its legislative body. Even more remarkable, Communists Peter Cacchione in Brooklyn and Ben Davis in Manhattan got elected with the second and fourth highest vote totals, together garnering 122,625 first-choice votes. Eugene Connolly, another ALPer, and Ira Palestin and Louis Goldberg, from the anticommunist Liberal party, which like the ALP had strong union backing, also served on the twenty-three person city council.[5]

Proportional representation facilitated minor party success, but even in winner-take-all elections the left made some strong showings. Congressman Vito Marcantonio had a voting record so left-wing that conservatives used it as the yardstick by which to judge other members of Congress.[6] In 1946 leftist RWDSU Local 65 organizer Kenneth Sherbell won election to the state assembly, and the next year Leo Isaacson, running on the ALP line, bested a New Deal Democrat in a Bronx special congressional election.[7]

These electoral feats both overstate and understate left strength. On the one hand, by running only a few candidates leftists could concentrate their resources on key races. If any left group had run a full slate of candidates, most would have suffered devastating defeats. On the other hand, since the mid-1930s the Communist-led left generally had not seen electing its own candidates as its main mode of exerting power. Rather, it followed one variant or another of the Popular Front policy of seeking coalitions with liberal and centrist forces and influencing policy by mobilizing pressure on established leaders.

The ALP served as a key vehicle for the Popular Front. The statewide party had been founded in 1936 by the garment unions to funnel votes to Roosevelt. Although on paper it barred Communists, over the years their influence within it grew. During World War II an anticommunist bloc, led by David Dubinsky of the ILGWU and Alex Rose of the Hatters, broke away from the ALP to form the Liberal Party, after losing a bitter primary fight.

In 1945, the ALP nominated Brooklyn Democrat William O'Dwyer for mayor before the Democrats themselves picked him, thereby helping to shape the ticket of the larger party. Because the election was a three-man race, O'Dwyer would have been elected even without the quarter of a million votes he received on the ALP line, but only with them did he achieve a majority. Once in office O'Dwyer gave the ALP (including the Communists within it) patronage appointments and, as an observer in *Commentary* put it, "could hardly have done more for the unions' cause had he been a labor or socialist mayor on the European model."[8]

Between electoral efforts, a dense web of institutions engaged leftists. Many left-wing newspapers came out in the city, including at least five dailies: the *Daily Worker*, the *Forward*, *Morgen Freiheit*, the *China Daily News* (*Meizhou Huaqiao Ribao*), and *PM*, an innovative paper founded in 1940 to give voice to the left-wing of the New Deal coalition.[9] Left-wing magazines were even more numerous. The city had left-wing schools, like the socialist Rand School (which had thirteen thousand students in 1946) and the communist Jefferson School (with five thousand students at its peak in 1947-48); left-wing arts and music groups; and even nightclubs with ties to the left, like Café Society.[10]

Some left-wing groups operated citywide, but many were neighborhood-based. The Liberal, American Labor, and Communist parties and the IWO all had neighborhood clubs or branches. In addition, scores of local, left-led consumer, tenant, and neighborhood associations could be found scattered around the city, like the Ocean Front Tenants League, founded in Brighton Beach in 1945, which claimed to have seventeen hundred members.

Women dominated neighborhood-based groups, unlike unions and political parties, which men generally led. In part this reflected the emphasis of these groups on consumption issues, particularly housing and food costs, the domain of women in working-class homes. Also, housewives could participate in neighborhood activities while juggling child care and household work, obstacles to traveling further afield. By their nature localistic, neighborhood groups occasionally banded together in citywide or even nationwide movements. New York consumer organizations, for instance, played a major role in several postwar meat boycotts designed to drive down prices. In 1951, Brooklyn housewives, led by Clara Lemlich Shavelson (who as a twenty-three-year-old had helped spark the famed 1909 shirtwaist-makers' strike), forced meat wholesalers to lower prices.[11]

The left so pervaded some neighborhoods that residents could engage in a broad range of social as well as political activities without straying beyond its realm. And when the neighborhood got to be too much, the left could offer at least temporary escape, to resorts and summer camps run by the IWO, the Socialists, and unions such as the ILGWU, Furriers, and UE. In a few areas, like Brownsville, the Communists had such influence that the life of a defector could be made truly miserable.[12]

In addition to its institutional network, the Popular Front left benefited from some extraordinary mass leaders. Benjamin Davis, Jr., for example, never shone quite as brightly as his onetime mentor and ally Adam Clayton Powell, Jr., but for a time he came close. An African-American, the son of a prominent Atlanta businessman and Republican official, Davis attended Amherst College and Harvard Law School before returning home to practice law. Drawn to the Communist Party in the course of defending black Communist Angelo Herndon, charged with insurrection for organizing unemployed workers, Davis was forced by death threats to flee Georgia. Settling in New York, he edited the *Harlem Liberator* and wrote for the *Daily Worker*, the *Amsterdam News*, and Powell's *People's Voice* while leading a series of anti-discrimination drives. In 1942, Davis helped Powell—the first African-American city council member—win a seat in Congress. In return, the following year Powell backed Davis's successful council bid (as did a host of musical luminaries including Billie Holliday, Teddy Wilson, Coleman Hawkins, and Ella Fitzgerald). An able speaker and writer, blessed with good looks, immense courage, and a Southern charm that appealed to the many ex-Southerners living in the city, Davis attracted a Harlem following perhaps dwarfed only by those of Powell and Davis's good friend Paul Robeson.[13]

Davis's fellow Communist councilman, Peter Cacchione, came from a more humble background. The son of Italian immigrants, he grew up in a small Pennsylvania town. For years he worked as a trainman and metal-worker. During the Depression he roamed the country, ending up in New York. Attracted to the Left through the Communist-led Unemployed Councils, Cacchione soon emerged as the head of the Brooklyn CP. Elected to the city council in 1941, he pressed such issues as maintaining New York's low transit fare and ending racial discrimination in housing and major league baseball. His combination of radical politics, attention to local issues, and down-to-earth manner won him reelection in 1943 and 1945, each time with a greater number of votes.[14]

Mike Quill, in holding both major union and electoral posts, continued a once-common practice that had become unusual by the mid-1940s. Born on a farm in western Ireland, into a home steeped in Irish nationalism, Quill enrolled in the Irish Republican Army as soon as he was old enough. After moving to New York in 1926, he took a job as a subway change maker. During the mid-1930s he joined a melange of Communists, Irish republicans, and militant workers in organizing the TWU. Quill's razor-sharp wit, ridicule of authority, and infectious high spirits made him a favorite among leftists, unionists, and Irish immigrants alike. Probably briefly a member of the CP, once he became president of the TWU, Quill avoided too close identification with the party. Nonetheless, he declared that he "would rather be called a Red by the rats than a rat by the reds."[15]

And then there was Vito Marcantonio, arguably the greatest popular tribune the New York left ever produced. Entering politics as a protégé of Fiorello La Guardia, Marcantonio inherited La Guardia's East Harlem political machine once the Little Flower moved to City Hall. Elected to Congress in 1934, Marcantonio repeatedly won reelection until 1950. While other New Deal–era radicals captured congressional seats, none had anywhere near his longevity.

Marcantonio's extraordinary career was in some ways a tribute to his ability, determination, and character. In private a reserved man, Marc, as everyone called him, in public became an electrifying figure, a masterful speaker in English or Italian and a competent one in Spanish (important in a district that over time grew more heavily Puerto Rican). Fiercely dedicated to his job, Marc familiarized himself with every detail of what went on in his district. Much of his success rested on his constituent service operation and personal intervention in the lives of East Harlemites, somewhat in the manner of a village patron, helping them get veterans benefits or medical services or legal assistance or even settling family disputes. Marc's integrity, modest lifestyle, and loyalty to community social norms won him the support of thousands of voters who did not share his leftism.

But if Marcantonio's success constituted a personal triumph, it also represented a collective achievement. Although Marcantonio himself was not a Communist, the Communist Party made his reelection a top priority, assigning cadres from throughout the city to work on his campaigns. The ALP and left-wing unions and fraternal groups pitched in with money and volunteers. Marcantonio especially benefited from ties to the United Public Workers (UPW), whose members, employed in the city's Department of Welfare, he could call on to assist his constituents. Concentrating resources on Marcantonio undermined other left-wing projects, including the growth of the ALP as a whole, but it helped sustain a national voice for the labor movement, the Popular Front, civil rights, and Puerto Rican independence without equivalence in mid-century America.[16]

For all the institutional density of the Popular Front-Left, and its leaders' abilities, it was the labor movement that made it a significant force in New York life. Without their labor base, the Communists would have been marginal figures, somewhat like the Trotskyists, whom C. Wright Mills acidly described as "bureaucrats without a bureaucracy."[17] At the end of World War II, in the New York–area CIO the Communists and their allies dominated the leadership of the UE, TWU, NMU, Furriers, American Communications Association, UOPWA, UPW, Shoe Workers, and Furniture Workers, and controlled Local 65 and most of the department store locals of the RWDSU. In the AFL they led locals of bakers, building service workers, and jewelry workers, the painters union district council, and Local 6 of the Hotel and Restaurant Employees (which had well over twenty thousand members). Also, some leaders of the unaffiliated International Association of Machinists worked with the Communists.[18]

In addition to individual unions, the Communist Party and its allies controlled the CIO Greater New York Industrial Union Council, which served three important, interrelated functions. First, it fostered interunion support and solidarity. Second, it acted as the political arm of the local CIO (although it could not truly speak for the whole CIO because many noncommunist and anticommunist unions refused to affiliate with it). And third, it represented labor before government bodies and in civil society. Though nominally led by its president—until late 1947, Joe Curran from the NMU—day-to-day responsibility for the council fell into the hands of its secretary-treasurer, Saul Mills, a former newspaper reporter, and the rest of its eleven-person paid staff.

In spite of sometimes chaotic methods, the council made itself a significant force in local politics. It organized mass demonstrations, sponsored voter registration drives, endorsed candidates, threw resources behind them, and sent lobbying delegations to Albany and Washington. The scale of the council's efforts could be staggering: it routinely issued leaflets in very large press runs—up to two million copies—and on election day in 1944 helped field 22,500 people in a joint CIO-ALP effort for the Roosevelt ticket.[19]

From 1940 through 1948 the council followed the political line of the CP, with only minor deviations. For the party, the council served as a channel of influence on local government and politics, allowing it to promote its positions and its people in the name of mainstream labor. Adherence to the CP line caused only occasional flareups between the council and the national CIO, because during the immediate postwar years their domestic programs did not differ greatly.[20]

Postwar CIO policy used as its jumping off point FDR's 1944 call for an economic bill of rights. The CIO interpreted this to require, above all else, maintaining price and rent controls so that postwar wage gains would not be eroded by inflation. Beyond that the CIO called for a massive housing construction program (the Wagner-Ellender-Taft Bill); national health insurance (the Wagner-Murray-Dingell Bill); national standards for public education and teachers salaries and federal grants to eliminate rural-urban and black-white inequities; improvements in the G.I. Bill; aggressive federal action against racial discrimination including an antilynching law, abolition of the poll tax, a permanent fair employment practices committee, and the ousting from Congress of members who incited racial violence; an increased minimum wage extended to uncovered low-income groups; price guarantees for farmers; antitrust action; aid to small business; and a shift of the federal tax burden from low to high earners. The CIO promoted this program on both moral and economic grounds, juxtaposing large corporate profits to declining real worker income and contending that without full employment, rising income, and tax redistribution to elevate national purchasing power, the country again would be plunged into a depression.[21]

The Greater New York Industrial Council tried to find concrete ways to press forward the CIO program. In 1945, for example, it sponsored a conference on postwar housing and community planning that featured Senator Robert Wagner, Eleanor Roosevelt, and Adam Clayton Powell, Jr. The council devoted a great deal of energy to fighting increases in consumer costs, pressing for the retention and enforcement of price and rent control laws (at one point debating but rejecting a proposal from RWDSU Local 65 for a four-hour general strike in support of price controls). The council also supported consumer boycotts aimed at checking price hikes. One UE local even bought eggs directly from Long Island farmers and resold them to members "to show that prices can be considerably lower than they are today." "Our food bills," it argued, "are not a solely economic but also a political matter." The council strongly opposed increases in the city sales tax and the subway fare, which directly impacted the working-class standard of living, and pressed for the use of state government surpluses to aid the deficit-ridden city government.[22]

The CIO Council involved itself in social services, relief, and charity, too. In 1943 the CIO organized its own United Way-type charity, the CIO War Chest, in order, as Amalgamated Clothing Worker leader Jacob Potofsky recalled, "to coordinate the giving by the CIO, and to get credit for it." "Before the advent of the War Chest," Potofsky noted, "credit for contributions from labor was given to employers." "By contributing to the various institutions," he continued, "CIO members will not have to consider themselves charity cases if the need arises for hospitalization or any personal service." To further help its members, the CIO Council worked with the Greater New York Fund to establish a Workers Personal Service Bureau as a bridge between unionists and welfare agencies, and itself ran a Veterans Service Bureau.[23]

The CIO Council leadership saw as its province all aspects of society

that affected workers, including politics, the economy, race relations, and social welfare. The AFL Central Trades and Labor Council differed dramatically. While leaders of the CIO Council conversed in the language of social
democracy, leaders of the rival AFL group remained rooted in an older tradition of "pure and simple unionism," that stressed immediate, job-related concerns of particular groups of workers.

Part of the difference was generational. Most CIO leaders—with the major exception of those from the Clothing Workers—were still young when
World War II ended. Quill, Curran, and Mills, for example, had not yet
reached forty. By contrast, the AFL council was a gerontocracy. Its secretary,
James C. Quinn, came out of the hatters union but had been a full-time council employee since the late 1920s. Martin T. Lacey, secretary-treasurer of
Teamsters Local 816 and council president from 1945 until his death twelve
years later, made Quinn look like a neophyte, having been a paid union official since 1903.[24]

The formal political positions the AFL council took to a surprisingly degree resembled those of its CIO counterpart. The AFL group backed the
Wagner-Murray-Dingell Social Security bill (as did the national AFL); supported Henry Wallace's confirmation as secretary of commerce; backed the
push for a permanent fair employment practices committee; and supported
President Truman's 1946 housing, minimum wage, and full employment proposals. Locally the council supported the Quinn-Ives antidiscrimination law
and generally opposed increases in transit fares, controlled rents, or the city
sales tax. In short, the council backed the same combination of Keynesian-
ism, expanded welfare measures, and an end to racial discrimination in employment that formed the heart of CIO left-liberalism.[25] However, in sharp
contrast to the CIO Council, the AFL group was vehemently anticommunist.
It did not share the CIO's internationalism, particularly its militant pro-UN
stance (it rarely addressed foreign policy issues at all),[26] and refused to work
with liberal groups like the Union for Democratic Action that allowed pro-
communist organizations to affiliate with them.[27]

In electoral politics, the AFL generally stayed out of primary fights and
then endorsed the Democratic ticket. Unlike the CIO, it rarely sponsored
mass mobilizations, demonstrations, or large-scale voter registration drives.
Some AFL unions operated politically outside the council framework. The
building trades unions, for example, had their own nonpartisan committee.
The ILGWU by itself could mobilize two thousand campaign workers.[28]

More than formal political position, however, style, priorities, and sense of purpose distinguished the two labor councils, especially the AFL's comparative parochialism and seeming remove from major social developments. Compared to the CIO, for example, the AFL council spent very little time on strike support. Reading its minutes from 1946, one would not realize that the greatest strike wave in the country's history was in progress. AFL unions actually conducted most of New York's largest postwar strikes, but the council seemed to see these as discrete, routine events, not part of a larger social conflict requiring broad mobilization or strategic solidarity. Similarly, economic reconversion, price controls, unemployment fears, international relations, and the other great postwar issues that the CIO Council extensively discussed rarely got mentioned at meetings of the AFL body. And while some AFL affiliates tried to organize just the types of workers the postwar labor movement often has been accused of ignoring—white-collar, sales, and service workers—the council itself played little role in these efforts.[29]

Rather than politics broadly construed, strike support, or organizing, the council concentrated on promoting the narrow interests of particular affiliates. This fell squarely in the AFL tradition. For most of its history, the AFL gave much higher priority to championing the minority of the workforce its affiliates represented—disproportionately male, white, and skilled—than the interests of the working class as a whole.

The AFL council paid particular attention to preserving unionized jobs. Often this involved serving as an advocate with the state apparatus. Usually depicted as more voluntarist than the CIO, the AFL was actually more entangled with the state than the younger labor federation, repeatedly intervening over the myriad rules, permits, and franchises that affected unionized workers, from the size of oil trucks allowed in the city to a proposed ban on electrical and neon signs advertising liquor (opposed on behalf of the electrical workers, sheetmetal workers, and signwriters) to a bill allowing milk and cream to be bottled in one gallon containers, which would have eliminated some teamsters' jobs.

Concern with job preservation led the AFL to deal with broad social issues from a remarkably parochial point of view. Its strong support for public works (including public housing) reflected as much its desire to keep construction workers employed as a commitment to expanded government services. The council (like the national AFL) opposed the St. Lawrence Seaway, which it feared would take away jobs from longshoremen and teamsters, and spent almost as much effort mobilizing against it as it did against Taft-Hartley. More extreme and more comical was AFL opposition to permanent voter registration on the grounds that it would reduce the amount of work for unionized printers! The council utilized its political connections to maintain a city government practice of hiring only unionized firms to do its printing, while the local branch of the AFL Union Label and Services Trade Department launched campaigns promoting patronage at unionized establishments and the purchase of union-made goods.[30]

In spite of the political differences between and within the citywide labor councils, union activists agreed about enough to significantly affect the politics of the city and region. During the 1940s, a kind of "New York exceptionalism" was cemented, a local polity that during coming decades came to symbolize the best or worst of urban liberalism, depending on one's point of view. National and international events to a great extent determined living and working conditions. But at least in some regards, working-class New Yorkers controlled their own fate.

Take the number one CIO priority, the control of living costs. While the battle to maintain price controls was fought and ultimately lost in Washington, the special case of rent controls played out differently. Imposed during the war in some areas, including New York, by the federal government as part of its anti-inflation program, after the war Washington gradually eased and then eliminated rent regulation. However, it allowed individual states to take over the control system, an option that New York, under immense popular pressure, took up. (In 1947, one organization alone, the Bronx Emergency Council to Save Rent Control, claimed forty-five thousand members in thirty-three neighborhood branches.) In 1950 the New York state government regulated 96 percent of the rental units and nearly 80 percent of housing of any kind in New York City. In the years that followed, while the rest of the state and those parts of the country that had not already done so shed rent controls—meant to be a temporary measure until postwar construction could ease a national housing shortage—in New York City they became, as Emanuel Tobier and Barbara Gordon Espejo put it, "a permanent part of the political landscape, ardently supported by a large and vocal constituency." Unions made up a significant part of that constituency, lobbying the board that controlled rents, winning representation on it, and, in the case of the CIO, establishing a "rent clinic" to provide advice for its members. A half-century after World War II ended, rent control remained ensconced in New York City, infuriating landlords and free market ideologues while tenaciously defended by tenant groups, some of which traced their roots to the 1940s left.[31]

Similarly, laborites, liberals, and leftists fought long, hard, and in the main successfully to maintain low transit fares. For nearly a half century after 1904, when the New York subway opened, popular pressure kept the fare on subways, trolleys, and most buses at five cents. In 1940 the city took over the operation of almost the entire rapid transit system and many bus and trolley lines, changing the political calculus of the fare. What had been primarily a matter of government regulation and antimonopoly populism became a municipal budget and tax issue. Faced with growing transit deficits, necessitating increased subsidies and higher taxes, Mayor O'Dwyer raised the fare to ten cents on the subway and seven cents on city buses and trolleys in 1948 after a long, complex struggle. The difficulty he had in doing so reinforced the belief of many conservatives and large property owners (interested in keeping down tax rates) that the transit tariff had to be removed from the political arena. They partially accomplished this in 1953 with the creation of the semiautonomous New York City Transit Authority, charged with running the transit system using passenger revenue alone, and authorized to raise the fare to do so. Still, the political climate was such that until 1970 fare hikes were modest and infrequent. This helped sustain an exceptional pattern of mass-transit use; in 1989 the New York subway carried one out of every nine mass-transit riders in the country.[32]

The case of transit illustrates the commitment of New York liberalism to using the state to both hold down living costs and provide extensive services. In housing, too, pressing the state to provide services as well as hold down costs was a key political goal; New York was not only the national center of rent control, it also was the national center of public housing. When World War II ended, the city was accommodating over fifty-eight thousand people in fourteen projects run by its housing authority. During the next five years the authority built twenty-one more projects. During the decade after that it added another 75,403 units.[33]

New York's unrivaled municipal college system provides another example of the unusual extent of its services. In 1945 the city's Board of Higher Education was running four tuition-free colleges. Over the next fifteen years, aided by collections from the federal government for students covered by the G.I. Bill, the system expanded to include four two-year colleges and two divisions of four-year schools that were soon to become independent colleges. Together the colleges enrolled 93,000 students, 36,000 full-time.[34]

The postwar years saw an expansion of other municipal services as well. In 1949 the city floated a $150 million bond issue to upgrade its public health facilities. The city broadcasting system grew from one radio station to three radio and two television stations (including those run by the Board of Education).[35]

New York even had a quasi-public arts center that brought high culture to working-class audiences. When in 1942 the city found itself in possession of a massive Shriners Temple on 55th Street as a result of a tax default, Mayor La Guardia decided to establish a nonprofit City Center for Music and Drama "to meet the demand for cultural entertainment at reasonable prices." Labor representatives played a major role in launching the new enterprise, attending planning meetings, serving as incorporators, and sitting on its board. The Clothing, Garment, and Musicians unions each lent the Center $5,000 and Workmen's Circle (a Jewish workers fraternal group) $2,500, a significant slice of the initial working capital. Almost immediately City Center began offering top quality, low-cost symphony, theater, opera, and ballet performances (in the latter two cases by its own companies) to "shirtsleeved audiences" that included many unionists, in a familial atmosphere far different from the stiff formality of traditional high-art venues.

In its early days, City Center's New York City Opera Company embodied the political spirit of the working-class that made its existence possible. With a top price of two dollars (compared to $6.05 for an orchestra seat at the Metropolitan Opera), it made a virtue of its financial constraints by hiring young American singers who had not yet achieved international reputations. "The prevailing audience attitude," one opera historian noted, "was one of encouragement for innovation." The September 1945 debut of baritone Todd Duncan presented for the first time an African-American in a leading role at a major American opera company. By contrast, the Met did not desegregate for another decade. Though over time the City Opera audience became increasingly middle-class, the company retained its innovative spirit and kept ticket prices at roughly a third those at the Met.[36]

Individually, few of the services New York City provided were unique. Other cities built housing and operated transit systems, colleges, hospitals, and even radio stations. But no city offered services of the scale and range of those in New York. In 1950 New York had twenty-two municipal hospitals; no other city had more than three.[37]

Organized labor played a critical role in creating the homegrown version of social democracy that made life in New York unlike anyplace else in the United States. Working-class pressure by no means alone accounted for the rise of this left-liberal polity, which had more in common with postwar European norms than with politics in contemporaneous United States cities. But with literally millions of New Yorkers living in a household with a union member in it, labor had potential clout at the polling place, in neighborhoods, and in the streets which, even when only partially mobilized, constituted an unrivaled force for progressive change in the city.

As labor groups and their allies fought to expand public services, they struggled to ensure that public resources and economic opportunities would be open to all, regardless of race or religion. Elements of the labor movement (though by no means all of it) allied with black groups and civil rights organizations in a persistent fight against discrimination. This, too, distinguished working-class New York from national norms.

The mid-1940s were an optimistic time for those hoping to change the country's long history of racial injustice. The war mobilization, the democratic rhetoric that surrounded it, and the growing African-American electorate in key northern states made racial discrimination a national political issue for the first time since Reconstruction. In most places, however, the immediate postwar period proved to be a false spring of racial liberalism, especially in the South, where the defense of white supremacy soon hardened. In New York, by contrast, antiracist efforts continued unabated. Remarkable were both the breadth of support for this struggle and the large role organized labor played in it.[38]

The 1945 Quinn-Ives Law exemplified New York's exceptionality. As World War II drew to a close, and the effort to make permanent the weak, wartime federal Fair Employment Practices Committee (FEPC) faltered, the New York state legislature passed the Quinn-Ives Bill, the first law in the United States to explicitly prohibit discrimination in private employment on the basis of race, creed, color, or national origins. Quinn-Ives did not pass without opposition; the Chamber of Commerce, Board of Trade, New York State Bar Association, three railroad brotherhoods, some real estate and manufacturing concerns, and multi-hatted public builder Robert Moses all came out against it. But more notable was the extent of backing for the bill, which passed with bipartisan support by overwhelming majorities. Active backers included the New York Federation of Churches, the YMCA, the Urban League, the American Jewish Congress, the National Negro Congress, the American Labor and Liberal parties, and the CIO. Even the state and city

AFL endorsed the bill, despite its ban on discrimination by unions, which was the kind of state interference in the affairs of organized labor that the federation in the past had vehemently opposed.[39]

The broad support for antidiscriminatory legislation in part reflected the sense of many New Yorkers besides African-Americans—most notably Jews—that they were being denied equal rights. Between July 1943 and December 1944, the most common complaint to the FEPC from New Yorkers was not racial discrimination (the cause of less than a fifth the complaints), but religious discrimination (over two-fifths the complaints), usually accusations of anti-Semitism. Reformers often joined the two issues; Mike Quill's literature for his 1943 city council race, for instance, called for "A City United Against Religious and Racial Discrimination."[40]

Quinn-Ives formed part of a broad postwar assault on segregation and racial inequality. In Brooklyn, for example, branches of the YWCA and YMCA, various church groups and hospitals, and, of course, the Dodgers desegregated. In the latter case, possible prosecution under Quinn-Ives, a growing population of potential black fans, an ongoing campaign by leftists and black activists demanding the integration of baseball, the desire to tap a new talent pool, and an inclination by Dodger general manager Branch Rickey to act fairly all came into play. The 1940s and early 1950s also saw a growing if still modest number of African-American officeholders. By the mid-1950s, New York City had an African-American congressman, city councilman, borough president, state senator, and five state assemblymen.[41]

New York unions regularly contributed to the Urban League, NAACP, and other civil rights groups; protested acts of racial violence in the region and the South; and futilely called for federal anti-poll tax, antilynching, and FEPC legislation.[42] Occasionally they supported racial quotas to ensure African-American representation within the labor movement and in the public sector. The bylaws of Local 6 of the Hotel Workers, for example, required that one black and one female officer be appointed if none was elected as a general officer of the union or to its board of vice presidents, while the NYC CIO Council called on Mayor O'Dwyer to appoint a "representative of Negro people" to a vacancy on the Board of Education.[43] But if nominal labor support for racial justice was widespread, action in its pursuit tended to be most vigorous among black unionists and those within the communist orbit.

From the 1920s on, African-American unionists formed a whole series of New York–based organizations to fight job discrimination and promote the unionization of blacks. Immediately after World War II—perhaps because of a perception that race issues had won a place on the mainstream liberal agenda—many of these groups became inactive.[44] In April 1949, however, class-wide black labor activism revived when a group of four hundred unionists—most but not all black, and many with ties to the CP—formed the Harlem Trade Union Council (later renamed the Greater New York Negro Labor Council). Led by Ewart Guinier of the United Public Workers, the council backed Local 968 of the International Longshoremen's Association, an almost entirely African-American Brooklyn unit, in its long battle for a fair share of waterfront jobs; publicized employment discrimination in the hotel, building, and printing trades; joined the fight against the whites-only policy at Metropolitan Life Insurance's giant housing project, Stuyvesant Town; campaigned for a hospital in Bedford-Stuyvesant (an African-American section of Brooklyn); and protested cases of racial violence. Along with a similar group in Chicago, it helped create what became its parent body, the National Negro Labor Council.[45] To try to counter these moves, anticommunist black socialist Frank Crosswaith—an ILGWU organizer—revived the Harlem Labor Committee, which he had founded in 1935.[46]

Among unions with a majority of white members, those that had or once had ties to the Communist Party tended to be the most active in pursuing racial justice. In a few industries—including retail pharmacies, hotels, and small machine and electrical shops—their efforts brought employment and promotion gains for nonwhites.[47] UE Local 475, for example, campaigned to get black and Puerto Rican workers into higher paid and more skilled jobs. Active in the National Negro Labor Council, the local, like UE nationally, promoted the council's model fair employment practices contract clause. In 1952 it got this language into forty-seven of its contracts. The union also set up its own Fair Employment Practices Committee. Like many left-wing unions, Local 475 sponsored Negro History Week activities (on one occasion a speech by W. E. B. DuBois) and membership meetings to discuss black, Puerto Rican, and women's rights. Another UE local, 1227, which like 475 had a mostly white membership, elected an African-American as its president in 1946.[48]

Even on the left, unions with large African-American memberships, like the National Maritime Union, tended to be the most attentive to the problems of black workers. However, some overwhelmingly white groups, like the Retail Drug Employees Union, Local 1199, had remarkable records of antiracist struggle. As part of a late 1930s organizing campaign, 1199 pressured Harlem drugstores into hiring black pharmacists and upgrading other African-

American employees. In 1947 it committed itself to opening up drugstores in the "entire city to negro employment in all capacities." While some unions used their hiring halls to block black employment, 1199 used its to promote it. When it suspected that an African-American sent out from the hall failed to get hired because of race, the union would "ask other members in the hiring hall to waive their seniority in order to send out another Negro member for the same job." Slowly, African-Americans workers—including pharmacists—began being hired by drugstores outside black neighborhoods.[49]

The high priority left-wing unions like UE, 1199, RWDSU Local 65, and the United Public Workers gave to what they called "the Negro Question" paralleled the policy of the Communist Party, which during the early 1950s made the struggle against "white chauvinism" a litmus test of loyalty (as well as a weapon in internal factionalism). However, even after unions like 1199 and 65 drifted away from the Communist Party, their commitment to racial justice stayed intense. In the case of 1199, its early grappling with racism helped prepare it for the extraordinary organizing drive it embarked on in the late 1950s that transformed it from a small, heavily-Jewish, largely-male New York drugstore union into a large, heavily nonwhite, largely female national health and hospital workers union. African-American and left-wing trade unionists helped sustain the citywide and national civil rights struggles during the 1950s, when support for them was thin, and they were to be an important source of leadership for the movement when it blossomed in the 1960s.[50]

In a variety of ways, then, labor—and particularly the left wing of the labor movement—helped set the optimistic, democratic tenor of postwar New York politics. The ramifications of the style of liberalism that labor helped sustain were concrete and far-reaching. For millions of New Yorkers, labor politics meant greater access to jobs, housing, health care, education, and culture.

The continued success of New York labor politics, however, was by no means assured as the 1940s drew to a close. The deepening Cold War, a national political shift to the right, an aggressive management campaign against unions, and a rising tide of anticommunism changed the terrain on which labor operated. Longstanding tensions within the labor movement soon exploded, with profound, long-range effects.

CHAPTER 5.

The Cold War in New York

For nearly a half century after World War II, an intense struggle against Communism structured the politics and culture of the United States. At its height, from the late 1940s through the early 1960s, the anticommunist campaign pervaded virtually every aspect of American life. Inquisitions, purges, patriotic displays, harassment, fear, religiosity, and righteousness gave these prosperous years a dark fervor.[1]

Nowhere was the battling over Communism more intense than in New York City. In much of the country, political radicals acted as gadflies or visionaries; in New York, the Communist left, through its presence in the labor movement, electoral politics, and the cultural apparatus, wielded considerable power. Its strength inspired fear and resentment among conservatives and liberals. Their counterattacks helped make New York an epicenter of anticommunism.

Nominally, the fight over communism concerned ideology, foreign policy, and national politics. But religious and racial conflict added fuel to the fire. Local struggles for jobs, political influence, and cultural hegemony gave the contest much of its ferocity.

The outcome of Gotham's Cold War had practical meaning for working-class New York: it determined who led its institutions, what policies they pursued, and what cultural and moral values they promoted. Into the late 1940s, the Communist-led left seemed on the ascendancy. In the years that followed, conservatives and liberals partially destroyed it. But leftists proved remarkably resilient, continuing to impart to working-class New York much of its particularity, even after their apparent rout.

World War II caused many working-class New Yorkers to feel under siege. The social disruption of the war mobilization, the population movements it set off, and the pluralist rhetoric used to justify the war threatened the insularity of their neighborhoods and their hold on occupational enclaves. Also, the massive influx of women into the workforce challenged the fixity of gender roles.

A dispute involving a junior high school history teacher named May Quinn dramatized the wartime cultural anxiety and social discord that set the

stage for Cold War battling. In January 1943, with New York awash in antifas-
cist sentiment, fourteen of Quinn's fellow teachers complained to their principal that she had engaged in "unbecoming" conduct by displaying
"intolerance and un-Americanism," disparaging Jews and Italians and telling
students that Hitler had done some good for Germany. The principal took no
action, but, determined to clear her name, Quinn filed a libel suit against her
accusers. In June 1945 a Brooklyn jury ruled against her. School Superintendent John E. Wade then suspended Quinn without pay, announcing that she
would face a Board of Education trial on charges of incompetence, prejudi-
cial conduct, and neglect of duty.

This obscure case soon became a citywide controversy. The Holy Name
Society of a Catholic Church near Quinn's Brooklyn school proclaimed that
the charges against the Catholic teacher had "their origin in a subversive or
Communistic group now operating in this part of our city." The Kings
County Board of the Ancient Order of Hibernians endorsed "Quinn's loyal
Americanism." From the other side, the Communist-led Teachers Union
charged that the *Tablet*, the conservative weekly newspaper of the Brooklyn
Catholic archdiocese, and "seditious forces throughout the country" had
made Quinn "a national test-case in the fight *for* or *against anti-Semitism*."

At her Board of Education trial, Quinn emerged as a parochial woman,
with conservative ideas and not uncommon prejudices, but school authorities failed to demonstrate gross classroom transgressions.[2] In late February
1946 the board reinstated her, fining her two months pay. The decision infuriated liberal, left, and Jewish groups, who became determined to drive her
from the schools. Parents picketed her school; civic and labor groups pa-
raded outside City Hall; and over a dozen organizations, including the
Teachers Union and its liberal, anticommunist rival, the Teachers Guild,
asked the state commissioner of education to review the case.[3]

In June, the commissioner of education upheld the Board of Education.
Quinn disappeared from the news until December 1949, when the superintendent of schools rebuked her for saying in class that "Negroes were happy
before they knew about racial discrimination," and "I would not go where I
was not wanted," but cleared her of any intent "to offend the Negro people or
to justify discrimination." Leftist and Jewish groups protested this "second
whitewash" of Quinn to no avail.[4]

The intensity of the Quinn controversy reflected conflicts that thread
through the history of Cold War New York. One pitted the two largest religious groups in the city—Jews and Catholics—against one another. As the

public-school teaching force became increasingly Jewish, many Catholics resented what they saw as their loss of power. Conversely, many Jews resented what they saw as undue Catholic influence on the schools. The heavily Jewish Teachers Union expressed dismay at calls for a system of affirmative action to keep up the proportion of Catholic teachers.[5]

Another conflict involved social values. One charge against Quinn was that she told a student "that woman's place was in the home and that she was against their taking defense jobs or joining the WACS." Quinn and many of her supporters felt discomfort with a world of working women (though Quinn, who was single, worked most of her life) and enforced contact with Jews, the foreign-born, and blacks. What had the United States been fighting for in World War II, the left-liberal, secular, pluralist Americanism embraced by Quinn's critics, or the openly religious, conservative Americanism of Quinn and her backers? Both sides sought to use the power of the state to enforce their claims.[6]

The social fault lines exposed in the school battle also rent the labor movement. Once World War II ended, the rhetoric of antifascism and Soviet-American cooperation no longer restrained anticommunism. In April 1946, the Hotel and Restaurant Employees (AFL) amended its constitution to bar Communist Party members or sympathizers from holding local offices and launched an investigation of communist influence in its New York affiliates.[7] Four months later, dissidents in the United Electrical Workers (UE) met in Pittsburgh to found UE Members for Democratic Action, dedicated to ousting Communists and their allies from control of the CIO's third largest affiliate.[8] Also in April 1946, National Maritime Union (NMU) president Joseph Curran, who had worked closely with the Communists, broke ranks, joining an odd alliance of ex-communists, Trotskyists, and anticommunists to battle the NMU officers who remained allied with the CP. By the spring of 1948, NMU members had voted every Communist official out of office.[9]

Labor's civil war unfolded in a rapidly changing political context. The November 1946 elections gave the Republicans control of both houses of Congress for the first time in sixteen years. In New York State, a significant number of Irish voters defected from the Democrats, tacitly encouraged by the Catholic Church as a way of protesting Democratic ties to the American Labor Party (ALP) and the CIO's Political Action Committee (CIO-PAC). As Soviet-American relations deteriorated, national politics kept moving to the right.

Under these circumstances, New York Democratic leaders, in alliance with the Republicans, launched a multifaceted campaign against the ALP. The two major parties refused to run joint slates with the ALP, transferred its partisans in city government away from their bases, and instituted changes in voting procedures to weaken the clout of minority blocs. The 1947 state Wilson-Pakula Law forbid a candidate from one party from entering the primary of another without permission of that party's county leadership. This targeted Vito Marcantonio's practice of entering (and usually winning) both the Democratic and Republican primaries. A Democratic-led drive against the proportional representation system, used since 1937 to elect the New York City Council, complemented Wilson-Pakula. Hammering away at the presence of two Communists on the council, the Democrats won support for district elections from the press, most Republicans, conservative veterans groups, and significant elements of the Catholic Church. The CIO defended proportional representation, while the AFL Central Trades Council supported repeal. The two-to-one defeat of proportional representation in a November 1947 referendum laid the basis for a half-century of near total Democratic control of the city council.[10]

Labor temporarily united to fight the Taft-Hartley Bill. Passed by Congress in June 1947, this omnibus revision of the 1935 National Labor Relations Act fulfilled the long-held desire by business leaders and Congressional conservatives to alter the balance of industrial power in the direction of employers. It forbid unions from organizing foremen, allowed skilled workers to opt out of industrial bargaining units, permitted employers to petition for elections to decertify unions, allowed unions to be sued for breach of contract, restricted union political contributions, empowered the president to get court orders suspending strikes that threatened national security, and enumerated a series of unfair practices by unions, including secondary boycotts. Particularly important for New York were restrictions on union security. Taft-Hartley outlawed closed shops, threatening the job control and hiring halls integral to many New York unions. In addition, it gave states the option of outlawing union shops, which a number of Southern states quickly took up, creating a two-tier system of labor law and an incentive for companies to move from the Northeast and Midwest to the South. Finally, Taft-Hartley required that in order to utilize the National Labor Relations Board (NLRB), unions had to file affidavits from their officers affirming that they did not belong to the Communist Party nor believe in the overthrow of the government by force or illegal means.[11]

In New York, both the CIO and AFL went all-out to pressure President

Truman to veto the Taft-Hartley Bill. On June 4, twenty-five thousand people packed an AFL-sponsored anti-Taft-Hartley meeting at Madison Square Garden, as thousands more gathered outside. Six days later came another Garden rally, sponsored by the CIO.[12] Mayor William O'Dwyer spoke at both rallies, declared June 4 "Veto Day," and denounced the labor bill in a national radio address sponsored by the AFL.[13]

Labor's consensus on Taft-Hartley proved short-lived. Truman vetoed the bill, but Congress overrode him, convincing most labor leaders of the need to cleave more closely to the Democrats in the hope that gains by them in 1948 would lead to repeal of the act. Liberals and leftists toying with the notion of a third-party presidential effort to check the Democratic drift toward the center and the increasingly anti-Soviet tenor of U.S. foreign policy found themselves isolated. Most non-CP unions, after initial defiance, submitted the noncommunist affidavits that Taft-Hartley required, while unions allied with the CP held out.[14]

As the government upped its pressure on the left, union battles over Communism grew more frequent. In the AFL Painters' Union, Louis Weinstock, a prominent Communist who had long led the union's New York district council, found himself unseated by a relative unknown, Martin Rarback, who, under the banner of anticommunism, pieced together a coalition that enabled him to just barely achieve victory.[15] In the CIO, the turning point in the treatment of Communists came with former Vice President Henry Wallace's decision, in late 1947, to launch a third-party presidential effort. At CIO president Philip Murray's urging, the October 1947 CIO convention voted to operate politically within the major parties. Nevertheless, the CP threw its resources behind Wallace. In response, Murray moved against the CIO's pro-communist minority.[16] In March 1948 the New York state CIO executive board replaced the ALP as its political representative with a newly formed political action committee. Soon thereafter, the national CIO authorized the committee to represent the CIO in the city as well.[17]

At the same time, the federal government intensified the pressure on left unions. In September 1947, government agents showed up at the headquarters of Local 6 of the Hotel and Restaurant Employees to arrest its president, Michael J. Obermeier, on charges of falsely denying Communist Party membership on his citizenship application. That same month, they rearrested John Santo, national director of organization of the TWU, on an old charge of staying in the country on an expired visa. The government next picked up Ferdinand Smith, secretary of the NMU, and Irving Potash, manager of the

Furriers New York Joint Council. All four eventually left the country as a result of deportation proceedings. Other, less well-known New York unionists were deported, too.[18]

In June 1948, the House Education and Labor Committee began investigating "communist infiltration" of New York unions. It used public hearings to build a case that Communist union control led to violence, industrial chaos, suppression of members rights, and contributions to pet Communist causes without membership approval. Committee members asked subpoenaed union officials if they were members of the Communist Party, leading most to take the Fifth Amendment. By portraying left-wing unionists as illegitimate and placing them in a position in which they appeared less than forthright, the congressional probe added to the sense of siege enveloping the Communist wing of New York labor.[19]

In union after union, anticommunist groups went on the offensive. In the Newspaper Guild, Popular Front and anticommunist blocs had long jousted, but the battling intensified after national union president Milton Murray testified before a Congressional committee in March 1947 that Communists dominated the New York Guild. In the next round of New York elections, anticommunists captured the top officer posts, though the CP and its allies retained control of the executive board. After months of intense warfare, in July 1948 eight leading "progressives" on the board, worn down by being "the whipping boy for all the failures and shortcomings of the administration," resigned. The CP denounced this "abdication," which gave control of the New York Guild to anticommunists for the first time in its history.[20]

The CP-left suffered a particularly grievous loss in the defection of TWU president Mike Quill. As the Cold War deepened, Quill became reluctant to gamble his political survival and that of his union on loyalty to a Communist leadership that he viewed as out of touch with political realities. Like Curran, he decided to switch sides before it became too late. His way was smoothed by a deal he made with the mayor, in which he supported a hike in the transit fare in return for a substantial pay boost for his members. With the majority of top TWU officials spurning Quill's path, a fight broke out for control of the union. Quill played the anticommunist card for all it was worth, easily carrying the day among the heavily Irish Catholic New York transit workers, who always had been somewhat uncomfortable with the leftism of their leaders.[21]

Simultaneous with the battle in the TWU, factionalism escalated in the UE, the most important national union allied with the CP. During 1947 the anticommunist opposition made significant gains in District 4 (New York–

New Jersey), capturing key offices in a number of locals. Adding to the pressure on the UE left, in September 1947 the War and Navy Departments barred UE members from holding certain jobs in factories making secret war material, including Sylvania and Sperry Gyroscope plants in Queens.[22]

In February 1948, Remington Rand announced that it would deal with UE only if it was certified by the NLRB (national UE refused to comply with Taft-Hartley). Almost immediately, a large bloc of members of Local 1237, which represented typewriter and business machine repairmen employed by Remington Rand and other New York companies, announced that they were leaving UE. Two small UE locals soon followed suit.[23]

In March 1948, the United Automobile Workers (UAW) executive board secretly authorized raids against UE. Targeted groups included Brooklyn-based Local 475. Four units of the local, which together represented over four thousand workers, quickly voted to bolt to the UAW. A second wave of defections included the eighteen-hundred-person unit at American Machine and Foundry Company. In less than a year, Local 475—the largest in UE—lost nearly half its membership.[24]

In other unions, too, Taft-Hartley compliance became a wedge. In August 1948 the Retail, Wholesale, and Department Store Union (RWDSU) international executive board ordered all locals to comply with the law. In September, when it began suspending local officers defying its decree, eight left-wing New York locals, including 1199 (drugstore workers), 65 (wholesale and warehouse workers), and several department store units, with a combined membership of thirty to forty thousand, disaffiliated, the first major defection from the CIO by unionists opposed to its anticommunist drift. That same month, the United Office and Professional Workers (UOPWA) local representing white-collar movie industry workers voted to affiliate with the AFL in an NLRB election in which the CIO union could not participate due to its Taft-Hartley stand.[25]

Until the 1948 presidential election, the pro-Soviet left defended itself against anticommunist attacks with a reasonable degree of optimism and a still strong institutional base. Henry Wallace's poor showing shattered both. Nationally, the former vice president received fewer than 1.2 million votes, 2.4 percent of the total cast, a meager result even by third-party standards. Truman's campaign turn toward the left and narrow, come-from-behind victory seemed to vindicate the wisdom of the CIO majority, while Wallace's frail backing exposed the CP-left as a marginal force in American politics.

New Yorkers, however, proved out of step with the rest of the nation, displaying the exceptionality of their political culture. Statewide, Wallace received more than a half million votes, over 8 percent of the total cast and nearly half of his entire national return. In the city, he did even better, winning over 13 percent of the vote, a figure consistent with ALP standard-bearers in prior postwar elections.[26]

Just weeks after the election, the CIO executive board revoked the charter of the Greater New York CIO Council for "slavish adherence" to the "line and dictates of the Communist Party."[27] The CIO convention that followed made it clear that unless the CP-led unions endorsed CIO policy, they would not long be tolerated.[28]

Outside the labor movement, too, the 1948 election, along with events abroad, especially the Communist coup in Czechoslovakia and the Berlin blockade, further upped the level of anticommunism. In New York, the Catholic Church, especially Francis Cardinal Spellman, played a leading role in turning it, briefly, into a mass movement. Two seemingly unrelated events raised Spellman's long-standing anticommunism to an even higher pitch. First came the arrest of Hungarian Cardinal Joszef Mindszenty, a symbol of Catholic resistance to Communism. In response, Catholics throughout the United States mobilized spiritually and politically. On February 6, 1949, designated by Spellman as a day of prayer for the Hungarian prelate, three thousand Fordham University students recited the rosary on his behalf, while four thousand Catholic Boy Scouts marched down Fifth Avenue to St. Patrick's Cathedral. Inside, Spellman called on government leaders to fight "Satan-inspired Communist crimes." Two weeks later, fifty-two thousand people marched in Jamaica, Queens, to protest Mindszenty's imprisonment, according to one police official the greatest public demonstration in the history of the borough. Later in the year, Spellman addressed twenty thousand Catholics at an Ebbets Field Mindszenty rally.[29]

The second event, a strike of nearly three hundred workers at Catholic cemeteries, linked Spellman's anticommunism to the CIO's anti-CP drive. First unionized in 1946, the cemetery men, when their contract expired at the end of 1948, sought a reduction of their forty-eight-hour week to forty hours without loss of income and time-and-a-half pay on Saturdays. The diocese rejected their demands, and on January 13, 1949, the men stuck.

Spellman never had been an enthusiastic supporter of unions but, a master politician, he maintained good relations with a number of labor leaders.

When it came to his own employees, though, he drew a firm line. The cemetery strike provided an opportunity for a show of strength.

Church negotiators first proposed submitting the dispute to a board of moral theologians, treating it as an internal church matter. They then accused the strike leaders of being Communists. The charge deeply wounded the union officers who, like most of the strikers, were anticommunist Catholics. But their local was affiliated with the Food, Tobacco, Agricultural and Allied Workers, a communist-led union that had come under attack at the recent CIO convention.

Amazingly, the strikers held firm in the face of Spellman's red-baiting and personal appeal to them at a meeting he convened. His use of contacts in the CIO and FBI to pressure the men likewise failed. Finally, in March, the cardinal ordered students at St. Joseph's Seminary to work as strikebreakers, personally leading them through picket lines into Calvary Cemetery in Queens, where over a thousand bodies lay unburied. Spellman's use of conscripted seminarians as scabs created considerable dismay among Catholic liberals and laborites, but it did the trick. The striking local repudiated its parent organization and, at Spellman's insistence, affiliated with the AFL Building Service Employees. Only then did the Church negotiate, quickly settling the strike with a wage increase and mediation of the hours issue.[30]

Spellman contributed mightily to the success of 1949 Loyalty Day, the most impressive display of popular anticommunism in the city's history. Loyalty Day had been the brainchild of William Randolph Hearst, an effort to counter Communist displays on May 1 by holding competing parades on the same day. The first Brooklyn and Manhattan Loyalty Day parades, held in 1948, attracted somewhat more marchers than the May Day parade. With the fortunes of the communist and anticommunist movements diverging, the gap grew. In 1949 the number of May Day paraders declined to under 20,000, while some 50,000 to 100,000 people marched in the Manhattan Loyalty Day parade and a smaller number in Brooklyn, with large crowds looking on.

Loyalty Day brought together the key players in the anticommunist drive. The Veterans of Foreign Wars and an ad hoc committee headed by businessman Charles Silver, a close Spellman ally (known in some circles as "Spelly's Jew"), cosponsored the Manhattan parade. Spellman himself marched up Fifth Avenue flanked by former Postmaster General James A. Farley. Contingents appeared from various unions, city departments, and federal agencies. The Truman administration sent the secretaries of labor and interior. Mayor O'Dwyer, who by then had thoroughly distanced himself from the Left, reigned on the reviewing stand. With ethnic and labor delegations, marching Catholic schoolchildren, bands from the fire department, post office, and Musicians Local 802, and contingents from many veterans and fraternal groups, the march had a populist air far removed from the narrow, mean-spirited aura of the prewar right.[31]

While Loyalty Day had a celebratory mood, events a few months later demonstrated the darker side of popular anticommunism. For several summers, Paul Robeson had given a fund-raising concert in Peekskill, New York, a blue-collar town north of the city, near which many New Yorkers vacationed. Already a controversial figure, Robeson gave a speech in Paris in April 1949 in which he was widely misreported as saying that African-Americans would refuse to fight against the Soviet Union. It set off a storm of criticism. Robeson's scheduled August 27 concert at a Peekskill picnic grounds never took place, as a mob of local veterans and Catholic high school students invaded the site, blocking its entrance, heaving stones at concertgoers, beating some up, burning a cross, and shouting anticommunist and anti-Semitic slurs while police stood by.

Three days later over three thousand people packed a Harlem ballroom to protest the riot. Under pressure from its black cadre, the Communist Party resolved to return to Peekskill. Left leaders recruited hundreds of guards armed with baseball bats from the Furriers, Local 65, and other unions. On September 4 a crowd of twenty thousand gathered to hear Robeson at a golf course near Peekskill. The concert itself went off without a hitch, but as concertgoers left the grounds along a narrow, uphill road, a rockthrowing crowd, unrestrained by police, ambushed them. At the concert site, civilians and police attacked the remaining union guards. By the time the riot ended, dozens of cars and buses had had their windows broken or had been overturned and 150 concertgoers required medical attention. For the Communists and their backers, the concert had been a cathartic refusal to cower in the face of their enemies, a moment of brave determination remembered and recounted in the years to come. But it also demonstrated the frightening potential for violence and vigilantism by a Negro-hating, red-hating, Jew-hating citizenry led by respected organizations, unchecked by state authority.[32]

In April 1949 the national CIO chartered a new New York City CIO Council. Many anti-communist unions that had spurned the old council affiliated with it, with only a third of the delegates coming from unions with CP ties. Like the old council, the new one devoted much of its energy to organizing and strike support. It continued the council's deep involvement in local politics, now on behalf of the Democratic Party rather than the ALP. In an unprecedented move, in 1949 it even joined forces with the AFL Central Trades Council to help reelect Mayor O'Dwyer and Senator Herbert Lehman.

In some respects, the new CIO Council, headed by a now anticommunist Mike Quill, operated more democratically than the old one, with more frequent debate and contested elections. But dissent went only so far. CIO leaders defined the council as a subservient body of the national CIO, obliged to hew to its policies and principles. These did not include tolerance of a pro-CP minority. Louis Hollander, from the Amalgamated Clothing Workers, charged by the CIO with relaunching the council, announced at its very first meeting that there was "no room under one roof for the Communist Party and CIO."[33] Within months, the CIO moved to rid itself of Communists and their allies by electoral challenges, raids, bans on officeholding, and, when necessary, mass expulsions.

It could be an ugly business, as demonstrated in the NMU. Even after Joe Curran's sweep of the 1948 NMU elections, the Communists retained considerable support among sailors, especially in New York. To clear them out, in May 1949, Curran got the NMU national council to propose expelling all Communists from the union under guidelines so broad that they could have been applied to almost any critic of his administration. Many Trotskyists and ex-Communists who had allied with Curran balked at this measure, leading to a war within the union. Curran's opponents seized the building housing the union's New York and national headquarters, but on Thanksgiving Day 1949 Curran and his allies physically ousted them with the aid of the police. Curran's victory in June 1950 union elections sealed his control. NMU leftists came under further attack after Congress's August 1950 passage of the Magnuson Act, which empowered the Coast Guard to deny waterfront workers deemed security risks the right to work. The NMU and other anticommunist unions supported the act and cooperated in its enforcement, which within three years pushed over eighteen hundred sailors from their jobs.[34]

In the summer of 1949, the increasing isolation of the Communist-bloc unions, the raids against them, and the difficulty of operating without the protection of federal labor law led the CP to reverse policy and allow its followers to sign Taft-Hartley affidavits. Communist labor leaders either resigned from their union posts or, much more commonly, from the CP.[35] This did not necessarily mean that unions stopped taking their lead from the party, but it did weaken CP control.

UE made this evident. By the time of its September 1949 convention, the anticommunist opposition had grown to the point that it controlled roughly 40 percent of the delegates. At the suggestion of the incumbent officers, the convention voted to comply with Taft-Hartley, becoming the last major CIO union to do so. But UE leaders ignored CP advice to fight a rearguard action within the CIO. Instead, UE stopped paying CIO dues and declined to send delegates to the November 1949 CIO convention.[36] In its absence, the CIO convention expelled UE and chartered a new union with the same jurisdiction, the International Union of Electrical, Radio, and Machine Workers (IUE). It also barred fascists or Communists from holding CIO office and set up a mechanism to expel unions that aligned themselves with the CP.[37]

In January 1950 the CIO began hearings on charges that ten of its affiliates consistently followed the Communist Party line. By the middle of the year its executive board expelled nine, including several heavily represented in New York: the Furriers, American Communications Association, United Public Workers (UPW), and United Office and Professional Workers (UOPWA). Only the Furniture Workers, by ousting its left-wing officers, escaped banishment.[38]

CIO officials pledged to win back the members of the expelled unions and organize the unorganized in their jurisdictions. But their efforts to do so proved halfhearted. In New York, the tight-knit Furriers faced no raiding; a severe fur industry slump, rather than defections, accounted for declining membership. AFL and CIO groups did raid the small American Communications Association, but it managed to retain most of its membership, including its large Western Union unit.[39]

It was a far different story for the white-collar union UOPWA. The insurance agents, who constituted nearly half its membership, had little sympathy for the CP, especially after the major insurance companies began refusing to bargain with UOPWA. At New York social service agencies, UOPWA members included a substantial number of anticommunist leftists and ex-leftists, tenacious in their opposition to Stalinism and experienced in factional warfare.

The Catholic Church helped coordinate the UOPWA opposition. The nerve center of its activities was Charles Owen Rice, the well-known, Pittsburgh-based labor priest. In the late 1940s, to add to his already formidable list of union contacts, Rice began publishing articles on Communism and labor in *Our Sunday Visitor*, a conservative Catholic weekly. Rice used the flood of letters he received in response to build union-by-union mailing lists. To these he sent periodic circulars encouraging anticommunist action and providing strategic advice. To delegitimize UOPWA, Rice publicly attacked the professed Catholicism of its president and secretary-treasurer.[40]

In 1949, UOPWA lost the bulk of its Prudential agents to an AFL rival. Then, after the CIO expelled the union, most of the remaining insurance agents decamped for a newly-established CIO unit. Many New York social service workers also left UOPWA to rejoin the CIO. Within a short time, little remained of an organization that only a few years earlier had seemed the best hope there was for bringing industrial unionism to the nation's rapidly growing clerical and professional work force.[41]

The fiercest effort to destroy an expelled union targeted UE. Initially, the CIO's new union, the IUE, concentrated on the giant electrical manufacturing firms. Since New York had relatively few large electrical factories, national IUE leaders devoted scant resources to the region. Nonetheless, the new CIO union made gains, especially at those large plants New York did have. At Sperry Gyroscope, future IUE president Paul Jennings and a number of other UE officers jumped to IUE as soon as it was founded, forming a local that defeated UE in a representation election. The Elizabeth, N.J., Phelps Dodge plant, scene of so much drama in 1946, also went IUE. By contrast, in small and mid-sized shops, UE held on to much of its membership. Even in this sector, though, it suffered defections. Local 1227, for example, remained solidly UE until the June 1950 outbreak of the Korean War, when a minority of the local's executive board, led by activities director James Trenz, backed a resolution supporting U.S. troops in Korea, while the majority, voted to condemn U.S. intervention. In short order Trenz left UE, got a charter from IUE, and wooed about 40 percent of Local 1227 to his new group.[42]

The United Public Workers (UPW) also came under heavy fire. What gave that battle broad significance was its close link to the purging of government employees. In an era when the legal right of public workers to unionize was at best shaky, nationally the UPW had had only spotty success in organizing federal, state, and local workers. In New York, though, it had made significant inroads in the city's Welfare, Sanitation, and Hospital departments, and, through its affiliated Teachers Union, the Board of Education.

The UPW's New York success testified to the talent and devotion of its youthful leadership, including welfare representative Frank Herbst, district president Jack Bigel, and Teachers Union legislative directors Bella Dodd and Rose Russell. The UPW's national president, Abram Flaxer, and its secretary-treasurer, Ewart Guinier, both came from New York. Guinier, a

Panamanian immigrant educated at Harvard, City College, and Columbia University, held the highest post of any nonwhite in a white-majority union. Committed to the Popular Front-Left—in 1949 he ran for Manhattan borough president on the ALP line—and the struggle for black advancement, Guinier helped push the UPW into the forefront of the struggle against racial discrimination.[43]

Government employment made UPW members exceptionally vulnerable to the national security scare that accompanied the Cold War. The Truman administration loyalty program, launched in 1947, decimated the federal membership of the union. Various cities, including Los Angeles, Detroit, and New York, soon began loyalty programs of their own that cost hundreds of UPW members their jobs.[44]

Though officially UPW's sin was supporting the Communist Party, at least in New York other issues lurked just below the surface. The O'Dwyer administration, like the La Guardia administration before it, nominally supported the right of municipal workers to unionize but sought to check the emergence of powerful unions outside its control which would drive up the cost of government and limit managerial authority. In the sanitation department, city officials openly sided with a group of friendly AFL locals in an effort to block CIO gains. In the welfare department, where the UPW and its predecessors had been ensconced since the mid-1930s, Commissioner Raymond Hilliard, upon taking office in 1948, launched fierce attacks on the union, arguing that its network of supporters extending into supervisory ranks undermined his ability to set and enforce policy. With ideas of their own about how the system should work, UPW activists fought efforts to reduce welfare costs and demanded less degrading procedures, looser eligibility requirements, and more generous benefits.[45]

Once O'Dwyer and the Democrats broke with the ALP, institutions aligned with the labor party, like the UPW, represented a political threat. Welfare Commissioner Hilliard began his anti-UPW campaign by banning all political activity by members of his department, an edict, by his own account, aimed at pro-Wallace electioneering. While purging his department of UPW activists, he hired two hundred Spanish-speaking workers so that Puerto Ricans in East Harlem would no longer have to go to Marcantonio's office for translators to fill out their home-relief applications.[46]

Hilliard's skirmishing with the UPW became a full-blown assault when, on March 1, 1950, the CIO expelled the union. Eight days later, Hilliard, quoting a CIO statement, declared the UPW an "instrument" of the Communist Party rather than a labor group, and withdrew the recognition it had long enjoyed as a representative of welfare department workers. Almost immediately, he began to transfer, suspend, and fire UPW activists. To ferret out leftists, Hilliard had twenty-four rookie policemen, posing as new welfare workers, join the UPW.[47]

Late in 1950, the Welfare Department ordered its employees to sign loyalty oaths and answer questions about the political groups they belonged to. Three hundred and sixty-one of the department's 7,790 employees refused, subjecting themselves to disciplinary action. By the time Hilliard resigned in April 1951, 191 workers had been fired as a result of his anti-red campaign, including many UPW leaders. By the next year, the left-wing union was dead at the agency that had spawned it nearly two decades earlier.[48]

Events in the school system paralleled those in Welfare. In June 1948 the board of education, in a brief to the state commissioner of education, argued that Communists and Communist Party supporters should be barred from the schools. The next year, the state legislature passed the Feinberg Law, designed to rout Communists from the schools through procedures for firing teachers who belonged to proscribed organizations. Almost immediately Superintendent of Schools Arthur Jansen began quizzing teachers about CP membership, but amid widespread protests against the Feinberg Law and a prolonged test of its constitutionality, the board took no further action.[49]

As in the Welfare Department, this changed once the CIO expelled the UPW. First, the board denied the Teachers Union the right—held by over sixty groups—to represent teachers in grievance and personnel matters. Second, Jansen called in eight members of the Teachers Union executive board, including its president, and demanded that they answer questions pertaining to their relationship with the Communist Party. When they refused, the board dismissed them.[50]

In the purge that followed, the board of education rarely applied the Feinberg Law or charged a teacher with being a Communist. Rather, as in the Welfare Department, it found it more expedient to fire suspected reds on other grounds, usually insubordination, conduct unbecoming a teacher, or violating a city charter requirement (designed to facilitate anticorruption probes) that city employees testify before authorized government bodies.[51] The AFL Central Trades Council pledged "wholehearted support in the justifiable move to rid the schools of communist teachers and communist ideology." The CIO Council restricted its comments to an insistence that *former* Communists not be discriminated against.

The board's anticommunist campaign forced at least three hundred teachers out of the schools. Though only a small percentage of the city's huge teaching force directly suffered from the inquisition, it had a widespread chilling effect.[52] All or virtually all the fired teachers were Jewish, which led many Teachers Union supporters to conclude that anti-Semitism played a large role in the purge. Some pointedly contrasted the treatment of the fired leftists with that of May Quinn. But the organized Jewish community largely failed to pick up the issue. The Teachers Union itself downplayed anti-Semitism, portraying the struggle against it as one of "thought control," anti-unionism, and Cold War mobilization.[53]

In early 1953, the UPW, with its main bases of support shattered, disbanded. The Teachers Union survived as a much-weakened, independent group. The few other remaining UPW locals affiliated with the Teamsters.[54]

The city loyalty program actually grew in scope and stringency after the demise of the UPW. The final flowering of municipal McCarthyism utilized the 1951 state Security Risk Law, which permitted the summary transfer or dismissal of employees in what were designated "security agencies" if their superiors had doubts about their "trust and reliability," believing that they might "endanger the security or defense of the nation." The state and city applied the law with breathtaking range, defining 81 percent of all city jobs as "security" positions. By February 1956, with the campaign still underway, sixty-two thousand city workers had undergone loyalty checks, resulting in the dismissal or resignation of fifty-three. Criteria for dismissal included refusal to answer questions about Communist Party membership on Fifth Amendment grounds, a policy validated by the Supreme Court in a 1958 decision involving subway conductor Max Lerner. While few Communists remained to be fired, the ongoing loyalty program helped insure that New York liberalism escaped the red tar.[55]

From the late 1940s on, the institutional base of the CP-left drastically contracted. The once vibrant Left and left-liberal press, for instance, rapidly shrank. The most significant blow came early, in 1948, when *PM* folded in the face of financial loses, disappointing circulation (averaging 165,000), and the breakup of the New Deal coalition needed to sustain it. The *China Daily News* weathered a fierce storm that included the 1955 jailing of three of its staff for violating the Trading with the Enemy Act (for accepting advertising from the Bank of China), but in the face of unrelenting pressure it began avoiding controversial political issues. The *Daily Worker* lost half its readership between 1950 and 1953, and in 1957 ceased publication.[56]

The problems of the left-wing press partly stemmed from diminishing public support, but the demise of the International Workers Order (IWO) resulted entirely from state action. With over 187,000 members in 1947, the IWO constituted one of the largest left-led organizations in American history. Its downfall came from one of its strengths, the low-cost insurance it provided to its members, which subjected it to regulation by the New York State Insurance Department. Although the department repeatedly found the IWO to be financially sound and efficiently run, in 1950 it recommended its liquidation on the grounds that it was a subversive organization whose activities exceeded those authorized in its charter and represented "a hazard to the public." A state judge, after hearing a parade of ex-communist witnesses, agreed. In December 1953, the state took over the IWO, transferred its insurance policies to a commercial company, and dissolved what remained.[57]

Anticommunism affected even the Brownsville Boys Club. In March 1954, newly-elected city council president Abe Stark fired eleven employees of the club, which the previous year he had arranged for the city to annex. With his political career beginning to take off, Stark, best-known for the Ebbets Field advertisement for his clothing store, "Hit Sign — Win Suit," apparently feared that the left-liberal views, community activism, and proactive integrationism of the club staff might leave him open to anticommunist attacks. His fears reflected the continuing strength of anticommunist sentiment. In April 1954, six thousand policemen attended a Holy Name Society Communion breakfast at which Senator Joseph McCarthy spoke. Later that year, while the Senate was considering his censure, a Madison Square Garden rally supporting McCarthy drew thirteen thousand.[58]

McCarthy's fall came too late to spark a revival of the left, at the polls or elsewhere. The ALP still exhibited impressive strength in 1949, when Vito Marcantonio, hoping to hold the party together, ran for mayor against O'Dwyer and Republican-Liberal Newbold Morris. Marc's 356,423 votes, nearly 14 percent of the total, exceeded the vote O'Dwyer received on the ALP line in 1945.[59] However, following the outbreak of the Korean War, the party suffered massive losses. In 1950 it received but 6.5 percent of the city vote. Three years later its mayoral candidate got only 54,000 votes.[60]

The last mass outpouring of New York's Popular Front left came in 1954, fittingly at Marcantonio's funeral. Just a few months earlier Marc had quit the dying ALP, frustrated with an increasing Communist emphasis on working within the Democratic Party. On August 9, on the eve of attempting a political comeback as an independent, he died of a heart attack. He was just fifty-one years old. Cardinal Spellman refused him a Catholic burial, so tens of thousands filed through a small funeral home in East Harlem where his body lay. At his funeral, W. E. B. DuBois hailed Marc for believing "in America when America no longer believed in itself." The gathered mourners, wrote the *National Guardian*, "were a rarely-seen cross section of New York's people—mostly the poor and toilworn, but of every national background, of every age. . . . from all corners of the city, but most . . . residents of Marc's own district."[61]

Fragmentation in its own ranks aborted CP moves toward establishing a new union federation.[62] The closest it got was the Distributive, Processing and Office Workers of America (DPOWA). In 1950 six locals that had left the RWDSU—four department store groups, 65, and 1199—joined with the UOPWA and the Food, Tobacco, Agricultural and Allied Workers to form the DPOWA. All the New York locals involved merged to form what was dubbed District 65, except 1199, which obstinately maintained its autonomy. With well over thirty thousand members, District 65 was the largest left union in the city. A young, ethnically diverse membership, which included many blacks and Puerto Ricans—groups becoming ever more important in the city's economy—gave the feisty union great promise. Its headquarters, a large building in downtown Manhattan housing the union's offices, hiring hall, security plan, credit union, shopping service, classes, cafeteria, and nightclub, buzzed with activity.

Successful as it was, District 65 almost immediately suffered from factionalism. Veterans of the old Local 65 dominated both District 65, led by David Livingston, and its parent DPOWA, headed by Arthur Osman. When they fired some Communist stalwarts, the CP criticized them for opportunism, white chauvinism, and other purported failings. Meanwhile, Osman began exchanging feelers with the CIO about reaffiliation, a path the CP opposed. In short order, full-scale war broke out between the CP and 65.[63] In early 1953, the DPOWA's convention resolved, "We love our country and oppose communism." In May, the CIO readmitted the union.[64]

By the time the DPOWA joined the CIO, the CP itself was moving away from advocating independent left formations. In line with this, in 1954 the Furriers union merged with the AFL Amalgamated Meat Cutters. Once in charge, the Meat Cutters began to "decommunize" the Furriers, shutting down its newspaper and summer camp and banning Communists and Communist sympathizers from office. That was not enough, however, for the AFL executive board, which disapproved the merger. Reluctantly, the Meat Cutters agreed to a far-reaching political rectification of its new division.[65]

In spite of these travails, Communist leaders interpreted the movement toward an AFL-CIO merger, consummated in late 1955, as a renewed opportunity for operating within the labor mainstream. They urged their followers to get into the AFL-CIO any way they could. Though the national officers of UE met with IUE leaders to discuss merging, they ultimately rejected the idea, holding IUE—and for that matter the AFL-CIO—in low regard. So Communist loyalists began fishing for deals for individual UE districts to join other unions.

Of all the UE districts, the Communists had the greatest influence in New York–New Jersey. When in the spring of 1956 the much-respected president of District 4, James McLeish, arranged its merger with the corresponding IUE district, there was, one UE official recalled, "really no internal resistance." For years UE activists had found it impossible to organize new members. Most had tired of the battle to survive. Furthermore, IUE agreed to accept the UE locals without purges, preconditions, or restrictions. UE thus found itself with virtually no New York members. New York's era of independent, left-wing unionism was over.[66]

What are we to make of the story of Communism and anticommunism in Cold War New York? Who won and who lost? And what difference did it make for the city and its working class?

The most peculiar part of the story, its ending, provides a starting point for understanding. How could the CIO—an organization that expelled a fifth of its members for belonging to red unions—welcome back the DPOWA after it gave only vague and perfunctory guarantees of its anticommunism? And how could the DPOWA so quickly build links to key anticommunist liberal institutions? Though it had long warred with the NAACP, for example, by 1954 the DPOWA had become so close to the group that it won its endorsement in a representation election against an AFL rival. Similarly, in 1953, Local 1199, still in many respects a Stalinist outfit, found itself solicited by the NYC CIO Council to work with it in Robert F. Wagner Jr.'s mayoral campaign, which it did with gusto.[67] The switch of New York UE to the IUE was even more remarkable, as the most Communist wing of the most vilified left-wing union was taken in by a rival whose very raison d'être was anticommunism.

Were Communism and anticommunism only outer raiment, put on and taken off as the occasion required? For some, undoubtedly yes.[68] But for many others, the key to their mercurial behavior lay in the complex relationship between Communism and anticommunism, their similarities as well as their differences.

Even at the height of the Cold War, the CP-left and the liberals who loomed so large in New York anticommunism put forth similar positions on most domestic issues. The CIO never abandoned (at least rhetorically) its "People's Program," while the AFL continued to back national health insurance, federally-funded public housing, rent control, and federal aid to education.[69] As Charles Maier pointed out, the post–World War II left, in Europe and America, shared with its liberal opponents a commitment to increased productivity and hierarchical workplace relations, unlike the World War I–era left, which challenged the fundamental social structure of industry. In the earlier period, a reconciliation between the radical Industrial Workers of the World and the AFL could not occur because of the gulf that separated them on basic issues. But, during the 1950s, Popular Front unionists could be welcomed back to the House of Labor after often-superficial rituals of renunciation because of a shared belief in progress through rationality, technology, and production.[70]

The very success of the Popular Front in disseminating its views eased reconciliation. The high priority that the CP-left gave to the struggle for black rights and cultural pluralism, for example, had become liberal orthodoxy by the mid-1950s. District 65 could easily switch its allegiance from the CP-linked National Negro Labor Council to the NAACP because the rival groups fundamentally agreed about racial equality, integrationism, and the importance of organized labor. Many left-wing social workers and teachers saw their careers and lives wrecked by anticommunism, but their approach to education and social service became widely adopted. The easing of religious tensions facilitated liberal absorption of fragments of the left. By the mid-1950s, the efforts of liberal interfaith groups, the assimilative effects of mass culture, the increasing secularization of society, and the careful orchestration of religious and ethnic harmony by the Democratic Party reduced the Catholic-Jewish friction so evident in the Quinn affair.

Of course, the CP-left and its opponents profoundly disagreed about international issues. For leftists to relegitimate themselves they had to either publicly renounce Soviet firstism — as DPOWA head Osman did — or at least maintain silence about foreign policy. By the early 1950s, however, many

Communist supporters, at least in private, no longer believed in Soviet infallibility or American original sin. When the Soviet Union invaded Hungary in 1956, the American CP conspicuously failed to back the socialist motherland.[71]

Even outweighing the Soviet issue among the motives for incapacitating the CP-left had been its autonomy from liberal control. Paralleling and infiltrating the structures of labor and liberalism, the CP and its allied groups — as liberals and socialists bitterly discovered — threatened at all times to hijack mass organizations and manipulate coalitions while remaining invulnerable to countermeasures short of all-out, antidemocratic action. CIO complaints about the CP stressed, above all else, its interference in CIO affairs. When the DPOWA reentered the CIO, one thing it did pledge was to "oppose and distrust all forms of totalitarianism and all forms of outside interference in the conduct of Union affairs." The greatest threat of the CP-left lay not in its program but in its structure, in its Leninism rather than its Marxism.[72]

Once the networks and institutions through which the CP operated were crippled or destroyed, ideas, organizations, and people associated with it could be absorbed into a hegemonic liberalism. When Communist control saturated an organization, as in the Furriers and Teachers unions, opponents demanded thoroughgoing purges or annihilation. But when leftism remained largely an indulgence of the leadership, as was the case in the UE, deals for wholesale absorption could be struck. In any case, by the mid-1950s the Communist left had been so shattered by state action, shifting political terrain, and internal disillusionment that even its stronger remnants represented little threat to the liberal center, which stood to gain by an infusion of capable but domesticated leftist cadre.[73]

What difference did the defeat of the old left make? For one thing, it left organizational voids. The liquidation of the IWO, for example, stripped many communities of centers of left ethnic culture (though some left fraternal groups, like the socialist Workmen's Circle, remained active), cutting off the transmission of egalitarian values to a younger generation and eliminating bases for working-class mobilization. The destruction of the UPW simply delayed by a few years the unionization of municipal workers, but the demise of the UOPWA, for all its failings, ended for decades any sustained effort to organize the city's private-sector clerical and professional workers. In some unions that did survive, corruption became a problem for the first time, as self-serving business unionists replaced relatively selfless, ideologically-driven radicals. The revelation that officials of the purged Furriers took payoffs from manufacturers to allow them to contract work to nonunion shops represented a sad coda to the history of this once Red union.[74]

For another thing, the Communist left did treat some issues quite differently than liberals. The defeat of the old left ended significant labor criticism of United States foreign policy. From the late 1940s on, organized labor operated as a government adjunct abroad, helping to sustain global Cold War while refraining from criticism of the military-industrial complex.[75] The CP-left also had a distinctive position on what it called the "woman question." It took the oppression of women more seriously than most labor and political groups. Though the Communist record was spotty, the few well-known female unionists in New York during the 1940s and 1950s mostly belonged to the party, including Dodd and Russell from the Teachers, Esther Letz, who ran Local 65 during World War II, and Ruth Young, secretary of UE District 4. (UE became particularly attentive to women workers in the early 1950s in an effort to win their loyalty in its rivalry with IUE.) The defeat of the old left retarded the advance of women in the labor movement while allowing a profound sexism to accompany the growth of the new left not so many years later.[76]

More than anything else, though, the rout of the CP-left removed from New York working-class politics the element most committed to winning and wielding social power. The Communists and their allies projected a totality of political vision, far surpassing in breadth the more parochial agendas of business unionists, liberals, and even most social democrats. Far more than their labor and working-class rivals, the reds considered themselves capable of anything and everything, believing in class rule—or at least in their own rule in the name of the working class—as both a theoretical and practical matter. As a matter of principle, they stuck their noses into every facet of city life. While the AFL and post-CP CIO councils took stands on issues such as juvenile delinquency, foreign policy, and housing not directly connected to the employer-employee relationship, they lacked the almost palpable hunger for class power that characterized the CIO Council in its left-wing heyday.

While the defeat (and self-destruction) of the CP-left transformed working-class New York in numerous ways, much didn't change. The Communist Party itself all but disappeared after 1956, but onetime CP members and sympathizers, and the worldview they shared, continued to influence working-class New York for decades to come. As Maurice Isserman noted, "If all the ex-Communists living in the United States in the mid-1950s had been gathered together in one radical organization, they would have consti-

tuted the largest movement on the Left in American history."[77] Nowhere did
left-wing and left-leaning ex-Communists have more influence than in New
York. Those in the know—who could recognize the habits of mind, modes of
operation, and circumspection that identified veterans of the Communist left
as clearly as class ties distinguished Ivy League graduates—could find them
holding positions of influence in the most likely and unlikely places.

Take the old United Public Workers crowd. UPW activists who managed to hang on in the Welfare Department played an important role in its
unionization in the 1960s and the general triumph of municipal unionism.
Jack Bigel, after driving a delivery truck, began a labor consulting firm that
eventually made him rich. After operating behind the scenes with the Uniformed Sanitationmen's Association, he reappeared in public view during
New York's mid-1970s fiscal crisis as the key strategist and negotiator for the
municipal unions, formulating with bankers and financiers the arrangements
that saved the city from bankruptcy. Ewart Guinier left the labor movement,
becoming an NAACP leader in Queens, an expert on urban affairs at Columbia University, and, finally, the first head of the Afro-American Studies Department at Harvard University. (Though Guinier never achieved national
renown, his daughter Lani did, by being nominated and then unnominated
by Bill Clinton to head the civil rights division of the Justice Department.)
Finally, the UPW legacy lived on, oddly, in professional sports. Marvin
Miller, the first executive director of the Major League Baseball Players Association (which broke the ground for unions in other sports), recalled that the
UPW's predecessor, the CIO State, County and Municipal Workers, which
he belonged to as a young New York welfare worker, "exerted a powerful influence on the way I viewed the world," while giving him "fundamental basic
training" in unionism.[78]

In some unions, like District 65 and 1199, incumbent leftists maintained
control for decades, largely without challenge. In others, leftists remained influential even after defeat. In the United Furniture Workers (UFWA), Max
Perlow, following his 1950 ouster as national secretary-treasurer, took a staff
job with a New York local. There, along with other Jewish leftists who had
founded the union, he nurtured two generations of new leaders, including
several African-Americans and Puerto Ricans who went on to national leadership. In his history of the Furniture Workers, Daniel B. Cornfield wrote
that this "mentoring process not only perpetuated the left-wing founders' ideology of working class unity among later generations of top UFWA leaders,
but it also created a new generation of minority union leaders, who as civil

rights activists mobilized for greater minority participation in UFWA governance."[79]

The union movement constituted but one arena in which the influence of
the old left long reverberated. Former *UE News* reporter Betty Friedan, who
in the early 1950s wrote union pamphlets attacking sexism, a decade later
achieved national renown as the author of *The Feminine Mystique* and a
founder of the modern woman's movement. In certain professions, like social
work and public health, in tenants groups and PTAs, in civil rights, antiwar,
women's, and senior citizen organizations, and in the Democratic Party, veterans of the postwar CP-left played important though often behind-the-
scenes roles into the 1990s. Their children helped lead the New Left, antiwar,
and feminist movements. Who could be surprised that the Rev. Jesse Jackson's 1988 presidential campaign manager was the proud son of an 1199
staffer?[80] Tough and tenacious, the old left, belatedly throwing off the dead
weight of Soviet allegiance, managed to snatch a degree of victory from its
awful defeat.

PART TWO
Labor's City

We have accepted, so to speak, a second Bill of Rights under which a new basis of security and prosperity may be established for all—regardless of station, race, or creed. Among these are:

The right to a useful and remunerative job in the industries, or shops or farms or mines of the Nation;

The right to earn enough to provide adequate food and clothing and recreation; . . .

The right of every family to a decent home;

The right to adequate medical care and the opportunity to achieve and enjoy good health;

The right to adequate protection from economic fears of old age, sickness, accident, and unemployment;

The right to a good education.

—Franklin D. Roosevelt, January 11, 1944

CHAPTER 6.

Big Labor

During the years roughly coinciding with the mayoralty of Robert F. Wagner Jr., 1954 to 1966, New York labor reached a zenith of power. Capitalizing on its long history of struggle and institution-building, and the impressive display of worker militance after World War II, organized labor wielded its influence in ways unrivaled in the city's history to make working-class life more pleasant and secure. To do so, it helped erect a social infrastructure that served New Yorkers far beyond its own ranks, including nonunion working-class families and many in the middle class. At a time when a national consensus condemned the evils of collectivism, working-class New Yorkers pushed their city toward a model as close to European social democracy as the country had seen.

From the mid-1950s through the mid-1960s, observers routinely portrayed "big labor," "big business," and "big government" as a triptych of social and economic power. In 1955, the country's seventeen million union members constituted a third of the workforce, with union penetration much higher in such vital sectors as manufacturing, construction, mining, and transportation. During the 1960s, the percentage of the workforce that belonged to a union slipped, but in absolute numbers union membership continued to grow. Union power contributed to a remarkable rise in the working-class standard of living, as a way of life once largely restricted to the middle class — car and home ownership, vacations and travel, routine health care and college education — became accessible to workers and their families.[1]

On December 5, 1955, fourteen hundred delegates crowded into the 71st Regiment Armory at Park Avenue and 34th Street for the founding convention of the AFL-CIO, created by the merger of the two, longtime rival, national labor federations. A photograph of AFL president George Meany (who headed the combined group) clasping hands with CIO president Walter Reuther appeared in newspapers and magazines throughout the country, personifying "big labor." Emblemizing the power unions had achieved, the AFL-CIO had its headquarters just up the street from the White House. When its executive board met, it literally looked down on the president's quarters.

The AFL-CIO merger solidified labor's national standing but marked a diminishment of its social ambition. The CIO's anticommunism paved the way for the amalgamation. On the one hand, the purge of Communists made the CIO acceptable to the larger, more conservative AFL. On the other hand, it accelerated the loss of much of what had made the CIO distinctive—its insistent demand on full social citizenship for all workers, its strategic daring, its critique of American society. By the early 1950s, the CIO had evolved into a junior partner in a stable system of industrial relations, beholden to the state for its status and expected, in return, to back the government in some of its most tawdry foreign adventures. Held together by little more than anticommunism, the CIO ran out of steam, while the once moribund AFL coopted some of its liberalism and did a better job at organizing.[2] Most union leaders portrayed the AFL-CIO merger as the beginning of a great new day for labor. Only one major figure, Mike Quill, argued otherwise. He characterized it as "the tragic liquidation" of the CIO, citing the failure to build into the new federation strong protection against racism, raiding, and racketeering.[3]

In holding the inaugural AFL-CIO convention in New York, the chieftains of labor made an appropriate choice, for no city better epitomized labor's success. Nationally, the AFL-CIO, as Quill feared, quickly settled into self-satisfied passivity. Locally, however, the merger reinvigorated labor, with the New York City Central Labor Council (created in 1959 by the merger of the AFL and CIO councils) displaying greater energy, imagination, and ambition than either of its immediate predecessors. The 1950s and early 1960s saw a whirlwind of labor activity in the city, as unionists and their allies built massive housing projects and huge health clinics, sponsored medical insurance programs, fought for shorter working hours and against the detrimental effects of automation, launched organizing drives, and sought to cope with the changing population makeup of the city and its working class.[4]

Organized labor went far beyond the traditional realm of collective bargaining in its efforts to assure decent, secure living for working-class New Yorkers. Its broad conception of the functions of unionism reflected the peculiarities of the region. New York's long, deep tradition of working-class leftism gave its labor movement a frame of reference quite different than that in most of the country, even after the Cold War took its toll. Socialist (or once-Socialist) and Communist (or once-Communist) unions played major roles in initiating programs to provide housing, health care, and other forms of social security for New York workers. However, some unions not usually associated with the left pioneered such programs, too. A general predilection toward social unionism informed New York labor as much as any particular ideological vision.

The structure of the New York economy encouraged this. With so many labor groups bargaining with small employers incapable of developing or administering welfare programs, unions had to take it upon themselves to do the job, breeding a more comprehensive sense of social responsibility than typically found in unions that bargained with huge employers with long records of offering extensive employee benefits. The spirit of creativity and innovation critical to such New York industries as garment manufacturing and electronics found its way into the realm of social welfare, while the density and sheer numbers of unionists in the city made possible approaches to service delivery impractical elsewhere.

A favorable political environment, partially of labor's making, facilitated union efforts. The size and electoral weight of the labor movement led politicians to pay obeisance to it. During a three-month period in 1961, Attorney General Robert Kennedy, Secretary of Labor Arthur J. Goldberg, and Governor Nelson Rockefeller each attended a meeting of New York City Central Labor Council executive board.[5] Having friends in Albany and City Hall proved indispensable for promoting labor's agenda.

The 1953 election of Mayor Wagner demonstrated the power of the labor-liberal alliance. Wagner had a perfect liberal pedigree: his father, New Deal Senator Robert F. Wagner Sr., authored the National Labor Relations Act, often deemed the "Magna Charta of Labor." As Manhattan borough president, the younger Wagner allied with the liberal wing of the Democratic Party, supporting tightly regulated rents and a low transit fare. He was not a charismatic figure, rather employing his blandness as a political strategy. Still, his primary fight against Mayor Impellitteri became a test of strength between liberal and conservative elements of the Democratic Party. A German Catholic, Wagner ran on a ticket that included a Jew for city council president, an Italian for comptroller, and an African-American for Manhattan borough president.

Wagner sought and received strong labor backing, promising, if elected, to recognize the right of municipal workers to engage in collective bargaining. Once victorious, he embraced organized labor to an extent that at least matched and in some respects surpassed any of his predecessors, acknowledging in both symbolic and practical ways the centrality of labor to his political future, the future of liberalism and the Democratic Party, and the future of the city. Shortly after taking office he even detailed his program to a special session of the New York City CIO Council, as if he was the winning candidate of a labor party reporting to his constituents.[6]

As mayor, Wagner, true to his New Deal patrimony, sponsored a massive, government-aided middle-income housing program, an expansion of public hospitals and other health services, new recreation facilities, increased assistance for the poor, and collective bargaining for city employees. Yet he also worked comfortably with business, embracing a vision of the city that left plenty of room for profitable, private development. Eager to preserve class harmony, Wagner often intervened in private-sector labor disputes, using mediator Theodore W. Kheel as a troubleshooter. Wagner lacked the populist charm of La Guardia, Marcantonio, or even O'Dwyer, but he proved a solid ally for New York's labor movement.[7]

Four-term Republican governor Nelson Rockefeller was a seemingly less likely collaborator for organized labor, coming as he did from one of the nation's wealthiest families, whose very name evoked images of antilabor plutocracy. However, like many moderate Republicans during the 1950s and 1960s, he enjoyed reasonably good relations with the labor movement. His familiarity with union leaders began early in his career, in the 1930s, when he assisted his father in supervising the construction of Rockefeller Center. One unionist he negotiated with was George Meany, with whom he kept in touch as the two men rose in power and position. To cultivate other labor leaders, Rockefeller put one of his poorer Dartmouth classmates, Victor Baretto, on the Rockefeller Center payroll. After Rockefeller's 1958 defeat of multimillionaire Averell Harriman to become governor, he continued to use Baretto as a liaison to the labor movement.

In a state with so many union members, it made political sense for an aspiring candidate or elected official to reach out to organized labor. But more than expediency shaped Rockefeller's relationship with labor. Rockefeller felt at ease with labor leaders, preferring their hearty, hail-fellow-well-met style to more prissy, upper-class ways. More important, he ardently embraced a productionist political economy, seeing government-stimulated economic growth as a way to upgrade living standards without redistributing wealth. He appreciated the many labor leaders who shared this vision.

Rockefeller took his productionism literally. One aide recalled that of all the aspects of being chief executive of what was then the nation's most populous state, "concrete excited him most." He rarely hesitated to expand the state budget or undertake massive borrowing to finance grandiose social programs or huge government structures. A shared commitment to bountiful public works cemented his relationship with the heads of the building trade unions, particularly Peter Brennan from the Painters union, who led the city's quarter-of-a-million member Building and Construction Trades Council, and Harry Van Arsdale, Jr., head of both Local 3 of the Electricians and the New York City Central Labor Council. But Rockefeller's policies aided more of working-class New York than just its skilled, white, male strata. Among other things, he won improvements in workers compensation, signed the nation's first state minimum wage law, oversaw a vast expansion of the state university, and greatly enlarged the state's involvement in mass transit.[8]

Organized labor, working with politicians like Wagner and Rockefeller and reformers of various stripes, erected a welfare state in New York far more robust than the national norm. It was not the "private welfare state" that some unions like the United Mine Workers and the United Automobile Workers won from employers. Their members received benefits and protections like health insurance, pensions, cost-of-living wage adjustments, and supplementary unemployment payments.[9] Many New York social benefits, unlike these employer provided programs, combined government and private resources and served more than just union members. However, neither was what developed in New York, strictly speaking, a public welfare state. Many of the benefits and protections that labor won in New York, like affordable housing and health care, did not come as universal entitlements, available to all, nor were they fully government funded. Rather, a hybrid form of municipal social democracy grew up in New York that included state action, an ever-increasing range of services provided directly by unions, and huge labor-linked cooperatives and service organizations. Some New Yorkers—disproportionately those with skills, union cards, and white skin—gained greater advantage from this experiment than did others, but literally millions benefited to some extent.

From the mid-1950s on, automation and an exodus of industrial employers out of the city reduced blue-collar employment, eroding key parts of the foundation upon which working-class power rested. Tackling the issue of jobs proved enormously difficult, because doing so meant challenging the free flow of capital and entrepreneurial rights, something liberal politicians and many union leaders shunned doing. At the same time, the makeup of the city population was changing as a result of the in-migration of African-Americans and Puerto Ricans and the outmigration of whites.

The combination of the decline of blue-collar jobs and the growth of the nonwhite population planted the seeds for a later social crisis. At the very moment that civil rights struggles promised to reduce employment discrimination, the kinds of entry-level jobs that had provided a level of economic stability for earlier waves of newcomers diminished in number, creating overlapping racial and economic divides within the city and its working class. As labor power reached its pinnacle, beneath the surface structural weakness spread, though the full implications of the shrinkage of blue-collar employment would only become evident when the great post–World War II economic boom ended in the early 1970s.

Even before then, New York labor welfarism began to stall. Changing economic conditions, especially inflation, made health and housing programs less viable. The geographic dispersion of the city's working class, a result of outer city development, suburbanization, and urban redevelopment, undercut important modes of service delivery. Meanwhile, institutions of what might be called the truly private welfare state—real estate companies, mortgage lenders, insurance companies, hospital complexes, and the American Medical Association—hemmed in labor's potential for independent action.

In the era of "big labor," the union movement had profound faults— racism and sexism, an inability to develop a strategy for dealing with the economic trends that eventually crippled urban America, and myopia about foreign policy and cultural change. Still, looking back from a later era of postliberalism, social meanness, and labor retreat, what New York workers accomplished during the quarter-century after World War II seems utterly breathtaking.

CHAPTER 7.

"A Decent Home"

In the three decades after World War II, the labor movement played a huge role in housing New Yorkers, massively intervening in a social sphere previously deemed the domain of the market. Labor's housing program transformed the physical face and social geography of New York, contributing to its distinctive character. It constituted one of the greatest and least-known achievements of working-class New York.

When World War II ended, New York's chronic housing problem reached crisis proportions. Many GIs left for war still living with their parents, but returned seeking homes of their own in which to begin families. To their frustration, vacant houses or apartments were impossible to find. The 1950 census found only eight-tenths of a percent of the city housing stock empty and available to rent, with another three-tenths of a percent unoccupied and for sale, the lowest known vacancy rates in the city's history.

A great deal of housing had been built in New York during the 1920s, but the Depression brought construction to a near halt. In 1940 nearly a fifth of the city's housing stock predated the 1901 Tenement Housing Law, which set minimal standards for multiple-unit dwellings. World War II saw a further decline in building, as defense production gobbled up labor and material. Immediately after the war, continuing shortages of material, rising costs, and other problems kept housing construction at Depression-era levels.

To meet the emergency, the New York City Housing Authority constructed 10,255 temporary housing units for veterans. But this just skimmed the surface of need. Tens of thousands of veterans — and non-veterans, too — found themselves doubled up with relatives or crammed into dilapidated structures. One analysis of 1950 census data concluded that New York had a shortage of 430,000 housing units. In the housing that did exist, well over 100,000 units lacked private toilets, while nearly a quarter of a million had no central heat. In 1947 the housing authority estimated that 272,720 new units were needed simply to replace substandard dwellings.[1]

Uncharacteristically, after World War II the ill-housed had considerable political clout. Never before or since have working people in need of housing been better organized, belonging as they did to myriad neighborhood, work-based, and ethnic organizations. Because so many were veterans, their demands had unusual moral urgency. In the feverish bout of building that ensued, two models of development competed, one emanating from the private sector, the other from working-class organizations and their allies. Their different approaches to housing corresponded to differing visions of how New York should be physically, socially, and economically organized.

The private sector stressed low-density development on the outskirts of the region. As soon as World War II ended, commercial builders began putting up large-scale developments of detached, single-family homes on the edge of the city and in adjacent suburbs. Levittown received the most publicity: 17,450 houses built between 1947 and 1951 in Hempstead, Long Island. Developer William Levitt, by designing simple, small structures, applying mass production techniques, employing nonunion labor, and depending on free news coverage for marketing, kept the prices for these homes extremely low—some cost less than eight thousand dollars—making them affordable to many blue-collar workers.[2]

Developers also resumed building "garden apartment" complexes, first popularized in the 1920s. Erected mostly on empty tracts in central and eastern Queens, these developments generally consisted of two and three story buildings set in park-like settings, with automobiles limited to their periphery. Some, like the 1,588-unit Oakland Gardens complex in Bayside, Queens, included small shopping centers. Monthly rents generally fell within working-class budgets.[3]

The concentration by private developers on suburban or semi-suburban housing reflected government policy. From the 1930s on, the federal government encouraged and subsidized the dispersal of middle-income city dwellers (including the upper strata of the working class) to racially segregated, suburban neighborhoods of single-family homes. In part it did this by funding highway and infrastructure construction that facilitated suburban growth and intraregional commuting. In New York, Robert Moses's growing empire of bridges, tunnels, and highways opened up the outer reaches of Queens and Brooklyn and suburban areas—especially on Long Island—to rapid development. Further, by making mortgage interest tax deductible, Washington provided a powerful financial incentive for home ownership (while giving no equivalent relief to renters). The Federal Housing Authority (FHA) and Veterans' Home Loan (VA) mortgage insurance programs allowed even families of modest means to borrow money for home purchases by eliminating lender risk. Federal lending guidelines encouraged racial discrimination and detached, single-unit dwellings. Government appraisers routinely gave poor ratings to African-American, ethnically-mixed, and densely settled areas, while favoring all-white suburban developments.[4]

Between 1945 and 1970, hundreds of thousands of white families moved from New York City to single-family homes in its suburbs, profoundly changing the character of the region. But suburbanization failed to solve the city's housing crisis. For one thing, the suburban building boom did not reach full stride until well into the 1950s. For another, not every New Yorker wanted to move away from their job, family, or old neighborhood. Finally, most new, single-family homes—Levittown notwithstanding—cost too much for working-class budgets. As New York State AFL president Thomas Murray complained in 1948, "private builders . . . are putting homes for sale at inflated prices most Americans simply cannot afford."[5] Acting from a position of strength, working-class organizations and their allies took matters into their own hands, promoting alternative solutions to the housing crisis that were at once more affordable, more urbanistic, and more collective.

Of all the working-class housing initiatives, the campaign by tenant groups, unions, and the American Labor Party (ALP) to make wartime rent controls permanent by far affected the most New Yorkers. In 1950, when New York State took over the federal rent regulation system, it took responsibility for capping rents in over two million New York City apartments. Rents in almost all pre-1947 buildings within the city could be increased only within strict guidelines.

Rent control allowed the working class to remain physically and culturally at the heart of the city. Families of modest means could stay put even at times of inflation and acute housing shortage. This helped sustain the dense working-class neighborhoods that bolstered labor solidarity and gave the city so much of its character. It also promoted the continuation of New York's unusually low rate of home ownership, so that most of its working class had little reason to concern itself with real estate tax rates and other property ownership issues that shaped the outlook of so many Americans.

Rent control had its flaws. It led many landlords, economically pinched or simply greedy, to neglect needed maintenance. By regulating only the pre-1947 housing stock, it locked many working-class families into older buildings and out of rapidly growing parts of the city. When run-down neighborhoods, like Yorkville, experienced a renaissance, landlords could evict rent-controlled tenants to erect new, more expensive apartments. Still, for millions of New Yorkers who had housing, rent control provided an unusual degree of economic and social protection.[6]

Restraints on rents, of course, did nothing to help those without housing. Working-class New Yorkers turned to the government for this, too, a measure of how deeply ingrained an expanded notion of state responsibility had become during the New Deal and war years.[7] In 1935 the newly formed New York City Housing Authority—a quasi-independent municipal agency—opened the first public housing in the nation on the Lower East Side. A decade later the city was accommodating over fifty-eight thousand people in fourteen housing authority projects, with plans on the books to more than double the number of units.

In mid-1946 a coalition of some forty labor, veteran, civic, and community organizations—including the normally conservative American Legion—protested delays in launching the city's postwar housing program. They demanded immediate construction of fifty thousand units. In a flamboyant demonstration in October 1946, seventy-four veterans, including many unionists, occupied the State Senate chamber for nearly a day demanding immediate action by the state, too, to provide new housing.

Politicians of all stripes could not ignore the broad push for new, decent, government-provided middle-income homes. Even Robert Moses, who vehemently opposed government spending on housing for the nonpoor, conceded that "we must meet the problem in some way." With his cooperation, in March 1948, Mayor William O'Dwyer announced a sweeping program of public housing construction aimed at veterans and middle-income families.

At the time that O'Dwyer unveiled his housing program, public housing, in its brief history, already had gone through several incarnations. The first federally-funded housing, built early in the New Deal, aimed not "at the poorest of the poor," as housing expert Peter Marcuse put it, "but at those able to pay a subsidized going rent." Organized labor strongly supported this initiative as a way to generate jobs for construction workers and material producers and to create decent homes for workers. In New York, a series of mayors acknowledged the importance of labor support for public housing by appointing and reappointing Frank R. Crosswaith, the African-American socialist, ILGWU organizer, and head of the Harlem-based Negro Labor Committee, as a member of the housing authority board.

The 1937 Wagner-Steagall Housing Act altered the character of public housing. Under pressure from developers and real estate interests, who vehemently objected to any government competition in potentially profitable segments of the housing market, the new federal law placed an income ceiling on public housing tenants and repositioned federal-funded construction to serve the impoverished rather than the working or lower-middle classes, with design standards lowered accordingly.[8]

O'Dwyer's 1948 housing program—which used city rather than federal funds—revived public housing for the nonpoor. To accommodate "families whose earnings are above income limits for present low-rent projects, but too low for new privately built housing," the city constructed a series of "no-cash subsidy" housing projects. Unlike previous government-owned projects, these were self-sustaining, covering costs, including debt service, out of rent rolls. Rents were kept low by using city borrowing power to finance the projects, exempting the buildings from real estate taxes, and erecting them on vacant lots, generally away from the heart of the city (which also avoided demolishing existing housing). By contrast, when the city resumed building subsidized housing for the poor, it generally did so in already dense neighborhoods like Brownsville and East Harlem, using land cleared of deteriorated buildings. In effect, the city created a two-tier public housing system within a stratified housing market, aiming to charge $12.50 to $15.00 a room per month for the no-subsidy projects, as opposed to $5.50 to $8.50 for subsidized projects, with limited-dividend housing costing $16.00 to $18.00 a room and private developments $25.00 and up.

With impressive dispatch, the housing authority built twenty no-cash subsidy projects, with a total of 21,094 units. Though a casual observer might not notice a difference between these projects and housing put up for the poor, they were built to different standards. Rooms in the no-cash subsidy projects, for example, were larger, bathrooms had showers, toilets came with seat covers, and closets had wooden doors (all deemed unnecessary for the poor).[9]

The no-subsidy projects did not carry the stigma generally associated with public housing. Many New Yorkers viewed them quite favorably. Basketball great Kareem Abdul-Jabbar's family stayed in a Harlem apartment it shared with six other tenants for an extra year-and-a-half so that they could move into the just-completed Dyckman Houses, a no-subsidy project in upper Manhattan, rather than accept a place in a subsidized project on the Lower East Side. Like their new neighbors, Abdul-Jabbar's parents were solidly working-class: his father worked as a Transit Authority policeman, while his mother checked prices at a department store. (Abdul-Jabbar's family exemplified the cosmopolitanism and fortitude that made the postwar New York working class so great. His Brooklyn-born father was a Juilliard-trained musician and avid reader. A Catholic, he spoke Yiddish from his days delivering ice to Jewish families in Brooklyn. His mother, a migrant from North Carolina, though not overtly political, fiercely protested acts of racial discrimination while drumming into her only child the importance of education and personal resolve.) Though he had his share of street fights and suffered occasional prejudice, Abdul-Jabbar recalled Dyckman Houses as a "little multinational enclave" without "the bunker mentality" that later ruled New York.[10]

At the same time that the city launched the no-subsidy public housing program, it promoted housing for the same population segment it served — veterans, workers, and the lower middle class — by a second means, tax breaks and assistance for housing cooperatives. In this form of housing, common in New York but unusual elsewhere, tenants jointly own their buildings. Labor played a critical role in originating and popularizing co-op housing.

Immigrants from Finland organized the country's first non-profit cooperative houses in Sunset Park, Brooklyn, during and just after World War I. A decade later, several Jewish worker organizations sponsored large cooperative housing projects in the northern Bronx, near subway lines running to the garment district. The first was the "Co-ops," a two-block complex housing over seven hundred families on Bronx Park East, built between 1926 and 1929. Sponsored by a group which had close ties to the Communist Party, the Co-ops were a self-contained political community, rich in educational, social, and cultural activities. The socialist Shalom Aleichem Houses and the labor Zionist Farband Houses opened soon after.

The 1926 New York State Limited Dividend Housing Companies Law facilitated co-op development by giving tax abatements to housing developers that agreed to limit their profits to 6 percent and target low-income tenants.[11] Union involvement with cooperative housing began shortly after the law went into effect with the construction of the Amalgamated Houses, near Van Cortland Park. The driving force behind this effort, and many subsequent labor cooperatives, was Abraham Kazan. A Russian immigrant, Kazan worked for the ILGWU before moving over to the Amalgamated Clothing Workers (ACW) in 1918. He and other Amalgamated activists recognized a desperate need for decent housing for garment workers, especially those crammed into slums on the Lower East Side. Kazan and the ACW toyed with the idea of building single-family homes or union-owned multiunit dwellings before settling on the idea of cooperatively-owned apartment buildings.

Most residents in the Amalgamated Houses, which began with six buildings containing 303 units but soon doubled in size, belonged to the Amalgamated or another union, but they did not have to; only employers were barred. Like the Co-ops, Shalom Aleichem Houses, and Farband Houses, the Amalgamated Houses contained extensive common facilities and sponsored a wide range of social and educational endeavors, including cooperative buying schemes. All four projects shared, as architectural historian Richard Plunz put it, "similar urbanistic ideals," rooted in working-class Jewish socialism and the enforced communalism of the shtetl and the Lower East Side. One "Coopnik," who grew up amid the throngs of children participating in sports activities, dances, marches, and political clubs, later contrasted the "relative isolation" of his own children's suburban youth.[12]

A second ACW project, the 36-unit Amalgamated Dwellings, completed in November 1930 on Grand Street on the Lower East Side, had more complex roots. It grew out of a movement for urban renewal situated largely outside organized labor. Since the nineteenth century, reformers had seen the congested, unsanitary, and unsafe conditions of inner-city slums as dangerous to the well-being not only of their residents but of the city as a whole. Real estate interests joined with them in seeking slum clearance out of a desire to protect and enhance land values.[13] The idea for the Amalgamated Dwellings apparently came from Franklin D. Roosevelt, at the time governor of New York, who was eager to apply the co-op method to rebuilding slums.[14]

The Depression halted the construction of co-op housing. Many reformers hoped that New Deal housing programs would promote its resumption. However, a fight to get provisions to that end into the 1937 Housing Act failed. Still, as Richard Plunz put it, with the cooperatives that were built in the 1920s, "the working class in New York City had achieved a vision of incredible dimensions."[15]

The post–World War II housing crisis rekindled interest in cooperative housing among unionists, housing reformers, government officials, veterans groups, and even some private developers. Many targeted undeveloped areas on the edge of the city, primarily in Queens. Others linked cooperative development to slum clearance.

The Lower East Side provided the setting for the first postwar cooperative effort, which established a set of alliances central to housing and redevelopment in the city over the next three decades. The impulse for the project came from the continuing deterioration of the area around the Amalgamated Dwellings, which led the ACW's Kazan to worry that the co-op would be "engulfed by the surrounding slum buildings." The Bowery Savings Bank—

which held the mortgage on the Dwellings—shared his concern, suggesting to the ACW that it sponsor new housing near the existing project to stabilize the neighborhood.

The New York State Redevelopment Companies Law, passed during World War II, provided a vehicle to proceed. It empowered the city to condemn slum property and resell it to limited dividend sponsors for housing redevelopment, with tax abatements on any improvements. In 1945, Kazan won Amalgamated backing for an extremely ambitious redevelopment plan for the sixteen blocks surrounding the relatively modest Amalgamated Dwellings. However, Robert Moses, in his capacity as a member of the city planning commission (one of many hats he wore that gave him extraordinary leverage over housing and redevelopment), rejected the plan in a typically scathing letter.

Screwing up his courage, several weeks later Kazan met with Moses, who to his surprise seemed eager to work with the union on a scaled-down plan. Though the Amalgamated had to make some concessions—most notably, acquiescing with the automobile-obsessed Moses's insistence on including a garage in the project, even though few prospective tenants owned cars, and those who did could not afford to rent garage space—in short order the two sides hammered out plans to demolish sixty-five tenements occupying four blocks adjacent to the Amalgamated Dwellings, replacing them with 807 units of housing and shopping facilities. Moses helped the union secure a mortgage and facilitated the condemnation process. Unlike the prewar coops, which positioned low-rise buildings around landscaped courtyards, the "Hillman Houses," as the ACW named its new project, consisted of three twelve-story buildings placed apart from one another on large superblocks created by closing several small streets, an early example of "the tower in the park" design both Kazan and Moses preferred for their postwar projects.[16]

At roughly the same time the Hillman Houses were rising, longtime reformer Louis Pink put together a group of prominent business and civic leaders—including former GE president Gerard Swope, Federal Reserve Bank of New York chairman Beardsley Ruml, IBM president Thomas J. Watson, and former Secretary of the Treasury Henry Morgenthau—to sponsor Queensview, a co-op redevelopment project in Long Island City. After completing the 726-unit complex in 1951, the group went on to sponsor a second co-op redevelopment project in Queens and another in Brooklyn.[17]

Farther out in Queens, other co-ops arose on vacant land. The most impressive was Electchester, located a few blocks away from Queens College.

Between 1949 and 1966, five non-profit corporations created by the Joint Industry Board of the Electrical Industry built thirty-eight buildings containing more than 2,400 apartments on a 103-acre site. Members of Local 3 of the International Brotherhood of Electrical Workers got the first chance to buy apartments in the complex, which eventually included a small shopping center, owned by the Joint Industry Board's Pension Committee, and a six-story office building, owned by the Board's Education and Cultural Fund, which housed Local 3, the Joint Board, a public library, a union-sponsored savings bank, a coffee shop, a cocktail lounge, a bowling alley, and a large auditorium used for union, industry, and community functions. Meanwhile, in Brooklyn, Butchers Local 234 sponsored three cooperative housing projects. City tax abatements, part of the city and state effort to deal with the postwar housing crisis, enabled co-ops to keep costs within the range of the working class.[18]

As historian Sylvia Murray has pointed out, O'Dwyer's decision to provide substantial tax abatements to both housing authority "no-subsidy" projects and limited-dividend co-ops provoked considerable opposition from real estate interests, homeowner groups, and politicians beholden to them. Queens homeowners worried that rapid development would overburden an already strained infrastructure. Existing schools, sewers, roads, libraries, and public transportation could not handle the burgeoning population of young families. But the emotional power behind the opposition to tax abatements came from the resentment of established homeowners toward newcomers, egged on by builders and real estate interests seeking to block state competition. Using language that was to become familiar two decades later, in 1948, Queens borough president James Burke opposed the no-subsidy housing program in the name of those who "bought their homes out of the savings of a lifetime. These homeowners are not rich but they are self-respecting, law-abiding citizens of our city and country. The people of Queens," he claimed, "feel that public housing should be restricted to slum clearance and be built only for low-income families." Protesting Queensview, the Astoria Heights Taxpayers Association argued that "many GIs and home owners are struggling to maintain the homes they purchased while people with larger incomes are enjoying living in tax-free houses."

Elsewhere, and in later years in New York, such appeals in the name of small property owners carried considerable punch. But in a city of renters, they had limited impact, except in Queens, with its unusually high proportion of single-family homes. The city continued its no-subsidy housing program and in coming years granted tax exemptions to ever bigger co-op projects. However, these projects tended not to be sited in areas of single-family homes, perhaps as a result of political considerations as well as the rising cost of vacant land. In any case, the 1949 passage of a new federal housing law brought powerful incentives for linking public housing and co-op construction to slum clearance.[19]

The 1949 Housing Act—which authorized the construction of 810,000 units of public housing—seemed like a rare, postwar liberal victory. In reality, though, public housing served as a veneer for provisions of the act promoting slum clearance. Under Title I of the law, local authorities could condemn slum areas, purchase the land at market value, clear it, and resell it at a reduced price to redevelopers, with the federal government picking up two-thirds of the cost. Redevelopers were not required to rehouse residents on the same site, nor to build residential structures at all.[20]

No one better understood the law or employed it more to his advantage than Robert Moses. Ohio Senator Robert Taft, while helping write the Housing Act, discussed its slum clearance provisions with Moses, his old Yale classmate. Knowing what was coming, Moses got the mayor to appoint him to head a new Slum Clearance Committee with broad powers and little accountability. From this base, Moses mapped the rebuilding of huge sections of working-class New York. His preferred approach sited low-income public housing and middle-income Title I projects near each other in slum areas that private capital spurned, thereby creating mixed income neighborhoods (a goal for which Moses is rarely given credit) while enabling him to use the public projects to house some of those displaced by Title I clearance.[21]

Moses needed private sponsors for the Title I projects he conceived. A main support group he turned to was labor. At first glance this seems odd, since Moses generally hated unions and held workers in contempt. But Moses, above all else, liked getting things done, and for that unions could be useful. The building trades made natural allies in the fight for his vast public works program. Other groups—like the garment unions—could provide a liberal facade for controversial projects. Also, through their pension funds, unions had access to cash that might be tapped for housing (as Local 3 did to finance Electchester), with some willing to take chances in neighborhoods private developers avoided. Finally, in Abraham Kazan, Moses recognized a soulmate of sorts, a hard-driving closet utopian, willing and able to make deals and overcome obstacles to get a job completed.

Almost as soon as the 1949 Housing Act passed Congress, Moses approached ACW president Jacob Potofsky about building new housing on the Lower East Side. Potofsky, Kazan, and other Amalgamated housing veterans quickly planned a thirteen-acre project on Grand Street between the Hillman Houses and the East River, in the center of a riverside strip Moses had long targeted for redevelopment.[22] To carry out this plan, Kazan launched a new organization that would play a major role in housing working-class New Yorkers in the coming decades, the United Housing Foundation (UHF).

Over the years, Kazan had been frustrated that "most of the people that moved into our developments were not cooperators ideologically speaking— they were looking for better housing." Once settled in, few residents or project sponsors had an interest in organizing new cooperatives. With the availability of Title I money, Kazan wanted a vehicle to maintain momentum from project to project, sponsor new projects, and promote the cause of co-operation. He designed the UHF to play this role, getting unions, existing cooperatives, and fraternal groups to affiliate with it.[23]

The first project the UHF completed took it back to its roots: a fourteen-story building near the Bronx Amalgamated Houses. But the Title I project on Grand Street, East River Houses, cosponsored by the ILGWU, provided its first real test. Finding new accommodations—as required under Title I—for the 878 families living on the site, many of them Puerto Rican and some not eager to move, presented one challenge. Financing presented another. With help from Moses, Kazan raised equity and lined up loans, but a crisis developed when the FHA refused to guarantee mortgages for the project, threatening to scuttle it. David Dubinsky saved the day by having the ILGWU provide half the needed money without mortgage insurance.

East River Houses was the first Title I project in the country to be completed.[24] By the time it opened in 1956, the UHF had entered high gear. That year it launched three new projects: Park Reservoir Housing, near the Bronx Amalgamated complex; Seward Park Houses, another Title I co-op on Grand Street; and Penn South Houses, also a Title I project, ten buildings between Eighth and Ninth Avenues from 23rd to 29th street. (The idea for the latter came from the ILGWU's Charles Zimmerman, who wanted housing from which garment workers could walk to work.)[25]

As the years went by, each successive UHF project eclipsed its predecessor in size, scale, and controversy. The original Amalgamated Houses had been five-story walk-ups, while the Hillman Houses had twelve stories. By contrast, the East River, Seward Park, and Penn South buildings had twenty to twenty-two stories, and the tallest buildings at Co-op City, a later UHF project, topped out at thirty-three. The early UHF projects had attractive outside appearances, with distinctive corner balconies recessed into brick facades, but from Penn South on the exterior design of UHF projects became banal. Furthermore, their ever larger, tower-in-superblock layouts left buildings floating in poorly planned open spaces, distancing residents from surrounding streets and neighborhood life.[26]

One architect, Herman Jessor, designed or helped design every UHF project. Probably no architect of equivalent obscurity had as much impact on the visual landscape of New York. Jessor began his career as an apprentice in the firm of Springsteen and Goldhammer, which designed the original "Co-ops" and the first Amalgamated Houses. When George W. Springsteen died in the course of construction of the East River Houses, Jessor took over as lead architect for the UHF.

A committed leftist, Jessor—who designed some forty thousand units of housing over the course of his career—valued function over aesthetics. Both he and Kazan placed the highest value on building comfortable housing at affordable prices, with exterior appearance secondary. Apartments in UHF projects were thoughtfully laid out, with plenty of light, cross-ventilation in most rooms, eat-in kitchens (with windows), and parquet floors. Most projects included stores, recreation facilities, and other amenities, and two had electrical cogeneration plants. But cost-cutting on decorative features left the post–Seward Park projects extremely unattractive from the outside.[27]

Kazan defended UHF design in class terms. In 1955 the UHF submitted plans for a redevelopment project adjacent to its Seward Park complex. The city Housing and Redevelopment Board rejected them, disapproving of the high-rise design. Instead, it suggested using a variety of building shapes and sizes, admitting that this would force up the carrying charges from $21 to $22 per room to $28 to $29. In response, the UHF pulled out. A furious Kazan wrote, "We do not now accept the theory that the exterior design of a building is worth the difference of $7.00 a room per month to the man of low and moderate income. . . . I consider it totally unfair and unjust to make the man who is in need of assistance to be able to live in a decent dwelling to pay $25.00 a month and more, to make the city supposedly more attractive architecturally." Acknowledging that "diversity and more artistic design . . . are valuable to the community," Kazan pointedly asked "why have we not demanded that luxury housing lead the way?"[28]

In adopting high-rise, tower construction, Jessor and the UHF went along with a broad postwar trend. Associated with modernism, and believed to be the most economical layout for housing, the tower-in-the-park attracted Jessor and Kazan for its contrast to the cramped, dark streets of old law tenement districts. Recalling the site selection for the first Amalgamated project, Kazan noted, "We wanted to have a location that would be around open spaces, parks . . . since all our lives we lived in congested areas." Absent the vacant land of the north Bronx, the tower-in-the-park provided an inner-city substitute for the open spaces and fresh air so valued in the European socialist tradition out of which the UHF sprung.[29]

Moses's Title I projects—especially those sponsored by labor—won praise from liberals and appreciation from residents, with turnover in some UHF projects practically nonexistent. Nonetheless, as the Wagner years progressed, they came under increasing attack. In part the battle reflected the emergence of an alternative vision of city planning and urban design, most famously associated with Jane Jacobs, who hated superblock projects, high-rises, and large-scale redevelopment. Instead, she called for small-scale projects, integrated into their surroundings, that preserved the existing streetscape. Her followers held up Penn South as an example of how not to design a housing development, contending that it lacked human-scale spaces and articulation with the surrounding community.[30]

Penn South and other Title I projects came under criticism on another front as well, the displacement of existing residents and businesses. Slum clearance, by definition, meant evicting people. Neither Title I nor housing authority rules required that they be rehoused on the same site. One study done in the early 1950s found that only 15 percent of families dislodged by Title I and housing authority projects could afford Title I rents, with another 35 percent meeting income requirements for public housing. Thus half had to be rehoused in the private market. But with an estimated 170,000 New Yorkers evicted during the first seven years after World War II to make way for public works, private housing could not absorb the flood of slum refugees. Furthermore, some areas they settled in themselves turned into slums. The rapid deterioration of East New York, for example, in part stemmed from a massive influx of poor families forced out of their homes in Brownsville and Harlem to make room for public housing.[31]

The population reshuffle caused by public works and slum clearance hit nonwhites hardest. Blacks and Puerto Ricans were disproportionately represented among the displaced and prevented by discrimination from relocating in many areas of the city. Some found new homes in public housing, but very few ended up in Title I projects. When the ILGWU agreed to fund the East

River Houses, the *Amsterdam News* expressed fears that it would be lily-white, since neither the Amalgamated Houses nor the Amalgamated Dwellings had any black residents, and Hillman Houses only a few. Kazan protested that the UHF never discriminated, but he declined "to solicit any particular groups." When opened, East River Houses had only about fifty black cooperators, while some labor-sponsored housing projects remained all or virtually all white.[32]

The relocation problem, growing opposition to racial segregation, a re-invigorated urbanism that celebrated heterogeneous neighborhoods and lively street life, and the beginning of a movement to preserve the architectural heritage of the city all contributed to mounting criticism of "bulldozer" clearance. For the first time, the UHF found itself on the defensive. After some soul-searching, Kazan launched a counterattack. Critics of slum clearance, he contended, were "far-removed from the actual conditions under which people in blighted areas spend their days." While they bemoaned neighborhood destruction, areas like Grand Street, Kazan claimed, had had little community spirit to them, in part because many residents had lived there only a short while. By contrast, UHF projects constituted real communities, with their extensive social activities and cooperative endeavors. Kazan spurned landmarks preservation: "It seems to us," he wrote in the UHF newsletter, "that history has always been made by people, not by buildings, and there certainly is not much point in saving old relics." Kazan dismissed the cast-iron district, rumored to be among the first targets of the newly established city Landmarks Preservation Commission, with the comment that "a finer collection of fire traps would be hard to find anywhere."[33]

In their open support for bulldozer clearance, Moses and Kazan were two of a kind. As Marshall Berman has argued, Moses belonged to a long procession of master builders, from Goethe's Faust to Paris's Georges Haussmann to the TVA's David Lilienthal, committed to overcoming all obstacles, human and natural, no matter the cost. The cult of construction, with its deep faith in progress and taste for gigantism, found an intellectual home in Marxism, a geographic home in the Soviet Union as well as New York, and an architectural home in the modernist, high-rise slab. Kazan and Moses both imbibed the early-twentieth-century faith in the perfectibility of society through systematic thought and technological advance, though for one it came linked to cooperation and socialism and for the other to elitism and anticommunism. To outsiders, Moses and Kazan may have looked very different, but they recognized each other as brothers under the skin.[34]

In spite of growing grumbling, the May 1962 inauguration of Penn South demonstrated continued liberal support for the UHF and its vision. Over ten thousand people attended the opening ceremony. Dignitaries included Eleanor Roosevelt, Wagner, Dubinsky, Nelson Rockefeller, and President John F. Kennedy.[35] Still, Moses and the UHF sensed the shifting winds. After Penn South, with one exception—a long-delayed project in Coney Island—the UHF never again built on occupied land.[36] Its next project, Rochdale Village, seemed designed specifically to respond to the critics of Title I.

The idea for Rochdale Village originated with Moses. Tired of being assailed over the relocation issue, "the bugbear of Slum Clearance," as he called it, he saw a golden opportunity for building new housing when he learned that the New York Racing Association might abandon its Jamaica Race Track. From the start, Moses conceived of a racially integrated project on the site. What made this especially unusual was that the neighborhoods surrounding the track were largely African-American, so integration meant enticing whites into a black neighborhood rather than convincing them to allow blacks into a white area. Moses raised his idea for a Jamaica Race Track project with the UHF in 1956. It took three years before the UHF and various public agencies agreed on final plans, and another six years after that before the project, with 5,860 units, was completed.[37]

By the criteria of its sponsors, Rochdale Village triumphed. When it opened, the sprawling complex—the largest co-op in the country—was about 85 percent white and 15 percent black. (Over time, it became more heavily African-American.) Rochdale seemed to embody everything the civil rights movement, then at its height, called for, an interracial community that promoted mutualism and mutual understanding through joint endeavors, including not only the housing project itself but two cooperative supermarkets, a cooperative pharmacy and optical center, recreation facilities, parent associations, and countless clubs and civic groups. Furthermore, the UHF and Moses achieved all this without displacing a single person. Yet oddly, few of their critics—or anyone except the residents—seemed to care much about this city of nondescript, fourteen-story, red-brick buildings in southern Queens, far from the homes and offices of the opinion-making class.[38]

Co-op City was the Vietnam of the nonprofit cooperative housing movement. The movement's leaders, blinded to criticism by hubris and faith in their own good intentions, marched straight into a quagmire, literal and figurative. The debacle rended labor liberalism, all but destroying the institutions that had done so much to house the working class.

Co-op City began as a Rockefeller-Moses brainchild, designed to speed up production of middle-income housing, thereby checking middle-class flight to the suburbs. Additionally, it would bail out builder William Zeckendorf, who had erected a vast amusement park, "Freedomland," on marshland in the northeastern Bronx in a failed effort to create an East Coast Disneyland. To build a city on the scale of the celebrated British and Scandinavian new towns, state officials turned to the UHF.

By this time, Kazan had developed doubts about gigantism, disappointed by what he perceived to be a lack of cooperative spirit in the larger UHF projects. The aging Kazan recognized that the UHF in effect had become a construction organization, putting little stress on cooperative education or self-help. Nonetheless, financial, political, and psychological imperatives pushed the UHF to take on ever-larger projects, and Co-op City was the humdinger of them all.[39]

In early 1965 state and UHF officials unveiled plans for the largest housing development ever attempted in the country. From that moment on, things did not go smoothly. Site planning proved trying and construction far more difficult than anticipated. Building on the swampy site required driving fifty thousand piles and expensive landfill. As the project proceeded, building costs and interest rates soared, part of the Vietnam War–induced inflation. Finally, the sheer scale of Co-op City—15,382 apartments, five schools, three shopping centers, a library, three community centers, indoor parking for ten thousand cars, and numerous recreational facilities—overwhelmed the UHF. Poor planning, shoddy construction, inadequate supervision, and widespread reports of corruption plagued Co-op City, unlike earlier UHF projects. To make matters worse, during construction Kazan suffered a stroke.[40]

In 1965, when the first cooperators put up equity for Co-op City, the UHF projected monthly carrying charges of $23 a room, but rising costs invalidated this estimate long before the first tenants moved in late in 1968. The next year the UHF set carrying charges at $31 per room, raising them to $38 by 1973, and $53 by mid-1975 (after the Arab oil boycott). As their housing costs unexpectedly doubled, furious and frightened Co-op City residents launched one of the most extraordinary tenant struggles in United States history.[41]

Friction between Co-op City residents and project sponsors did not arise only from rising carrying charges. Kazan and his colleagues, first at the Amalgamated and then at the UHF, always had been decidedly paternal in their treatment of co-op residents. Generally they did not distribute stock in the co-op corporations immediately, instead themselves selecting initial co-op boards, putting on them prominent nonresidents (often union leaders). When cooperators received their shares (and with them voting rights), they usually backed incumbent boards.

In the 1960s, UHF paternalism, like so many other structures of authority, began to be challenged. The first assault came at Penn South where, to the utter consternation of the UHF, David Smith, a veteran of the CP labor-left, led a dissident slate to victory in a board election. While this might have been written off to ancient left factional battles, rumblings of trouble occurred elsewhere. Disgruntled co-op members picketed the 1969 UHF annual meeting, demanding lower carrying charges and tenant control in projects where the UHF retained member stock. Then, in the early 1970s, about a fourth of the residents of Rochdale Village joined a rent strike protesting rising charges.

To UHF stalwarts, such "divisiveness and irresponsible conduct" reflected a lack of cooperative spirit. The residents of Co-op City had a "rent control mentality," a UHF vice president complained, carried over from years of battling landlords. Still thinking of themselves as tenants rather than property owners, "they were philosophically tuned to the idea that rents are political." Perhaps the fact that many of the fifty thousand Co-op City residents at one point or another had belonged to left-wing organizations contributed to their deep hostility to all building managers, including the UHF. Charlie Rosen, a thirty-three-year-old printer who emerged as the most prominent tenant leader, grew up in a Communist household and had been active in the Maoist Progressive Labor Party. Rosen viewed UHF leaders as trade union bureaucrats who pushed around workers they held in contempt: "They were the same Social Democratic whores I've hated all my life."[42]

In July 1972 a UHF official appealed to the executive board of the Central Labor Council to try to convince unionists living in Co-op City to stop attacking the UHF, but to no avail. Two months later, Co-op City residents sued the UHF for stock fraud, charging that it had failed to keep its promises on carrying charges made to purchasers of co-op shares. With massive penalties possible, the UHF saw the suit as a threat to its very existence. Over the years the UHF had begun providing a variety of technical and administrative services to member co-ops to take advantage of economies of scale. Now it began its own dismemberment, selling its insurance subsidiary to pay legal costs and spinning off other units to protect them if a court defeat brought down the parent organization.

In a key ruling, the United States Supreme Court sided with the UHF, declaring stock in a low-cost housing corporation not to be a security subject to federal regulation. The case bounced back to the state courts, where it ground on for over a decade.[43] Meanwhile, in June 1975 Co-op City tenants turned to another tactic, withholding their carrying charges, or as most thought of it, their rent.

Over the next thirteen months, the rent strikers—over 80 percent of Co-op City residents—waged a tenacious battle. As veteran unionists and tenant activists, small businessmen, workers, and technicians—most products of the densely communal life of the Bronx working class—they had the skills, experience, and political savvy needed for an audacious effort. Ironically, in the course of it they developed precisely the community spirit Kazan had bemoaned as lacking in other UHF endeavors. When their leaders, slapped with court injunctions, faced the possibility of jail, eviction, and impoverishment, they picked second-line cadres to take over if necessary. Fearing that authorities would seize strike steering committee equipment, tenants secreted printing machinery in the project to keep literature flowing. And most important, a network of building captains collected over fifteen million dollars in withheld rent checks, putting them in green plastic garbage bags that strike leaders hid in the attics and homes of secret sympathizers. The *Wall Street Journal* decried the strike as "mass neurosis," an illustration of how a "generous government subsidy somehow becomes converted into a vested right."

When the rent strike began, the UHF—stunned by recent developments—gave up; the labor members of the Co-op City board resigned, ceding control to the state, which held the project mortgage. By then, Nelson Rockefeller had gone on to the vice presidency, leaving Democratic governor Hugh Carey holding the bag. At first, state officials and Bronx Democratic regulars tried to smash the strike, but as it wore on the dishonesty, malfeasance, and even criminal corruption of the Bronx Democratic machine became exposed. Meanwhile, reform Democrats, eyeing fifteen thousand almost exclusively Democratic families, sided with the strikers. Finally, in June 1977, the strikers and the state signed a truce: in return for handing over the withheld rent, the strike committee would take over the co-op board and manage the project for a six-month trial period, during which rents would be frozen. At a victory rally, Charlie Rosen, now head of the board of a corporation with five hundred million dollars in assets, gleefully shouted, "We beat the bastards!"[44]

For Co-op City residents, this was the beginning of a long, largely successful effort to force the state to take responsibility for construction defects and subsidize a return to financial stability. But for the UHF, the end had come. In 1967 it had announced another giant project to be built on swampland on the edge of the city, "Twin Pines Village." Landfill at the Canarsie site began in 1970, but inflation and delays drove up costs. By early 1972 projected carrying charges exceeded what the UHF felt its constituency could afford. Fearful of Co-op City redux, the UHF sold its land and plans to a commercial developer, which using Jessor's design (his last) built "Starret City." Dispirited by the Co-op City and Twin Pines debacles, the UHF went into prolonged dormancy, never again building even a single unit of new housing.[45]

The demise of the UHF virtually ended union housing efforts. All along, a few unions had sponsored cooperative housing outside the UHF umbrella. But only one major project followed Co-op City, 1199 Plaza, a 1974 East Harlem co-op sponsored by the Drug and Hospital Workers Union. The changed financial and political climate proved inhospitable to similar endeavors. A final co-op effort, Manhattan Plaza, sponsored by seven entertainment industry unions, ran into such financial problems that the city foreclosed on its mortgage, turning it into a rental complex. After the 1970s, the only labor-sponsored housing built in New York were small, federally-aided projects for the elderly.[46]

All told, individual unions and the UHF erected nearly forty thousand units of cooperative housing in New York City, the vast majority between the mid-1940s and the mid-1960s. In 1970, a median of three persons lived in each unit of New York City rental housing, which suggests that roughly 120,000 people lived in New York labor's housing empire.[47]

In housing the population of a midsized city, labor-sponsored cooperatives revealed and reinforced New York's exceptionality. No thorough national account of labor-sponsored housing exists, but in all likelihood, a more complete count would show that labor groups built more units of housing in New York City than they did in the entire rest of the country.[48]

During the postwar years, Americans of all classes equated social and economic success with single-family, suburban homeownership. For workers this often brought self-identification as middle-class rather than working-class. In New York, however, a significant fraction of the working and middle classes sought and found what they believed to be the good life in urban cooperatives. This contributed to New York's relative success compared to other old cities in maintaining its population and tax base, while helping to perpetuate the unique culture of the city.[49]

By 1965 the housing situation in New York had significantly improved compared to twenty years earlier. The vacancy rate for rental units—one indication of the supply-demand relationship—reached a postwar high of 3.2 percent. In both rental and owner-occupied buildings, New Yorkers had significantly more living space (measured by rooms per person) than in the immediate postwar years. Furthermore, the overall quality of the housing stock had been considerably upgraded.[50]

Between 1946 and 1970, 785,100 units of housing were built in New York. With demolitions and conversions, this resulted in a net gain of 612,200 units. Labor-sponsored cooperatives accounted for nearly 5 percent of the new units; public housing another 16 percent. (By the early 1970s, well over a half million New Yorkers lived in public housing.) Taken together, various types of government-subsidized housing—including public housing, Title I, Mitchell-Lama, and tax-abated limited dividend projects—comprised an estimated 30 percent of the dwelling units built in the city during the quarter-century after the war. A majority of all housing units either had been erected with government assistance or fell under rent control.[51]

For working-class New Yorkers, the root of the housing problem lay in the gap between their income and the market cost of decent shelter. Organized labor helped lessen the gap by promoting government housing subsidies, sponsoring nonprofit projects, supporting rent control and public housing, and raising wages. In a sense, the last measure—boosting working-class income—constituted labor's greatest housing program.

CHAPTER 8.

"Adequate Medical Care"

During the two decades after World War II, New York workers erected a comprehensive health care system that brought medical service and insurance to groups previously at the mercy of fate and charity. In doing so, they took a different path than the rest of the country. As Cold War America turned rightward, liberal hopes for a national health system hit a stone wall of political and professional opposition. Almost alone among advanced industrial societies, the United States remained wedded to individual, self-employed doctors in fee-for-service practice, with commercial firms providing most medical insurance.[1] Unwilling to accept this rejection of socialized medicine, New York labor developed health care systems operated directly by unions or by labor-influenced, nonprofit institutions. It also pioneered the unionization of medical industry employees.

In many respects, the story of New York labor and health parallels that of housing. Faced with an enormous social need, inadequately addressed by the private market, workers and their allies pressed the state to intervene. At the same time, working-class institutions launched initiatives of their own along collectivist lines. Doing so required building alliances with business and government leaders, in some cases the same men labor dealt with about housing. In spite of impressive success, labor eventually had to scale back its direct provision of services. Like housing, health security illustrates the limits of working-class power as well as its extent.

For most of American history, ill health meant disaster for working-class families. Dangerous working conditions, crowded housing, and poor living standards made accidents and disease common. The financial repercussions could be catastrophic. Many working-class families never used doctors, and until World War II those who did usually faced only modest charges. But few workers had sufficient savings to cover lost income even for a brief while.

The collective quest for protection from the consequences of ill health is as old as the working class itself. One reason workers founded ethnic societies, fraternal groups, and unions was to provide sickness and death benefits. However, self-insurance often had serious problems, with actuarial principles unknown, fund misuse common, and benefits too small to make much difference.[2]

During the early decades of the twentieth century, a few New York unions and fraternal groups experimented with directly providing medical care. In 1913 several ILGWU locals founded a Union Health Center that offered diagnostic and preventive services and later added ambulatory treatment. Small user payments and union subsidies financed the center.[3] In 1930 the International Workers Organization (IWO) organized a medical plan along different lines. In return for a small monthly payment, plan members could utilize the services of a panel of doctors, located throughout the city, without fee. In addition, the IWO offered discounts on specialist visits, obstetrical care, surgery, x-rays, drugs, optical services, and dental work, and a birth control clinic, which both members and nonmembers could use for a yearly fee. The Transport Workers Union (TWU) launched a similar medical plan in 1939.[4]

Impressive as they were, the ILGWU, IWO, and TWU programs, along with a few other union and fraternal medical plans, covered only a small fraction of the city's working class. Some additional workers received medical care through their employer. But until World War II, most working-class New Yorkers, when sick or injured, received either very modest cash benefits or no help at all.[5]

The Second World War altered the social, economic, and political framework for health care delivery. While in the short run it reduced working-class health security, in the long run it paved the way for new modes of mass medical care. The social disruption and ethnic assimilation stemming from war mobilization accelerated the decline of benefit programs sponsored by local ethnic and fraternal groups. Also, as physicians entered the armed services and economic recovery increased doctor utilization, it became difficult to find or retain personnel for IWO-TWU type programs. At the same time, the positive experience millions of soldiers and sailors had with military medicine undermined the medical profession's repeated assertions that only individual doctor-patient arrangements could deliver quality care. So did the widely-publicized, prepaid medical service that Henry J. Kaiser provided for workers at his West Coast shipyards and defense plants. Furthermore, the 1942 Beveridge report in Britain, which called for a comprehensive system of state social benefits and a national health service, stimulated liberal interest in a government-sponsored medical program.[6]

The Roosevelt administration had considered including medical insurance in its 1935 social security proposal, but dropped the idea. During the war it revived it as part of a plan for a broad expansion of social security. Embodied in the Wagner-Murray-Dingell bill, first introduced into Congress in 1943, the proposed comprehensive, universal federal insurance scheme remained the favored approach to medical security among liberals and unionists for the next decade. But even with support from Roosevelt and later Truman, fierce opposition from the American Medical Association (AMA) and congressional Republicans made its passage a formidable challenge.[7]

In 1944, Mayor Fiorello La Guardia, anticipating the possible failure of Wagner-Murray-Dingell, proposed the creation of a regional, nonprofit health delivery system. La Guardia argued that a national health system was preferable to a local one, just as a compulsory plan was preferable to a voluntary one. But given political and practical considerations, the best way to begin, he felt, was with a local, voluntary program that could demonstrate the advantages of comprehensive medical insurance.

La Guardia's proposed Health Insurance Plan of Greater New York, or HIP, departed from established medical practice in several respects. First, it was a prepaid service plan, rather than indemnity insurance. In return for a fixed annual fee, HIP members would be entitled to comprehensive doctor services without additional charges. Second, subscribers could only see doctors who belonged to group practices associated with HIP. HIP assigned the groups, which included family practitioners and specialists, specific geographic regions and paid them a fixed amount per patient (capitation), rather than reimbursing for particular services. HIP planners hoped that the combination of no patient fees and capitation would encourage doctor visits and preventive medicine while holding down costs. State law forbid insurers from covering both doctor and hospital costs, so HIP required subscribers to enroll in Blue Cross, a nonprofit hospital insurance plan.

Although the city government played a critical role in initiating it, HIP was not a government entity but a nonprofit corporation. Its board of directors reflected the corporatist inclination of the group around La Guardia that launched it, including liberal bankers and businessmen, prominent doctors and hospital officials, and three labor representatives. To give HIP an initial subscriber base, the city agreed to pay half the cost of a combined HIP–Blue Cross package for any municipal employee who wanted to sign up.[8]

HIP did not help workers deal with their loss of income when they became sick or injured, as the Murray-Wagner-Dingell Bill would have done. For this, unions turned to state government. Rhode Island passed the first state disability insurance law in 1942, followed by California and New Jersey. These plans used payroll taxes to fund cash payments for those unable to work due to non-work-related sickness or injury. (Workmen's compensation — established in New York State in 1914 — covered work-related injuries and disease.) New York employers opposed disability insurance if mandatory or state-run. They won on the latter issue but not the former: in 1949 New York State required all employers to provide payments for non-employment-related disability, with up to thirteen weeks of benefits at a rate up to twenty-six dollars a week, through contracts with insurance companies, self-insurance, or participation in state-approved plans. Financing came from employer and employee payroll contributions.[9]

With disability in place, most New York workers received cash payments, for a few months anyway, in the event of job loss (unemployment insurance), work-related accidents or disease (workmen's compensation), or non-work-related ill health (disability). These mandates went a long way toward reducing the catastrophic effects of temporarily stopping work. A 1949 bill called for further protection in the form of state medical and hospital insurance, to be financed through a payroll tax, but this and subsequent, similar proposals failed. With the possibility of action in Albany or Washington diminishing, unions experimented with other ways of ensuring medical care for their members.[10]

While World War II stimulated discussion of an expanded state role in medicine, it simultaneously promoted another approach to health security, employee benefits achieved through collective bargaining. Only a few unions had bargained for employer-financed medical benefits before World War II. During the war their number rapidly grew, largely as a result of federal policy. A National War Labor Board rule allowing employers to contribute up to five percent of their payrolls for "fringe benefits," such as vacation pay, shift differentials, sick leave, and health benefits, without violating the wartime freeze on wages provided a way for employers and unions to address worker discontent with wage stagnation. Because the federal government treated contributions for medical and insurance benefits as tax-deductible business expenses, they cost employers little during a period of high corporate taxes.[11]

Even before the war ended, a flood of union contracts included employer-financed health benefits. Though many accounts of fringe benefits (or "social benefits" as they were often called at the time) stress the role of large industrial unions, particularly the Mine Workers, Auto Workers, and Steelworkers, in institutionalizing them, many local unions, including craft outfits, won health benefits before the industrial behemoths. In New York, the Amalgamated Clothing Workers, Fur Dyers, Furniture Workers, Hatters,

Hotel and Restaurant Employees, construction electricians, Garment Workers, and drugstore workers negotiated health benefits during the war.[12]

Several postwar developments accelerated the trend toward negotiated health benefits. First came the realization that Wagner-Murray-Dingell would not pass soon. Most unionists hoped and expected that eventually a plan like it would be enacted, but, until then, they saw negotiated benefits as a stopgap. Second, in 1949 the Supreme Court ruled health benefits a mandatory subject of negotiation under federal labor law; companies could not simply refuse to discuss them. Finally, in an era of "pattern bargaining," when the giant industrial unions did win health benefits in the late 1940s, many smaller labor groups felt compelled to follow suit.[13]

National corporations generally insisted on keeping control over money allocated for bargained benefits. However, smaller firms—the norm in New York—generally had neither the desire nor the ability to organize benefit programs. Instead, unions, with greater resources and sophistication about welfare issues, took the prime responsibility. Typically employers agreed to pay 2 or 3 percent of their payroll into benefit trust funds which they jointly administered with labor or which unions ran alone (until Taft-Hartley made this illegal for multi-company funds). With this money, unions pursued several paths toward health security.[14]

Perhaps most impressively, during the fifteen years after World War II, New York workers erected an enormous medical system under their own control in the form of union health centers. Elsewhere in the country, few unions (with the notable exception of the Mine Workers) set up their own medical facilities. For one thing, it required densely clustered members, common in New York but not so in many areas. For another, the AMA and local medical societies fiercely opposed prepaid group practices like union clinics, making it difficult to recruit doctors. New York atypically had so many doctors, including a large cadre of liberals and leftists, that unions could staff health facilities.[15]

Unions liked running their own clinics for several reasons. Medically, clinics allowed proactive care, including yearly physicals, preventive health programs, and health education, rather than simply reactive therapy. Financially, they allowed direct control over costs. And organizationally, they strengthened and stabilized the labor movement, providing a strong incentive for workers to remain in unionized jobs and tangible evidence of the advantages of unionism.

The ILGWU health center served as a model for other unions. During

World War II, the ILGWU bargained for employer-financed benefit funds, which it used to support the center, replacing dues money and user fees. Eliminating charges for visits contributed to an over fourfold increase in utilization between 1944 and 1952. By the end of the 1940s, the center occupied six stories of its own large, garment-center building. To handle the nearly half-million visits a year, most after work or on weekends, it employed 148 physicians, thirty-five nurses, five pharmacists, twenty-seven technicians, and 150 clerical workers.[16]

The Amalgamated Clothing Workers, following the path of its longtime rival, opened its Sidney Hillman Health Center in 1951, jointly financed by employers and the union. It, too, provided diagnostic, therapeutic, and preventive services. Indicative of the union's social and medical ambitions, the center earmarked a quarter of a million dollars for research into cardiovascular disease and arthritis.[17] Three years later, the Laundry Workers Joint Board, affiliated with the Amalgamated, opened its own health center in a building it constructed near the Empire State Building, an extraordinary accomplishment for workers in an industry notorious for low wages, poor conditions, and ill health.[18] Other New York unions that opened health centers included the Hotel Trades Council, Building Service Employees Local 32B, Longshoremen, and United Wire Workers.

Through the late 1950s, the union clinic model of health care thrived in New York. By 1958, thirteen union health centers provided care to a half-million New Yorkers. The centers instilled in their patients the notion that health services were "a matter of absolute right," making all but impossible a return to the days when working families had to fend for themselves in the medical marketplace.[19] Yet in spite of this seeming success, direct union provision of health care proved an abortive experiment. Other modes of servicing workers ultimately proved dominant.

HIP was the closest cousin to the union clinics, sharing with them a stress on group practice, disease prevention, and health education at odds with mainstream medicine. HIP envisioned itself as a close ally of the labor movement. Its very first subscribers were 2,643 members of Chefs, Cooks, Pastry Cooks and Assistants Local 89. In the mid-1950s, 70 percent of HIP's half-million members worked for the city government and another 15 percent enrolled through a union.

Union leaders liked the comprehensive nature of HIP coverage. They also appreciated its pro-labor stance. Following its ad hoc effort in 1950 to provide medical care to striking telephone workers, HIP developed a plan to regularly provide emergency care to strikers and their dependents. Also, when in the late 1940s it began bargaining with its clerical and sales staff, HIP became the first nonprofit health insurer to recognize a union of its employees.[20]

In the late 1950s, then, roughly a million New Yorkers got some or all of their health care through a union clinic or HIP. Nonetheless, in New York, as elsewhere, the most common health benefit for workers was Blue Cross. New York hospitals founded the area's Blue Cross plan in the mid-1930s to ensure themselves a steady income stream from insured patients while providing subscribers cost-protection in case of hospitalization. In return for an annual fee, Blue Cross guaranteed subscribers twenty-one days of free hospitalization in a semiprivate room, with a 50 percent discount for an additional ninety days. (Blue Cross did not cover doctors' fees, even for in-hospital services.) Individual middle-class subscribers made up the initial Blue Cross base, but the plan soon began working with employers to sign up workers through payroll deductions.

As they began bargaining fringe benefits, unions found Blue Cross attractive because it relieved them of the complex challenges of initiating and administering their own hospitalization plans. After discussions with labor leaders, Blue Cross took a number of steps to attract union subscribers, adding AFL and CIO representatives to its board and tailoring its plan to the needs of particular union locals. By the late 1950s, a majority of all union members in the region had Blue Cross coverage, contributing to the plan's meteoric growth.[21]

Though little noted at the time, the labor-aided growth of Blue Cross negatively impacted the municipal hospital system, a major health provider for the working class and the poor. Because Blue Cross paid for semiprivate rooms, which most of the municipal hospitals lacked (they had old-fashioned wards), insured patients preferred going to the nonprofit "voluntary" hospitals, bringing to them a very substantial stream of working-class assets while starving the city system of needed funds. Some voluntaries exacerbated the situation by "dumping" chronically-ill patients into municipal hospitals once their insurance coverage expired. As the voluntaries thrived, the municipal system deteriorated.[22] The failure to win universal health insurance thus exacted a subtle price, as advances by the unionized and better-paid sectors of the working-class undermined services for those beneath them.

Though largely ignoring this problem, labor leaders, even as they signed up their members with Blue Cross, became increasingly uncomfortable with the insurance provider. They did not like the limited nature of its benefits, their cost, and the meager labor role in the organization's governance. Every time Blue Cross rates went up, as they frequently did in the late 1940s and 1950s, labor protested, demanding more comprehensive benefits and greater representation on the insurer's board of directors. Blue Cross tried to mollify labor, for example in 1953 putting a member of the Communications Workers on staff to serve as a liaison with the CIO. But union dissatisfaction grew. In the late 1940s, Local 65, having left RWDSU, set up its own hospitalization plan modeled on Blue Cross but costing less. The Furniture Workers pulled out of Blue Cross in the mid-1950s. Meanwhile, CIO leaders discussed forming their own health insurance company.[23]

The CIO deliberations were part of a broad union reconsideration of health benefits. By the mid-1950s, unions had a decade or more experience providing health security. Through bargaining gains and rising wages (to which employer fringe contributions often were pegged), they saw the possibility of expanding coverage. At the same time, many complained about available options.

Some unions grew disillusioned with directly providing health care, even as others continued to build clinics. As early as 1948, Local 1199 dropped a free doctors' service it provided after finding that many eligible members failed to use it.[24] A far more significant defection came in 1956, when three locals affiliated with the Dress and Waistmakers Joint Board pulled their nearly forty-five thousand members out of the ILGWU health center. The dispersion of garment workers out of neighborhoods close to the center in part motivated the move. But other factors also came into play. Some ILGWU leaders criticized the large size of the center and the quality of its care. Others focused on the extent of benefits their money bought. In 1954 the joint board expended $44.04 per member for health benefits, which included health center services and disability payments but not hospitalization insurance. HIP cost $36.36 a year. By pressing employers to increase their welfare contributions and to completely take over disability insurance, the union could purchase both Blue Cross (at $19.20 per person) and HIP for its members, providing far more comprehensive coverage than in the past.

This benefits realignment, proposed by Cutters union manager Charles Zimmerman, faced opposition. Luigi Antonini, head of the Italian dressmakers, feared losing the close bond between the union and its members created by the direct provision of sick benefits and health services. But Zimmerman's argument that "doctor and hospital bills create havoc in the hearts of people [facing serious illness] . . . and our objective should be to help overcome this situation" carried the day.[25]

Initially the dress board intended to replace health center services only with HIP, but it ultimately offered members a choice between HIP and Group Health Insurance (GHI). GHI was the oldest prepaid medical plan in the city, having been founded in 1939 as an offshoot of the cooperative movement. Like HIP, it had close ties to labor, with significant union representation on its board. After experimenting with several medical and surgical plans, in 1956 it introduced a highly popular "Family Doctor Plan." For an annual premium about the same as HIP's, GHI covered the full cost of home, office, and hospital care by any physician who agreed to accept its fee schedule. (Subscribers using nonparticipating doctors had to pay any costs over the schedule.) Thus, like HIP, GHI provided comprehensive, prepaid coverage, but whereas HIP depended on its own group practices, facilitating preventive health and quality control programs but narrowing the choice of doctors, GHI gave subscribers virtually unlimited doctor choice while exerting little control over medical practice.[26]

Many, though by no means all, workers eligible for HIP objected to its system of closed physician panels. Some found the location and hours of HIP doctors inconvenient. Others wanted to continue using doctors they saw before HIP coverage became available. By the mid-1950s, many city workers and members of unions contracting with HIP demanded that indemnity insurance be offered as an alternative. Starting with the dressmakers, HIP reluctantly acquiesced to such "dual insurance" plans, which soon became common.

To its chagrin, HIP discovered that under dual plans a majority of unionists chose indemnity insurance (typically GHI). Furthermore, when unions allowed members to transfer between plans subsequent to their initial enrollment, HIP consistently suffered a net loss of subscribers. A particularly telling blow came in 1958 when the Furriers' union introduced a dual HIP-GHI plan. In spite of an extensive education effort, a union leadership predisposed to HIP, and membership, as HIP put it, "probably more idealogically oriented in favor of HIP than any other union group we have enrolled in the past," HIP signed up only a third of the Furriers.[27] HIP's problems extended beyond limited doctor choice. Clients complained of impersonal or rude service, long waits, and other inconveniences. To some extent, these resulted from a long, vicious campaign by local medical societies against HIP. Seeing HIP as a threat to individual practitioner, fee-for-service medicine, New

York-area county medical societies at various times declined to admit HIP doctors, socially and professionally ostracized them, declared group practice unethical, and lobbied for legislation making closed physician panels illegal. The refusal of hospitals in Staten Island and parts of Nassau County to grant HIP doctors admitting privileges made it extraordinarily difficult for the plan to take root in those growing areas, to which workers were beginning to move.

The relentless attack by organized medicine gave HIP a somewhat unsavory image among doctors and potential subscribers. Originally, HIP hoped that its doctors would work exclusively in HIP centers. However, in many areas it could not recruit staff on that basis, so it ended up depending on physicians who worked out of their own offices seeing both HIP and private patients, with the former often feeling they received inferior treatment. The cumulative effect of all this was a widespread belief that HIP provided second-class medicine. When offered the possibility of using, without financial penalty, practitioners who served all types and classes of patients, many workers jumped at the chance.[28]

Responding to changing circumstances and the desire of many union members for a free choice of doctors and hospitals near their homes, unions in New York became less idiosyncratic, increasingly offering the same type of benefit packages as labor elsewhere, a combination of indemnity insurance for doctors' bills, either from a commercial carrier, GHI, or Blue Shield (a plan sponsored by the local medical societies) and Blue Cross for hospital costs. Union clinics and HIP continued to operate, but no longer as the clear favorite modes of labor health security.

Labor's strategic shift had its downside. As New York unions deemphasized the direct provision of medical services, they found themselves dependent on organizations largely outside their control, unable to assure the quality of care delivered or control rapidly escalating costs. With more and more health care taking place in hospitals, Blue Cross became the prime focus of their frustration. The depth of the problem became evident in 1957, when Blue Cross applied for a 40 percent rate hike. The AFL and CIO councils strenuously opposed the increase, which they feared would drain union benefit funds or force renegotiation of employer contributions. The underlying problem, in labor's view, was that "commercial thinking and standards have begun to creep into Blue Cross policy making"; rather than representing the interests of its subscribers, monitoring the quality and cost of care, too often Blue Cross simply acted as a collection agent for the hospitals. In the face of a labor-led campaign, state regulators rejected the Blue Cross rate request, but the next year granted a smaller increase. When Blue Cross asked for another rate hike in 1959, labor reacted more vehemently than ever, for by then another issue had become conflated with health costs, the unionization of health care workers.[29]

Given the huge revenue stream it directed toward Blue Cross and Blue Shield, the fact that none of the insurers' two thousand employees was unionized irritated labor, particularly Office and Professional Employees Local 153, which represented many HIP clerical workers.[30] But this never became a major issue. By contrast, resistance to the unionization of hospital workers created a deep schism between labor and the medical establishment.

In 1957, Local 1199, the druggist and drugstore union, hired Elliot Godoff, who had been trying to unionize hospital workers since before World War II, to begin a hospital organizing campaign. At the time, the voluntary hospitals were entirely nonunion. Explicitly exempted from federal labor laws and uncovered by state statute, they subjected their nonprofessional staff to atrocious conditions. Newly hired workers received less than the minimum wage. Poverty forced some full-time hospital employees to go on public relief. Managers were paternal and sometimes autocratic. Furthermore, they were almost all white, while more and more service and support workers were Puerto Rican or black.

Godoff first targeted Montefiore Hospital in the Bronx, where he had led earlier, unsuccessful organizing efforts. Concentrating on the mostly Caribbean and African-American service workers, by mid-1958, 1199 signed up a majority of the hospital's nine hundred employees. Ineligible to use legal mechanisms to force recognition, the union instead mobilized support within the labor movement and from such leading liberals as Eleanor Roosevelt and Herbert Lehman.[31]

Critical to 1199's success was the surprisingly strong support it received from Harry Van Arsdale Jr. The tough head of IBEW Local 3—before the war he was found guilty of shooting an opponent and inciting a picket line riot but managed to get both convictions overturned—Van Arsdale emerged in the late 1950s as the city's most powerful unionist, and one of its most open-minded and dynamic. Under his leadership Local 3 developed an extraordinary range of programs, situating its members' lives within the framework of unionism to an unusual degree. Pushing the benefit fund model to its limit, by the early 1960s the local provided (jointly with management) pensions; disability, medical, surgical, hospitalization, and optical benefits; free dental care; educational benefits for members and college scholarships for their children; a Long Island estate housing a convalescent home and week-long courses on "critical thinking"; and, of course, Electchester. While this all-encompassing benefit package reinforced a certain insularity among unionized electricians, Van Arsdale himself increasingly looked outward, sometimes to the chagrin of his colleagues. When he made Local 3 officials sit through a screening and two-hour discussion of *Viva Zapata*, to illuminate how power can make a leader forget his origins, many left stupefied.[32]

Following the death of Martin Lacey in late 1957, Van Arsdale took over the leadership of the AFL Central Trades Council. Immediately he began breathing life into an organization that, like its CIO counterpart, had become somnambulant. When the AFL and CIO councils merged in early 1959, they elected Van Arsdale president of the new AFL-CIO Central Labor Council, making him in title as well as reality the leading unionist in the city. Symbolic of the energy the merger and Van Arsdale's leadership unleashed, in 1959, 115,000 New Yorkers marched in the city's first Labor Day Parade in twenty years.[33]

Van Arsdale saw in 1199 a way to demonstrate a commitment to black and Hispanic workers at a time when, nationally, organized labor was coming under fire for discriminatory practices. His backing gave 1199 far greater legitimacy than it would have had on its own, neutralizing efforts to tar it with its red past. Van Arsdale also provided 1199 with access to the highest levels of local power. His intervention with Mayor Wagner helped 1199 secure a victory at Montefiore. After the union threatened to strike the hospital in December 1957, Wagner called an emergency collective bargaining session. With Van Arsdale representing the hospital workers, Montefiore agreed to recognize 1199 as their sole bargaining agent and negotiate a collective bargaining agreement. To help finance the settlement, Wagner increased by 25 percent the rate at which the city reimbursed voluntary hospitals for the care of charity ward patients.[34]

Following its Montefiore victory, 1199 moved quickly to organize other hospitals. Seeing an opportunity, other unions jumped in, too, with Building Service Employees Local 144 eventually organizing a sizable bloc of workers at nursing homes and small hospitals. At many hospitals, workers eagerly greeted 1199 organizers, most full-time drugstore workers helping out before or after work. Their reception testified to the positive image unionism held among black and Puerto Rican New Yorkers, who filled most hospital service and maintenance jobs.

1199 quickly built a large following at a half-dozen major voluntaries, but the hospitals it targeted, unlike Montefiore, dug in their heels against union recognition. Unable to legally force recognition elections, on May 9, 1959, 1199 struck five hospitals. (A sixth walked out later.) Though a high percentage of workers—thirty-five hundred altogether—struck, the hospitals, by reassigning staff, using volunteers, and hiring new workers, maintained normal operations while standing fast in their antiunionism.

Only massive backing from the city labor movement—the greatest display of labor solidarity New York had seen since the post–World War II strike wave—allowed 1199 to survive. District 65 lent the hospital union ten organizers and gave it $10,000 in cash; the ILGWU contributed $15,000; the Clothing Workers $11,000. Many smaller unions donated money and food. The greatest support, though, came from Van Arsdale and the IBEW. Local 3 gave 1199 $28,000, loaned it another $50,000, and halted construction work at three hospitals. The mostly white, virtually all-male electricians marched on hospital picket lines and, at one point, assessed themselves a dollar a week to support the heavily female and nonwhite hospital strikers. The executive board of the Central Labor Council urged council delegates to "not only endorse the strike but take the strike over so that it will become that of the labor movement in New York City and not Local 1199 itself." To some extent, just that occurred. In negotiations, for example, leaders of the Central Labor Council and District 65 represented the hospital workers, rather than 1199 officials.

In spite of strong labor and liberal backing, 1199 could not overcome the determination of the voluntary hospitals to keep out unions. Collectively, the trustees of these institutions represented an extraordinary assemblage of wealth and power: leaders of the German-Jewish aristocracy; successful Eastern European Jewish businessmen, like Charles Silver; the Catholic hierarchy; and pillars of the Protestant establishment. After forty-six days on strike, the best the union could do was a face-saving formula worked out under Wagner's prodding, which required the hospitals to take back the strikers and institute some new labor-management procedures, without recognizing the union.[35]

When during the hospital strike Blue Cross requested a 34.2 percent rate hike, infuriated labor leaders bitterly attacked the insurer. Why, they asked, should Blue Cross get more money to give to the hospitals at the very moment that they were denying their underpaid "involuntary philanthropists," as 1199 liked to call hospital workers, the right to unionize? Blue Cross, they believed, tolerated excessive hospital costs for everything but nonprofessional labor. Furthermore, in their view, Blue Cross continued to deny the one million unionists and their dependents who subscribed to the plan adequate representation in its governance.

Some union leaders also questioned the quality of care their members received. Teamsters Joint Council 16, which negotiated benefits for some 250,000 workers and members of their families, in early 1959 established a joint committee with management to consider self-insuring and running its own hospitals. The committee commissioned Dr. Ray Trusell, director of the Columbia University School of Public Health, to conduct a study of the medical care received by Teamsters and their families under Blue Cross. Trusell found that 9 percent of sampled Teamsters patients were unnecessarily hospitalized and nearly a quarter received "poor" care.[36]

Unhappy as they were with Blue Cross and the voluntary hospitals, few labor leaders seriously considered breaking away from the medical delivery system they had literally and figuratively bought into. Rather, they used public threats to try to reform it, with some success. In August 1959, Blue Cross established a public advisory group, which included labor representatives, to strengthen its relationship with subscribers. Also, it began increasing labor representation on its board, hiring unionists for important staff positions, and assuming a more adversarial relationship with the hospitals.[37]

The medical establishment, too, increasingly recognized labor's importance. In 1959 leaders of the local county medical societies, once spear-carriers for doctor autonomy and individual, fee-for-service medical practice, admitted to the ILGWU's Charles Zimmerman (in his words) "that their attitude towards medical services to the mass of the people had been wrong and that they were earnestly desirous of correcting this situation." When in late 1960 the Central Labor Council formed a Professional Advisory Committee to help it address the cost and quality of medical care, the heads of many key medical institutions—the city Health Department; Mt. Sinai, Bellevue, Montefiore, and the Catholic hospitals; the State Medical Society; and Blue Cross and Blue Shield—agreed to participate.[38]

Labor's political and financial muscle allowed it to revive corporatist health planning. Governor Rockefeller's predilection towards corporatism and desire for labor backing furthered this trend. In the early 1960s, Rockefeller strengthened the State Hospital Review and Planning Council, a group made up of representatives (including Van Arsdale) of nongovernmental groups, hoping that it would rationalize the health delivery system.[39]

Corporatist planning and monitoring, however, failed to check the sharply rising cost of medical and hospital care. All through the 1960s, the cycle of increased hospital costs, Blue Cross rate hike requests, and vehement labor protests continued. Between 1960 and 1965 alone, Blue Cross rates increased 124 percent.[40]

Unable to fundamentally reform the dominant, doctor-hospital controlled mode of health care delivery, and unwilling to go it alone, the labor movement, nationally and locally, turned once more to the state. Strong labor support helped win, over fierce AMA opposition, the 1965 passage of the federal Medicare and Medicaid programs.[41] In New York State, labor tried to go farther, backing compulsory employee health insurance to protect workers whose unions or employers did not already provide such coverage. A 1965 state AFL-CIO insurance plan, however, failed to win enactment.

Two years later, the Central Labor Council revived its campaign for a state health insurance mandate. A Rockefeller aide reported that several business groups, including the Commerce and Industry Association and the Retail Merchants "could probably go with a decent plan," but Associated Industries found the notion "totally abhorrent." Again, no state action resulted. In the meantime, city unions helped implement a state Medicaid program backed by the governor.[42]

The city labor movement and Rockefeller collaborated on another matter as well, the unionization of hospital workers. Though 1199 lost the 1959 hospital strike, its members did not see themselves as defeated. To the contrary, many gained confidence from the act of having stood up to their bosses and lived to tell the tale. Following the strike, 1199 worked hard to solidify its organization at the hospitals it had struck. Meanwhile, it won recognition at a number of smaller institutions. Equally important, the union launched a campaign to have hospital workers placed under state labor law.

In 1962, 1199 stuck two voluntary hospitals with the specific aim of getting Rockefeller to support labor law revision. Increasingly portraying its hospital organizing as an adjunct of the civil rights movement, 1199 used veteran black leader A. Philip Randolph, head of the Brotherhood of Sleeping Car Porters, as a conduit for pressure on the governor. Even more important was the ubiquitous Van Arsdale. The strategy worked; the governor backed an extension of collective bargaining rights to hospital workers, leading 1199 to end its walkout.

Once the legislature passed the labor law revision (which applied only to New York City, banned hospital strikes, and called for binding arbitration in cases of impasse), 1199 could win recognition through state-supervised elections. But in many cases that proved unnecessary, as hospitals and nursing homes acknowledged the groundswell of support for unionization. By January 1968, 1199 had twenty-three thousand hospital and nursing home members. Many large voluntaries, like Mt. Sinai, recognized the union, though some of the most powerful (including Columbia-Presbyterian, Roosevelt, and the Catholic hospitals) managed to hold off the union for some years, and a few (most notably New York Hospital) defeated all efforts by 1199 and Local 144 to gain recognition. [43]

1199's expansion into hospitals and nursing homes was, with the exception of the unionization of public employees, New York labor's most important organizing success in the post–World War II era. For one thing, it gave labor a major inroad to the rapidly growing service sector of the economy. (Private-sector medical and health service jobs in the city increased by 50 percent between 1960 and 1970, to 145,700.) For another, it brought tens of thousands of African-Americans, Puerto Ricans, and West Indians into the union movement, a critical development given the increasing importance of these groups in the city's working class. [44]

The triumph of 1199 reflected the ingenuity, tenacity, and political commitment of the union's ex-Communist leadership, the selflessness of its drugstore members who sacrificed time and money to make themselves an occupational and ethnocultural minority within their own union, the extraordinary show of solidarity from other unions, the liberality of the region's political culture and the sensitivity of politicians to a united labor movement, and the spirit and determination of the hospital workers themselves. This was New York at its finest. Ironically, though, the rise of 1199 further complicated labor's effort to gain health security.

All along, hospital executives had argued that unionization would drive up hospital costs. Union leaders either pooh-poohed the idea or argued the injustice of keeping down costs through the extreme exploitation of one of the poorest elements of the working class. But, of course, hospital executives were right. In bargaining its first hospital contracts, 1199 stressed union security and grievance procedures. But in 1966 it won a 24 percent wage hike, and two years later another major raise. Hospital executives quickly realized that jumps in labor costs could be used to win higher reimbursement rates from the increasing number of government-run or regulated insurance programs (including Medicare and Medicaid), enabling them to cover wages hikes while increasing their total budgets. By the end of the decade, 1199 and the hospitals at least tacitly conspired to use bargaining crises to bring more third-party money into the health care system. Taxpayers and insurance subscribers ultimately paid the freight.[45]

Once unions began representing both consumers and providers of health services, their outlook on health policy fragmented. In the mid and late 1960s, most unions continued to press for hospital cost containment, but 1199 opposed efforts that were "little more than a freeze on the wages of people who work in hospitals." Unions also divided over whether or not Blue Cross should be allowed to offer experience-rated contracts (which based premiums for subscriber groups on their hospitalization rates, lowering costs for healthy groups but raising them for the old and sickly). Such disagreements weakened labor's overall influence on the health care system, even as individual unions and unionists remained powerful.[46]

By the end of the 1960s, with the government ever more involved in the health system, the hospital–medical school complexes growing in size and power, health insurers controlling astronomical amounts of capital, and unions holding conflicting views, the labor movement found itself but one of many groups pursuing its interests on the tricky terrain of health economics. However, if labor leaders felt frustrated by their limited ability to control the health care system their members used, many had been around long enough to know what a large role labor, and they themselves, had played in creating it. After all, it had been the decision of unions to begin bargaining for "fringe benefits" that provided the vast flow of money to health providers and insurers necessary for the spectacular postwar growth of American medicine.

In many ways, labor's postwar health policies had served its members and society well. In large part as a result of labor action, by the end of the 1960s sickness and accidents no longer meant financial catastrophe for working-class New Yorkers. Disability payments provided partial income replacement, while through union clinics, collectively-bargained health benefits, benefits offered by nonunion companies in part to forestall unionization, and government-sponsored programs passed with labor backing, most New Yorkers had ready access to modern medicine. This gave a much greater sense of security to the working class (though how much it actually affected its health is uncertain).[47]

In most of the country, from the start labor's efforts to provide the working class with health security involved subordination to other players in the health industry: doctors, hospitals, insurers, and government. In New York, the density of the unionized working class and the presence of doctors willing to buck the medical establishment allowed labor to construct an exceptional health care delivery system, partially under its control, based on prepaid, capitated, group practice and preventive medicine rather than on individual practitioner, therapeutic, fee-for-service. By the end of the 1960s, though, as the city's working class began dispersing geographically, the complexities and prestige of medicine grew, and the ideology of "free choice" of doctors achieved hegemony, labor increasingly threw in its lot with a medical establishment over which it had only limited influence. In a segmented medical system, working-class New Yorkers wanted the best services they could obtain, even if that meant abandoning the progressive institutions they themselves had helped to establish.

Ironically, just a few years later, the mode of medical practice New York labor helped develop, now dubbed Health Maintenance Organizations (HMOs), became a favored solution among liberals and conservatives alike to the ever-escalating cost of medical care. But when in the 1990s HMOs finally extinguished the cherished ideal of organized medicine—the individual practitioner as petty capitalist—most provider plans belonged neither to labor nor to government but to huge, highly profitable corporations. Labor had pointed the way to the future, but had lost control of the throttle before the train of history arrived.[48]

CHAPTER 9.

"A Useful and Remunerative Job"

From the mid-1950s through the late 1960s, working-class New York confronted the challenge of deindustrialization, as runaway shops and automation eroded the blue-collar job base on which its culture and power rested. Slowly but relentlessly, the goods production and distribution sectors shrank. The stories of five groups of New Yorkers—garment workers, electrical and metal manufacturing workers, construction electricians, printers, and longshoremen—illustrate how unions fought with some success to protect the jobs of their members but had less success preserving blue-collar jobs for future generations.

In 1954, Mayor Robert Wagner Jr.'s first year in office, New York City lost forty-one thousand manufacturing jobs. These constituted only a small fraction of the city's total manufacturing employment, which stood near its all-time high, providing a livelihood for well over a million men and women. Still, the combination of a national recession, the decision by several large firms to move production out of the region, and threats by others to do so caused a wave of anxiety about blue-collar job loss.[1]

Industrial relocation entailed two related developments, decentralization of industry within the New York region and movement away from it. Throughout the postwar period, New York City's share of regional manufacturing jobs diminished, as companies left the city for suburban areas and more manufacturing jobs were created there than in town. The change took place gradually; in 1953, New York City had 56 percent of the region's manufacturing jobs; in 1960, 54 percent. By 1966 a majority of the jobs lay outside the city.[2]

As factories migrated outward, so did workers. When at the end of World War II, Sperry Gyroscope moved from Brooklyn to Nassau County, many of its employees moved with it, as did its union, which began organizing other plants in the area.[3] In 1952, Helena Rubinstein relocated her main cosmetics factory—which had been in Queens—to Nassau County, too. The union that represented her employees set up a private bus system to bring workers from the city to the suburban plant. It continued for seven years, until enough workers moved near the factory or bought automobiles to make it unnecessary.[4]

Workers could not always move with their companies; some firms left specifically to escape them. In the late 1940s, following two strikes by New York Teamsters, many trucking firms relocated to New Jersey, where Teamsters locals had lower wage scales and less vigilantly enforced contracts. To stem the exodus, Local 807, the largest Teamster local in New York (and the country), cracked down on wildcat strikes, accepted greater use of arbitration, and pushed for an area-wide wage equalization.[5]

Unions followed and tried to organize firms that moved away in order to diminish the incentives for suburbanization and check downward pressure on wages and conditions in the city. UE Local 1227, for example, aggressively pursued the electronics industry as it moved out of New York. When Yardley Electric, a maker of nickel-cadmium batteries, responded to city complaints about its dumping of toxic chemicals into the sewer system by shifting most of its operation to Connecticut, the local sent agents who unionized the new plant. In the city, Local 1227 business agent James Garry recalled, most electronics workers lived close to work, rooting the union in tight-knit communities and laying the basis for a strong class sensibility. By contrast, companies that moved outward generally set up shop in isolated industrial parks. Almost all workers drove to work, most from some distance, making the company parking lot their only common space outside the plant itself.[6]

The flight of industry to the suburbs hurt the city. First, it diminished the tax base. Second, workers entering the city job market, especially with limited skills, found fewer employment possibilities. The 1954 decline in manufacturing employment hit Puerto Rican workers particularly hard, given their clustering in low-skilled jobs and lack of seniority. Third, job relocation deepened the lines of racial segregation. Since housing markets in areas to which industry moved generally discriminated against nonwhites (in 1960, Levittown, near Nassau County's burgeoning defense industry, did not have a single African-American among its eighty-two thousand residents), blacks and Puerto Ricans could not easily follow manufacturing outward. Nonwhite urban newcomers found themselves locked out of the industrial jobs that had provided ladders of social mobility for previous generations. Fourth, the industrial exodus excluded the city, already largely outside the Fordist economy, from important sectors of economic growth. The relocation of electronic and aircraft equipment manufacturers to Long Island, for example, meant that New York benefited little from the Cold War boom in armaments spending. In 1963 only 3.5 percent of New York's manufacturing employees engaged in defense-oriented production, in contrast to over half in Nassau County.[7]

In spite of these effects, New York business and political leaders remained sanguine about the suburbanization of industry. With overall city employment remaining steady, many argued that job losses to relocation were counterbalanced by growth in other sectors.[8] Many prominent real estate owners, businessmen, planners, and politicians actually wanted manufacturing to move from Manhattan and downtown Brooklyn to either outlying areas of the city or its suburbs. Real estate owners believed that central city land values would go up if office buildings and housing replaced manufacturing. Many architects, planners, and politicians scorned the grime, pollution, and working-class ambiance of industry, preferring civic buildings, office towers, housing, or parks.[9]

Industrial movement out of the entire area gave New York leaders greater pause than suburbanization. It threatened to weaken the regional economy while providing little opportunity for workers to move with their jobs. But even in this case, government and civic reaction to job loss proved muted, while labor's efforts, though extensive, had limited and ironic consequences.

The apparel industry, as the largest component of New York manufacturing, presented a key test of the area's ability to retain blue-collar jobs. In some ways, its peculiarities made it unusually susceptible to job retention efforts. When most industries moved, they did so in toto. In apparel, by contrast, design, sales, and fabric cutting usually remained in the city, giving unionists and businesses leverage over those parts of the industry that had left or were contemplating leaving. Well before World War II, the ILGWU began requiring New York-based manufacturers and jobbers to give preference to local contractors in the belief that union organization and labor standards could more easily be preserved in a geographically compact industry than a dispersed one. In 1951 the cloakmakers held a brief strike to force employers to agree to an "equitable" distribution of work between New York and out-of-town shops. In some sectors of the industry, the ILGWU even won the right to dictate to jobbers which contractors they could use, insisting that firms setting up operations outside of the city also establish shops within it.[10]

During the 1950s, the ILGWU made serious, somewhat successful efforts to unionize garment shops in the hinterland of the New York market, particularly Pennsylvania, New Jersey, New England, and Puerto Rico. (The union made fewer efforts in the South, which in 1950 accounted for 17 percent of apparel employment, and ten years later 28 percent.)[11] However, even when the ILGWU unionized shops in the rural areas, small cities, and coal mining towns that relocating firms favored, it generally allowed them to pay wages below New York scale. Given the sharp differences between the labor markets and living costs in these locales and in the city, to do otherwise probably would have been impossible. Nonetheless, this left a residual wage gap that the union addressed by giving wage concessions and contract exemptions to New York companies threatening to relocate or claiming hardship. The practice became so common that employers routinely ignored their contracts, forcing the New York Joint Dress Board to hold its first strike in twenty-five years in 1958 to end what Local 22 activist Maida Springer called "gunka-munka business" in contract enforcement.[12]

Even after the strike, ILGWU leaders continued to grant concessions to New York employers out of a belief that only a policy of wage moderation would slow their exodus. The ILGWU's Gus Tyler argued that external economies helped keep manufacturing in New York, but a large pool of low-wage labor was more important. Some ILGWU locals urged manufacturers to take advantage of the city's growing Puerto Rican and African-American workforce by switching from the tailor system to less skilled section work, already dominant outside the city.[13]

In part as a result of these policies, earnings in the garment industry fell sharply relative to other manufacturing sectors. In 1950, New York City apparel production workers received an average hourly wage ten cents more than the city manufacturing average. Ten years later they made twelve cents an hour less. By 1965 the gap had widened to twenty-two cents. Economist Leon Keyserling, in a report on the New York dress industry, noted that between 1952 and 1962 "virtually no progress was registered either in average real weekly earnings or in average annual earnings." Keyserling attributed part of the wage stagnation to low productivity growth, but he also blamed the ILGWU's "lack . . . of sufficiently uniform and up-dated wage policy" and inadequate contract enforcement.[14]

The low-wage policy of the ILGWU probably retarded the exodus of jobs, but at a high price. By the mid-1960s, many low-skilled garment workers made little above the minimum wage. ILGWU endorsement of section work helped constrict opportunities for upward mobility just as Puerto Ricans and African-Americans entered the industry in large numbers. And while union policy may have slowed industrial dispersion, it did not stop it. Employment in the New York apparel industry dropped from 340,700 in

1950 to 267,400 in 1960 and 241,300 in 1965. The limited results of the sacrifices workers made indicated how difficult it was to influence industrial location decisions.[15]

Electrical and metal manufacturing provides another case in point of the difficulty of checking deindustrialization. In the early the 1950s, electrical, appliance, and metalworking firms began moving work out of New York and northern New Jersey to be closer to national markets and away from centers of labor militancy. Local leaders of the International Union of Electrical Workers (IUE) implored their national union to end its "complacency" and engage the rank and file in a national campaign "to stalk the runaway shops into the southland and the sagebush." Dick Lynch, the head of an IUE local in Bloomfield, N.J., called for strict federal controls over plant relocation. In 1955, IUE president James Carey called on the governors and senators of the northeastern states to act together to stop industrial flight. But plants continued to leave the region, and New Jersey IUE leaders remained critical of their national union's failure to devote sufficient resources to runaway shops and the resulting partial deunionization of the industry.[16]

A dramatic 1954 struggle between IUE's rival, the United Electrical Workers (UE), and the American Safety Razor Company made evident the difficulties faced by even the most militant workers in trying to deny management the right to relocate. American Safety Razor made razor and surgical blades, employing fourteen hundred workers at its main factory in downtown Brooklyn. During World War II, the City Planning Commission announced plans for a grandiose civic center in Brooklyn that would entail the redevelopment of industrial space for office and residential use. American Safety Razor lay within an area designated for housing. Although the city never moved to take over the site, the company had understandable fears about its ability to continue to operate, let alone expand, at its current location.[17]

In 1953, as the civic center plan inched forward, American Safety Razor commissioned a relocation study. Once word went out that it was contemplating a move, communities—particularly in rural, low-wage areas—inundated it with offers, many including substantial subsidies. The company considered relocating within the New York region, but may have found moving far away more attractive because of its stormy relations with UE Local 475, which had struck the company in 1951 and 1952.[18]

In July 1954, American Safety Razor announced its intention to move to a modern plant that it bought in Staunton, Virginia, offering to pay the expenses of any worker who wanted to go with it. Local 475 vigorously opposed the relocation. A committee it sent to Staunton reported that wages there were 50 percent below those in New York, housing inadequate, and segregation prevalent, making it an inappropriate home for most incumbent workers, 85 percent of whom were women, 20 percent black or Puerto Rican, and most over age forty. However, facing a company threat to relocate immediately, the union did agree in mid-August to a package of severance, early retirement, and relocation benefits in return for maintaining normal production until the transfer actually took place, which the company said would not be until May 1955 at the earliest.[19]

This verbal accord soon broke down. When Local 475 continued its campaign to stop the move, American Safety Razor insisted that the union cease its agitation before it would sign a contract incorporating the August agreement. Local 475 refused, believing that it still had a chance of stopping the company—its largest shop—from leaving.

On October 1, six hundred workers tried to force the company to put its pledges into writing by occupying its plant, a rare example of a post–World War II sit-down strike. After two weeks, the sit-downers left the plant, but the strike continued. On October 21 the company announced it would not honor the agreement to stay put until May nor provide pension, severance, and relocation payments. On November 3, police cleared pickets from in front of the plant so that the company could begin moving its machinery to Virginia. Local 475 launched a nationwide boycott of American Safety Razor products to force the company to pay the contested severance and pension benefits, but to no avail. In the end, the company transferred only eighteen production workers to the new plant. A UE study found that six months after the Brooklyn plant closed, 74 percent of its members surveyed were still unemployed. The most militant effort in the city's history to stop a factory relocation had, if anything, negative consequences for the affected workers.[20]

Both the AFL and the CIO avoided involvement in the American Safety Razor battle—UE's unreconstructed leftism made it a pariah—but over the course of 1954 the New York City CIO Council expressed growing concern over runaway shops. Its leaders raised the issue, which particularly affected the Lithographers and the Furniture, Clothing, and Shoe Workers, with the mayor and set up a permanent council subcommittee on runaway shops that kept pressing Wagner for action.[21]

In the past, the city government had paid remarkably little attention to manufacturing. However, a 1954 jump in unemployment, along with pressure from labor, brought new attention from city officials, the press, and civic groups. Well-publicized plant relocations kept the issue alive. In June 1954, the Alexander Smith Carpet Works, the oldest and largest company in Yonkers (just north of the Bronx), announced a move of all its operations to Greenville, Mississippi. Capitalizing on the ensuing fear, Otis Elevator Company threatened to close its 102-year-old Yonkers plant unless it received cost-reducing concessions from its union and the local government.[22]

As apprehension grew, various private and public agencies undertook studies of plant relocation. The resulting reports stressed the overall health of the city economy and minimized the problem of industrial exodus. Nonetheless, their surveys proved revealing about why businesses left the city. Some companies cited a desire to take advantage of interregional differences by moving away from militant unions to areas with lower costs. But the most commonly cited motive was the difficulty in finding suitable buildings in the city when forced to vacate existing facilities or seeking to expand. Mid- and large size companies with extensive, integrated operations — Fordist production — found it nearly impossible to find the large, one-story buildings with good road and rail connections they preferred. Small manufacturers could efficiently operate in multistory loft buildings, but they had a hard time finding such space at affordable rents, especially in Manhattan, where virtually no lofts had been built in decades and some had been converted to showrooms or offices. Additionally, manufacturers expressed frustration with high shipping costs stemming from poor transportation connections and traffic congestion.[23]

To a considerable extent, the city itself created the problem of inadequate space. According to historian Joel Schwartz, between 1945 and 1955 redevelopment projects along the East River alone, including the Brooklyn Civic Center, United Nations, NYU-Bellevue medical complex, Stuyvesant Town, Peter Cooper Village, public housing, and the UHF's East River Houses, resulted in the demolition of buildings housing nearly eighteen thousand jobs. Slum clearance, public housing, and highway construction displaced tens of thousands more jobs in East Harlem, Greenwich Village, Lincoln Square, and elsewhere. Once forced to move, many companies left the city entirely. Furthermore, many manufacturers, fearing inclusion in a future redevelopment site, refrained from expanding or modernizing their buildings.[24]

Little concrete government action resulted from the industrial relocation studies. Not until 1959 did the city launch even a modest effort to create new industrial space. Using its power of condemnation, it assembled a ninety-six-acre site in the Flatlands section of Brooklyn for use as an industrial park. However, when Wagner left office six years later, the park had not yet materialized, as litigation, rising costs, and inattention led to repeated delays. A proposal by a mayoral committee for a "World Fashion Center" just south of Herald Square, with over four million square feet of new loft space, never got off the ground. A nonprofit corporation set up by the city as a conduit for cheap, state industrial mortgages did help finance the construction of twenty-two plants during Wagner's regime, but only thirty-five hundred jobs were saved or added, a modest figure considering that New York lost over two hundred thousand manufacturing jobs during the mayor's twelve years in office.[25]

The state government, too, did little to address the problem of industrial flight. One study found that during Nelson Rockefeller's governorship "no bureaucrat or politician of consequence seemed to care, or to care very much, whether business came or went." By contrast, other states, especially in the South, mounted aggressive programs to attract industry, offering industrial development bonds, tax exemptions, industrial parks, and other inducements.[26]

The diversity and fragmentation of New York's manufacturing sector partially explains the inattention to its needs by government leaders. With financiers and real estate operators dominating the most powerful business associations, no citywide organization promoted the particular interests of manufacturers. The Rockefellers, whose Manhattan real estate holdings led them to favor industrial decentralization, heavily influenced both the Commerce and Industry Association and the Downtown–Lower Manhattan Association which, like the Chamber of Commerce, generally backed redevelopment of industrial zones for non-industrial use. A few business groups, like the Brooklyn Chamber of Commerce, did fight to preserve industrial space, but pro-redevelopment coalitions of real estate interests, bankers, retailers, and local politicians usually outgunned them. The 1961 citywide zoning revision reflected the balance of power: it diminished areas designated for manufacturing, required a strict separation between residential and manufacturing districts, and established "performance standards" limiting noise, fumes, and noxious odors created by industrial activity.[27]

In 1955, the AFL proposed a congressional investigation into the use of public inducements to lure companies to move, an end to the federal tax exemption for local development bonds, gradual elimination of geographical wage differentials, nationalization of unemployment insurance, and repeal of state "right-to-work" laws permitted by Taft-Hartley, but little action resulted.[28] New York unionists fought to raise the federal minimum wage sufficiently to narrow the wage gap between New York and the South but failed. Though they pressed national unions to step up organizing in nonunion areas to eliminate incentives for relocation, the South remained overwhelmingly nonunion.[29]

Forced to craft local approaches to job retention, New York unionists confronted their own differing interests. Perhaps the sharpest (though rarely articulated) conflict pitted the building trades against manufacturing unions. While the latter had an interest in freezing the physical development of the city to preserve industrial zones, the former saw construction of every sort—the bigger the better—as their very lifeblood. Fear of displacing manufacturing jobs proved no obstacle to the building trades' backing for a vision of a rebuilt New York in which industry would be pushed outward, to be replaced by giant office and residential complexes which would boost land values and replace blue-collar jobs with white-collar ones. Manufacturing unions had more members than the building trades, but they lacked their attentiveness to employment issues, their unity of interest, and their structure for united action. Production unions tended to worry about jobs for their members only when a crisis arose, whereas the building trades, given the short duration of construction projects and the prevalence of union hiring halls, did so routinely. Thus construction unions proved to be the key labor voice on land use issues.[30] During the debates leading up to the 1961 zoning revisions, the only unions to speak up were the building trades, who opposed restrictions on permitted building size that would inhibit development.

Wage policy also divided labor. No union liked to admit that it tempered wage and benefit demands as a strategy for retaining jobs, but many did just that. At the venerable Steinway & Sons piano factory in Queens, veteran members of the Furniture Workers kept reelecting as their business agent James Cerofeci, who pursued a policy of wage restraint in the face of company pleas of poverty and periodic threats to move. Only after the older generation of workers began retiring in 1960s did younger activists, promising greater militancy, oust him. Similarly, in UE Local 475, younger workers, with few responsibilities and confident that they could get jobs elsewhere, wanted to press even marginal firms to upgrade wages, while older workers, with more responsibilities and fewer options, preferred wage restraint to risking that their employers might move or go bankrupt.[31]

The fear that excessive demands might drive firms out of business re-flected bitter experience. Many workers remembered the 1949 strike against the city's fourteen breweries, which gave giant, out-of-town beer companies an opportunity to expand their presence in the city. Within two years, three of Brooklyn's seven breweries closed; over the next three decades they all did. Though poor rail connections and high costs for land, water, electricity, sewerage, and taxes all played a role, so did the high cost of labor. Similarly, a 1955 strike by the Newspaper Guild demanding that the *Brooklyn Eagle* pay its members the same wages as the Manhattan-based dailies led to the paper's demise.[32]

Wage restraint, even when in the best interest of a particular group of workers, hurt the city workforce as a whole. A 1962 study by Nicholas Kis-burg of Teamsters Union Joint Council 16 charged that the low-wage policy of the garment unions had depressed the earnings of unskilled New Yorkers across-the-board in comparison to their peers in other cities. In 1950 the av-erage hourly and weekly earnings of manufacturing production workers in New York exceeded the national average; by 1957 the hourly advantage had been eradicated while weekly earnings had fallen below the national aver-age.[33]

Many unionists and civil rights leaders saw government action as a way to counteract the erosion of wages. In addition to pressing for a higher federal minimum wage and its extension to such exempt groups as retail workers, they asked the legislature to establish a state minimum above the federal level. A NAACP representative testified in 1952 that "Negroes and members of other minority groups . . . especially need the protection provided by such legislation." But in spite of sustained lobbying, the state legislature did not establish a state minimum until 1960, and then set it at the federal level, thus helping only those workers not already covered by federal statute.[34]

Frustrated by inaction in Albany, in 1959 a coalition of African-American and Puerto Rican groups proposed that New York City establish its own minimum wage of a $1.50 an hour, fifty cents above the federal floor. A city-sponsored study found that a local minimum wage would most help retail, hotel, hospital, nursing home, and laundry workers, groups with high per-centages of women and nonwhites. Many unionists backed the idea, dis-tressed by the sinking city wage level and eager to address the widely decried "exploitation" of Puerto Ricans, who made up a growing segment of the un-skilled work force. The rub was the opposition of the ILGWU. Although the average hourly wage in the New York garment industry easily exceeded $1.50, a large spread between the highest and lowest paid workers meant that a considerable number of ILGWU members—by one estimate 15 to 20 percent—made less than that. Seeing the proposed city minimum as a threat to their job retention strategy, garment union leaders maneuvered to prevent its enactment.

For Mayor Wagner, the minimum-wage proposal presented a political nightmare. Having broken with Tammany leader Carmine DeSapio, he faced a 1961 reelection bid in which he needed the support of both the Liberal Party, controlled by the ILGWU, and labor, black, and Puerto Rican groups. Only after the election, did Wagner, under growing pressure, take a first step toward a city minimum wage; he signed a city council bill requiring all firms selling goods or services to the municipal government to pay their workers at least $1.50 an hour. But he hesitated about going farther, instead appointing David Livingston from District 65 and Luigi Antonini from the ILGWU to a committee to study the city economy. With Commerce Commissioner Louis Broido, a key leader of the Liberal Party, as its chair, the committee first stalled and then drafted a toothless report. But Livingston—backed by the bulk of the union movement—succeeded in substituting a recommendation for a $1.50 city minimum wage, which the city council promptly passed and Wagner reluctantly signed.[35]

Undoubtedly to Wagner's relief, the New York State Court of Appeals declared the new city law invalid. In response, labor and civil rights leaders, shifting their focus back to Albany, demanded both an increase in the state minimum and legislation enabling local governments to pass minimums of their own. However, in spite of heavy lobbying and a mass demonstration in Albany, the Republicans only agreed to raise the state minimum in synch with the federal minimum. The Central Labor Council kept plugging away at the issue, but when in 1965 the legislature finally did pass a $1.50 minimum, Governor Rockefeller vetoed the measure. Thus a dozen years of labor and civil rights efforts to use the power of state and local government to raise the wage floor led to what Van Arsdale termed "complete failure," in part because of the rift within labor's own ranks.[36]

Surprisingly, even as debate continued over issues associated with runaway shops, industrial exodus per se disappeared as a major political issue. After 1955 it rarely got discussed by labor leaders or politicians, until the 1970s when the city economy and its manufacturing sector took a devastating plunge. Yet during the intervening years some of the city's biggest and best-known industrial concerns moved away. Pharmaceutical maker E. R. Squibb, founded in Brooklyn in 1858, transferred its manufacturing operation to New Jersey in 1956. Soon thereafter, the Mergenthaler Linotype Company decamped from Brooklyn to Nassau County and Pennsylvania.[37]

No doubt a rapid recovery from the 1954 recession helped assuage fears about joblessness. Between 1954 and 1956, New York gained nearly one hundred thousand jobs. Even manufacturing showed modest growth before resuming its slide.[38] When in 1958 the jobs issue did reemerge in the face of a new recession, the worst in two decades, New York unionists and public officials highlighted automation as a threat to economic security rather than runaway shops.

Elsewhere in the country, "automation hysteria" had begun earlier. Employers had been introducing labor-saving technology since the country's earliest days, but the post–World War II spread of mechanized material transfer systems and sophisticated, self-regulating electronic controls raised widespread fear of mass unemployment.[39] In April 1958, over five hundred New York unionists attended a conference on unemployment sponsored by the AFL and CIO councils, which called for federal antirecessionary action. Shortly thereafter, Harry Van Arsdale convened a small group of AFL leaders to discuss automation, its effect on employment, and the need for a shorter workweek, laying the basis for his creation of an ongoing AFL-CIO Shorter Work Week Committee. Automation fulfilled Van Arsdale's desire for an issue that would unite the local labor movement at a time when a long, difficult effort to merge the city AFL and CIO councils neared fruition.[40] Unlike industrial relocation, which largely affected manufacturing, automation impacted almost every type of economic activity.

The labor movement long had seen reducing work hours as a way to both create jobs and lessen the burden on working people. No doubt Van Arsdale got the idea for his committee from the national AFL, which had had its own shorter workweek committee. During the post-Korea recession, the AFL had called on Congress to reduce the workweek to thirty-five hours without loss of pay. Some elements within the CIO also had advocated a shorter week, seeing it as a way to forestall technological unemployment. But UAW and CIO president Walter Reuther opposed them, portraying reduced work time as at most a distant goal. Reuther argued that an immediate cut in hours would reduce the nation's output, threatening its military security and ability to provide ever-greater consumer bounty.[41]

Because of New York's industrial mix and the strength of its union movement, workers in the city generally worked fewer hours a week than those elsewhere. Between 1950 and 1964, New York manufacturing production workers averaged between 37.3 and 38.1 hours of work a week, compared to 39.7 to 40.7 nationally. New York lithographers cut their workweek to thirty-five hours in 1946, while brewery workers, as a result of their 1949 strike, won a thirty-seven-and-a-half hour week. Privately employed bus workers—not covered by the Fair Labor Standards Act—won the forty-hour week only in 1953, after a twenty-nine day strike. That same year, the ILGWU made the thirty-five-hour week an industry-wide goal, which it achieved within three years.[42]

In the late 1950s, at Van Arsdale's prodding, New York unionists began to systematically link the issues of working hours and automation. Van Arsdale promoted shorter hours not only among local unionists, but to state and city labor councils throughout the country. His June 1958 call for a four-hour work day garnered extensive publicity. Nevertheless, his drive initially had little practical effect.[43]

In some industries, where automation was wiping out whole categories of work, shorter hours seemed irrelevant. Between 1950 and 1970, for example, the introduction of passenger-operated elevators reduced the number of elevator operators in the city by 55 percent from over 24,000 to 11,000. The Building Service Employees had some success winning termination pay, pensions, and retraining programs for laid-off workers, but could not stop the rapid elimination of a group of workers who when World War II ended had brought the city to its knees simply by withdrawing their labor.[44]

Other unions facing automation gave short shrift to shorter hours because of their confidence that industry growth would compensate for technological job displacement. The massive expansion of telephone service, for instance, allowed workers in jobs being automated—most notably telephone operators—to find other positions in the industry. The Communications Workers of America (CWA) never opposed technological innovations nor aggressively fought to shorten hours, seeing the higher productivity that came with automation as "a lever" for improved pay, benefits, and security.[45]

Few business or political leaders endorsed shorter hours, as evident at a June 1960 conference on automation organized by Nelson Rockefeller. In his keynote address, Rockefeller came much closer to Reuther's approach to automation than Van Arsdale's. "We should welcome automation," the governor said, "because our problem over the coming decade promises to be not one of creating enough jobs but one of creating enough production." Job displacement, he argued, could best be addressed though "accelerated economic growth." Rockefeller opposed any cut in working hours as undermining economic expansion, hoping to see a "moratorium on increased leisure."[46]

In a newspaper editorial, Van Arsdale's union praised Rockefeller's call for faster economic expansion without mentioning his opposition to a shorter workweek. When the Central Labor Council held an automation conference of its own in November 1960, union leaders reiterated many of Rockefeller's themes, including the benefits of automation if linked to faster growth. But they devoted far more attention than he did to the need for increased protection for displaced workers.[47]

Van Arsdale also kept pushing for shorter hours. In the months following the conference, he canvassed unions to support a four-hour workday and convinced thirty-nine locals to set up shorter workweek committees.[48] But it was his own local that catapulted the workweek issue to national prominence. In December 1961, Van Arsdale announced that the construction electricians would strike on January 1 unless employers agreed to reduce their workweek to five, four-hour days, from their current five-day, thirty-hour workweek, with a mandatory hour a day of overtime (paid at time-and-a-half).[49]

Local 3's demand raised a storm of criticism. As the Building Trades Employers Association pointed out, the electricians faced no shortage of work with their current schedules. A New York Times editorial argued that by driving construction costs "prohibitively high," the shorter workweek would create joblessness rather than alleviate it. It noted President Kennedy's recent pronouncement that the United States needed the forty-hour week to meet the Soviet industrial challenge, keep its goods competitive, and prevent inflation.[50]

A threat by a second major union to strike for shorter hours at the very same time as Local 3 made the situation especially ominous to business leaders. In June 1961, TWU Local 100 officials announced their intention of making a four-day, thirty-two-hour workweek their main demand in negotiations to replace contracts with the Transit Authority (TA) and seven private bus companies expiring at the end of the year. Between 1955 and 1960, the TA, with the tacit approval of the union, had cut its workforce through attrition from 42,068 to 34,360. Now it was preparing to test an automated, crewless subway train on the 42nd Street shuttle line, raising the specter of even greater job loss. Terming this newest move "a terrific threat" to the union,

TWU president Michael J. Quill resolved to block crewless operations and seek a shorter workweek to preserve jobs.[51]

In mid-December, the TA drive to automate nearly shut down the city; when the agency scheduled a test of its crewless shuttle while negotiations for a new contract were taking place, Quill threatened an immediate, general transit strike. Arbitrator Theodore W. Kheel defused the crisis by ordering the TA to postpone its test.[52] Still, with the TWU insisting on a thirty-two-hour week, for a brief moment it looked like two of New York's most powerful labor leaders would simultaneously lead their troops to battle for less work time.

Appearances, though, proved deceptive. The TWU and IBEW actually viewed the hours issue quite differently. Though nominally the transit union had been committed to shorter hours as a cure for automation since 1955, it used the demand tactically. By contrast, for Van Arsdale shorter hours represented an end in themselves.

On December 28, the Transit Authority and the TWU signed a two-year contract that provided a pay raise and improved benefits but no hours reduction. Instead, the union won a guarantee of no layoffs during life of the contract and agreement that during a trial period of the automated shuttle a motorman would be on board, with a final resolution of the manning issue to be negotiated later. With alternative means of dealing with automation in place, the TWU's pursuit of shorter hours all but ended. As promised, the TA had motormen standing by when it tested the automated shuttle, which it found disappointing in its cost savings and eventually abandoned. Meanwhile, the size of the TA workforce stabilized. In the next round of contract talks, the TWU again demanded a thirty-two-hour week only to drop the issue in the final stage of negotiations, making clear its status as a bargaining ploy rather than a serious goal.[53]

By contrast, on January 11, 1962, nine thousand construction electricians began Local 3's first general strike since 1941, after the contractors with whom it normally had a harmonious relationship refused to budge on the hours issue. Eight days later the strikers returned to work with victory in hand: the employers agreed to a twenty-five-hour workweek, the shortest ever stipulated in a major union contract.[54]

Electricians did not actually work only five hours a day under the new pact. Rather, the preexisting system of an hour a day overtime continued, so that electricians minimally worked thirty hours a week. Furthermore, during peak building season many worked two hours overtime a day, leading some contractors and union critics to charge that the shorter workweek merely had served as a cover for boosting earnings. Ted Kheel, appointed by Mayor Wagner to monitor the pact, reported that it did create new jobs in spite of a drop in the volume of construction, but not as many as originally antici- pated.[55]

Such subtleties got lost in the blare of publicity attendant to the contract settlement. A few labor leaders, like Quill, hailed the agreement, but criticism came from many quarters. A *New York Times* editorial bemoaned "unjusti- fied excess payments," while national AFL-CIO leaders, the same paper re- ported, found the pact "an embarrassment." The sharpest comments came from the Kennedy administration, which hoped to keep union settlements at what it deemed a non-inflationary level and opposed workweek reductions. At a press conference in late January, the president scorned the Local 3 pact for failing to meet either standard.[56]

The electricians contract had an important, unexpected result. To help finance shorter hours, the agreement loosened restrictions on the use of ap- prentices, who received lower pay than journeymen. Van Arsdale pledged to recruit a thousand new trainees, doubling the apprenticeship pool. Almost immediately, the NAACP, seeing an opportunity to open up the notoriously racist construction trades to nonwhite workers, called on Local 3 to recruit "a substantial number of Negro apprentices." Local 3 had a few nonwhites in its construction division (along with many in its manufacturing divisions), which put it a cut above most of the building trades. However, by admitting mostly sons of construction electricians to apprenticeships, it perpetuated the disproportionate hold whites had on the best jobs in the industry. (The 1960 census found only seventy-nine black electrical apprentices in the whole country.)

Politically shrewd, and in his own way committed to civil rights, Van Ar- sdale quickly claimed that it had been Local 3's intention all along "to incor- porate as many Negroes as possible" into its enlarged training program, though little evidence indicated that to have been true. In any case, the union recruited over two hundred African-Americans and Puerto Ricans to be among the 1,020 apprentices it signed up in 1962. Union leaders kept tight control over the desegregation process, as those with family ties to the union continued to receive favored treatment. Nevertheless, the implementation of the 1962 contract constituted a major step toward desegregating the electrical trade. Its exceptionality heightened awareness of the deep racist streaks within organized labor, especially in the construction unions.[57]

Ironically, though the Local 3 contract had notable unanticipated effects, the widespread push for shorter hours that many expected would come in its wake never materialized. The Central Labor Council held conferences on automation in 1962 and 1963, with Van Arsdale claiming that since 1958, sixty-three of its affiliated locals had won shorter hours. None, however, had achieved breakthroughs like Local 3. Within a few years, the council's Shorter Work Week Committee slipped into inactivity.[58]

The shorter hours movement petered out amid a general decline in concern over automation. A robust economy, stimulated by heavy government spending on the Vietnam War, all but erased fears of mass unemployment. In New York City, the unemployment rate fell from 5.3 percent in 1963 to just 3.1 percent in 1969. With jobs there for the taking, and academic experts claiming that automation would not lessen the demand for labor, only exceptional groups of workers fretted about the long-term effects of technological change. At the moment when the bargaining power of New York labor reached its historic high, most workers and unionists did not see the need for structural innovations to ensure economic security for themselves or the city. Those who did were generally those who faced imminent crisis.[59]

Nowhere did the struggle to protect workers' livelihoods prove more complex or capture greater public attention than at the city's daily newspapers. Proud of its status as part of the country's oldest labor organization, Local 6 ("Big Six") of the International Typographical Union (ITU) held extraordinary control over the composing rooms of New York's newspapers: foremen belonged to the union, members with steady jobs ("situation holders") could hire a substitute for themselves whenever they liked, seniority dictated assignments, and strict rules regulated the division of labor with members of the many other newspaper unions. Publishers in other cities introduced new technologies after World War II to circumvent worker control, provoking bitter strikes. In New York they shied away from taking on Local 6, which retained a virtual veto over automation. Only gingerly—after negotiations with the union—did they introduce new equipment such as teletypesetters, which allowed linotype machines to be operated by punched paper tapes produced off-site.[60]

In the early 1960s, New York newspaper publishers sought a freer hand to use teletypesetting and convert to "cold type" (photocomposition and computerized typesetting). In response, newly elected Local 6 president Bertram A. Powers put together an alliance of ten newspaper unions for mutual support. On December 8, 1962, after the ITU and the newspapers failed to resolve wage, benefit, and automation issues, Big Six struck four of the city's dailies, whereupon the publishers of the four remaining papers locked out their employees.

In a city addicted to the word, the newspaper strike left a palpable void. Television stations beefed up their news programs, while several leading literary figures took advantage of the walkout to found the *New York Review of Books*. (Edmund Wilson remarked, "The disappearance of the *Times* Sunday book section . . . only made us realize it had never existed.")

Both sides proved capable of waging an extended battle. All the papers except the *News* had strike insurance, diminishing their losses. The printers received extremely generous strike benefits, financed in part by a three percent assessment on the earnings of ITU members throughout the country, provoking resentment among members of the other newspaper unions who received more modest benefits or none at all. Though rife with tension, the union coalition held together as Van Arsdale, whose union represented about 150 newspaper electricians, pushed hard for unity. When in early January the Publishers Association hinted that the struck papers might resume publishing without Big Six members, the Central Labor Council mobilized twenty-five thousand people to circle the *New York Times* headquarters, possibly the largest picket line in the city's history. In late February, the Publishers Association itself cracked, with the *New York Post* announcing plans to end its lockout.

As the strike dragged on, criticism of Local 6 grew. At a February 21 press conference, President Kennedy upbraided Bertram Powers and his local for excessive demands, the second time in just over a year that he took a New York union to task. But it took more than a month longer for Ted Kheel, once again acting on behalf of the mayor, to craft a settlement that included a token shortening of the printers' workweek, improved wages and benefits, strict limits on the use of typesetting tape, a ban on layoffs due to its use, and the sharing of savings generated by it. After 114 days, the presses finally rolled again.[61]

The 1962–63 walkout proved to be just the first of a series of newspaper strikes involving automation issues. In 1965, when the *New York Times* refused a Newspaper Guild demand that like Local 6 it be given a veto over the introduction of new equipment, the white-collar union struck the paper. All the other dailies except the *Post* stopped publishing in sympathy. This time it took twenty-five days to settle the dispute, with the Guild failing to get its veto.[62]

The final resolution of composing room automation issues did not come until 1974. That year, after *Daily News* printers started a slowdown, management succeeded in producing the paper without them, a measure of how far automation had advanced and how disunited the newspaper unions had become. After being locked out for eighteen days, the printers signed a pathbreaking contract with the *News* and the *Times*. Running for an unprecedented eleven years, it provided lifetime job guarantees for all eighteen hundred situation holders and substitutes at the papers. In return, the printers granted management the unlimited right to automate and freed them to disregard seniority in assignments and retraining, reduce the workforce through attrition, and eliminate longstanding work rules. To lessen the number of unneeded printers, the newspapers offered a twenty-five-hundred-dollar bonus to those agreeing to retire and granted each worker a six-month paid "productivity leave" (while refusing to shorten the workweek, fearing that other unions would demand the same).

The 1974 printers contract embodied one solution to the dilemma of automation: trading job guarantees for an incumbent workforce for management's right to eliminate future jobs through technology. Within just a few years, the extraordinary increase in productivity that came with cold type and computerization turned newspaper composing rooms into "ghost towns." The ITU survived only through a merger with the much larger Communications Workers of America, while rapid automation made it possible for management to put out a paper even when most workers struck, opening the way for fierce attacks by the *News* and *Post* on their unions two decades later.[63]

The waterfront exemplified how automation could change the very character of the city. When World War II ended, all interested parties agreed that New York's docks—about half of which the city government owned—needed massive renovation. However, various business and labor interests disagreed about who should take charge. Although the Port Authority of New York, which had been established in 1921 to coordinate port activity in New York and New Jersey, seemed like the most logical choice for port development, waterfront businessmen, International Longshoremen's Association (ILA) leaders, and mobsters with ties to the Democratic Party blocked its participation, fearing any threat to their existing arrangements. Left to its own devices, the city invested tens of millions of dollars on shipping facilities, but by the mid-1950s had constructed only one new dock, at ten times its original estimated cost.[64]

While the city let its docks become outmoded, the state stepped in to address other problems that were driving away business, namely worker militancy and dockside corruption. Longshoremen held wildcat strikes in 1945, 1947, and 1951, and an official strike in 1948, giving the port a reputation for worker strife and high labor costs. Organized crime, especially a truck loading racket and massive pilferage, added to shipping expenses. Rank-and-file militants, some working with Father John M. Corrigan of the Xavier Labor School (the model for the Karl Malden character in *On the Waterfront*), helped publicize mob control of the docks, feeding journalists information about loan-sharking, kickbacks needed to get work, and violence against union dissidents. In 1951, Governor Thomas Dewey ordered the state Crime Commission to investigate the waterfront. Its hearings and reports documented pervasive mob influence, rooted in an oversupply of labor and the shape-up system. At its urging, in 1953, New York and New Jersey formed a Waterfront Commission empowered to require that all waterfront hiring take place through government-run hiring halls. To decasualize labor, the commission allowed only longshoremen who put in a set number of hours a year to continue working. To get rid of troublemakers, it banned convicted felons and those whose presence endangered "public peace or safety" (in practice, Communists) from the industry.[65]

Many longshoremen disliked the Waterfront Commission, which they called the "Gestapo" or "N.K.V.D." (Soviet secret police). However, within a few years it succeeded in reducing the workforce, leading to steadier work and rising incomes for the those who remained.[66] But just as longshoremen began enjoying improved conditions, two new technologies threatened their livelihood, jet airplanes and containerization.

Commercial jets, which began flying in 1958, revolutionized the airline industry. From 1960 to 1966, the tonnage of air freight passing through New York increased fivefold. In 1967 it accounted for a quarter of all foreign trade in the metropolitan area. Flights to and from John F. Kennedy Airport—by the end of the 1960s the largest air freight center in the world—carried everything from fur coats to flowers to war dead from Vietnam.

Air passenger travel increased even more dramatically. In 1955 an equal number of people crossed the Atlantic by plane as by boat; by the late 1960s they outnumbered them twenty to one. Within a few more years, regular transatlantic passenger ship travel ended altogether, with only a rump cruise industry remaining of the bustling passenger trade that for decades had given New York so much of its feel.[67]

Though less visible, containerization had as dramatic an effect. Sea-Land Services introduced the first commercial container service in 1956, serving the New York to Puerto Rico run. Packing goods into large, standardized metal containers that could be lifted by crane onto and off of ships, trains, and trucks offered enormous savings in time, labor, and breakage over the traditional method of loading loose cargo by sling. Since containerization required specialized ships and port facilities, it spread slowly, so that in 1966 it accounted for only 3 percent of the general cargo in the port. But the potential productivity gains had become apparent well before then.

Containerization raised two major questions: what arrangements would be made with labor to permit its deployment, and where would container facilities be built? The ILA at first resisted employer pressure to decrease the size of work gangs as mechanization changed labor requirements. But in 1964, after a strike by Atlantic and Gulf Coast longshoremen, the union agreed to a phased reduction in gang size, while the employers agreed to guarantee a minimum of sixteen hundred hours a year pay for longshoremen who regularly reported to the hiring halls, regardless of the amount of work actually performed, to be financed by a tonnage assessment on goods passing through the port.[68]

The combination of decasualization and containerization drastically decreased the size of the waterfront workforce. In 1954 over 35,000 men registered with the Waterfront Commission. By 1970, only 21,600 longshoremen and checkers remained; by 1980, only 13,177. Nine years later, some 8,000 longshoremen moved 50 percent more goods than 35,000 men had handled thirty-five years earlier.[69]

Containerization helped shift the center of port activity away from New York. In 1958, New Jersey accounted for just 18 percent of portwide longshore hirings; by 1989, 78 percent. Manhattan, which as late as 1960 handled a quarter of the cargo in the port, lacked the open space and rail and road connections optimal for containerization, whereas the Jersey shore had plenty of available land for sprawling facilities, less congested traffic, and superior rail connections. But politics played a role, too. Having been spurned by New York while embraced by Newark, the Port Authority invested hundreds of millions of dollars developing the New Jersey waterfront, building the first berth designed specifically for container operations in Port Elizabeth in 1962. Eventually the Port Authority developed a container port in Brooklyn, but at the end of the 1970s its facilities in Newark and Elizabeth handled seven times as much cargo as its New York City operations.[70]

There is little reason to pine for the days when tens of thousands of New Yorkers worked on the docks. Though some longshoremen derided work at the highly mechanized containerports as unmanly—"Clean it may be, interesting it isn't," said one—during its heyday the waterfront had been a dangerous, grueling, insecure world, a "pirates' nest" as veteran labor journalist Mary Heaton Vorse termed it, that few survived without physical or spiritual scars. Furthermore, as longshore work disappeared, air transportation generated a greater number of jobs; between 1958 and 1969 employment in air transportation in New York City nearly doubled, from 29,600 to 56,700 (with Kennedy Airport inheriting from the docks the distinction as the mob's favorite hunting grounds).[71]

Still, changes on the waterfront divorced the city from its past. When ships began docking at New Jersey piers far from Manhattan, and staying only a day instead of the better part of a week, many sailors stopped going into the city at all, depriving it of a presence that went back to the colonial Jack Tar. The ships chandlers, rope works, and saloons that had lined the shores of Brooklyn and Manhattan since the days of Melville disappeared. The maritime unions, once so important in the labor politics of the city, imploded, as containerization and the end of the passenger lines drastically diminished the need for sailors as well as longshoremen, and more and more shipping lines used foreign crews.[72]

Nothing better symbolized the passing of maritime New York than the closing of the Brooklyn Navy Yard, a vast facility with six drydocks, eight piers, 270 buildings, nineteen miles of streets, and thirty miles of railroad track. In operation since 1761, the yard's workers had built the Navy's first oceangoing steamship during the War of 1812, outfitted the *Monitor* during the Civil War, and constructed the battleships *Maine*, whose sinking in Havana led to war with Spain, and *Missouri*, on whose deck Japan surrendered, ending World War II. At its height, in 1944, the yard employed seventy-one thousand women and men, making it the Navy's biggest shipyard and the largest industrial enterprise in the city. After the Korean War, however, work contracted sharply, as the Navy shifted production elsewhere. In 1965 fewer than seven thousand workers still toiled there. The next year, the Navy shut down the yard.[73]

By the 1970s much of New York's glorious waterfront lay abandoned. Decaying piers on Manhattan's West Side routinely burnt up in spectacular fires. Some docks were used as parking lots, others as bus barns and sanitation department garages. A few served as impromptu sunbathing decks. City officials and private interests continued to discuss the need for new waterfront investment, but no longer to serve industry or transportation. Instead, they envisioned high rise offices, luxury housing, and recreation facilities to service corporate New York, the "headquarters town" that had grown and grown during the decades when industrial New York reached its peak and began its long decline.[74]

When Mayor Wagner left office at the end of 1965, New York still had a massive goods producing and distributing economy. But relative to the past, blue-collar labor had diminished. In 1946, 41 percent of the city labor force had consisted of craftsmen, operatives, laborers, foremen, and kindred workers; in 1970, only 29 percent, nearly matched in number by clerical and secretarial workers, who made up 27 percent of the labor force.[75]

Elements of the labor movement recognized early on the economic trends that transformed the city. Some unions proved extraordinarily adept at protecting their members in the face of the relentless change so characteristic of capitalism. A generation of printers and longshoremen lived out their lives with economic security and personal dignity even though their occupations underwent near extinction, a magnificent accomplishment of trade unionism.[76] Unions in the garment, electrical, metalworking, construction, and transit industries, too, managed to provide at least some job protection for their members through hours reductions, seniority systems, manning level guarantees, subcontracting rules, and other devices. The fate of these workers sharply differed from that of the millions of Americans—workers and managers alike—who had to fend for themselves under the impact of deindustrialization and corporate restructuring.

New York unions, however, generally proved unable to protect jobs for future generations from the impact of industrial relocation and the shrinkage of the blue-collar trades. Probably unions, no matter what they did, at most could have had a modest effect on the evolution of the New York economy, given suburbanization, automation, and the increasing ability of business to flee high costs and well-organized workers. Most major northeastern and midwestern cities suffered postwar declines in manufacturing employment as steep or steeper than New York's, a measure of the national and international scope of the forces at work.[77] Still, a number of factors undercut what influence working-class New Yorkers might have had.

First, on some key issues they had few allies. Most civic, business, and political leaders favored the redevelopment of industrial zones into office and residential districts, while even labor-backed liberals like John Kennedy viewed as utopian or misguided the notion that workers should have more leisure as a way to preserve jobs and as an end in itself. Second, disagreements among workers along industrial and political lines undercut their ability to intervene in or create debates over macroeconomic issues. Third, many working-class leaders simply did not see it as their place to try to shape the long-run future of the region.

Finally, few working-class New Yorkers found the shift in the city economy distressing, except to the extent that it threatened their own jobs. Instead, they commonly saw the shift from blue-collar to white-collar work as a natural, positive progression. Told over and over again by businessmen, the mass media, academics, and political leaders that "post-industrialism"—the world of offices, service work, and white-collar employment—promised an easier, more lucrative, more secure way of life than blue-collar labor, most saw little reason to bemoan its displacement of industry. Workers in some trades, like construction, longshoring, and printing, encouraged their children to follow their path, as long as jobs remained. However, most men and women who made, moved, or maintained things—practical-minded and committed to progress—hoped that their children if not themselves would escape manual toil. One veteran needle trades worker—a strong union supporter— pointedly asked an interviewer in the early 1970s, "Would *you* want your children to work in the garment industry?"[78]

From 1955 through 1969 nonagricultural employment in the city rose in every year but three, with a net gain of 321,500 jobs over the fifteen-year period. The city unemployment rate fell below the national rate every year except one from 1958 through 1970.[79] As long as employment opportunities in other domains grew, evolution away from manual work did not seem terribly threatening. Few anticipated the severe economic difficulties that the city would begin experiencing as the 1960s ended. But none could miss noticing what a different place New York had become.

CHAPTER 10.

Goodbye Molly Goldberg

As the number of manual jobs in New York fell, two developments further diminished the social weight of blue-collar New York. The first was the growth of the corporate headquarters economy. The second was the dispersion of working-class families. New York by no means stopped being a working-class city. In 1970 it still had a million blue-collar workers and a larger number of white-collar employees.[1] But the nature and status of its working class had changed, and with it the character of the city.

The 1950s and 1960s witnessed the greatest commercial construction boom in New York's history. Nearly two hundred major new buildings added sixty-seven million square feet of office space, twice that in the next largest nine cities combined. This burst of construction—largely mediocre, modernist, high rises—transformed the visual and social landscape of downtown and midtown Manhattan, coming as it did at the very moment when the waterfront and manufacturing were going into decline. Lower Manhattan—which in the mid-1950s looked much the way it had before the Great Depression, with narrow streets, eighteenth- and nineteenth-century buildings, food and leather merchants, hardware stores, and docks—saw one boxy office building after another rise along its shores, blotting out the spires of the first generation of skyscrapers, built during the early years of the century.[2]

A strengthening of New York's role as the headquarters for world capitalism largely accounted for this developers' dream. After World War II, upper-class New Yorkers—men like Dean Acheson, John McCloy, Robert Lovett, Averell Harriman, and Paul Nitze—helped shape a foreign policy of anticommunist liberal internationalism. As the national center of banking, finance, advertising, and entertainment, the city rode the crest of postwar prosperity and United States global hegemony. Blue-collar New York economically benefited from neither the high level of military spending nor the increased volume of world trade associated with the postwar economic order, but New York–based banks and corporations thrived in it, expanding their operations abroad and their power within the United States.[3]

In the mid-1960s, 136 of the nation's 500 largest goods-producing corporations had their headquarters in the city. So did dozens of major financial and communications firms.[4] The growth of the corporate headquarters complex, which included both corporate offices and businesses that served them, such as advertising agencies and law firms, helped offset employment losses in goods production and distribution. So did substantial growth of the city government, the nonprofit sector, hospitals and medical services, and, during the go-go years of the late 1960s, the securities industry. Between 1955 and 1970 service industry employment rose by 46 percent; finance, insurance, and real estate jobs by 36 percent; and government employment by 44 percent. By contrast, employment in manufacturing fell by 25 percent and in transportation and public utilities by 2 percent.[5] One expert estimated that in the late 1940s an equal number of blue- and white-collar workers could be found in Manhattan south of 61st Street, where half of all New York jobs were located. By the end of the 1960s, white-collar workers outnumbered blue-collar employees two-to-one.[6]

Many celebrated this change. In 1956, developer William Zeckendorf called the decline of New York manufacturing a "magnificent thing." "Our destiny is in the service field," he proclaimed. "As we have lost industrial workers from the population, we have gained higher-paid, higher-educated administrative personnel that make New York an unparalleled consumer's market." But white collars did not necessarily mean higher pay. In 1965, New York service industry employees on average grossed less than manufacturing workers, while finance workers only matched them. Many of the fastest growing occupations—for example low-skilled health industry jobs—ranked among the most poorly paid.[7]

Many white-collar jobs—particularly those held by women—were more proletarianized than the typical New York blue-collar job. Manufacturing workers tended to work for small firms involved in flexible production; finance, service, and government workers tended to work for larger, highly-structured operations. In 1969, three-quarters of the employees in the banking, insurance, and securities industries (including 170,000 clericals) worked for firms with five hundred or more workers.[8]

Banks, insurance companies, telephone companies, and other large employers of female, white-collar workers instituted degrees of work regimentation and supervision unusual in industrial settings, leaving little if any room for individual initiative. Advanced electronic devices allowed managers to continuously supervise the work pace of typists, keypunchers (who entered data for computers onto punch cards), telephone operators, and even telephone sales representatives. Individual output could be calculated in precise detail and any unauthorized work cessation instantly acted on. Though these workers often worked in large numbers side-by-side, many felt isolated: their tasks required no interaction with one another, and some employers had rules against talking on the job.

The large size of many white-collar employers made it economical for them to institute personnel practices far more sophisticated than anything employed by small or midsized manufacturers, trucking firms, construction contractors, or stevedore companies. New York Telephone, for example, had manuals and procedures for every aspect of employee relations. It encouraged a pervasive paternalism and routinely recruited supervisors and managers from among lower-level workers, building loyalty to the company. After working in the company's commercial department, writer Elinor Langer reported that the female sales representatives "do not see themselves as 'workers' in anything like the classical sense." Carefully-wrought approaches to human resources helped large employers keep out white-collar unions or, in the case of New York Telephone, restrict them to largely toothless independent outfits.[9]

Workers sought out low-level, white-collar jobs, in spite of their drawbacks. Black women, with few choices because of racial discrimination, eagerly abandoned housecleaning for clerical work, when they could get it. Young Italian women came to prefer clerical to factory work, even when it did not pay as well, prizing the superior working conditions, shorter hours, and decreased susceptibility to seasonal and cyclical downturns and layoffs. By the 1940s, Italian-American families, once renowned for discouraging education for their children, began urging girls to finish high school in order to prepare for clerical careers.[10]

The rapid expansion of the corporate headquarters complex made it increasingly important as a path of upward mobility for the children of working-class homes. (Older paths, including teaching, civil service jobs, contract construction, buying a truck or delivery route, and the military continued to provide options for social and economic advancement). By 1970, New York had nearly as many managerial, professional, and technical workers as clerical and secretarial employees.[11]

Like the growth of the corporate headquarters sector, residential changes diminished the cultural presence of working-class — especially blue-collar — New York. During the twelve years Robert Wagner served as mayor, rising income, new home construction, and widely available mortgages made it possible for hundreds of thousands of New Yorkers to leave older working-class neighborhoods. All around the city, people were moving out and moving in.

Because the apartment units that typically housed working-class New Yorkers could not be enlarged as residents' space needs or spending power increased, finding larger or more luxurious quarters often meant leaving the old neighborhood. Sometimes it meant leaving the city altogether. To find sufficient room, many cramped apartment dwellers reluctantly plunged into home ownership and years of indebtedness. (In one skit on his New York–based television show, Sid Caesar played the madcap scientist Ludwig von Space Brain who, when asked what was the most important single problem in space, replied "closet space.") Three-quarters of recent Queens home purchasers claimed in a 1947 survey to have been "forced to buy in order to have a decent place to live."[12]

Urban renewal and public works projects demolished the homes of hundreds of thousands of New Yorkers, leaving them no choice but to relocate, even if they had no desire to do so. On Manhattan's West Side, Irish tenement and brownstone dwellers fought a series of projects, including Park West Village, Lincoln Center, and Penn South, that markedly reduced their demographic and cultural presence in the heart of the city. In East Tremont, housewives and store owners fought a tenacious but futile struggle against the Cross-Bronx Expressway. Bay Ridge residents tried but failed to stop the approach roads for the Verrazano Narrows Bridge from gobbling up a huge chunk of their neighborhood.[13]

Necessity, though, was only part of the story. In his 1951 masterpiece, *A Walker in the City*, Alfred Kazin lovingly recalled the Brownsville of his youth, capturing its look and feel along with the ironic sensibility of the neighborhood itself. But Kazin was not describing a neighborhood he still lived in; he had left Brownsville a decade earlier. Central to the culture of Brownsville, Kazin argued, was the desire to leave it. "We were Brownsville," he wrote, "*Brunzvil*, as the old folks said—the dust of the earth to all Jews with money, and notoriously a place that measured all success by our skill in getting away from it." Irish-American fireman Dennis Smith lived with his wife and three children in a three-room walk-up apartment in the city. When his wife inherited some money, they bought a four-bedroom house on a half-acre lot in a small town sixty miles north of New York. "After living in tenements all my life," Smith wrote in *Report from Engine Co. 82*, "I want to give my three sons a little more space than I had, a place where they can ride a bicycle and breathe clean air." For all the rhetoric of neighborhood attachment, most working-class New Yorkers had only recent roots in their immediate communities, two generations or less. During the 1950s and 1960s, commercial culture, at the height of its romance with suburban living, celebrated wealth, consumption, and change. Many working-class New Yorkers accepted the idea that mobility measured success, believing, as in Philip Roth's tale of Jewish suburbanization, *Goodbye, Columbus* (set in Newark and its environs), that staying put meant being a loser.[14]

Some families—almost always white—moved in response to racial and ethnic change. After World War II, for example, African-American and Puerto Rican families began moving from Harlem to nearby Washington Heights. Their arrival undermined the sense of ease and neighborhood possession of the large (though always minority) Irish population. Growing crime (still modest by post-1960s standards) and gang warfare, stemming in part from ethnic tension and unstable neighborhood borders, made streets that once seemed like extensions of home and community feel threatening.

The death of a local teenager, Michael Farmer, in a 1957 gang fight greatly sharpened the fears of the uptown Irish while illustrating the complexity of ethnic and racial identity. All the gangs involved in the incident were multiracial: the local Jesters, though predominantly Irish, had some African-American members, while the mostly Puerto Rican Egyptian Kings and Dragons, which had come up from Harlem for the brawl, included a sprinkling of whites and blacks. Nonetheless, white Washington Heights residents thought of the Jesters as "Irish boys" and the invaders, as a dying Michael Farmer told the police, as "the Niggers." Many Irish, reducing a complex clash over territory, racial pride, group loyalty, and individual honor to simply a racial battle, took the extensively publicized case as a signal that the time had come to get out, joining an exodus already underway to other parts of the city and nearby suburbs, particularly Bergen and Rockland Counties, short drives from Washington Heights across the George Washington Bridge.[15]

The large-scale exodus of the prosperous and energetic sapped the vitality of working-class neighborhoods. Writer Pete Hamill recalled that in the mid-1950s, his native Park Slope, "its streets already emptied at night by television, began to reel from departures to the new suburbs and the arrival of the plague of heroin." "[A]mong those who stayed," he reported, "money was still short. . . . In the daytime, there were more men in the bars, drinking in silence and defeat." Though *Marty*, Paddy Chayefsky's celebrated 1953 television drama, had only scattered references to families moving out of the Bronx neighborhood in which it was set, it foreshadowed the loneliness and sense of failure of the staybehindniks, in this case an Italian-American butcher.[16]

During the 1940s nearly a half million white New Yorkers left the city; during the 1950s, 1.2 million; and during the 1960s another half million, an outmigration on a scale associated in world history with forced departures or natural disasters. Most of those leaving settled nearby. Between 1950 and 1960, the population of Nassau County jumped 93 percent, to 1.3 million. Suffolk County, farther out on Long Island, grew by 142 percent. Westchester, Bergen, Middlesex, Monmouth, and Union counties each added at least one hundred thousand residents. Whereas in 1940, New York City accounted for nearly two-thirds of the population of the metropolitan region, by 1970 it housed less than half.

Many departing New Yorkers continued to work in the city. In 1960, over 40 percent of employed Nassau County residents traveled to jobs in New York, as did a substantial if smaller portion of the workers living in other nearby counties. In the past, outside of executive ranks, the women and men employed in New York City and those living there were essentially the same group, but during the postwar years a growing part of the city workforce no longer resided in Gotham. Though executives and professionals were more likely to be commuters than lower-paid workers, by the early 1960s, 20 percent of the people working in Manhattan's central business district left the city at night, including 14 percent of the clerical workers and 10 percent of "labor."[17]

Probably more working-class families relocated within the city than moved to the suburbs. Municipal employees and those who hoped to get jobs with the city government had no choice. The Lyons Law, a city ordinance passed during the Depression to protect established residents from job competition from suburbanites and newcomers, required three years of city residence for appointment to most municipal jobs and continued city residence to maintain them. Other New Yorkers stayed within the city limits to remain close to family, friends, and jobs.

Inner-city redevelopment provided new homes for some of these families, but many moved to the outer fringes of the city, where vacant land helped keep housing costs down. Rapidly developing peripheral areas included eastern Queens, the Queens and Brooklyn marshlands abutting Jamaica Bay, and the northern Bronx. Queens became a "haven" for city employees, drawn to its semi-suburban ambience and nonprofit co-ops, garden apartment complexes, and middle-income public housing. Its population soared to nearly two million by 1970, surpassing Manhattan and the Bronx to become the city's second most populous borough (after Brooklyn).

Builders erected several types of housing in newly developed areas. Canarsie, in southeastern Brooklyn, consisted largely of detached houses on small lots and multifamily row houses. The northeast Bronx grew with a similar mix, but also some very large apartment complexes. Extensive garden apartment development gave eastern Queens its particular feel, but builders interspersed tracts of detached homes and apartment buildings.[18]

New circumstances inevitably changed the way working-class New Yorkers lived and how they viewed the world. In many cases, the neighborhoods they moved to had greater occupational and social heterogeneity than those they left. In northeastern Queens, managers, craftsmen, professionals, clerical workers, machine operatives, sales, and service workers lived intermingled with one another. In 1950 about three-fifths of the labor force living in the area held white-collar jobs, while one-fifth had blue-collar jobs (many quite skilled) and another fifth managerial positions. Similarly, Canarsie had a mix of blue-collar workers (many skilled craftsmen or machine operators), schoolteachers, sales, and clerical workers. Many upwardly mobile young couples stayed in the area only briefly before moving on to better accommodations on Long Island. Here, as in other "settler" areas, roughly equivalent spending power masked differences in workplace status and social trajectory.

The union movement facilitated working-class mobility by raising income, sponsoring affordable housing in outer reaches of the city, and providing social benefits and insurance that lessened dependence on family and neighborhood networks in times of trouble. Decentralization, though, tended to undermine union-mindedness. Construction union leader Peter Brennan attributed declining attendance at union meetings in part to the outward dispersion of members. IBEW Local 3, which imposed fines for missed membership meetings, saw a rise in absenteeism from 1960 on, which one study postulated partly reflected an exodus of electricians to the suburbs. Residential dispersion eroded the viability of social benefit delivery through central facilities, like union health clinics, and made it less likely that workers and their families would go to union halls for entertainment and recreation.[19]

Meanwhile, in the growing periphery of the city, community bonds less frequently developed around work issues than in older, more homogeneous, more central neighborhoods. Schools and traffic problems and threatened overdevelopment more often drew neighbors together than work-related issues. In many burgeoning areas, ethnicity provided an organizational and social armature, joining together the working and middle classes. Residents of Howard Beach and South Ozone Park, single-family home areas in southern Queens to which many Irish and Italian families moved during the postwar years, proved as ethnically oriented and hostile to outsiders as inhabitants of the most densely immigrant areas of the inner city.

Working-class homeowners were particularly likely to develop political and psychological ties to their more middle-class neighbors. Having scraped together all of their savings and then some to buy a home, many feared anything that threatened the value of their new possession and the status it brought, including racial integration, high density development, and higher property taxes.

New suburbanites who still worked in the city often found their identification with it quickly diminished. After he moved out of New York, Dennis Smith wrote, "I am still a part of it, yet I feel removed, like a broken jockey who grooms horses." Moving to a new neighborhood did not necessarily break old attitudes and activities. Historian Sylvie Murray documented a high degree of political activity in northeastern Queens, as newcomers brought concerns over civil rights, a rent strike habit, and even battling between ALP and Liberal Party adherents to the freshly-seeded courtyards of garden apartment complexes and the auditoriums of overcrowded local schools.[20] Still, over time new circumstances subtly transformed the self-understanding of the upwardly and outwardly mobile.

The economic and spatial restructuring of New York contributed to a gradual diminishment of a distinctly working-class presence in the cultural life of the region and the nation. In 1954, the Goldbergs, the quintessential fictional Jewish family that gave its name to a long-running radio and television drama, moved from an apartment in a working-class district of the Bronx to a single-family home on Long Island. Left behind were plot lines revolving around rent strikes, Lewisohn Stadium concerts, and other city doings. Deracination soon followed; in 1955 *The Goldbergs* was renamed *Molly*. But this was not enough to save a series whose working-class New York Jewishness—even moderated—stood out like a skyscraper on a television landscape increasingly suburban and distant from the East Coast. Within a year, the show went off the air.

New York-based performers and shows had dominated early network television, when most television set owners lived in the northeast. In 1948, television's first star, Milton Berle, brought to the *Texaco Star Theater* a comedic style rooted in Yiddish vaudeville. However, as television grew into a truly national medium, the urban, ethnic sensibility Berle embodied became less acceptable to audiences and sponsors. Under criticism for his New York parochialism and raucous manner (replete with risque jokes and cross-dressing), Berle survived by toning down his act. When more structured "situation comedies" eclipsed vaudeville-style variety shows, many of the new series had New York settings. However, over time their characters relocated or new shows, set elsewhere, replaced them. By 1957, working-class New Yorkers, once seen in *The Goldbergs*, *The Life of Reilly* (about a Brooklyn family resettled in Los Angeles), *Amos 'n' Andy*, *Hey Jeannie*, and *The Honeymooners*, had disappeared from TV-land. That year Jackie Gleason, Sid Caesar, and Milton Berle all saw their shows canceled. As the fictional characters who populated television America left New York, so did the industry that created them, migrating to Los Angeles.[21]

In New York itself, comedic styles changed, as increasingly the "higher-paid, higher-educated administrative personnel" whom Zeckendorf celebrated set the cultural mood of the city. In 1961, Daniel Bell noted that "the raucous-tone, vulgar, smart-aleck jokes of a George Jessel, a Myron Cohen, or a Joe E. Lewis reflected the wise-guy quality of the old garment trades. Today, the new sophisticates — raconteurs and satirists like Shelley Berman, Mort Sahl, Elaine May and Mike Nichols — reflect the new face of New York, a white-collar dominance of the large corporation and its advertising-media satellites."[22]

For many New Yorkers, the 1958 flight of the Brooklyn Dodgers proved more painful than television's departure. Gothamites commonly viewed the team's move west as a tale of moral turpitude, in which the team's owner, banker Walter O'Malley, spurned the loyalty of ordinary Brooklynites and destroyed a quintessential symbol of working-class New York in his quest for greater wealth. Dodger fans had a distinctive plebeian rowdiness, egged on by Hilda Chester and the Sym-phoney Band, overlaid by the tense interracialism of the Jackie Robinson era. How sharply Ebbets Field, situated amid apartment houses and shopping streets, near the Brooklyn Public Library, the Botanical Gardens, and Prospect Park, differed from the comfortable but antiseptic Chavez Ravine stadium, floating in a sea of parking lots, that O'Malley built for the Los Angeles Dodgers.

National League baseball returned to the city in 1962. The New York Mets illustrated Hegel's comment (via Marx) about "the first time as tragedy, the second as farce." The Mets inherited the Dodger exuberance, but as

loopy ineptitude (the team lost 120 games its first season) rather than the med-
ley of skills and backgrounds that made the "Boys of Summer" both an athletic and cultural triumph. By the time the Mets achieved greatness, with their
1969 world championship, they had distanced themselves from the urban,
everyman tradition of New York baseball. For one thing, the team moved
from the upper Manhattan Polo Grounds to Shea Stadium, in Queens, where
they attracted more affluent fans from Long Island. For another, their foremost player, pitcher Tom Seaver, looked more comfortable in wealthy suburbia than on city streets.[23]

Dispersed, assimilated, fractured, and overshadowed, by the early 1960s
working-class New York, though still economically and even politically vital,
no longer held a central position on the cultural stage. As a national cultural
presence, the New York working-class had virtually disappeared, gone from
television, only episodically appearing in literature and cinema, gone from
the visual arts (except in the work of a few idiosyncratic figures like Jacob
Lawrence, Romare Bearden, and Edward Hopper), and gone from the theater.[24]

But the history of working-class New York did not travel in straight lines.
The decade after Robert Wagner left office saw a burst of labor militance that
equaled and in some ways surpassed the postwar strike wave and once again
brought national attention to New York workers. To a considerable extent,
this reanimation of working-class New York came from newcomers to the
city, from those who had moved in as others moved out, and from the long,
hard struggle they waged for their civil rights.

PART THREE
Strike City

We want no condescending saviors to rule us from their judgment hall. We workers ask not for their favors. Let us consult for all.

— "The International"

CHAPTER 11.

Freedom Now

The vast demographic changes of the 1950s and 1960s—especially the influx of African-Americans and Puerto Ricans to the city and the outflow of whites—profoundly changed working-class New York. Newly arriving workers and their families faced different and more formidable challenges than those they replaced. Their fight against racial discrimination injected a language of rights, a spirit of militance, and a heightened degree of political mobilization into a working class that had become less of a presence in the city. The civil rights struggles of the 1950s and early 1960s set the stage for the decade of extraordinary, working-class self-assertion that followed.

Many African-Americans and Puerto Ricans came to New York specifically because, compared to most parts of the country, it seemed a pocket of racial liberalism. Nevertheless, even when they inhabited the very houses that departing whites had lived in or held the very same jobs, their experiences were never identical, for persistent discrimination and racism made their New York profoundly different from the city upwardly mobile white workers were leaving behind.

Take the Whitmans, a black family Joseph P. Lyford described in his 1966 study of the Upper West Side. In many ways, the family found New York to be an enormous improvement over Atlanta, where they had lived previously. In New York, Mr. Whitman recounted, "You're more free; you can get into an argument and call each other names and you don't go to jail and get beat up or turn missing. . . . you can sit where you want to and eat what you want to." In addition to its lack of legal segregation and lower level of police brutality, the family prized New York for its higher wages and the much better public education their daughter was getting than she had in Georgia. Still, the lives of the Whitmans were constrained by discrimination.

Arthur Whitman, raised on a farm, worked as a plumber's helper when he first arrived in New York, but discovered that the plumbers' union did not accept nonwhites as journeymen. He ended up at a Queens car wash. On good days he could earn decent money but, because no one wanted their car washed when it was raining or snowing, he rarely worked a full, six-day week. Arthur's wife, Catherine, worked as a hotel chambermaid (and belonged to a union), but her work, too, tended to be intermittent.

Even with two family members working, the Whitmans could get only a two-room apartment (for a family of five), infested with insects, with peeling paint, holes in the kitchen floor, and no running water in the bathroom sink. The Whitman's landlord, by supplying a few pieces of furniture, could rent their apartment as "furnished," charging higher rent than otherwise allowed under rent control. The family's fondest hope was to get into public housing.

The Whitmans were not unusual. The blocks Lyford studied, 82nd to 106th Streets between Central Park and the Hudson River, though far from the city's poorest, housed a large number of unemployed adults and many workers with irregular jobs paying too little to support "a minimal standard of living." While a lack of education and skills contributed to the plight of poor West Siders, so did dark skin.[1]

In spite of the state prohibition against discrimination in employment by race, religion, or nationality and years of campaigning by civil rights groups, black organizations, and a few unions, well into the 1960s race and ethnicity played a major role in hiring and promotion decisions. During that decade, federal studies found a total or near total absence of African-Americans from the New York banking, insurance, advertising, and communications industries. The skilled building trades remained overwhelmingly Caucasian. Many private employment agencies coded applications by race, enabling them to comply with illegal but common employer requests for whites only. The state's own employment service engaged in the same practice.

When industries did hire blacks or Puerto Ricans, they often restricted them to less desirable positions. The hotel and restaurant industry, for example, was a major employer of nonwhite workers: without their labor it could not have operated. But expensive hotels rarely allowed African-Americans to hold jobs that involved interaction with guests, like bartender or waiter. Instead, most were relegated to housekeeping and cleaning departments. Similarly, though nonwhites made up a growing percentage of the garment industry workforce, few held the more skilled or better paid positions. Young Harlemites referred to a garment industry job as "a slave." "A guy who worked in the garment center," memoirist Claude Brown recalled, "wouldn't say he had a job; he'd say, 'Man, like, I got a slave.' . . . I had seen old men down there, old colored cats. . . . they looked like they were about sixty years old, but they were still pushing trucks through the snow."[2]

In 1959, the annual income of New Yorkers averaged $6,091, but for nonwhites it was only $4,437 and for Puerto Ricans $3,811. In Washington Heights, nearly half of all employed blacks and Puerto Ricans earned less than $3,000, compared to a quarter of the Jews and Irish. Citywide, in 1960, 34 percent of white Puerto Ricans and 27 percent of nonwhites lived below the poverty line (family income less than $3,000), compared to just 12 percent of non–Puerto Rican whites.[3] Low levels of education hurt African-Americans and Puerto Ricans, but even when they had the same educational achievements as mainland whites they generally got paid less. Similarly, though African-Americans and Puerto Ricans were disproportionately represented in lower-paid occupations, even when they worked in the same jobs as non–Puerto Rican whites they generally made less.[4] Unemployment figures also capture glaring differences in the positions of whites, blacks, and Puerto Ricans. In 1960, when the overall unemployment rate in the city was just over 5 percent, the rate for nonwhites (including non–white Puerto Ricans) neared 7 percent and for Puerto Ricans equaled 10 percent.[5]

Long-term changes in the city's economy reduced opportunities for those with few skills, poor education, little work experience, poor English, or dark skin. The exodus of manufacturing from the city diminished what had been the largest source of employment and economic advancement for new New Yorkers. Though many whites lost jobs when manufacturers moved, the disproportionate concentration of African-Americans and Puerto Ricans in blue-collar work meant that they suffered the most from industrial relocation.

Automation also disproportionately hurt blacks and Puerto Ricans. Herman Badillo, who came to New York from Caguas, Puerto Rico, in 1941, and went on to become the first Puerto Rican borough president (1966) and congressman (1971), put himself through City College and law school by working as a bowling alley pin boy, an elevator operator, and a dishwasher, all jobs soon automated nearly out of existence. The post–World War II mechanization of southern agriculture led many African-Americans to move north, only to find automation of industry, transportation, and some types of service work restricting opportunities there.

The full impact of changes in the local economy was not felt until the 1970s, when the city underwent a severe economic crisis. Still, well before then a pattern had emerged in which white workers had the strongest foothold in economic sectors showing robust growth, like finance or corporate headquarters activity, while blacks and Puerto Ricans tended to be clustered in either declining sectors, like manufacturing, or in the lowest, least skilled jobs in expanding service industries, like health care and restaurants and hotels.[6]

When faced with discrimination in the private sector, New Yorkers long had used municipal employment as a path of upward mobility. However, after World War II, city leaders, backed by the business community, complained that under the Lyons Law—requiring city residence for municipal employees—they could not recruit top managers from out of town without seeking waivers from the City Council. They also pointed to the difficulty residency requirements caused in hiring engineers and policemen. In 1960 the state legislature created a loophole, allowing city policemen to live in nearby suburbs, a right extended to sanitation men the next year. In 1962, Mayor Wagner engineered the law's removal.

The issue of race and ethnicity rarely came up in discussions of the Lyons Law, but it lurked nearby. At a public hearing before Wagner signed the repeal bill, the most vocal opposition to it came from two Puerto Rican Democratic activists, who complained that because of bigotry the city failed to properly utilize nonwhites already working for it. Several years later, Ewart Guinier—the former public unionist, by then self-reinvented as an academic urbanist—noted that repeal came "at a time when blacks and other nonwhites lived in New York City in large numbers and were an untapped resource to fill the very jobs that were allegedly unfilled for want of applicants." Once residency requirements were lifted, the workforce in some city jobs— especially fireman and policeman—became increasingly made up of white suburbanites, servicing and policing an increasingly nonwhite city. Not without reason, many residents of black and Puerto Rican neighborhoods came to see the police as an occupying army.[7]

Public education represented another traditional route to economic and social mobility that blacks and Puerto Ricans could not take full advantage of, in part because of discrimination. Compared to black schools in the South, New York public schooling represented a very marked improvement. However, within the New York school system de facto segregation was widespread and growing, with white schools getting more resources and more experienced teachers than schools predominately black or Puerto Rican. Dropout rates for black and Puerto Rican children were much higher than for whites. At the municipal colleges, in 1960 minorities made up only 5 percent of the student body, the same percentage as ten years earlier, even though the African-American and Puerto Rican population of the city had increased by over 70 percent.[8]

Through the late 1960s, the continued economic strength of the city benefited African-Americans and Puerto Ricans. Between 1960 and 1970 all ethnic groups saw their unemployment rates drop, with the Puerto Rican drop larger than that for the city population as a whole. Some blacks and Puerto Ricans were able to take advantage of structural changes in the city economy—including the growth of the corporate headquarters complex—to escape drudgery. In 1940, two out of three employed black women living in Brooklyn worked in domestic service; in 1950, one out of three; in 1960, one out of five; and in 1970, fewer than one in ten. One study concluded that the "occupational distribution of Brooklyn blacks and whites was significantly more similar in 1970 than in 1940," with the gap between black and white income decreasing. Still, the labor market remained segmented along overlapping ethnic, racial, and gender lines.[9]

Discrimination in housing tended to be even more intractable than employment discrimination. Even when nonwhites had sufficient income to afford decent housing, they often could not obtain it because of the widespread, generally illegal refusal of building owners to rent or sell to them. As their numbers swelled, Puerto Rican and African-American New Yorkers were penned into either areas in which they already were heavily represented or a few, largely poor neighborhoods being abandoned by whites.

Though Harlem was the historic center of black New York, after World War II most of the growth of the African-American population took place outside Manhattan. During the 1940s, the black population of Bedford-Stuyvesant, a north central Brooklyn neighborhood of brownstones and solid brick buildings, more than doubled to 137,436. During the 1950s and 1960s, black population growth centered in nearby Crown Heights, where African-Americans had lived since the 1830s, and in the much poorer neighborhoods of Brownsville and East New York to the east. By 1970, "Greater Bedford-Stuyvesant" had become New York's largest African-American community.[10]

Growing African-American communities tended to be in areas being emptied by the outmigration of whites. The influx of nonwhites accelerated white exodus, as fear spread that once predominantly white neighborhoods were becoming poor and black, a distressing notion to many if not all white residents. Predatory real estate agents engaging in "blockbusting" fueled the process. First they scared whites into selling their houses. Then they unloaded them on nonwhites at inflated prices they could ill afford. Rapid foreclosure and housing deterioration resulted. Meanwhile, apartment building owners reduced or eliminated services, taking advantage of the lack of housing alternatives for nonwhites and, in some cases, hoping that the city would buy them out in the course of urban renewal.[11]

City housing policy exacerbated the problems of blighted areas. Rather than scattering subsidized public housing, the Housing Authority clustered it in massive assemblages. In Brownsville, for example, it followed the low-rise 1947 Brownsville Houses (1,338 units) with the adjacent high-rise Van Dyke Houses (1,453 units) and Tilden Houses (998 units). Nearby it built Boulevard Houses (1,441 units), Howard Houses (815 units), and Linden Houses (1,590 units). These projects replaced severely deteriorated tenements, but such massive reconstruction over the course of a dozen years created social chaos. Brownsville public housing, one study concluded, "rather than stemming the tide of decay, seemed to accelerate it." As movement into and out of the area became frantic, many landlords stopped even routine maintenance or abandoned their buildings altogether. Families lived in houses stripped bare by vandals, in some cases without heat or hot water.[12]

Given the discrimination and deficiencies of the private housing market, many black New Yorkers, like the Whitmans, saw public housing as their salvation. Between 1951 and 1957, the percentage of public housing units occupied by African-Americans rose from 30 to 39 percent. Yet the scale, architectural brutality, and penny-pinching construction standards of public housing for the poor bred deep resentment. "The projects in Harlem," wrote James Baldwin, "are hated almost as much as policemen, and . . . for the same reason: both reveal, unbearably, the real attitude of the white world, no matter how many liberal speeches are made, no matter how many lofty editorials are written, no matter how many civil-rights commissions are set up. The projects are hideous . . . there being a law, apparently respected throughout the world, that popular housing shall be as cheerless as a prison."[13]

Puerto Ricans faced many of the same housing problems as blacks. East Harlem served as a cultural capital for Puerto Rican New York, much as central Harlem did for black New York. However, the neighborhood lacked sufficient housing to accommodate the massive flow of postwar migrants, even with the movement of Italian-Americans out of the area for more prosperous neighborhoods in the city and Westchester. As a result, as the Puerto Rican population of the city swelled, it decentralized. In 1950 a majority of Puerto Rican New Yorkers lived in Manhattan, but ten years later, with the Puerto Rican population of the city having more than doubled, from 245,900 to 612,600, only 37 percent still lived there. By 1970 both Brooklyn and the Bronx had larger Puerto Rican populations than Manhattan.

Many areas in which Puerto Ricans clustered suffered severe deterioration. The South Bronx, where the largest Puerto Rican settlement developed, had acre after acre of tenement buildings in advanced states of decay. Landlords subdivided apartments to increase their rent rolls while investing little in maintenance. As whites moved out, the city stopped maintaining parks and reduced services, from garbage collection to health care. Large-scale public housing projects, while providing badly needed living units, created social strains in what became one of the largest concentrations of poor people in the country.[14]

In 1960, 17 percent of New York families renting their homes lived in what the census bureau deemed dilapidated or deteriorating buildings, but among nonwhite renters the figure was 35 percent, and among Puerto Ricans 41 percent. Citywide, 9 percent of renting families had to share a bathroom with others or had none, but 18 percent of black families and 15 percent of Puerto Ricans lived with this daily ordeal. Yet 40 percent of black and 34 percent of Puerto Rican families who rented their homes had to spend a quarter or more of their income on housing, compared to 30 percent of all city renters.[15]

Postwar New York never had legally mandated segregation. To the contrary, state and city laws passed during the 1940s and 1950s forbid various types of discrimination in housing and employment. But the lived experience of blacks and Puerto Ricans proved the limits of legal protections unaccompanied by the social will to enforce them, and the hollowness of opportunities for those lacking the economic and social wherewithal to take advantage of them. For all of New York's rhetorical commitment to equality and racial justice, during the decades after World War II patterns of occupational discrimination, school segregation, and ghettoization endured and deepened.

Throughout the 1950s and 1960s, working-class African-Americans, Puerto Ricans, and their allies protested against discrimination in employment, schools, and housing. Their attacks on local racism intertwined with efforts to support the civil rights movement in the South. The battle for racial equality — though rarely described in class terms — constituted a mobilization by workers and their families in defense of their rights and interests and for justice for all.

In the mid-1950s, the *Brown v. Board of Education* Supreme Court decision, the racist murder of Emmett Till in Mississippi, and the Montgomery, Alabama, bus boycott energized New York civil rights supporters. Following the 1955 acquittal of Till's murderers, the Brotherhood of Sleeping Car Porters sponsored a Harlem rally attended by ten thousand people, where representatives of the ILGWU, the Catholic Church, and the NAACP spoke. A second demonstration, organized by District 65, the NAACP, and the Jewish Labor Committee, attracted twenty thousand protesters. When in 1956, Martin Luther King Jr. spoke at Brooklyn's Concord Baptist Church, ten thousand people tried to squeeze their way in. Reacting to events in the South, the New York City CIO Council called on the president to send troops to Mississippi and South Carolina "to protect American citizens" and on Congress to reduce representation from states which disenfranchised blacks.[16]

Even while mobilizing against Southern injustice, civil rights supporters protested discrimination closer to home. In 1954, before the Supreme Court announced its decision in *Brown v. Board of Education*, psychologist Kenneth Clark, who helped prepare a brief for the court case, began protesting the de facto segregation of New York schools. Segregation, by economic status or by race, Clark argued, "becomes a force in solidifying undemocratic class cleavages."

While Clark carefully marshaled facts and used his ties to various elites to press for school integration, grassroots efforts began as well. In Brooklyn, Junior High School 246 PTA president Annie Stein—a longtime Communist and former union staffer (who was white)—took up the issue inside the Brooklyn NAACP, enlisting the support of Milton Galamison, the black pastor of the Siloam Presbyterian Church in Bedford-Stuyvesant. By 1956, Stein and Galamison had drawn four hundred members to their NAACP Parents' Workshop, including leaders of sixty-four PTAs. Through meetings with school officials, rallies, and publicity, the committee pressed for desegregation and the upgrading of schools serving predominantly nonwhite students. Galamison demonstrated the support for his militant approach by winning a contested election for the presidency of the Brooklyn branch of the NAACP.

As Galamison's prominence grew, so did his frustration. In October 1958, he charged that in the four-and-a-half years since *Brown v. Board of Education*, segregation in the New York schools had actually increased, and siting plans for new schools made it likely that the future would bring still greater racial separation. That year, in Bedford-Stuyvesant, the parents of seven children refused to send them to their local school, arguing (along the lines of the *Brown* decision) that segregation made it inferior. In Harlem, five families took similar action.[17]

As the 1960s began, protests by African-Americans against discrimination and exploitation grew louder and more frequent. The Southern civil rights movement helped inspire a new wave of tenant activism. Starting in

1959, one-time National Maritime Union and ALP activist Jesse Gray organized a series of highly publicized protests against Harlem landlords and city housing policy, repopularizing the use of rent strikes. In the early 1960s, other groups launched similar campaigns. Fearful of escalating demonstrations, in 1964 Mayor Wagner "virtually endorsed 'legal' rent withholding," while pressing for state measures to aid tenants. Though by the mid-1960s the firestorm of rent strikes had largely burned itself out, it was the largest display of mass housing action since the fight to retain rent control in the 1940s, and unlike that struggle it explicitly linked housing problems to racism and racial discrimination.[18]

The southern struggle similarly spurred protests against job discrimination. The Brooklyn chapter of CORE—the Congress of Racial Equality—with a racially integrated, working- and middle-class membership, took the lead in fighting hiring inequities using direct action tactics. In 1962, its members blocked trucks at Ebbingers bakery in Flatbush, demanding that the company begin hiring African-Americans. Protesters also targeted a Sealtest-Sheffield Farms milk plant in the middle of Bedford-Stuyvesant, which had only seven black employees among its 367-person workforce, Bond Bread, and A & P supermarkets, in each case winning improved job opportunities for nonwhites.[19]

Organized labor played a complex role in the swelling campaign for racial equality, supporting it in the abstract but coming under increasing criticism for its own discriminatory practices. Backing civil rights in the South provided a way for New York unions to embrace racial justice without threatening arrangements in which they themselves were involved. In 1960, for example, during the sit-downs at segregated southern lunch counters, the Central Labor Council organized union support for picketing of New York Woolworth stores. One day the ILGWU provided eight hundred picketers. New York unions supported federal civil rights legislation and donated substantial amounts of money to civil rights groups, including fifteen thousand dollars the ILGWU gave to the Southern Christian Leadership Conference in 1965.[20]

The August 1963 March on Washington marked the zenith of New York labor's support for civil rights. The idea for the march came from A. Philip Randolph, the veteran New York-based head of the Brotherhood of Sleeping Car Porters, who in 1941 had threatened to hold a similar demonstration, calling it off only after President Roosevelt agreed to establish a wartime Fair Employment Practices Committee (FEPC). Randolph found early backing for a new march among fellow members of the Negro American Labor Council—a group he helped found in 1960—including the Jamaican-born secretary-treasurer of District 65, Cleveland Robinson, who ultimately chaired the protest's administrative committee. After the spring 1963 demonstrations in Birmingham, Alabama, Martin Luther King, Jr. and other civil rights leaders agreed to cosponsor Randolph's march, seeing it as a way to up the pressure on the federal government to make a dramatic move against discrimination. Indicative of its roots in the black labor movement, it was to be a "March on Washington for Jobs and Freedom," demanding not only the passage of the civil rights bill proposed by the Kennedy Administration but also a higher minimum wage, a federal public works program, and a revived permanent FEPC (which was added to Kennedy's bill, as finally passed, in the form of the Equal Economic Opportunities Commission). Though at the urging of its president, George Meany, the AFL-CIO refused to endorse the march, its Industrial Union Department—essentially the old CIO unions—did. In New York, both the Central Labor Council and the state AFL-CIO backed the demonstration. Van Arsdale's union, IBEW Local 3, assigned a staffer full-time to mobilizing support and sent a four-hundred-member delegation. The nearly all-white cutters local of the ILGWU also sent members. So did ILA Local 1814, which represented Brooklyn longshoremen. Unions with large numbers of black members, left-wing traditions, or both provided the greatest support. District Council 37 of the American Federation of State, County, and Municipal Employees, which was beginning to make breakthroughs in organizing city workers, sent a delegation of twenty-five hundred. Local 144 of the Building Service Employees—whose black and Puerto Rican membership mushroomed once it began organizing nursing homes and hospitals—sent four hundred members. Local 1199 arranged transportation for one thousand, and then had to turn away additional members who wanted to go. And most impressive of all, District 65, whose secretary-treasurer, Cleveland Robinson, chaired the protest's administrative committee, sold two thousand tickets for two trains it chartered and estimated that an equal number of its members traveled to Washington by other means. These latter four unions alone provided 2 to 3 percent of all those present at the historic march.[21]

Even as New York labor leaders basked in the glory of that great day, many felt rising pressure on their own institutions to end discriminatory practices. As early as March 1960, as black students were sitting down at segregated lunch counters across the South, the Central Labor Council executive board devoted most of a meeting to a discussion, led by Van Arsdale and

Charles Zimmerman of the ILGWU, of the need to support the Southern movement *and* end union discrimination against blacks.[22]

Zimmerman's own union provided a cautionary tale of the consequences of ignoring this advice. Though the ILGWU long had been a political and financial supporter of the civil rights movement, in 1959, NAACP leaders began including it in their denunciations of labor union discrimination. NAACP labor secretary Herbert Hill emerged as the union's most vocal and persistent critic. In 1961, with the aid of Hill, garment worker Ernest Holmes filed a charge with the state Commission for Human Rights claiming that ILGWU Local 10, the cutters local, had refused to admit him because he was black. An initial decision in favor of Holmes and subsequent court proceedings brought the ILGWU a great deal of negative publicity. As charges and countercharges flew, it became obvious that blacks and Puerto Ricans were woefully underrepresented among the cutters. In 1962, Congressman Adam Clayton Powell, Jr., head of the House Committee on Education and Labor, convened hearings on alleged discrimination by the ILGWU. Though ILGWU leaders vigorously defended themselves, the episode tarnished the union's liberal reputation.[23]

The stand-pat racial exclusivity of most construction unions also threatened to create a political crisis for New York labor. On June 12, 1963, the Joint Committee for Equal Employment Opportunity—a coalition of CORE, the NAACP, the Negro-American Labor Alliance, the Workers Defense League, the Urban League, and the Association of Catholic Trade Unionists—launched a summer-long offensive against discrimination in the construction industry by throwing up a picket line at the building site for an annex to Harlem Hospital. The demonstration at 136th Street and Lenox Avenue—the center of Harlem—drew throngs of spectators (including Malcolm X), some of whom began chanting, "If we don't work, nobody works." Fearing disorder, the city shut down work on the project while a committee investigated racial discrimination in the building trades.[24] Recognizing a tinderbox, Van Arsdale once again initiated a discussion among leaders of the Central Labor Council on the need to take concrete steps "so that equal opportunity is available to all workers in all unions." But, as was the case three years earlier, agreement on this proposition led to few changes in practice.[25]

The Joint Committee resumed its campaign for more construction jobs for blacks and Puerto Ricans on July 9 with a sit-in at Mayor Wagner's office and picketing at a Lower East Side housing project construction site. The next day it added a sit-in at Governor Nelson Rockefeller's New York City

office and a picket line in Bedford-Stuyvesant, where the state university
was building Downstate Medical Center. The picketed projects presented
tangible symbols of injustice, publicly-funded buildings going up in largely
nonwhite neighborhoods that were providing very good jobs for white
workers—some of whom commuted in from far outside the city—while
neighborhood residents remained largely locked out of the skilled trades because of their color.[26]

The decision of a group of leading Brooklyn ministers to back the Downstate Medical Center protest elevated the antidiscrimination campaign to a
new level. On July 15, fourteen ministers, including Gardner C. Taylor, a
former member of the Board of Education and a close colleague of Martin
Luther King, Jr., were among forty-two persons arrested for blocking a truck
from entering the Downstate site. Black Brooklyn was electrified. Nightly
church rallies, attended by thousands, generated a charged spiritual and political air much like that in Montgomery and Birmingham at the height of the
civil rights crusades there.

On July 21, over twelve hundred protestors surrounded the Downstate
construction site. Police took into custody 211 people for blocking entry
ways, the largest mass arrest in New York City since the Harlem riot of August 1943. By the end of the month six hundred people had been arrested at
Downstate, and scores more at other locations, while the sit-ins at the offices
of the mayor and governor continued.

At Downstate, however, the ministers discovered that sustaining their
drive was more difficult than launching it. With building trades leaders and
politicians endorsing their goals even as they evaded concrete steps toward
realizing them, with the police avoiding the brutality so often used against
southern demonstrators, and with adult churchgoers needing to be at work,
the number of protesters quickly dwindled. Not wanting a prolonged, futile
campaign, in early August the ministers called off their protests. The Joint
Committee continued protests on its own, but the campaign petered out. In
mid-November the city resumed construction on the Harlem Hospital annex,
recognizing that the heat was off. Leaders of the summer protests—among
the largest civil rights protests ever held in the North—expressed deep dis-
appointment that, in spite of various new committees and programs, only a
few blacks and Puerto Ricans had obtained work in the construction industry.[27]

Immediately following the building trades campaign, the focus of civil
rights activity shifted to the schools. In the summer of 1963, local chapters of

Striking longshoremen under police watch on the Manhattan waterfront in 1951. Within a generation their jobs would disappear from the Manhattan scene.

(Photo by Daniel Nilva, courtesy of the Tamiment Institute Library, New York University.)

The huge, union-sponsored Penn South Housing Cooperative in the heart of Manhattan, opened officially by President John F. Kennedy, Jr. in 1962.

(Photo by Sam Reiss, courtesy of the Tamiment Institute Library, New York University.)

An aircraft carrier being built at the Brooklyn Navy Yard.
Once the largest industrial facility in New York, the yard was closed in 1966.

(Photo by Sam Reiss, courtesy of the Tamiment Institute Library, New York University.)

The changing image of working-class New York on television:
The Goldbergs, The Honeymooners, and *All in the Family.*

(© Baldwin H. Ward and Kathryn C. Ward/CORBIS, © Bettmann/CORBIS, and © Bettman/CORBIS)

Michael J. Quill, the most charismatic of New York's postwar labor leaders,
asking transit workers to vote on a job action in 1950.

(Photo by Ossie LeViness, courtesy of the *New York Daily News*.)

Nelson A. Rockefeller campaigning for governor at a baseball game in 1958.
Despite his background and wealth, he worked closely with many leading New York unionists.

(Reproduced from the collections of The Library of Congress.)

Harry Van Arsdale, leader of the International Brotherhood of Electrical Workers
and long a force in the New York labor movement, at his home in Queens in 1957.
(Reproduced from the collections of The Library of Congress.)

Robert Moses, who single-handedly changed daily life in New York
for half a century, in his office in 1963.
(Reproduced from the collections of The Library of Congress.)

In the mid- to late 1960s, massive labor unrest—such as the transit strike in 1966 and the Ocean Hill/Brownsville teacher conflict in 1968—threatened to rend the fabric of New York.

(Photos by Sam Reiss, courtesy of the Tamiment Institute Library, New York University.)

UFT President Albert Shanker's in-your-face style was emblematic of the New York labor movement in the late 1960's.

(Photo by Sam Reiss, courtesy of the Tamiment Institute Library, New York University.)

Mayor Abraham Beame holding the famous "Ford to City: Drop Dead" issue of the
New York Daily News, October 1975. Just after the photograph was taken Beame ripped up the paper.

(Photo by Bill Stahl, Jr., courtesy of the *New York Daily News*.)

By the late 1970s, arson and widespread abandonment of housing had left large swaths of New York —like the South Bronx—in rubble. (Photo by Mel Rosenthal.)

In the late 1990's, working-class militancy continues on: tens of thousands of construction workers shut down Madison Avenue in 1998 to protest use of non-union labor.

(Photo by Robert Rosamilio, courtesy of the *New York Daily News*.)

CORE and the NAACP joined with Galamison's Parents' Workshop and the Harlem Parents Committee in threatening a school boycott unless the Board of Education moved decisively toward desegregation. The agreement by Bayard Rustin, fresh from coordinating the March on Washington, to help organize the boycott brought it credibility. Desperate to forestall an embarrassing demonstration, the board promised to develop a plan and timetable for integration by December. When it failed to do so, the civil rights coalition scheduled a one-day boycott, with the Urban League and the National Association for Puerto Rican Civil Rights joining the original sponsors. The United Federation of Teachers did not back the boycott, but it promised to defend any teacher who stayed home.

On February 3, 1964, 464,361 students — 45 percent of those enrolled — stayed out of school, far more than the usual 100,000 absentees. Eight percent of the teachers were absent, compared to the usual 3 percent. Arguably it was the largest civil rights demonstration ever held in the United States. Though absenteeism was highest in African-American and Puerto Rican neighborhoods, some 20 percent of the boycotters were white.

This extraordinary display yielded few gains. When the president of the Board of Education dismissed it as a "fizzle," Galamison announced plans for "fizzle number two," a second boycott, but did so without consulting his coalition partners. Many of them, including the NAACP, the Urban League, and Rustin, declined to back the demonstration (though Malcolm X — who had not been involved in the first boycott — did). According to the Board of Education, an impressive 267,459 students stayed out of school on March 16, but the movement had lost its unity and momentum. While the Board of Education continued to issue plans, statements, and reports, and civil rights and liberal groups, along with a few labor leaders, tried to keep up the pressure for integration, the schools grew more segregated.[28]

An incident coincident with the school boycotts seemed emblematic of the fear and contempt that authorities had for black New Yorkers. In March 1964, Bedford-Stuyvesant's Boys High School — the city's oldest secondary school and a perennial athletic powerhouse — won the Public School Athletic League (PSAL) men's basketball championship at the annual tournament in Madison Square Garden. A melee among student fans, which escalated to seat slashing and bottle throwing, marred their victory. Though the Garden had seen worse, the PSAL announced an end to its tradition of holding its championship there, moving it to small, neutral gyms. What this meant, noted sportswriter Pete Axthelm, was that "the black stars who dominate

high school ball in the city were swept quietly out of sight. . . . While the
media fall in love with the Knicks, a top high school star searches in vain for a
paragraph or two in the *Times* on his team's victories." A former Boys High
coach commented, "By ignoring these kids, you strangle them at the most
basic level. And then people wonder why they get bitter."[29]

The bitterness exploded just a few months later. On the morning of July
16, 1964, some African-American summer school students at a junior high
school in Yorkville got into an altercation with a building superintendent who
had sprayed them with water. An off-duty white police lieutenant who came
upon the scene shot and killed fifteen-year old James Powell. Police and city
officials justified the slaying, claiming that Powell had come at the officer with
a knife, but witnesses disputed many aspects of this account.

On the evening of July 18, a protest in Harlem against Powell's shooting
ended in a march to a nearby police station. There pushing and shoving escalated into running battles between demonstrators and police, accompanied
by widespread smashing of store windows. The next night violence intensified, with one person killed and over one hundred injured. On the third day,
fighting between police and young African-Americans spread to Bedford-
Stuyvesant, where it reached its highest pitch before dying down five days
after it began.[30]

For Kareem Abdul-Jabbar, then a high school student spending his summer working at a Harlem antipoverty program, James Powell's killing "spot-
lighted not the uniqueness but the absolute commonness of the crime. . . .
It was not the death—that happened all the time—but the lie that was intol-
erable. It made all of Harlem face the fact that they didn't even have the
strength to exact an acceptable apology." Kenneth Clark found the "revolts"
"a weird social defiance." "Small groups of young people seemed to take delight in taunting the police . . . 'Here's a nigger, kill me.' . . . [They]
would die rather than be ignored." Martin Luther King, Jr., who rushed to
the city at the request of Mayor Wagner to help restore calm only to find the
mayor unwilling to make any concessions to the black community, concluded
that "the major problem remains one of economics . . . the need for millions of dollars now for full employment and for the elimination of slums." He
left the city more optimistic about prospects for racial justice in the South
than in the North.[31]

As Gay Talese noted in the *New York Times*, neighboring East Harlem remained quiet during what came to be known as the Harlem Riot of 1964.

Talese attributed this to a "Peace Patrol" organized by the East Harlem Action Committee. Deeper differences, however, distinguished the Puerto Rican and African-American communities. While worse off economically than African-Americans, Puerto Ricans suffered less social discrimination, such as in housing. Coming from a society in which race mattered less than in the mainland United States, many remained optimistic that they could reproduce the pattern of European immigrants, achieving upward mobility and social acceptance free of the damning taint of racial otherness imposed on African-Americans. Others saw their time in New York as an interlude before returning to the island.[32]

Puerto Rican New Yorkers did not have the long history of self-organization that black New Yorkers had. The Puerto Rican government's 1948 establishment of a Migration Division in New York reinforced a clientistic political tradition and inhibited the growth of mainland-based groups. Low levels of voter registration and geographic dispersion meant that well into the 1960s, Puerto Ricans had very little clout in electoral politics.[33]

Like black New Yorkers, with whom they episodically allied, Puerto Rican New Yorkers protested discrimination and demanded equal opportunity. However, given their different situations, the two communities did not always have the same priorities. In the 1950s and into the 1960s, job-related issues received the most attention in the Puerto Rican community, outweighing protests against housing discrimination and school segregation.

As early as 1950, the New York AFL and CIO, joining with the mayor's office, set up a committee "to see if something could be done to be helpful . . . relative to the labor situation of Puerto Ricans in Harlem." Puerto Rico's Migration Division saw unionization as the best way to stop "unscrupulous employers" from preying on "the ignorance of the Puerto Rican both of English and of labor history and labor organizations." Like the union movement and the New York City government, it saw labor market exploitation, not discrimination, as the essential problem that Puerto Ricans faced.[34]

Before World War II, the small Puerto Rican community in New York had had a strong tradition of unionism, leftism, and political activism, transmitted through fraternal groups, left-wing newspapers, and campaigns for Vito Marcantonio and Puerto Rican independence. Ida Torres, who became a top officer of the Bloomingdales local of the Department Store Workers, recalled going as a child with her parents—both unionists—to the Mutualista Obrera Puertorriqueña, an IWO lodge on Third Avenue and 104th Street, where she learned that "workers . . . help each other." Many post–World War II migrants shared her positive view of organized labor.

Unfortunately, the unions that signed up Puerto Rican workers often had little regard for their welfare and little interest in assimilating them. Some, like the International Jewelry Workers Union, were little more than criminal enterprises run by longtime racketeers. Signing sweetheart contracts with employers, they never held meetings nor provided workers with benefits. Others, like some ILGWU locals, engaged in bona fide collective bargaining but refused to have Spanish translators at meetings, translate contracts, or hire Spanish-speaking staff, effectively locking Puerto Rican members out of decision-making and union life. A few unions, including UE Local 475 (later IUE Local 485) and District 65, brought Puerto Ricans into leadership and fought for their rights, recognizing that they suffered from discrimination as well as exploitation. But they were exceptions that proved the rule.

By the mid-1950s, many Puerto Rican workers had grown disillusioned with unionism.[35] As complaints from workers and pressure from the Puerto Rican government grew, in 1954 the AFL and CIO central labor councils created a Labor Advisory Committee on Puerto Rican Affairs. But with little funding and minimal staff, the committee had "no real influence to make member unions take heed of Puerto Rican shop problems."[36]

Two developments led to more serious efforts to address the exploitation of Puerto Rican workers: a congressional investigation, and a series of demonstrations and wildcat strikes. In 1957 the Senate established a select committee chaired by Arkansas' John McClellan to study improper labor activities. Armed with the largest investigative staff any congressional committee had ever employed, its televised hearings—particularly the confrontations between committee counsel Robert F. Kennedy and Teamsters Dave Beck and Jimmy Hoffa—made union corruption a national issue. In August 1957 the committee held hearings on unions that victimized Puerto Ricans. A representative of the Association of Catholic Trade Unionists (ACTU), several Hispanic workers, and a reporter from the largest Spanish-language newspaper in New York, *El Diario*, exposed collusion between a number of AFL-CIO locals and employers at the expense of Puerto Rican workers.

The McClellan committee hearings scared AFL-CIO leaders into action. Hoping to forestall government oversight of their organizations, they launched a yearlong housecleaning that culminated in the expulsion of the Teamsters. As part of this effort, in mid-1957, George Meany sent his assistant, Peter McGavin, to New York to address the plight of Puerto Rican workers. In one case, McGavin helped coordinate raids by District 65 and IUE Local 485—leftist unions Meany normally would have shunned—against a corrupt Retail Clerks local. Meany agreed to provide additional staff to the Labor Advisory Committee on Puerto Rican Affairs, and personally gave the main speech at a conference it sponsored. Meanwhile, prodded by the congressional hearings, Mayor Wagner appointed a Committee on Exploitation of Workers with labor, city, and business representatives.[37]

As labor and city officials flurried about denouncing "racket unions," Puerto Rican members of what was widely deemed a "legitimate" union, the ILGWU, became increasingly public in expressing their dissatisfaction with it. In 1957, four hundred African-American and Puerto Rican workers from a Bronx factory picketed the ILGWU offices, protesting what they saw as its failure to adequately represent them. Later they tried to get the union decertified. The next year, two hundred largely Puerto Rican workers at a Brooklyn knitwear company, under contract with the ILGWU, held a wildcat strike to protest extremely low wages. That same year, two hundred members of Local 132 (Button and Novelty Workers) picketed the ILGWU's international headquarters, protesting what they charged were "back-door deals" with employers and the union's failure to hold meetings in Spanish.

ILGWU officials displayed little empathy for the protesters. Never acknowledging any underlying problem in their relationship with Puerto Rican workers, they presented legalistic arguments demonstrating that, at least in some cases, their critics had failed to understand or utilize existing union procedures. Such responses did not satisfy the press. One *El Diario* editorial criticized the low wages of Hispanic ILGWU members and the union's lack of high-level Hispanic leaders, calling on David Dubinsky "to dedicate less time to the [Liberal] Party . . . and pay more attention to the workers who belong to . . . substandard [ILGWU] locals." The ILGWU figured prominently in Peter Braestrup's October 1958 series in the *Herald Tribune* on the exploitation of Puerto Rican workers.[38]

The formation of the AFL-CIO New York City Central Labor Council in early 1959 brought a more serious labor push to help Puerto Rican workers. Its standing committee on Exploitation of Minorities, chaired by Paul Jennings from the IUE, sought out Spanish-speaking unionists to join its effort. Meanwhile, the council shifted attention away from the touchy issues of poor representation and union discrimination by focusing on the minimum wage issue. It also launched a campaign to organize low-paid workers, concentrating on the service and wholesale sectors, which helped increase Puerto Rican

union membership.[39] In 1965, forty-nine locals affiliated with the Central Labor Council reported significant Puerto Rican membership, while forty Puerto Ricans held elective union office. Many Puerto Rican workers continued
to be frustrated in their dealings with unions. But through the council's organizing efforts and its co-optation of the independent Spanish Labor Committee (later renamed the Hispanic Labor Council) to serve as an advisory group,
it went a long way toward bringing the most militant and articulate elements
of the Puerto Rican working class into the official labor movement.[40]

The postwar expansion of the black and Puerto Rican populations, and the
accelerating drive for civil rights and racial justice, led to countermobiliza-
tions by white New Yorkers committed to maintaining their separation and
their privileges. The resulting conflicts deepened fault lines within the working class. The 1963 drive to desegregate the construction industry provides a
good example. Union intransigence about procedures for admitting apprentices and journeymen brought increasing bitterness on both sides. During the
campaign, building trades leader Peter Brennan began using rhetoric that
soon would become common in New York and elsewhere, charging that demands for the immediate admission of blacks and Puerto Ricans to apprenticeship programs amounted to "unfair and un-American" racial
discrimination in reverse, since whites on existing waiting lists would be by-
passed. Even the *New York Times* found this argument strained, noting that
one union under state investigation, Sheet Metal Workers Local 28, had
never had even a single nonwhite member and routinely took sons and neph-
ews of members into apprenticeships ahead of other, longer-waiting applicants. (When in 1964, New York State ordered all apprenticeship programs
to undertake open recruitment, the greatest beneficiaries were whites shut
out by past nepotism, not African-Americans.)

Many construction workers saw efforts to open up apprenticeship programs and job opportunities as threatening their immediate interests and
those of their friends and family. Preferential access to jobs, training, and
union membership represented a kind of social capital that could be passed
on to (and held over) kin. For whites who lacked other kinds of resources, the
devaluation or elimination of ethnic job monopolies and nepotistic hiring
systems represented a social menace. Richard Gambino argued that Italian-
Americans defended exclusionary practices with particular vehemence because as a group they had "used their efforts to build the labor unions rather
than other organized means of economic progress, for example an educated

class or mass political or social movements." But in the ILGWU and Amalgamated Clothing Workers, Jews as well as Italians limited access by others to
skilled jobs, going so far as to block proposals in the 1960s for federally-
funded job-training programs.[41]

Clashes over job discrimination by no means precluded cooperation between organized labor and nonwhites. The New York union movement included many African-Americans, Puerto Ricans, Afro-Caribbeans, and white
unionists committed to racial justice. Working-class New Yorkers generally
had more contact at work with people of other racial and ethnic backgrounds
than better-off city dwellers, creating practical motives for working together.
Relative to most sectors of New York society, the labor movement remained
an arena of interracial cooperation. Still, fights over discriminatory union
practices divided the labor movement, alienated many nonwhites from it, and
lessened its ability to shape the future of the city.[42]

Housing desegregation proved an even more explosive issue. A September 1964 poll of white New Yorkers found two-thirds supporting the ban in
the recently-passed Civil Rights Act on employment discrimination, but 40
percent indicated that they would "feel uncomfortable about having a number of Negro families" living near them. Many white workers who were willing, perhaps reluctantly, to toil besides nonwhites, fiercely resisted efforts by
blacks or other minorities to move into their neighborhoods.[43]

Fear that racial integration would lower property values, as it often did,
accounted for much of the opposition. One retired Queens shipyard worker
told the *New York Times*: "I would be the first to move out if a Negro family
moved into this neighborhood. Property devaluates as soon as a Negro moves
into an area." Working-class homeownership generally represented a lifetime — or several lifetimes — of savings. With so great a physical and emotional toll invested in their homes, many working-class families defended
their monetary value with a fierceness rivaling the most monomaniacal robber
baron.

But property values formed only part of the story. Many whites feared
that having African-American or Puerto Rican neighbors would lead to
physical and cultural decay. A Brooklyn utility worker spoke for tens of thousands when he told a reporter: "As soon as they move into a neighborhood
the place turns into a slum." To support this view, whites pointed to neighborhoods like Brownsville, where, most believed, population change had
been the cause of deterioration, overlooking such factors as city policy, the
impact of urban renewal, the dynamics of a dual housing market, the greed of

landlords, the consequences of poverty and discrimination, and the cumulative effects of aging buildings and disinvestment.

Recent working-class arrivals in outer city neighborhoods had a particularly strong stake in resisting integration. Many had left neighborhoods undergoing disorderly processes of ethnic succession, and desperately sought to avoid going through the experience again. Equally important, many had a psychological investment in exaggerating the extent to which the neighborhoods they left had changed, and the role of racial and ethnic succession in their decision to leave. As Jonathan Rieder noted in his study of Canarsie, "minorities were used as a scapegoat by a younger generation ready to cut its ties to the past." Deeply ambivalent about their abandonment of a highly-valorized and much-mythologized old-neighborhood way of life, recent departees found psychological and moral relief in portraying themselves as having been forced to leave by nonwhite newcomers.[44]

Resistance to residential integration remained a neighborhood by neighborhood affair, but resistance to school integration became a citywide movement. Organized opposition first arose in 1959. The Ridgewood-Glendale section of Queens was a neighborhood of working-class and lower-middle-class homeowners of Irish, German, Romanian, Italian, and Slovene descent. When the Board of Education proposed to bus in black students from overcrowded elementary schools in Bedford-Stuyvesant, parent and civic groups objected, expressing the same fear of lowered property values that sparked opposition to residential desegregation. They also contended that school integration would bring lowered educational standards and increased crime and delinquency. Some said they feared that white children would be "contaminated" by the newcomers.

For several years the Ridgewood-Glendale anti-integration movement remained anomalous because the Board of Education launched so few efforts at desegregation. However, in the fall of 1963, as civil rights groups grew more militant and the Board of Education experimented with pairing white and black schools as a way to desegregate them, local groups opposing school integration sprung up around the city, linked by a newly formed organization, Parents and Taxpayers (PAT). PAT grew through the mobilization of existing civic, taxpayer, and parent associations. Its very name reflected the importance of concerns about property values (in New York City, "taxpayers" generally connoted property tax payers), as did the prominence in its leadership of real estate lawyers.

PAT's greatest support came from lower and lower-middle-class white homeowners—not necessarily with children in public schools—in areas with expanding black populations or adjacent to nonwhite neighborhoods. Though the opponents of school integration never mobilized as many activists as integrationists did, they proved just as militant and ultimately more successful. In March 1964, following the pro-integration school boycott, PAT brought some fifteen to twenty thousand demonstrators to City Hall. The next September, PAT and its allies sponsored their own two-day school boycott, during which a quarter of the city's schoolchildren stayed home, fewer than during the integrationist protest but still a massive showing. In some neighborhoods, opponents of busing for desegregation even held sit-ins, adopting tactics from the civil rights movement.

David Rogers, a close observer of the school integration battle, concluded that with its extensive base in preexisting, local groups, the "neighborhood schools movement" proved more effective in mobilizing sustained support than did desegregation advocates. A September 1964 *New York Times* survey found 80 percent of whites opposing a Board of Education school pairing plan. Many more respondents viewed PAT favorably than unfavorably. In the face of such sentiment, the Board of Education and the city leadership rapidly backpedaled from any commitment to desegregation, especially when it involved the mandatory transfer and busing of students. As middle-class whites, unwilling to risk having their children involved in desegregation efforts, pulled their children from the public school system, integration became an ever less practical goal. By the fall of 1965, the campaign for school integration effectively ended in obvious failure, as the Board of Education abandoned desegregation as a major objective. The retreat from the argument informing *Brown v. Board of Education*—that integration was both necessary for social justice and a way to improve education—laid the basis for a fierce and ugly battle over community control of schools just a few years later.[45]

The demographic changes that took place after World War II, and the social and political conflicts that accompanied them, weakened and strengthened working-class New York. Many of the hundreds of thousands of black and Puerto Rican workers who came to New York for jobs and freedom joined the labor movement and struggled through it for workplace advances and social gains. But organized labor did not serve as their primary vehicle for pursuing racial equality, and sometimes presented an obstacle to it. The resistance by white workers and unionists to desegregation tarnished the labor movement and pitted workers against one another. In resisting desegregation, some white workers deepened their ties with more middle-class neighbors with links to the real estate industry, antitax groups, and conservative politicians.

Though the civil rights movement often failed to achieve its goals, it nonetheless transformed the city and its working class. Most important, it fostered a rebirth of mass politics—of direct popular political engagement—on a scale not seen since the demise of the Popular Front left. Civil rights struggles forged a new style of politics, fusing the language of rights and morality with mass mobilization and direct action. Though some of the movement's most celebrated tactics and symbols—like the sit-in and the song "We Shall Overcome"—had been borrowed from labor, their renewed use represented a break from the corporatist liberalism the New York labor movement increasingly had relied on during the 1950s to advance its interests.[46]

For workers, their spouses, and their children, the civil rights movement and the opposition to it taught and retaught a basic lesson: power could be found in the streets. From the mid-1960s through the mid-1970s, New York workers would act on that lesson, over and over again, in causes both progressive and reactionary. In doing so, they carried forth the long legacy of working-class New York and the particular contribution of the new New Yorkers.

CHAPTER 12.

Municipal Unionism

Histories of American labor generally portray worker militancy peaking during the Gilded Age or the Progressive Era or the New Deal. In New York City, that moment arguably came from the mid-1960s through the early 1970s, when a series of strikes matched, and in some ways surpassed, the post–World War II strike wave in scale and consequences. Industrial conflict intensified nationally during the Vietnam War era. Workers, emboldened by low unemployment, sought a larger share of the rewards of a booming economy, while managers, distressed by decelerating productivity and falling profit rates, sought to check their power.[1] In New York, industrial workers joined the strike wave, but the most dramatic strikes involved government employees, who sought meaningful collective bargaining and pay scales matching those in private industry.

After World War II, the number of public-sector workers in New York— employees of the city, state, and federal governments and public agencies like the Transit Authority—ballooned. In 1950 they totaled 347,400; in 1960, 408,200; and in 1970, 563,200. By far the largest group worked for the city, which in 1970 had more employees than the garment, banking, and longshore industries put together.[2]

New York's political culture accounted for its exceptionally large municipal workforce. About half of it performed functions common to most municipalities: elementary and secondary education, police, fire, sanitation, highways, parks, and general administration. The other half were employed in New York's version of social democracy, providing services other cities did not offer or offer on the same scale: hospitals, public housing, higher education, and mass transit.[3]

Historically, workers had been drawn to public-sector jobs for the security they provided. Government workers rarely got laid off, and they received pensions before they became common in the private sector. The civil-service system provided an element of protection against arbitrary, unfair, or discriminatory treatment, since hiring and promotions depended, theoretically, on objective measures, like examinations.

But public-sector jobs had disadvantages. Generally they paid less than equivalent jobs in the private sector. Some provided fewer opportunities for advancement. Also, sometimes they were controlled by politicians.

To address these problems, as far back as the nineteenth century a few New York City employees had joined unions and gone on strike. However, until the 1930s most municipal worker organizations were not true unions but benevolent associations that encouraged social ties among workers, used connections to supervisory personnel and politicians to help individuals with promotions and transfers, and lobbied the state legislature and the city council for higher wages and better conditions, but did not engage in collective bargaining. Only in the 1930s did actual unions begin to aggressively organize public workers. Rivalries among these groups and the anti-red crusade limited their growth, but by the early 1950s several thousand New York City employees (not counting transit workers, who had a well-established union) belonged to a labor organization.[4]

Even as they grew, public-employee unions remained in legal limbo. The 1935 National Labor Relations Act, which gave private-sector workers the right to join unions without reprisal, specifically exempted public employees. In 1947 the New York state legislature, in response to a teachers' strike in Buffalo, enacted the Condon-Wadlin Law, which made strikes by state and local government workers illegal. Under the law, strikers were considered to have terminated their employment. If rehired, they could not receive a pay raise for three years.[5]

In 1953, while campaigning for mayor, Robert Wagner Jr. promised to upgrade conditions for city workers and create "a genuine pattern of collective bargaining." Seven months after taking office, he instituted a "Career and Salary Plan" that rationalized job titles, promotion paths, and salaries and standardized pensions, health benefits, personnel practices, and working conditions. Additionally, he ordered city agencies to establish grievance procedures and labor-relations committees and directed agency heads to meet with representatives of employee organizations to discuss wages, hours, and working conditions.[6]

During the years that followed, Wagner slowly gave city workers more rights. In November 1955, over two thousand Sanitation Department employees, led by District Council 37 (D.C. 37) of the American Federation of State, County and Municipal Employees (AFSCME), held a one-day strike to protest miserable working conditions and autocratic discipline imposed by Parks Commissioner Robert Moses. Prodded by Wagner to do something, Moses ordered a representation election, perhaps believing AFSCME would not get much support. But D.C. 37 garnered 4,117 votes out of 4,290 cast, greatly enhancing its stature and that of municipal unionism in general. Soon thereafter Wagner allowed unions the right to have their members' dues collected by the city (dues check-off) and established a forty-hour workweek for those city employees working longer hours.[7]

Wagner went farther in 1958 when he issued Executive Order 49, which allowed the city to certify exclusive bargaining agents for particular groups of workers, a major step toward private-sector-style labor relations. That year the Uniformed Sanitationmen's Association became the first union outside of the transit system to sign a contract with the city. (During the mid-1930s, when private companies operated most New York transit lines, their workers unionized. After the city took over the transit system, the TWU successfully fought to maintain collective bargaining.)[8]

In 1962 the city tried to stop a trend among its workers toward job actions by invoking the Condon-Wadlin Act to fire sixteen striking motor vehicle operators. The effort boomeranged when thousands of workers rallied in their support and private-sector labor leaders pressured Wagner to return the men to their jobs and settle the ten-day strike on terms favorable to the union.[9]

The municipal union activists of the 1950s—Parks workers, motor vehicle operators, sanitationmen, and laborers—tended to be Irish and Italian men in occupations that in the private sector were unionized and better paid. Unions like the United Public Workers that had organized heavily white-collar, female, Jewish, and nonwhite elements of the city workforce had been decimated by the anti-red crusade.[10] Only in the early 1960s did new efforts begin to unionize these sectors.

Advances came first in the schools. The Cold War persecution of the Teachers Union left a host of small, ineffective teacher groups fighting one another. High school teachers displayed the greatest militancy, dissatisfied with a 1947 state law that equalized their pay with the traditionally lower-paid (and much more heavily female) elementary school teachers, as well as the lack of compensation for supervising extracurricular activities. A series of boycotts of after-school activities, led by the High School Teachers Association, culminated in a 1959 strike by evening-school teachers. The three-week walkout forced the Board of Education to shut down its evening programs and offer the strikers a huge pay hike.

In March 1960 the Teachers Guild absorbed part of the high school group and renamed itself the United Federation of Teachers (UFT). When

the Board of Education made no move to meet the union's demand for a vote
to select an exclusive bargaining agent for teachers, the UFT called a strike
for the day before the 1960 general election. Five thousand of the city's forty
thousand teachers stayed home. National and local labor leaders—including
George Meany and Harry Van Arsdale, Jr.—opposed the idea of a teachers'
strike, especially one that might disrupt the election (most voting took place
in schools). Once it occurred, Van Arsdale maneuvered to end it quickly by
getting Wagner to agree to a fact-finding committee stacked with union representatives, which eventually recommended a representation vote.

In June 1961, teachers voted three-to-one for collective bargaining
through an exclusive representative. The broad support for this notion represented a remarkable turnabout in attitudes. Through the 1950s, both the
American Federation of Teachers (with which the UFT was affiliated)
and the much larger National Education Association (NEA) opposed
teachers' strikes and were at best ambivalent about private-sector-style labor
relations.[11]

In December 1961, the UFT defeated an NEA-led coalition and the
Teachers Union to win bargaining rights for New York's teachers. The following April, when contract talks with the city stalled, UFT members voted
to strike. This time half of the city teachers walked out. Local and national
labor leaders again opposed their action, fearing that government worker
strikes would erode public support for unionism. They managed to end the
strike after a day by getting Governor Rockefeller to help finance a contract
somewhat better than the last prestrike offer. Though the improvements were
modest, the 1962 walkout set off a national wave of teacher strikes and gave
public-sector union organizing a major boost.[12]

The UFT combined militancy with a sense of professional responsibility. In its next round of negotiations, the union won an agreement from the
Board of Education to limit class sizes (the city routinely violated state-
mandated limits) and to make greater teacher recruitment efforts in the
South, seen as a way to increase the number of African-American instructors.
In 1967, the UFT pushed for a More Effective Schools (MES) program to
upgrade education in the worst schools through smaller classes and extra resources. When the city and the union could not reach a contract agreement,
46,000 of the city's 58,000 teachers stayed away from their jobs for over two
weeks, until the city agreed to a substantial pay boost and modest funding of
the MES program. In less than a decade, New York teachers had embraced
unionism, won collective bargaining rights, convinced themselves and others

of the legitimacy of teacher job actions, and held a massive walkout for better conditions for themselves and for New York City children.[13]

Social workers went through a similar process of recovering from the effects of McCarthyism, melding professional and trade union concerns, and embracing militancy. The Welfare Department, once a union stronghold, had been so thoroughly purged of leftists and union leaders that through the 1950s it hosted little labor activity. Supervisors and clerical workers rather than social workers dominated AFSCME Local 371 (part of D.C. 37), which tried to fill the gap created by the destruction of the United Public Workers but which developed a reputation of closeness to management verging on company unionism.

In 1959, a former UPW member, Sam Podell, set out to reform Local 371 into a "more militant and representative union." Within two years, he and a group of activists at the Brownsville Welfare Center gave up on AFSCME and formed the unaffiliated Social Service Employees Union (SSEU). Changes in the welfare system drew social workers to the brand of militant, socially conscious unionism SSEU advocated. A rapid rise in the number of welfare recipients pushed caseloads far above mandated levels, requiring harried social workers to spend more time on paperwork and less time with clients. Many new welfare workers—hired at an extraordinary clip to deal with expanding rolls and high turnover—had experience in the civil rights movement or the student left which inclined them toward sympathy with their clients and sharp criticism of the political establishment.[14]

In October 1964, SSEU defeated Local 371 in an election to represent the social work titles at the Welfare Department, leaving AFSCME with only the supervisors and clerks. Contract talks with the city broke down when SSEU demanded not only a substantial boost in the low salaries its members received, paid overtime, and other benefits, but also improved training opportunities and a cap on caseloads. The city considered many of the union demands—especially a caseload limit—inappropriate subjects for collective bargaining. Some AFSCME leaders agreed but, in a key strategic decision, the newly installed reform leadership of Local 371 decided to ally with SSEU.

On January 4, 1965, some eight thousand welfare workers went on strike, forcing the city to close two-thirds of its welfare centers. Because the strikers sought improvements for welfare recipients as well as themselves—for example, streamlined procedures for issuing clothing grants—they received widespread backing from civil rights and social service advocates, including

Martin Luther King, Jr. and CORE executive director James Farmer (who had once worked as a D.C. 37 organizer).

For over a decade, Mayor Wagner had prevented any serious, labor-caused disruption in city services through a combination of gradualism, personalism, and political machination. With these no longer sufficing, the city fired five thousand strikers for violating the Condon-Wadlin Act and jailed nineteen leaders of SSEU and Local 371. But the Welfare workers stuck it out for twenty-eight days, returning to work only after Wagner agreed to a fact-finding board empowered to consider all issues including caseloads. The mayor also agreed to seek a stay of Condon-Wadlin penalties.

The report of the fact-finding panel and a subsequent contract with the city brought welfare workers a substantial wage increase, funds for additional education, and full city payment for health insurance. The city also agreed to cap caseloads and hire additional personnel. Finally, it established a new panel to reconsider its entire approach to labor relations.[15]

In January 1968, Mayor John V. Lindsay put into effect a series of recommendations that established a new legal and procedural framework for municipal labor relations. Previously, the city had dealt with unions as both an employer and a labor relations referee. The new setup transferred the latter function to an Office of Collective Bargaining (OCB), run by a board jointly picked by the city and its unions. In few other private or public jurisdictions did unions play so large a role in regulating labor relations. The OCB had authority to determine bargaining units, run representation elections, certify bargaining agents, and intervene in contract and grievance impasses. The law setting it up limited the scope of bargaining to wages, hours, and working conditions, explicitly banning bargaining over the level of services city agencies delivered. However, it did allow bargaining over the impact of managerial decisions on working conditions, a backdoor through which unions forced bargaining on manning levels and other issues seemingly outside their province.

Though SSEU's militancy and political panache led to the OCB, its own future proved troubled. Internal discord and difficulty getting the city to abide by its contract and negotiate a new one led to a 1969 decision to merge with Local 371. The three-way battle between SSEU, Local 371, and the city had provided a rich breeding ground for union leaders, schooling them in organizing, collective bargaining, debate, factionalism, and compromise, and bestowing on a good number the mantle of sacrifice from eleven days spent in jail during the 1965 strike. For three decades to come, onetime social workers like Al Viani, Stanley Hill, and Charles Ensley played a leading role in D.C. 37 and the New York labor movement.[16]

Just after the 1965 Welfare strike, D.C. 37 became involved in another jurisdictional battle, this time for the right to represent twenty-one thousand municipal hospital workers. Under Wagner's bargaining rules, a union that represented a particular group of workers could negotiate the terms of employment that applied strictly to those workers, including wages rates. However, the city withheld the right to bargain over working conditions that affected all its employees—like benefits, vacations, hours of work, overtime rules, and pensions—until one union achieved recognition for a majority of all city workers, no matter what agency they worked for. Only two unions had a reasonable chance of obtaining that status, D.C. 37 and Teamsters Local 237. Whichever won the contest to represent city hospital workers almost certainly would achieve an overall majority and become the dominant municipal union.

Municipal hospital aides, cooks, cleaners, and other support personnel suffered from very low pay, terrible working conditions, and an almost total lack of respect from supervisors and professional coworkers. The city would have been hard-pressed to fill their jobs if not for discrimination elsewhere in the labor market, which made it difficult for nonwhites to find better positions. By one estimate, Puerto Ricans and African-Americans (many recent arrivals from the South) held 85 percent of nonprofessional city hospital jobs.

The UPW had had a significant following in the hospitals, where it targeted black workers. Its destruction left AFSCME as the leading public hospital union, but in 1951, D.C. 37 leader Henry Feinstein bolted with many members to the Teamsters, where he established Local 237. Though D.C. 37 made some advances in the hospitals, through the mid-1960s, Local 237 had more worker support.

Following the 1965 Welfare strike, the Teamsters decided to cement their advantage in the hospitals by seeking a representation election. The Teamsters had a highly popular leader in former hospital worker Bill Lewis, one of the highest ranking African-Americans in the New York labor movement. Lewis assumed that the Teamsters would win easily. AFSCME, knowing it was behind, launched an all-out campaign, led by newly-appointed D.C. 37 executive director Victor Gotbaum. For help, Gotbaum brought in a unionist he had worked with in Chicago, Lillian Roberts. Roberts had grown up in a family on welfare. At eighteen she became the first African-American nurse's aide at the University of Chicago Lying-In Clinics. A decade later she got active in the AFSCME local at her hospital, eventually going on union staff. In New York, Roberts proved skilled at speaking to and for hospital workers—especially the large number of black women among them— melding the languages of civil rights and unionism in a campaign that promised greater respect and upgrading opportunities for aides, messengers, cooks, and clerks.

When it appeared that the Teamsters would win the election, AFSCME succeeded in getting George Meany to intervene with Wagner to postpone the vote, allowing them time to catch up. (Since the AFL-CIO had expelled the Teamsters, its leaders felt free to favor AFSCME.) When the election finally took place in December 1965, D.C. 37 narrowly won the largest unit, hospital aides, and carried the messengers and clerks, leaving Local 237 with only the cooks.[17]

D.C. 37's hospital success ushered in a series of representation election victories that brought into the union school lunch workers, school aides, and building cleaners (all heavily black groups), chemists, librarians, actuaries, lifeguards, court reporters, and even institutional barbers. Having won representation rights for a majority of all mayoral agency workers, D.C. 37 entered negotiations for the first citywide contract in mid-1967. After prolonged discussions, in February 1969 the city and the union signed an agreement that provided eleven paid holidays, cash pay for overtime, shift differentials, and an upgraded pension plan that allowed workers to retire after twenty-five years at 55 percent of their final salary.[18]

As municipal unions began transforming the lives of city workers, some New Yorkers resented their growing power. For one thing, better pay and benefits for city workers meant higher taxes. For another thing, as their power grew, municipal unions seemed to be diminishing the sovereignty of elected government, for example winning more generous treatment of welfare recipients and establishing rules about what city workers could or could not be asked to do. Many of their critics associated the municipal unions with the city's system of Democratic party rule, in which interest groups won favors from government in return for political support.

In 1966, liberal Republican John V. Lindsay took office as mayor promising to end such arrangements. His ascension reflected chaos within the Democratic Party. Shortly before the 1961 election, Mayor Wagner, under pressure from a middle-class, Manhattan-based reform movement, broke with the political bosses who had helped him win power. Labor gave the mayor crucial support. The garment unions ensured that he kept his Liberal Party endorsement (important for attracting Jewish voters), while the Central Labor Council, anticipating Wagner's possible loss in a Democratic primary, set up the Brotherhood Party as a vehicle for him to attract working-class Catholics unlikely to vote Liberal. In the end, Wagner got the Democratic endorsement and won the general election, but with only 51 percent of the vote.[19]

By 1965 the Democratic Party had become so fractious that it took a four-way primary to pick a mayoral candidate, a lackluster Brooklyn regular, Comptroller Abraham Beame. David Dubinsky and Alex Rose, fearing a return of Tammany influence, and eager to enhance their own power, engineered a Liberal Party endorsement for Lindsay, the congressman from the Upper East Side's "Silk Stocking" district. Lindsay's nomination by the Republicans sparked William F. Buckley Jr. to enter the race as a candidate of the Conservative Party. The only difference between Lindsay and Beame, Buckley quipped, was biological; Lindsay stood six-feet, four inches tall, while Beame topped out at five-foot-two.

Lindsay's election measured how much New York had changed during the dozen years that Wagner held office. For the first time, people of color determined the outcome of a mayoral race. Disaffection with their limited gains under the Democrats, and attraction to Lindsay's strong civil rights record, led more than four out of ten black voters and a quarter of Puerto Rican voters to back the Republican-Liberal candidate, giving him his margin of victory.[20]

Lindsay took office as the "Golden Age of Capitalism"—the years of rapid, post–World War II economic growth—peaked, imparting an effervescent air to centers of money and power like London and New York. Recruiting young, energetic assistants, Lindsay promoted a sophisticated urbanism that positioned New York, or at least Manhattan, as an animated alternative to suburban torpor. Parks Commissioner Thomas Hoving, the thirty-four-year-old son of the chairman of Tiffany's, sponsored "happenings" in Central Park: kite flying, meteor watching, discos, a "paint-in." Meanwhile, Lindsay received national attention for his efforts to reach out to nonwhite New Yorkers, walking the streets of their neighborhoods in a largely successful effort to keep the rioting that gripped urban America from recurring in New York. New York, declared the newly-elected Mayor, was "a fun city."[21]

Not everyone, though, shared Lindsay's sense of fun, for he first used the phrase amid a transit strike that paralyzed New York. At 5:00 A.M. on January

1, 1966, just hours after Lindsay took office, thirty-five thousand municipal bus and subway employees stopped work. For the next twelve days New Yorkers endured the most disruptive strike of the entire post–World War II era. In spite of staggered rush hours, greater use of commuter trains, and makeshift corporate transit systems, the city suffered the worst traffic jams in its history. Hundreds of thousands of people could not get to their jobs, with the absentee rate ranging from 20 percent in the printing trades to 65 percent in the clothing industry. A *New York Times* editorial described the strike as probably the greatest alteration in normal city life since the Civil War draft riots (an almost identical characterization as that used by the paper for the tugboat strike twenty years earlier).[22]

Though transit workers long had been unionized, they remained poorly paid. In 1965, only with overtime and supplementary allowances did the average annual earnings of municipal transit workers—$7,179—better what the Bureau of Labor Statistics deemed an adequate budget for a family of four. As the TWU contract approached expiration at the end of 1965, union president Mike Quill, faced with an increasingly restive membership, insisted on a major wage hike. Normally, Quill quietly worked out a deal with the mayor while going through a public display of strike threats, theatrics, and last-minute agreement. This time both outgoing Mayor Wagner and Mayor-elect Lindsay avoided participation in the negotiations, not wanting responsibility for a strike or an agreement that might force the Transit Authority to raise the bus and subway fare.[23]

A clash of class and culture exacerbated the conflict between Quill and Lindsay. For Quill, who had spent a lifetime rhetorically jabbing at the ruling class, the patrician, Yale-educated Lindsay, with his matinee-idol looks, presented an irresistible target. In one of his milder ripostes, Quill told Lindsay he was "nothing but a juvenile, a lightweight, and a pipsqueak. . . . You don't know anything about the working class." Lindsay's only close advisers in the labor movement, David Dubinsky and Alex Rose, urged him to take a tough stand with Quill, believing—quite wrongly—that his threat to call a strike was mere bluff. The *New York Times*, whose editorial support had been an important factor in Lindsay's election, called Quill a "union czar," enjoining the new mayor to demonstrate "that the city will not capitulate to . . . tyranny." Picking up the cue, Lindsay declared that the city would not give in to "power brokers." By touring strikebound black neighborhoods, Lindsay highlighted the fact that it was poor New Yorkers, without cars and unable to afford taxis, who suffered the most from the strike, tacitly positioning strikers and nonwhites as opposing interests (though the TWU itself was roughly a quarter black and Puerto Rican).[24]

On the fourth day of the strike, Quill and eight other union leaders were arrested for defying a court injunction forbidding the walkout. Before going to jail, Quill announced, "The judge can drop dead in his black robes and we would not call off the strike." Then, reflecting back on his years of peacefully settling contracts, he added: "We became labor statesmen. But we're labor leaders now. . . . It is about time that someone, somewhere along the road ceases to be respectable." Just hours later, Quill collapsed in jail of congestive heart failure and was transferred to a guarded room in Bellevue Hospital. He died two weeks after the strike concluded.

In the end, Lindsay agreed to a generous package to end the crippling walkout, a two-year contract providing a staged 15 percent pay increase along with improved working conditions and pensions. Because the settlement exceeded a federal anti-inflationary wage increase guidepost of 3.2 percent a year, President Lyndon Johnson denounced it at a press conference. To circumvent a taxpayer lawsuit demanding enforcement of the Condon-Wadlin Act, the state legislature, under heavy pressure from Governor Rockefeller, passed a retroactive waiver of the law. (Rockefeller reportedly cut a deal with the TWU for their neutrality in the upcoming gubernatorial election.)

The transit strike effectively destroyed Condon-Wadlin. In 1967 the state legislature passed a replacement, following the recommendations of a panel Rockefeller appointed after the walkout. The new law, dubbed the Taylor Law after George W. Taylor, the panel chair, recognized the legitimacy of public-sector collective bargaining and set up mechanisms for public employees throughout the state to win bargaining rights. Like Condon-Wadlin, the Taylor Law outlawed public employee strikes, but it replaced the draconian and unenforceable Condon-Wadlin penalties with more moderate sanctions.[25]

The transit tie-up began a series of city employee strikes that created tumult during Lindsay's first term. To some extent, the mayor himself was responsible. Lacking Wagner's ties and debts to the burgeoning municipal unions, Lindsay took a confrontational stance toward city workers. Municipal unions, feeling no reason to temper their demands, responded with ever greater militance. But national conditions also came into play.

Nationwide, the annual number of strikes rose steadily after 1963, peaking in 1970 and remaining at a high level for another half decade. In New York

City in 1966, construction, airline, newspaper, cemetery, and taxi workers struck, while 1968 saw an East Coast longshoremen's strike along with major strikes against United Parcel Service, Consolidated Edison, and painting contractors. One strike, a walkout by oil truck drivers, left thousands without heat. Across the country, workers turned against their own union leaders as well as employers, as wildcat strikes and insurgent movements became more common. The number of instances of unionists rejecting contracts recommended by their leaders — once a rarity — rose steadily during the 1960s.[26]

The strike wave of the 1960s and early 1970s reflected a combination of worker assurance and insecurity. With the unemployment rate low and falling, workers felt emboldened to engage in job actions. Many became infected by the same antiauthoritarian spirit so widely noted among student radicals, counterculturists, and the burgeoning social movements of the 1960s. Simultaneously, as the inflation rate began to rise after 1965, they feared that price hikes would undermine whatever wage gains they made and threaten their standard of living.[27]

A 1968 walkout by sanitationmen that left the city, as writer Willie Morris recalled, "so laden from days of uncollected garbage that even the Upper East Side reeked of a thousand Yazoo civic garbage dumps," illustrated how totally the mechanisms of conflict containment broke down. Though the head of the Uniformed Sanitationmen's Association, John DeLury, had a long, impressive record of gains for his members, when in February 1968 he presented to them a proposed new contract, they booed him off the stage, pelted him with eggs, and rejected his call for a mail ballot on the agreement, instead voting for an immediate strike. Hostility to the mayor partially accounted for their reaction. The sanitationmen resented Lindsay's failure to pay them the kind of symbolic respect Wagner always had shown city workers, a touchy issue among hardworking men sensitive about their low status as "garbagemen." Like many other unionists, the sanitation workers saw Lindsay as a patrician uninterested in their world. One union leader told the *New York Times*: "Lindsay is a WASP. He treats labor with contempt. He cares only for the very rich and the very poor. The middle class bores him."[28]

Lindsay, having come into office determined to check the power of municipal unions, only to endure the 1966 transit strike and a 1967 strike by teachers, decided to stand tough against the sanitationmen. First the city secured an injunction that sent DeLury to jail. Then Lindsay ordered other municipal workers to man the sanitation trucks, which they refused to do. After six days the mayor asked Governor Rockefeller to mobilize the National

Guard to rid the city of its growing piles of garbage. In response, the New York Central Labor Council set up a committee "to demonstrate that under no conditions will the Council tolerate use of the National Guard against workers." Van Arsdale threatened a general strike.

Rockefeller—whose family name was forever besmirched by the 1914 Ludlow Massacre, in which Colorado militiamen called out to crush a strike against a Rockefeller-controlled company killed over a dozen women and children—refused to use troops. Instead, the governor got DeLury freed and negotiations resumed. When mediators proposed modest improvements in the prestrike agreement, Rockefeller endorsed their plan, but Lindsay demurred, calling it "blackmail" to end the walkout. With that, the governor moved against his fellow presidential aspirant and rival for leadership of the liberal wing of the Republican Party, asking the state legislature to allow him to take over the city sanitation department and impose the mediators' package, a move that got the strikers back to work. But as public opinion turned against the strikers, the legislature balked. Binding arbitration finally produced a new contract.

Though materially the sanitationmen come out well from their struggle, politically the municipal union movement suffered a clear defeat. Unlike during the strike wave of 1945-46, when many New Yorkers suffered inconvenience in good humor, believing that employers could and should treat their workers better, during the municipal worker strikes of the 1960s and 1970s the public feared the price they would have to pay through taxes to finance higher wages and benefits, benefits that in many cases they themselves did not receive. A growing segment of the city population, angered by the vulnerability it felt, came to view city workers and their unions as greedy, seeking to benefit themselves at public expense without consideration of the general good. By the late 1960s, city workers already had lost much of the moral standing they once had had as overworked, underpaid public servants.[29]

But while others might not have liked their effect, for city workers unions proved a boon. A minimum wage negotiated by D.C. 37 in 1969 boosted the pay of lower-level clerical and hospital workers by over 20 percent, bringing many of them above the poverty line for the first time. The starting salary for teachers went up an average of nearly 13 percent a year between 1966 and 1972. Firemen and policemen saw their base pay go up from $8,483 to $12,800 during the same period. Many city workers saw their wage rates match or exceed those of their private-sector equivalents.[30]

Even city workers who remained poorly paid—hospital support work-

ers, clerical workers, and school aides—benefited substantially from unionization. Organization brought meaningful grievance procedures, critical to
ending abuse and arbitrary action by supervisors, and a greater measure of
dignity. To supplement the pay and benefits the city provided, unions bargained for city contributions to welfare funds, which they used to provide additional member services. Former UPW leader Jack Bigel, working as a union
consultant, popularized this approach, which had been pioneered by the garment unions. In 1962 the Uniformed Sanitationmen's Association won the
first city welfare fund contributions. By the late 1970s, more than two hundred such funds had been set up, to which the city gave well over one hundred million dollars a year. D.C. 37 developed the most extensive array of
member services. It provided medical benefits beyond those the city offered,
including catastrophic medical insurance, dental care, a prescription drug
plan, and free eye examinations and eyeglasses; free legal assistance with
housing and credit problems, divorces, and wills; and personal counseling.
The union also developed a massive educational program—largely paid for
by city contributions—that included civil service test preparation, occupational training to upgrade low-skilled workers to better jobs, high school
equivalency courses, and a four-year, accredited college program.[31]

When World War II ended, garbagemen, bus drivers, hospital aides, and
other low-skilled city workers could afford to live only the most constrained
lives—cramped apartments, few possessions, old ages in poverty. Three decades later, many of their successors had acquired elements of what was once
considered a middle-class way of life: car and perhaps home ownership, vacations and sometimes vacation homes, comfortable retirements. Municipal
unionism provided city workers and their families with a range of social benefits and protections that, even in the age of the Great Society, remained rare
elsewhere. Through their unions, public workers had created a revolution in
their way of life.[32]

CHAPTER 13

"A Man by the Name
of Albert Shanker"

One event stands out like a huge, garish, insistent neon sign on the historical skyline of public worker unionism, the 1968 teachers' strike. Keeping the city in chaos for half a year, the walkout rent the civic body, creating wounds that remained raw decades later. Nationally, the conflict marked a turning point in the history of the civil rights movement, liberalism, and black-Jewish relations. Locally, it cast a pall of ill-humor and distrust over social and political relations. Working-class New York was never the same thereafter.

The teachers' strike revealed the complexity of the connections between the municipal union and civil rights movements. Both mobilized ordinary citizens to demand enforced and expanded rights, material uplift, and respect. Both utilized direct, mass, disruptive action, including lawbreaking in the name of justice, to achieve their goals. Both taught the downtrodden and discriminated against to refuse to accept their lot. Often they actively supported one other. Sometimes, though, struggles for civil and public worker rights came into conflict.

With 36,000 of the 62,000 jobs added by the New York City government between 1963 and 1971 filled by African-Americans or Puerto Ricans, municipal unionism to a considerable extent became a movement of and for non-whites. The father of Charles Ensley, the long-serving president of the merged SSEU Local 371, during the 1950s led black workers at the *Birmingham* [Alabama] *News* in a fight for equal pay. Ensley himself graduated from Howard University at a time when it teemed with civil rights activism, working with CORE before taking a job as a New York City caseworker. As more and more black workers joined municipal unions, they brought into them a heightened sensitivity to civil rights issues. TWU leaders rushed to Selma, Alabama, in 1965 to join the blocked voter registration march to Montgomery, no doubt reflecting, at least in part, their awareness of the concerns of the large and growing number of African-American transit workers.[1]

While some city workers were mobilizing their unions to support civil rights, others used unionism to fight against efforts for racial justice. A flagrant case came early in the Lindsay administration, an effort to block a civilian board to review police behavior. The issue was not new. Since the early 1950s, civil rights and civil liberties groups had been proposing an independent, civilian board to review alleged police misconduct. In 1964 CORE again pressed the issue, winning support from liberal and good government groups but sparking fierce opposition from the Patrolmen's Benevolent Association (PBA). When the city council held a hearing on the subject, the police union mounted a five-thousand-member picket line in protest.

During the 1965 mayoral campaign, John Lindsay came out for a civilian review board. Once in office, unable to get city council approval for a new board, he added four civilians to an existing three-person Police Department review board which had limited, advisory powers. Immediately a fierce reaction began. The *Daily News* dubbed the board "the property of bleeding hearts and cop-haters." Both the PBA and the Conservative Party circulated petitions to hold a referendum on an amendment to the City Charter to limit membership on any police review board to members of the Police Department. The PBA proposal won a place on the ballot.

The police department constituted a reservoir of racism within the city workforce. With the repeal of the Lyons Law and rising police salaries, a growing proportion of the force lived outside the city. Many of those who left the city looked down upon it, particularly its nonwhite population. An explicitly white, male self-identity served to bond policemen to one another.

While American Legion posts, homeowner, civic, and business groups, and the Conservative Party actively campaigned to eliminate Lindsay's review board, the PBA took the lead in financing and coordinating the effort. The Lindsay administration pulled together a coalition to defend the review board that included the New York Civil Liberties Union, the Guardian's Association (an organization of black policemen), the American Jewish Committee, the B'Nai B'rith Anti-Discrimination League, the Liberal Party, and New York's two senators, Republican Jacob Javits and Democrat Robert F. Kennedy. In a "stunning" result, though, as one study put it, the referendum delivered "a rout for civil rights forces." Sixty-three percent of the electorate supported the PBA measure, which carried in every borough except Manhattan. A survey of Brooklyn voters found massive working-class opposition to the civilian board. Only one out of five voters holding blue-collar, clerical, or sales jobs opposed the PBA measure. Only in black and Puerto Rican neighborhoods did the board win heavy backing.

The police union and its allies displayed impressive power, at a high cost to the city. In making a symbol out of a review board with few practical powers, they exacerbated racial tensions and brought an in-your-face quality to political discourse. When less than two years later civil and municipal worker rights again came into conflict, this time in the school system, the aggressive, self-righteous stance adopted by all parties nearly destroyed the city.[2]

The paramount cause of the school conflict was the city's failure to desegregate its schools in spite of a decade of demands for compliance with the law of the land, which deemed racially separate education inherently unequal. By 1966, many black parents and activists had given up any expectation of integration, hoping in its absence to improve the schools in their communities by winning greater control over them. The issue first came to a head at a new school in East Harlem, Intermediate School (I.S.) 201. The Board of Education promised that it would be integrated, but then chose its siting and catchment area so that half the students would be Puerto Rican and half black. Local parents, furious with the board, demanded that either it assign some white students to I.S. 201 or give them substantial say in the school's operation and staffing. The board did not bring in white students and, in a pattern of vacillation and incompetence that contributed greatly to the school crisis of the coming years, first appointed a white principal, then acceded to community demands to replace him with a black administrator, and then reversed itself, further angering the parent activists and their allies.[3]

In the wake of the I.S. 201 controversy, many parents, educators, and political activists embraced "community control" of schools. For some, this represented a turn away from integration, part of the general resurgence of nationalism in black America during the late 1960s. Community control, its proponents argued, would allow African-Americans to run the institutions that served (or mis-served) them and introduce ideas, methods, and role models that would advance the abilities, social development, and political consciousness of their children. One parent, defending the call for a black principal at I.S. 201, said, "We're not champions of segregation" but "we feel the need of an image reflecting the community." For others, community control constituted what Kenneth Clark called a "strategy of despair" growing out of a belief that the school system, including its teachers, had failed black children, that no nonblacks much cared, and that nothing short of a radical redistribution of power would improve things. Another I.S. 201 parent declared, "I don't want any more teachers who make excuses for not teaching, who act as if they're afraid of a seven-year-old child because his color is different. I don't want to be told that my daughter can't learn because she comes from a fatherless home or because she had corn flakes for breakfast instead of eggs." Community control also meant jobs. As Milton Galamison noted, it would ensure that "Non-resident whites could not reap the economic benefits of working in the Black Community while Black children suffered the degradation of unwantedness."[4]

No one really knew how much popular support existed for community control. Though it had many enthusiastic backers, the movement for it, unlike the drive for integration, never mobilized massive numbers of students, parents, or community residents.[5] Nonetheless, the push for community control set the agenda for school reform because it was not simply a movement from below; many government leaders, philanthropists, and educational professionals also came to advocate school decentralization and greater community involvement.

Mayor Lindsay was the most important backer of decentralization. He had a narrow motive; splitting the Board of Education into smaller districts would yield greater state funding. But more important, the mayor recognized that the school system did not work. No friend of the board, which he did not control, nor of the teachers' union, he did not object to giving parents a role in picking principals and school administrators.

Following the I.S. 201 controversy, Lindsay appointed a panel headed by Ford Foundation president McGeorge Bundy to draft a plan for greater community involvement in school governance. While some panel members had experience in public education, Bundy did not; until late 1965 he had been the president's national security adviser and a leading exponent of escalating the war in Vietnam. Lindsay appointed no labor representative to the group, a measure of how much the city's ruling coalition had changed with the passing of Wagner and the defeat of the Democrats.[6]

The Ford Foundation's involvement with community control extended beyond Bundy's advisory role. Its leaders sympathized with the plight of African-Americans and urgently sought a formula for urban peace in the wake of the 1965 Watts riot and the growing militancy of dissatisfied blacks. Called in by the Board of Education during the I.S. 201 affair, Ford officials met repeatedly with the activists who had demanded local control of the school. Bundy personally tried, without success, to win over members of the Council of Supervisory Associations (CSA)—an organization of assistant principals, principals, and other supervisors—to community control. Ford also prodded the Board of Education to announce in February 1967 small steps toward decentralization. The foundation then helped organize and fund planning groups for three "demonstration districts" to experiment with the devolution of power, one at I.S. 201, one on the Lower East Side, and one in Ocean Hill–Brownsville, which became the epicenter of citywide controversy.[7]

Ocean Hill, a small black neighborhood between Bedford-Stuyvesant and Brownsville, had little community organization until terrible conditions in local schools drove parents to activism. A failed experiment at integration inclined many of them toward community control. During the 1965–66 school year, three thousand Ocean Hill students took buses to schools in white areas. Many did not receive a warm reception. Some schools assigned the new students to separate classes from local whites. In Bay Ridge, hostile crowds confronted them. Before the year ended, half the bused children opted to return to schools in Ocean Hill.[8]

John Powis, associate pastor of Saint Benedict's Roman Catholic church, took the lead in getting Ocean Hill designated an experimental decentralization district. With money from the Ford Foundation, a planning group hired Rhody McCoy—a veteran black assistant principal—as district administrator and held an election among local parents for a governing board to take charge of the area schools in September 1967. As this burst of activity took place, the Board of Education failed to spell out what powers the demonstration district boards would have, sowing the seeds of disaster. However, it did make clear its position on one key issue; when the Ocean Hill–Brownsville board asked for the power to control its own money and to directly seek outside funding, the board refused, saying that it wanted decentralization to be a controlled experiment, in which the independent variable would be local control, not added resources. For the same reason, the central board would not allow all the schools in the district to participate in the expensive, UFT-sponsored More Effective Schools (MES) program. Here lay the evil genius of decentralization, the use of the issue of control to absolve the board, the city, and ruling elites of the responsibility for devoting more resources to public education.

In part because the local board did not press for MES, UFT support for the Ocean Hill–Brownsville experiment waned even before school opened in September 1967. The two-week citywide teachers' strike at the start of that school year deepened tensions. The UFT did not see its strike as against decentralization. The local board, however, believed that the union was undermining the community control experiment by walking out at the very moment it began. Furthermore, the board, like some civil rights and black teacher groups, saw the UFT demand that teachers be given greater power to remove disruptive students as pointed at African-American youngsters. Accordingly, the Ocean Hill board not only refused to back the strike, it actively worked to keep its schools open.

During the months that followed, relations between the bulk of white Ocean Hill–Brownsville school personnel and the governing board deteriorated. For one thing, a large group of principals and assistant principals asked to be transferred, beginning a pattern in which school veterans, by seeking to leave the district midyear, threatened to seriously disrupt education. For another thing, the UFT joined the CSA in suing to block the Ocean Hill board's appointment of principals who had not been on the ranked civil service list, a tactic aimed at integrating the supervisory staff. Meanwhile, relations between a group of black teachers who had worked during the strike and UFT loyalists remained acrimonious.[9]

The stakes in the success or failure of the demonstration districts went up in November 1967, when the Bundy panel issued a report recommending that the school system be broken up into thirty to sixty autonomous districts, to be run by local boards, with a majority of their members elected by parents. The new districts would assume most of the Board of Education's power over personnel, budget, and curriculum. The UFT launched a furious attack on the proposal, labeling it a plan for "Balkanization" which would "increase administrative costs and reinforce segregation." While agreeing to some decentralization, the union wanted far fewer districts and the retention by a central board of power over collective bargaining and teacher tenure.

Events in Ocean Hill now converged with developments in Albany. After making some modifications in the Bundy plan, Lindsay asked the state legislature to enact it. Meanwhile, the United Parents Association, the Public Education Association, the CSA, and the New York State Board of Regents all offered their own decentralization plans.[10] In early May, while legislative deliberations proceeded, the Ocean Hill–Brownsville board ordered the involuntary transfer of nineteen teachers and administrators out of the district, without any formal charges against them. Though the board, the UFT and CSA, and other parties endlessly debated whether these were permissible reassignments or impermissible firings, the underlying issue clearly stood out: would community boards have the power to hire and fire their own personnel?

Superintendent of Schools Bernard Donovan ordered Rhody McCoy to reinstate the transferred employees, but McCoy refused. When some of the teachers tried to return to their classrooms, a crowd of activists, parents, local board members, and students blocked them from doing so. Each day the crowds, police presence, and potential for violence grew. Donovan vacillated, reversing himself by ordering the transferred teachers out of the district, then, on the very next day, again ordering the district to take them back. When the Ocean Hill–Brownsville board balked, 350 of the district's 556 teachers went on strike and remained out until the end of the school year, leading McCoy to try to terminate or discipline them all. Few parents had much enthusiasm for either side; a poll in the experimental districts found only 29 percent of those sampled supported McCoy and the community boards, while 24 percent supported the teachers.

Though UFT president Albert Shanker did not provoke the Ocean Hill crisis, it proved a godsend to his effort to block enactment of any "strong" decentralization plan. The actions of the Ocean Hill board enabled the UFT to portray the community control conflict as over the right of teachers to due process, an issue that elicited considerable sympathy from other workers. Scenes of African-American crowds blocking white teachers from going to work allowed Shanker to play on the fears of many whites that militant black activists represented a threat to their own safety. A full-page UFT ad in the *New York Times*, recounting events in Ocean Hill, read "The Legislature's Decentralization Plan Will Mean More of the Same. Don't let our school system be taken over by local extremists." Shanker's lobbying campaign worked; the legislature put off enacting a permanent decentralization plan, while authorizing a continuation of the existing experiments and giving Lindsay additional appointments to the Board of Education, allowing him to control it for the first time.[11]

When the new school year began, the community control conflict resumed, at a higher pitch than ever. Over the summer a trial examiner dismissed all the charges McCoy belatedly filed against the transferred teachers. Meanwhile, Ocean Hill recruited new teachers to replace the 350 who had gone on strike, ending up with an inexperienced but highly enthusiastic staff, about 70 percent white. For its part, the Board of Education adopted an interim decentralization plan, which, though far weaker than the Bundy proposal, would have allowed local boards to make interdistrict personnel transfers without prior central board approval.[12]

UFT members struck all the city schools at the start of the fall 1968 term, demanding that Ocean Hill take back the teachers exonerated by the summer hearings and that the Board of Education guarantee that various informal arrangements—like teacher sabbatical leaves—be preserved in the course of decentralization. After two days, superintendent Donovan gave in, granting concessions on the issue of teacher transfers, promising back pay for the teachers who had struck the previous term, and again ordering McCoy to take back the transferred teachers. But the Ocean Hill board—not party to the agreement—stood its ground. When the transferred teachers and several score of those who McCoy had terminated for striking tried to return to their schools, parents and activists—including Powis and Brooklyn CORE head Sonny Carson—blocked their way. Later, the district ordered the teachers to attend an "orientation" in the Junior High School (J.H.S.) 271 auditorium, where a boisterous crowd—including many without formal connection to the schools—harassed and threatened them, with the apparent approval of district officials. Almost immediately the UFT resumed its citywide strike.

The UFT's second strike aimed to rein in the Ocean Hill board (and any similar boards set up in the future) by establishing a mechanism for enforcing central directives. After two weeks, Donovan and the UFT reached a settlement that would have guaranteed the return of all the disputed teachers to Ocean Hill while allowing the district to retain its newly hired staff as well. But once again, amid demonstrations and chaos, the Ocean Hill board refused to yield. The Board of Education suspended the local board, McCoy, and the district's principals, and Donovan shut down J.H.S. 271. But when the superintendent announced his intention to reopen the junior high school and reinstate the principals without solid guarantees that the disputed teachers would be given classroom assignments, UFT members voted 6,000 to 2,100 to strike yet again.

The third teachers' strike (or fourth counting the spring walkout in Ocean Hill) lasted a month, during which the city seemed to come apart at its seams. For the parents of a million students, faced with a school year that would not start, life became a shambles, a desperate effort to improvise childcare arrangements and keep bored children out of trouble. For the city as a whole, the walkout became the seed crystal for long-present social tensions. "Like a vortex," wrote one of its chroniclers, "it drew in almost everyone—city agencies, labor groups, Jewish communities—not only pitting them against each other but splintering them within, wheels within wheels, spinning sparks long after the strike was over." All sense of authority seemed to evaporate, as city, state, and Board of Education officials repeatedly issued directives that were immediately ignored, and then issued new, superseding orders that were ignored, too. In a year that had already seen the Tet offensive in Vietnam, the assassinations of Martin Luther King Jr. and Robert F.

Kennedy, the student takeover of buildings at Columbia University, the police riot at the Chicago Democratic convention, and a strong, racist presidential bid by George Wallace, the strike seemed truly apocalyptic.[13]

The UFT now openly sought the destruction of the Ocean Hill–
Brownsville experimental district. When early in the third strike the Ocean
Hill board finally indicated a willingness to take back the disputed teachers,
Shanker rejected the offer as too little too late. For the teachers—and especially Shanker—the walkout had become a way to show once and for all that
the UFT could and would bring the education system to a halt whenever it
deemed it necessary to protect the interests of its members. The specifics did
not matter. Over the course of the strike, Shanker repeatedly changed his demands, sometimes casually raising whole new issues just as others seemed
close to resolution.[14]

Shanker and the UFT self-consciously followed a policy of overkill, shutting down the whole school system for almost two months over a dispute involving just eight schools. Rather than trying to minimize racial polarization,
the UFT—overwhelmingly white and about 85 percent Jewish—embraced it
as a way to shore up support within its own ranks, in the legislature, and
among a large segment of the pubic. Most notoriously, the union (and the
CSA) reprinted and widely circulated a few anti-Semitic leaflets that had been
distributed in Ocean Hill in an effort to create the false impression that extensive black anti-Semitism existed there. Little mention was made of the fact
that half the white teachers the experimental district had hired the previous
summer were Jewish.[15]

Over the course of 1968, Al Shanker came to personify the intransigence
of the UFT and its willingness to pursue its interests at any cost. Shanker's
rise—he had been elected UFT president only four years earlier—marked
the reemergence of the tough Jew in New York civic life. Before World War
II, tough Jews had populated the urban stage: prizefighters, gangsters, left-
wing heavies, and trade unionists, especially in the rough and tumble worlds
of garment manufacturing and construction. (Shanker's father delivered
newspapers, his mother worked in a clothing factory.) After the war, as the
Jewish, blue-collar working class shrunk, other stereotypes—the brainy but
wimpish professional, the pale scholar or office worker, the peace-loving
liberal—eclipsed images of Jews as fighters.

The 1967 Six Day War between Israel and its Arab neighbors changed
that. As Paul Breines wrote in his pathbreaking study *Tough Jews*: "It is no
exaggeration to say that suddenly—literally overnight in numerous cases—

many American Jews took genuine delight in being Jewish for the first time in their lives. . . . inspired to do so by a display of Jewish military might and skill." Behind the transformation of 1967 lay the shadow of the Holocaust, not yet the center of Jewish identity that it would become but for many the darkest (though half-repressed) possible lesson about the limits of Jewish assimilation and reasonableness. So when in 1967 "little David slew the Arab Goliath," many New York Jews concluded that they could and must fight like hell for themselves, and stop worrying if others saw them as pushy, rude, or unreasonable.[16]

Urban riots and demands for greater black political power frightened many Jewish New Yorkers, who saw them as endangering their own recently achieved economic and political standing. Shanker embodied the Jewish mood of fear and assertiveness and used it to shore up support for the strike from teachers, many of whom held liberal views on race but feared antiwhite violence, including from their own students. Not all teachers backed Shanker or the walkout. By the fall of 1967, almost all the members of the small African-American Teachers Association, founded three years earlier by UFT members, had left the union. Its leaders became vehement supporters of community control and bitter antagonists of the UFT. Then, shortly before the fall 1968 strike, remaining African-American UFT leaders formed a caucus which opposed the walkout, though some black teachers stuck with the strike until its end. Many white teachers, particularly Teachers Union veterans and younger New Leftists, felt torn between support for the union and for black advancement. Shanker stripped two white UFT vice presidents—perhaps significantly neither Jewish—of their posts for calling for an end to the walkout. As the strike went on, a growing number of teachers returned to work, ultimately over eight thousand out of fifty-seven thousand. Ironically, the one part of the city where schools operated with near normality was Ocean Hill, which had a large cadre of anti-UFT teachers hired the previous summer.[17]

At first, the UFT had the near-unanimous support of the labor movement. In September 1968, the Central Labor Council executive board voted to back the teachers union in its struggle with the Ocean Hill–Brownsville board, viewing the central issue as contract violations. Black unionists took out a newspaper advertisement supporting the UFT. The next month, when the third UFT strike began, the Central Labor Council executive board asked its affiliates to give the teachers union financial as well as picket line support. The council itself contributed fifty thousand dollars.[18]

As the strike dragged on, however, labor's solid front began to crack. In early November, according to the *New York Times*, some union leaders began pressuring the UFT to end the walkout, fearing that its continuation would incite antilabor feeling among the public and lead the legislature to enact more drastic restrictions on public employee strikes. (The UFT strike violated the Taylor Law, and Shanker eventually served fifteen days in jail for leading it.) But the key break followed racial lines, as leaders of three left-leaning unions with large black and Puerto Rican memberships, D.C. 37, District 65, and Local 1199, began pressing Van Arsdale to push Shanker toward compromise, fearful that the school strike would create a deep rift between organized labor and nonwhite New Yorkers. At first Van Arsdale rebuffed their efforts, telling the hospital workers' Leon Davis: "I'm going to write a book called 'War and Peace,' war in the hospitals and peace in the schools. It's a terrible thing to upset the community—when someone else is doing it."

On November 13, the dispute broke into public view. District 65's Cleveland Robinson asked Van Arsdale to meet privately with him, David Livingston, Davis, Victor Gotbaum, and others to discuss their criticism of the strike. During or after that meeting, a group of nearly fifty black and Puerto Rican leaders from a dozen unions, either unaware of the other meeting or unsatisfied by it, sat in at the Central Labor Council office for five hours, until Van Arsdale agreed to meet with them. One 1199 vice president told Van Arsdale that unless he used his influence to bring the teachers' strike to an end, "those of us who are black and Puerto Ricans and Hispanic will set up our own labor movement." Van Arsdale defended Shanker against the charge of racism, but agreed that "we would all be better off if we got this strike terminated immediately." Later, back at the private meeting, Van Arsdale came under more pressure to end the walkout, including from Bayard Rustin, who in public had steadfastly supported the UFT (taking a great deal of heat for doing so), and TWU president Matthew Guinan (who had succeeded Quill), a Central Labor Council insider, who like Davis, Livingston, and Gotbaum headed a union with a very substantial nonwhite membership.[19]

On November 18, with his labor support eroding and his call for a special legislative session on the school crisis rejected (a rare miscalculation), Shanker agreed to a settlement that provided for a state trustee to oversee the Ocean Hill–Brownsville district, continued suspension of the local board, classroom assignments for all the disputed teachers, and the appointment of a three-member board with the power to suspend any Board of Education employee accused of harassing a teacher. Though the UFT got almost everything it wanted, it was not enough for many members of the union's delegate assembly, who denounced Shanker as a "sell-out." But the membership as a whole overwhelmingly endorsed the settlement, bringing the long, night-marish strike to an end.[20]

The full extent of the UFT victory became evident the following spring, when the state legislature passed a weak decentralization plan fully acceptable to the UFT. The act denied local boards the power to hire or fire, folded the existing experimental districts into larger entities, restricted involuntary teacher transfers, and replaced the existing, pro-community control Board of Education with an interim board appointed by the borough presidents. Meanwhile, the UFT signed a new contract with the city that provided major salary boosts.[21]

The teachers' strike added greatly to racial tensions in the city. But at least within the working class, the conflict may not have been as racialized as commonly portrayed. Initially, a substantial number of black New Yorkers shared the UFT's outrage over the treatment of teachers by the Ocean Hill–Brownsville board. That support dissipated during the third strike, when the UFT tactics and rhetoric alienated many nonwhites. Still, except among those immediately involved in the community control experiments, not much passionate support ever materialized for the idea. At the height of the contro-versy, a citywide pro-decentralization rally mobilized only 5,000 to 6,000 people, while two days later a UFT rally drew 40,000. The UFT's behavior did not put off nonwhite workers from seeking to benefit from its clout. Shortly after the school strike ended, the UFT and D.C. 37 began signing up school paraprofessionals. In a showdown vote, the UFT emerged victorious, in part because of strong support it won among black and Puerto Rican para-professionals in Ocean Hill–Brownsville.

In February 1970, when the first elections for the local school boards set up by the state decentralization act were held, only 14 percent of those eligible voted. Ironically, many members of the new boards represented either the Catholic Church or religious schools. In future years, as turnout fell even lower, the UFT, D.C. 37 (which represented aides, clerks, and some blue-collar workers in the schools), the Catholic Church, and local political ma-chines emerged as the key forces controlling the boards. To some extent, this represented an assertion of working-class power, but of the worst sort, paro-chial interests seeking power over public institutions largely to protect nar-row self-interests. Community control—posited as a way to increase democratic participation and improve schools—proved largely a dead end, while integration faded into the past as an abandoned goal, far more utopian than either its supporters or critics had realized.[22]

The unionization of public employees proved a godsend for organized labor. Coming at time when heavily unionized industries such as mining, manufacturing, and transportation were growing far more slowly than nonunionized sectors like service work, the burst of organization among government workers helped maintain—or at least slow the decline—in the proportion of the workforce that carried a union card. In New York, the growing prominence of Shanker and Gotbaum as public faces of labor signaled the changing composition of the union movement.

The social alchemy that mixed the rise of municipal unionism with a revolution in race relations yielded complex results. Sometimes, as in the 1968 school strikes, it generated poisonous fumes. But other times, quite different compounds resulted. D.C. 37, for example, displayed a remarkable degree of internal harmony and cultural pluralism, as Italian, Irish, Jewish, and African-American workers, in jobs ranging from civil engineer to hospital attendant, built a structure that provided local autonomy and broad solidarity.

Organized labor paid a price for the pugnaciousness of the municipal unions—growing public disgust. In late 1968, Van Arsdale fretted about what he called a "lynch labor" atmosphere in the city. At a special meeting of the Central Labor Council executive board called in early 1969 to discuss the situation, several unionists expressed concern over "strike fever," suggesting greater efforts to educate the rank and file about responsible unionism and avoidance of "strikes which had no 'specifics'." In a measure of labor's clout, Governor Rockefeller attended part of the meeting, joining in brainstorming about how to prevent an antilabor backlash. A couple of board members went so far as to suggest cooling-off periods before strikes or compulsory arbitration.[23]

The expanding sense of rights and entitlement that swept through New York and the nation during the 1960s, and the conflicts swirling around municipal unionism, reinforced a loud, unyielding style of political action and social relations among working-class New Yorkers. In Woody Allen's masterpiece *Sleeper*, a character who had been frozen in 1973 finds upon awakening two hundred years later that his civilization had been destroyed. When he asks what happened, he is told that "a man by the name of Albert Shanker got hold of a nuclear warhead."

CHAPTER 14.

Longhairs and Hardhats

When the 1968 teachers' strike ended, few New Yorkers imagined that the pitch of social conflict it generated could continue for long without the city blowing apart. But in the years that followed, civic tumult grew, as layer upon layer of the population politically mobilized. Though scholars and memoirists usually associate the social activism of the 1960s with African-Americans and middle-class youth, by the end of the decade working-class New Yorkers of all ages, creeds, and backgrounds had forcefully injected themselves into public life. Taking to the streets, they demanded new rights and benefits from public and private authorities, while fighting with one another over a cascading series of political and cultural issues.

Many of the forces that mobilized working-class New York during the mid and late 1960s continued to do so into the early 1970s: confidence stemming from years of declining unemployment and a powerful labor movement, worries over inflation and status, and a continuing quest for racial equality. But new factors came into play as well, including rifts over the war in Vietnam, challenges to established sexual norms, and an economic downturn.

Less than a year after the 1968 UFT strike, the public education system again plunged into turmoil, as student activists demanded that the City University of New York (CUNY) open its doors to nonwhites. Their campaign coincided with an effort by educational, business, and political elites to address changes in the labor market. From these two drives came a radical democratization of the municipal college system.

By the late 1960s, changes in New York's industrial mix and a booming economy resulted in selective but critical labor shortages. With service, finance, trade, and government employment growing, employers had difficulty filling white-collar jobs, especially positions requiring "subprofessional training" or advanced clerical skills. Labor insufficiencies threatened the city's plan for economic development based on the expansion of "national center functions," corporate headquarters and business services.

In the mid-1960s, CUNY began an expansion program designed to satisfy the manpower needs of city employers, adding two community and three senior colleges. Even so, white-collar jobs remained unfilled. One study found over sixteen thousand clerical vacancies in mid-1968. As Wall Street's "go-go years" rolled on — between 1964 and 1969 the number of shares sold on the New York Stock Exchange more than doubled — the financial industry found itself hard-pressed to find clerical help. Many clerical and service jobs did not require higher education, but the failure of the public schools to provide decent basic education to the burgeoning nonwhite student population left many labor market entrants ill-prepared for employment. One state report bemoaned that "inadequate basic skills and poor work attitudes and habits make it difficult to fill clerical jobs even where the number of jobseekers is adequate to meet the need."[1]

In 1966 the Board of Higher Education, which ran CUNY, committed itself to offering some form of further education to all high school graduates by 1975. University chancellor Albert Bowker declared, "We want the children of the newer migrations to rise to fill the newer [labor market] needs!" The board proposed a three-tiered system, a dumbed-down version of the celebrated California hierarchy of public universities, colleges, and two-year community colleges. In the board plan, the four-year CUNY colleges would constitute the upper tier, community colleges the middle tier, and new "educational skills centers" providing vocational training the bottom tier.[2]

The board's slow movement toward universal access to postsecondary education failed to satisfy the small, increasingly politicized, nonwhite CUNY student body. As demand outstripped available classroom seats, the high school average needed for CUNY admission rose, making free college education a receding possibility for many aspiring students. In 1969, African-Americans made up just 14 percent of the entering CUNY class, and Puerto Ricans 6 percent. At City College, the most prestigious CUNY school, only 13 percent of freshmen were nonwhite.

In February 1969, black and Puerto Rican students demanded that admissions to City College reflect the racial composition of the city's high schools, at the time roughly half nonwhite. In addition, they wanted a separate school of Black and Puerto Rican Studies, a voice in running the SEEK program, which recruited and provided remedial help for students from disadvantaged backgrounds, and a requirement that all education majors — many of whom ended up teaching in local public schools — study the Spanish language and black and Puerto Rican history. To draw attention to their demands, they took over a campus building for four hours.

At first, the admissions demand provoked surprisingly little controversy. Demands other students had made, such as an end to on-campus recruiting by the military and defense contractors, commanded as much attention. Some students objected to instituting "a quota system," but even conservatives acknowledged that City College had drifted away from its original mission of educating the poor. The administration seemed sympathetic to the demands of the black and Puerto Rican students, but it moved slowly in considering them.[3]

The student activists soon lost their patience. On April 21, a thousand students, the majority white, from City College and several Manhattan high schools, rallied in support of the five demands and three more added by white leftists, including "Open admission for all." The next day, two hundred African-American and Puerto Rican students blocked the gates to the campus. City College president Buell Gallagher ordered the school closed.[4]

While City College remained shuttered, demonstrations rocked other City University campuses. At Brooklyn College, several hundred students issued eighteen "non-negotiable demands," including admission of all black and Puerto Rican applicants. After protesters disrupted a Faculty Council meeting, vandalized the president's office, started several small fires, and scuffled with police, the college president shut the campus. When he reopened it, over sixteen hundred students signed petitions protesting violence and threats of violence by supporters of the eighteen demands, whose tactics sparked more opposition than their program.[5]

At Queens College, SEEK students had pressed for control of their program since winter. On May 1 and 2 some broke windows, smashed furniture, and overturned card catalogs. Meanwhile, members of Students for a Democratic Society (SDS) occupied a building, demanding that criminal charges stemming from an earlier protest be dropped. These demonstrations sparked a backlash among students affronted by the disruption of classes and what they saw as a hijacking of the campus. Some sat in at the registrar's office, protesting the college's failure to call police to evict the SDSers. Meanwhile, a crowd of white students pursued the window-breaking SEEK students, shouting racial epithets and demanding that black students leave the campus.[6]

With turmoil sweeping across the City University and a fall 1969 mayoral election coming up, politicians jumped into the fray. Staten Island state senator John J. Marchi, who was challenging Lindsay for the Republican mayoral nomination from the right, attacked the mayor "for not taking swift police action" to deal with the municipal college demonstrations. Bronx Democratic congressman Mario Biaggi obtained a writ requiring CUNY officials to explain in court why they should not be required to reopen City College. The Jewish Defense League and City Comptroller Mario A. Procaccino, a City College alumnus and contender for the Democratic mayoral nomination, obtained similar court orders. Giving in, the Board of Higher Education ordered City College reopened.[7]

Ugly trouble came quickly. On May 7, black students trying to reshut the campus disrupted classes and assaulted students and professors. President Gallagher closed the campus again. But several hundred white students refused to leave. At that point, some twenty-five young African-Americans, some but apparently not all students, armed with two-by-fours and heavy tree branches, approached the whites. A vicious free-for-all ensued that sent seven white students to the hospital. Though the following day the Board of Higher Education formally approved one of the student demands—the added requirements for education majors—it announced a belated determination to keep City University campuses open even if that required massive police presence, a decision that led Gallagher to resign.

As City College closed, opened, closed, and opened again, the black and Puerto Rican students, the administration, and the faculty held sporadic negotiations. By the end of May, the administration and faculty approved programs that gave students almost everything they sought. To achieve racial balance, the faculty endorsed a "dual admissions" system: half of an enlarged freshman class would be chosen using existing, grade-based criteria, while the other half would be filled with students from designated high schools in poverty areas, who would not have to meet any grade standard.[8]

A groundswell of opposition followed. Unless City College dramatically expanded—an open question in a year when the governor had tried to cut the state appropriation for CUNY—reserving half its places for students from designated, poverty-area high schools would have the effect of lessening the number of slots available to whites. Few voiced opposition to increasing opportunities for blacks and Puerto Ricans, per se. A poll of Brooklyn College students, for example, found 54 percent supported accepting students from "underprivileged areas . . . under a discretionary admissions program." But the possible restriction of opportunity for whites as a consequence of dual admissions generated extensive criticism. Governor Rockefeller, former Mayor Wagner, and the CUNY Faculty Senate all opposed the dual admissions proposal. So did organized labor. A delegation from the Central Labor Council which met with the Board of Higher Education condemned "the proposed settlement by CCNY which would . . . [block] the sons and daughters of the labor movement from an education merely because they did not come from the ghetto." The labor leaders portrayed this as not a racial issue, calling the proposed admissions system "unfair to our black and Puerto Rican members who do not live in the ghetto [and whose children therefore would not be attending high schools designated for special admissions]." As an alternative, Harry Van Arsdale suggested "enactment of a master plan [guaranteeing higher education for all high school graduates] not in 1975 but in 1970."

Norman Mailer, running a quixotic campaign for the Democratic mayoral nomination, predicted that "The moment white boys can't get a free education in this city is the moment we are going to get open admissions for all . . . Not before. So long as Black boys are denied, you're going to have the same buck-passing and complaints about expenses." Mailer proved prescient. As pressure from all sides grew, the Lindsay administration and CUNY officials became increasingly amenable to an immediate, huge expansion of the City University system to accommodate all comers. The alternative was politically and socially disastrous, an ongoing battle among ethnic and racial groups over the allocation of access. By boldly democratizing CUNY through a color-blind initiative, the Lindsay administration could give something to working-class whites while increasing opportunities for nonwhites; lowering CUNY admission standards would benefit the former even more than the latter. Accordingly, on July 9, 1969, the Board of Higher Education approved a proposal to offer "some University program" to all high school graduates starting in the fall of 1970, with enough remedial services to maintain academic standards.

In spite of the radical thrust of open admissions, the suddenness with which it was implemented, and its potential cost, the program won broad support, including from the American Jewish Congress, the Central Labor Council, the City College alumni association, and the college teachers' unions. When Buell Gallagher suggested that CUNY could survive a drastic expansion only by imposing tuition, Van Arsdale, the UFT, and others successfully argued that to do so would make a mockery of the expanded access the new admissions policy was meant to provide.[9]

In a mad scramble to gear up for open admissions, the City University increased its staff by nearly 30 percent. Even so, the system lacked the personnel and physical facilities to accommodate its expanded student body, as the freshman class jumped from 20,000 to 35,000 in a single year. CUNY registration turned into a nightmare of long lines and closed-out courses. Classrooms had not enough seats, cafeterias too few tables, bookstores not enough books. In high-rise buildings, crowds waited in front of hopelessly inadequate elevators. Many incoming students found themselves in community colleges with a heavily vocational orientation, studying stenography or data processing rather than literature or philosophy.[10]

Still, in many respects open enrollment accomplished what it set out to do. Of the 100,000 students who entered the City University during the first three years of open admissions, 48,000 would not have qualified under prior admission standards. Between 1969 and 1972 the percentage of minority students in the freshman class nearly tripled. But in absolute numbers, the jump in white students easily surpassed the increase in minority entrants. Of all the ethnic groups in the city, Italian-Americans made the greatest gains. When Richard Gambino went to Queens College in 1957, he was one of only a handful of Italian-Americans in the student body, even though Italian-Americans made up a quarter of the city's population. With open admissions, the number of incoming Italian-American CUNY freshmen doubled, from 4,989 in 1969 to 9,803 in 1971.

The City University had a hard time coping with the dramatic change in its student body, just as many students admitted through open admissions had a hard time handling college. Many of the new CUNY students faced far more severe academic, financial, and social hurdles than their predecessors. Still, more than half those admitted under open admissions during the first three years of the program eventually received a B.A. degree (though in some cases only many years later).[11]

In years to come, CUNY suffered severe underfunding, crippling its ability to fulfill its mission, but open admissions continued to provide a path of enlightenment and upward mobility for working-class New Yorkers, helping to preserve the cosmopolitan tradition of the city. Though not without faults, open admissions represented a significant advance toward equal opportunity and the ideal of liberal education for all. It was one of the great triumphs of working-class New York.

Well before the results of open admissions became evident, the student protests that helped bring about the policy sparked a political backlash, much as the school decentralization battle had the year before. The term "backlash"—more fully "racial backlash"—entered the political vocabulary in 1964, when Alabama governor George Wallace, running in the Democratic presidential primaries, won 30 percent or more of the vote in Maryland, Wisconsin, and

Indiana. Wallace garnered substantial support from white blue-collar workers, who were reacting, many believed, to the gains and demands of the civil
rights movement. In the congressional elections two years later, the Democrats lost forty-seven House seats, including many held by staunch labor supporters. Major defections of white, working-class voters contributed to the
debacle. The worst losses occurred in neighborhoods close to areas where
racial disturbances had taken place. A post-election poll of union members
found many, especially under age forty, deeply concerned over property
taxes, crime, and zoning, issues to which the AFL-CIO paid almost no attention, while caring little about issues like the minimum wage and right-to-work
legislation, dear to the national labor leadership. Backlash politics appeared
in particularly virulent form in local elections in cities rocked by school busing conflicts, rising crime, or race riots. In New York, the growing draw of
conservative mayoral candidates—Lawrence Gerosa in 1961 and William F.
Buckley Jr. in 1965—in part reflected white lower- and middle-class reaction
to the civil rights revolution.[12]

"Backlash was a disorderly affair," noted sociologist Jonathan Rieder,
"that contained democratic, populist, genteel, conspiratorial, racist, human-
ist, pragmatic and meritocratic impulses." Many whites presented themselves
as more upset by the violence and disorder associated with social protest than
with aims such as racial equality. In a society engaged in a losing war overseas, racked by urban riots, where assassination had come to play a major role
in politics, and in which established cultural and sexual norms seemed to be
dissolving, racial conflict appeared as one more sign of a world gone haywire.

With backlash came a note of self-pity and self-righteousness not previously evident in the culture of working-class New York. Many working-class
whites came to see themselves as victims, as much or more so than African-
Americans, to whom they believed government gave special favors. Economically, workers were doing better than ever, yet a sense of being put-upon
seeped into white working-class social halls and living rooms, from Canarsie
to Inwood. Although organized labor exerted considerable clout, many white
workers felt powerless and alienated. Even the normally irrepressible Harry
Van Arsdale seemed in a black mood. In late 1968 he complained, "Nobody
cares about New York City anymore. They all want to get out of it. You go to
a meeting of a hundred of the biggest names in New York and the first thing
you find out is that at least 60 of them live outside the city. It's the same thing
with the policemen and firemen and everyone else." The electricians' leader
derided press "glorification" of militant protesters, while bemoaning high

taxes and crime. Proud that George Wallace did not get a large vote from New York unionists in that year's presidential election, Van Arsdale nonetheless proclaimed, "Wallace said a lot that was true."[13]

Many working-class New Yorkers resented the nihilist side of late 1960s protest, such as the destruction of property at the city colleges. Dismay sometimes slipped into racism. At Queens College, after some SEEK students ransacked a dean's office, a student newspaper reported: "You hear it over and over again from people who complain that 'they're ungrateful; they get in here without the marks everyone else has to have, and some of them are even getting paid—it's amazing that they're the ones that are causing all the trouble.'" One middle-aged secretary shouted, "They all should be sent back to Africa."

Antistatism riddled backlash politics: resentment against government leaders who seemed to care little about the average citizen, who pandered to protesters (actually a rather rare breed), and who imposed experiments in liberal social engineering on those of modest means while leaving the upper classes unaffected. Behind such railing often lurked racial fears and hatreds. Columnist Jimmy Breslin once wrote: "To the people of a place like Queens . . . 'government' does not mean City Hall or Washington. A true crisis in government is not Nixon in Watergate. It is Sonny Liston in your daughter's class."[14]

In the 1969 mayoral race, the local, race-related controversies of the previous three years—over the civilian police review board, school decentralization, and the City University—gave punch to the national racial backlash. Lindsay provided a perfect foil for the resentment, fear, and envy of white workers, homeowners, and shopkeepers. His patrician manner and apparent belief that poor blacks and Puerto Ricans had greater claim to government resources than moderately successful whites offended the sense of fairness of many working-class voters.

The mayor's obvious political vulnerability roused a swarm of challengers. Staten Island's John Marchi ran as a law and order candidate, gaining the endorsement of the Conservative Party and launching a primary fight for the Republican nod. Five prominent Democrats, including former mayor Robert Wagner, trying to make a comeback, vied for their party's nomination.

Lindsay had little chance of winning Republican renomination, given the conservative bent of the party rank and file. Only a large infusion of money from upper-crust liberal Republicans made it a close contest, with Marchi barely edging out the mayor. Lindsay's hope always lay with the Liberal Party nomination, which Hatters Union leader Alex Rose handed to him over the objection of the ILGWU and other longtime party backers. Rose, believing that "New York had become a political Stalingrad" where the forces of backlash had to be turned back, refused to hold a party primary, which Wagner might have won. Rose's staunch backing for Lindsay—who provided him with access to power and patronage—proved critical to the mayor's reelection, but hastened the decline of the Liberal Party from a vehicle for labor politics into a vote and job getting machine for a small coterie of political operatives.

For many union officials, Wagner symbolized an era before liberalism shattered against the hard knots of race, war, and cultural conflict, a time when labor had considerable power and encountered relatively little criticism. In a seemingly desperate effort to roll back time, early in the election season the Central Labor Council endorsed the former mayor—the first time it ever took a stand in a primary—and pledged "to spend whatever money is necessary" to promote his election. But Van Arsdale could not deliver anything like united labor backing, with D.C. 37's Victor Gotbaum immediately disavowing the Central Labor Council endorsement.[15]

Gotbaum's dissent reflected a surprising election-year rapprochement between Lindsay and the municipal unions. In the months prior to the election, the Lindsay administration signed a series of generous contracts with city unions, winning their political backing or at least neutrality, while avoiding strikes that might have alienated voters. This stunning political reversal revealed how much even the more ideologically-driven municipal unions saw local politics as a way to advance immediate, narrow interests. It also revealed the growing gulf between the city's public- and private-sector unions.[16]

The hope of many private-sector union leaders, to bring back the past through the political resurrection of Robert Wagner, remained just that. Though relatively unknown, Mario Procaccino, an Italian-born lawyer and longtime politico, rode the backlash wave to victory in the Democratic primary with a third of the votes, as his four more-liberal opponents divided the rest. Procaccino, Norman Mailer's campaign manager recalled, "sang the same teary refrain of how only *he* had stood up to *them* and reopened City College." Mailer's running mate for city council president, Jimmy Breslin, grew so disgusted with such posturing that he blurted out during a televised debate that the way to win office in New York City was "to kick a black, preferably a welfare mother, in the shins two weeks before election day."[17]

After the primary, the Central Labor Council unenthusiastically stuck with the Democratic party, even as many prominent Democrats and Republicans, repelled by the conservative stands of both Procaccino and Marchi, endorsed the mayor. Procaccino tried to rid himself of his image as a racist, launching populist attacks on Lindsay for running what he called a "Manhattan arrangement" that served the city elite while giving short shrift to the middle-class majority living in the outer boroughs. In backlash talk, working people belonged to the middle class, not a separate working class; backlash spurned class-specific politics even as it fueled itself on resentment of the rich. Procaccino added to the backlash lexicon when he dubbed Lindsay's supporters "limousine liberals." Like Marchi, he pounded away at the rising crime rate, aided by John J. Cassese, president of the Patrolmen's Benevolent Association and coordinator of the campaign against the civilian review board, who resigned his post to campaign for the conservative Democrat.

Having a three-way contest gave Lindsay the opening he needed. Running a shrewd, efficient campaign, he solidified his base among nonwhites and committed liberals while wooing a small but sufficient slice of the white middle class. Lindsay's vocal opposition to the war in Vietnam helped him among Jewish voters, a key swing bloc, many of whom had become disenchanted with the mayor on other grounds, such as school decentralization. In the end, Lindsay took home 42 percent of the vote, with African-American and Puerto Rican voters again proving critical to his victory. New York re-elected a mayor associated with racial liberalism and cultural change, even as a clear majority of the voters gave their support to backlash candidates.[18]

In the spring of 1970, the mixture of student protest, political backlash, working-class mobilization, and divisions over the war in Vietnam exploded. The spark came on Friday, May 8, when a thousand college and high school students rallied on Wall Street to demand the withdrawal of American troops from Indochina, the release of all "political prisoners in America," and the end of war-related work on university campuses, part of a wave of protests following the United States invasion of Cambodia and the National Guard killing of four student demonstrators four days before at Kent State University. Just before noon, two hundred workers from nearby construction sites, marching behind American flags, converged on the rally. Pushing aside a thin line of police, the workers waded into the crowd, hitting the students with fists, hardhats, and tools and chasing them through the narrow streets of the financial district. The workers then headed up to City Hall, where Mayor Lindsay had ordered the flag flown at half-mast to honor the slain Kent students. A postal worker somehow got onto the roof of the building and raised the flag. When a mayoral aide relowered it, the crowd charged the building. Hoping to calm a riotous situation, city officials reversed themselves and reraised the stars and stripes, giving the construction men a victory. Not yet done, part of the crowd moved on to nearby Pace College, where they broke windows and beat up students, antiwar protestors, and anyone who tried to stop the attacks. Meanwhile, other workers twice charged Trinity Church, where injured antiwar protesters had taken refuge. By the time the flag-carrying crowd dispersed, seventy people had been injured, including dozens hospitalized. The police, having done little to stop the assaults, arrested only six people.[19]

The following Monday, a crowd of two thousand construction workers, longshoremen, and Wall Street clerks snarled the financial district as they marched, chanted "U.S.A. Alla Way" and anti-Lindsay slogans, and got showered with ticker tape and computer punch cards by admirers. Over the next two weeks, almost every lunch hour saw similar demonstrations. Though violence on the scale of the first day did not recur, workers occasionally beat up taunting bystanders or those making v-fingered peace signs. On May 18, workers on a construction site across the street from the Board of Education threw eggs and bags of water at students demonstrating against the Vietnam War and police killings at Jackson State University.

The pro-war demonstrations peaked on Wednesday, May 20, when an estimated 60,000 to 150,000 people held a midday march through lower Manhattan. "Flags, fervent oratory, patriotic tunes and a river of yellow, red, and blue hard hats," wrote the *New York Times*, marked the demonstration. Some workers rode on a concrete mixer with a sign reading "Lindsay for Mayor of Hanoi." Unlike the previous demonstrations, which had no open sponsorship (though they were not spontaneous; newsmen and the police had been told a day ahead of time of plans for the first, violent march), the climactic parade was sponsored by the Building and Construction Trades Council of Greater New York.[20]

The New York demonstrations made construction workers—"hard-hats," as they came to be called—prime symbols of "Middle America," the "silent majority" that the Nixon administration posited as the moral and political salvation of a nation beleaguered by enemies abroad and protest at home. On May 26, the president, quick to take advantage of a rare instance of demonstrative support for the invasion of Cambodia, hosted a delegation from the New York Building and Construction Trades Council. Council president Peter Brennan pinned a metal American flag on Nixon's lapel and gave him a hardhat with a presidential seal and another with four stars for the commander of U.S. forces in Vietnam. Nixon briefed the group on the war and the economy and "was visibly moved" when Michael Donovan, a delegation member whose son had been killed in Vietnam, said "if someone would have had the courage to go into Cambodia sooner, they might have captured the bullet that took my son's life."

Encouraged by the hardhat demonstrations, the Nixon administration worked hard to woo union support, hoping to use right-wing populism as a prybar to break up the already crumbling Democratic coalition. The strategy paid off when the AFL-CIO remained neutral in the 1972 presidential election, the only time in its history that it failed to back the Democratic nominee. Shortly thereafter Nixon appointed Brennan secretary of labor.[21]

The May 1970 events made the hardhat—both the apparel and the person wearing it—a symbol of masculinity. Journalists, politicians, social scientists, and novelists portrayed construction workers as the rudest, crudest, and most sexist of all workers. At a time when the incipient women's and gay movements were bringing dominant patterns of gender relations into question, the stereotyped image of the construction worker—hard-drinking, hard-fighting, and ultrapatriotic—became a rallying point for those nostalgic for a putative time when men were men, women knew their place, and social and familial authority remained unquestioned. In movies like *Saturday Night Fever* and *Bloodbrothers* (both set in New York) and the *Rocky* series, "the blue-collar world . . . replaced the Old West as the mythical homeland of masculinity." Companies trying to convince men that drinking a particular brand of beer would confirm their manhood began featuring hardhat-wearing actors in their advertisements. Political candidates, worried that they were perceived as "wimps," donned hardhats and posed near industrial equipment.[22]

The hardhat demonstrations laid the basis for the rediscovery of the working class—and specifically the New York working class—by television. In 1971, Norman Lear's *All in the Family* took to the air, turning backlash politics and intergenerational tensions into weekly comedy. This brilliant chronicle of a Queens loading dock worker and his family brought issues of race and ethnicity back to the airwaves for the first time in nearly two decades. Earlier situation comedies set in working-class New York, like *The Goldbergs*, portrayed the tension between assimilation and ethnic or racial identity as heartwarming or comic, but *All in the Family* reveled in parochialism and prejudice. Archie Bunker shared Molly Goldberg's predilection for mala-propisms, but while Molly was a warmhearted neighbor to all, Archie became the preeminent symbol of working-class bigotry.[23]

While nationally the construction worker demonstrations became a pivot for political and cultural realignments, locally they widened fissures within the labor movement and the working class. The hardhat demonstrations manifested, and deepened, disagreements over the war in Vietnam. Throughout the Indochinese conflict, the AFL-CIO backed U.S. policy. In May 1967, the seventy thousand marchers at a "Support the Boys" parade down Fifth Avenue included large contingents from the National Maritime Union, Carpenters, Teamsters, Motion Picture Mechanics, Bricklayers, Composition Roofers and Waterproofers, Tile Layer Helpers, Longshore-men, and Patrolmen's Benevolent Association.[24]

The AFL-CIO executive board, however, did not speak for all of orga-nized labor, let alone for all workers. Polls taken in the mid- and late 1960s generally indicated that working-class Americans were as or slightly more likely to oppose the war than the population as a whole. A Gallup poll found that by the end of the Johnson presidency a majority of "manual workers" opposed U.S. policy in Vietnam.[25] While until 1970 most labor organizations that took a stand on the war supported it, a minority of unions and union leaders, disproportionately based in New York City, criticized American ac-tion.

In February 1965, Health and Hospital workers Local 1199 became the first sizable union in the country to officially oppose the war. Several other New York unions with roots in the old left soon joined it, as did the Negro American Labor Council. The next year, when New York critics of the war formed the first significant labor peace group in the nation, the Trade Union division of SANE, their ranks expanded to include Victor Gotbaum and Albert Shanker. Top officials of the Amalgamated Clothing Workers also began speaking out against the war.

The Vietnam War threatened to cleave New York labor, much as debates over World War II and the Cold War had done. At the 1967 AFL-CIO con-vention, the NMU's Joe Curran, whose son had just completed two years ser-vice in Vietnam, caustically criticized 1199's Leon Davis for speaking up against the war.[26] The invasion of Cambodia and the hardhat demonstrations embittered the divide. Though Brennan disavowed any union involvement with the hardhat violence, he made clear his sympathy with the marauding workers. Van Arsdale, who supported administration war policy, remained silent about the violence, for which he was criticized by Gotbaum and others. For their part, leaders of a dozen antiwar unions, in response to the Cambodia invasion and the hardhat action, jointly sponsored a peace rally with student groups. The demonstration, held on May 21, attracted a reported twenty thousand people, considerably fewer than at the previous day's pro-war rally but still an impressive turnout.

Though pro- and antiwar stands did not exactly correlate with industrial sectors, the building trades and maritime unions generally backed the war while D.C. 37, the city's largest public-sector union, joined left-leaning wholesale, retail, and service unions like District 65 and 1199 at the antiwar forefront. This divide and the ill-feeling attending it hastened the decline of the Central Labor Council. Van Arsdale had brought into the council groups like the construction trades which had previously stayed aloof, using the council's augmented power to help the organization of low-wage and public-sector unions. By 1970, however, 1199 and the public-sector unions no longer depended on support from older, private-sector groups. The split over the war, coming just after disagreements about the 1969 mayoral election, pushed labor toward fragmentation, with the public-sector and construction unions going their separate ways.[27]

The depth of the divide became evident at the fall 1970 State Federation of Labor convention, in a contest over its gubernatorial endorsement. Democratic candidate Arthur J. Goldberg had long, deep ties to labor, having served as the general counsel of the AFL-CIO before becoming secretary of labor and a justice of the Supreme Court. Nonetheless, Nelson Rockefeller, seeking a fourth term, retained the loyalty of his allies in the building trades by promising to continue his extensive program of public works. To ensure a Rockefeller endorsement, State Federation president Ray Corbett—a business agent for Iron Workers Local 40—worked with Van Arsdale to pack the convention, held at a Catskills hotel. When Gotbaum demanded a roll call vote, Corbett refused, instead holding a standing vote which he declared went for Rockefeller. Over Gotbaum's protests, Corbett quickly adjourned the session and shut off the lights, as infuriated delegates heaved ashtrays at the dais.[28]

The hardhat demonstrations seemed to confirm a common, middle-class view of manual laborers, that held them to be one-dimensional, inarticulate, and intolerant. In reality, though, many participants in the hardhat demonstrations had more complex views than union leaders like Brennan, who became their spokesman. Some of the demonstrators believed in deferring to elected officials on foreign policy issues. One excavation worker at the World Trade Center—under construction near Wall Street and from where many of the demonstrating hardhats came—told the *New York Times*: "I figure the big leaders should know what they're doing. I support the President." But other hardhats had their doubts about the war and expressed a degree of tolerance for opposition to it. What infuriated them was what they saw as contempt among antiwar protesters for the nation, its symbols, and its soldiers. An elevator constructor, arrested on the second day of the demonstrations, told a reporter, "I don't care if a person stands on a street corner and tells everybody 'I don't like the war.' I don't like it either. But when they try to ruin the country and desecrate the flag, I can't stand it."

Class resentment fueled the anger of the hardhats, many of whom had served in the armed services or had children then serving. One building tradesman recalled: "Here were these kids, rich kids, who could go to college, who didn't have to fight, they are telling you your son died in vain. It makes you feel your whole life is shit, just nothing." A Wall Street worker, married to a longshoreman arrested for assaulting a detective, explained that she and her husband had been watching the hardhat-student battle from her office and "wanted to go get down there with them. We wanted to tell off those kids. They have too much."[29]

The swagger and abandon of the hardhats reflected both confidence and anxiety. Construction workers had thrived during the post–World War II era. A labor shortage, strong unions, and an extended building boom had enabled them to raise their hourly wages to the point that the overpaid construction worker became a stock figure in postwar culture. More than other workers, building tradesmen seemed to enjoy their work, with the independence it afforded them and the pride it allowed them to take in their skills and the structures they erected. Yet while construction workers had an acute sense of the social contributions they made, they saw little outside recognition. While in earlier eras manual workers were celebrated in murals, songs, and statues, in the postwar years they virtually disappeared from the mass media and official iconography, to the building tradesmen's chagrin.[30]

In 1970, New York City had plenty of work for construction workers, as a long orgy of speculative office development entered its final phase. Thousands of out-of-town workers—"permit men" whose unions gave them leave to work outside their home regions—flocked to the city. Yet even in good times, construction workers fretted about where the next job would come from. And they had reason to worry. Faced with labor shortages and declin-

ing profits, some contractors had begun using less skilled workers, standard-
izing tasks, and training men for particular specialties rather than as all-
around craftsmen. At the same time, accelerating inflation—a by-product of
the Vietnam War—threatened to wipe out wage gains. To press for lower
construction labor costs, the largest purchasers of new buildings, the major
national corporations, formed the Construction Users Anti-Inflation Roundtable. In September 1969, President Nixon suspended most federal construction spending as an anti-inflationary measure, insisting that labor and
management find a way to control costs before money would be released. In
1972, the Construction Users group merged with another to become the
Business Roundtable, a leading force in what one journalist called "the political rearmament of the business community." It pressed for pro-business labor law and tax reform, deregulation of industry, and lower levels of social
service spending.[31]

In the short run, New York construction workers proved quite capable of
defending themselves. In the summer and fall of 1969, steamfitters, sheetmetal workers, hoisting engineers, rigging and machinery movers, and construction material teamsters struck for higher wages, improved benefits, and
restrictions on the use of prefabricated components. Their display of
power—which idled dozens of high-rise projects—contributed to the self-
confidence evident the following year.[32] But fear contributed to their lashing
out as well.

Many construction workers worried that the push to racially integrate the
skilled building trades was finally getting serious after a decade of stalling and
token gestures. In 1964, James Haughton, son of a black bricklayer, founded
Fightback, a Harlem-based group that pressed construction contractors to
hire African-American and Puerto Rican workers, whether or not they belonged to a union. Meanwhile, the State Committee Against Discrimination,
which normally favored conciliation over prosecution, took one of the city's
most recalcitrant unions—Sheetmetal Workers Local 28, which did not have
a single black member—to court for violating the Quinn-Ives Act. And more
ominously, in September 1969 the Nixon administration announced the
Philadelphia Plan, a model program requiring contractors to set specific goals
for minority hiring. To avoid federal imposition of a similar plan, in March
1970—just months before the hardhat demonstrations—Mayor Lindsay and
Governor Rockefeller announced a voluntary New York Plan, approved by
the Building Trades Council and the U.S. Department of Labor, which

promised jobs for eight hundred minority "trainees" on government-sponsored or subsidized projects.

Construction workers opposed the desegregation of their industry for a variety of reasons. Suburban residents and permit men feared that the hiring of nonwhite city residents would force them out of their own positions at a time when construction—except in New York City—had entered a slump. Building tradesmen who lived in the city wanted to reserve training and job slots for their kin. Some white workers did not want to work with nonwhites simply because of racial prejudice. Furthermore, many construction workers believed that their own early struggles—real or imagined—would be rendered meaningless if African-Americans were given new, supposedly easier ways to enter the industry.[33]

On the surface, the hardhat demonstrations had nothing to do with race, yet those familiar with the construction industry immediately made the connection. A few black construction workers participated in the demonstrations, but most stayed away in disapproval. One young African-American sheetmetal worker, noting that "We've had political confrontations with these cats before," predicted that "it's going to get worse now." An older black carpenter, who wore an American flag pin on one collar and black nationalist buttons on the other, denounced the workers who beat students as "make-believe patriots and cowards." Assistant Secretary of Labor Arthur A. Fletcher suggested that the pro-war activity had "an ulterior motive." "I believe they feel that if they can support the President on this one issue," he said, "they can get inside the White House and be a formidable opponent of the Philadelphia Plan." Lindsay's visible support for the New York plan and construction trades desegregation undoubtedly contributed to the particular venom with which the hardhats attacked him. At the May 21, 1970, student-labor antiwar rally, International Union of Electrical Workers' district leader William Bywater (a future national president of the union), asked, "Will those labor leaders who say they support our boys in Vietnam give jobs to black vets when they come back? That's the true test of patriotism." As secretary of labor, Peter Brennan did what he could to ensure that the answer was no, successfully choreographing resistance to the desegregation of the construction industry.[34]

Like shifts in race relations, changing gender relations and notions of sexuality caused anxiety among white, male construction workers. Unlike African-American men, women did not present a threat of job competition. The female labor participation rate in New York City during the 1950s had been above the national average, but over the next ten years it barely crept upward, from 40 percent in 1960 to 41 percent in 1970, while the national figure climbed to 43 percent.[35] A significant push to open up the construction trades to female employment did not come until the late 1970s. But if construction workers did not face a threat from women on the job, everywhere else—in the streets, in the media, and in their homes—they confronted a drive for legal and sexual equality.

The hardhat persona emerged against the background of sweeping changes in the place of the sexes in society. Parents and children routinely fought over what it meant to be a man or a woman. In Richard Price's novel *Bloodbrothers* (the basis for the later movie), about a construction electrician and his family living in Co-op City in the early 1970s, Tommy De Coco says when his son announces that he is going to work in a hospital, "Ah grow up Stony. That's woman's work," to which Stony mockingly replies: "Oh yea, right, sorry, you're right. I should be runnin' aroun' in my T-shirt with a screwdriver and a red [hard] hat on. Yeah, then I'd be a real man."

Only days before the 1970 hardhat demonstrations, the Senate, under pressure from women's groups, held the first hearings on the Equal Rights Amendment in twelve years, the prelude to its passage two years later. As everything from marriage roles to beauty pageant notions of female worth came under attack, the very structure of patriarchy seemed to be at stake. Exaggerated—even brutal—assertions of masculinity were one reaction. When at the first hardhat protest a young, female city employee grabbed the jacket of a construction worker about to join three others in pummeling a student, the worker responded: "If you want to be treated like an equal, we'll treat you like one" and proceeded with two other tradesmen to punch the woman, break her glasses, and bruise her ribs so badly she was taken to the hospital.[36]

If new notions of womanhood were seen as threatening by many construction workers, new notions of manhood were likewise unsettling. On popular music stages, at "be-ins," on college campuses, and at political demonstrations, longhaired young men rejected the idea that manhood meant physical strength and aggressiveness. Instead these counterculturists linked manhood to such traditionally female notions as sensuality and sensitivity. Even more startling were the growing number of men, particularly after the June 1969 Stonewall Inn riot in Greenwich Village, who proudly proclaimed their homosexuality.

Initially the new images of manhood had a particular class content; they were associated with privilege, with those who did not have to labor all day in the heat and cold as hardhats did, with those who used their class position to dodge the draft and the war in Vietnam (though in reality the Stonewall crowd had been heavily working-class). It was the combination of class resentment and perceived threat to patriarchal notions of manliness that gave the hardhat demonstrations their explosive character. While many of the hardhats used the hoary language of Cold War anticommunism ("Kill the Commie bastards!"), homophobic jibes ("America wasn't made to have these pansy-assed creeps running around wild") seemed just as common. Pro-war construction workers singled out for assault male antiwar protesters with the longest hair and shouted at New York's patrician mayor that he was a "faggot."[37]

Yet even as they resented and attacked student protesters and counterculturists, some hardhats undoubtedly envied them, for during the course of the 1960s many young Americans had discovered the joy of breaking rules, defying conventions, and playing hooky from the responsibilities of daily life. Construction workers, too, got a kick out of thumbing their nose at bourgeois order. Many deliberately flouted middle-class notions of decorum by wearing rough work clothes as a badge of honor, riddling their speech with curses, and harassing women who passed by construction sites. Ironworker Mike Cherry recalled his pleasure at the "weekly dumb show" when his coworkers building a midtown skyscraper went to cash their checks, evoking "the uncomprehending, often half-frightened stares of Chase Manhattan's more typical customers as the . . . hoards of construction workers—variously oily, muddy, or dusty and all irrepressibly and vulgarly gregarious—poured in."

By the mid-1970s, a longhaired young man was more likely to be a construction worker than a college student, as the counterculture migrated from its predominantly middle-class origins to working-class youth. In the process, it lost much of its expansive, optimistic character; no longhaired construction worker ever thought that the Age of Aquarius was dawning. By the time the center of countercultural gravity had shifted down the socioeconomic ladder, the country had entered a long, deep recession. As middle-class youth scurried for the shelter of conventional careers and social acceptability, the counterculture made its last stand among working-class youth, for whom it became a statement of difference and diffidence, a rejection of the norms of a middle class they had diminishing chances of joining.[38]

*   *   *

Having learned from the civil rights, antiwar, and student movements that, as a longshoreman who joined the hardhat demonstrations put it, "protest is the only thing that works today," workers of the late 1960s and early 1970s felt little need to abide by hierarchical procedures or even the law in seeking what they saw as justice and equity.[39] Rapidly rising prices from 1968 on, combined with low (though rising) unemployment and widespread politicization, kept labor strife at a high level through the mid-1970s. Workers demanded pay and benefit increases and greater respect from both management and union leaders.[40] In November 1970, John Brady, a dissident candidate for president of United Financial Employees Local 205, which represented stock exchange workers, issued a ten-point program that captured the complex challenges unionists faced. Brady promised "Protection and safety precautions in lieu [sic] of the recent bomb scares"; "A decent salary where a man does not have to work two jobs or need overtime in order to support his wife and children"; "arbitration because of unrealistic rules pertaining to hair, beards, etc."; and no contract "without a cost of living clause in the salary and in the pension."[41]

The range of workers engaged in labor conflict indicated the deep roots of the strife. In 1969 one of the most prominent labor clashes involved the employees of the Metropolitan Opera Company. When negotiations with the orchestra, soloists, chorus, and dancers failed to yield agreements, Met general manager Rudolph Bing began a lockout, canceling summer rehearsals and postponing the fall season. Met artists wanted higher wages and guarantees of more weeks of work, difficult demands for the financially pressed opera organization in an era before substantial government subsidies. But issues of hierarchy and work culture prolonged the conflict, as worker tolerance for Bing's autocratic style of management ended. "Mr. Bing and the [Met] board," said one baritone, "are as out of touch with the artistic members of the Metropolitan as the administration at Columbia was out of touch with students. The chorus and ballet people are asking for respectability." Other strikers in 1969 and 1970 included longshoremen, taxi drivers, and building service workers.[42]

The most dramatic strike of the era involved postal workers. Forbidden by federal statute from striking, post office employees had not walked off their jobs since 1868. In the late 1960s, discontent in the postal service simmered, especially in New York. Postal wages, set by Congress, had slipped way behind equivalent private-sector and local government pay. Workers in large cities suffered the most, since wage rates were uniform throughout the country but living costs were not. A New York City postal worker with twenty-three years experience made 25 percent less than what the federal government deemed necessary to maintain a "moderate standard of living" for a family of four. Some full-time postal workers were eligible for supplementary welfare benefits. Many held second jobs.[43]

A 4 percent postal pay hike in July 1969 — less than the inflation rate and a tenth the boost Congress had voted for itself — sparked scattered protests, including a sickout at the Kingsbridge Post Office in the Bronx. In its wake, a group of postal workers began organizing a revolt in New York Branch 36 of the National Association of Letter Carriers (NALC) against what they viewed as a complacent union leadership. Most of the rebels had been postal workers since the 1930s or 1940s. A sprinkling of younger workers — longhaired, with some college education and past contact with the civil rights and antiwar movements — seasoned their ranks.

Postal officials, members of Congress, and the president recognized the inadequacy of postal pay. Efforts at redress, though, got delayed by a Nixon administration plan to convert the postal service from a cabinet department to a semiautonomous, federally-owned corporation. The administration won support from NALC president James Rademacher for its postal reorganization bill — which would have granted workers the right to collective bargaining but not to strike — by including in it a retroactive 5.4 percent pay hike. Leaders of some other postal unions (nine different unions represented postal workers) and many NALC members fiercely opposed what they called the "Rat-emacher bill," seeing its pay provisions as grossly inadequate and rejecting the ban on strikes. As an alternative, the dissidents in NALC Branch 36 demanded an immediate pay hike, improved benefits, area wage differentials, and the right to strike.

Postal employees had watched New York municipal workers achieve far greater gains through illegal strikes than they had won through Congressional lobbying. Now many were prepared to strike themselves in spite of the possible consequences (striking federal employees could be fined up to a thousand dollars and imprisoned for up to a year). One New York letter carrier told *Newsweek* that a strike would "be well worth going to jail for."[44]

In spite of such grumbling, a postal strike seemed so improbable that almost no one paid attention when on March 12, 1970, rank-and-file members of NALC Branch 36 forced their local president to schedule a strike vote. Five days later, branch members voted 1,555 to 1,055 to stop work. Late that night a few letter carriers began picketing the main New York Post Office. The next day the strike spread through the metropolitan region, helped by a recommendation from the leaders of the Manhattan-Bronx Postal Union (M-BPU) that their twenty thousand members respect NALC picket lines. M-BPU president Moe Biller, a veteran post office activist who during the 1950s had been forced off his job as a result of an internal security sweep, led his union officially out on strike three days later. By then the walkout had spread, generally without formal union involvement, to cities throughout the country. Before anyone except the postal workers realized what was happening, nearly two hundred thousand letter carriers, postal clerks, truck drivers, mail sorters, and the like had joined the first major, national strike by federal employees. To date, their walkout remains the largest public-employee strike and the largest wildcat (or at least semi-wildcat) strike in U.S. history.

Two federal court injunctions against the strike failed to have any effect. Nor did informal talks among postal union leaders, post office officials, and leaders of the congressional postal committees. At Nixon's behest, Secretary of Labor George Shultz stepped in, offering unprecedented collective bargaining on all issues (with the tacit assumption that Congress would approve the final agreement) if the strikers returned to work. Though Shultz convinced Rademacher and other union officials to urge the strikers to resume work, their entreaties infuriated postal workers, leading some who had kept working to stop.

Determined to show his resolve, on March 22 the president announced that he would send troops to New York City, the epicenter of the strike, to restore postal service. Nixon's announcement, along with preliminary meetings between Shultz and the unions, prompted a back-to-work movement, first in rural and suburban areas and then in some cities. In New York the strike remained solid.

On March 24, twenty-five thousand unarmed National Guard members and Reservists occupied the major New York postal facilities, apparently the first time federal troops had been used to break a walkout blocking mail delivery since the 1894 Pullman strike. Though no violence occurred and little mail moved, Nixon's show of force helped turn the tide. On March 25 the strike ended when Biller, in light of reports that a highly favorable settlement, including amnesty for strikers, had been worked out by Shultz, congressional leaders, and the unions, recommended a return to work. The terms finally set by the Postal Reorganization Act were not as generous as the reported deal, but they did provide a 14 percent pay increase, fewer years to reach top rates, and collective bargaining. However, Congress prohibited postal strikes or a union shop and did not grant regional pay differentials, a major blow to New York workers.

While New York postal employees did not get all they wanted out of their strike, the spirit of working-class New York they embodied permanently altered labor relations at the nation's second largest employer. In a ratification of New York–style militant unionism, Vincent Sombrotto, a leader of the Branch 36 dissidents, quickly rose through the ranks of the NALC, becoming its national president in 1978. Two years later Moe Biller assumed the presidency of the American Postal Workers Union. The two strike leaders reunited in a bargaining alliance which negotiated for 80 percent of the nation's postal workers. In one extraordinary moment, a handful of New York workers had launched a revolution that left the nation's largest nonmilitary government agency changed forever.[45]

In other unions, too, rank-and-file workers challenged established leaders. Harry Van Arsdale, Jr., for example, hard on the heels of the controversies over the pro-war violence and the 1970 state AFL–CIO convention, faced a revolt in the thirty-six thousand member Taxi Drivers' Union. In November 1970, Van Arsdale, who in addition to his other jobs had headed the city's taxi worker union since its organization by the Central Labor Council in 1965, led a two-week strike supposedly to increase the percentage of the fare that drivers kept for themselves. But the strike ended with an agreement to *reduce* the percentage for new drivers while keeping it the same for veterans, an early example of the kind of two-tier wage settlements that became common in the 1980s. In theory, a steep fare increase, supported by both the union and management, would boost revenue for drivers as well as owners. However, when the fare hike went into effect, "overnight, the passengers seemed to disappear" and tips plummeted.

At an April 1971 taxi union meeting, thousands of angry taxi workers literally forced Van Arsdale and his fellow officers out of the hall. Afterward, some veteran workers joined a group of drivers new to the industry but with experience in the antiwar, woman's, and civil rights movements in forming the Taxi Rank & File Coalition, dedicated to rejecting the still unratified (but implemented) contract and reforming the union. Over the next six years, Van Arsdale faced mounting opposition as the taxi dissidents issued a newspaper, held petition drives, demonstrations, and wildcat strikes, and won a federal court order forcing more democratic union procedures. The kind of paternalistic unionism that Van Arsdale had spent a lifetime advancing no longer held the same sway. In 1974, Van Arsdale won reelection in a three-way con-

test with only a minority of the vote, quite a rebuff for the nominal leader of
New York labor. Three years later he called it quits, handing over the Taxi
Union presidency to one of his lieutenants (though he hung on to his more
important posts with the Electrical Workers and the Central Labor Council).[46]

In some unions, the line between rank-and-file militants and the official
leadership proved porous. Unions representing New York City law enforcement and fire department personnel, for instance, tacitly supported illegal job
actions, as militant critics repeatedly and often successfully challenged incumbent leaders. In January 1971 the police held a six-day, wildcat job action,
a combination sickout and slowdown. That same year firefighters launched a
series of slowdowns, during which they performed only emergency services.
Two years later, the firefighters actually went on strike for most of a shift.
(It later came out that their union's president had falsely reported that the
membership had voted to hold the walkout when in fact a mail ballot had
gone the other way.) Just a few years earlier, such actions by public safety officers would have been unthinkable.[47]

In 1971 the number of workdays lost in New York City as a result of strikes
peaked at 4.2 million, over twice the previous year's figure. Yet even as the
most significant strike wave since the immediate postwar years zenithed, the
economic and political conditions that sustained it were rapidly changing. After years of growth, from 1969 on the number of jobs in New York City declined. An accelerated shrinkage of manufacturing accounted for much of the
loss. Between 1969 and 1974, 51,900 jobs in apparel manufacturing alone disappeared. At the same time, port employment continued to contract. And in
1971 construction began a decline that soon turned into a near freefall.

Unlike in the past, when new white-collar jobs more than compensated
for the loss of jobs making and moving things, as the 1960s ended, the financial and business headquarters sectors began contracting, too. The securities
industry shed thirty-five thousand jobs between 1969 and 1974, to a large extent as a result of the computerization of backroom operations. From 1970 to
1972, the city suffered a loss of 17,200 jobs in manufacturing administrative
offices, as companies moved elsewhere. A huge growth in local government
employment (up 37,500 jobs from 1969 to 1974) and medical and health services (up 38,800 jobs) partially cushioned the job losses elsewhere. Still, the
city unemployment rate rose from 3.1 percent in 1969 to 4.8 percent in 1970
and 6.7 percent in 1971, when for the first time in six years the New York fig-

ure exceeded the national rate. Furthermore, inflation increased faster in the New York region than it did nationally. Whereas most of the country quickly recovered from the 1969 recession, New York continued to slide.[48]

Workers had embraced militant action in part because low unemployment made them less fearful of company reprisals. After 1971, with jobs harder to get, the number of strikes declined sharply. In 1974 only 55,000 New York workers took part in walkouts, compared to 199,000 in 1970.[49] Two strikes that began in 1971—one in the public sector, the other in the private—made evident the rapidly changing calculus of industrial relations.

In mid-1970, D.C. 37 negotiated a citywide contract covering many of its own members and members of Teamster Local 237 that provided for generous pensions: workers with twenty years of service could retire at age fifty-five at half pay, while workers with forty years service would receive their full salary upon retirement. Because many of the covered workers made quite low salaries, the high salary percentages they would receive at retirement did not translate into opulent golden years. Nonetheless, with few employees in the private sector receiving pensions anywhere near as generous when calculated on a percentage basis, opposition to the new pact quickly arose, stirred by the daily press.

Under New York State law, any public-sector pension plan more generous than the state's own plan had to be approved by the governor and the legislature. Both turned down the city plan. Partisan factors came into play: the Republicans controlled the state assembly, senate, and governorship, while D.C. 37 had thrown its money and clout behind the Democrats. Also, state officials came under pressure from private-sector employers, unable or unwilling to match municipal pay and benefits for low-paid workers, like clericals. Of the city's newspapers, only the *Civil Service Chief* and the *Amsterdam News* criticized the Republicans for blocking the new pension plan.

In an effort to reverse the Albany decision, D.C. 37's Victor Gotbaum and Local 237's Barry Feinstein made a spectacular political blunder. Hoping to put the heat on suburban commuters, who in turn might pressure their legislators (New York City Democrats were not the problem), Gotbaum and Feinstein called a selective strike of their members on June 7, 1971. On one of the hottest days in June, eight thousand sewer treatment plant workers, drawbridge operators, and other unionists walked off their jobs, allowing raw sewage to flow into area waterways and leaving drawbridges locked in the up position.

A firestorm of criticism ensued, including from pro-labor liberals. Although the unions called off the strike after two days, the damage had been done. Many residents of both the city and the suburbs, viewing the walkout as an illegal attempt at blackmail by workers who already had more generous benefits than they themselves received, turned against municipal unionism. In Albany, legislators got flooded with messages saying, as a magazine summarized them, "screw the g.d. union." The legislature again refused to endorse the negotiated city pension plan and, in 1973, removed pensions from the scope of public-sector collective bargaining and made them subject to direct legislative control. The era of pension improvements for city workers ended, as the legislature rolled back pension provisions for incoming workers.[50]

A month after the "drawbridge strike," tens of thousands of New Yorkers joined colleagues throughout the country in striking the nation's largest private employer, AT&T. Over the previous few years, the various AT&T subsidiaries in the New York area had been hotbeds of worker activism. Quickie strikes—with or without union backing—had become a common resort for dissatisfied workers. Some involved as many as fifty thousand employees. Ballooning demand for telephone services and a severe company labor shortage emboldened the workforce, particularly the growing number of young, nonwhite, and female workers. Younger workers, with experience in leftwing student politics, helped organize several rank-and-file caucuses within the Communications Workers of America (CWA), which stressed issues of race and gender inequality and called for greater union militancy.

Faced with rising inflation and rank-and-file mobilization, national CWA leaders sought a major wage and benefit package in their 1971 AT&T negotiations. To that end—and probably also to defuse membership discontent—the union called a national telephone strike on July 14, 1971. After four days, national union president Joseph Beirne and AT&T officials announced a settlement that included a one-third boost in wages over three years, a cost-of-living-adjustment, and other contractual improvements. Beirne ordered the strikers to return to work immediately, in spite of a prior pledge to end the strike only after the membership ratified a settlement.

Nationally, CWA members endorsed the strike settlement two-to-one, but CWA members at New York Telephone, dissatisfied with the first-year wage hike and the pact's failure to address a series of locally-raised issues, turned it down, 11,405 to 9,734. The strike at New York Telephone dragged on for half a year. Because of automation and the company's ability to deploy a vast cadre of supervisory personnel, many of whom had worked their way up from the ranks and therefore knew how to do various jobs, the AT&T subsidiary succeeded in maintaining normal phone operations. The strikers, though not starved out—many took temporary jobs in addition to getting strike benefits and unemployment insurance—never found a lever to exert crippling pressure on the company. In late January 1972, management agreed to a settlement with only very minor improvements over the July 1971 pact. Over the opposition of the rank-and-file groups, the membership voted to accept the offer, returning to work in mid-February. The strike, according to historian Aaron Brenner, had been "an unqualified defeat for the workers and a smashing victory for management, and both sides felt the impact for many years."[51]

Through an extraordinary social mobilization, working-class New Yorkers significantly improved their lot during the 1960s and early 1970s, boosting their salaries and benefits and increasing their educational opportunities. Yet as the era drew to a close, an increasingly sour tone characterized the city's working class, especially white workers. The economy set the mood, as inflation ate away at the gains workers made. Between 1967 and 1972, the real, net spendable earnings of New York City factory production workers essentially plateaued, though nominal wages rose. Rising unemployment and slowing growth frightened those fighting to win or maintain a middle-class lifestyle—a car, a home, intergenerational mobility. Noneconomic factors, too, contributed to social dyspepsia: rising crime (between 1965 and 1972, the number of reported crimes in New York City more than doubled, while the number of reported murders nearly tripled), divisions over the losing imperial effort in Indochina, cultural gulfs, and the tension and violence associated with efforts to achieve (and resist) racial and gender equality.

The hardhat demonstrations provided the most visible symbol of the conservative current that had enveloped segments of the white working class. Though the construction workers themselves had an exuberance about them, many working-class conservatives exhibited a defensiveness, fearfulness, even bewilderment. The generosity of spirit once characteristic of working-class New York seemed to have shriveled.[52]

For many working-class New Yorkers, the 1960s and early 1970s had been an era of liberation—from cramped opportunity, racial and sexual discrimination, cultural claustrophobia, and economic want. Early in the Lindsay administration, a heady, liberatory atmosphere surrounded working-class New York, in spite of rancor over issues like police brutality and school decentralization. But years of battling, fear, and resentment took their toll. By the time Lindsay left office at the end of 1973, a darker, more defensive, parochial mood pervaded the city and its working class. Even before the full effects of economic contraction hit the city, the fractiousness, chaos, and uncertainty that accompanied social mobilization took their toll. Worse was yet to come.

CHAPTER 15.

The Fiscal Crisis

For New Yorkers of a certain age, the phrase "fiscal crisis" has a very specific meaning, the extended moment in the mid-1970s when the city seemed on the verge of bankruptcy and social collapse, when daily life became grueling and the civic atmosphere turned mean. As a recession settled over the country, a municipal budget squeeze became the occasion for a broad reordering of city life as bankers, financiers, and conservative ideologues made an audacious grab for power. Normally opaque class relations became shockingly visible. So did a national distaste for the city, its residents, and their way of life. Though working-class resistance slowed the counterrevolution from above, it could not stop it. Within a few years, many of the historic achievements of working-class New York were undone.

Though sweeping in its effects, New York's fiscal crisis began narrowly, in the 1975 refusal of major financial institutions to continue to lend the city money. For decades, New York's municipal debt had grown. Long-term bonds to finance capital construction accounted for much of the borrowing, but, from the mid-1960s on, more and more of it consisted of short-term notes, used to fill holes in the city budget. The municipal worker drive for better pay and benefits, the cost of expanded services demanded by a mobilized working class, and expenses associated with an aging population and a growing number of poor pushed up the cost of municipal government. Tax revenues, negatively impacted by suburbanization and job relocation, grew more slowly. By mid-1974 the city had a debt of $11 billion, including $3.4 billion in short-term notes. Over 11 percent of city spending went to debt service.[1]

A worldwide recession that began in 1973 deepened the city's budgetary woes. The number of jobs in the city, falling since 1969, declined steadily through 1977. With employment opportunities diminishing, the population of the city, which had held steady for a quarter-century, dropped from 7.9 million in 1970 to 7.1 million ten years later. Even with the labor force shrinking, the city's unemployment rate jumped from under 5 percent in 1970 to 8.5 percent at the end of 1974 and 12 percent in mid-1975. Population and job shrinkage left the city government with flattening revenue just as the recession increased demand for social services. Rather than cutting back on spending, the city kept adding to its workforce.[2]

The mid-1970s recession led the municipal government's largest creditors, the commercial banks, to reconsider their lending practices. For years, banks had urged state and local governments to increase their borrowing. Banks made money off such debt in two ways, underwriting the offerings and holding notes and bonds in their own accounts. Municipal paper paid high interest, entailed low risk, and was exempt from federal income taxes. New York City debt had the additional attraction for local institutions of being exempt from city and state taxes.

The banks, however, sought to shift funds out of municipal bonds and lessen their exposure to questionable loans just as New York's borrowing needs spun out of control. In the mid-1970s, loan losses, foreign tax credits, and equipment leasing provided alternative tax shelters for banks and other large investors. At the same time, many banks became concerned about their liquidity. The bankruptcy of department store chain W. T. Grant, severe problems in the airline and real estate industries, and heavy Third World lending left them with massive potential losses, threatening their capital base. New York commercial banks had loaned the city (as of early 1975) well over a billion dollars, and now they wanted some of it back.[3]

In order to roll over its debt and remain solvent, the city needed to borrow nearly five billion dollars over the fall of 1974 and winter of 1975, a staggering sum. During these months, the large commercial banks quietly sold off some of their New York paper. To bring in more individual investors, the city reduced the denominations of the smallest municipal notes from $25,000 to $10,000. To stimulate sales, underwriters kept pushing up the interest rate.[4]

As they reduced their exposure to city debt, New York's top financial institutions pressed the municipal government to address its budgetary problems. The banks and brokerage houses first used a standing committee, the City Comptroller's Technical Debt Management Committee, for this purpose. But in January 1975 the leaders of the city's financial community, including David Rockefeller, chairman of Chase Manhattan Bank, Ellmore Patterson, chairman of Morgan Guaranty Trust, William T. Spencer, president of First National City Bank (later Citibank), John F. McGillicuddy, president of Manufacturers Hanover, Donald T. Regan, chairman of Merrill Lynch, and William Salomon, managing partner of Salomon Brothers, formed the Financial Community Liaison Group as a vehicle for pressuring city leaders to adopt reforms that would reassure investors—especially themselves—of the city's solvency, thereby keeping open a market for New York paper. Some proposed reforms were technical: having the city provide accurate financial information; ending gimmicks like putting operating expenses in the capital budget; and restructuring the city's debt. But from the start, the financial community also pressed for a program of municipal austerity, including a freeze or cutback in the number of city workers, an increase in their productivity, reductions in capital spending, cutbacks in city services, and increased fees and taxes.

In the recession and the budget crisis, financial leaders saw an opportunity to undo the past, to restructure New York along lines more to their liking than those drawn by decades of liberalism and labor action. They wanted less and less costly government, fiscal probity, and the desocialization of services and protections for the working class and the poor. They also wanted humbled municipal unions that no longer would enable government workers to have superior benefits and a less intense pace of work than private-sector workers. The banks had not been able to effect such a program during the post–World War II years, a testament to the strength of labor and its allies. But as the city began sliding toward insolvency, they saw a greater need and a greater possibility of carrying out their financial and social agenda.[5]

In October 1974, facing an unexpectedly large budget deficit, Abraham Beame, the Brooklyn clubhouse Democrat who had succeeded Lindsay as mayor at the start of the year, ordered a freeze on most city hiring and merit pay increases. In December, as the city's financial situation deteriorated and pressure from the banks increased, he ordered large-scale layoffs and other cutbacks. However, when the municipal unions protested, Beame partially reversed himself, rehiring some of the laid-off workers. Also, it came out that some of the workers he claimed were laid-off had been shifted to state-funded positions. As of February 1975, only 1,700 of the city's nearly 300,000 employees had been let go.

Beame's modest and misleading efforts to address the city's deteriorating financial situation, rather than reassuring the bankers, convinced them that he was unwilling and unable to provide honest financial information or to embark on a sufficient program of austerity. In January, City Comptroller Harrison Goldin and the banks canceled a planned note sale. A lawsuit caused a February sale to be canceled as well. Late that month, the Urban Development Corporation, a semiautonomous state authority, defaulted on its debt, sending shock waves through the municipal bond market. Two weeks later the city received no bids to underwrite a planned, half-billion-dollar note sale, forcing it to negotiate an extraordinarily high interest rate with a syndicate of banks and brokers. Soon thereafter, the banks made it clear that they considered New York notes unmarketable, effectively closing municipal access to private capital.[6]

The bank refusal to underwrite city bonds pushed New York toward the precipice of default, as it lacked the cash needed for upcoming interest and principal payments on the money it already had borrowed. Vast uncertainty loomed; no one knew what would happen if an unpaid creditor tried to throw the city into bankruptcy, or what bankruptcy would mean for city employees, bondholders, and residents. To avoid finding out, in early May, Beame, Governor Hugh Carey, and bankers David Rockefeller, Ellmore Patterson, and William Spencer traveled to Washington to ask Secretary of Treasury William Simon for short-term federal loan guarantees, to enable the city to meet its immediate borrowing needs. When Simon turned them down, Carey and Beame appealed to President Gerald Ford. But Ford, too, rejected federal guarantees, stating that they would "merely postpone" the city coming to grips with its fiscal problems through needed budget slashing.

Ford and Simon found New York's plight a vehicle for pursuing ideological and political ends. Simon was implicated in the creation of New York's debt. Before coming to Washington in late 1972, he had headed the municipal bond division at Salomon Brothers and served on the Comptroller's Technical Debt Management Committee. Though he later claimed that at the time he had no inkling of the city's fiscal problems—a startling admission coming from the nation's chief financial officer—he felt no compunction about denouncing irresponsibility and ineptitude among city officials. But Simon's real beef was with the city's social policies, not its financial practices. Deeply conservative—almost social Darwinian in his defense of the free market—Simon believed that "absurd" municipal worker salaries and "appalling" pensions were the root cause of the fiscal crisis, along with city subsidies to what he termed the middle class: the City University, middle-income housing, rent control, and the like. New York civic liberalism, Simon believed, had shaped the national "philosophy of government" to the country's woe. Making an object lesson out of New York could serve as a national curative for overly generous social programs and attendant fiscal irresponsibility. Any federal aid to New York, Simon testified in October 1975, should be on terms "so punitive, the overall experience made so painful, that no city, no political subdivision would ever be tempted to go down the same road."

Ford shared Simon's hostility to New York–style liberalism. Hoping to retain the presidency he had obtained without an election, he feared a challenge within the Republican Party from his right, in the figure of Ronald Reagan. Beating on New York might prove useful in courting conservatives.[7]

New York fared no better in Congress. "Cities are viewed as the seed of corruption and duplicity," Delaware senator Joseph Biden told a reporter. "There is a general negative feeling toward New York City." North Carolina representative Richardson Preyer said, "New York City has a certain overtone of sinfulness about it."

New York Times reporter Fred Ferretti claimed that "the resistance in Washington to helping the city was grounded largely in the view that the city was a haven for 'welfare cheats' (read that 'lazy niggers'), people with an overabundance of *chutzpah* (read that Jews), for 'minorities who want a free ride' (read that Puerto Ricans and other Hispanics), for arrogant smart-asses who didn't give a damn about the rest of the country." America always had had antiurban and anticosmopolitan currents, but over the course of the postwar years New York City seemed to have gone from a place of allure to a symbol of profligacy, moral laxity, and social chaos.[8]

With the federal government refusing to help, the state stepped in. Governor Carey, fearful of a city default and its implications for state access to credit, turned for advice to four pillars of the business establishment: former federal judge Simon H. Rifkind, investment banker Felix Rohatyn, Richard Shinn, president of the Metropolitan Life Insurance Company, and Donald B. Smiley, the chief executive of R. H. Macy. In doing so, he was asking leaders of large capital, who had a national and international orientation that left them normally oblivious to day-to-day city affairs, to shape a solution to the fiscal crunch. They, in turn, while mainly concerned with ensuring that the city's creditors got their money back, feared the civil dangers of bankruptcy. A city default, Rohatyn told the *Wall Street Journal*, would create "a social and cultural catastrophe. We'd probably have to bring the troops home from Germany to keep order."[9]

Working in consultation with the banks, Carey's advisers came up with a structural device to get the city the cash it needed to stay solvent, the Municipal Assistance Corporation, or "Big MAC." As authorized by the state legislature in early June, MAC could sell up to three billion dollars in bonds, using the proceeds to retire city notes. To ensure that MAC bonds themselves could be sold, the agency got direct control over the city sales and stock transfer taxes. MAC did not have to lend money to the city if its board did not believe that the city was making progress toward reforming its budgetary practices. This gave the board—made up of business leaders, brokers, and bankers—enormous leverage over the city's affairs.[10]

While MAC was being put in place, Mayor Beame, under intense pressure from the financial community, proposed a series of drastic steps to reduce city spending, targeting the gains municipal employees had won through their unions and, more broadly, the social democratic achievements of working-class New York. Beame first called on city workers to forgo a 6 percent pay increase scheduled for July 1 or accept, with proportional pay reductions, a four-day workweek. When their unions rejected the proposal, he called for a huge reduction in CUNY admissions, closing library branches and health facilities, and the immediate elimination of thirty-eight thousand city jobs.[11]

The formation of MAC and Beame's "austerity" budget set off a wave of protests. The municipal unions, which had not been major actors in the deepening crisis, took a sharp turn to the left. In late May, the leaders of the Municipal Labor Committee (MLC), a coalition of most of the unions that bargained with the city, denounced First National City Bank as the "No. 1 enemy" of the city, charging that it had orchestrated pressure on the city government to cut services and fire workers. MLC chairman Victor Gotbaum attacked First National chairman Walter Wriston for calling on the mayor to withhold 6 percent raises due workers making $8,000 and $9,000 a year, while he himself took home $425,000. The MLC called for a boycott of the bank and, on June 4, sponsored a spirited lunchtime demonstration that brought ten thousand protestors to the narrow, downtown streets surrounding a First National building.

The bank demonstration frightened First National executives and other business leaders, who were not used to direct, populist attacks on their institutions and themselves. Felix Rohatyn later recalled that he found pictures of Gotbaum "picketing Citibank—a very, very scary kind of experience." The success of the demonstration and the anger it revealed seemed to frighten Gotbaum, too, who soon became one of the strongest union advocates of seeking an accommodation with the city and business leaders to avoid default.[12]

As layoff slips began to be handed out, groups of workers took actions on their own. On June 28, two hundred sanitation men staged a one-day strike to protest layoffs. That same day, several hundred residents of City Island protested a drastic reduction in the number of firefighters assigned to it. The real action, though, began on July 1, when thousands of layoffs went into effect. In reaction to the firing of nearly three thousand of their number, ten thousand sanitation workers walked off their jobs, in what the union claimed was a wildcat strike. Meanwhile, five hundred newly laid-off policemen demonstrated at City Hall and blocked the nearby Brooklyn Bridge. In a frightening scene, the ex-policemen let the air out of tires of cars on the bridge, threatened motorists who argued with them, and "hurled beer cans and bottles at uniformed officers and commanders who pleaded with them to clear the roadways." The next day a wildcat strike by highway workers snarled rush-hour traffic on the Henry Hudson Parkway.[13]

City Hall and other government buildings came under siege. The police stopped bothering to take down the sawhorses they had erected to control crowds. On July 11, for example, two hundred people demonstrated in front of fire department headquarters to protest the closing of an engine company on the Lower East Side. On July 24, four thousand doctors, nurses, other hospital workers, and even patients, all taking their cue from the police, blocked the Manhattan entrance to the Brooklyn Bridge to protest cuts in the municipal hospital budget.

But even the most impressive displays yielded few results. The sanitation strike, for example, ended in a peculiar agreement, in which the city temporarily rehired the laid-off workers using $1.6 million in union funds, pending a study of how many might be permanently kept on as a result of new taxes authorized by the state legislature. Two weeks later, half the rehired men were again let go.[14]

Beame's cuts led to escalating demands. All through the first weeks of July, leading bankers told MAC that the city had not taken sufficiently bold steps for investors to accept city or MAC bonds. On July 17, a delegation that included Wriston, David Rockefeller, Donald Regan, and William Salomon met with the MAC board. The bankers and loan underwriters criticized the city for still doing "business as usual" and argued that only MAC—and not the mayor—could reestablish city credibility with investors. Immediately after the financial leaders left, the MAC board met with the mayor, pressing on him the need for dramatic action. After a discussion of a wage freeze and across-the-board service cuts, Rohatyn said that "an 'overkill' was required if for no other reason than that of 'shock impact'. . . . The possibility of revenue increases such as fare increases and [CUNY] tuition increases should be examined. . . . It was apparent from what the banking community had said that the city's way of life is disliked nation-wide."

Rohatyn's message could not have been clearer: to reenter the credit markets and avoid bankruptcy, the city would have to rachet down the social benefits it provided its citizens to the more meager national level deemed appropriate by the financial community. New York exceptionalism had to be ended, quickly and dramatically. MAC and city officials immediately began drafting a financial plan that included a wage freeze, more layoffs, four-week unpaid furloughs, a transit fare hike, tuition at CUNY, a complete halt to all capital construction, and a cut in welfare benefits.[15]

Union leaders initially rejected any wage freeze that canceled increases their members were scheduled to receive under existing contracts. Some preferred to see the city default, which they believed would hurt the banks as much as the workforce. But that was a minority view. By July, Gotbaum and other key labor officials had come to believe that bankruptcy would have disastrous implications for city workers, since it would void their contracts, threaten their pensions, and leave their fate in the hands of the judiciary. Two priorities emerged in their thinking: preserving collective bargaining and preventing default.[16]

In late July, the municipal unions began intense negotiations with the city about a package of concessions as an alternative to a unilateral wage freeze. MAC leaders joined the discussions. Offstage the banks got involved, too, promising the city bridge loans it needed if acceptable budget reforms were instituted. Thus began an unprecedented level of formal corporatism that would continue for the next few years.

In the end, the union coalition agreed to defer all or part of 6 percent wage increases that had gone into effect on July 1, with the lowest paid workers giving up 2 percent, mid-level workers 4 percent, and the highest-paid workers all 6 percent. The city committed itself to repaying the deferred wages after fiscal year 1978 with money saved through productivity gains, if and when the city's budget was balanced and it regained access to the bond market. In the meantime, workers would continue to receive scheduled cost-of-living increases. The unions also agreed to change various work rules to increase productivity. For its part, the city pledged to try to minimize job loss among permanent employees by firing non-civil service workers, ending contracting out of work, and using funds from a federal job creation program, the Comprehensive Employment Training Act, to hire laid-off workers. Finally, the banks agreed to provide $250 million in bridge loans and exchange $700 million in short-term city notes for MAC bonds.

Some unionists balked at giving back what they already had won. Leaders of the firemen's and policemen's unions rejected the coalition pact, worried about rank-and-file anger. The teachers union, which was on a different contract cycle, also rejected the agreement. Meanwhile, within D.C. 37 opposition groups popped up, denouncing the deal. But none of this mattered. Gotbaum succeeded in getting his members to ratify the pact, while the city simply imposed a wage freeze on the uniformed worker unions that rejected the give-backs.[17]

With labor costs being scaled back and union contracts reopened, MAC and the financial community moved on to other sacred cows of New York social democracy. Under intense pressure, in late July, Mayor Beame proposed an increase in the transit fare from thirty-five to fifty cents, a plan put into effect the following month by the Metropolitan Transportation Authority, with approval from MAC. What was extraordinary about the fare hike was that it had little impact on the city budget, since the transit agency was an autonomous entity. Rather than a response to specific fiscal needs, the fare increase was political symbolism, a visible sign of a willingness to break pre-existing social arrangements and impose austerity on working-class New York. In short, it showed who was boss. Donna Shalala, the only nonbusiness person on the MAC board—at the time she was a professor at Columbia University—recalled a perfunctory discussion, without staff papers or background work, before the group approved the hike. "We had no hard facts. . . . We were told this decision would open up the market [for MAC bonds]." She nonetheless voted for the increase.[18]

Free college education and rent control stood out as other prominent targets for critics of New York ways seeking to take advantage of the opportunities created by the debt crunch. Vice President Nelson Rockefeller, who as governor periodically had tried to get CUNY to impose tuition, pressed the idea on the president and the mayor at the start of the fiscal crisis. William Simon urged the elimination of rent control and the addition of tuition at CUNY. Some of the younger, more ideological bankers took a similar line.

Instituting CUNY tuition and ending rent control proved more difficult than jacking up the transit fare. In the summer of 1975, the city cut the CUNY budget by $32 million, the equivalent of what the university would receive if it charged tuition at the State University rate. However, the Board of Higher Education resisted imposing tuition, seeing it as a massive retreat from the historic mission of the city college system. Only in June 1976, after ever-mounting pressure from Albany and Washington and a year in which CUNY literally ran out of funds, forcing a shutdown before the academic year ended, did the board—with new members appointed after others resigned in protest—approve the end of the 129-year tradition of free tuition at the city colleges. The repeal of rent control, though episodically discussed, never took place, primarily because it required action by the state legislature rather than by a politically insulated entity like MAC or the Board of Higher Education.[19]

Damaging as they were to the fabric of New York life, the creation of MAC, the city's austerity budget, the fare hike, and the CUNY cuts failed to satisfy investors. MAC succeeded, with difficulty, in selling two one-billion-dollar bond issues, but it found little interest in a planned, subsequent offering. By the end of August 1975, the city again faced fiscal catastrophe. In another effort to reopen private capital markets, Carey and his coterie of establishment advisers, including MAC chairman William Ellinghouse (whose day job was president of New York Telephone), Simon Rifkind, Rohatyn, and several commercial bankers, sought even more stringent outside controls over city finances. An omnibus bill they drafted called for additional state aid to the city to be linked to the creation of an Emergency Financial Control Board (EFCB) with control over all city revenue, a mandate to develop a financial plan for the city, broad powers to reject city spending and labor contracts, and even the power to remove the mayor and other officials if they defied its policies. Though developed in secret, at the last minute Carey sought backing from municipal labor leaders for the bill, believing their support necessary to get it through the legislature. Gotbaum led other union leaders in endorsing the EFCB legislation in return for two concessions, that collective bargaining would continue and attrition would be used before layoffs in workforce reductions.[20]

The EFCB, on which sat the mayor, governor, city and state comptrollers, and three private members appointed by the governor, Ellinghouse, Rohatyn, and Colt Industries head David Margolis, quickly demonstrated its political will. Over the summer of 1975 the city laid off over eight thousand teachers and school paraprofessionals, creating an extremely difficult atmosphere for contract negotiations between the UFT and the Board of Education. Shanker—like Gotbaum a student of realpolitik—sought relatively little, mainly the preservation of benefits in the expiring contract. Still, when school began in September, the board and the union had not finalized an agreement. Returning teachers found chaos: massive understaffing, wholesale transfers necessitated by layoffs, oversized classes, and new work rules. Rank-and-file fury forced the UFT to call a strike. In spite of solid support, after five days the union settled for a contract very similar to what had been on the table before the walkout: a continuation of most existing benefits, a freeze of wage rates, and elimination of extra preparation periods in certain schools. The EFCB refused to accept the pact, arguing that longevity pay increases and other provisions in it violated the city's financial plan. In a warning to other unions, the EFCB sat on the contract for seventeen months before approving it with minor modifications.[21]

Like MAC, the EFCB elbowed the city toward budgetary discipline and tightened the vise around municipal labor but failed in its ostensible purpose, reopening the municipal bond market to city paper. By the early fall it was clear that nothing the city, MAC, or the EFCB could do would attract sufficient private capital to prevent the city from defaulting. The ability of the banks and underwriters to set city policy diminished, as they would not or could not deliver their end of the bargain, cash to prevent bankruptcy. City and state leaders and fixers like Rohatyn had to search for new sources for the billions the city needed.[22]

They again looked to Washington. During the late summer and early fall, congressional and Ford administration opposition to bailing out the city softened, as a host of influential figures began stressing the wide ramifications of a New York bankruptcy. In mid-September, the mayors of fifteen cities appealed to the president to prevent a New York City default and the havoc it would wreak on the entire municipal bond market. Later that month, at a meeting between Ford and key New York bankers, David Rockefeller indicated that Chase Manhattan, reversing its position, now wanted federal intervention in the city's crisis. Within days, Rockefeller's younger brother, the vice president, began moving away from his opposition to federal assistance. In early October, Federal Reserve Board Chairman Arthur F. Burns likewise eased his opposition to federal help, worrying that a default "could trigger a recession." Concern also grew overseas. German Chancellor Helmut Schmidt warned that a New York default would ripple beyond U.S. shores, disrupting international financial markets. French president Valery Giscard D'Estaing summoned a partner of Lazard Frères & Co., Rohatyn's firm, to indicate his alarm about the possibility of a New York default.[23]

William Simon remained dead set against federal aid. In early September, he had the Treasury Department develop a plan for dealing with what he recognized might well come to pass without it, a New York City default. Simon set two priorities, "avoiding civil unrest and preserving confidence in the financial structure, particularly the banking system." Simon was willing to bail out the banks, but only after a city bankruptcy, which would provide the legal context for voiding municipal union contracts and radically revamping the city government.[24]

With Simon's position winning the day in the executive branch, a variety of plans to aid New York emerged in Congress. However, on October 29, the president, in a speech televised live by the national networks, announced that he was "prepared to veto any bill that has as its purpose a Federal bailout of New York City to prevent default." Attacking free CUNY tuition, the municipal hospital system, the way New York City had managed its finances, and the salaries, fringe benefits, and pensions of city workers, Ford suggested bankruptcy as a way for the city to reorganize its finances. The next morning, in huge 144-point type, the *Daily News* summed up the president's speech in the most famous headline ever run by a New York City newspaper, "FORD TO CITY: DROP DEAD."[25]

Even as New York officials pressed Washington for help, they began exploring another source of funds, the New York City employee retirement funds, which had nearly eight billion dollars in assets. By the end of the summer, city and state pension funds had committed $750 million to purchases of city and MAC paper. With the possibility for federal aid looking bleak, Governor Carey eyed a much more massive tapping of pension money, using it as the primary source of capital to pay back holders of city securities.[26]

This required delicate political maneuvering. Unions appointed half the trustees of most of the pension funds, giving them an effective veto over investments. At the very moment that Carey was considering making pension money the centerpiece of a city bailout, Mayor Beame, in an effort to cut two hundred million dollars out of the city budget, proposed a new round of layoffs and a three-year wage freeze. Having seen the city lay off 13,500 employees, municipal union leaders reacted with fury. Several floated the idea of a general strike. Their bold words, however, remained just that. Gotbaum opposed a general strike, having adopted a strategy of accommodation and doubtful that city workers would solidly support what would be a very dangerous clash. Shanker declared: "A general strike is a political weapon associated with the communist unions of Europe. For us to use it would be irresponsible."[27]

Shanker instead tried to regain some lost power by using pension money as a lever. In mid-October, the city found itself in a sudden cash crunch, unexpectedly short of funds to redeem an upcoming loan obligation. As part of an emergency funding package, Rohatyn and Carey asked the pension funds to complete MAC bond purchases they had pledged to make. Three retired teachers who served as trustees of the Teachers Retirement System balked. Though they worried about their fiduciary responsibilities, their holdout largely represented an effort by Shanker to pressure the EFCB into approving the contract that ended the September teachers' strike. Conceivably the city might have gotten money elsewhere, but Carey, Rohatyn, and Rifkind mounted an extraordinary campaign to pressure Shanker to reverse his stand, warning him in a nonstop series of meetings that if the city defaulted the blame would fall on his head. As the city began going through the motions of preparing for default, Shanker caved. "It was blackmail and unfair," he told the *New York Post*, "but the price of not acceding to it would have been the destruction of the city and we didn't want to shoulder that responsibility."[28]

With the immediate crisis averted, city and state officials returned to constructing a longer-range financial plan using money from the retirement funds to roll over city debt until private markets reopened. Until the early 1960s, the bulk of the assets of the retirement systems had been kept in city securities. This kept down the cost of city borrowing but hurt the funds, which had no need for the tax advantages of municipal bonds yet paid the price for them in the form of lower interest rates. When the municipal unions won representation on the retirement fund boards, they pushed to diversify investments. By 1974, less than 5 percent of the retirement money was in city securities. Now, the city and the state asked the unions to reverse that trend and again put the bulk of pension fund assets into municipal bonds.

For the unions, such a course had obvious disadvantages. Most importantly, it put the money needed to fund their members' retirements at risk; if MAC defaulted or the city went bankrupt, some or all of it might be lost. Furthermore, if the pension funds became major creditors of the city, the unions would come under enormous pressure to do whatever was necessary to avoid default, since the chief victims would be their own members. Using the pension funds to solve the fiscal crisis would irrevocably link the unions to the cause of city solvency, no matter what the social cost.

Nonetheless, municipal union leaders agreed to invest $2.5 billion from the pension funds in MAC securities over a two-and-a-half year period. They justified the decision in terms of the very fiduciary responsibilities that seemingly pointed the other way. Jack Bigel, the former UPW leader, who as the head of a consulting firm emerged as the key technical adviser and strategist for the municipal unions during the fiscal crisis, prepared detailed studies showing the impact of default on the ability of the retirement funds to meet their obligations to current and future retirees. If a bankrupt city stopped making payments into the funds, and city employees facing layoffs retired at a greater than normal rate, the retirement system would go broke in a half-dozen years. Thus, Bigel claimed in 1976, the decision to use pension fund assets to buy city paper "was made solely because it was the only way of protecting solvency in the retirement system." Twenty years later he admitted that "we shot crap with the assets of 350,000 pension fund members."[29]

Some municipal union leaders, like Gotbaum and Bigel, shot crap as part of a general corporatist approach toward surviving the fiscal crisis. Having seen the power of the financial community, the hostility of the federal government, and the divisions within the union movement, they shied away from a militant, independent labor strategy which might have led to them being blamed for a city bankruptcy. Instead, they preferred to make concessions and invest their members' pension money in city debt in return for a place at or near the table where decisions about the city's future were being made by financiers, businessmen, and state and federal officials. Gotbaum became so entranced by the power elite—not mayors or city councilmen but men of real international clout—that within a few years he and Rohatyn were calling each other best friends, even holding a joint birthday party in Southampton. Other union leaders, without Gotbaum's or Bigel's sophisticated understanding of the retirement system, social aspirations, or ideological vision, went along with the pension deal out of fear, confusion, and a lack of obvious alternatives. City workers, having won through hard battle a massive accumulation of capital to ensure secure lives in their old ages, now saw that money being used to allow some of the world's richest institutions to disinvest from New York City. By the spring of 1978, the six major New York banks had less than 1 percent of their assets in city paper, while the city pension funds had 38 percent of their assets so invested.[30]

With union agreement for pension fund investments in hand, Carey put together a new bailout package that he hoped would lead the Ford administration to provide seasonal loans to help the city manage fluctuations in its cash flow. Without these, bankruptcy still seemed like a certainty. Acceding to a demand from Simon, the state legislature raised taxes in the city by two hundred million dollars. It also imposed a "moratorium" on the repayment of $2.6 billion in short-term city notes, offering instead to exchange them for long-term bonds in a kind of controlled default which the banks and pension funds, though not individual note holders, agreed to. (A year later, the state court of appeals found the moratorium unconstitutional.) Finally, some of the cost of future pension fund contributions was shifted from the city to employees. Meanwhile, the EFCB produced a plan for a city budget surplus within three years through ever-greater austerity.

With these pieces in place, the president ended his die-hard opposition to federal assistance. Polls indicated that his "Drop Dead" speech had not been well received by the public, even outside New York. Many Republicans viewed his harsh rhetoric and punitive stand as an albatross to bear in upcoming elections. After negotiations with Carey and Congress, Ford agreed to a program of up to $2.3 billion in short-term loans. The secretary of treasury had to approve each loan, giving him powerful leverage over the city.

With Ford's signing of the Seasonal Financing Act of 1975, the key structures for navigating the fiscal crisis were in place—MAC, the EFCB, pension fund investments, and federal seasonal loans.[31] Though periodic new crises arose over the next several years, in a wild season of capitalist creativity the banks, state government, and financial community had found a way to retrieve the money investors had lent to New York City, in the process stripping the city government, the municipal labor movement, and working-class New Yorkers of much of the power they had accumulated over the previous three decades. The results could be seen on every street and in every institution of working-class New York.

The fiscal crisis of the 1970s affected all New Yorkers, but the poor and working class were hit hardest. For one thing, they depended more on public services—schools, parks, public transportation, and neighborhood police— than the well-off who could afford private schools, health and country clubs, automobiles, and private security. For another thing, any diminishment in the quality of life, be it from higher taxes or reduced services, had greater effect on those living close to the margins than on those with a cushion of ease and security.

City employees took the most severe blow. During the first three years of the crisis, the city laid off twenty-five thousand employees. It eventually rehired many or transferred them to federally-funded job-training positions, but some never regained city employment. Adding in attrition, largely through retirements, the city government shed over sixty-three thousand jobs—a quarter of its total—between 1975 and 1980. The workers who remained faced impossible workloads, working harder than ever while failing to maintain previous levels of service.[32]

With funding and manpower levels dramatically decreased, the level and quality of city services plummeted. The Board of Education suffered some of the worst cuts. Between 1974 and 1976 it reduced its teaching force by nearly 25 percent, while the number of students remained steady. The system-wide teacher-pupil ratio shot up, and classes of forty or more students were not unusual. With most young teachers laid off, the average age of the instructional staff soared. The staff also became much whiter; layoffs reduced the percentage of African-American and Spanish-surnamed teachers from 11 to 3 percent, setting back the long effort to integrate the school system. Guidance counselors, crossing guards, sports programs, adult education, summer school, and bilingual education became luxuries, reduced or eliminated. The principal of one elementary school, in a working-class neighborhood in upper Manhattan, wrote the mayor in late 1975 that "There was a love and a spirit and a dedication at PS 98 that was apparent to almost everyone who walked through our doors—that is, until last June. Now there is tension everywhere, fighting constantly. Now we're just about holding our own, and not too well at that."[33]

CUNY suffered even more grievous harm. The imposition of tuition, in spite of tuition assistance programs, led to a 62,000 student decline in enrollment. By 1980 the university had 50 percent fewer black and Hispanic freshman than four years earlier. The university halted capital construction, stopped all library and laboratory acquisitions, and laid off 3,294 faculty members. One scholar termed the cutbacks "an orgy of official vandalism." With the economy undergoing a prolonged recession and unemployment high, business no longer needed CUNY to train a stream of new employees. Business leaders who once saw CUNY as a boost to the economy now saw it as an unneeded luxury, a squandering of tax money, a giveaway to the poor.[34]

And so it went, from service to service. Subways and buses not only cost more than before the fiscal crisis, they came less frequently, suffered more service breakdowns, arrived late more frequently, and caused more injuries as a result of faulty equipment. Crime against subway passengers rose sharply. Service deterioration and fear led riders to switch to automobiles, adding to traffic congestion. On Manhattan side streets, the average speed bogged down to just 4.4 miles an hour. With street resurfacing all but ended, potholes bloomed like flowers in the spring. Perhaps no industry benefited more from the fiscal crisis than auto repair.[35]

Some deleterious effects of the fiscal crisis proved short-lived. For example, layoffs, made in the order of seniority, undid much of the progress the city had made toward integrating its workforce; African-Americans and Hispanics typically had entered civil service later than whites, and as a result lost their jobs in disproportionate numbers. Over time, though, attrition had the opposite effect, since most retirees were white. By the end of the 1970s, many city agencies had a higher percentage of non-white employees than when the crisis began. Similarly, the city eventually restored some services to or above their pre-crisis levels.[36]

Nonetheless, the damage caused by the fiscal crisis to the idea and reality of an expansive, democratic, state sector was immediate, strong, and irreversible. The ideological attacks on the city and the massive cuts in spending had the effect of repositioning the city's schools, hospitals, and university as second-rate entities. Deprived of resources, they found themselves constantly on the defensive, in difficult, demoralizing fights to maintain even inadequate levels of funding and service. Things considered essentials elsewhere — gym classes and gym teachers in public schools, offices and office supplies in colleges, modern hospital buildings — came to be considered unattainable and unnecessary luxuries in New York.

As public-sector institutions were increasingly attacked, damaged, and discredited, those who could afford to buy their way out increasingly did so — by sending their children to private or parochial schools, by going to NYU or St. John's or Hofstra instead of CUNY, by seeking treatment in a private hospital rather than a public one. Public institutions once attractive to all sorts of New Yorkers became subnormal institutions of last resort. Starved of needed funds, and then attacked for failing to accomplish their mission, many never fully recovered.

The fiscal crisis constituted a critical moment in the history of privatization, spreading the belief that the market could better serve the public than government, that government was an obstacle to social welfare rather than an aid to it, that the corporate world, if left alone, would maximize the social good. Because New York served as the standard-bearer for urban liberalism and the idea of a welfare state, the attacks on its municipal services and their decline helped pave the way for the national conservative hegemony of the 1980s and 1990s. Working-class New York led the way in both the rise and the fall of social democracy in America.[37]

The same recession that triggered the fiscal crisis amplified its effects. Unlike most of the country, New York never recovered from the economic slump at the end of the 1960s, so the next recession to hit the country proved exceptionally virulent there. A Port Authority study reported that in 1975 the "worst economic downturn since the 1930's swept through the New York-

New Jersey Metropolitan Area." That year alone New York City registered a decline in jobs of over 3 percent, bringing total employment to its lowest level in a quarter century.[38]

All told, between 1969 and 1977, when an economic recovery at last began, New York lost over six hundred thousand jobs, a 16 percent drop. Though the downturn hit all aspects of the city economy, the majority of the lost jobs were in goods-producing industries. Construction employment plunged in the face of a surplus of office space and a drastic drop in residential building. Manufacturing employment shrank by 35 percent, as the city lost over a quarter of its printing and publishing jobs, nearly a third of its jobs in apparel and textile production, and almost half its jobs making food and beverages.[39]

The decline of the once-huge garment industry had the greatest impact. Longstanding conditions—comparatively high wages, unionization rates, rents, taxes, and shipping costs—kept pushing garment jobs out of the city. The deterioration of city services and rising crime gave employers further reasons to leave. Well into the 1960s, most apparel production that left New York was replaced by production elsewhere in the country. During the late 1960s and 1970s, however, imports grew rapidly, ballooning from 6 percent of the market in 1967 to over 20 percent in the late 1970s.

As competition with low-cost foreign manufacturers intensified, conditions in New York deteriorated. Unionized shops pressed employees to work faster and harder, ignoring contractual work rules and wage rates. Meanwhile, nonunionized shops sprang up by the hundreds in the South Bronx, Brooklyn, Queens, and New Jersey, in many cases owned by Chinese or Hispanic entrepreneurs who hired their co-nationalists. The ILGWU spent millions of dollars on newspaper, radio, and television advertisements urging consumers to "look for the union label," with few tangible results. It did make efforts to appeal to new workers, especially Chinese women, whose presence in the New York garment industry grew rapidly. But even when the ILGWU signed contracts with new shops, lax contract enforcement meant that often the union benefited from fee and dues collection while workers received very low wages and suffered numerous, often illegal abuses.[40]

While the recession hit those who worked with their hands the hardest, it cast a wide pall over the whole metropolitan economy. Employment at brokerage houses and securities dealers plummeted during the early and mid-1970s. So, with the fiscal crisis, did government employment. Employment in the administrative offices of manufacturing firms also declined. The social

changes in New York, and the impact of the fiscal crisis, repelled many executives. Shortly before Union Carbide's widely publicized 1977 decision to
move out of New York, a company official said, "It is an image we have to
contend with. And it isn't just crime and high living costs. It's the city's
changing ethnic mix, which makes some people uncomfortable, and the graffiti on the subways, the dirt on the streets, and a lot of other things," things
that did not plague nearby western Connecticut, where many corporate executives lived and where many companies, including Union Carbide, built
new headquarters.[41]

The recession, declining population, and the fiscal crisis took a heavy
toll on working-class neighborhoods. At best, a greater shabbiness came to
characterize them. In March 1976, a newspaper in Elmhurst, Queens, reported that "burglaries and muggings have been on the rise. . . . Sanitation
pickups have dwindled to one a week in some sections and overall our streets
are filthy." The local public library opened only three days a week.[42] At
worst, whole neighborhoods literally dematerialized, going from bustling (if
not thriving) communities to acres of rubble-strewn lots in just a few years.

Though at first not much noticed outside of the affected areas, New York
had begun experiencing significant housing abandonment during the late
1960s, as landlords walked away from their buildings rather than pay out-
standing mortgages, taxes, and other expenses. Initially confined to a few
neighborhoods, like the South Bronx, Brownsville, East New York, Harlem,
East Harlem, and the Lower East Side, during the 1970s abandonment
spread to the central Bronx, parts of Crown Heights and Flatbush, and other
neighborhoods that until recently had seemed economically and socially
solid. One study estimated that 200,000 housing units were abandoned between 1965 and 1975. Government officials and housing experts put the abandonment rate at its peak, in the mid-1970s, at somewhere between 20,000 and
60,000 units a year.

A growing gap between the income of the lower strata of the working
class and the cost of profitably operating rental housing underlay abandonment. On the one hand, high inflation, especially soaring energy prices and
interest rates, drove up landlords' costs. On the other, high unemployment
and a depressed economy reduced working-class spending power. Suburbanization and development on the edge of the city already had lured upwardly mobile whites out of many older neighborhoods. As the city
population declined, remaining families with steady incomes could improve
their situation by moving to better off areas of the city, leaving their old neigh-

borhoods heavily populated by those at the bottom of the economic hierarchy, the unemployed, underemployed, and welfare recipients. Landlords and their ideological allies blamed the deterioration of New York's housing stock on rent control, but in neighborhoods suffering abandonment the control system had little effect, since residents could not afford even legally allowable rents.

An owner's decision to abandon a building usually followed the deterioration of its immediate surroundings due to crime, drug dealing, prior abandonment, or arson. Most abandonment occurred in African-American or Hispanic neighborhoods, with white landlords' negative views of their tenants adding to their pessimism about the long-term opportunities for profit. So did the heightened tenant activism of the civil rights and post–civil rights movement years.

Even when landlords wanted to upgrade their buildings or buy new ones, they often could not do so because banks virtually stopped mortgage lending in large expanses of the city. In 1975, Dollar Savings Bank, the largest bank in the Bronx and the fifth largest savings bank in nation, gave only thirty-two mortgages in its entire home borough. Such "redlining" reflected lenders' calculations that particular areas were on a downward slide, making investments there a risky proposition. But equally important, a series of regulatory changes allowed bank deposits—including the savings of working-class New Yorkers—to flow out of local housing: in 1966 New York State eased its rule banning mutual savings banks from making conventional mortgages outside the region, and it subsequently liberalized restrictions on investments in commercial paper and GNMA securities. Banks found that they could make as much or more money through other types of investments as they could through local residential lending.

Unable to make money through ongoing operations or refinancing, landlords began disinvesting, stopping tax and mortgage payments and most or all tenant services, while continuing to collect rents for as long as possible. Often the final act of abandonment was arson, to collect insurance.[43] In neighborhoods experiencing abandonment, hundreds of thousands went to bed each night in terror of being woken by sirens and the possible loss of all they owned, or their very lives. Landlords and their hired agents—often local youngsters—set fires. So did "finishers," seeking to drive out residents to ease the job of stripping buildings of their plumbing and other fixtures. Sometimes tenants burnt their own buildings, hoping to take advantage of a rule that gave priority placement in public housing to those made homeless by fire. Rival gangs seeking revenge, or kids simply looking for fun, torched buildings, too.[44]

The plague of abandonment and arson consumed large chunks of the city before it received national acknowledgment in 1977. In March of that year, CBS televised a documentary by Bill Moyers entitled "The Fire Next Door" about arson in the South Bronx. Then, on the evening of July 13, lightning knocked out a major electrical transmission line near the Indian Point nuclear plant, north of New York City. Cascading equipment failures plunged the city into darkness. Twelve years earlier New York had experienced a similar blackout. That time, when the electricity went back on after thirteen hours, New Yorkers patted themselves on the back for the orderly, even jolly, way they coped with the crisis. Folklore had it that nine months later the birth rate spiked. The second time around, however, events unfolded very differently. Within minutes of the electrical shutdown, looting broke out in widespread parts of the city, including the Upper West Side, East Harlem, and downtown Brooklyn. Police cars careened through dark streets, scattering crowds helping themselves to clothing, groceries, and furniture. In the South Bronx and Bushwick, fires burned out of control. By the time Consolidated Edison restored power the following evening, looters, rioters, and arsonists had caused an estimated three hundred million dollars in damages and the police had arrested more than three thousand people.

The carnival of theft and disorder during the blackout brought national attention to New York, sparking President Jimmy Carter into action, or at least to gesture. Worried that his administration would be deemed inattentive to urban problems (as it largely was), in October, Carter, in New York for a UN appearance, made a surprise visit to a rubble-strewn block on Charlotte Street in the South Bronx. Pictures of the president standing amid devastation of the sort most Americans associated with bombed European cities during World War II shocked people throughout the country and made the South Bronx the national emblem of urban collapse. The ABC network drove home the message the following week, when during its telecast of World Series games at Yankee Stadium it repeatedly cut to aerial shots of flames arising from the nearby South Bronx. Sportscaster Howard Cosell, whose nasal voice, racial liberalism, and in-your-face demeanor personified New York to many outlanders, kept intoning "the Bronx is burning."[45]

In the wake of his visit to the South Bronx, President Carter pledged federal assistance to rebuild the area, and the city hastily produced a plan for its revitalization, but federal and city promises proved to be largely posturing.[46]

In 1976, the city's housing and development administrator, Roger Starr, had come closer to characterizing the actual city policy toward neighborhoods like the South Bronx suffering abandonment. In a series of speeches, interviews, and articles, Starr suggested that the city follow the lead of private capital and walk away from Brownsville, the South Bronx, and other troubled areas, reducing police and fire service and shuttering schools, hospitals, and subway stations to let whole stretches of the city "lie fallow until a change in economic and demographic assumptions makes the land useful once again." Starr argued that with the New York population declining, it made more sense to concentrate resources on selected neighborhoods than spread them throughout the city. Not that Starr bemoaned the reduction in population. Rather, he proposed using government inducements and service withdrawals to move residents of declining neighborhoods not only to other parts of the city but to other parts of the country, "where economic opportunities are opening up." He had particular population groups in mind, blacks and Puerto Ricans. "Our urban system," said Starr, "is based on the theory of taking the peasant and turning him into an industrial worker. Now there are no industrial jobs. Why not keep him a peasant?"[47]

Most city officials publicly rejected Starr's program of "planned shrinkage," but in practice they endorsed a version of it, a kind of planned shrinkage "lite" that gave priority in public investment, tax relief, and economic development to the central business district, while leaving outlying areas, including those undergoing devastation, to fend for themselves. Foundation officials and business leaders encouraged this approach, placing their hopes for city survival on attracting more white-collar employers, particularly those linked to national and global activities.

Many union officials also supported this strategy.[48] The economic plight of the city and the fiscal crisis spawned a flurry of initiatives in which business and labor leaders joined together to promote economic development. In these corporatist efforts, the two wings of the labor movement—private sector and public sector—dealt separately with the business establishment.

Only private-sector unions took part in the Business/Labor Working Group on Jobs and Economic Revitalization in New York City (B/LWG), formed in early 1976. Chaired by David Rockefeller and cochaired by Harry Van Arsdale, the B/LWG included such business luminaries as Edgar Bronfman of Seagram, Gabriel Hauge of Manufacturers Hanover Trust, *Daily News* publisher W. H. James, Pfizer chair Edmund T. Pratt, Richard R. Shinn from Metropolitan Life, *New York Times* publisher Arthur

Sulzberger, P. Robert Tisch, president of Loews Corporation, and Cyrus Vance, who was nominated to be secretary of state as the group completed its deliberations. In addition to Van Arsdale, three labor leaders served on the B/LWG coordinating group: Peter Brennan from the Building Trades, Sol Chaikin from the ILGWU, and Murray Finley from the Amalgamated Clothing Workers.

The B/LWG gave a corporatist gloss to an agenda of government aid to business. Its recommendations included lower business and individual taxes, regulatory simplification, federalization of welfare (eliminating a large burden on the New York City budget), ending rent control, and reductions in energy costs by loosening environmental standards. While some recommendations—like better marketing of the city—spoke to the overall business climate, others—like a reduction in taxes on commercial banks—met the needs of particular group participants. The B/LWG education committee provided a particularly crass example of how, in the fiscal crisis atmosphere, private interests attempted to grab public resources in the name of efficiency. Comprised of the presidents of Columbia, Fordham, Pace, Pratt, and N.Y.U., and a representative of the Rockefeller Brothers Fund (but no unionists or public-sector educators), the committee sought to lessen CUNY's ability to compete with private colleges for students, faculty, and public resources. It urged that CUNY "concentrate on education at the junior college level allowing the 33 private colleges and universities . . . to concentrate on full undergraduate and graduate level education." Complaining that "City University has highest faculty compensation levels negating competition from private institutions," the group suggested "contracting public-sector educational services to independent schools where feasible and when the costs are lower."

The endorsement of the B/LWG report by leaders of unions once associated with plans of social grandeur and class self-reliance reflected how defensive and deferential labor had become. Faced with massive unemployment in their industries, Van Arsdale, Brennan, Chaikin, and Finley accepted a heavily corporate view of economic development in return for business support for steps that they hoped would protect or generate jobs for their members. Unlike many New York business groups, the B/LWG paid attention to the needs of manufacturing, for instance supporting trade restrictions to aid domestic clothing production. And it gave its highest priority to pushing two massive public works projects that would generate construction jobs while upping the value of Manhattan real estate: a controversial new convention center, which was completed in 1986, and Westway, an even more controver-

sial highway and landfill scheme, which after relentless resistance by environ-
mentalists and neighborhood activists was abandoned in 1990.[49]

As the B/LWG wound down its operation, the public-sector unions got
involved in a corporatist effort of their own, the Municipal Union – Financial
Leadership Group (M.U.F.L.G.). It grew out of renewed fighting among city,
union, and bank officials over municipal debt repayment plans, particularly a
demand by the banks for even more stringent and longer-lasting controls over
city finances than already imposed. Furious at this new bid for power, the
municipal unions for a while suspended pension fund purchases of city
bonds.[50]

In the spring of 1977, Jack Bigel approached Citibank's Walter Wriston
about holding ongoing discussions between leaders of the financial community and the municipal unions to minimize future clashes. M.U.F.L.G. resulted, joining together bank heads, top municipal unionists, and several
members of the MAC board. Meeting once a month, the group developed
positions on municipal issues such as taxation and welfare and familiarized
bankers and unionists with the imperatives each felt. Like the B/LWG,
M.U.F.L.G. led unionists to back such business-promoted development
steps as lower state personal and corporate income taxes and construction of
the convention center and Battery Park City. For their part, the banks eased
off in their call for worker givebacks in municipal labor contracts.[51]

While the B/LWG and M.U.F.L.G. had some influence on public and
private policy makers, neither group had the capacity to carry out fundamental social or industrial restructuring that would significantly increase productivity, rejuvenate the regional economy, or maintain consensual social peace.
Efforts to streamline the operations of the New York City government demonstrated the difficulties of overcoming bureaucratic inertia and resistance by
a still feisty workforce. In the years after 1975, both the EFCB and the federal
government placed intense pressure on the city to roll back labor costs and
increase worker productivity. When it negotiated new labor contracts, the
city generally granted no general wage increases, required that cost-of-living
adjustments (COLAs) be paid for through productivity gains, and in some
cases reduced fringe benefits. Union leaders reluctantly went along, but many
of their members saw no reason why they should carry the burden of remedy-
ing the city's fiscal plight.[52]

To implement its productivity program, in 1976 the city set up an elaborate structure of labor-management committees. However, resistance by
workers and managers alike frustrated efforts to redesign municipal jobs or

otherwise increase efficiency. The agreement widely cited as a model for improving productivity, in which the Sanitationmen's union allowed the introduction of two-man trucks to replace three-man vehicles in return for sharing the savings between the city and the participating workers, stood out for its exceptionality.[53]

Worker opposition to austerity contracts had the potential to undermine the municipal unions. Membership in them was optional, so worker dissatisfaction could quickly translate to declining ranks and revenue. D.C. 37 took the lead in plugging up the escape route. It had long sought passage of an "agency shop" bill in Albany that would allow it to sign contracts requiring all covered workers to pay union dues or their equivalent, whether or not they chose to join the union. The fiscal crisis gave a new urgency to the effort, while creating an opening for reaching out to politicians not previously aligned with organized labor but now interested in working with unions to maintain social stability. To do this, D.C. 37 abandoned its policy of only endorsing Democrats, building relationships with key moderate Republicans. In August 1976—soon after a coalition of municipal unions signed a contract offering no raises—D.C. 37's effort paid off with the enactment of an agency shop law.[54]

Agency shop gave the municipal unions a guarantee of financial stability, but episodic flare-ups of worker militancy still occurred. The day after Governor Carey signed the agency shop bill, 18,000 workers struck the city-run hospitals to protest the layoff of 1,350 of the number. Two years later, TWU leaders barely succeeded in getting ratified an austere contract they negotiated with the Transit Authority, facing mass rank-and-file opposition which included demonstrations at the union's headquarters and City Hall.[55]

If 1975 had been a blitzkrieg by financial leaders and conservative ideologues against working-class New York, what followed was a war of attrition. Repeated demonstrations by service users—parents seeking to reverse school cutbacks or stop day care center closings, communities sitting down in firehouses to keep them from being shuttered, hospital workers and community activists seeking to keep city-owned health facilities open and adequately funded—made each step toward austerity laborious.[56] Meanwhile, the municipal unions slowly regained some initiative. In 1978 the city agreed to pay retroactive COLA payments as part of its next municipal union contract without a requirement for offsetting productivity gains. Soon thereafter, the city unions, by using their clout in local electoral politics, effectively ended the EFCB's ability to block collective bargaining agreements and won wage gains that partially recouped the ground they had lost during the fiscal crisis. Still, working-class New Yorkers remained on the defensive, forced to justify every service and benefit in a discourse that accepted governmental solvency as the highest social goal and left unchallenged the notion that there were insufficient economic resources available to undertake even the most obviously needed and beneficial government programs.[57]

By the end of the 1970s, New York had become quite a different city than when the decade began. It had been a hard ten years, for New York and the country. President Carter catalogued some of the disillusioning events of the recent past in July 1979, when the energy crisis became an occasion for him to inquire into what he dubbed a "crisis of the American spirit":

> We were sure that ours was a nation of the ballot, not the bullet, until the murders of John Kennedy and Robert Kennedy and Martin Luther King, Jr. We were taught that our armies were always invincible and our causes were always just, only to suffer the agony of Vietnam. We respected the Presidency as a place of honor until the shock of Watergate. We remember when the phrase 'sound as a dollar' was an expression of absolute dependability, until ten years of inflation began to shrink our dollar and our savings. We believed that our Nation's resources were limitless until 1973, when we had to face a growing dependence.[58]

In New York, a round of reappraisals had come in the wake of the 1977 blackout looting. In an op-ed article in the *New York Times*, historian Herbert Gutman decried the use of animal terms—"vultures," "a jackal pack"—to describe the looters and compared it with the way newspapers had described Jewish women taking part in a 1902 kosher meat riot as "animals" and "beasts." The flood of letters protesting Gutman's article revealed how hardhearted many New Yorkers had become in the harsh climate of prolonged recession and austerity politics. Over and over, the letter writers proclaimed how different their impoverished forbearers had been from the current poor, how the 1902 rioters were engaged in legitimate protest, while the blackout looters "sought only selfish gain." A *Times* editorial characterized the letters as raising "the 'my grandfather' question: 'My grandfather pushed a pushcart all over the Lower East Side to earn enough to feed and raise his family. He worked to make it. Why can't *they*?'" It left unaddressed the utter lack of empathy among the letter writers for New York's poor, the meanness and self-satisfaction that pervaded their outrage at Gutman's linkage of their ancestors with contemporary rioters in his effort to show that the animal metaphor always "separates the *behavior* of the discontented poor from the *conditions* that shape their discontent."[59]

Midge Decter tried to give intellectual substance to the niggardly spirit of the *New York Times* letters in an article in *Commentary*. Taking on liberal punditry about the blackout looting, including Gutman's "truly disgraceful" article, Decter argued, "It is cant to call the looters victims of racial oppression and it is still worse cant to say that their condition is the result of our apathy." The real culprits of the looting, Decter proclaimed, were "liberal racists," who in their hearts believed blacks inherently inferior, and therefore did not hold them to the same moral standards or social expectations to which they held others.

Directing her greatest fury not at the looters but at liberals, Decter at times seemed to have a certain amount of sympathy for poor, young blacks. Still, she treated the blackout thieves with precisely the dehumanization Gutman protested. The looters, she wrote, suggested not animals but "urban insect life." The looting left the feeling "in the city . . . of having been given a sudden glimpse into the foundations of one's house and seen, with horror, that it was utterly infested and rotting away. No one will be at ease in the edifice again for a long time, if ever."

The implication that before the blackout New Yorkers were at ease in their urban edifice reflected the parochialism of Decter and her like, who had come to equate their view and their experience, the view and experience of the white middle-class, risen from the working class and dining off of it forever, with the view and experience of the city as a whole. An ideological structure of "them and us" emerged from the economic strictures and social disorder of the 1960s and 1970s. Thus Decter could write an article seeking to explain looters, who she herself noted came from quite varied backgrounds, that rested on a long discussion of liberal attitudes toward African-Americans, as if that would do to explain all of *them*. *They* had no particularity. At one point, Decter even lumped Puerto Ricans among "immigrants" who "go to any lengths not to be sent home."[60]

Decter's casual use of a voice of *us*, which excluded so much of the city, reflected an indifference that emerged during the 1970s among opinion-makers and the powers-that-be toward the growing number of New Yorkers who lived outside the economic mainstream. With a shrinking number of jobs in the city, soaring unemployment, and long-term changes in the industrial and occupational structure, population groups once valued by business as reserve armies of labor came to be seen as unneeded and expensive human surplus, best ignored in the hope that they would go away. Thus, business and government leaders looked on with near indifference as large sections of the city literally burned down.

Some young New Yorkers refused to accept the social invisibility to which they had been relegated. In 1971, a young Greek-American began writing his nickname, Taki, followed by 183, for the street he lived on in upper Manhattan, on subway cars and station walls all over the city. Though teenagers had been scrawling nicknames on neighborhood walls for some time, graffiti writing soon exploded, especially on the walls and cars of a subway system in deep decline, whose filth and failures exuded contempt for its ridership. At first graffiti writers wrote simple "tags," their initials or nicknames in small black letters. Soon the tags got larger, more stylized, and more colorful. By the mid-1970s, as spray paint replaced marking pens, some "writers" had taken to painting the entire sides of subway cars with what in effect were rolling murals. A few crews of "masters" even managed to paint entire, ten-car trains.

Teenage boys made up the bulk of the graffiti writers, though some girls and men in their twenties wrote, too. They were a cosmopolitan lot. Writers came from every conceivable economic, ethnic, and racial background, though the poor predominated, and much of the writers' graphic and personal style came from black and Latin culture. Young New Yorkers who wrote graffiti, unlike many of their peers, roamed all over the city, forming bonds with writers from areas geographically and culturally distant from their own. In the process they created a new subculture replete with its own argot, hierarchy, aesthetic, and sense of history. The graffiti writers helped propel hip-hop into national prominence.

Almost from the start, city and transit officials hated graffiti. It represented, Metropolitan Transportation Authority (MTA) chairman Richard Ravitch said, "a symbol that we have lost control." Rider reactions were harder to gauge. When applied to ugly, old, shabby cars, graffiti could provide a cheering sight. When it covered subway car windows or defaced the new cars that eventually began to be bought, the antisocial side of graffiti seemed more evident. For years, the MTA and the city waged war against graffiti, trying special police anti-graffiti squads, new types of car paints and washing solvents, and stiffer penalties for those caught in the act. But as the 1970s drew to an end, little progress had been made.[61]

*   *   *

Edward I. Koch got elected mayor of New York in the fall of 1977 by capitalizing on the mood of meanness and parochialism evident in the writing of
Decter and other critics of Gutman's blackout looting piece. Koch, a congressman from Greenwich Village with a reputation for liberalism, began as
one of the lesser-known of seven candidates in the Democratic primary. Hoping to win over middle-class voters in Brooklyn, Queens, and the Bronx, during the campaign he took a sharp turn to the right, making his prime issue
support for the death penalty, a matter over which the mayor had no say. The
day after the blackout, Koch announced that if he had been mayor he would
have asked the governor to call up the National Guard. Positioning himself as
the defender of a put-upon middle class, Koch adopted the emotional vocabulary, if not the open racism, of backlash politics. Though Congress-
woman Bella Abzug, another Democratic contender, had the strongest pro-
labor positions, most unions backed either incumbent mayor Abe Beame or
Secretary of State Mario Cuomo. Koch won the Democratic nomination and
then the general election owing little to organized labor.[62]

Once in power, Koch institutionalized in the city government itself—as
opposed to watchdog agencies—the agenda of the financial elite which had
played so large a role in the fiscal crisis. Koch emphasized fiscal prudence,
municipal austerity, and economic development through government assistance for large white-collar employers and tourist attractions. He also sought
to counter the sense of disorder felt by many New Yorkers. In an effort to end
graffiti, in September 1981 he appropriated $1.5 million dollars to build two
parallel fences, topped with razor wire, around the Corona subway yard, with
six German shepherds let loose between them. The MTA painted the subway cars stored in the yard all white, and white they stayed.

Koch's handling of a 1980 strike by transit workers revealed how much
the political terrain of the city had been changed by the fiscal crisis. The
strike represented the last major effort by New York workers to challenge the
postulates of austerity. Following the narrow ratification of the TWU's 1978
contract, at least seven groups opposed to the union's leadership began meeting, attracting several thousand members. In addition to the poor contract,
workers complained of union deference to management, grievances unat-
tended to, insufficient attention to health and safety problems, and a union
leadership still dominated by whites, though blacks and Hispanics had come
to make up half the workforce.

In late 1979, TWU Local 100 president John Lawe had the good fortune to face not one but three opponents in his reelection bid, enabling him to return to office with only 43 percent of the vote. However, opposition candidates won nearly half the seats on the local's executive board. By the end of March 1980, when the union's contract with the Transit Authority expired, the dissidents had managed to cobble together a one-vote executive board majority.

Pressed hard by the opposition, Lawe demanded a 30 percent wage hike, even as the MTA, which controlled transit system funding, declared that it faced a record deficit. Privately, Lawe and MTA chairman Richard Ravitch arranged to orchestrate a last-minute settlement that would make Lawe look good: a "final" management offer of 6 percent wage increases for two years, to be followed by a Lawe demand for 7 percent hikes, which Ravitch would accept. But the deal fell apart because, unlike in the past, the union executive board did not act as a rubber stamp. At a climactic meeting, just as the old contract expired, the board not only rejected Ravitch's offer but Lawe's proposed counteroffer, electing instead to begin a strike of the city's buses and subways that morning, April 1, 1980.[63]

For eleven days, the workers held steady. Their walkout disrupted nearly every aspect of city life, just as the 1966 transit strike had done, but the intervening years and changed political scene the fiscal crisis brought about made its effects dramatically different. To be sure, this strike occurred during the spring, not the winter, making walking and bicycling easier. And over the years since 1966, the city had become more dependent on cars, somewhat lessening the centrality of mass transit. But most importantly, the attitude of political and business leaders by the time of the 1980 strike, and their resultant actions, were starkly transfigured.

In 1966, Mayor John Lindsay had urged unessential workers to stay home. By contrast, in 1980, Ed Koch urged businesses to stay open and employees to get to work if at all possible. To encourage them, he took to personally greeting commuters entering Manhattan by foot and bike via the Brooklyn Bridge and the Staten Island Ferry. Koch, who faced an upcoming round of negotiations with city workers in which the transit pact would undoubtedly set precedents, denounced the union's demands as outrageous. He portrayed New Yorkers coming to work as active resisters to a union effort to blackmail the transit system into a contract it could not afford. In 1966, the business community urged Lindsay to end the transit strike as quickly as possible; this time it pressed Koch (whose back, in any case, probably needed no stiffening) and the MTA to hold out for what it considered a reasonable settlement. B/LWG members David Rockefeller and Richard Shinn were among those who publicly opposed the strike, a measure of how quickly their corporatist inclinations dissolved when class conflict erupted. Having a Democrat like Koch position himself as a cheerleader for antiunionism reflected the changed, post–fiscal crisis power relations in the city and the dramatic weakening of pro-labor sentiment.[64]

The strike ended bizarrely. On its eleventh day, the MTA made a new contract offer, which included a 9 percent wage hike the first year, an 8 percent hike the second, and a COLA that could bring the wage gain above 20 percent over two years. (Since consumer prices rose 13.5 percent in 1980, the offer was not as generous as it might seem. High inflation was a little-noted key to the city's fiscal recovery, pushing up tax revenues while interest costs on long-term bonds remained fixed and the real wages of municipal workers fell.) The agreement also called for some union givebacks, including a reduction in break time and lower salaries for new workers during their first two-and-a-half years on the job. When Lawe presented this proposal to his executive board, the board split down the middle. The dissidents would have been able to block the pact, but one of their number had gone off for the weekend for reserve army training. After the tie vote, Lawe unilaterally ordered the strikers to return to work immediately. Lawe's opponents screamed foul, but the strikers quickly resumed work and several weeks later ratified the contract by a three-to-one margin that surprised even its backers.

In some respects, the transit workers won their strike. The contract they achieved exceeded by a considerable margin what the MTA had offered before the walkout, and by even more what Koch deemed appropriate. In carrying out an extended strike, in defiance of both the state Taylor Law and the prevailing austerity climate, the transit workers displayed remarkable resolve. Yet, as columnist Murray Kempton noted, "Everyone was dead certain . . . that the transit workers had beaten the public officials except apparently the transit workers." For one thing, fines imposed under the Taylor Law—two days pay for each day out on strike—effectively wiped out the first-year wage hike under the new contract. For another thing, the disarray among the insurgents that marked the end of the strike had the effect of relegitimizing John Lawe and other old-guard union officials while undermining confidence among transit workers—and no doubt other workers, too—about the desirability of rank-and-file leadership. Though in a narrow sense the transit workers won the battle, they and the old world of working-class New York they represented lost their war against the post–fiscal crisis political order.[65]

By the end of Koch's first term, with the federal loan program expiring and the city having achieved balanced budgets, the mayor and the press declared the fiscal crisis over. Its effects, though, were far from over. For one thing, MAC and a restructured Financial Control Board remained as its institutional residue. For another, and more importantly, the social, ethical, and political environment of the city had been forever changed. In a few short years, financial leaders, politicians allied with them, and conservative intellectuals had succeeded in at least partially prying the city away from its working-class, social democratic heritage. Compared to the results of the anticommunist crusade a quarter-century earlier, this was a mighty victory indeed.[66]

PART FOUR
Trump City

If a man has flair and is smart and somewhat conservative and has a taste for what people want, he's bound to be successful in New York.

—Donald J. Trump

Our idea of a just society is one in which honest labor raises the standard of living for all, rather than creating enormous wealth for just a few. And our notion of a moral nation is one that cares for its young, its old, and its poor, and leaves the rich to fend for themselves.

—John J. Sweeney

CHAPTER 16.

Global Dreams and Neighborhood Realities

New York regained some of its economic shimmer during the 1980s. Investors, academics, and policymakers hailed New York as a "global city." The city, they proclaimed, had emerged from its fiscal crisis era of woe by becoming a dominant control center for transnational economic activity, positioning itself to thrive in a world in which capital, goods, and people flowed across international borders in growing volume.

Celebrants of global New York oversold the importance of international activity to the city and overstated the break from past patterns of capitalist activity.[1] Still, as anyone walking the streets of Manhattan could attest, the growth of international business and an influx of foreign money, businessmen, and tourists transformed the character of New York. A culture of celebrity came to dominate public life that had little place in it for the ordinary toilers and their kin, who seemed increasingly alien to the well-traveled but socially blindered tastemakers of the city and the nation.

During the fiscal crisis, working-class New York had been highly visible. To a great extent, the crisis had been *about* the working class, an effort to lower its living standards, expectations, and political power. Once a new stasis had been achieved, workers as a class faded from view. The fiscal crisis established a set of seemingly self-evident necessities—a balanced city budget, a more attractive climate for business, a paring down of social benefits—that inhibited discussion of alternative policies, much the way President Ronald Reagan's creation of a massive deficit squelched discussion of federal initiatives. The widespread acceptance of the view that overly-liberal government policies and overly-paid workers caused the fiscal crisis kept unions and their allies on the defensive.

No one better symbolized the spirit of the new New York than real estate developer Donald Trump. In the mid- and late 1980s, his name seemed to be everywhere. The developer of several super-luxurious Manhattan apartment buildings, at one point he owned the Plaza Hotel, a football team, an airline, three casinos, a historic mansion in Florida, a 282-foot yacht, and the largest piece of undeveloped land in Manhattan. A relentless self-promoter who

named most of his buildings after himself, Trump appeared in the press almost daily, denouncing politicians, squiring his wife or girlfriend, meeting
with this or that celebrity, announcing ever-grander plans. When in 1986 he
rebuilt Central Park's ice-skating rink in five months, after the city had spent
six years bungling the job, the media hailed him as the embodiment of one of
the lessons of the fiscal crisis: let the genius of private enterprise replace the
morass of government bureaucracy. Trump himself touted his genius in a
best-selling account of his rise to fortune that he wrote while barely in his forties.[2]

Like many ambitious New Yorkers, Trump had moved to Manhattan
from the outlands of the city to make his mark. His father, Fred Trump, had
made a modest fortune housing upwardly-mobile New Yorkers. The senior
Trump targeted the same market as the labor-sponsored cooperatives, well-
paid workers and the lower strata of the middle class. He built his largest
project, Trump Village in Coney Island, by piggy-backing on a planned
United Housing Foundation project; Trump got political allies to block tax
abatements for the labor cooperative until he won control over half the site
and tax breaks for a development of his own.[3]

Donald Trump had contempt for the proletarian city in which his father
thrived. "Plenty of other people could buy and sell little brownstones or build
cookie-cutter red-brick buildings," he wrote. He wanted only "the best location," Manhattan, where he won fame and fortune as a bottom-feeder during
the recession of the 1970s. His first projects involved properties optioned
from the bankrupt Penn Central railroad, two huge rail yards on the west side
of Manhattan and the Hotel Commodore, adjacent to Grand Central Station.
Trump first envisioned repeating his father's formula at the rail yards, building government-financed middle-income housing. When the fiscal crisis
dried up state and city housing money, he marshaled his political connections to convince the city to buy one yard as the site for its new convention
center. Trump then took advantage of the desperate desire begot by the fiscal
crisis for visible signs of municipal revival to win an unprecedented forty-year
tax abatement for the Commodore, which he renovated in partnership with
the Hyatt hotel chain. Trump's next project, Trump Tower, a high-rise retail,
office, and residential building on Fifth Avenue, secured his place as a leading
developer.

Trump perfected a personal and architectural style that local and national media associated with New York's revival: glitzy, superficial, and ultimately provincial. In redoing the Commodore, Trump wrapped its sober

stone exterior with reflective glass and lined its lobby with expanses of brown marble. To gain the right under zoning regulations to build a larger structure, he put a shopping plaza in Trump Tower with an indoor waterfall and even more marble, this time pink. Though hailed by Trump and others as the epitome of sophistication, the atrium merely brought the suburban shopping mall to New York, as the city stopped setting trends and began playing catch-up.

Trump's rail yard was emblematic of the changes in the city's economy that altered New York's culture and feel during the 1980s and 1990s. An I. M. Pei-designed convention center, a palace of meeting and selling filled with men and women in smart suits, replaced what had been a major freight handling center, where longshoremen, teamsters, and railroad men held sway. As New York wealth came increasingly from activities far from the city itself, upper- and middle-class concern for (let alone interaction with) the local working class diminished.[4]

The New York economy had bottomed out in 1977, after eight years of decline. Then employment in the city expanded every year (except 1982) until 1989, when New York had 3.7 million jobs, up from 3.2 million in 1977. Gotham's recovery rested almost entirely on the service sector, as the long-term decline in goods production and distribution continued. The number of manufacturing workers in the city dwindled from 538,600 in 1977 to 360,600 in 1989. Employment in wholesale trade and goods transportation also dropped. Even employment at manufacturing headquarters fell, as goods-producing corporations continued to move their offices out of New York. Meanwhile, financial and corporate services boomed. Between 1977 and 1989 the securities industry added 67,000 jobs, the banking industry 53,000, legal services 37,000, management consulting 11,000, and accounting 10,000. The entertainment, culture, and tourism industries gained 68,000 jobs, health and social services added 110,000 workers, and a post-fiscal crisis expansion pushed up the local government payroll by 50,000.[5]

Many thriving sectors of the economy were internationally oriented. Multinational corporations headquartered in New York earned nearly half their revenue abroad, much more than multinationals located elsewhere in the country. New York-based law firms, banks, advertising agencies, and consulting firms likewise earned much of their money overseas. Meanwhile, foreign capital, capitalists, and tourists poured into the city, finding it a cheap and relatively safe haven from political and economic threats. When in 1981 French voters chose socialist François Mitterand as their president, a flurry of nervous, rich Frenchmen bought condominiums at Trump Tower (or so claimed Donald Trump).[6]

From the late 1970s on, a series of foundation- and government-sponsored commissions asserted that the best opportunity for local prosperity lay in coordination functions for a globalizing economy. This meant concentrating municipal resources on central business district development. Saskia Sassen and other academics argued that international economic restructuring, while decentralizing production, increased the demand for centralized financial and producer services. As companies relocated manufacturing facilities to low-wage regions throughout the world and moved their headquarters out of old center cities, they became more dependent than ever on specialized services concentrated in a handful of cities like London, Tokyo, and New York.

New York's globalization, though, affected only limited economic strata. A very small proportion of the goods manufactured in post–fiscal crisis New York was exported. (Foreign trade, like foreign investment, actually played a larger role in the New York economy during the 1880s and 1890s than a hundred years later.) Similarly, the huge growth in health care and government employment had little to do with the global economy. Still, the late-twentieth-century growth of internationally-oriented finance, real estate, tourism, and business services imparted to New York—or at least midtown and downtown Manhattan—a renewed sense of power, prosperity, and centrality.[7]

The new New York featured a widening income gulf between the upper class and everyone else. In part this stemmed from the growing importance of service industries. Though securities, banking, insurance, advertising, accounting, and corporate law firms employed fleets of well-paid and very well-paid executives, managers, and professionals, many service workers—like janitors, day care workers, and security guards—received low salaries and had little security, few benefits, and scant opportunities for advancement. The high and low sides of the service economy depended on one another. The proliferation of expensive and hip restaurants, hotels, bars, and clubs serving corporate employees and tourists required an army of low-paid dishwashers, maids, laundry workers, and food preparers, many newly-arrived immigrants.[8]

Real median household income rose more rapidly in New York than in the country as a whole, but so did income inequality. In 1977 the top 10 percent of New York earners received fifteen times the income of the bottom 10 percent; in 1986 they took home twenty times as much. In the latter year, Wall

Street firms paid out two *billion* dollars in bonuses. Meanwhile, the number of city residents officially deemed living in poverty soared from 1.1 million in 1975 to 1.7 million in 1984. Homelessness reached record levels, as every night thousands of men and women slept on the streets, in the subways, and in public buildings.[9]

Most New Yorkers who fell between the extremes of rich and poor saw their real household income inch upward between 1977, when the economic recovery began, and 1989, when a stock market collapse ended it. However, rising housing costs, deteriorating public services, and pervasive crime meant that many workers with secure jobs found it hard to maintain a lifestyle that earlier New York workers had grown accustomed to.[10]

The changing economy did not preclude upward mobility. Once New York got over the worst of its budgetary woes, civil service resumed its role as a path of working-class advancement. Black New Yorkers made the greatest use of this route, gravitating to the public sector because they faced less racial discrimination there than in private employment. Many white New Yorkers, by contrast, spurned municipal jobs once the fiscal crisis led to a relative decline in city wages.

Government jobs made possible a substantial increase in the size of New York's black middle class, which between 1977 and 1989 grew faster than the white middle class. Southeastern Queens, an area favored by black civil servants, grew into one of the largest black middle-class neighborhoods in the world, with a homeownership rate over double that of the city as a whole. (In 1986, New York City reimposed a residency requirement for most of its non-teaching, nonuniformed employees.) In 1990, the median household income of black residents of Queens exceeded that of white residents.[11]

The expanding health and hospital industry provided another upward path for workers, particularly for those who took advantage of union-sponsored training programs and other educational opportunities. West Indian, Filipino, Indian, and Soviet immigrants and native-born blacks disproportionately turned to health services for employment. Women made the greatest gains; health care, like government work, presented them with more opportunities and fewer obstacles than most private industry.[12]

Entrepreneurship provided still another route upward favored by immigrants seeking to circumvent problems getting work as a result of discrimination or limited command of English. By mobilizing family and community resources, some nationalities came to dominate particular niches, such as the Korean fruit and vegetable stores which became ubiquitous during the 1980s.

The success of immigrant entrepreneurs—Korean greengrocers; taxi and limousine operators from the Middle East, the Caribbean, and Africa; South Asian newsstand operators—depended on a high degree of self-exploitation and exploitation of family members, just as it had for earlier generations of European immigrants.[13]

Even as some routes to economic security and betterment remained open, others narrowed. For decades, jobs in goods production and distribution had enabled working-class New Yorkers to achieve a measure of financial security. The economic shifts of the 1970s and 1980s eliminated many of those jobs. This put an even greater premium than in the past on education and access to capital as prerequisites to economic advancement. Groups with low levels of both, like Puerto Ricans, saw their situation decline.[14]

For those without the education, connections, ambition, or luck to escape the low-end service jobs that proliferated, or to get work at all, New York in the 1980s could be grim. The economic polarization of the era increased the already great differences in living conditions between affluent neighborhoods and the rest of the city. New York's version of the Reagan boom had a distinct spatial dimension: prosperity and gentrification in parts of Manhattan and nearby sections of Brooklyn coexisting with stagnation and even decline elsewhere. In 1977, per capita personal income in the boroughs other than Manhattan was 52 percent of the Manhattan level; by 1988 it had fallen below 50 percent. Meanwhile, some suburbs experienced extraordinary affluence as a result of the revival of the city economy, with commuters holding an increasing percentage of the jobs in New York City in the economic sectors with the greatest income growth. Commuters to New York from most suburban counties took home an average income exceeding that of Manhattan residents. Those coming in from Connecticut doubled it.[15]

Even as commuters occupied an expanding place in New York's economy, a sizable number of professionals, managers, and executives sought to reside in the city. The growth of business and professional services, combined with long-term trends toward greater female workforce participation, smaller families, and later childbearing, created a cohort of young white-collar workers, with plenty of disposable income, eager to partake of the joys of the city. Top corporate executives overwhelmingly preferred the suburban life. But many lawyers, advertising executives, marketers, media workers, and the like rejected what they saw as a 1950s version of the American dream, drawn instead to the convenience, excitement, and social cachet of downtown living. Their quest for housing transformed the social geography of New York, as gentrification hit one neighborhood after another.[16]

Gentrification had a natural history. Where large industrial spaces were available, artists generally served as the "pioneers" who "opened up" areas to middle-class settlement. Elsewhere, gentrification involved the middle-class reclaiming once elegant neighborhoods which had become rundown. After World War II, for example, Brooklyn's Park Slope lost many of its wealthier residents to the suburbs. Poorer families replaced them, with many owners converting large brownstones into rooming houses. In the 1970s, the process reversed, as young professionals began pricing the poor out of the area.[17] Once gentrification began, real estate agents and speculators quickly got into the act, renaming neighborhoods to distance them from their gritty past: part of Red Hook became Carroll Gardens, Hell's Kitchen became Clinton, and the acronyms SoHo, NoHo, and TriBeCa got attached to industrial districts. Finally came the main army of gentrifiers, as urban economist Emanuel Tobier described them, "a blend of a raffish Bohemian lot and straight-on careerists."[18]

Gentrifying neighborhoods served as arenas for cultural exchange, where artists, merchants, clothing designers, and advertising executives picked up on the latest developments in black and Puerto Rican music, dress, and lingo, which they embraced, coopted, and retransmitted to national and international audiences. During the late 1970s and 1980s, fashion bubbled upward. What was hot on the streets of the South Bronx, Harlem, or the Lower East Side one month could be seen in downtown clubs and discos a few months later, and in exquisitely photographed store catalogs and magazine advertisements a few months after that.[19]

Gentrification provided a visual exclamation of how far New York had moved away from its working-class roots, even as it helped preserve the city's architectural past. Buildings that had once been sites of toil—trolley garages, wholesale markets, factories, and docks—got recycled as elegant restaurants, luxury apartment buildings, film studios, college libraries, and high-end sports emporia. The charm and financial value of these beautifully refurbished structures lay in their social and physical patina, their origins in a bustling world of making and trading. Their preservation and prettification proclaimed a new social reality; workers of the type who once created the wealth of Gotham in these very buildings could not afford to enter their portals, nor would they be made to feel welcome if they could.

While gentrifiers were transforming some working-class neighborhoods, longtime building owners and residents transformed others. Most notably, they spread owner-occupancy. This happened in two ways, the conversion of rental units to individual ownership and the construction of new, owner-occupied homes. In 1950, fewer than two out of ten city households owned their home. By 1993, three out of ten did. While compared to most of the country, New York remained exceptional in its degree of rental housing, the gospel of homeownership belatedly evangelized Gotham.

Starting in the 1970s, many landlords in better-off working-class neighborhoods (and middle-class neighborhoods, too), chose to cash out their investments by converting multiunit buildings into cooperatives or, less commonly, condominiums, selling off individual apartments. (Unlike in non-profit cooperatives, owner-residents in these buildings could resell their apartments at market prices and keep any profit.) From 1981 through 1984 alone, building owners filed plans to convert nearly 150,000 units to individual ownership.[20]

At the same time, on a smaller scale, new owner-occupied units were built in poor neighborhoods. In this, the government played only a modest role. In 1973, the Nixon administration placed a moratorium on federal funding for housing construction. Shortly thereafter, the fiscal crisis led the city and state to suspend their housing programs as well. New federal programs, begun after 1973, proved short-lived, undergoing severe cutbacks during the Reagan years. Compared to previous decades, very little public housing got built in New York during the 1970s, 80s, and 90s.[21]

In the past, organized labor had been a major force in supplementing and leveraging government housing programs. After the Co-op City debacle, however, unions shied away from substantial involvement. In their stead came organized religion. In the 1960s and early 1970s, church groups used subsidies from the Model Cities program to build thirty-three thousand units of housing. Churches also got involved in neighborhood preservation efforts, in part to protect their property. In 1974, the Catholic Church, which had massive investments in Bronx churches, schools, and Fordham University, took the lead in establishing the Northwest Bronx Community and Clergy Coalition, which set up neighborhood groups and mobilized the local population to pressure banks, insurance companies, and the city to keep abandonment and community devastation from spreading further northward in the borough.[22]

The most influential church-sponsored housing effort, the Nehemiah Plan, named after the Old Testament prophet who rebuilt Jerusalem, took place in east central Brooklyn. Developer I. D. Robbins, who built the Big Six housing cooperative for the Typographer's union, had long advocated an inner-city version of Levittown, modest single-family homes to be sold to low- and moderate-income families. Robbins argued that costs could be kept down by using standardized plans, efficient building techniques, and essentially worthless vacant land in devastated neighborhoods. His plan went nowhere until the East Brooklyn Churches (EBC), a church alliance formed in 1979, took it up.

The Robbins-EBC plan required considerable outside funding. The seed money came from the religious establishment: the Lutheran Church–Missouri Synod and the Episcopal Diocese each provided one-million-dollar interest-free loans and the Brooklyn Catholic Archdiocese lent five million dollars. Once the churches committed their money, the state and city got on board, offering subsidized mortgages, free land, and loans that made possible the construction of one thousand units of row housing. Another thirteen hundred units followed, allowing working-class families—nearly half living in public housing projects—to buy homes in Brownsville and East New York.[23]

The Nehemiah housing embodied different values than the nonprofit cooperative housing of earlier years. Although the product of community mobilization and substantial government assistance, Nehemiah at least implicitly promoted individual values of discipline and self-sacrifice as roads to betterment, rather than the intense collectivity that underlay the labor co-op movement. Nehemiah rejected the model of multiunit housing, which had long been dominant in working-class New York, believing that individual homes created a greater sense of accountability. It promoted home ownership as a kind of empowerment, a way of breeding responsibility and freedom through financial risk. In this regard, Nehemiah reflected a social conservatism that could be found in many politically active black churches.[24]

While Nehemiah went a long way toward bringing the suburban model of housing to the inner city, the most-publicized government housing effort of the 1980s, Charlotte Gardens, went even further. A massive municipal plan, designed to make Jimmy Carter fulfill his pledge to rebuild the South Bronx, collapsed under the weight of questionable planning, squabbles among city politicians, and doubts about the extent of federal commitment. Eventually, Washington provided money for a much smaller project on the Charlotte Street lot where Carter and later Ronald Reagan stood amid rubble. In constructing attached houses, the Nehemiah Plan retained at least an element of urbanism. By contrast, Charlotte Gardens consisted of ninety-four ranch houses, complete with front lawns and fenced back yards, a surreal enclave of suburbia surrounded by apartment buildings and ruination. As the gentrifying upper class rejected suburban values, government planners for the urban poor saw them as the way to reclaim the country's most notorious urban place.[25]

In 1986, Mayor Koch began an ambitious housing program for poor and working-class neighborhoods, partially in response to criticism that his administration had failed to adequately deal with the growing number of homeless people, insistent reminders of the underside of global New York. Rather than bulldozer redevelopment, in the Moses or Kazan mode, the city put the bulk of its resources into rebuilding thirty-nine thousand units in abandoned or severely deteriorated apartment buildings. The twelve thousand units of city-financed new housing consisted of one-, two-, and three-family houses, in-filled on scattered, vacant, city-owned lots, that were sold to working families.[26]

In effect, the physical design notions of Jane Jacobs, combined with the longstanding national preference for owner-occupancy, to which New York City had stood as an exception, proved triumphant. In many cases, those buying newly-built low- and moderate-income houses fulfilled longstanding dreams. But the number of such homes that church and government efforts provided proved very modest compared to both earlier rates of public and nonprofit housing construction and the demand for decent, low-cost shelter. Furthermore, the largely self-contained Nehemiah and Charlotte Gardens projects did little to upgrade conditions in the surrounding communities. One housing expert concluded in 1987 that "the resources required to meet New York City's housing needs exceed by far the amounts currently spent or planned for in the future."[27]

As economic polarization transformed New York, socially and physically, so did immigration. Following passage of the 1965 Hart Cellar Act, which loosened immigration restrictions, the number of foreigners moving to the city increased steadily. New York's officially-recorded foreign-born population rose from 1.4 million in 1970 (18 percent of the population) to 1.7 million in 1980, and 2.1 million in 1990 (28 percent of the population). Including undocumented immigrants—who numbered in the hundreds of thousands—by the latter year the foreign-born probably neared a third of New York's population, still below the proportion during the first decades of the century but high by post–World War II standards.[28]

Immigration reversed New York's population decline. During the 1980s the city gained a quarter of a million residents. Until the early 1960s, most immigrants had come from Europe. The Hart Cellar Act, however, ended the racist prejudices built into immigration law, eliminating special bars against Asians and distributing quota slots evenly, rather than assigning the bulk to Western Europe. Meanwhile, the globalization of the world economy, the spread of American culture via movies, radio, and television, and declining transportation costs made temporary or permanent relocation to the United States attractive and feasible to groups for whom it was once unthought of.[29] Between 1983 and 1989, the nations from which the largest number of immigrants moved to New York were the Dominican Republic, Jamaica, China, Guyana, and Haiti, in that order. Other groups that heavily emigrated to the city after 1965 included Greeks, Italians, Colombians, Ecuadorians, Indians, Koreans, Irish, and Soviet Jews. In 1990, New York had eighty foreign-language and ethnic newspapers, including twenty-two dailies, half of which had been founded during the previous two decades.[30]

Immigrants coming after 1965 differed from their predecessors in economic status as well as country of origin. Prior to World War II, virtually all immigrants were working-class. Most post-1965 arrivals were, too, but a substantial minority consisted of professionals and technicians, contributing to a wide range in income and living standards among New York's newcomers. Koreans, many of whom came from middle-class backgrounds, had a median family income not much below the citywide figure. Jamaicans earned less, but still exceeded the median family income of native-born black New Yorkers, benefiting from a high level of female work force participation and facility in English. Dominicans, by contrast, had a median family income significantly below that of native-born blacks, and a poverty rate significantly above them.

Most new immigrants worked in manufacturing, service, or construction jobs. The garment, health care, and hotel and restaurant industries all made extensive use of immigrant labor. Some immigrant-held jobs required considerable skill—a third of West Indian women workers, for instance, were nurses or nurse's aides—but most did not. The most vulnerable immigrants depended on casual labor markets, like the Eastern European and South and Central American men, many in the country illegally, who congregated on street corners and in parking lots in Brooklyn and Queens hoping for a day's work in demolition, landscaping, or construction.[31]

A score of neighborhoods were transformed by immigration. Crown Heights and Flatbush developed as centers for Afro-Caribbeans. Flushing emerged as the city's second Chinatown, as well as a home to Japanese, Korean, Indian, and Pakistani communities. Sunset Park revived as Hispanic and Asian immigrants, along with some white professionals, moved in.[32]

In some neighborhoods, one nationality dominated. Nearly a third of the Dominicans who emigrated to New York during the mid and late 1980s settled in Washington Heights or Inwood, replacing and displacing the diminishing Irish community. By the end of the decade, Dominicans set the ambience of upper Manhattan. Most Dominican New Yorkers worked at low-skilled jobs, with an exceptionally large proportion—over a quarter—employed in manufacturing, leaving them vulnerable to that sector's continuing decay. At the same time, an entrepreneurial stratum emerged, as Dominicans supplanted Puerto Ricans as the leading owners of bodegas, car services, travel agencies, and music stores serving the Hispanic community. Even in non-Hispanic neighborhoods, Dominican-owned food stores helped fill the void created by the decision of the national supermarket chains to stop servicing inner-city neighborhoods. Dominicans also played a major role in the illegal drug trade, with Washington Heights providing an ideal location for servicing customers from New Jersey, who could quickly zip into and out of the neighborhood via the George Washington Bridge.[33]

Immigration utterly transformed the Queens neighborhoods of Jackson Heights, Elmhurst, and Corona, making them among the liveliest and most ethnically heterogeneous in the country. By the time of the Hart Cellar Act, the German, Irish, Italian, Jewish, and Polish working- and lower-middle-class apartment dwellers and homeowners who had long inhabited the area had aged. Many of their children had moved to Long Island or elsewhere outside the city. Streets and stores had grown dingy. Cutbacks in city services during the fiscal crisis further diminished the quality of life.

After 1965, a growing stream of newcomers, from Colombia, Argentina, Ecuador, Peru, Cuba, the Dominican Republic, China, the Philippines, Japan, Korea, Haiti, Pakistan, and India, brought a teeming vibrancy and new generation of young people to the area. By 1980, the Latin American population of Elmhurst-Corona outnumbered the native white population. Ten years later, so did the Asian population. Along Roosevelt Avenue in Jackson Heights, Indian, Korean, Argentine, and Colombian restaurants sprang up, sharing the streets with "telefonereas" offering discount telephone calls to Asia and South America and grocery stores selling produce most Americans would have had difficulty identifying. Periodically, neighborhood lampposts got covered with posters for candidates running for office in Colombia or the Dominican Republic.[34]

Immigration pushed the typical New York neighborhood toward greater ethnic and racial diversity. In 1990 significantly fewer New Yorkers lived in racially homogeneous areas and significantly more in places characterized by some mixture of whites, blacks, Asians, and Hispanics than twenty years earlier. There was, however, an important "cross-cutting trend," the growth of neighborhoods occupied exclusively by blacks and/or Hispanics. Over half the African-Americans in Elmhurst-Corona, for example, lived in a single, large, heavily-black apartment complex, Lefrak City.[35]

All things considered, the city absorbed the surge of post-1965 immigration with remarkably little strife. In the long run, immigration meant an infusion of cultural and political vitality to working-class New York. In the short run, though, it further fragmented it. Typically, during their first years in the country, newcomers stayed out of local (as opposed to home-country) politics and rarely got involved with institutions other than the schools that transcended their own national or ethnic group. Instead, they directed their organizational energy toward building cross-class fraternal, cultural, and religious entities within their national communities.[36]

Outside of immigrant neighborhoods, many New Yorkers did not pay attention to the rapid diversification of the city's population and culture. Partially, this reflected the indifference of the media. But it also reflected the intensification of an old problem that continued to dog the city, racial conflict.

Race dominated political discourse during the 1980s, pushed to the forefront by a series of horrifying incidents of interracial violence, which became the occasion for extensive, sensational media coverage and angry protests and counterprotests.[37] Whites and blacks seemed locked in a discourse that, in a perverse way, kept them in a dominant cultural and political position even as their demographic importance declined. Between 1980 and 1990, non-Hispanic whites went from a majority of the city population — 52 percent — to a minority of 43 percent. Though the native-born, non-Hispanic black population grew modestly, together native-born whites and blacks dropped from 70 percent of the population to 63 percent. Yet even as the city moved away from its postwar demography, in which whites, native-born blacks, and Puerto Ricans made up the vast majority of the population, most immigrant groups received little media attention and had little political clout.[38]

Politicians and media-made celebrities worked, with differing degrees of self-consciousness, to maintain a bipolar (black-white) or tripolar (black-white-Hispanic) construction of New York politics and race relations. As mayor, Ed Koch relished taking on liberal taboos about race, denouncing black leaders, closing a Harlem municipal hospital (Sydenham) which provided poor health care but had great historic importance to the black community, and releasing an interview in which he said "blacks are anti-semites." Koch made little effort to court the native black vote (though he did woo Caribbeans), counting on white and Hispanic support for reelection. The mayor's race talk allowed him to maintain the backing of many white working-class voters who had liberal economic ideas but feared the city's black populace, even as Koch himself moved to the right, allying with the real estate and securities industries and overseeing a city of growing economic inequality.[39]

Koch found perfect collaborators for upping the heat of race relations in a small group of freelance activists, including Al Sharpton, Alton Maddox, Vernon Mason, and Sonny Carson, who capitalized on incidents of racial violence to project themselves as leaders of black New York. During the late 1980s, when white Jewish men held nine of the eleven votes on the city's Board of Estimate in an extraordinary mismatch with the population makeup, the activists' sharp nationalist rhetoric—much of it aimed at Koch—won them extensive media attention and considerable support among blacks, including those skeptical of their claims but admiring of their feisty stance toward white authority. Operating with little institutional base, the "professional provocateurs," as one historian dubbed them, managed to partially displace the mainstream black political leadership in the public eye, as the latter's ineptitude, factional squabbles, and tense relationships with Hispanic politicians undermined efforts to depose Koch or construct countervailing power.[40]

As the 1980s drew to a close, Tom Wolfe's best-selling novel, *The Bonfire of the Vanities*, became the most talked about New York book in a generation. With dark humor, Wolfe chronicled the chasm between the rich and everyone else; the city's cult of celebrity; its racial tension; the desolation of huge swaths of New York; the victims and criminals of the lower class; and the unclothed greed of Wall Street, which set the moral tone for the metropolis and the decade. Almost completely missing were ordinary working people. The closest Wolfe came were the mother of the victim around which his plot revolves and the detectives and court officers he portrayed unflatteringly, "*brutes* from the outer boroughs" in the mind of the novel's bond-broker protagonist.[41]

Wolfe caught New York in the 1980s, and missed it. Most of the city's population lived between the social extremes of the Upper East Side and the South Bronx. The city's working class had changed, become more fragmented and less visible, and wielded less influence than in the past. But it had not disappeared. Nor had the labor movement, which during the 1980s and 1990s struggled to recapture the centrality it once had had in the politics, economy, and social life of New York.

CHAPTER 17.

Hanging On

The globalization of New York—part fact, part fiction—seemed to leave organized labor behind, an atavism of a time, rapidly receding into the past, when factories and warehouses, deep-sea docks and great railroad yards served as the armature for city life. The vast flows of people and money, coming into and out of the city by jet plane and wire transfer, made local struggles of this or that group of workers seem parochial and puny. Yet even in the adverse circumstances of the 1980s, organized labor displayed a surprising durability in New York, particularly compared to elsewhere. But labor's victories tended to be defensive. By the 1990s, working-class New Yorkers, while by no means bereft of power, were no longer the major force they once had been in setting the trajectory of the city.

On September 7, 1981, some 200,000 New Yorkers marched in the city's first Labor Day parade in thirteen years. In reviving this ninety-nine-year-old tradition, the Central Labor Council recognized how much labor's standing had slipped. Labor leaders sought to reconnect with a past when working people thought of themselves as a distinct class that annually showed its colors.

Dusting off the parade was part of an effort by the union movement nationally to wake itself up. The alarm clock was Ronald Reagan's firing of over twelve thousand striking air traffic controllers in early August 1981, a signal to business that the shibboleths of postwar industrial relations no longer held sway. In response, the AFL-CIO called for a "Solidarity Day" demonstration in Washington in mid-September, which ended up being one of the largest gatherings that city had ever seen. New York's Labor Day parade served as a preview of the Washington demonstration and its local equivalent, a display of power to friends, enemies, and members alike.

Measured by numbers, spirit, and organization, the parade proved a great success. Four thousand air traffic controllers led a seven-hour procession up Fifth Avenue. (To blunt the parade's impact, President Reagan flew to New York that day to deliver an eighty-five million dollar check to Mayor Koch for construction of the Westway highway project.) In a tradition harking back to the very first labor demonstrations, union delegations displayed symbols, tools, and products of their trade. The electricians showed off multicolored blinking signs, building trades workers brought heavy construction equipment, and the Transport Workers drove two New York City buses. Typesetters wore aprons, nurses white uniforms, and teachers mortarboards. Bands, floats, mimes, and clowns created a festive air.[1]

Traditionally the mayor marched at the front of the Labor Day parade, but in 1981 that honor went to Democratic state assemblyman Frank Barbaro, who was challenging Ed Koch in the upcoming election. The Central Labor Council's decision to back Barbaro's candidacy constituted another effort to reinject itself into the center of New York life. Barbaro disrupted what otherwise might have been an unopposed recoronation of the mayor. Koch, fearing a possible challenge from disenchanted liberals, was running in the 1981 Republican primary as well as the Democratic contest. Barbaro's Democratic primary race represented the one serious effort to deny Koch reelection by acclamation.

Frank Barbaro came out of the labor left. As a young man he campaigned for Henry Wallace. During fifteen years as a longshoreman, he opposed the mob-dominated leadership of his union. While still on the docks, he attended law school at night. Active in his Bensonhurst neighborhood as an opponent of the war in Vietnam and a tenant organizer, in 1972 he successfully ran for the state assembly. In Albany, he fought the Democratic leadership until a compromise won him the chairmanship of the Assembly Labor Committee.

For the aging Harry Van Arsdale, Jr., supporting Barbaro represented a final effort to harness the energy of the left on behalf of mainstream labor, much as he had, years earlier, in backing Local 1199's hospital organizing drive. Barbaro's key advisers came out of the old Popular Front, like Henry Foner, who headed what remained of the furriers' union, and Lou Gordon, a Spanish Civil War veteran who led a Brooklyn-based paperworkers local. Koch's hostility to organized labor allowed Barbaro to win the backing of many unions that normally would be uncomfortable with someone of his ilk.

Though they had grown weaker in other respects, New York unions had as much or more clout than ever in the electoral arena. For one thing, at a time of falling voter turnout they could mobilize their own members to go to the polls, a significant boost for candidates those members favored. (Unions had greater success in getting people to vote than in telling them who to vote for.) For another thing, in an era when political clubs had atrophied, unions— with their large staffs, fleets of volunteers, phone banks, print shops, and other resources—had a greater capacity for mounting electoral field operations than any other local institutions, filling a role played by the Christian right elsewhere in the county.

Barbaro's mayoral quest had serious problems. Little known outside the labor movement and his neighborhood, the media ignored him, while Koch's every doing got massive coverage. With little money (union backing for him went only so far), Barbaro could not use advertising to get out his pro-tenant, antiracist message, while Koch had a large war chest, raised from real estate developers, investment bankers, and lawyers. Barbaro failed to win the backing of white, liberal political activists outside the labor movement, and even within labor his support was far from unanimous; most of the municipal worker unions remained neutral or backed Koch, as did the ILGWU, the longshoremen, and the Operating Engineers.[2]

With Koch an assumed shoo-in, voting in the mayoral primary was the lightest since World War II. Koch won the Republican contest with two-thirds of the vote and captured 60 percent of the Democratic ballots to Barbaro's 36 percent. Koch and most observers hailed this as an extraordinary triumph, but given the mismatch of resources and Barbaro's obscurity, it revealed the mayor's weakness as much as his strength. Even Koch recognized that his defeat by Barbaro (who was white) in every single minority assembly district represented an extraordinary level of disaffection among nonwhite New Yorkers. Though it could not defeat the mayor, labor put on an impressive show.[3]

The Labor Day parade and the Barbaro campaign testified to the continuing institutional strength of New York unionism. No accurate citywide membership figures exist, but in all likelihood at least a million New Yorkers carried a union card during the late 1980s and early 1990s, roughly the same number as forty years earlier. Since 1990 employment only slightly exceeded the earlier level, the proportion of workers who belonged to a union remained about the same, between a quarter and a third. By contrast, the percentage of workers nationally who belonged to a union fell by nearly half between 1950 and 1990, from 31.5 percent to 16.1 percent.[4]

The makeup of the New York labor movement differed markedly in the late 1980s from the immediate postwar years. Manufacturing unions no longer held the dominant position they once had. From World War II through the mid-1960s, the ILGWU had been the largest union in the city, with a local membership that peaked near 200,000. By 1989, it had shrunk to 70,000 members. Meanwhile, AFSCME had taken its place as the city's largest union, with D. C. 37 alone claiming 120,000 members, emblematic of the dramatic growth of unions representing public employees.[5] In the metropolitan region, two out of three public-sector workers (in 1988) belonged to a union, compared to one out of five workers in the private sector.[6] New York unionism's sustained density, even as union strength plunged elsewhere, reflected this success in signing up government workers along with continuing high membership in transportation, construction, and utilities, and some important gains in the service sector, especially among health care workers.

Sheer numbers, however, overstate the degree of working-class self-organization. Though most unions made serving their members their primary goal, corruption and mob influence turned some into organizations devoted above all else to enriching their leaders or outsiders who effectively controlled them. The measures that the labor movement and the federal government took in the 1950s to attack corruption—most notably the establishment of the AFL-CIO Ethical Practices Committee and the passage of the Landrum-Griffin Act, which provided union members with a bill of rights—seemed irrelevant to the day-to-day practices of New York labor. For long stretches of time, leading unionists, businessmen, and government officials willed themselves blind to union corruption and illegality. In the late 1980s and 1990s, a series of investigations by law enforcement agencies exposed gross corruption, criminality, and autocracy in a whole series of New York unions. The hard, violent side of working-class New York had not disappeared.

The building trades had the most serious problems, a result of a long-standing, systematic effort by organized crime to infiltrate them. Gangsters used construction unions to make money in a variety of ways. They took payments from employers in return for guaranteeing labor peace or allowing violations of union contracts. They bilked money from employee benefit funds. And union control facilitated bid-rigging schemes that benefited mob-controlled contractors. When threatened by rank-and-file opponents or mob rivals, gangsters unleashed extreme violence.[7]

District Council 9 of the Painters Union provides a case in point. In the late 1970s, when dissident union members charged council secretary-treasurer Jimmy Bishop with mismanaging union funds, the international union appointed a trustee over him. Seeking to win back his autonomy, Bishop approached the Luchese crime family for help, arranging for the trustee to be beaten at union headquarters so badly that he spent three months in the hospital. Back in charge, Bishop became a member of the executive board of the Central Labor Council and president of the Metal

Trades District Council, and chaired the Labor Day parade two years in a row. Meanwhile, the Luchese family began receiving payoffs from the union. By one account, the mob took a rakeoff of nearly 10 percent on large union painting contracts. Employers who paid kickbacks got labor peace, were allowed to hire nonunion workers at subunion wages, and could make reduced welfare fund payments.

A shift of power within the Luchese family led to Bishop's undoing. In 1989 mob threats led him to resign. Embittered, he began talking to the Manhattan District Attorney's office. In May 1990, after word of his cooperation got out, mobsters killed him outside the Queens apartment complex where his mistress lived. Six weeks later, two contractors and nine district council officials, including Bishop's successor, were indicted on bribery and extortion charges. Ten of the eleven pled guilty.[8]

The Mason Tenders, Cement and Concrete Workers, Carpenters, Laborers, and the Teamsters local which had jurisdiction over construction supply deliveries also had serious problems with corruption and mob control.[9] Some unions in other industries experienced similar difficulties. A federal sting operation caught officials of ILGWU Local 10 asking for bribes in return for looking the other way at the use of nonunion workers who were paid low salaries and given no benefits. Hotel and Restaurant Employees Local 100 president Anthony R. Amodeo Sr. took payoffs from restaurant owners in return for allowing them to reduce wages and skip health and pension fund payments for waiters, busboys, and other workers. As was often the case, internal autocracy accompanied corruption; the federal government charged Amodeo with rigging union elections, threatening violence against complaining union members, and hiring relatives for union posts. In yet another case, the Manhattan District Attorney documented extensive racketeering by members of the Newspaper and Mail Deliverers Union, including the systematic theft of newspapers and magazines.[10]

While corruption and mob infiltration weakened particular unions, internal divisions weakened the movement as a whole. The death of Harry Van Arsdale, Jr., in February 1986, became the occasion for a public display of personal animosity, institutional rivalry, and ideological disagreements among the city's labor leaders. The previous summer, as Van Arsdale's health began failing, he temporarily stepped down as head of the Central Labor Council, allowing his son, Thomas Van Arsdale, a colorless IBEW Local 3 business agent, to assume the acting presidency. The elder Van Arsdale's death set off a contest to permanently succeed him between his son and D.C. 37's Victor Gotbaum.[11]

Cosmopolitan in his outlook and grand in his ambitions, Gotbaum long had been restless for broader horizons. In 1979 he launched an unsuccessful effort to oust Jerry Wurf as AFSCME's international president. He found some satisfaction in his later election to the presidency of Public Service International, a worldwide federation of public-sector unions, but that post rotated after one term.[12] Gotbaum already had announced his plan to retire from D.C. 37 when Van Arsdale died.

The opening at the Central Labor Council seemed a godsend for Gotbaum and an opportunity for the city's labor movement to gain a highly prominent, articulate spokesperson. But the younger Van Arsdale, unknown except among electricians and labor insiders, would not step aside for the abrasive Gotbaum, who over the years had rubbed many unionists the wrong way. The result was a rare public showdown, a contested election for the Labor Council presidency.

Ideological differences played a role in the Gotbaum–Van Arsdale contest; Gotbaum opposed Reagan-era U.S. foreign policy, while Van Arsdale lined up with AFL-CIO president Lane Kirkland in supporting it. But the election also revealed the importance of personal, often petty issues to New York's labor leadership. The private-sector unions generally supported Van Arsdale, with some exceptions. The public-employee unions generally supported Gotbaum, but key defections cost him the election: the Teachers, Postal Workers Metro Branch, and public-employee locals of the Communications Workers supported Van Arsdale, apparently because of their leaders' rivalries with Gotbaum over the years. Furthermore, some unions that seemed on ideological grounds natural backers of Gotbaum, most notably 1199, surprised him by backing Van Arsdale. Equally costly, several unions backing Gotbaum, including District 65 and some locals of D.C. 37, failed to pay their back dues to the Central Labor Council, making them ineligible to participate in the election, an extraordinary act of incompetence by the Gotbaum camp.[13]

The election outcome suggested that a majority of union leaders preferred a fragmented movement, in which individual unions went their own way, to a more active, more public, more central leadership like Gotbaum promised. In spite of the decline of labor's fortunes, a majority of unions voted against rocking the boat. Which is what they got; for a decade under Thomas Van Arsdale, the Central Labor Council remained a passive, ineffective, low-profile organization, playing little significant role in the life of the city.[14]

Along with ideological disagreements and personal feuding, racial and ethnic change undermined labor unity. Some unions did reach out to new immigrant groups. A 1982 strike by garment workers in Chinatown, directed against Chinese-owned factories, accelerated ILGWU efforts to organize Chinese workers, prodded by a new generation of Asian-American activists. In 1990 the union set up a Garment Workers Justice Center in Sunset Park, where many Chinese garment workers lived, offering English lessons and workshops on immigration rights, domestic violence, and welfare reform. As an increasing number of Asians began taking jobs with the city government as engineers, architects, and planners, AFSCME Local 375, which represented them, began sponsoring celebrations of Diwali, a Hindu festival, and Chinese New Year, along with its established celebrations of Jewish and Hispanic Heritage months. Most unions, however, only slowly responded the remaking the New York's workforce, making it difficult for them to convincingly speak for the working class as a whole.[15] More positively, many unions did belatedly open up top offices to African-Americans and Puerto Ricans. In the 1980s, a cohort of nonwhite labor leaders emerged, as African-Americans and Hispanics assumed posts that had a substantial impact on the economic and political life of the city.

Among the city's major labor groups, D.C. 37 provided a model of racial harmony, or at least peaceful coexistence. With a membership highly heterogenous in racial and ethnic background, type of work, skill level, and income, the union's survival depended on sensitivity to internal diversity and the creation of broad solidarity. Anticipating an increasingly African-American membership, Victor Gotbaum decided early on that his successor should be black. Lillian Roberts long appeared to be the heir apparent, but when she got caught up in a nasty internal union battle her prospects ended. Governor Hugh Carey provided Roberts with a graceful way out, appointing her head of the state Labor Department. To replace her as associate director, Gotbaum chose black staffer Stanley Hill. When Gotbaum retired at the end of 1986, the D.C. 37 executive board elected Hill without opposition to succeed him. As head of the city's largest union, Hill immediately became one of New York's most prominent African-American leaders.[16]

Hill grew up on the predominantly white Lower East Side, developing, as a survival strategy, a conciliatory style he unabashedly displayed as a labor leader. Attending heavily white Iona College on a basketball scholarship,

Hill, like his childhood hero, Jackie Robinson, found himself at the center of a racial sports drama. In December 1956, the University of Mississippi basketball team walked out of the All-American City tournament in Owensboro, Kentucky, because its opponent, Iona, had a black player, Stan Hill.

A knee injury ended Hill's dream of pro ball. After graduating college he went to work for the Department of Welfare, rising to a supervisory position. Meanwhile, he became active in the Social Service Employees Union, taking part in the 1965 and 1967 welfare strikes. After SSEU and D.C. 37's Local 371 merged, the combined group elected Hill its president. In 1972, following a lost bid for reelection, Hill went on D.C. 37 staff.

A product, through and through, of working-class New York (his father was a truck driver and mechanic), Hill had plebeian tastes. Gotbaum owned a townhouse in Brooklyn Heights and relaxed at a second home in eastern Long Island. Teamsters Local 237 president Barry Feinstein lived on a rural estate north of New York, with an apartment in the city. (His use of union funds to maintain a lavish lifestyle ultimately led federal officials to force him to resign.) Hill, by contrast, lived in Rochdale Village, the labor-sponsored cooperative in southern Queens, where he moved with his wife, a college secretary, in 1965 and remained even when as executive director of D.C. 37 he received a quarter-of-a-million dollars a year.[17]

Hill had an instinctual sympathy for the left. But at times he acted as if his most important achievement was winning a seat at the table where decisions about city labor relations and Democratic politics were made. Once there, he seemed reluctant to launch all-out battles. In his own institution, Hill deferred to the leaders of the large affiliated locals, looking the other way as a culture of financial self-serving developed. In 1998, in the face of revelations of kickbacks from vendors, embezzlement, and vote rigging, D.C. 37's parent union, AFSCME, placed it in trusteeship, leading to Hill's retirement.

Hill's smooth ascension and political moderation masked the significance of his rise. As head of D.C. 37, he became one of the few black New Yorkers to lead a major, racially-integrated institution, one of a handful of African-Americans outside of electoral politics with whom local, state, and even national political leaders had to deal. (Among his many positions, Hill sat on the Democratic Party national committee). Within his union, he did not stand alone; during the 1980s and 1990s, throughout D.C. 37, African-Americans, and to a lesser extent Hispanics, moved into positions of power.[18]

Health and Hospital Workers District 1199 also went through a process of generational and ethnic leadership change during the 1980s, but it went horribly awry, nearly destroying the union. 1199 president Leon Davis had long recognized the need for African-American leadership in his union. In the 1960s, he began grooming two black, rank-and-file recruits. Henry Nicholas, an orderly at Mt. Sinai hospital, eventually organized and headed a ten-thousand-member Philadelphia branch of the union. Doris Turner, a dietician at Lenox Hill Hospital, became head of the union's New York hospital division.

Although they saw the need for change, Davis and other veteran, white, leftist 1199 leaders proved reluctant to give up power. Davis later rued that he underestimated "the frustration that blacks had for the role of leadership . . . . for actual control."[19] Only when Davis's health deteriorated in the late 1970s did union officials finally address succession. Then they made two decisions that proved disastrous. First, they split Davis's jobs as head of the national union and of its New York district between Nicholas and Turner. Second, they negotiated a plan for 1199 and the union with which it was loosely affiliated, the Retail, Wholesale, and Department Store Workers Union (RWDSU), to merge with the Service Employees International Union (SEIU), a much larger group that also organized health care workers. The merger would have brought together the country's two largest health care unions and provided a financial and institutional base for an invigorated national organizing drive. But in the eyes of Turner and many others, it seemed that the old guard had decided, just at the long-awaited moment when African-Americans assumed the leadership of 1199, to submerge it in a white-led institution.

The succession process literally split 1199 apart. Allying herself with the president of the RWDSU, Turner succeeded in blocking the SEIU merger. In the process, her relationships with Davis and Nicholas—who supported the merger—became irreparably damaged. After intense battling, the Turner and Nicholas camps agreed to go their separate ways, with the New York district of 1199 remaining in RWDSU, while 1199 elsewhere became a new, AFL-CIO chartered union.

In New York, the fight continued. To consolidate her power, Turner forced dozens of staffers and officers out of their jobs. Simultaneously, she moved the union away from its longstanding leftism, secularism, and multiculturalism. She encouraged Bible reading among the staff, started a gospel chorus, argued against abortion and for capital punishment, and distanced the union from left-wing causes.[20]

Turner's course reflected personal beliefs and resentments to which Davis and other longtime colleagues had been oblivious. But it also reflected the changed economic and political environment in which the union functioned. The child of a left-liberal polity, when Jews and blacks joined together for civil rights and progressive change, by the time of Davis's retirement 1199 operated in a city and nation in which liberalism was in decline, Jewish-black relations strained, and racial conflict rife. The recession of the early 1980s hit African-Americans especially hard. Unemployment soared and business became increasingly antiunion, while in the labor movement top-level black leaders remained rare. Under those circumstances, some African-American activists saw their best course as continuing to promote interracialism and strengthening ties to mainstream labor. Henry Nicholas and Turner's critics in New York embraced that course, as did Stan Hill at D.C. 37. Turner and some others, like James Butler, head of AFSCME Local 420, which represented municipal hospital workers, took a more a parochial path, aimed at preserving hard-won power bases. While cutting pragmatic deals with white leaders, they reached out to groups in the black community not traditionally linked to labor and used race pride and calls for racial solidarity to maintain internal support.[21]

Turner might have maintained power if she had not been so arrogant, and if hospital managers had not seen in the 1199 turmoil an opportunity to regain power that they had lost to the union. In April 1984, Turner and her supporters stuffed the ballot boxes in order to avoid a runoff in an election she would have won anyway. Soon thereafter, with little membership preparation, the local called a strike against the voluntary hospitals. The hospitals stood tough. In some, new labor relations managers, rejecting the existing balance of power and no doubt influenced by the national antiunion climate, already had begun playing hardball with the union. Hospital executives saw the strike as a golden opportunity to cut 1199 down to size. "There was a dawning realization," one labor relations official recalled, "that we could maybe change the whole show, that we could run the hospital without them." Unable to find a politically acceptable way to end the strike, Turner let it go on and on. Finally, after forty-seven days, she settled on terms the hospitals had offered much earlier, a 10 percent wage increase over two years and improved benefits in return for a package of givebacks to be agreed upon by the union. At a highly-charged Madison Square Garden meeting, Turner denied that she had agreed to givebacks and failed to tell union members that no actual contract existed, only a memorandum of agreement.

Once the strike ended, the roof fell in on Turner's head. The hospitals refused to give workers their pay increase until Turner designated givebacks, which she refused to do. Meanwhile, one of her closest aides, disgusted with her performance, went to federal authorities with a detailed account of the election fraud. As the Department of Labor pressed an investigation of the election and U.S. Attorney Rudolph Giuliani began looking into charges of financial irregularities at the union, Turner agreed to an election rerun. A multiracial "Save Our Union" coalition mounted a vigorous campaign against the Turner forces. In April 1986, Georgianna Johnson, a black social work assistant, defeated Turner by 18,972 votes to 16,039.[22]

The Save Our Union coalition, an amalgam of Communists (at this late date New York City might have been the only place in the country where Communist Party members could influence the internal life of a union), noncommunist leftists, and longtime militants, repeated the mistakes of the Davis leadership in its dealings with Johnson. Johnson had been chosen as the coalition standard-bearer to counter the advantages Turner's race and gender gave her, since black women made up the largest demographic bloc within 1199. No one expected Johnson to actually run the union. But once in power, she grew tired of being a figurehead.

Lacking a base of her own, Johnson found allies in two quarters, RWDSU president Lenore Miller and, ironically, Doris Turner. Like Turner, Johnson came to see the union's factional fighting in racial and gender terms, as an effort by white men to control a union made up largely of black women. Once again 1199 found itself in a demoralizing round of election battles, lawsuits, race-baiting, and brawling. Finally, in a membership referendum, the anti-Johnson group managed to just barely put through a series of structural reforms.

After that, the battle ended. Miller cut a deal with the anti-Johnson executive board, leading Johnson to bitterly complain, "She abandoned me like all the other whites." In 1989, executive vice president Dennis Rivera challenged Johnson for the union presidency. With the incumbent barely campaigning, Rivera swept into office by a nine-to-one margin.[23]

In his own way, Rivera represented a second coming of Leon Davis–style left labor leadership. Ironically, Rivera's parents met because of antiunionism; his father, an Irish-American from upstate New York, had been sent to Puerto Rico to find a low-wage site for a women's underwear factory, where it would be safe from unionization. In the small town of Aibonito he built the factory and married the innkeeper's daughter. Their oldest son,

Dennis, as a student in San Juan, got swept up in opposition to the war in Vietnam, campus radicalism, and the Puerto Rican independence movement. Quitting college, he worked for a series of left-wing Puerto Rican unions before moving to New York in 1977, where he landed a job as an 1199 organizer.

Though Rivera lacked the oratorical power and personal charisma of Davis and Turner, as head of 1199 he quickly emerged as New York's most dynamic, surefooted, and media-loved labor leader. Like Davis, he combined an idealistic aura and left-inclination with tactical flexibility and political pragmatism. Almost immediately after his election, he helped orchestrate a brilliant campaign of publicity and short strikes that won 1199 a first-rate hospital contract, in spite of the union's still weakened state. Critical to Rivera's success was an alliance he forged with the city's socially conservative, pro-union cardinal, John O'Connor, who controlled many Catholic-run hospitals and nursing homes. With a new contract in hand, Rivera became a power in New York Democratic politics and one of the nation's most prominent Hispanic unionists.[24]

The ascension of Stan Hill and Dennis Rivera brought the leadership of two of the city's largest and most influential unions in line with the increasingly black and Hispanic workforce in government and service jobs. For all the difficulties of racial and generational succession, in many respects the service and public-sector unions that arose in the postwar years better accommodated membership change than the manufacturing unions they displaced at the forefront of New York labor. By the mid-1990s, D.C. 37, 1199, TWU Local 100, and Teamsters Local 237 all had African-American or Hispanic heads. The garment unions, by contrast, decades after going from predominantly Jewish and Italian to heavily black, Hispanic, and Asian memberships, still had white leaders.

In one respect, though, the public-sector and service unions reproduced the record of the garment unions: men held a monopoly on the top positions even when women made up the bulk of the membership. The failure of heirs apparent Lillian Roberts in D.C. 37 and Doris Turner and Georgianna Johnson in 1199 to achieve or maintain top office exemplified the greater difficulties women faced in seeking union leadership than men. By the 1980s and 1990s, many women held important jobs in the New York labor movement, but they tended to be clustered in support areas, such as benefits, education, and public relations, or in mid-level membership service posts. At the very highest levels, they were few and far between. Sandra Feldman, who succeeded Albert Shanker as the head of the UFT, was the only woman leading a major New York union during the 1990s, even though women made up a majority of the members of many substantial groups, including 1199, D.C. 37, and the ILGWU.[25]

As the Reagan-Bush years came to a close, two major events signaled how robust organized labor remained in New York compared to the rest of the country, though weakened compared to its own past. One involved the political arena, a mayoral election, the other the industrial realm, a bitter strike at the *Daily News*.

In 1989, organized labor made possible the election of New York's first African-American mayor, David Dinkins. A confluence of factors undermined Ed Koch's bid for an unprecedented fourth term. Early in his third term, massive corruption in his administration by the Democratic bosses with whom he had allied became exposed. At the same time, Koch's general insensitivity toward minorities took its political toll. At a time when horrific incidents of racial violence came at regular drumbeats, the mayor inflamed race relations with his blistering rhetoric, such as a 1988 declaration that Jews and supporters of Israel "would have to be crazy" to vote for Jesse Jackson.

In his ongoing attacks on black leaders, Koch proved out of touch with the city. Many New Yorkers of all races sought an end to racial polarization, something Koch could not plausibly offer. Meanwhile, African-Americans gained electoral clout because of demographic changes and a major voter registration increase stimulated by Jackson's 1984 and 1988 presidential campaigns.[26]

David Dinkins proved an ideal candidate for taking on Koch. A product of the Harlem Democratic Party and a lifelong political regular, he could count on support from significant elements of what remained of the Democratic machine as well as from white liberals and the black community. His personal dignity, political moderation, and lifelong commitment to interracialism and Israel convinced many whites and Latinos that he would be even-handed and bring to New York a level of social harmony that it sorely lacked.

Still, Dinkins faced an uphill battle in a city where whites held most major public offices. His modest record of achievement in past posts and questions about his personal finances did not help. Labor gave him the edge he needed. With the Democratic Party in disarray, unions provided Dinkins with money, organizational resources, and volunteers.

The enthusiastic support Dinkins won from important New York unions reflected both the changing makeup of the labor movement and its disgust with the incumbent mayor. For black unionists like Stanley Hill, the Dinkins campaign took on the air of a crusade, driven by race pride as well as institutional interests. But white unionists proved at least as important to Dinkins. His endorsement by the city's most visible Jewish labor leaders, Sandra Feldman and Barry Feinstein, proved particularly important in keeping Jewish Democrats who had not supported Dinkins in the primary from defecting to the Republican candidate, Rudolph Giuliani, in the general election. Dinkins's campaign manager, Bill Lynch, a former union organizer, made full use of labor's resources and social movement–style mass mobilization. It made all the difference; after beating Koch handily in the primary, Dinkins's superior get-out-the-vote operation gave him his victory over Giuliani in the closest mayoral election in the city's history.[27]

Less than a year after Dinkins took office, the most important New York strike in over a decade broke out at the *Daily News*. At first, the clash seemed to fit a new national pattern, in which determined company managers provoked or weathered strikes by seemingly powerful unions, using careful preparations and replacement workers to force striking employees to sue for surrender or deunionize. Labor's loss of a series of widely publicized walkouts—the 1981 air traffic controllers strike, the Phelps Dodge and Continental Airlines strikes in 1983, and strikes against the Hormel meatpacking plant in Austin, Minnesota, in 1985, International Paper in 1987, and Eastern Airlines in 1989—set the cadence for what seemed organized labor's march toward marginality or demise.[28]

The parent of the *Daily News*, the Tribune Company, helped lead the corporate turn toward union-busting. In 1985 it used replacement workers to defeat a strike by printers, pressmen, and mailers at its flagship paper, the *Chicago Tribune*. Only after the walkout had dragged on for three years, during which time the paper continued to publish, introduced new technology, eliminated four hundred jobs, and committed numerous labor law violations, did it settle with the strikers. With that victory under its belt, the company turned to New York, where it hoped to apply the same formula to the *Daily News*, which in spite of massive circulation was losing tens of millions of dollars a year.

Well before the labor contracts at the *News* expired on March 31, 1990, management began preparing for a showdown, hiring a notorious antiunion law firm, stationing armed guards at its printing plants, training managers and replacement workers at off-site shadow facilities, and demanding that its unions grant it the unilateral right to determine staffing levels, schedules, work assignments, overtime, and layoffs. Many observers felt that the paper sought a strike, either to bust its unions, paving the way for huge cost reductions (one report indicated that the *News* hoped to eliminate 1,000 of its 2,800 jobs), or as an excuse to close the paper without having to meet all its severance and pension obligations.

The *Daily News* unions, having seen what happened elsewhere, tried to avoid a strike when their contracts expired, continuing to work for seven months without new agreements. But in an atmosphere of growing tension, an early morning incident on October 25, 1990, at the *News*'s Brooklyn printing plant set off a walkout. A supervisor suspended a member of the newspaper drivers union, assigned to a bundling machine while recovering from a knee injury, for refusing to work standing up. When some thirty of his colleagues gathered outside the building, management would not let them back in, leading another 230 workers to leave the plant. Within an hour, the *News* tried to bus in replacement workers, only to have them stopped by milling unionists. By dawn, four delivery trucks had been firebombed. When the paper fired sixty drivers and announced it had hired permanent replacements for them, the drivers union declared itself on strike, followed in short order by seven other unions and, after some hesitation, by the Newspaper Guild, which represented reporters and other white-collar workers.[29]

Amazingly, given the long buildup to the strike, the unions initially seemed befuddled, lacking a coherent strategy. Many reporters and photographers, the only strikers the *News* courted, had deep doubts about the walkout, feeling little identification with the drivers, whom some considered featherbedding roughnecks, and believing that they had been trapped into a conflict they had little chance of winning. The *News* management, using replacement workers and staff from other newspapers owned by its parent, managed to put out a slimmer-than-normal paper in a reduced press run, which frightened and demoralized the strikers, especially members of the Guild.

For a moment, it seemed as if all that stood between the Tribune Company and quick victory was striker violence. Using rocks, baseball bats, bottles, eggs, firebombs, and traffic blockages, strikers tried to stop scabs from entering the *News* printing plants and from delivering papers. Historically, newspaper delivery workers were a tough lot, hired in part for their ability to outmuscle drivers from competing papers. With pleas, threats, and sometimes brutality, they and their allies pressured newsstand and store op-

erators not to sell the struck paper, a tactic that proved extremely effective as
the strike wore on.[30]

While the war in the streets raged, the striking unions began to mobilize
in other ways, with leadership from unexpected quarters. At the Guild meeting which voted to strike, the most effective plea for backing the other unions
came from columnist Juan Gonzalez, who during his years at the *News* had
attended only one other union meeting. But of all the strikers, Gonzalez had
the greatest experience at mass mobilization. As an undergraduate at Columbia University he helped lead the 1968 building takeovers. The Puerto
Rican–born, New York–raised Gonzalez went on to cofound the Young
Lords party, a militant Puerto Rican group that, for a brief moment, had had
considerable presence in East Harlem and the Bronx. When the Young Lords
collapsed, Gonzalez moved to Philadelphia, where he became a reporter with
the *Philadelphia Daily News* before joining the *Daily News*. Gonzalez's
whirlwind of activity, democratic manner, and ability to articulate a rationale
for worker solidarity helped buck up the morale of the white-collar strikers
and made him the leader of the strike within the Guild. Although several hundred Guild members, including most of the sportswriters and photographers, crossed picket lines to return to work, the city desk reporters by and
large remained loyal to the union.

Gonzalez brought another player into action, Dennis Rivera. Well before
the walkout began, the AFL-CIO had designated the *Daily News* struggle as
of national importance, and it provided substantial resources to the unions
involved. But when the strike started, local labor leaders seemed uncertain
how to proceed. Rivera showed the way. Days after the strike began, he
brought five hundred 1199 members to the *News* picket line. At the same
time, he began prodding the striking unions and the Central Labor Council
toward more aggressive, systematic efforts to build public support and put
pressure on the paper. On November 1, ten to fifteen thousand people attended a strike-support rally in front of the *News* headquarters on 42nd
Street. The next day, a smaller crowd rallied to hear Jesse Jackson, whom
Rivera arranged to come, back the strikers. Four more rallies took place that
month, while the union movement began raising a very large strike fund and
launched a boycott of *Daily News* advertisers.

National and local labor leaders saw the *News* strike as pivotal to the future of labor. If the Tribune Company could bust unions in an exceptionally
strong labor town like New York, it could happen anywhere. In the city itself,
one unionist said, it "would mean it's open season on unions." But even rec-

ognizing the stakes, many veteran union leaders, after a decade of strike losses and declining power, seemed fatalistic when the conflict began. More than anything else, Gonzalez and Rivera brought to the struggle faith that it could be won.[31]

Gonzalez, Rivera, and Jesse Jackson played another vital role, helping to neutralize a *News* effort to racialize the strike. *News* officials portrayed the conflict as pitting atavistic, racist unions, trying to preserve monopolistic privileges, against a forward-looking management using an unfortunate strike as an opportunity to hire more nonwhites and women. For many years, the newspaper unions had been white male preserves, and at least one striking union, the pressmen, remained strictly that. But the *News* race card did not play well. First, as a result of legal pressure, the drivers union had begun to change, to the extent that twenty-nine of the sixty workers fired in the incident that set off the strike were African-American, Latino, or Asian. Second, though the *News* did hire many nonwhites and women as replacement workers, its interest in affirmative action seemed hypocritical, since just three years earlier it had been found guilty of racial discrimination in its newsroom promotion practices. When the *News* recruited the homeless to hawk the paper in an effort to circumvent its strike-related distribution problems, many New Yorkers were repelled by this cynical exploitation of human misery. Having well-known civil rights advocates and nonwhite unionists line up behind the strike helped ensure that the effort to whip up antilabor sentiment in nonwhite communities failed.[32]

The Tribune Company seriously underestimated the extent to which support for labor still permeated the political, social, and moral structure of New York. During the strike, circulation of the paper fell by hundreds of thousands of copies. Major advertisers deserted the paper due to the circulation drop and the union boycott. The police did not treat threats and violence against scabs and news vendors as a high priority, and the public seemed indifferent to the widespread pro-union lawlessness. If anything, the violence seemed to spark interest, locally and nationally, in laws to ban the use of replacement workers. When *News* officials complained about union lawbreaking at a state legislative hearing, they found themselves being scolded by its cochairman, Frank Barbaro. Leading public figures, including Governor Mario Cuomo, Mayor Dinkins, and Cardinal O'Connor supported the strikers at union rallies and benefits, with the latter calling the use of replacement workers "immoral." Two generations of entertainers, including Pete Seeger and Lou Reed, volunteered their services to the Guild, a culture front spanning old left folk sentimentality and hard-edge, urban social realism.

In the end, the Tribune Company, losing $700,000 a day at the *News*, and with no prospect of victory in sight, gave up. On the 147th day of the walkout it sold the paper, *paying* British publisher Robert Maxwell sixty million dollars to take over the *News* and most of its liabilities. In a whirlwind of negotiations, Maxwell forged agreements with all the striking unions. New York labor had won, showing that at least in one corner of America workers could defend themselves from the no-holds-barred corporate antiunionism that had proved so devastating elsewhere.[33]

The *Daily News* strike and the election of David Dinkins demonstrated both the continued power of New York labor and how circumscribed that power had become. By the 1990s, winning did not bring much for working-class New York. Generally it meant, at best, the preservation of the status quo. Often it simply slowed the erosion of working-class living standards and say-so.

Though the *Daily News* strikers frustrated the Tribune Company's union-busting, costing its stockholders a reported $785 million, their victory brought little joy. In order to convince Maxwell to buy the paper, the *News* unions agreed to the elimination of eight hundred jobs, largely through voluntary buyouts but in some cases through layoffs (with severance pay). In November 1991, Maxwell's body was found floating near the Canary Islands, where he had been cruising on his yacht. Investigations revealed that he had faced ruin, having kept his publishing empire afloat through illegal financial maneuvers. The *News* quickly slid into bankruptcy. The paper was sold again, this time to real estate developer and publisher Morton Zuckerman. Zuckerman demanded another round of cutbacks and ended supposed lifetime job guarantees for the typographers. Most of the *News* unions, having few alternatives, reached agreements with Zuckerman, but the Newspaper Guild balked at his plan to cut the editorial staff by a third. The new owner then unilaterally fired 170 Guild members and reduced the pay of those who remained. When Rupert Murdoch repurchased the *New York Post* in 1993 (he had owned it from 1976 to 1988), he copied Zuckerman's strategy, first reaching agreements with the production unions, then smashing a weeklong Guild strike and deciding himself which members of the union to rehire. New York's newspaper unions survived through tenacity and broad support when their equivalents elsewhere suffered annihilation, but they did so defanged, capable of mounting only fighting retreats.[34]

David Dinkins's election had a bittersweet quality similar to the *News* strike victory. After years of racial roiling from City Hall, Dinkins's celebration of New York as a "gorgeous mosaic" and his debts to organized labor promised a new era of social calm, mutual respect, and reordered priorities. But his four years in office proved disappointing even to many of his staunch supporters. Dinkins appointed Bill Lynch as a deputy mayor, giving labor, black activists, and the political left an accessible liaison. But Dinkins's first deputy mayor, Norman Steisel, a second-string, second-rate financier from Lazard Frères, wielded more power, steering the administration on a course acceptable to the real estate industry and Wall Street. Dinkins failed to depart in any serious way from the post–fiscal crisis consensus that city government best served the populace by creating a pro-business climate through tax breaks, zoning, and spending priorities. Incompetent as a manager, Dinkins suffered the burden of the severe economic downturn that followed the 1987 stock market plunge. During his administration, the city lost nearly 400,000 jobs, leading to widespread misery, evident in homelessness and begging on a scale unseen since the Great Depression.

Organized labor did not get the payoff from Dinkins they hoped for. Municipal union leaders grew disenchanted with the mayor over contract negotiations and his failure to consult them on important matters, while private-sector unions bemoaned the failure of the city to check the economic free fall. Many of Dinkins's key labor backers, like Sandra Feldman, declined to endorse him for a second term. Even in the realm of race relations, the mayor could not deliver what he promised; the city suffered grievous blows when blacks battled Hasidic Jews in a Crown Heights riot and Dominicans fought police in Washington Heights, events which contributed to Dinkins's narrow defeat in his reelection bid.[35]

If labor's bright hopes for Dinkins proved unrealized, so did their worst fears about his successor, Rudolph Giuliani, who squeaked by the incumbent in their 1993 rematch. Giuliani came into office with bold words about reinventing government and privatizing huge chunks of the public sector, including the municipal hospital system. But in the face of persistent labor and community opposition and formidable organizational and legal hurdles, the mayor quietly retreated. Meanwhile, he spurned antilabor rhetoric and consulted frequently with top unionists.

Giuliani's cordial relations with Stanley Hill and other municipal union leaders helped him extract tough contracts from their organizations, five-year pacts with no raises for the first two years. In return, the city promised no layoffs for most city workers, a significant concession coming at a time when New York had yet to benefit from the 1990s economic recovery. Even so, the "two zeros" proved so unpopular with the rank and file that D.C. 37 leaders resorted to the shameful act of rigging the contract ratification vote.

By the time the vote-tampering became exposed, Giuliani had been easily reelected to a second term. A slowly improving economy and a drastic drop in crime had brought notable betterment to much of working-class New York, for which Giuliani received credit. Fearful of crossing the notoriously vindictive mayor, and comfortable with their relationships with him, the Central Labor Council and several municipal unions, including D.C. 37, in 1997 endorsed him against veteran liberal Ruth Messinger.[36]

The experience of the Dinkins and Giuliani years made evident the stability of the balance of forces that emerged from the fiscal crisis. The real estate and financial sectors remained the most powerful groups directing the city, pushing it toward an ever-greater concentration on white-collar service and finance jobs and upper-income center-city redevelopment. Labor remained potent, unlike most of the country, but largely defensive, rarely putting forth a vision of an alternative path of development or a set of values outside the dominant consensus. Occasionally magazines and newspapers ran stories asking whether or not New York still was a "labor town." Often they answered yes, as they should have. By the 1990s, however, the resonance of that once-mighty term, "labor town," had been dampened by the economic and social transformations of the previous quarter century. Working-class New York no longer formed the heart of the city.[37]

CHAPTER 18.

The Ghost of Class

On June 30, 1998, 40,000 construction workers, protesting the use of a non-union firm to build a subway communications center, blocked Madison Avenue, where the Metropolitan Transportation Authority had its headquarters, and marched crosstown to shut down nonunion construction sites. Traffic congealed, sidewalks became blocked, and thousands of people found themselves unable to enter stores and offices. When outnumbered police tried to contain the protest using barricades, mace, pepper spray, and horses, the mostly white building tradesmen shouted obscenities, threw bottles, blew high-pitched whistles, and fought back. In shades of *Blazing Saddles*, one worker got arrested for punching a police horse.

All three New York newspapers featured the demonstration as their lead story, with pictures of construction workers, some carrying flags, others bare-chested, on their front pages. The *Daily News* devoted eight pages to the event. The protest startled editors and reporters, as it did government officials and passersby, not just because of its size and raucousness but because it did not jibe with their sense of what New York was. In Rudolph Giuliani's city, white men who lived in Staten Island and Queens and Rockland County, as many of the protesters did, were supposed to share with the police a sense of "us" versus "them," not throw things at officers, assault their mounts, and shout "police state."

To many mid-town regulars, the construction workers seemed an alien presence. A *New York* magazine editor, commissioning an article about the demonstration, described them as "an invading army," an odd description for a group which probably had a higher proportion of native New Yorkers and in-city residents than the advertising, media, and corporate executives working along Madison Avenue whose lives they momentarily disrupted. A full-page article in the *New York Post*, headlined "Hunk Heaven," treated the protesters as sexual exotica. "In a neighborhood dominated by men in suits who usually confine themselves to loosening their tie at the end of the day," the paper commented, "the sight of guys ripping off wet muscle shirts or stuffing flannel shirts in torn jean pockets was something of a revelation."[1]

In the late 1990s, denizens of a corporatized, globalized, white-collarized Manhattan did not have a social category in which to place the people and events they witnessed on the hot June day when building tradesmen took their stand to check the spread of nonunion construction work. New York's union movement had not disappeared, but when labor showed its militant face many New Yorkers either blotted it out or saw it as something different. In the month prior to the construction protest, two other major labor demonstrations had taken place. In the first, taxi drivers, led by an independent Pakistani drivers' association, had snarled the city by using their cabs to slow traffic in a protest against harsh new regulations cracking down on driver misconduct. Rather than as a labor dispute, the conflict was widely characterized as a struggle between the forces of order and those of chaos and lawlessness, the latter sometimes identified, by implication, with the third worldization of New York. The police commissioner went so far as to call the taxi drivers "terrorists." Soon after, a Manhattan rally of twenty thousand hospital workers received only modest media attention. In a season of extraordinary working-class mobilization, the city's political leaders and media failed to recognize it as such.[2]

In the rest of the country, too, workers no longer figured prominently in images and notions of New York. In the 1970s and 1980s, one television producer recalled, "One of the Ten Commandments was, no one wants to see a show set in New York."[3] By the 1990s, that reversed, as dozens of television series had New York settings. But unlike in the eras of Ralph Kramden and Archie Bunker, working-class New York rarely appeared. Rather, upper-class professionals and young, middle-class singles dominated shows like CPW, The Cosby Show, Spin City, Veronica's Closet, and Friends. The decade's most popular show, Seinfeld, did hark back to an earlier generation's ethnic culture, in George's and Jerry's parents. But working-class life consistently appeared only in what had long been its main, popular culture redoubt, police dramas like N.Y.P.D. Blue.

A variety of developments help explain the virtual disappearance of the notion of a working class—in spite of the continued presence of a huge working population and a still powerful labor movement—from public discourse, popular culture, and the mental maps New Yorkers had of the city. For decades, there had been a national predilection to spurn the language of class. By 1990s, even the labor movement shied away from it, with the AFL-CIO turning to the inoffensive, inclusive phrase "working families," which piggybacked on the cult of "family values" that became so prominent in the Reagan and post-Reagan eras. When classes got discussed at all, they usually were a broadly-defined middle class, presumed to include most Americans, and "the underclass," a polite version of "us" and "them."[4]

In New York, an economic group rarely labeled a class, the rich, dominated civic life to a greater extent than in the recent past. New York's very slow recovery from the recession of the early 1990s brought an increasingly disproportionate share of wealth and power to the upper class, particularly to those profiting from the long stock market boom. One government study found that between 1991 and 1996 low-income New York families saw very modest real income growth, middle-income families even smaller gains, while the income of upper-income families went up by a third. Wall Street employed less than 5 percent of the city work force, but accounted for over half the increase in aggregate earnings between 1992 and 1997.[5]

The white light of new money, radiating from Wall Street, made other economic groupings look pale, difficult to discern. New York financiers did not have to have any relationship with working-class New York to exert economic and political power. Economically, they depended on global markets, not local production. Politically, their national influence rested not, as in the past, on political parties or coalitions that required attention to the interests of varied bases, but on direct ties to the Treasury Department and the Federal Reserve Bank. The ups and downs of the financial markets became much-watched referenda on particular government policies; when President-elect Bill Clinton contemplated his administration's economic initiatives, his foremost concern was how the New York–based bond markets would react, for a minor move in interest rates might sabotage a robust recovery from the recession that had enabled him to defeat George Bush. Bond traders—once thought of as a breed as boring as shoe salesmen—became cultural stars, the protagonists of books like *The Bonfire of the Vanities* and Michael Lewis's *Liar's Poker*.[6]

As this escalation of upper-class presence overshadowed working-class New York, changes in the working class itself further diminished its social and cultural impact as a class. For many workers, the politics and culture of racial and ethnic identity overweighed working-class identification. Nothing better emblemized this than the fate of New York's Labor Day Parade.

After its successful revival in 1981, the Central Labor Council sponsored a labor parade most years. However, enthusiasm for it slowly drained away. Many workers preferred to extend their summers with a long weekend away or to spend time with their families, rather than marching through the largely deserted streets of midtown Manhattan. Without a sharp challenge, like

Ronald Reagan's firing of the air traffic controllers, it proved difficult to galvanize fervor for the march outside the ranks of committed activists.

Meanwhile, another event, held on the same day, Brooklyn's West Indian American Day Carnival, grew in size and popularity. Though modeled after Trinidad's Carnival, the New York celebration, begun in 1967, was not a traditional festival. By scheduling it in September rather than just before Lent, the Catholic norm, its organizers freed Carnival from its original religious and geographic moorings and opened it up to emigrants from throughout the Caribbean, including from predominantly Protestant islands without a Carnival tradition. As the Caribbean population of New York grew, so did Carnival. By the early 1980s, attendance at the event, which featured Caribbean food, elaborately prepared floats and costumes, intricate dance routines, and numerous bands, reached an astounding 800,000 people, what sociologist Philip Kasinitz dubbed "the nation's largest block party." Yet few non–West Indians noticed, as the news media and leading politicians rarely ventured to Eastern Parkway, where Carnival took place.

In the late 1980s, that began to change. In 1988, Mayor Edward Koch, who was feuding with union leaders, attended Carnival rather than the labor parade. Meanwhile, the news media, which traditionally used Labor Day as the occasion for state-of-the-labor-movement stories, began paying less attention to the parade, part of a general decline in labor coverage which included a period when, for the first time in decades, the *New York Times* had no reporter assigned specifically to the labor beat. Simultaneously, newspapers and especially television began paying more attention to Carnival, which provided glorious visual images on a traditionally slow news weekend. By the mid-1990s, Carnival was outshining the Labor Day Parade.

In 1996, the Central Labor Council threw in the towel and began scheduling the Labor Day Parade for the weekend after Labor Day. That way it did not have to compete with the West Indian celebration, nor with end-of-summer plans. Furthermore, the weekend after Labor Day had many more shoppers and tourists on midtown streets to witness the workers' procession than found on the holiday weekend.[7]

Labor's ceding of its own holiday, Labor Day, to Carnival told the obvious story of labor's eclipse. But the tale was not simple. Many participants in Carnival themselves were active unionists, not surprising since many unions in the city—including 1199 and D.C. 37—had large Caribbean memberships. West Indian unionists who attended Carnival rather than the labor parade were not rejecting an identification of themselves as workers or members of the labor movement, but they were expressing a priority, a stronger bond with an ethnic identity than a work-based identity. (The fact that Carnival was a much livelier event than the labor parade no doubt also played a role in decisions about where to spend the holiday.) Once the Central Labor Council switched its parade date, workers participating in Carnival could more easily do so as unionists. Several unions, including the Teamsters, 1199, the UFT, and D.C. 37, became official sponsors of Carnival bands, providing financial support and having their banners, hats, and tee-shirts on display.[8]

Ethnic, racial, and class identification did not preclude one another. Rather, they coexisted in complex relationships to one another. Growing "pan-West Indian consciousness"—and its equivalent among workers from other regions—did not necessarily weaken organized labor. The rescheduling of the Labor Day Parade actually came at a time of signs of a labor revival. The election of a new AFL-CIO president, John Sweeney (the son of a New York bus driver, who once headed SEIU Local 32B—the building service workers union that in 1945 had tied up the city) reflected deep dissatisfaction among workers and unionists with the passivity of the old guard. In New York, immigrants played an important role in the labor resurgence, pumping new life into the Hotel Employees, units of the Teamsters and Machinists, and other unions. For its part, the Central Labor Council made active efforts "to bridge relationships with the multi-ethnic communities of our city." One of the main groups behind the 1998 construction worker protest was Local 79 of the Laborers' Union, which undertook a highly successful drive to organize demolition workers, asbestos removers, and hod carriers, largely Polish and Latino newcomers. (To protest the use of nonunion workers, the local set up giant inflatable rats in front of construction sites and company offices.)[9] Still, the strength of ethnic identity and organization, bolstered by the city's post-1965 wave of immigration, tended to leave class identity—and the very notion of a working-class New York—in the shadows.

Changes in consumption patterns, too, contributed to the bleaching out of a distinct, working-class New York. Class identity came not only from the workplace; it came from dwelling and consumption patterns as well. These were particularly important for those outside the paid workforce, disproportionately women, the young, and the old. The type of clothing and food and other stores a person frequented, and the items they purchased, helped situate them in the economic and social hierarchy.

New York long had an idiosyncratic pattern of retailing, characterized by a myriad of small, specialty stores. In much of the city, virtually every block or intersection had, at a minimum, a candy store, selling newspapers, magazines, cigarettes, candy, stationery, and soda fountain treats, or a small grocery store. Many had a definite ethnic character. Shopping in such stores reinforced a particular sense of being, broadly plebeian if not working-class per se. Yet for all the affection for the egg cream or the batido, many New Yorkers found local shopping infuriating. New York stores, especially groceries, tended to be small, dirty, and expensive, with staff more surly than helpful, and sometimes racist.

For years, New York remained relatively insulated from the growth of national chain stores, especially the so-called big box stores.[10] New York's high price of land, high cost of labor (due in part to unionization), zoning, and other regulations led retail corporations to avoid the city, in spite of its huge market. Many New Yorkers with cars, seeking bigger stores and lower prices, took to going to malls and superstores in New Jersey, lower Westchester, and on Long Island.

In the 1980s and 1990s, more options opened up in the city proper, as the national and international chains—like Rite-Aid, CVS, Home Depot, Tower Records, HMV, Blockbuster, Barnes and Noble, the GAP, and Pathmark grocery stores—began making inroads. New shopping centers and national retailers even began appearing in what the *New York Times* termed "areas that became retail wastelands as the Bronx burned." Increased size helped reduce the number of retail establishments in the city from over 100,000 in the late 1940s to only 40,000 in the early 1990s.

Eateries reflected the same trend. After a slow start, the national fast-food chains moved into New York in a big way, adapting their usual freestanding designs for dense city settings. Even Seattle-based Starbucks belatedly made it to a city where the term "coffee shop" meant something other than a dispensary of high-quality, high-cost coffee variations.[11]

In some respects, the corporatization of New York retailing improved the quality of working-class life, as residents in areas like Harlem and western Queens got access to cleaner, better-stocked, lower-priced, more service-oriented stores than previously available. But the new retailing had consequences that went beyond the individual shopping experience. First, it pushed New Yorkers toward greater dependency on cars, for many of the new superstores were far from public transit, which in any case was inconvenient for carrying home bulky purchases. Second, national and international retailing undercut, as it already had in much of the country, a sense of place, of particularity, of exceptionality. One Home Depot looked pretty much like any other Home Depot. The coffee bar in the television show *Friends*, ostensibly in New York, could be in any American city, unlike the coffee shop in the slightly earlier *Seinfeld*, which had a distinctly New York ambience. Third, big box retailing blurred lines of social hierarchy and class, as New Yorkers of varied economic backgrounds became more likely to shop in the same stores, buy the same things, and eat in the same restaurants.[12]

The swelling of the hyper-rich, the new blossoming of ethnicity, and the homogenization of selling all served to diminish consciousness of class. This had political as well as cultural consequences. Even as New York suffered through a prolonged economic downturn, issues related to employment and economic policy rarely came to the fore in electoral politics, political discourse, or the major media.

New York City was much harder hit by the recession of the early 1990s than most of the country. Between January 1989 and December 1992, it lost 13.5 percent of its jobs, compared to a national decline of only one percent. Even more ominously, recovery came later and weaker in New York than elsewhere. In 1997, the city had an unemployment rate of 9.4 percent (down from over 13 percent in early 1993), nearly twice the national rate of 4.9 percent. In 1998, fewer New York City residents had jobs than in 1989. In the mid-1990s, while most of the United States experienced an economic boom, the typical New Yorker, outside of the upper ranks of finance, real estate, and business services, lived in a recession.[13]

New York City's economic performance suggested deep structural problems. A shortage of jobs, especially secure, well-paying jobs for those without advanced skills or education, cast a pall over the city. By national standards, New York had an exceptionally low level of labor force participation. In 1997—generally considered an unusually flush moment in the country's history—only two-thirds of New Yorkers of working age had a job or were looking for one. The percentage of working-age New Yorkers holding a job was 9 percent below the figure for all city dwellers in the country. The employment situation for youth was especially dreary; in 1996, just 16 percent of New York teenagers had a job, compared to 40 percent nationally. Furthermore, many New Yorkers with jobs found themselves downwardly mobile, as corporate downsizing and the continued exodus of manufacturing forced them into lower-paying, part-time, or temporary positions.[14]

In spite of this gloomy picture, in neither the 1993 mayoral election, when Rudolph Giuliani defeated David Dinkins, nor in the 1997 election, when he defeated Ruth Messinger, did economic issues play a significant role. Liberals and conservatives alike rarely acknowledged that working-class New York was stuck in something that looked like permanent stagnation, even as wealthy New York and the rest of the nation gorged at an end-of-the-century barbecue. Even some labor leaders seemed to succumb to the hegemonic outlook of the 1990s, which posited individual behavior and cultural values as the key to economic success or failure, rather than structural factors and class relations. While in 1996 the labor movement opposed federal welfare reform — the "Personal Responsibility and Work Opportunity Reconciliation Act" — few unions broke with President Clinton or congressional supporters of the bill for ending "welfare as we know it." Their timid opposition did little to counter the widely held view that the problem of poverty lay in the morality and habits of the poor, rather than in a lack of appropriate jobs. In New York, two major unions, D.C. 37 and TWU Local 100, acquiesced to the use of welfare recipients to do work once performed by unionized workers. In return, they won job security for their own members and a vague commitment to put some welfare recipients into civil service jobs.[15]

In the history of the United States, a diminishing sense of class and an inactive or ineffective labor movement have tended to reinforce one another. Conversely, collective action often has created or recreated a sense of shared group interest, of cultural and political mutuality. Very large economic and social forces contributed to the attenuated presence, by the 1990s, of a distinct, working-class New York, forces difficult to challenge or reverse. But possibilities remained, as the twenty-first century begins, for ordinary folk, through action, to turn the ghost of working-class New York back into a living organism, and allow it once again to play the morally and socially salutary role it traditionally held in the great city.

Conclusion:
New York and the Nation

In the decades after World War II, labor unions brought a measure of prosperity and security and a sense of entitlement to tens of millions of Americans. Unions brought higher pay, nicer homes, decent medical care, and retirement in comfort and dignity.[1] Politically they acted as a liberal force (at least on domestic matters), protecting and in limited ways extending the legacy of the New Deal. But what labor accomplished, impressive as it was, fell short of the hopes and dreams many Americans had when the war ended, expressed in President Franklin D. Roosevelt's Economic Bill of Rights and the CIO's People's Program, with their calls for full employment, universal, government-guaranteed health care, affordable housing, racial equality, and checks on corporate power, a social democratic program rooted in shared sacrifice and a commitment to communal responsibility. As things turned out, corporate power increased in postwar America, as a more prosperous but individualistic way of life grew out of the soil of the Cold War, suburbanization, mass culture, and free market ideology.

New York City took a different path. New York workers and their allies put in place a far more extensive web of social benefits than elsewhere. This New York social democracy, which encompassed housing, health care, education, the arts, and civil rights, was intensely urban in its origins, strategies, and beliefs. Integral to it was the labor movement, a civilizing force in a city dedicated to wealth and power, and one that remained relatively strong even as unionism elsewhere weakened.

New York's exceptionality had multiple roots. New York had a long history of liberalism and leftism. Communists, socialists, and liberals built institutions and spread values that allowed their movements to replicate themselves long after the national political trajectory turned in a more conservative direction. The fact that the vast majority of New Yorkers were Catholic, Jewish, African-American, or Puerto Rican—outsiders in a country and a city in which white Protestants controlled the most important levers of power and wealth—helped sustain a political culture of dissent and struggle, an openness to ideas and movements outside the national mainstream.

New York's unusual housing pattern contributed to its social and political exceptionality. Dense neighborhoods promoted communal cultures and an inclination toward collective solutions for shared problems. A low level of home ownership kept at bay the politics of property taxes and real estate values, elsewhere poisonous to expansive notions of government and neighborhood heterogeneity.[2]

The structure of New York business facilitated labor power and liberal reform. Small New York employers might fight particular unions, but they had neither the wherewithal nor the inclination to launch an antiunion movement. In some industries, employers came to depend on unions for a flexible supply of skilled workers. Meanwhile, the small scale of most New York businesses left it up to unions and left-liberal professionals to take the lead in developing benefit programs, which they did in pathbreaking ways.

Eventually, working-class New York's progress down a road not taken by most of the country halted. Nationally, Cold War anticommunism checked the power of labor and all but destroyed its left wing. In New York, some left-wing unions managed to survive, and a few, like 1199, even expanded their influence. But almost across the board, labor abandoned radical, utopian, or social democratic rhetoric, spurning even the language of class. Impressive, innovative labor advances got described in the bland, bloodless language of mainstream liberalism, one reason why working-class New York's extraordinary achievements remain unheralded and unknown outside of labor's ranks.

When in the 1970s, images and discussion of New York workers as members of a distinct class again become common, they were associated with marauding hardhats and Archie Bunker, symbols of Vietnam-era backlash. By then, shifting residential patterns and changing housing and health economics had reduced the ability of the labor movement to serve its members and their families. Internal disputes, over racial integration and foreign policy and over who should wield power, further robbed the movement of momentum. Soon after came the fiscal crisis, which proved more damaging to New York social democracy than the Cold War. Beneath the cover of assumed economic necessity, a wholesale shift in power and normative values took place.

In spite of the changes in New York that resulted from the fiscal crisis, many outsiders still saw it as aberrant. In the mid-1990s, House Speaker Newt Gingrich proclaimed that "the malignant combination of machine politics, bankrupt welfare statism, and rapacious unionism" was contributing to

the city's "slow-motion suicide." A commissioner of Cobb County, in Gingrich's congressional district outside of Atlanta, told a *New York* magazine reporter, "We're the power now. These suburbs, built on white flight, are only
going to become more conservative and more powerful. New York has been
deposed." In a set of "Bad, Worse & Worst" jokes in a *Betty* comic book, one
entry read: "Bad: lost tooth; Worse: lost homework; Worst: lost in New
York."[3]

Yet even as the age-old use of New York as a negative definer of America
continued, in many respects the city had become less exceptional. Like everywhere else, brand name consumption and culture reigned, with the once
raunchy Times Square turned into a benign amusement center where locals
and tourists attended Disney shows and bought food and souvenirs at restaurants and stores owned by Disney, Warner Brothers, ESPN, and other national corporations. Simultaneously, as in much of the country, the politics
and culture of racial and ethnic identity seemed to overwhelm outlooks and
mobilizations resting on class identification. When World War II ended, New
Yorkers took for granted the sight of manual workers and labor protests in the
heart of the city, even if they opposed what labor stood for and how it acted.
By the late 1990s, many Manhattanites were startled by the mere presence of
protesting workers.

While in some respects New York had become more like the rest of the
country, the rest of the country, in some respects, had become more like New
York. Nationally, during the 1980s and 1990s, the most robust economic
growth occurred in the service industries, while manufacturing declined in
relative importance. And within the manufacturing sector, many companies
turned away from the standardized, mass production methods of the Fordist
heyday for more flexible approaches to production of the sort long characteristic of New York.[4] At the same time, foreign-born workers became increasingly vital to industries far from New York and other ports of entry. Slowly
and unevenly, the United States moved toward the ethnic and racial diversity
long present in New York. Ethnic foods — like bagels — once available only in
a handful of cities, by the mid-1990s could be found in grocery stores and
fast-food outlets from one end of the country to the other.[5]

At the end of the twentieth century, working-class New York no longer
had the dominant role it once possessed in shaping the social organization,
politics, and sensibility of the city. But New York labor had proved remarkably stubborn, balking at leaving history's stage. Its persistence, and its continuing vitality, perhaps augur well for the new century. Working-class New

York represents America's past, a survival from the days when most Americans made or moved things for a living, from when social ambitions were large and class conflict openly acknowledged. But it also may represent America's future, the future of a country that has come to look more like its largest city.[6] Working-class New York may still have more to contribute to American democracy.

ACKNOWLEDGMENTS

At every stage of work on this book, I received generous assistance. Like all historians of New York labor, I am in debt to the Robert F. Wagner Labor Archives at New York University, which under the leadership of Debra E. Bernhardt has done so much to preserve the labor history of the city. There and elsewhere, archivists went out of their way to be helpful, including Denise Conklin, Historical Collections and Labor Archives, Penn State University; David Ment, Special Collections, Teachers College; Jim Quigel, International Union of Electrical Workers Archives, Rutgers University; David Rosenberg, UE/Labor Archives, University of Pittsburgh; and Richard Strassberg, Kheel Center for Labor-Management Documentation & Archives, Cornell University. Gerald Finkel and Robert Delaney of Local 3 of the International Brotherhood of Electrical Workers; Jack Bigel, of Program Planners, Inc.; and Kier Jorgensen of the Amalgamated Clothing Workers (now part of UNITE) facilitated my access to important historical material. So did Ken Wray of the United Housing Foundation, who also shared his deep knowledge of cooperative housing. Several veteran New York unionists generously allowed me to interview them; Robert Delaney, James Garry, and Ida Torres, in particular, gave me a far richer sense of New York labor than documents alone could provide.

Over the years I enjoyed help from some very able research assistants. My thanks go out especially to Scott Gac, Mark Higbee, Angus Johnston, and Kevin Kenny. I also need to thank the remarkable students — many now teachers themselves — from whose work I learned a great deal about working-class New York: Martha Biondi, Aaron Brenner, Venus Green, Anne Kornhauser, Billy Massey, Sandra Opdyke, Christine Philliou, Gail Radford, Michael Spear, and Emily Straus. Two marvelous reference books, *The Encyclopedia of New York City*, edited by Kenneth T. Jackson, and the *Encyclopedia of the American Left*, edited by Mari Jo Buhle, Paul Buhle, and Dan Georgakas, stayed at my elbow as I worked away.

Comments and suggestions from colleagues who read sections of this book in draft proved invaluable. For their time and insight, I thank Alan Brinkley, Eric Foner, Kenneth T. Jackson, Deborah Levenson, Bruce Nelson, and Steve Rosswurm. In addition to reading the manuscript, David Rosner, in an act of extraordinary generosity, gave me a mountain of documents and newspaper clippings that he collected, which form much of the basis for chapter 8.

Fellowships from the National Endowment for the Humanities and the American Council of Learned Societies gave me invaluable time to work on this book. A reduction in my teaching load at Queens College facilitated its completion. I would particularly like to thank Donald Scott and Frank Warren for their strong support for scholarly endeavors by myself and my Queens colleagues.

As work on this project progressed, I became ever more dependent on what I came to think of as my "team," which read each chapter as I completed it. Without the detailed comments, sharp criticism, and warm encouragement I received from Jack Metzgar, Elizabeth Blackmar, and Deborah Bell, I would not have finished this book. Reading the manuscript of Jack Metzgar's own splendid book, *Striking Steel: Remembering Solidarity*, and poring over his comments on my chapters, kept me from wavering in my belief that it is terribly important that ordinary working people not be left out of the narrative of modern America, as they so often are. Betsy Blackmar provided me with a model of what a scholar should be: smart, searching, scrupulous, and unbelievably generous with time and ideas. From Deborah Bell, I learned much of what I know about labor. Her lifetime engagement in the struggles of working-class New York has given her a profound understanding of unionism. Her healthy realism checks the romantic flights about labor to which outsiders are prone, while enabling her to repeatedly find opportunities to promote social justice.

I had the unusual pleasure of working with two wonderful editors on this project. From its inception, Steve Fraser provided me with a much-needed sense that I was on to something important, something that would work. His faith in the book, combined with his unrelenting push for a deeper view of its subject, led me to a more ambitious and broader conception than I otherwise would have had. Working with such a dear friend, superb editor, and superlative historian was a privilege for which I am deeply grateful. Matt Weiland picked up where Steve left off. He and André Schiffrin "got" what this book was about, and gave me the boost I needed to complete it. All authors should be as lucky as I have been in the close attention, intelligence, and forbearance that Matt has provided. Eugenia Bell deserves the credit for finding the marvelous photographs.

Finally, I need to thank those who put up with me during the years I worked on this book. It took its toll, in time and temper. Friends looked interested as I droned on. Colleagues urged me forward. But my greatest gratitude goes to my family, Deborah, Julia, and Lena Bell, whose love and tolerance have been gifts from heaven.

NOTES

Abbreviations

1199	Health and Hospital Workers Union 1199 Papers, Kheel Center for Labor-Management Documentation & Archives, Cornell University, Ithaca, N.Y.
ACW	Amalgamated Clothing Workers Collection, Kheel Center for Labor-Management Documentation & Archives, Cornell University, Ithaca, N.Y.
AFL Min	Minutes of the Central Trades and Labor Council of Greater New York City, Robert Wagner Labor Archives, New York University, New York, N.Y.
AFL Ex Min	Minutes of Executive Board, Central Trades and Labor Council of Greater New York, Robert Wagner Labor Archives, New York University, New York, N.Y.
AFL-CIO Ex Min	Minutes of Executive Board, New York City Central Labor Council, Robert Wagner Labor Archives, New York University, New York, N.Y.
Bd of Ed	Records of the New York City Board of Education, Special Collections, Milbank Memorial Library, Teachers College, Columbia University, New York, N.Y.
CIO Min	Greater New York CIO Council, "Digest of Council Minutes," Robert Wagner Labor Archives, New York University, New York, N.Y.
CIO Ex Min	Greater New York CIO Council, "Executive Board Minutes," Robert Wagner Labor Archives, New York University, New York, N.Y.
CIO (NYC) Min	Minutes of the New York City CIO Council, Robert Wagner Labor Archives, New York University, New York, N.Y.
CIO (NYC) Ex Min	Minutes of the Executive Board, New York City CIO Council, Robert Wagner Labor Archives, New York University, New York, N.Y.
DN	*Daily News*
EncLeft	Mari Jo Buhle, Paul Buhle, and Dan Georgakas, eds. *Encyclopedia of the American Left* (Urbana, 1992)
EncNY	Kenneth T. Jackson, ed. *The Encyclopedia of New York City* (New Haven, 1995)
Guinier Papers	Ewart Guinier Papers, Schomburg Center for Research in Black Culture, New York Public Library, New York, N.Y.
HT	*New York Herald Tribune*
ILGWU	Records of the International Ladies Garment Workers Union, Kheel Center for Labor-Management Documentation & Archives, Cornell University, Ithaca, N.Y.
IUE	Records of the International Union of Electrical Workers, Rutgers University, New Brunswick, N.J.
J-A	*New York Journal-American*
La Guardia Papers	Fiorello La Guardia Papers, Municipal Archives Research Center, New York, N.Y.

MARC   Municipal Archives Research Center, New York, N.Y.

NYCHA   Records of the New York City Housing Authority, La Guardia-Wagner Ar-
                        chives, La Guardia Community College, Queens, N.Y.

NYP   *New York Post*

NYT   *The New York Times*

O'Dwyer Papers   William O'Dwyer Papers, Municipal Archives Research Center, New York,
                        N.Y.

RAC   Rockefeller Archives Center, North Tarrytown, New York

RWLA   Robert Wagner Labor Archives, New York University, New York, N.Y.

UE   Records of the United Electrical, Radio and Machine Workers of America,
                        UE/Labor Archives, University of Pittsburgh, Pittsburgh, Pennsylvania

VV   *Village Voice*

Wagner Papers   Robert F. Wagner Jr. Papers, Municipal Archives Research Center, New York,
                        N.Y.

WSJ   *The Wall Street Journal*

W-T   *New York World-Telegram*

Xavier   Records of the Xavier Institute of Industrial Relations, Fordham University,
                        Bronx, New York

Unless otherwise indicated, all interviews were conducted by and are in the possession of the author.

INTRODUCTION: WHAT MADE NEW YORK GREAT

1. E. B. White, *Here Is New York* (New York, 1949); V. S. Pritchett, *New York Proclaimed* (New York, 1965); Jan Morris, *Manhattan '45* (New York, 1987); Truman Capote, "A House on the Heights," in Andrea Wyatt Sexton and Alice Leccese Powers, eds., *The Brooklyn Reader: Thirty Writers Celebrate America's Favorite Borough* (New York, 1994); Willie Morris, *New York Days* (Boston, 1993).

2. A recent exception is Debra Bernhardt and Rachel Bernstein, *Ordinary People, Extraordinary Lives* (New York, 2000).

3. See, for example, David Brody, *Workers in Industrial America: Essays on the 20th Century Struggle* (New York, 1980), chapters 5 and 6; Nelson Lichtenstein, "From Corporatism to Collective Bargaining: Organized Labor and the Eclipse of Social Democracy in the Postwar Era," in Steve Fraser and Gary Gerstle, eds., *The Rise and Fall of the New Deal Order, 1930-1980* (Princeton, 1989); and Kim Moody, *An Injury to All: The Decline of American Unionism* (London, 1988).

4. Union membership in New York and the nation are detailed in chapters 3 and 17.

5. R. Emmett Murray, *The Lexicon of Labor* (New York, 1998), 187. The literature on class is vast; a useful introduction is Ira Katznelson, "Working-Class Formation: Constructing Cases and Comparisons," in Katznelson and Aristide R. Zolberg, eds., *Working-Class Formation: Nineteenth-Century Patterns in Western Europe and the United States* (Princeton, 1986).

6. Particularly influential in this regard were a series of studies sponsored by the Regional Plan Association during the 1950s. The summary volume is Edgar M. Hoover and Raymond Vernon, *Anatomy of a Metropolis* (Cambridge, 1959).

CHAPTER 1: A NON-FORDIST CITY IN THE AGE OF FORD

1. *HT*, Sept. 20–30, 1945; *PM*, Sept. 26, 1945; *NYP*, Oct. 1–2, 1945; *NYT*, Feb. 4, 1946; and Grace Palladino, "When Militancy Isn't Enough: The Impact of Automation on New York City Building Service Workers, 1934–1970," *Labor History* 28 (spring 1987), 196–220.

2. United States Department of Labor, *Handbook of Labor Statistics 1975 — Reference Edition* (Washington, D.C., 1975), 390.

3. For the painters strike, see *PM*, Sept. 13, 1945; Sept. 14, 1945; and *HT*, Sept. 20, 1945; for Western Union, see *NYT*, Feb. 5 and 9, 1945; and Jos. L. Egan to William O'Dwyer, Jan. 28, 1946, box 158, subject files, O'Dwyer Papers; for Mergenthaler, see *UE News*, March 9, March 16, and July 27, 1946; for the trucking strikes, see *J-A*, Jan. 20, 1946; *NYT*, Feb. 2, 1946, Feb. 3, 1946; "The O'Dwyer Plan for Industrial Peace," folder 1682, box 158, and Commerce and Industry Association of New York, Inc., "Effect of Trucking Strike on New York City Business," file 1722, box 161, subject files, and press release of Sept. 11, 1946, box 2, department letters, O'Dwyer Papers.

4. *NYP*, Oct. 2, 1945; John T. McManus and John F. Ryan to William O'Dwyer, Jan. 18, 1946, box 158, subject files, O'Dwyer Papers; *NYT*, Feb. 3, 1946.

5. Accounts of the strike can be found in Vernon H. Jenson, *Strife on the Waterfront: The Port of New York Since 1945* (Ithaca, 1974), 36–53, and George Lipsitz, *Class and Culture in Cold War America: "A Rainbow at Midnight"* (South Hadley, Mass.: 1982), 40–45.

6. Alan Block, *East Side-West Side: Organized Crime in New York, 1930–1950* (Cardiff, 1980), 183–95; Allen Raymond, *Waterfront Priest* (New York, 1955), 2–3, 9–12, 23–28, 41–42; Jenson, *Strife on the Waterfront*, 86–87.

7. Raymond, *Waterfront Priest*, 70–71; Jenson, *Strife on the Waterfront*, 41–53.

8. *NYT*, Feb. 2 and 3, 1946; William O'Dwyer, "Proclamation," Feb. 6, 1946, in subject files, box 161, folder 1723, O'Dwyer Papers.

9. Statement by Mayor O'Dwyer, Feb. 4, 1946, box 161, folder 1723, and Edward C. Maguire to William O'Dwyer, Feb. 4, 1946, "Strikes and Labor Problem," box 158, subject files, O'Dwyer Papers; *NYT*, Feb. 5, 1946, and Feb. 13, 1946; Patrick Renshaw, *American Labor and Consensus Capitalism, 1935–1990* (Jackson, Miss., 1991), 74–88.

10. *NYT*, Feb. 6, 7, and 9, 1946; William O'Dwyer, "Proclamation," Feb. 6, 1946, and Paul L. Ross, Report to The Mayor, Feb. 9, 1946, both in subject files, box 161, folder 1723, O'Dwyer Papers.

11. *NYT*, Feb. 13 and Feb. 14, 1946; *W-T*, Feb. 12, 1946; Office of the Mayor, Statement, Feb. 13, 1946, and Joint Statement of James P. McAllister and Joseph P. Ryan, subject files, box 161, folder 1723; and "Summary of Newspaper Editorials and Comments," box 161, folder 1724, O'Dwyer Papers.

12. U.S. Department of Labor, Bureau of Labor Statistics, *Work Stoppages Caused by Labor Management Disputes in 1945*, BLS Bulletin 878 (Washington, 1946), 19–21, and *Work Stoppages Caused by Labor Management Disputes in 1946*, BLS Bulletin 918 (Washington, 1947), 29–32; *W-T*, Jan. 15, 1946; *J-A*, Jan. 22, 1946; and CIO Min, Jan. 17, 1946.

13. CIO Min, Mar. 21, 1946; Marcel Sherer to William O'Dwyer, box 160, file 1696, subject files, O'Dwyer Papers; *UE News*, Feb. 9, June 6, June 15, June 22, July 6, July 13, Aug. 3, Sept. 14, and Sept. 28, 1946; Joe Klein, *Woody Guthrie: A Life* (New York, 1980), 232–34.

14. CIO Min, Jan. 17, 1946; *J-A*, Jan. 22, 1946.

15. *NYT*, May 24 and 25, 1946; Renshaw, *American Labor and Consensus Capitalism*, 85–86.

16. Bureau of Labor Statistics, *Work Stoppages in 1946*, 10–11, 31–32; Art Preis, *Labor's Giant Step* (New York, 1972), 294–96; Ray Denison, "The Seafarers Union Remembered: A Retrospective Log, 1946–1963, *Labor's Heritage* 3 no. 3 (April 1991): 6–9; *NYP*, Oct. 11, 1946; Herman M. Strum, "Postwar Labor Relations in the Maritime Industry," in Colston E. Warner, et al., *Labor in Postwar America* (Brooklyn, 1949), 478–81.

17. Bureau of Labor Statistics, *Work Stoppages in 1946*, 12; State of New York, Department of Labor, *Annual Report of the Industrial Commission for the Twelve Months ended June 30, 1920* (Albany, 1921), 159.

18. Calculated from State of New York, Department of Labor, *Handbook of New York Labor Statistics, 1948* Special Bulletin No. 226 (1949), 5.

19. Jan Morris, *Manhattan '45* (New York, 1987), 7; *EncNY*: "television," 1159–60, and "United Nations," 1214.

20. Sails: Morris, *Manhattan '45*, 237; horses: Lloyd Ullman, *The Beautiful Bronx, 1920–1950* (New York, 1979), 54, and Elliot Willensky, *When Brooklyn Was the World, 1920–1957* (New York, 1986), 119; DC current: *Meyer Berger's New York* (New York, 1960), 18, and Sandra Opdycke, "Private choices, public obligations: New York City and its hospitals since 1900," Ph.D. diss., Columbia University, 1995, 361; gas light: Morris, *Manhattan '45*, 73; potbellied stoves: Andreas Feininger, *New York in the Forties* (New York, 1978), 113; ice: E. B. White, *Here Is New York* (New York, 1949, reprinted 1988), 24, and Milton Jonathan Slocum, *Manhattan Country Doctor* (New York, 1986), 103.

21. Nelson Lichtenstein, "The Making of the Postwar Working Class: Cultural Pluralism and Social Structure in World War II," *The Historian* 51 (Nov. 1988): 42–63; Lipsitz, *Class and Culture*.

22. Calculated from State of New York, Department of Labor, *Handbook of New York Labor Statistics, 1948*, 5; United States Department of Commerce, Bureau of the Census, *County and City Data Book 1952* (Washington, D.C., 1953), 474. On the categorization of blue-collar workers, see Andrew Levison, *The Working-Class Majority* (New York, 1975), 22–23. Service here is used as an occupational category, a way of characterizing workers by the tasks they performed. Elsewhere the term service is also used as an industrial category, a way of dividing up workers by what their employers produced.

23. John Gunther, *Inside U.S.A.* (New York, 1947), 553; Bureau of the Census, *County and City Data Book 1952*, 479.

24. Regional Plan Association, Inc., *The Economic Status of the New York Metropolitan Region in 1944* (New York, 1944), 4.

25. Regional Plan Association, *Economic Status*, 9; Bureau of the Census, *County and City Data Book 1952*, 3, 476; Edgar M. Hoover and Raymond Vernon, *Anatomy of a Metropolis* (Cambridge, 1959), 26–28.

26. Bureau of the Census, *County and City Data Book 1952*, tables 1 and 4; State of New York, Department of Commerce, *New York State Business Facts: New York City* [1951], 15.

27. The population figure was calculated using the United States Census New York–Northeastern New Jersey Standard Metropolitan Area. U.S. Department of Commerce, Bureau of the Census, *Census of the Population: 1950. Volume II: Characteristics of the Population. Part 32, New York* (Washington, 1952), 100, 369; Hoover and Vernon, *Anatomy of a Metropolis*, 36–39; N.Y.S. Department of Commerce, *New York State Business Facts: New York City* [1951], 15.

28. Max Hall, ed., *Made in New York: Case Studies in Metropolitan Manufacturing* (Cambridge, 1959), 4.

29. Hoover and Vernon, *Anatomy of a Metropolis*, 21; N.Y.S. Department of Commerce, *New York State Business Facts: New York City* [1951], 15; New York City Planning Commission, *Planning for Jobs* (New York, 1971), 38, 40; Jason Epstein, "The Tragical History of New York," *New York Review of Books* (April 9, 1992): 47; Joshua Brown and David Ment, *Factories, Foundries, and Refineries: A History of Five Brooklyn Industries* (New York, 1980), 54; Berger, *Meyer Berger's New York*, 70; *NYT*, June 12, 1992.

30. Bureau of the Census, *Census of the Population: 1950. Volume II: Characteristics of the Population. Part 32, New York*, 369; Regional Plan Association, *Economic Status*, xvi, 17–18.

31. Calculated from U.S. Department of Labor, Bureau of Labor Statistics, *Employment, Hours, and Earnings, States and Areas, 1939–82, Volume II* (Washington, D.C., 1984), 578, 579, 582, 584, 585, and unpublished historical data from the U.S. Department of Labor, Bureau of Labor Statistics.

32. U.S. Department of Labor, Bureau of Labor Statistics, *Employment, Hours, and Earnings, States and Areas, 1939–82, Volume II*, 579, 581, 586, 587.

33. Calculated from Bureau of the Census, *Census of Manufactures: 1947, Volume III: Statistics by States*, 22, 417.

34. Bureau of the Census, *Census of Manufactures: 1947, Volume III*, 447–48; United States Department of Commerce, *Business Establishments, Employment and Taxable Pay Rolls, First Quarter 1947, Part II: New York* (Washington, D.C., 1948), 16.

35. Calculated from Bureau of the Census, *Census of Manufactures: 1947, Volume III*, 22, 435-42. The New York City figures do not include Staten Island.

36. Hoover and Vernon, *Anatomy of a Metropolis*, 25-31.

37. Hall, *Made in NY*, 8, 10-11. David A. Hounsell, *From the American System to Mass Production, 1880-1932: The Development of Manufacturing Technology in the United States* (Baltimore, 1984), and Philip Scranton, "Diversity in Diversity: Flexible Production and American Industrialization, 1880-1930," *Business History Review* 65 (spring 1991): 27-90, provide good introductions to mass production and small batch/custom production respectively. See also Michael J. Piore and Charles F. Sabel, *The Second Industrial Divide: Possibilities for Prosperity* (New York, 1984), esp. chapter 2.

38. B. J. Stern, "An Industrial and Occupational Survey of Selected Industries in the City of New York with Particular Reference to Job Openings for the Graduates of Our Vocational High Schools," Board of Education, City of New York [1945], 25; *W-T*, Jan. 15, 1946; Hall, *Made in NY*, 279; *J-A*, Aug. 5, 1945.

39. On piecework among garment makers, see *Labor Chronicle* XLI no. 3 (March 1947): 5, and Research Department, Amalgamated Clothing Workers of America, "Equal Pay for Equal Work Among Members of the Amalgamated Clothing Workers of America, CIO," March 24, 1952, box 245, folder 1, ACW; on section and tailor work, see Hall, *Made in New York*, 81-83. Skilled to semiskilled ratio calculated from U.S. Department of Commerce, Bureau of the Census, *Census of the Population: 1950. Volume II: Characteristics of the Population. Part 22, Michigan* (Washington, 1952), 236-37 and *Part 32, New York*, 274-75, using the category "operatives and kindred workers, manufacturing" for semiskilled manufacturing workers and "craftsmen, foremen and kindred workers," subtracting foremen, for skilled blue-collar workers. The contrast between New York and Flint is far greater when only male workers are counted, a measure of the radical differences in the occupational structures of men and women in New York blue-collar jobs, as discussed below.

40. Jesse Thomas Carpenter, *Employers' Associations and Collective Bargaining in New York City* (Ithaca, N.Y., 1950), ix-xi; Bureau of the Census, *Census of Manufactures: 1947, Volume III*, 23-24; Hall, *Made in New York*, 26-40; *NACLA's Latin America & Empire Report* XI no. 3 (March 1977): 3-8.

41. Hall, *Made in New York*, 23-24, 64; Stern, "Industrial and Occupational Survey," 16-17.

42. Hall, *Made in New York*, 12-13; Piore and Sable, *Second Industrial Divide*, 28-31.

43. Hall, *Made in New York*, 3; Hoover and Vernon, *Anatomy of a Metropolis*, 248; N.Y.S. Department of Commerce, *New York State Business Facts: New York City* [1951], 8; Bureau of the Census, *County and City Data Book 1952*, 455.

44. Morris, *Manhattan '45*, 257; Hoover and Vernon, *Anatomy of a Metropolis*, 61, 77; Philip S. Foner, *The Fur and Leather Workers Union* (Newark, 1950), vii; Hall, *Made in New York*, 100.

45. Harry Kelber and Carl Schlesinger, *Union Printers and Controlled Automation* (New York, 1967), 185-89; Hall, *Made in New York*, 149, 162-73; Hoover and Vernon, *Anatomy of a Metropolis*, 65.

46. Morris, *Manhattan '45*, 128; Helen Worden, *Round Manhattan's Rim* (Indianapolis, 1934), 88-92; New York City Planning Commission, *Planning for Jobs* (New York, 1971), 12-13, 16-17, 38-79; Hoover and Vernon, *Anatomy of a Metropolis*, 14, 69-71; Federal Writers' Project, *The WPA Guide to New York City* (New York, 1939; reprinted 1982), 574-75.

47. Hoover and Vernon, *Anatomy of a Metropolis*, 11, 91-94; Federal Writers' Project, *WPA Guide to New York City*, 71-72, 74, 122, 164; The Editors of Look, in collaboration with Frederick Lewis Allen, *Look at America: New York City* (Boston, 1948), 52, 119.

48. On the general significance of industrial districts, see Piore and Sabel, *Second Industrial Divide*, 28-33, and Scranton, "Diversity in Diversity," 33-34.

49. Hall, *Made in New York*, 7-9; Hoover and Vernon, *Anatomy of a Metropolis*, 25-31.

50. Hall, *Made in New York*, 255-89.

51. Regional Plan Association, *Economic Status*, 43; Harold Underwood Faulkner, *American Economic History*, 5th ed. (New York, 1943), 608-9; Robert Reich, *The Next American Frontier* (New York, 1983), 6; Hoover and Vernon, *Anatomy of a Metropolis*, 210; United States Department of Commerce, Bureau of the Census, *Statistical Abstract of the United States, 1972* (Washington, D.C., 1972), 7, 545.

52. On antebellum New York manufacturing, see Sean Wilentz, *Chants Democratic: New York City & the Rise of the American Working Class, 1788-1850* (New York, 1984), chapter 3.

53. Hall, *Made in New York*, 279-282, 294-305; Hoover and Vernon, *Anatomy of a Metropolis*, 48.

54. Charles F. Sabel, *Work and Politics: The Division of Labor in Industry* (Cambridge, Eng., 1982), chapter 5; Piore and Sabel, *The Second Industrial Divide*; Reich, *The Next American Frontier*.

55. Robert Schrank, *Ten Thousand Working Days* (Cambridge, Mass., 1978), 1-9, 69-84; *NACLA's Latin America & Empire Report* XI no. 3 (March 1977): 7-8.

56. Hall, *Made in New York*, 30-32; Gus Tyler, "Marginal Industries, Low Wages, and High Risks," *Dissent* VII no. 3 (summer 1961); Block, *East Side - West Side*, 163; Reich, *Next American Frontier*, 246.

57. Hall, *Made in New York*, 41-42; Foner, *Fur and Leather Workers*, 648; Research Department, N.Y. Cloak Joint Board [ILGWU], "Survey of the Annual Earnings of the Workers in the New York Women's Coat and Suit Industry, 1950," box 20-20, folder 3, ILGWU; Christine Philliou, "Greek Local 70 of the International Fur and Leather Workers' Union, 1925-1966: Crossing the Lines, unpublished essay, May 1994, copy in possession of the author, 9. My own work experience and that of family members in the cosmetic, taxi, and fur industries made me familiar with patterns of seasonal work and dual occupations.

58. Altagracia Ortiz, "Puerto Ricans in the Garment Industry of New York City, 1920-1960," in Robert Asher and Charles Stephenson, eds., *Labor Divided: Race and Ethnicity in United States Labor Struggles 1835-1960* (Albany, 1990); Philliou, "Greek Local 70," 7.

59. Gender breakdown of the workforce calculated from N.Y.S. Department of Labor, *Handbook of New York Labor Statistics, 1948*, 44, 103-4, and U.S. Department of Commerce, Bureau of the Census, *Census of Manufactures: 1947, Volume I* (Washington, D.C., 1950), 70; craft to operative ratios calculated from Bureau of the Census, *Census of the Population: 1950. Volume II: Characteristics of the Population. Part 32, New York*, 274-75, as in n. 41. For a critique of the standard skills categorization, see Harry Braverman, *Labor and Monopoly Capital: The Degradation of Work in the Twentieth Century* (New York, 1974), 424-49.

60. Mike Cherry, *On High Steel: The Education of an Iron Worker* (New York, 1974); Piore and Sabel, *The Second Industrial Divide*, 115-18; U.S. Department of Commerce, *Business Establishments, Employment and Taxable Pay Rolls, First Quarter 1947, Part II: New York*, 16; Bureau of the Census, *Census of the Population: 1950. Volume II: Characteristics of the Population. Part 32, New York*, 108; Roger Waldinger and Thomas Baily, "The Continuing Significance of Race: Racial Conflict and Racial Discrimination in Construction," *Politics & Society* 19 (September 1991): 295-302; Anne Kornhauser, "Craft Unionism and Racial Equality: The Failed Promise of Local 3 of the International Brotherhood of Electrical Workers in the Civil Rights Era," MA essay, Columbia University, 1993; Temporary Commission on City Finances, *Economic Trends in New York City: The Outlook for the Future* (New York, 1977), 85.

61. Wilentz, *Chants Democratic*, 23-35, 134-37; John I. Griffin, *The Port of New York* (New York, 1959); Jan Morris, *The Great Port: A Passage through New York* (New York, 1969); Press release announcing Joint Committee on Port Industry, April 29, 1950, subject files, box 136, O'Dwyer Papers; Benjamin Chinitz, *Freight and the Metropolis, the Impact of America's Transport Revolutions on the New York Region* (Cambridge, 1960), 19; New York City Department of City Planning, *New York City Comprehensive Waterfront Plan* (New York, 1992), 83-85.

62. These figures include workers throughout the bistate port district; employment levels in New York City proper obviously were lower. Also, in a few occupations counting only full-time workers would significantly change the figures; a third of all longshoremen worked less than 100 hours over the course of a year. Griffin, *Port of New York*, 9-10, 101; Press release announcing Joint Committee on Port Industry, April 29, 1950, 1; Bureau of the Census, *Census of the Population: 1950. Volume II: Characteristics of the Population. Part 32, New York*, 269.

63. Bruce Nelson, *Workers on the Waterfront: Seamen, Longshoremen, and Unionism in the 1930s* (Urbana, 1988), 26-30; Truman Capote, "A House on the Heights," in Andrea Wyatt Sexton and Alice Leccese Powers, eds., *The Brooklyn Reader: Thirty Writers Celebrate America's Favorite Borough* (New York, 1994), 38-39; Morris, *Great Port*, 42-45.

64. N.Y.S. Department of Commerce, *New York State Business Facts: New York City* [1951], 10; U.S. Department of Commerce, *United States Census of Business: 1954. Vol. IV Wholesale Trade—Area Statistics* (Washington, 1956), tables 1a, 105; Regional Plan Association, *Economic Status*, 43-44; Jay Tabb, "A Study of White Collar Unionism," Ph.D. diss., University of Chicago, 1952, 30-32, 250; U.S. Department

of Commerce, *Business Establishments, Employment and Taxable Pay Rolls, First Quarter 1947, Part II: New York*, 16; Bureau of the Census, *Census of the Population: 1950. Volume II: Characteristics of the Population. Part 32, New York*, 370.

65. Arthur Miller, *Arthur Miller's Collected Plays* (New York, 1957), 138.

66. N.Y.S. Department of Commerce, *New York State Business Facts: New York City* [1951], 12–13; Bureau of the Census, *Census of the Population: 1950. Volume II: Characteristics of the Population. Part 32, New York*, 276, 370; U.S. Department of Commerce, *Business Establishments, Employment and Taxable Pay Rolls, First Quarter 1947, Part II: New York*, 17; C. Wright Mills, *White Collar: The American Middle Classes* (New York, 1951; pbk. 1956), 28–33; Bernard Malamud, *The Assistant* (New York, 1957).

67. I adopted the category "goods production and distribution" from Matthew P. Drennan, "The Decline and Rise of the New York Economy," in John H. Mollenkopf and Manuel Castells, eds., *Dual City: Restructuring New York* (New York, 1991). Drennan used detailed employment statistics from the U.S. Bureau of Labor Statistics. Since these are unavailable for the period I am discussing, I used the occupational breakdown in Bureau of the Census, *Census of the Population: 1950. Volume II: Characteristics of the Population. Part 32, New York*, 369–70.

68. Thomas McCormick, *America's Half-Century: United States Foreign Policy in the Cold War* (Baltimore, 1989), 3.

69. Matthew Drennan, "The Economy," in Charles Brecher and Raymond D. Horton, eds., *Setting Municipal Priorities, 1982* (New York, 1981), 63.

70. Total employment in finance, insurance, and real estate, counting both New York City residents and those who commuted into the city, was somewhat higher, around 313,000. Bureau of the Census, *Census of the Population: 1950. Volume II: Characteristics of the Population. Part 32, New York*, 370; U.S. Department of Commerce, *Business Establishments, Employment and Taxable Pay Rolls, First Quarter 1947, Part II: New York*, 17; Regional Plan Association, *Economic Status*, xviii; Hoover and Vernon, *Anatomy of a Metropolis*, 92–93.

71. Bureau of the Census, *Census of the Population: 1950. Volume II: Characteristics of the Population. Part 32, New York*, 270, 370; N.Y.S. Department of Labor, *Handbook of New York Labor Statistics, 1948*, 5.

72. Bureau of the Census, *Census of the Population: 1950. Volume II: Characteristics of the Population. Part 32, New York*, 370; Bureau of the Census, *County and City Data Book 1952*, 1980.

73. Andreas Feininger, *New York in the Forties* (New York, 1978).

74. Hall, *Made in New York*, 63–65; Frank Lee Donoghue to William O'Dwyer, "Statistical material on television," July 17, 1950, box 162, folder 1737, subject files, O'Dwyer Papers.

75. Editors of Look, *Look at America: New York City*, 52.

CHAPTER 2: WORKING-CLASS NEW YORK

1. David A. Hounshell, *From the American System to Mass Production, 1800–1932: The Development of Manufacturing Technology in the United States* (Baltimore, 1984), 303–30; Quentin Hoare and Geoffrey Nowell Smith, eds., *Selections from the Prison Notebooks of Antonio Gramsci* (New York, 1971), 277–318; Nelson Lichtenstein, "From Corporatism to Collective Bargaining: Organized Labor and the Eclipse of Social Democracy in the Postwar Era," in Steve Fraser and Gary Gerstle, eds., *The Rise and Fall of the New Deal Order, 1930–1980* (Princeton, 1989), 143–44; Harvey Swados, "The UAW—Over the Top or Over the Hill?," in Swados, *A Radical at Large: American Essays* (London, 1968), esp. 70–72; and Swados, *On the Line* (1957; reprinted, Urbana, 1990).

2. On *The Honeymooners*, see James Bacon, *How Sweet It Is: The Jackie Gleason Story* (New York, 1985). On the heroic image of the worker, see Eric Hobsbawm, *Workers: Worlds of Labor* (New York, 1984), 81–102; Barbara Melosh, *Engendering Culture: Manhood and Womanhood in New Deal Public Art* (Washington, D.C., 1991); and Elizabeth Faue, *Community of Suffering & Struggle: Women, Men and the Labor Movement in Minneapolis, 1915–1945* (Chapel Hill, 1991).

3. Geoffrey D. Neeleer, "Kings English: Facts and Folklore of Brooklyn Speech," 181, in Rita Seiden Miller, ed., *Brooklyn USA: The Fourth Largest City in America* (New York, 1979); *Lifeboat*, Twentieth Century Fox Film Corporation, 1944; directed by Alfred Hitchcock.

4. *NYP*, Oct. 12, 1945; CIO Min, Jan. 17, 1946; Art Preis, *Labor's Giant Step* (New York, 1972), 293; *UE News*, Sept. 28, 1946; *NYT*, May 30, 1946; Oct. 11, 1946.

5. James J. Matles and James Higgins, *Them and Us: Struggles of a Rank-and-File Union* (Englewood Cliffs, N.J., 1974), 144–45; *UE News*, Feb. 2, 1946; March 16, 1946.

6. CIO Min, Jan. 3, 1946, Jan. 17, 1946, Feb. 21, 1946.

7. *UE News*, July 13, 1946.

8. Steven Fraser, *Labor Will Rule: Sidney Hillman and the Rise of American Labor* (New York, 1991), 565–66.

9. Population figures calculated from Ira Rosenwaike, *Population History of New York City* (Syracuse, 1972), tables B-1 and B-2, and United States Department of Commerce, Bureau of the Census, *Census of Population: 1950. Volume II, part 1* (Washington, D.C., 1953), 101; John H. Mollenkopf and Manuel Castells, eds., *Dual City: Restructuring New York* (New York, 1991), 7.

10. Rosenwaike, *Population History*, 151–52, 155, 159, 163–64, 205; Deborah Dash Moore, *At Home in America: Second Generation New York Jews* (New York, 1981), 3, 243; Norman Podhoretz, *Making It* (New York, 1967), 83.

11. William E. Leuchtenberg, *The Perils of Prosperity, 1914–32* (Chicago, 1958), 226; *Annie Hall*. United Artists, 1977; directed by Woody Allen; Thomas McGrath, *This Coffin Has No Handles* (New York, 1988), 46–47; *The New Yorker*, March 29, 1976.

12. Prior to 1930 and after 1960 there was significant black immigration, but not during the years discussed here. Rosenwaike, *Population History*, 140, 143; Harold X. Connolly, *A Ghetto Grows in Brooklyn* (New York, 1977), 135; Katherine Trent and Richard D. Alba, "Population," in Gerald Benjamin and Charles Brecher, eds., *The Two New Yorks: State-City Relations in the Changing Federal System* (New York, 1988), 86.

13. While there had been a Puerto Rican community in New York City since the early years of the century, as late as 1940 it constituted less than one percent of the population. History Task Force, Centro de Estudios Puertorriqueños, *Labor Migration Under Capitalism: The Puerto Rican Experience* (New York, 1979), 15–26; Trent and Alba, "Population," 87; C. Wright Mills, Clarence Senior, Rose Kohn Golden, *The Puerto Rican Journey: New York's Newest Migrants* (New York, 1950), 44–45; United States Department of Commerce, Bureau of the Census, *Census of Population: 1950. Volume IV: Special Reports. Part 3D* (Washington, D.C., 1953), 12; [Lois S. Gray], U.S. Department of Labor, Bureau of Labor Statistics, Middle Atlantic Regional Office, *A Socio-Economic Profile of Puerto Rican New Yorkers* [Regional Report 46] (New York, 1975), 9, 24.

14. E. B. White, *Here Is New York* (New York, 1949; reprinted 1988), 10–11.

15. City of New York, City Planning Commission, *New York City: A Study of its Population Changes* (New York, 1951), 1; Rosenwaike, *Population History*, 131, 135, 138, 140, 143; Temporary Commission on City Finances, *Economic Trends in New York City: The Outlook for the Future* (New York, 1977), 67, 85.

16. In absolute numbers the foreign-born population of the city peaked in 1930, while as a percentage of the city's population it crested even earlier, in 1910, at 41 percent. United States Department of Commerce, Bureau of the Census, *Census of Population: 1950. Volume II, part 1*, 101; City Planning Commission, *New York City: A Study of Its Population Changes*, 12; Temporary Commission on City Finances, *Economic Trends*, 67. Age distribution calculated from Rosenwaike, *Population History*, tables B-1 and B-2.

17. "William O'Dwyer," *Dictionary of American Biography*, supplement 7 (New York, 1981); Chris McNickle, *To Be Mayor of New York: Ethnic Politics in the City* (New York, 1993), 85; Henry J. Browne, *One Stop Above Hell's Kitchen: Sacred Heart Parish in Clinton* (South Hackensack, N.J., n.d.), 32; Michael Weisser, *A Brotherhood of Memory: Jewish Landsmanshaftn in the New World* (New York, 1985), 220; newspaper clippings in Records of the Board of Transportation, New York Transit Museum Archives, Brooklyn, N.Y.

18. Moore, *At Home in America*; Robert Anthony Orsi, *The Madonna of 115th Street: Faith and Community in Italian Harlem, 1880–1950* (New Haven, 1985); Bacon, *How Sweet It Is*, 2–3; Sid Caesar,

with Bill Davidson, *Where Have I Been? An Autobiography* (New York, 1982), 9–10; Alfred Kazin, *A Walker in the City* (New York, 1951); Podhoretz, *Making It*; Irving Howe, *A Margin of Hope: An Intellectual Autobiography* (San Diego, 1982).

19. Rosenwaike, *Population History*, 143–49; Emanuel Tobier, "Population," in Charles Brecher and Raymond D. Horton, eds., *Setting Municipal Priorities, 1982* (New York, 1981), 32–36.

20. Bureau of the Census, *Census of Population: 1950. Volume IV: Special Reports. Part 3D*, 12; Mills, et al., *Puerto Rican Journey*, 25, 30–37, 51–53, 60, 69–75; History Task Force, *Labor Migration Under Capitalism*, 128, 145–48, 119–20, 198, 228, 230–31; BLS, *A Socio-Economic Profile of Puerto Rican New Yorkers*, 15–18, 23, 89–90, 110.

21. Oscar Handlin, *The Newcomers: Negroes and Puerto Ricans in a Changing Metropolis* (Cambridge, 1959), 52.

22. Handlin, *Newcomers*, 61–62; Rosenwaike, *Population History*, 174; Temporary Commission on City Finances, *Economic Trends*, 70–71; *J-A*, Aug 5, 1945, section B.

23. Elliot Willensky, *When Brooklyn Was the World, 1920–1957* (New York, 1986), 58; Miller, ed., *Brooklyn USA*, 27, 31; Moore, *At Home in America*, 66; "East Harlem," "Harlem," and "Yorkville," in *EncNY*, 356, 523–25, 1284–85; Peter Kwong, *Chinatown, N.Y.: Labor & Politics 1930–1950* (New York, 1979); Handlin, *Newcomers*, 88; Kazin, *A Walker in the City*, 35. On neighborhood-based industry see, for example, Gerald Sorin, *The Nurturing Neighborhood: The Brownsville Boys Club and Jewish Community in Urban America, 1940-1990* (New York, 1990), 11, and Will Anderson (with the assistance of Judy De Sena), "The Breweries of Brooklyn: An Informal History," in Miller, ed., *Brooklyn USA*.

24. Browne, *One Stop Above Hell's Kitchen*, 32; Orsi, *The Madonna of 115th Street*, 47.

25. See, for example, Podhoretz, *Making It*, 83, and Jerry Della Femina and Charles Sopkin, *An Italian Grows in Brooklyn* (Boston, 1978), 8, 24 (quote), 65.

26. In Philadelphia and Baltimore, like New York, fewer than 10 percent of residential dwellings were detached, single-family homes. However, row housing and small multifamily houses rather than large apartment buildings typified working-class districts in those cities. Richard Harris, "Working-Class Home Ownership in the American Metropolis," *Journal of Urban History* 17 no. 1 (Nov. 1990): 56; United States Department of Commerce, Bureau of the Census, *County and City Data Book 1952* (Washington, D.C., 1953), 445, 453, 461, 469, 477, 493; United States Department of Commerce, Bureau of the Census, *Census of Housing: 1950. Vol. 1, General Characteristics, Part 4* (Washington, 1953), table 17; Ann Petry, *The Street* (Boston, 1946), 68; Evelyn Gonzalez, "City Neighborhoods: Formation, Growth, and Change in the South Bronx, 1840-1940," Ph.D. diss., Columbia University, 12 (quote), 322. For an example of the willingness of labor groups and their allies to seek higher real estate taxes to finance city services, see Joshua B. Freeman, *In Transit: The Transport Workers Union in New York City, 1933-1966* (New York, 1989), 288.

27. The data on Jewish neighborhoods is from 1930, but there is no reason to believe that the situation was substantially different twenty years later. Moore, *At Home in America*, 52-53, 66; Dan Wakefield, *Island in the City: Puerto Ricans in New York* (New York, 1959), 17; Miller, ed., *Brooklyn USA*, 31; Connolly, *A Ghetto Grows in Brooklyn*, 132-34; Jim Sleeper, *The Closest of Strangers: Liberalism and the Politics of Race in New York* (New York, 1990) 136; Larry King, with Marty Appel, *When You're From Brooklyn, Everything Else Is Tokyo* (Boston, 1992), 35, 37-38, 44.

28. Edward Rivera, *Family Installments* (New York, 1982); Joseph P. Fitzpatrick, *Puerto Rican Americans: The Meaning of Migration to the Mainland* (Englewood Cliffs, N.J., 1971), 124-25; Willensky, *When Brooklyn Was the World*, 131.

29. Kitty Hanson, *Rebels in the Streets: The Story of New York's Girl Gangs* (Englewood Cliffs, N.J., 1964), 15; Juvenile Delinquency Evaluation Project of the City of New York, "Interim Report No. XIV," excerpted in *Dissent* VIII no. 3 (summer 1961): 338 (includes quote); Wakefield, *Island in the City*, 125-26; Leonard Bernstein, *West Side Story: A Musical* (New York, 1958).

30. "Red Hook" and "Sunset Park," in *EncNY*; Arthur Miller, *A View from the Bridge: A Play in Two Acts with an Introduction* (New York, 1960); Willensky, *When Brooklyn was the World*, 108; Budd Shulberg, "Joe Docks," in Alexander Klein, ed., *The Empire City: A Treasury of New York* (New York, 1955).

31. Gus Tyler, "Marginal Industries, Low Wages, and High Risks," *Dissent* VIII (summer 1961): 323.

32. Emanuel Tobier, "The Bronx in the Twentieth Century: Dynamics of Population and Economic Change," *The Bronx County Historical Society Journal* 25 no. 2 (fall 1998), 72–75, 78; Leonard Kriegal, "In the Country of the Other," *Dissent*, fall 1987, 618–19; Willensky, *When Brooklyn Was the World*, 87; Edgar M. Hoover and Raymond Vernon, *Anatomy of a Metropolis* (1959; reprint, Garden City, N.Y., 1962), 149, 154, 167–68; 173–4; Harris, "Working-Class Home Ownership," 62.

33. Sorin, *Nurturing Neighborhood*, quotes on 36, 41; Kazin, *A Walker in the City*, 37–39.

34. Marcantonio did once visit Puerto Rico. Kenneth Waltzer, "The American Labor Party: Third Party Politics in New Deal–Cold War New York, 1936–1954," Ph.D. diss., Harvard, 1977, 182, 203–206; Gerald Meyer, *Vito Marcantonio: Radical Politician 1902–1954* (Albany, 1989), quote on 142.

35. Della Femina and Sopkin, *An Italian Grows in Brooklyn*, esp. 8, 52–53, 65; Marianna De Marco Torgovnick, *Crossing Ocean Parkway* (Chicago, 1996), 3–34, 159–74 (quote on 7); Jonathan Rieder, *Canarsie: The Jews and Italians of Brooklyn* (Boston, 1985), 27, 138.

36. Harold Freeman to Beatrice Freeman, Nov. 13, 1944, copy in possession of the author. See also, Howe, *A Margin of Hope*, 90–103.

37. Nelson Lichtenstein, "The Making of the Postwar Working Class: Cultural Pluralism and Social Structure in World War II," *The Historian* 511 (Nov. 1988): 42–63; Richard Polenberg, *One Nation Divisible: Class, Race, and Ethnicity in the United States since 1938* (New York, 1980), 54–57; Edward Pessen, "A Young Industrial Worker in Early World War II in New York City," *Labor History* 22 (spring 1981): 276–77; Al Nash, "A Unionist Remembers: Militant Unionism and Political Factions," *Dissent* (spring 1972): 181–89.

38. Polenberg, *One Nation Divisible*, 50–54; Mark Naison, "Remaking America: Communists and Liberals in the Popular Front," esp. 57–64, in Michael E. Brown, et al., *New Studies in the Politics and Culture of U.S. Communism* (New York, 1993); Robbie Lieberman, *"My Song Is My Weapon": People's Songs, American Communism, and the Politics of Culture, 1930–1950* (Urbana, 1989), 40–41; Mary L. Douzma, "Desegregation as a Cold War Imperative," *Stanford Law Review* 41 (Nov. 1988): 68–69. Frank Sinatra can be heard singing "The House I Live In" on his album *Best of The Columbia Years: 1943–1952*, Sony, 1995.

39. Carl E. Prince *Brooklyn's Dodgers: The Bums, the Borough, and the Best of Baseball, 1947–1957* (New York, 1996), 134, 190; Neil J. Sullivan, *The Dodgers Move West* (New York, 1987), 14–19 (quote on 18), 25–26, 38–40. See also Roger Kahn, *The Boys of Summer* (New York, 1973).

40. Clifton Hood, *722 Miles: The Building of the Subways and How They Transformed New York* (New York, 1993), 215–20; *The Cool World*. Wiseman Film Company, 1963; directed by Shirley Clarke.

41. Vernon W. Boggs, *Salsiology: Afro-Cuban Music and the Evolution of Salsa in New York City* (New York, 1992), esp. 97–105, 127–64, 239–59; *New York Newsday*, July 26, 1993; Max Salazar, "The Development of Latin Music in New York City," [WBAI] *Folio*, Jan. 1976.

42. *NYT*, July 31, 1997, section C.

43. On the contributions of ordinary New Yorkers to language, see Irving Lewis Allen, *The City in Slang: New York Life and Popular Speech* (New York, 1993).

44. Milton Klonsky, "The Trojans of Brighton Beach: Life on the Old Block," *Commentary* 3 no. 5 (May 1947): 466. As Irving Lewis Allen explains in *The City in Slang* (p. 20), the phrase "smart Aleck" itself came from the New York streets, probably derived from the name of a 1840s thief.

45. Daniel Bell, "The Three Faces of New York," *Dissent* 8 no. 3 (summer 1961): 222–32.

46. White, *Here Is New York*, 21–22; Klonsky, "Trojans of Brighton Beach," 463–64; Amanda Dargan and Steven Zeitlin, *City Play* (New Brunswick, 1990); King, *When You're from Brooklyn*, 174–77.

47. Lionel Abel, "New York City: A Remembrance," 255, and Irving Howe, "New York in the Thirties: Some Fragments of Memory," 242–43, both in *Dissent* 8 no. 3 (summer 1961).

48. Nash, "A Unionist Remembers," 182; Jack Metzgar to author, March 20, 1995.

49. Howe, "New York in the Thirties," 242; Della Femina and Sopkin, *An Italian Grows in Brooklyn*, 98.

50. Jerry Wexler with David Ritz, *Rhythm and the Blues: A Life in American Music* (New York, 1993), 12–13, 35–37; Kahn, *Boys of Summer*, 23–68; Studs Terkel, *"The Good War": An Oral History of World War II* (New York, 1984), 143; AFL Min, Mar. 4, 1946; King, *When You're from Brooklyn*, 206;

Program for 50th Anniversary of Local 10 [Cutters Union], ILGWU, at Carnegie Hall, Oct. 5, 1952, box /2-308, folder 3A, ILGWU.

51. Allen Raymond, *Waterfront Priest* (New York, 1955); Nicholas Pileggi, *Wiseguy: Life in a Mafia Family* (New York, 1985); Della Femina and Sopkin, *An Italian Grows in Brooklyn*, 48–66; Sorin, *Nurturing Neighborhood*, 20–25, 89–90. Fulton, who eventually became an international vice president of Transport Workers Union, discussed his early career and aspirations with me at the New York Transit Museum, Feb. 6, 1993.

52. *The Hawsepipe: Newsletter of the Marine Workers Historical Association* 2 no. 2 (May 1984): 22.

53. Elliot Gorn, *The Manly Art: Bare-Knuckle Fighting in America* (Ithaca, 1986), 11.

54. Miller, *A View from the Bridge; On the Waterfront*. Columbia Pictures Corporation, 1954; directed by Elia Kazan. Hubert Selby Jr., *Last Exit to Brooklyn* (New York, 1964).

55. For an overview of the cultural influence of postwar New York, see Leonard Wallock, ed., *New York: Cultural Capital of the World, 1940–1960* (New York, 1988). Michael Denning makes interesting comments about the relationship between the so-called New York intellectuals and the working class from which they sprung in "New York Intellectuals," *Socialist Review* (Jan.-Mar. 1988): 136–47. Pete Hamill discusses Sinatra's social importance in *Why Sinatra Matters* (Boston, 1998).

CHAPTER 3: LABOR DAYS

1. For an introduction to the history of labor, see the American Social History Project's *Who Built America? Working People & the Nation's Economy, Politics, Culture & Society*, vols. 1 and 2 (New York, 1989–1992).

2. State of New York, Department of Labor, *Directory of Labor Unions in New York State* (Special Bulletin Number 223), New York, 1948 lists private-sector unions and employee associations (including those like TWU Local 100 that represented both public- and private-sector employees). There is no equivalent listing of public employee unions, but see Greater New York CIO Council, *New York Trade Union Directory, 1948* (New York, [1948]), 68, 92–93, and Ralph T. Jones, "City Employee Unions: Labor and Politics in New York and Chicago" (unpublished manuscript in possession of the author), 156–65. On TWU Local 100, see Joshua B. Freeman, *In Transit: The Transport Workers in New York City, 1933–1966* (New York, 1989); on Local 802, Robert D. Leiter, *The Musicians and Petrillo* (1953; reprint, New York, 1974), 94–111. Washington D.C. was the only city with more national union headquarters than New York. See Colston E. Warner, et al., *Labor in Postwar America* (Brooklyn, 1949), 717–45.

3. According to Leo Troy, "Distribution of Union Membership among the States 1939 and 1953," Occasional Paper 65, National Bureau of Economic Research, New York, 1957, 18–19, in 1953 there were just over two million unionists in New York State. In a telephone conversation with the author on July 23, 1993, Troy estimated that half were in New York City. In 1950, Cornell University industrial relations expert Jesse T. Carpenter, in his *Employers' Associations and Collective Bargaining in New York City* (Ithaca, New York, 1950), viii, estimated that total union membership in the New York metropolitan area "may well exceed 1,500,000." In January 1946, the Greater New York CIO Council publicly claimed that there were 600,000 CIO members in the New York area, but an internal CIO estimate from two years later placed the figure at 350,000. In the late 1940s the Central Trades and Labor Council claimed 750,000 AFL members in the city, undoubtedly a considerable exaggeration. In addition there were a number of independent unions, most important the Machinists and the railroad brotherhoods. CIO Min, Jan. 3, 1946; "New York City Industrial Union Council," March 15, 1948, "Greater New York IUC, Z-235—New York" file, CIO Papers, Catholic University of America, Washington, D.C.; AFL Ex Min, May 23, 1945. Union organization rate for NYC calculated from Troy and Carpenter estimates and U.S. Department of Labor, Bureau of Labor Statistics, *Employment, Hours, and Earnings, States and Areas, 1939–82. Volume II* (Washington, 1984), 578.

4. N.Y.S. Department of Labor, *Directory of Labor Unions, 1948*, 17–47.

5. I estimated the relative size of union membership in various industrial sectors using a database I assembled of individual unions' membership.

6. For examples of union-run hiring halls, see Joseph Curran Oral History, Columbia University Oral History Research Office, 136–48; *New York Age Defender*, April 17, 1954; Retail Drug Employees Union Local 1199, D.W.U., "Employment Department Guide" [c. 1951], box 3-4-5-6-6A; David Livingston letter of Aug. 29, 1958 and "An Employment Office Guide to applicants for membership in District 65," box 59-60-61, "Hiring Hall Data" file, 1199. Some unions, like IBEW Local 3, ran job referral agencies jointly with the employers. See Gerald Finkel, "The Determination of Wages for Unionized Construction Electricians, in New York City, 1953–1983," Ph.D. diss., New School for Social Research, 1990, 33. On closed shops and job control, see Alice H. Cook and Lois S. Gray, "Labor Relations in New York City," *Industrial Relations* (May 1966): 91; Warner, et al., *Labor in Postwar America*, 446–47; "Investigation of Communism in New York City Distributive Trades," Hearings before a Special Subcommittee of the Committee on Education and Labor, House of Representatives, 80th Congress, 2nd sess. (Washington, D.C., 1948), 452–53, 462–64; *Fortune*, Nov. 1948, 203; Jan. 1953, 64; interview with Robert Delaney, March 3, 1994; *Electrical Union World*, Jan. 6, 1945; *UE News* , Nov. 9, 1948; Harry Kelber and Carl Schlesinger, *Union Printers and Controlled Automation* (New York, 1967), 37–42; "Union-Made Bagels," Industrial Bulletin [N.Y.S. Department of Labor], March 1963, 9–12.

7. Bernard Elliot Budish, "Office Worker Unionism in the United States: Origin, Present Status, and Future," Ph.D. diss., NYU, 1956, 111; Dorothy Fennell, "The Union's Inspiration: Making Industrial Unionists among New York City's Wholesale Workers, 1933–1937," unpublished paper in possession of the author, 54–57; *Amsterdam News*, Sept. 23, 1950.

8. *NYT*, Feb. 7, 1946; Puerto Rican & Negro Members, ILGWU, New York City Locals, December 1952," folder 1c, box 2-280, and "Comparative Membership Census, June 30 and January 1, 1963, New York City Area," folder 1, box 2-439, ILGWU; *Fortune*, July 1950, 34.

9. Broadus Mitchell, "Industrial Relations in the Men's and Women's Garment Industries," in Warner, et al., *Labor in Postwar America*, 510; N.Y.S. Department of Labor, *Directory of Labor Unions, 1948*, 24–25; folder 1 and 6b, box 2-308, ILGWU; Robert Laurentz, "Racial/Ethnic Conflict in the New York Garment Industry, 1933–1980," Ph.D. diss., SUNY Binghamton, 1980, 217.

10. State of New York, Department of Labor, *Directory of Labor Unions, 1948*, 25, 38–40; *NYT*, Feb. 8, 1946; *Report to the General Executive Board and Proceeding of the Fourteenth Biennial Convention of the Amalgamated Clothing Workers of America, May 5–19, 1944*, 188, 193; *HT*, Sept. 30, 1945; Philip S. Foner, *The Fur and Leather Workers Union* (Newark, 1950), 637.

11. N.Y.S. Department of Labor, *Directory of Labor Unions, 1948*, 9, 13; "Joint Board of Cloak Suit Skirt and Reefer Makers' Unions of Greater New York" [1952], file 7, box 20-20, ILGWU; Amalgamated Laundry Workers Joint Board, "'To Serve Our Members': Thirty Years of Progress," box 289, ACW.

12. District councils or joint boards acted as the prime bargaining agents for the Brewers, Shoe Workers, Carpenters, Mason Tenders, Hod Carriers, and Painters. Cook and Gray, "Labor Relations in New York City," 90; *Electrical Union World*, Jan. 6, 1945; Apr. 7, 1945; June 9, 1945; Oct. 11, 1946; N.Y.S. Department of Labor, *Directory of Labor Unions, 1948*, 31–32; Carpenter, *Employers' Associations and Collective Bargaining*, 15–16, 144, 246, 257; Robert D. Leiter, *The Teamsters Unions* (New York, 1957), 119–20; "New York City Hotel Unions," *Industrial Bulletin* (Feb. 1951): 20–23.

13. Carpenter, *Employers' Associations and Collective Bargaining*, 9–10, 66fn, 152; Warner, et al., *Labor in Postwar America* , 22.

14. Herbert Hill, "Guardians of the Sweatshops: The Trade Unions, Racism, and the Garment Industry," in Adalberto Lopez and James Petras, eds., *Puerto Rico and Puerto Ricans: Studies in History and Society* (New York, 1974), 403–4.

15. N.Y.S. Department of Labor, *Directory of Labor Unions, 1948*, 17, 30, 37.

16. Files 7b and 7c, box 2-312, 2-213 ILGWU; Ronald L. Filippelli, "Luigi Antonini, The Italian-American Labor Council, and Cold-War Politics in Italy, 1943–1949," *Labor History* 33 (winter 1992): 102–25; and Hill, "Guardians of the Sweatshops," 404.

17. Steve Fraser, " *Landslayt* and *Paesani*: Ethnic Conflict and Cooperation in the Amalgamated Clothing Workers of America," in Dirk Hoerder, ed., *"Struggle a Hard Battle": Essays on Working-Class Immigrants* (De Kalb, Ill., 1986), 280–303; Puerto Rican & Negro Members, ILGWU, New York City Locals, December 1952," folder 1c, box 2-280, and "I.L.G.W.U. Membership, January 1, 1962," box 2-439, folder 1; box 20-23, file 10; and box 14-26, ILGWU; Hill, "Guardians of the Sweatshops"; Alta-

gracia Ortiz, "Puerto Ricans in the Garment Industry of New York City, 1920-1960," in Robert Asher and Charles Stephenson, eds., *Labor Divided: Race and Ethnicity in United States Labor Struggles 1835-1960* (Albany, 1990); Barbara M. Wertheimer and Anne H. Nelson, *Trade Union Women: A Study of their Participation in New York City Locals* (New York, 1975), 63. Complaints about discrimination against African-American and Puerto Rican workers are scattered throughout the ILGWU records. The ILGWU did establish a Spanish-language edition of its newspaper, hire some Puerto Rican business agents, allow a Spanish "club" inside one large local, and provide English classes for Spanish speakers.

18. Carpenter discusses the variety of relationships between craft locals and union alliances in *Employers Association and Collective Bargaining in New York City*, esp. chapters 7-9. On TWU Local 100, see Freeman, *In Transit*, 130-31, 329-330.

19. Jack Barbash, "The I.L.G.W.U. as an Organization in the Age of Dubinsky," *Labor History* 9 (spring 1968): 112.

20. There are very few statistics on female union membership in New York City, especially for the immediate postwar decades. However, see Roy Helfgott, "Survey of Shops and Workers in New York Coat and Suit Industry," July 1953, box 20-20, file 3, ILGWU; Research Department, ACWA, "Equal Pay for Equal Work Among Members of the Amalgamated Clothing Workers of America, CIO," March 24, 1952, box 245, folder 1, ACW; Mitchell, "Industrial Relations in the Men's and Women's Garment Industries," 510; interview with Ida Torres, Sept. 8, 1993; *NYT*, Oct. 2, 1947; Dorothy Sue Cobble, *Dishing It Out: Waitresses and Their Unions in the Twentieth Century* (Urbana and Chicago, 1991), 108, 180-84; Lisa Kannenberg, "The Impact of the Cold War on Women's Trade Union Activism: The UE Experience," *Labor History* 34 no. 2-3 (spring-summer 1993): 310-11, 313-14, 316-17; Aaron Michael Brenner, "Rank and File Rebellion, 1966-1975," Ph.D. diss., Columbia University, 1996, 158; Deborah E. Bell, "Unionized Women in State and Local Government," in *Women, Work & Protest: A Century of Women's Labor History*, ed. Ruth Milkman (Boston, 1985), 280-82.

21. Wertheimer and Nelson, *Trade Union Women* (especially 84-120, 130-32) discusses this issue at length, though for a somewhat later period. See also Elaine Leeder, *The Gentle General: Rose Pesotta, Anarchist and Labor Organizer* (Albany, 1993), 85-102.

22. Wertheimer and Nelson, *Trade Union Women*, 20, 122; J. B. S. Hardman, "David Dubinsky, Labor Leader and Man," 45, and Joel Seidman, "The I.L.G.W.U. in the Dubinsky Period," 57, both in *Labor History* 9 (spring 1968); Cobble, *Dishing it Out*, 80-84.

23. Interviews with James Garry, July 7 and Aug. 2, 1994.

24. *Electrical Union World*, July 4, 1945; Grace Palladino, *Dreams of Dignity, Workers of Vision: A History of the International Brotherhood of Electrical Workers* (Washington, D.C., 1991), 208-09.

25. "Report to the G.E.B. on the Recent Organization Drive in the Dress Industry, Aug. 29, 1953," box 14-13, folder 9; "Report of the Organization and Patrol Department [Joint Cloak Board], June 1, 1954," box 20-29, folder 11; and Roy Helfgott to General Manager Naler [Joint Cloak Board], Aug. 2, 1954, box 20-20, folder 3, ILGWU; *NYT*, Sept. 29, 1948; Oct. 8, 1948; Oct. 16, 1948; Feb. 3., 1949; May 11, 1949; July 24, 1952; July 30, 1952; Aug. 30, 1952; *Fortune*, Sept. 1952, 70-73.

26. Budish, "Office Worker Unionism," 91; Sharon Hartman Strom, "'We're No Kitty Foyles': Organizing Office Workers for the Congress of Industrial Organizations, 1937-50," in Milman, ed., *Women, Work & Protest*, 211-15; Warner, et al., *Labor in Postwar America*, 26-27, 573-74; *Fortune*, April 1950, 51, 54; Mar. 1952, 49-50; Everett M. Kassalow, "White-Collar Unionism in the United States," in Adolf Sturmthal, ed., *White-Collar Trade Unions: Contemporary Developments in Industrialized Societies* (Urbana, Ill., 1967), 306, 317-29.

27. *Report of the General Executive Board and Proceeding of the Fourteenth Biennial Convention of the Amalgamated Clothing Workers of America, May 15-19, 1944*, 183, 187; N.Y.S. Department of Labor, *Directory of Labor Unions, 1948*, 24; Daniel J. Leab, *A Union of Individuals: The Formation of the American Newspaper Guild, 1933-1936* (New York, 1970); Mark McColloch, *White Collar Workers in Transition: The Boom Years, 1940-1970* (Westport, Conn., 1983), 45-46; Budish, "Office Labor Unionism," 118-20, 187, 207, 215; Strom, "'We're No Kitty Foyles'," 221, 226; and Herman Liveright to Arthur Wallander, July 12, 1946, and Norman Aronson to William O'Dwyer, July 20, 1946, box 158, O'Dwyer Papers.

28. Strom, "'We're No Kitty Foyles'," 221-24; Budish, "Office Labor Unionism," 97-98, 101-3,

108, 116; Paul Jacobs, *Is Curly Jewish?* (New York, 1965), 149–51; Al Nash, "Local 1707, CSAE: Facets of a Union in the Non-Profit Field," *Labor History* 20 no. 2. (spring 1979): 257.

29. Budish, "Office Labor Unionism," 117–18; William Frankfurt, "Dear Sir and Brother," Jan. 13, 1949, "Unions—Correspondence, 1948, 1949," box 50-51-52, 1199; CIO Min, May 20, 1943; Strom, " 'We're No Kitty Foyles'," 215–17; Vera Shlakman, "The Status of Clerical and Professional Workers," in Warner, et al., *Labor in Postwar America*, 579.

30. Budish, "Office Labor Unionism," 99–100, 113–15; McColloch *White Collar Workers*, 42–43.

31. At some banks UOPWA won bargaining rights only for security, maintenance, and building service workers. McColloch, *White Collar Workers*, 49–50; *NYT*, Jan. 11, 1947.

32. The Brooklyn Trust strike can be followed in CIO Min, May 8, 1947, and *NYT*, July 17–19, 1947; July 26, 1947; July 30–31, 1947; Aug. 6–7, 1947; Aug. 14, 1947; Aug. 17, 1947; Aug. 19–20, 1947.

33. Budish, "Office Labor Unionism," 124, 172–73; *Labor Leader*, Apr. 12, 1948; *NYT*, Feb. 23, 1948; Mar. 4, 1948.

34. *NYT*, Jan. 21, 1948; Feb. 7, 1948; Feb. 26, 1948; Feb. 29, 1948.

35. Emil Schram, "To Members, Member Firms and Branch Offices," Apr. 4, 1948, box 4, "UFE Union Local 204, Strike-Correspondence, 1947–49, ND" folder, New York Stock Exchange Archives, New York, N.Y.; Joseph P. Fitzpatrick, S.J., "The White Collar Worker on Wall Street: A Sociological Study of Employer-Employee Relationships," Ph.D. diss., Harvard University, 1948, 383, 396, 440.

36. Budish, "Office Workers Unionism," 175–76; Fitzpatrick, "White Collar Workers on Wall Street," 225, 277, 300–60, 440; AFL Min, May 3, 1948; UFE Strike Committee, "In our corner," file 1658, box 159, subject files, O'Dwyer Papers; *Labor Leader*, April 12, 1948; *NYT*, April 3, 1948; April 24, 1948.

37. *W-T*, March 30, 1948; *NYT*, March 30–31, 1948.

38. "UFEU Local 205 Strike—Emergency Procedures 1947–48, ND," box 4, NYSE Archives; *NYT*, April 3, 1948; April 6, 1948; April 8, 1948; April 11, 1948; April 15–17, 1948; April 19, 1948; April 29–30, 1948; May 7, 1948; June 17, 1948; AFL Ex Min, April 12, 1948; Budish, "Office Labor Unionism," 188–89; Fitzpatrick, "The White Collar Worker on Wall Street," 439.

39. For a discussion of the Protocols of Peace, see Arthur A. Goren, *New York Jews and the Quest for Community: The Kehillah Experiment, 1908–1922* (New York, 1970), 196–207.

40. *NYT*, June 5, 1949; Carpenter, *Employers' Associations and Collective Bargaining*, 256.

41. Joint Industry Board of the Electrical Industry, *History and Organization of the Joint Industry Board of the Electrical Industry: 40 Years of Labor Management Relations, 1943–1983* (New York, 1983), 3–16.

42. Cook and Gray, "Labor Relations in New York City," 101–2; Jack Altman, et al. to William O'Dwyer, folder 1682, box 158; Thomas Jerrson Miley to O'Dwyer, June 3, 1947, and Arthur Reis to O'Dwyer, June 5, 1947, both in folder 1732, box 162, subject files, O'Dwyer Papers.

43. See O'Dwyer Papers: subject files, box 158, esp. Edward C. Maguire to William O'Dwyer, Feb. 4, 1946, and "The O'Dwyer Plan for Industrial Peace"; Executive Secretary to Mayor to Civil Service Commission, Nov. 25, 1946, and Maguire to O'Dwyer, Nov. 20, 1946, Department Letters, box 3; and "Mayor O'Dwyer's Report on the Division of Labor Relations, 1946–1949," folder 1001, subject files, box 95 (includes quote).

44. Robert Moses to Edward C. Maguire, April 18, 1947 and May 10, 1947, folder 1683, box 158; "Broadcast Over W.J.Z., interview with Edward C. Maguire," August 3, 1947, folder 1681, box 158; and Theodore W. Kheel to William O'Dwyer, Sept. 15, 1948, folder 1686, box 159, subject files, O'Dwyer Papers; *News and Opinion* [Building Trades Employers Association of the City of New York], February 1948; *New Republic*, Jan. 26, 1948, 12–13.

45. Press release, April 29, 1950, box 136, and press release, Dec. 10, 1947, file 1394, box 135, subject files, O'Dwyer Papers; AFL Ex Min, Jan. 31, 1949.

46. Minutes of 4th Annual Meeting of Board of Directors of the CIO Relief Fund, July 31, 1946, and minutes of the CIO Services Conference, Nov. 9, 1946, both on microfilm R5336, RWLA; Saul Mills to Members of the Executive Board [NYC CIO Council], Dec. 13, 1945, box 2, folder 8, Saul Mills Papers, RWLA.

CHAPTER 4: THE RISE OF A SOCIAL DEMOCRATIC POLITY

1. Larry King, with Marty Appel, *When You're from Brooklyn, Everything Else Is Tokyo* (Boston, 1992), 206.

2. Excerpts from [NYC CIO] "Council Digests," folder 2, box 3, Saul Mills Papers, RWLA; *Production Front* [UE Local 1227], Jan.-Feb. 1945; CIO Ex Min, Apr. 30, 1945; *PM*, Sept. 9, 1945; *NYT*, Sept. 19, 1945, Jan. 16, 1946, Sept. 20, 1946, and Nov. 1, 1946; *HT*, Sept. 27, 1945; Jervis Anderson, "A. Philip Randolph, 1889-1979," *Labor's Heritage*, fall 1992, 28; AFL Ex Min, March 18, 1945, and March 4, 1946, and CIO Min, May 16, 1946; Martin Bauml Duberman, *Paul Robeson: A Biography* (New York, 1989), 305, 673.

3. *NYT*, May 2, 1946; *PM*, May 2, 1946.

4. Joshua B. Freeman, *In Transit: The Transport Workers Union in New York City, 1933-1966* (New York, 1989), 229; *Electrical Union World*, Oct. 6, 1945; Norman Markowitz, "A View from the Left: From the Popular Front to Cold War Liberalism," in Robert Griffith and Athan Theoharis, eds., *The Specter: Original Essays on the Cold War and the Origins of McCarthyism* (New York, 1974), 105.

5. City of New York, *Official Directory, 1946* (New York, 1946), 65-66.

6. Gerald Meyer, *Vito Marcantonio: Radical Politician, 1902-1954* (Albany, 1989), 22-46, 80.

7. CIO Min, Oct. 17, 1946 and Nov. 7, 1946; Norman D. Markowitz, *The Rise and Fall of the People's Century: Henry A. Wallace and American Liberalism, 1941-1948* (New York, 1973), 268.

8. Kenneth Waltzer, "The American Labor Party: Third Party Politics in New Deal-Cold War New York, 1936-1954," Ph.D. diss., Harvard University, 1977, 305-9; Chris McNickle, *To Be Mayor: Ethnic Politics in the City of New York* (New York, 1993), 53-67 (*Commentary* quote on 66); Charles Garrett, *The La Guardia Years: Machine and Reform Politics in New York City* (New Brunswick, 1961), 294-300, 395; Paul O'Dwyer, *Counsel for the Defense: The Autobiography of Paul O'Dwyer* (New York, 1979), 112-13.

9. Entries on "*Daily Worker*" and "Yiddish Left" in *EncLeft*; Renqiu Yu, *To Save China, To Save Ourselves* (Philadelphia, 1992), 94-96; Paul Milkman, *PM: A New Deal in Journalism, 1940-1948* (New Brunswick, 1997).

10. Maurice Isserman, *If I Had a Hammer . . . The Death of the Old and the Birth of the New* (New York, 1987), 79-89; on schools, see entries on "Jewish Workers University," "Jefferson School of Social Science," "Rand School of Social Science," and "Yiddish Schools" in *EncLeft*; Robbie Lieberman, *"My Song Is My Weapon": People's Songs, American Communism, and the Politics of Culture, 1930-50* (Urbana, 1989); David W. Stowe, "The Politics of Café Society," *Journal of American History* 84 no. 4 (March 1998): 1384-1406.

11. Joel Schwartz, "Tenant Power in the Liberal City, 1943-1971," in *The Tenant Movement in New York City, 1904-1984*, edited by Ronald Lawson with the assistance of Mark Naison (New Brunswick, N.J., 1986), 141-48; Annelise Orleck, *Common Sense and a Little Fire: Women and Working-Class Politics in the United States, 1900-1965* (Chapel Hill, 1995), 57-61, 267-69.

12. Thomas H. E. Walker, *Pluralistic Fraternity: The History of the International Workers' Order* (New York, 1991), 62; "Summer Camps" and "Rand School of Social Science," *EncLeft*; Raymond Munts and Mary Louise Munts, "Welfare History of the I.L.G.W.U.," *Labor History* 9 (spring 1968): 87-88; *NYT*, March 27, 1955; *Labor Front* [UE Local 1227], June-July 1947. A letter from Les Finnegan to James B. Carey, Aug. 30, 1949, describing the fears of an ex-communist UE official of what would happen to him in his neighborhood (Brownsville) if he publicly denounced the CP, can be found in folder A2.05, "Communist Party. Sidney Mason, 1949 Affidavits and Explanation," IUE.

13. Mark Naison, *Communists in Harlem during the Depression* (Urbana, 1983), 109-11, 148, 258-59, 299, 312-313; Harry Haywood, *Black Bolshevik: The Autobiography of an Afro-American Communist* (Chicago, 1978), 381-82, 403-06; Will Haygood, *The King of the Cats: The Life and Times of Adam Clayton Powell, Jr.* (Boston, 1993), 54, 88, 94, 98, 101; Duberman, *Paul Robeson*, 230, 283-84, 310; George Charney, *A Long Journey* (Chicago, 1968), 148-51.

14. Simon W. Gerson, *Pete: The Story of Peter V. Cacchione, New York's First Communist Councilman* (New York, 1976); Paul Buhle, "Peter Cacchione," in *EncLeft*.

15. Freeman, *In Transit*, 55-57, 137.

16. Meyer, *Vito Marcantonio*; Waltzer, "The American Labor Party," 182-206, 272-78. See also Alan Schaffer, *Vito Marcantonio, Radical in Congress* (Syracuse, 1966), and Patrick Watson, *Fasanella's City: The Paintings of Ralph Fasanella, with the Story of His Life and Art* (New York, 1973), 104-07.

17. C. Wright Mills, *The New Men of Power: America's Labor Leaders* (New York, 1948; reprinted, 1971), 16.

18. *Fortune*, June 1952, 71; House of Representatives, "Investigation of Communism in New York City Distributive Trades," Hearings Before a Special Subcommittee of the Committee on Education and Labor, 80th Congress, 2d session (Washington, D.C., 1948), 533; "Local 144: 'A Miniature U.N.'," *Industrial Bulletin*, March 1963, 18; Robert Schrank, *Ten Thousand Working Days* (Cambridge, 1978), 101, 114.

19. Memo on "New York City Industrial Union Council," March 15, 1948, "Greater New York Inc,—New York file, CIO Papers, Catholic University, Washington, D.C.; Jack Altman et al. to William O'Dwyer, Oct. 16, 1946, folder 1682, box 158, subject files, O'Dwyer Papers; CIO Ex Min, April 4, 1944, May 2, 1944, Aug. 8, 1944, Aug. 29, 1944, and May 11, 1946; and CIO Min, March 21, 1945, Jan. 3, 1946, and Oct. 17, 1946; unlabeled history of the NYC CIO Council, 2, 15-16, and Saul Mills to Members of Executive Board of the NYC CIO Council, Dec. 13, 1945, box 2, folder 8; Mills to Charlotte Carr, Nov. 13 [1944], and miscellaneous political literature, box 2, folder 15, Saul Mills Papers, and Oral history of Saul Mills, esp. p. 10, RWLA.

20. Disagreements did develop between the CP and CIO liberals over foreign policy, but not in a major way until late 1947. Saul Mills Oral History, 15-19. For a good discussion of CIO politics during this era, see Nelson Lichtenstein, *Labor's War at Home: The CIO in World War II* (Cambridge, Eng., 1982).

21. CIO Political Action Committee, *People's Program, 1946* (New York, n.d.); Congress of Industrial Organizations, *1947 Facts for Action: Raise Wages not Prices!*, CIO Publication #142 (Washington, D.C., n.d.); Greater NYC CIO Council, "MAY DAY, 1946 — Statement," microfilm R5336, RWLA; Steven Fraser, *Labor Will Rule: Sidney Hillman and the Rise of American Labor* (New York, 1991), 506-10.

22. CIO Min, March 21, 1945, May 2, 1946, July 18, 1946, July 25, 1946, March 4, 1948; and CIO Ex Min, March 28, 1945, Aug. 6, 1946; *Labor Front*, Dec. 1947.

23. Greater New York CIO Council, *New York Trade Union Directory and Manual* (New York, 1946), 24, 34-37; Minutes of 4th Annual Meeting of Board of Directors of the CIO Relief Fund, July 31, 1946, and Minutes of the CIO Services Conference, Nov. 9, 1946, microfilm R5336, RWLA; Saul Mills to Members of the Executive Board, NYC CIO Council, Dec. 13, 1945, box 2, folder 8, Mills Papers, RWLA.

24. Freeman, *In Transit*, 55; Nelson Lichtenstein, ed., *Political Profiles: The Kennedy Years* (New York, 1976), 105; Henry Foner, "Saul Mills and the Greater New York Industrial Union Council, CIO," *Labor History* 31 no. 3 (summer 1990): 347; AFL Min, March 9, 1953; Dec. 15, 1955; AFL Ex Min, May 23, 1945, Nov. 19, 1957. On Lacey, see *NYT*, Aug. 17, 1957 and Nov. 14, 1957, and Robert D. Leiter, *The Teamsters Union* (New York, 1957), 119-27. ,

25. AFL Min, Feb. 26, 1945, and AFL Ex Min, Feb. 13, 1945, July 16, 1945, Jan. 14, 1946, Jan. 3, 1947, Jan. 15, 1951, April 2, 1951, and Jan. 3, 1952.

26. The one notable exception to this was Israel: the AFL council strongly backed both the Israeli state and Histradrut. With the CIO also strongly supporting Israel, this was one of the few matters on which the two labor councils cooperated. See AFL Ex Min, passim, esp. Dec. 12, 1948, Oct. 18, 1954.

27. AFL Ex Min, Jan. 14, 1946, Jan. 31, 1949.

28. AFL Ex Min, Oct. 15, 1945 and Jan. 31, 1955; *Fortune*, Feb. 1952: 60.

29. The AFL council had a standard financial contribution that it gave striking affiliates and would appeal to its member unions for additional funds. Beyond that, the council rarely engaged in strike support activities. AFL Min, May 7, 1954, and AFL Ex Min, Aug. 16, 1948, May 23, 1949, and Dec. 8, 1952.

30. *NYT*, April 10, 1977; AFL Min, Dec. 15, 1955, and AFL Ex Min, March 30, 1953, July 15, 1954, Dec. 12, 1955.

31. Emanuel Tobier and Barbara Gordon Espejo, "Housing," in Gerald Benjamin and Charles Brecker, eds., *The Two New Yorks: State-City Relations in the Changing Federal System* (New York, 1988), 452-58; Schwartz, "Tenant Power," 134-53. For more recent developments, see Ronald Lawson with the

assistance of Rueben B. Johnson III, "Tenant Responses to the Urban Housing Crisis, 1970-1984," also in Lawson, ed., *The Tenant Movement in New York City*. On labor support for rent control, see CIO (NYC) Min, Sept. 12, 1949; CIO (NYC) Ex Min, June 14, 1951 and Sept. 17, 1957; AFL Ex Min, Jan. 15, 1951. In 1993 over a million apartments in New York City—about 56 percent of the rental stock—was under some form of rent regulation. See New York State Division of Housing and Community Renewal, Office of Rent Administration, *Rent Regulation after 50 Years: An Overview of New York State's Rent Regulated Housing, 1993* (n.p., n.d.), 12.

32. Federal Writers' Project, *The WPA Guide to New York City* (New York, 1939; reprinted, 1982), 406; Clifton Hood, *722 Miles: The Building of the Subways and How they Transformed New York* (New York, 1993), 107, 182, 184, 219-21, 240-54; Freeman, *In Transit*, 286-94, 303-04, 311, 325.

33. Joel Schwartz, *The New York Approach: Robert Moses, Urban Liberals, and Redevelopment of the Inner City* (Columbus, Ohio, 1993), 59, 120; and Richard Plunz, *A History of Housing in New York City* (New York, 1990), 261, 274.

34. Charles R. Morris, *The Cost of Good Intentions: New York City and the Liberal Experiment, 1960-1975* (New York, 1980; reprinted 1981), 43-45; The Newt Davidson Collective, *Crisis at CUNY* (n.p., 1974), 54-55.

35. Morris, *Cost of Good Intentions*, 39; Harold H. Hart, *Hart's Guide to New York City* (New York, 1964), 963-64, 1235; *NYT*, Aug. 1, 1999, section 13.

36. Martin L. Sobol, *The New York City Opera: An American Adventure* (New York, 1981), 6-13, 58, 63-64, 116, 124-25, 168, 201-3; Thomas Kessner, *Fiorello H. La Guardia and the Making of Modern New York* (New York, 1989), 553; Nimit Saba Habachy, "Family Portrait: Fifty Years of New York City Opera," *Opera News* 58 no. 1 (July 1993): 28; Jay R. S. Teran, "The New York Opera Audience: 1825-1974," Ph.D. diss., New York University, Oct. 1974, 153-67, 193.

37. Sandra Opdycke, "Private Choices, Public Obligations: New York City and its Hospitals Since 1900," Ph.D. diss., Columbia University, 1995, 304.

38. For overviews of race relations during this period, see Jack M. Bloom, *Class, Race & the Civil Rights Movement* (Bloomington, 1987), chapters 2-4, and Harvard Sitkoff, *The Struggle for Black Equality, 1954-1992* (New York, 1993), chapter 1.

39. Martha Biondi, "The Struggle for Black Equality in New York City, 1945-1955," Ph.D. diss., Columbia University, 1997; Merl E. Reed, *Seedtime for the Modern Civil Rights Movement: The President's Committee on Fair Employment Practice, 1941-1946* (Baton Rouge, 1991); *Fortune*, Sept. 1950, 50, 52; New York State Federation of Labor, *Proceedings, Executive Council Regional Meetings, Aug. 13 to 17, 1945* (Albany, 1945), 5, 49, 101-2; AFL Ex Min, Feb. 13, 1945.

40. Cheryl Lynn Greenberg, *"Or Does It Explode": Black Harlem in the Great Depression* (New York, 1991), 202-3; "Mayor LaGuardia Endorses Michael J. Quill" [palm card] (N.Y., 1943), Maurice Forge Papers, RWLA.

41. Harold X. Connolly, *A Ghetto Grows in Brooklyn* (New York, 1977), 146-49; Jules Tygiel, *Baseball's Great Experiment: Jackie Robinson and His Legacy* (New York, 1983), 36-38, 53-54, 69; "Data from notes taken from Ewart G," folder 20, Guinier Papers.

42. See, for example, AFL Ex Min, April 30, 1945, Jan. 14, 1946, March 18, 1946, and Feb. 18, 1952; Greater New York CIO Council Executive Board, "May Day, 1946—Statement," microfilm R5336, RWLA; CIO (NYC) Ex Min, May 18, 1955 and Oct. 10, 1955; box 20-23, file 10, and box 14-26, ILGWU; and United Public Workers, "International Executive Board Meeting, Feb. 15-16, 1952," 35, Guinier Papers; Joseph F. Wilson, *Tearing Down the Color Bar: A Documentary History and Analysis of the Brotherhood of Sleeping Car Porters* (New York, 1989), 217-31; Dave Montgomery, "Local Protests Murder of Till Youth in South," *475 News* [UE Local 475], Sept. 1955; *Labor Front* (Oct.-Nov. 1946); "Report on Convention of Distributive Workers Union," "Distributive Workers Union—1950" folder, box 56,57,58, 1199 (5206-D).

43. Dorothy Sue Cobble, *Dishing It Out: Waitresses and Their Unions in the Twentieth Century* (Urbana and Chicago, 1991), 182; CIO Min, March 7, 1946.

44. Greenberg, *"Or Does It Explode?"*, 108-39; Philip S. Foner, *Organized Labor and the Black Worker, 1619-1973* (New York, 1974; pbk. 1976), 293.

45. *New York Age*, April 16, 1949; *New York Amsterdam News*, May 26, 1951; March 22, 1952; United Public Workers, "International Executive Board Meeting, Feb. 15–16, 1952," 30, folder 2, and Greater New York Negro Labor Council, "Jobs Action Conference," March 8, 1952, folder 6, Guinier Papers.

46. Lionel C. Barrow to Charles P. Gross, Feb. 11, 1946, "Discrimination to 1957" file, New York Transit Museum Archives, Brooklyn, N.Y.; Naison, *Communists in Harlem*, 262–63; *New York Age*, Jan. 29, 1949; Sept. 5, 1953; *New York Amsterdam News*, Jan. 7, 1950, Jan. 14, 1950, March 8, 1952, and March 28, 1953; *NYT*, March 2, 1952; Greater New York Negro Labor Council, "Jobs Action Conference," 2–3.

47. Greater New York Negro Labor Council, "Jobs Action Conference," 7; Foner, *Organized Labor and the Black Worker*, 304; Ewart Guinier, "A New Wind Is Blowing," folder 7, Guinier Papers.

48. UE Local 475, "Officers Report to the Membership," Nov. 16, 1952, 29–35, 68–71, FF1057, UE; Foner, *Organized Labor and the Black Worker*, 304; *475 News*, June 1953; Feb. 1954; March 1954; *Labor Front*, Dec. 1946.

49. Donald T. Critchlow, "Communist Unions and Racism," *Labor History* 17 no. 2 (spring 1976); Leon Fink and Brian Greenberg, *Upheaval in the Quiet Zone: A History of Hospital Workers' Union, Local 1199* (Urbana, 1989), 21, 24; "The Union Democracy Built," May 26, 1957 [phonograph record], taped copy in possession of the author; Executive Board Meeting, May 7, 1947 (first quote); Executive Council, May 6, 1950 (second quote), Oct. 29, 1951, Nov. 12, 1951, box 3,4,5,6,6A; Ted Mitchell, "Report for June 4th Negro Affairs Membership Meeting," Negro Affairs Committee, 1951-52 folder," box 75; and "Report on Employment Department for the years 1956 and 1957," "Hiring Hall Data" folder, box 59,60,61, all 1199.

50. On Local 65, see *New York Amsterdam News*, Sept. 23, 1950 and April 21, 1951; on the United Public Workers, see United Public Workers, The New York City Joint Anti-Discrimination Committee, "First Annual Report," and Teachers Union, Local 555, UPW, "Bias and Prejudice in Textbooks in Use in New York City Schools: An Indictment," both in folder 4, Guinier Papers; Joseph Starobin, *American Communism in Crisis, 1943–1957* (Berkeley, 1975), 198–201.

CHAPTER 5: THE COLD WAR IN NEW YORK

1. Good overviews of anticommunism include Ellen Schrecker, *Many Are the Crimes: McCarthyism in America* (Boston, 1998); and David Caute, *The Great Fear: The Anti-Communist Purge Under Truman and Eisenhower* (New York, 1978).

2. *NYT*, June 20, 1945, Oct. 25, 1945, Oct. 31, 1945, Dec. 18, 1945, Dec. 20, 1945, Dec. 22, 1945, Jan. 3, 1946; *J-A*, Dec. 17, 1945; *The Tablet*, Nov. 24, 1945, Dec. 8, 1945, Dec. 15, 1945, Dec. 29, 1945, Jan. 5, 1946; Teachers Union, "Dear Union Member and Friends," [Dec. 6, 1945], and United Parents Association, Day Letter, Dec. 4, 1945, folder 149, box 66, United Parent Association records, Special Collections, Milbank Memorial Library, Teachers College, Columbia University.

3. *NYT*, Feb. 28, 1946, March 1–3, 1946, March 6, 1946, March 11, 1946, March 15, 1946, April 18, 1946; Parent Association Public School 206, "Dear Parent Member" folder 149, and folder 154, box 66, United Parent Association records; *Tablet*, March 30, 1946, April 6, 1946, June 29, 1946.

4. *NYT*, June 14, 1946, Dec. 17, 1949, Dec. 19, 1949, Dec. 23, 1949; Files of Superintendent William Jansen [III.A.1], box 5, Bd of Ed.

5. An informal quota system gave a third of the seats on the Board of Education to Catholics, a third to Jews, and a third to Protestants. Patrick J. McNamara, "Anti-Communist Catholic Activity in the Diocese of Brooklyn from the Depression through the Post-War Years," paper presented at the Middle Atlantic Historical Association of Catholic Colleges and Universities 19th Annual Conference, La Salle University, March 27, 1993; John Cooney, *The American Pope: The Life and Times of Francis Cardinal Spellman* (New York, 1984), 180; "Highlights of To-Day's Mail," May 17, 1948, Files of Superintendent William Jansen [III.A.1], Bd of Ed.

6. *J-A*, Dec. 17, 1945; McNamara, "Anti-Communist Catholic Activity"; Caute, *Great Fear*, 437–38; Michael Kazin, *The Populist Persuasion: An American History* (New York, 1995), 173–78.

7. Transcript of Hotel and Restaurant Employees investigation, Bd of Ed, IV.E.8.d. (subject files related to hearings), box 23, mislabeled as "Central Trade and Labor Council Investigation of Communism." See also *NYT*, Oct. 16, 1947, Nov. 4, 1947, and Jan. 29, 1948.

8. Ronald L. Filippelli and Mark D. McColloch, *Cold War in the Working Class: The Rise and Decline of the United Electrical Workers* (Albany, N.Y., 1995), 91-94.

9. The NMU battle can be followed in: Murray Kempton, *Part of Our Time: Some Monuments and Ruins of the Thirties* (New York, 1955), 83-104; "The Reminiscences of Joseph Curran" and "The Reminiscences of M. Hedley Stone" Oral History Research Office, Columbia University; Harvey A. Levenstein, *Communism, Anticommunism, and the CIO* (Westport, Conn., 1981), 253-59; Art Preis, *Labor's Giant Step: Twenty Years of the CIO* (New York, 1972), 325-26, 359; *NMU Pilot*, July 6, 1946, Dec. 27, 1946, Jan. 3, 1947, Jan. 14, 1947; *President's Report on the State of the Union, Sixth National Convention of the National Maritime Union of America, CIO*, Sept. 22, 1947, 54, 57, 106-14, box 92, Records of the NMU, Rutgers University Library.

10. Warren Moscow, *Politics in the Empire State* (New York, 1948), 46; Martin Shefter, *Political Parties and the State: The American Historical Experience* (Princeton, 1994), 203-19; Joshua B. Freeman, *In Transit: The Transport Workers Union in New York City, 1933-1966* (New York, 1989), 282-83; CIO Ex Min, Oct. 21, 1947, and AFL Ex Min, July 21, 1947.

11. Robert H. Zieger, *American Workers, American Unions, 1920-1985* (Baltimore, 1986), 108-114; Christopher L. Tomlins, *The State and the Unions: Labor Relations, Law, and the Organized Labor Movement in America, 1880-1960* (Cambridge, Eng., 1985), 282-300; Patrick Renshaw, *American Labor and Consensus Capitalism, 1935-1990* (Jackson, Miss., 1991), 88-93.

12. CIO Ex Min, April 17, 1947; AFL Ex Min, April 17, April 28, May 12, and June 16, 1947; *Labor Chronicle*, June 1947.

13. In denouncing Taft-Hartley, O'Dwyer incurred the wrath of major New York business groups, while winning plaudits from the left. Folders 1732, 1733, and 1734, subject files, box 162, O'Dwyer Papers.

14. Zieger, *American Workers*, 110-18; Irving Richter, *Labor's Struggles, 1945-1950: A Participant's View* (Cambridge, Eng., 1994), 96-133; Levenstein, *Communism, Anticommunism, and the CIO*, 217-18.

15. "Case Painting Union Loc 51," "Painters Unions Jan. 10, 1955," and Rank and File of Local 905, "Rank and File Newsletter," Sept. 1965, folder 33, box 3, Xavier; Caute, *Great Fear*, 197-99, 226-27.

16. Preis, *Labor's Giant Step*, 344; "Proceedings — State Executive Committee, American Labor Party, Jan. 7, 1948," in "ALP Campaigns — Misc. Corresp., 1939-53; NY State Exec. Comm." file, box 25, Vito Marcantonio Papers, New York Public Library; Freeman, *In Transit*, 292-93; Proceedings of the International Executive Board of the Congress of Industrial Organizations, Washington, D.C., Jan. 22-23, 1948 (copy in AFL-CIO Library, Washington, D.C.); Levenstein, *Communism, Anticommunism, and the CIO*, 224-26.

17. Freeman, *In Transit*, 294, 296; *NYT*, April 28, 1948.

18. Potash served five years in federal prison, for violating the anticommunist Smith Act, before being deported. Caute, *Great Fear*, 234-36; *NYT*, Oct. 16, 1947, Nov. 2, 1947; Philip S. Foner, *The Fur and Leather Workers Union* (Newark, 1950), 649; Freeman, *In Transit*, 232-33, 283-84, 320, 344.

19. United States House of Representatives, Hearings before a Special Subcommittee of the Committee on Education and Labor, 80th Congress, 2nd sess., "Investigation of Communism in New York City Distributive Trades"; "Investigation of Communist Infiltration Into the Fur Industry"; "Investigation of Communist Infiltration of UERMWA"; and "Investigation of Teachers Union Local No. 555, UPWA-CIO" (Washington, 1948).

20. *Post Guildsman*, April 4, 1947; *Daily Worker*, July 15, 1948; *Labor Leader*, Dec. 27, 1948.

21. Freeman, *In Transit*, 286-317.

22. Filippelli and McColloch, *Cold War in the Working Class*, 96-97, 104, 109-110.

23. *NYT*, Feb. 8, 1948; *W-T*, Feb. 9, 1948; Bill B. [William Bolton] to Harry [Block?], Feb. 12, 1948, UE District 4, Local 1237 file, box 2021, and John E. Dillon to Les Finnegan, Sept. 7, 1949, A.205, IUE; Filippelli and McColloch, *Cold War in the Working Class*, 104, 109, 111; District 4, UE, "Officers Report," Oct. 24, 1948, FF142, UE.

24. Filippelli and McColloch, *Cold War in the Working Class*, 118; Daily Worker, Jan. 26, 1948, Jan.

14, 1949; *NYT*, April 2, 1948, July 14, 1948, Aug. 11, 1948, Aug. 31, 1948, Oct. 7, 1948; Irving Abramson to Philip Murray, Aug. 27, 1948, UE Local 475 file, and John E. Dillon to Les Finnegan, Sept. 7, 1949, A.205, IUE; "A Year to Remember" and "Jack Sario's Open Letter of Members of UE Local 475," Dillon-2 folder, box D, John Dillon papers, Walter Reuther Library, Wayne State University.

25. "Resolution adopted by Executive Board—Local 1199—August 18th, 1948," "Special Executive Board Meeting Held Sept 17th, 1948," and "Special Membership Meeting," Sept. 23, 1948, box 3-6A, 1199; Levenstein, *Communism, Anticommunism, and the CIO*, 277; *NYT*, Sept. 29, 1948.

26. Kenneth Waltzer, "The American Labor Party: Third Party Politics in New Deal-Cold War New York, 1936-1954," Ph.D. diss., Harvard University, 1977, 417-28.

27. Preis, *Labor's Giant Step*, 372-73; Henry Foner, "Saul Mills and the Greater New York Industrial Union Council, CIO," *Labor History* 31 no. 3 (summer 1990): 347-360.

28. Levenstein, *Communism, Anticommunism, and the CIO*, 280-83.

29. Donald F. Crosby, "American Catholics and the Anti-Communist Impulse," in Robert Griffith and Athan Theoharis, eds., *The Specter: Original Essays on the Cold War and the Origins of McCarthyism* (New York, 1974), 25-30, 37; Cooney, *American Pope*, 160, *Catholic News*, Jan. 1, 1949, Jan. 15, 1949, Feb. 19, 1949; Jim Tuck, *McCarthyism and New York's Hearst Press: A Study of Roles in the Witch Hunt* (Lanham, Md., 1995), 45, 54-58.

30. Cooney, *American Pope*, 187-95; *Catholic News*, March 5, 1949, March 12, 1949, March 19, 1949; Cemeteries," in folder 38, box 3, Xavier; Freeman, *In Transit*, 275; Richter, *Labor's Struggles*, 63n; *The Catholic Worker*, April 1949; and Thomas J. Shelley, "Francis Cardinal Spellman and His Seminary at Dunwoodie," *The Catholic Historical Review* 80 no. 2 (April 1994): 289-93.

31. *J-A*, May 1 and 2, 1949; *NYT*, May 2, 1948, May 1 and 2, 1949. On Charles Silver, see Cooney, *American Pope*, no. 5, 163, 172, 300-01.

32. Martin Bauml Duberman, *Paul Robeson: A Biography* (New York, 1989), 341-50, 364-75; Griffin Fariello, *Red Scare: Memories of the American Inquisition: An Oral History* (New York, 1995), 74-80.

33. CIO (NYC) Min, April 25, 1949, June 22, 1949, and Sept. 12, 1949; CIO (NYC) Ex Min, May 19, 1949, Aug. 16, 1949, Feb. 9, 1950, and March 9, 1950.

34. "Reminiscences of Joseph Curran," 86, 162-64; *President's Report on the State of the Union, Seventh National Convention of the National Maritime Union of America, CIO*, Sept. 12, 1949, 69-72 Records of the N.M.U., Rutgers University Library; Levenstein, *Communism, Anticommunism, and the CIO*, 248; Philip Taft, "Civil Rights in the National Maritime Union," August 1950, American Civil Liberties Union, copy in possession of the author; *Fortune*, May 1950, 155-56; "Reminiscences of M. Hedley Stone," 289-90, 294-95; Caute, *Great Fear*, 393-400, 605.

35. Levenstein, *Communism, Anticommunism, and the CIO*, 290-91; Ellen W. Schrecker, "McCarthyism and the Labor Movement: The Role of the State," in Steve Rosswurm, ed., *The CIO's Left-Led Unions*, (New Brunswick, N.J., 1992), 148-54.

36. Joseph R. Starobin, *American Communism in Crisis, 1943-1957* Berkeley, 1975), 202-3; Filippelli and McColloch, *Cold War in the Working Class*, 134-39; Levenstein, *Communism, Anticommunism, and the CIO*, 292-94; James J. Matles and James Higgins, *Them and Us: Struggles of a Rank-and-File Union* (Englewood Cliffs, N.J., 1974), 194.

37. Levenstein, *Communism, Anticommunism, and the CIO*, 298-302; Filippelli and McColloch, *Cold War in the Working Class*, 137-40.

38. Levenstein, *Communism, Anticommunism, and the CIO*, 302-6; Daniel B. Cornfield, *Becoming a Mighty Voice: Conflict and Change in the United Furniture Workers of America* (New York, 1989), 102-18; Rosswurm, "Introduction: An Overview and Preliminary Assessment of the CIO's Expelled Unions," in Rosswurm, *The CIO's Left-Led Unions*, 2.

39. Robert H. Zieger, *The CIO, 1935-1955* (Chapel Hill, 1995), 290-91; "Haywood, Allan S(haw)," *Current Biography, 1951-1952* (New York, 1953), 251-53; F. S. O'Brien, "The 'Communist-Dominated' Unions in the United States since 1950," *Labor History* 9 no. 2 (spring 1968): 193-94, 197; *Fortune*, June 1952, 71-74; folder 21, box 3, Xavier.

40. Ignatius Brennan to Allan Haywood, Dec. 13, 1948, and Edward T. Lowry to Nash, Dec. 13, 1948, reel B; Paul McDonald, Dear Brother and Sister, Jan. 13, 1949, reel C; and Robert L. Ponsi and

Kenneth O'Dell to James Durkin, May 11, 1949; Ponsi and O'Dell "To Our Fellow Members of U.O.P.W.A., C.I.O.," June 4, 1949; and The Agents Ticket, "Local 30 — Election Times," reel D, microfilm edition, Charles Owen Rice Papers, Pennsylvania State University; *NYT*, March 1, 1948, Oct. 8, 1948, Oct. 18, 1948; *Fortune*, Feb. 1949, 170; Paul Jacobs, *Is Curly Jewish?* (New York, 1965), 149–53; Al Nash, "Local 1707, CSAE: Facets of a Union in the Non-Profit Field," *Labor History* 20 no. 2 (spring 1979): 257. See also, Charles Owen Rice, "Special to Members of the UOPWA, the UPW and other small, inefficient Communist Led Unions"; Rice, "To Members of the UOPWA"; Rice to James H. Durkin, Dec. 31, 1948; "ACTU; Exchange," all reel C, and [Rice] to Edward P. Agnew, May 22, 1948; Carl Schoenberg to Rice, Dec. 30, 1948, reel D, Rice papers; *Our Sunday Visitor*, April 23, 1950; *W-T*, Jan. 28, 1949.

41. *Fortune* (March 1952): 49–52; Nash, "Local 1707, CSAE," 257; CIO (NYC) Min, March 15, 1950 and Jan. 17, 1951; American Federation of Labor, News Distribution Organizing Committee, Jan. 14, 1949, "Unions — Correspondence, 1948, 1949" file, box 50-52; Distributive, Processing and Office Workers of America, National Executive Board Meeting, April 12–14, 1951, 10, and attached Report on District 65, 1, 3; Min, General Executive Board Meeting, April 15–17, 7, in Distributive, Processing and Office Workers of America file, box 56-57-58, 1199.

42. Ronald W. Schatz, *The Electrical Workers: A History of Labor at General Electric and Westinghouse, 1923–60* (Urbana, 1983), 225–40; Filippelli and McColloch, *Cold War in the Working Class*, 141–58; Stanley Aronowitz, *False Promises: The Shaping of American Working Class Consciousness* (New York, 1973), 346–49; Minutes of the Meeting of the Administrative Committee of UE-CIO [IUE], October 1, 1950, 65–66; "Tentative Draft Report on UE Convention" [1949], 9, both reel 3, Harry Block Papers, Pennsylvania State University; Albert Fitzgerald to James McLeish, Nov. 9, 1949; David Scribner to James Matles, March 29, 1950; and "GO CIO" [leaflet, 1949], all FF885, UE; interviews with James Garry, July 7, 1994 and Aug. 2, 1994; "District 4 — Local 441: 1950, 1952" file, box 2004, IUE.

43. There is no history of UPW, but see Subcommittee to Investigate the Administration of the Internal Security Act and other Internal Security Laws of the Committee on the Judiciary of the United States Senate, "Subversive Control of the United Public Workers of America," 82nd Congress, First Session (Washington, 1952); Mark Henry Maier, "The City and the Unions: Collective Bargaining in New York City, 1954–1973," Ph.D. diss., New School for Social Research, 1980, 68, 163; Leon Fink and Brian Greenberg, *Upheaval in the Quiet Zone: A History of Hospital Workers' Union, Local 1199* (Urbana, 1989), 17–18; "City Hospital Organizing Plan"; "No Retreat on Discrimination!"; and UPW, New York City Joint AntiDiscrimination Committee, "First Annual Report," all in folder 4, Guinier Papers; *New York Age*, May 20, 1950. On Guinier, see *NYT*, Feb. 7, 1990; UPW, "For Immediate Release," June 9, 1950, folder 7, and Ewart Guinier To Mrs. Howard L. Reiner, Feb. 13, 1952, folder 8, Guinier Papers; *PM*, July 16, 1941.

44. Caute, *Great Fear*, 268–70, 339–45; Senate Internal Security Subcommittee, "Subversive Control of the United Public Workers of America," 51, 70; Schrecker, "McCarthyism and the Labor Movement," 145–46; *Levenstein, Communism, Anticommunism, and the CIO*, 180, 243–44.

45. On Sanitation, see James V. King to William O'Dwyer, Jan. 23, 1946, box 158, and James Griese and Michael Garromone to O'Dwyer, Jan. 20, 1948, file 1687, box 159, subject files, O'Dwyer Papers; *NYT*, Jan. 25, 1948; CIO Min, July 18, 1941, March 4, 1943, and Feb. 15, 1945; AFL Ex Min, Jan. 14, 1946; and Maier, "The City and the Unions," 68. On Welfare, see Raymond M. Hilliard, "We Threw the Commies Out," *Saturday Evening Post*, June 30, 1951; *NYT*, March 10, 1950.

46. Hilliard, "We Threw the Commies Out," 21, 114–15. See also James Griese and Michael Garromone to William O'Dwyer, Jan. 20, 1948, file 1687, box 159, subject files, O'Dwyer Papers.

47. The city also pressured nonprofit social service agencies it funded to stop dealing with the UPW. Hilliard, "We Threw the Commies Out," 21, 114–17; Frank Herbst to William O'Dwyer, Sept. 17, 1948, file 1686; Jack Bigel to O'Dwyer, May 16, 1950, and Herbst to O'Dwyer, June 28, 1950, file 1690, box 159, subject files, O'Dwyer Papers; Raymond M. Hilliard, Executive Order No. 291, folder 7, box 5, Xavier; *NYT*, March 10, 1950, March 31, 1950, May 16, 1950, Feb. 3, 1951.

48. *NYT*, Nov. 21, 1950, Jan. 17, 1951, Jan. 21, 1951, Feb. 3, 1951, May 4, 1951, May 12, 1951, Aug. 8, 1951; Ewart Guinier, "The Union They Couldn't Break," folder 6, Guinier Papers; Maier, "The City and the Unions," 163–64.

49. *NYT*, June 29, 1948; Caute, *Great Fear*, 433–34; House of Representatives, Hearings before a

Special Subcommittee of the Committee on Education and Labor, 80th Congress, 2nd sess., "Investigation of Teachers Union," 94; Celia Lewis Zitron, *The New York City Teachers Union, 1916–1964* (New York, 1968), 212–17; Majorie Murphy, *Blackboard Unions: The AFT & the NEA, 1900–1980* (Ithaca, 1990), 187; *J-A*, May 2, 1949. Hundreds of postcards protesting the Feinberg Law are in the Files of Superintendent William Jansen (III.A.1.a), boxes 4 and 6, Bd of Ed.

50. *Teachers Bulletin* [National Teachers Division of UPW], April 1950, May 1950; Zitron, *Teachers Union*, 224–36; Caute, *Great Fear*, 435–37.

51. Caute, *Great Fear*, 434–37; Zitron, *Teachers Union*, 228–52; AFL Ex Min, June 12, 1950; CIO (NYC) Min, Nov. 28, 1951.

52. Caute, *Great Fear*, 441. See also Abraham Barnett to Dr. Theobold, Oct. 28, 1959, "Feinberg Law" folder, box 3, subject files related to hearings (IV.E.8.d.), Bd of Ed; Mildred Grossman, "On the '33 teachers'," *Rights* [National Emergency Civil Liberties Committee], Feb. 1977, 4–5.

53. Postcards in box 5, files of Superintendent William Jansen (III.A.1.a), Bd of Ed; Murphy, *Blackboard Unions*, 190–92; Caute, *Great Fear*, 437–38; *Teachers Bulletin*, May 1950.

54. Zitron, *Teachers Union*, 45–52; O'Brien, "The 'Communist-Dominated' Unions," 191; *NYT*, April 20, 1953, Dec. 12, 1956, Dec. 14, 1956, Dec. 23, 1956; *J-A*, May 17, 1953; *WSJ*, March 7, 1979; Fink and Greenberg, *Upheaval in the Quiet Zone*, 18–19.

55. *NYT*, May 8, 1953, June 26, 1953, Dec. 11, 1953, Nov. 25, 1954, June 24, 1955, Sept. 22, 1955, Nov. 22, 1956, Feb. 15, 1956, Feb. 16, 1956, March 1, 1957, July 1, 1958; Caute, *Great Fear*, 344–45.

56. Dan Georgakas, "*PM*" and Paul Buhle, "*Daily Worker*," in *EncLeft*; Roy Hoopes, *Ralph Ingersoll: A Biography* (New York, 1985), 328–32; Renqiu Yu, *To Save China, To Save Ourselves* (Philadelphia, 1992), 187–91, 198–99; David A. Shannon, *The Decline of American Communism* (New York, 1949), 218.

57. Arthur J. Sabin, *Red Scare in Court: New York versus the International Workers Order* (Philadelphia, 1993); Roger Keeran, "International Workers Order," in *EncLeft*.

58. Gerald Sorin, *The Nurturing Neighborhood: The Brownsville Boys Club and Jewish Community in Urban America, 1940–1990* (New York, 1990), 147-48; Caute, *Great Fear*, 109; Tuck, *McCarthyism and New York's Hearst Press*, 157–58.

59. Chris McNickle, *To Be Mayor of New York: Ethnic Politics in the City* (New York, 1993), 70–82, 332; Gerald Meyer, *Vito Marcantonio: Radical Politician, 1902–1954* (Albany, 1989), 39–41; Waltzer, "American Labor Party," 441–42; Shefter, *Political Parties and the State*, 210–15, 219–20.

60. Tuck, *McCarthyism and New York's Hearst Press*, 158; Waltzer, "American Labor Party," 446–449; Meyer, *Vito Marcantonio*, 83.

61. *National Guardian*, Aug. 23, 1954; Meyer, *Vito Marcantonio*, 82–86, 182–84; W. E. B. DuBois Papers, microfilm collection, Columbia University, reel 81, frames 916–20.

62. "Once upon a Shop Floor: An Interview with David Montgomery," *Radical History Review* 23 (spring 1980): 39, 42; George Charney, *A Long Journey*, (Chicago, 1986), 166–70; *Fortune*, Mar. 1951, 38–41; Levenstein, *Communism, Anticommunism, and the CIO*, 308–9; Save the Union Committee, "Clean Them All Out!!," folder 59, box 3, Xavier; *NYT*, Jan. 12, 1951, Aug. 14, 1990.

63. "That these people tolerated our arrogance and stupidity for so long," New York State CP head George Charney later wrote, "is testimony to their devotion and youth." "Report on Convention of Distributive Workers Union," "Distributive Workers Union - 1950" file; and "Arthur Osman, et al., "To: All Local Unions," Oct. 13, 1950; DPOWA National Executive Board Meeting, April 12–14, 1951; Minutes, General Executive Board, DPOWA, April 15–17, 1952, all in "Distributive, Processing and Office Workers of America" file, box 56-57-58; "Minutes of Special Meeting Executive Board, March 16, 1949, and Executive Council Minutes, May 16, Aug. 18, Sept. 16, and Oct. 2, 1950, box 3-4-5-6-6A, 1199; *Fortune*, Nov. 1950, 50, 52; March 1952, 54; George N. Spitz, "The Struggle for Control in the DPOWA," *The New Leader* (March 3, 1952): 8–9; Spitz, "DPOWA Goes Anti-Communist," *The New Leader*, June 9, 1952, 10–11; Alex H. Kendrick and Jerome Golden, "Lessons of the Struggle Against Opportunism in District 65," *Political Affairs*, June 1953, 26–37; *Union Voice*, April 19, 1953; Moe Foner Oral History, Oral Research Office, Columbia University, 82, 155–58, 161–65, 172, 185, 196–205, 223–24; Charney, *A Long Journey*, 170–71.

64. Walter Reuther to Irving Simon and Arthur Osman, May 13, 1953, and Jack Paley to Local 1199 — DPO, April 4, 1954, "Distributive, Processing and Office Workers of America" file, box 56-57-58, and Executive Council Minutes, May 11, 1953, box 3-4-5-6-6A, 1199; *NYP*, April 3, 1953.

65. Shannon, *Decline of American Communism*, 258-60; Levenstein, *Communism, Anticommunism, and the CIO*, 314, 323-25; *Women's Wear*, March 25, 1955; *NYT*, March 27, 1955, Aug. 10, 1955; Philip Taft, *The A.F. of L. From the Death of Gompers to the Merger* (New York, 1959), 434-35; O'Brien, "The 'Communist-Dominated' Unions," 193-94; Ben Gold, *Memoirs* (New York, n.d.), 184-91.

66. Schatz, *Electrical Workers*, 230-32; Matles and Higgins, *Them and Us*, 227-31; Filippelli and McColloch, *Cold War in the Working Class*, 158-59; James J. Matles to Clifton Cameron, July 25, 1955, FF988; Cameron to Matles, Aug. 11, 1955, FF993; and "Statement of Local 475 Executive Board on Labor Unity and Merger," Apr. 11, 1956, FF1053, UE; interview with James Garry, Aug. 2, 1994.

67. Walter Reuther to Irving Simon and Arthur Osman, May 13, 1953, "Distributive, Processing and Office Workers of America" file, box 56-57-58, and 1199 Executive Council Minutes, Oct. 19, 1953 and Oct. 26, 1953, box 3-4-5-6-6A, 1199; Moe Foner oral history, 203; Roy Wilkins to District 65, Feb. 26, 1953; Cleveland Robinson to Walter White, March 20, 1953; Henry Hamilton to Herbert Hill, July 27, 1953; Hill to Hamilton, Sept. 15, 1953; Robinson to White, Jan. 5, 1954; Robinson to Hill, April 19, 1954; "Press Release — issued by District 76, D.P.O.-C.I.O., May 19, 1954," all Papers of the NAACP, microfilm edition, part 13, series A, reel 15.

68. Ronald Schatz noted (*Electrical Workers*, 226-27) that in the IUE "[i]deologically and religiously motivated people tended to drop out of leadership in the union's early years," leaving ambitious young careerists in charge.

69. CIO (NYC) Min, March 29, 1951; CIO (NYC) Min, Jan. 28, 1955; *Fortune*, Oct. 1949, 197; Freeman, *In Transit*, 333.

70. Charles S. Maier, "Two Postwar Eras and the Conditions for Stability in Twentieth-Century Western Europe," *American Historical Review* 86 (April 1981): esp. 338-39.

71. Spitz, "Struggle for Control in the DPOWA," 8; *NYP*, April 4, 1953; Maurice Isserman, *If I Had a Hammer . . . The Death of the Old Left and the Birth of the New Left* (New York, 1987), 8-9, 29-30.

72. Len De Caux, *Labor Radical: From the Wobblies to the CIO, A Personal History* (Boston, 1970), 473-75; Zieger, *The CIO*, 270-71; Walter Reuther to Irving Simon and Arthur Osman, May 13, 1953, "Distributive, Processing and Office Workers of America" file, box 56, 57, 58, 1199.

73. Rosswurm, "Introduction," 8; interview with James Garry, July 7, 1994.

74. Rosswurm, "Introduction," 5, 8, 12; Gold, *Memoirs*, 191-92.

75. Zieger, *The CIO*, 306, 328-32; Anthony Carew, "The American Labor Movement in Fizzland: The Free Trade Union Committee and the CIO," *Labor History* 39 (Feb. 1998): 25-42.

76. Sara Evans, *Personal Politics: The Roots of Women's Liberation in the Civil Rights Movement & the New Left* (New York, 1979), esp. ch. 5; Rosalyn Baxandall, "The Question Seldom Asked: Women and the CPUSA," in Michael E. Brown, et al., eds., *New Studies in the Politics and Culture of U.S. Communism* (New York, 1993); Spitz, "Struggle for Control in the DPOWA," 9; Lisa Kannenberg, "Impact of the Cold War on Women's Trade Union Activism: The UE Experience," *Labor History* 34 no. 2-3 (spring-summer 1993).

77. Isserman, *If I Had a Hammer*, 32-33; Shannon, *Decline of American Communism*, 290-91, 360.

78. Maier, "The City and the Unions," 161-88; *WSJ*, March 7, 1979; *DN*, Feb. 17, 1980; April 3, 1994; *NYT*, Feb. 7, 1990, April 30, 1993; Marvin Miller, *A Whole Different Ball Game: The Sport and Business of Baseball* (New York, 1991), 20.

79. Fink and Brian Greenberg, *Upheaval in the Quiet Zone*; Cornfield, *Becoming a Mighty Voice*, 199-208 (quote 207-8).

80. See, for example, Daniel Horowitz, "Rethinking Betty Friedan and *The Feminine Mystique*: Labor Union Radicalism and Feminism in Cold War America," *American Quarterly* 48 no. 1 (March 1996); Annelise Orleck, *Common Sense and a Little Fire: Women and Working-Class Politics in the United States, 1900-1965* (Chapel; Hill, 1995), 270-71; *Public Employee Press*, June 14, 1996; *NYT*, Oct. 13, 1997, section D (Albert Blumberg obituary); Fink and Brian Greenberg, *Upheaval in the Quiet Zone*, 242.

CHAPTER 6: BIG LABOR

1. U.S. Bureau of the Census, *Historical Statistics of the United States, Colonial Times to 1970*, Electronic edition edited by Susan B. Carter, et al. (Cambridge University Press, 1997), Series D 946-951; American Social History Project, *Who Built America? Working People & the Nation's Economy, Politics, Culture & Society, Volume 2* (New York, 1992), 503-12; Richard H. Freeman, "Can American Unions Rebound," *WSJ*, Dec. 8, 1987.

2. Robert H. Zieger, *The CIO, 1935-1955* (Chapel Hill, 1995), 328-32, 357-71; Patrick Renshaw, *American Labor and Consensus Capitalism, 1935-1990* (Jackson, Miss., 1991), 145-51.

3. Robert H. Zieger, *American Workers, American Unions, 1920-1985* (Baltimore, 1986), 357-77; Michael J. Quill, address to the final session of the CIO Convention, New York City, Dec. 1955, copy in "MJQ Stand Against AFL-CIO Merger, Feb.-Dec. 1955" file, records of the Transport Workers Union of America, RWLA.

4. The merger of the AFL and CIO New York City central bodies was delayed by jurisdictional claims by the Teamsters and building trades against CIO groups. CIO (NYC) Ex Min, May 17, 1956; CIO (NYC) Min, Jan. 24, 1957, Dec. 2, 1957, and Feb. 5, 1959; AFL-CIO Ex Min, Feb. 19, 1959.

5. AFL-CIO Ex Min, June 6, 1961, July 19, 1961, and Aug. 17, 1961.

6. Chris McNickle, *To Be Mayor of New York: Ethnic Politics in the City* (New York, 1993), 91-108; Warren Moscow, *What Have You Done For Me Lately? The Ins and Outs of New York City Politics* (Englewood Cliffs, N.J.), 37-42; Fred Ferretti, *The Year the Big Apple Went Bust* (New York, 1976), 21; Joshua B. Freeman, *In Transit: The Transport Workers Union in New York City, 1933-1966* (New York, 1989), 325; CIO (NYC) Ex Min, July 28, 1953, Oct. 5, 1953, and Dec. 1, 1953; CIO (NYC) Min, Sept. 30, 1953 and Jan. 25, 1954; AFL Min, Oct. 28, 1953.

7. McNickle, *To Be Mayor*, 98-101, 116-21, 152-58; Charles R. Morris, *The Cost of Good Intentions: New York City and the Liberal Experiment, 1960-1975* (New York, 1980), 15-22; Nelson Lichtenstein, ed., *Political Profiles: The Johnson Years* (New York, 1976), 331-32.

8. Joseph E. Persico, *The Imperial Rockefeller: A Biography of Nelson A. Rockefeller* (New York, 1982), 122-25, 201-4 (quote on 201), 215; Robert H. Connery and Gerald Benjamin, *Rockefeller of New York: Executive Power in the Statehouse* (Ithaca, 1979), 218-41, 274-80, 292-327. The close relationship Rockefeller had with Brennan and Van Arsdale can be discerned in his correspondence with them, on reels 34 and 316 respectively, Nelson A. Rockefeller Gubernatorial Microfilm name file, RAC.

9. Nelson Lichtenstein, "From Corporatism to Collective Bargaining: Organized Labor and the Eclipse of Social Democracy in the Postwar Era," in Steve Fraser and Gary Gerstle, *The Rise and Fall of the New Deal Order, 1930-1980* (Princeton, 1989), 140-44.

CHAPTER 7: "A DECENT HOME"

1. United States Department of Commerce, Bureau of the Census, *Seventeenth Census of the United States: 1950, Housing, Volume II, Part 4* (Washington, D.C., 1953), 101-68; Cleveland Rodgers and Rebecca Rankin, eds., *The World's Capital City. Its Development and Contributions to Progress* (New York, 1948), 292-93; United States Department of Commerce, Bureau of the Census, *Sixteenth Census of the United States: 1940, Housing, Volume II, Part 4* (Washington, D.C., 1943), 275; *EncNY*, 567; Frank S. Kristof, "Housing: Economic Facets of New York City's Problems," in Lyle C. Fitch and Annmarie Hauck Walsh, eds., Agenda for a City: Issues Confronting New York (Beverly Hills, 1970), 299; Richard Plunz, *A History of Housing in New York City: Dwelling Type and Social Change in the American Metropolis* (New York, 1990), 274.

2. Gwendolyn Wright, *Building the Dream: A Social History of Housing in America* (New York, 1981), 251-53; Plunz, *History of Housing*, 275-77; Sylvie Murray, "The Shaping of 'Forgotten America': Workers and Taxpayers in Post-World War II New York," Paper presented at the Fifteenth Annual North American Labor History Conference, Wayne State University, Detroit, Oct. 16, 1993, 7.

3. *J-A*, May 1, 1949; "Privately Operating Housing Developments Now Accepting Applications" [May 1948], series 06, box 0060D6, folder 35, NYCHA.

4. Kenneth T. Jackson, *Crabgrass Frontier: The Suburbanization of the United States* (New York, 1985), 190–218; Plunz, *History of Housing*, 227–28, 260; Wright, *Building the Dream*, 246–48; Leonard Wallock, "The Myth of the Master Builder: Robert Moses, New York, and the Dynamics of Metropolitan Development Since World War II," *Journal of Urban History* 17 no. 4 (Aug. 1991): 346–48.

5. Michael Musuraca, "Organized Labor and Public Housing in New York City, 1934–1986," unpublished paper in possession of the author; *Electrical Union World*, April 8, 1946.

6. New York State Division of Housing and Community Renewal, Office of Rent Administration, *Rent Regulation after 50 Years: An Overview of New York State's Rent Regulated Housing, 1993* (n.p., n.d.), 2–4; Joel Schwartz, "Tenant Power in the Liberal City, 1943–1971," in Ronald Lawson with the assistance of Mark Naison, ed., *The Tenant Movement in New York City, 1904–1984* (New Brunswick, N.J., 1986), 141–53; Kristof, "Housing," 303–23; Sylvie Murray, "Suburban Citizens: Domesticity and Community Politics in Queens, New York, 1945–1960," Ph.D. diss., Yale University, 1994, 249–59.

7. *UE News*, Oct. 26, 1946; Greater New York CIO Council, "Digest of Council Minutes," Resolution on Housing, May 2, 1946, and Statement on Veterans Housing, May 16, 1946, microfilm R5016, RWLA; AFL Ex Min, May 14, 1951; Joel Schwartz, *The New York Approach: Robert Moses, Urban Liberals, and Redevelopment of the Inner City* (Columbus, Ohio, 1993), 59, 119–20; Charles Garrett, *The La Guardia Years: Machine & Reform Politics in New York City* (New Brunswick, 1961), 184–87; Wallock, "Myth of the Master Builder," 349–54; Wright, *Building the Dream*, 248; Robert Moses to William Charney Vladeck, Nov. 10, 1948, series 6, box 0069E4, folder 7, NYCHA; Murray, "Shaping of 'Forgotten America'," 7, 11; and *New York Age*, Sept. 5, 1953.

8. Peter Marcuse, "The Five Lives of Public Housing in New York," presentation at the Columbia University Seminar on the City, Dec. 10, 1992; Musuraca, "Organized Labor and Public Housing"; Gail Radford, *Modern Housing for America: Policy Struggles in the New Deal Era* (Chicago, 1996); Wright, *Building the Dream*, 223–32.

9. New York City Housing Authority, "Housing without Cash Subsidy" [1948]; *Staff Bulletin* [NYCHA], March 23, 1948; and draft Board of Estimate resolution [c. 1953], all in series 01, box 0064C6, folder 3, NYCHA; Rodgers and Rankin, eds., *World's Capital City*, 293–96; Murray, "Shaping of 'Forgotten America'," 6, 11; Wright, *Building the Dream*, 228.

10. Kareem Abdul-Jabbar and Peter Knobler, *Giant Steps: The Autobiography of Kareem Abdul-Jabbar* (New York, 1983), 1–47.

11. Landmarks Preservation Commission, "United Workers' Cooperative Colony," June 2, 1992, Designation List 245; Jacqueline Leavitt, "The Interrelated History of Alternative Housing Tenure: Cooperatives and Public Housing from the Thirties to the Fifties," in Allan Heskin and Leavitt, eds., *The Hidden History of Housing Cooperatives* (Davis, Ca., 1995); Richard Plunz, *A History of Housing in New York City* (New York, 1990), 151–59; Abraham E. Kazan, "Union cooperative housing," in J. B. S. Hardman and Maurice F. Neufeld, *The House of Labor: Internal Operations of American Unions* (New York, 1951), 320–26.

12. Amalgamated Clothing Workers, *30 Years of Amalgamated Cooperative Housing, 1927–1957*, copy on box 294, ACW; Oral History of Abraham Kazan, Oral History Research Office, Columbia University, New York, N.Y., 1–213; Plunz, *History of Housing*, 159; *NYT*, May 2, 1977.

13. Marc A. Weiss, "The Origins and Legacy of Urban Renewal," in Pieer Clavel, John Forester, and William W. Goldsmith, eds., *Urban and Regional Planning in an Age of Austerity* (New York, 1980); Schwartz, *New York Approach*, 1–32.

14. Amalgamated Clothing Workers, *30 Years of Amalgamated Cooperative Housing*; 284–304; Plunz, *History of Housing*, 155; Kazan, "Union Cooperative Housing," 321.

15. Leavitt, "The Interrelated History"; Plunz, *History of Housing*, 158.

16. Kenneth G. Wray, "Abraham E. Kazan: The Story the Amalgamated Houses and the United Housing Foundation," MA thesis, Columbia University Graduate School of Architecture, Planning, and Preservation (real estate program), 1991, 15–18; Amalgamated Clothing Workers, *30 Years of Amalgamated Cooperative Housing*; Oral history of Abraham Kazan, 284–304; Schwartz, *New York Approach*, 90–

93, 134-35. Plunz discusses the origin and evolution of the tower in the park in his *History of Housing in New York City*.

17. Louis Pink, "Queensview," *The American City*, April 1952; Schwartz, *New York Approach*, 126-28, 137-38; *Co-op Contact* [United Housing Foundation], Nov. 1964, 8-9.

18. James J. Munro to James H. Englan, folder 5, and Robert Moses to Herman Stichman, May 19, 1950, folder 10, series 06, box 0060D6, NYCHA; Murray, "Shaping of 'Forgotten America'," 11-12; *Co-op Contact*, Nov. 1964, 6-7; Joint Industry Board of the Electrical Industry, *History and Organization of the Joint Industry Board of the Electrical Industry: 40 Years of Labor Management Relations, 1943-1983* (New York, 1983), 36-42, 96-97; Interviews with Robert Delaney, Mar. 3 and 18, 1994; Frank Parente, *AFL-CIO Survey of Union-Sponsored Housing* (Washington, 1991).

19. Murray, "Shaping of 'Forgotten America'," 12-17; "Statement by Borough President Burke on the $200,000,000 Housing Program," series 01, box 0064C6, folder 3, and Astoria Heights Taxpayers Association, Inc. to Thos F. Farrell, series 06, box 0060D6, folder 2, NYCHA.

20. As things turned out, during the next eleven years only 322,000 units of public housing were actually funded. Weiss, "The Origins and Legacy of Urban Renewal"; Jackson, *Crabgrass Frontier*, 224.

21. Robert A. Caro, *The Power Broker: Robert Moses and the Fall of New York* (New York, 1974), 707, 777-78; Schwartz, *New York Approach*, 108-75.

22. Schwartz, *New York Approach*, 133-37; Caro, *The Power Broker*, 735-38. Moses's respect for Kazan is evident throughout his correspondence, for example in his letter to John J. McCloy, April 30, 1958, a copy of which is in the "R. Moses" file concerning Rochdale Village, in the Archives of the United Housing Foundation, New York, N.Y.

23. Abraham Kazan oral history, 316; Wray, "Abraham E. Kazan," 22-29; United Housing Foundation, *Twenty Years of Achievement* (n.p., n.d.), 2.

24. United Housing Foundation, *Twenty Years of Achievement*, 11; Schwartz, *New York Approach*, 177; Wray, "Abraham E. Kazan," 30-36; Abraham Kazan oral history, 341-43.

25. United Housing Foundation, *Twenty Years of Achievement*, 10-16; Abraham Kazan oral history, 37-40, 404-7.

26. Data on and pictures of UHF projects appear in *Co-Op Contact*, Nov. 1964, 6-9, and United Housing Foundation, *Twenty Years of Achievement*. On Co-op City, see *NYT*, Nov. 20, 1994, section IX.

27. Tony Schuman has done pioneering research on Jessor, from which I have greatly benefited. See his unpublished paper "Labor and Housing in New York City: Architect Herman Jessor and the Co-operative Housing Movement," copy in possession of the author. See also Landmarks Preservation Commission, "United Workers' Cooperative Colony"; Abraham Kazan oral history, 341, 396-97, 401-43, 473; "The Cost of Variety in Architecture," *Co-op Contact*, summer 1965, 19; Wray, "Abraham E. Kazan," 48-49; and *The Story of Amalgamated Warbasse Houses*, 20 (copy in box 294, ACW).

28. Abraham E. Kazan, "A New Trend in Slum Clearance?", *Co-op Contact*, April 1963, 2; Abe [Kazan] to James Felt, Dec. 18, 1961, series 6, box 0073C4, folder 22, NYCHA.

29. Plunz, *History of Housing*, 184-90, 243-45, 267-70, 280-81; Abraham Kazan oral history, 72.

30. Schwartz, *New York Approach*, 201, 303-5; Wray, "Abraham E. Kazan," 35; Jane Jacobs, *The Death and Life of Great American Cities* (New York, 1961); Plunz, *History of Housing*, 289-93.

31. Schwartz, *New York Approach*, 199; Caro, *The Power Broker*, 967-69; Richard Rogin, "This Place Makes Bedford-Stuyvesant Look Beautiful," in Joseph Bensman and Arthur J. Vidich, eds., *Metropolitan Communities: New Forms of Urban Sub-Communities* (New York, 1975), 112.

32. Caro, *The Power Broker*, 967-68, 972; Schwartz, *New York Approach*, 175, 202-3; *New York Amsterdam News*, May 12, 1952.

33. Schwartz, "Tenant Power," 160-64; Abe [Kazan] to James Felt, Dec. 18, 1961, series 6, box 0073C4, folder 22, NYCHA; Wray, "Abraham E. Kazan," 42-44; *Co-Op Contact*, fall 1965, 12.

34. For the similarity of their views on slum clearance, compare Kazan's letter to James Felt, Dec. 18, 1961, series 6, box 0073C4, folder 22, and Moses's to William Charney Vladeck, Nov. 10, 1948, series 6, box 0069E4, folder 7, NYCHA. Marshall Berman, *All That Is Solid Melts Into Air: The Experience of Modernity* (New York, 1982).

35. Oral history of Abraham Kazan, 443.

36. The delay in building the Coney Island project resulted from an effort by Brooklyn developer

Fred Trump to win control of the site. See *Story of Amalgamated Warbasse Houses*, and oral history of Abraham Kazan, 474–82.

37. Moses's involvement in Rochdale Village can be followed through letters in the file marked "R. Moses," stored with other material on Rochdale in the UHF Archives. Moses's "bugbear" comment comes from an interview broadcast over radio station WNYC, Oct. 17, 1957, a copy of which is in this file. See also oral history of Abraham Kazan, 493–515.

38. A search of the *New York Times Index* and the *Readers Guide to Periodic Literature* revealed only one article on Rochdale Village published between 1964 and 1966, a fine piece by radical writer Harvey Swados in the *New York Times Magazine*, Nov. 13, 1966, "When Black and White Live Together." See also Wray, "Abraham E. Kazan," 49–50.

39. Jack Newfield and Paul DuBrul, *The Abuse of Power: The Permanent Government and the Fall of New York* (New York, 1977), 296–301; Ada Louise Huxtable, *Will They Ever Finish Bruckner Boulevard? A Primer on Urbicide* (New York, 1972), 77–78; Kazan oral history, 471; Wray, "Abraham E. Kazan," 56.

40. United Housing Foundation, *Twenty Years of Achievement*, 17–23; Harold Ostroff to Board of Directors of Community Services, Inc., June 17, 1968, UHF Archives; Betsy Brown, "Co-opting a Dream: The Making of a Financial Nightmare," *Empire State Report*, March 1977, 106–7; Huxtable, *Will They Ever Finish Bruckner Boulevard?*, 79–80; Newfield and DuBrul, *Abuse of Power*, 301–3.

41. Brown, "Co-opting a Dream," 107; Newfield and DuBrul, *Abuse of Power*, 303.

42. Kazan oral history, 451, 453; Minutes of Annual Meeting, United Housing Foundation, March 22, 1969, and leaflet "United Housing Fraud," UHF Archives; Newfield and DuBrul, *Abuse of Power*, 300, 303–6; Brown, "Co-opting a Dream," 107–8; *In These Times*, Nov. 15–21, 1976.

43. AFL-CIO Ex Min, July 13, 1972 (Special Meeting); Wray, "Abraham E. Kazan," 58–59; United Housing Foundation, *Twenty Years of Achievement*, 34–43; interview with Ken Wray, Jan. 17, 1996.

44. Newfield and DuBrul, *Abuse of Power*, 295–96, 303–10; Brown, "Co-opting a Dream," 108; *WSJ*, May 24, 1976; *In These Times*, Nov. 15–21, 1976.

45. United Housing Foundation, *Twenty Years of Achievement*, 21–27; Harold Ostroff to Board of Directors of Community Services, Inc., June 17, 1968; Minutes of Special Meetings of Board of Directors of Twin Pines Village, Inc., Sept. 11, 1969, Jan. 11, 1971, Jan. 6, 1972, and May 4, 1972; and Ostroff to Donald H. Elliot, May 24, 1968, June 5, 1968, and June 6, 1968, all in UHF Archives.

46. *NYT*, March 12, 1995, 41; Parente, *AFL-CIO Survey of Union-Sponsored Housing*, 7–8; Plunz, *History of Housing*, 301–2, 312; interview with Ken Wray, Jan. 17, 1996.

47. I calculated the total number of labor-sponsored units in New York from a database I constructed of individual projects. The median number of occupants comes from U.S. Bureau of the Census, *1970 Census of Housing: Metropolitan Housing Characteristics, New York, N.Y. SMSA* (Washington, D.C., 1972), 64; city sizes from U.S. Bureau of the Census, *Statistical Abstract of the United States, 1972* (Washington, D.C., 1972), 21–23.

48. Parente, *AFL-CIO Survey of Union-Sponsored Housing*, 2–3.

49. Leavitt, "Interrelated History"; Jackson, *Crabgrass Frontier*, 231–45, 325.

50. Kristof, "Housing," 299–303; New York City Council on Economic Education, *1980–81 Fact Book on the New York Metropolitan Region* (New York, 1979), 113, 115.

51. Calculated from NYC Council on Economic Education, *1980–81 Fact Book*, 116, 120; Elizabeth Roistacher and Emanuel Tobier, "Housing Policy," in Charles Brecher and Raymond D. Horton, eds., *Setting Municipal Priorities, 1981* (Montclair, N.J.), 149–52, 172–74; my union-sponsored housing database; and Roger Starr, "Housing: Prospects for New Construction," in Fitch and Walsh, eds., *Agenda for a City*, 350. Estimate for total public-assisted housing from Kristof, "Housing," 334.

CHAPTER 8: "ADEQUATE MEDICAL CARE"

1. Jennifer Klein, "The Business of Health and Welfare: The Growth of Commercial Health Insurance, 1940–1955," paper delivered at "Labor and the Welfare State" conference, George Meany Memorial Archives, Silver Springs, Maryland, Nov. 17–18, 1996.

2. Paul Starr, *The Social Transformation of American Medicine* (New York, 1982), 236, 245; Gerald Markowitz and David Rosner, "Seeking Common Ground: A History of Labor and Blue Cross," *Journal of Health Politics, Policy and Law* 16 no. 4 (winter 1991): 696–98; Helen Backer and Dorothy Dahl, *Group Health Insurance and Sickness Benefit Plans in Collective Bargaining* (Princeton, 1945), 11–16; Abraham Weiss, "Union Welfare Plans," in J. B. S. Hardman and Maurice F. Neufeld, eds., *The House of Labor: Internal Operations of American Unions* (New York, 1951), 277–80.

3. "Statement by Frederick F. Umley before the House Interstate and Foreign Commerce Committee," Jan. 15, 1954, box 5-1, folder 5, ILGWU; Ruth Glazer, "Unions and Health Care," in Hardman and Neufeld, eds., *House of Labor*, 309–13; *NYT*, April 10, 1949.

4. National Executive Committee of the International Workers Order, *Five Years of International Workers Order, 1930–1935* (New York, 1935), 109–112; New York District, International Workers Order, Medical Department, "At Your Service 365 Days a Year," box 48, International Workers Order Collection, Kheel Center for Labor- Management Documentation & Archives, Cornell University, Ithaca, New York; interview with Lewis Fraad, June 30, 1980; Joshua B. Freeman, *In Transit: The Transport Workers Union in New York City, 1933–1966* (New York, 1989), 120–21.

5. "Prospectus, The Health Insurance Plan of Greater New York," folder 9, box 2, Saul Mills Papers, RWLA; Starr, *Social Transformation*, 309, 312.

6. Markowitz and Rosner, "Seeking Common Ground," 700; Freeman, *In Transit*, 121; Backer and Dahl, *Group Health Insurance*, 56; Starr, *Social Transformation*, 280, 320–21; "Prospectus, The Health Insurance Plan of Greater New York."

7. United States House of Representatives, "H.R. 2861," 78th Congress, 1st Session; Starr, *Social Transformation*, 266–89; Alan Derickson, "Health Security for All? Social Unionism and Universal Health Insurance, 1935–1958," *Journal of American History* (March 1994): 1333–56.

8. "Prospectus, The Health Insurance Plan of Greater New York"; The Committee for the Special Research Project in the Health Insurance Plan of Greater New York, *Health and Medical Care in New York City* (Cambridge, 1957), 4–8; *NYT*, April 2, 1947.

9. Workmen's Compensation Publicity Bureau, *Digest of Workmen's Compensation Laws in the United States and Territories, with Annotations*, 7th ed. (New York, c. 1921), 11; Walter Hoving to Members of the Commerce and Industry Association of New York, Inc., Feb. 17, 1949, and Commerce and Industry Association of New York, Inc., Albany News-Bulletin, April 14, 1949, both in folder 1563, box 148, subject files, O'Dwyer Papers; Weiss, "Union Welfare Plans," 284; AFL Ex Min, Jan. 31, 1949.

10. *NYT*, Jan. 11, 1949, Jan. 15, 1953, Nov. 14, 1955.

11. Weiss, "Union Welfare Plans," 281–82; Backer and Dahl, *Group Health Insurance*, 16–19, 23–27; Nelson Lichtenstein, *Labor's War at Home: The CIO in World War II* (Cambridge, Eng., 1982), 211–12, 240–41.

12. Starr, *Social Transformation*, 312; Nelson Lichtenstein, "From Corporatism to Collective Bargaining: Organizing Labor and the Eclipse of Social Democracy in the Postwar Era," in Steve Fraser and Gary Gerstle, eds., *The Rise and Fall of the New Deal Order, 1930–1980* (Princeton, 1989), 140–44; Robert H. Zieger, *American Workers, American Unions, 1920–1985* (Baltimore, 1986), 148–53; David Brody, *Workers in Industrial America: Essays on the 20th Century Struggle* (New York, 1980), 192–93; Backer and Dahl, *Group Health Insurance*, appendix A; Philip S. Foner, *The Fur and Leather Workers Union* (Newark, 1950), 620; Dorothy Sue Cobble, *Dishing It Out: Waitresses and Their Unions in the Twentieth Century* (Urbana, 1991), 148; IBEW Local 3, minutes of regular membership meeting, April 12, 1945, microfilm reel R5112, RWLA; United States Department of Labor, Bureau of Labor Statistics, *Union Health and Welfare Plans* [Bulletin No. 900], (Washington, D.C., 1947), 16–18; Report to Executive Board by President Davis, Aug. 1, 1945, box 3-4-5-6-6A, 1199.

13. *NYT*, March 29, 1949; Weiss, "Union Welfare Plans," 283; Backer and Dahl, *Group Health Insurance*, 80–83; Derickson, "Health Security for All?," 1344–52; Zieger, *American Workers, American Unions*, 150; Starr, *Social Transformation*, 312–17; Lichtenstein, "From Corporatism to Collective Bargaining," 143–44.

14. Bureau of Labor Statistics, *Union Health and Welfare Plans*, 2; Starr, *Social Transformation*, 314.

15. John H. Simons, "The Union Approach to Health and Welfare," *Industrial Relations* 4 (May 1965): 62; Leo Price, M.D., "Statement for: Cooperative Health Federation of America" [July, 1948], folder 6, box 5-1, ILGWU; Starr, *Social Transformation*, 302–06, 323–27.

16. Glazer, "Unions and Health Care"; "Statement by Frederick F. Umley before the House Interstate and Foreign Commerce Committee"; *NYT*, April 10, 1949, 57; Bureau of Labor Statistics, *Union Health and Welfare Plans*.

17. Amalgamated Clothing Workers of America, Press release, April 14, 1951, folder 8, box 237, and *Fiftieth Anniversary Souvenir History of the New York Joint Board* (New York, 1964), 27–28, copy in box 289, ACW.

18. *N.Y. Age Defender*, Oct. 16, 1954; Amalgamated Laundry Workers Joint Board, *1937–1957: The Remarkable Twenty-year History of Amalgamated Laundry Workers Joint Board, Amalgamated Clothing Workers of America, AFL-CIO*, copy in box 289, ACW.

19. *NYT*, Oct. 22, 1950; *Industrial Bulletin*, Feb. 1951, 22–23 (includes quote); William L. Wheeler Jr., "What Is Labor's Attitude Toward Health Insurance?" *New York State Journal of Medicine*, Sept. 15, 1960, 2929; AFL Min, May 1, 1958.

20. AFL Ex Min, May 24, 1948, Feb. 13, 1951; CIO (NYC) Min, Dec. 20, 1950; Committee for the Special Research Project in the Health Insurance Plan of Greater New York, *Health and Medical Care in New York City*, 8; George Baehr, "Group Health Plans," *Connecticut Federationist* (1954); *NYT*, April 10, 1949, Sept. 10, 1950; *HIP News*, May 1955, Nov. 1955, March 1956, July–Aug. 1958; Meeting of the Executive Committee of the Board of Directors of the Health Insurance Plan of Greater New York, Oct. 25, 1955, in folder 1691, box 114, and minutes of the Board of Directors of HIP, Nov. 6, 1958, file 1700, box 115, subject files, Wagner Papers; Columbia University School of Public Health and Group Health Insurance, Inc., *Hearings on the Extension of Voluntary Health Insurance* (New York, 1955), 24, 45; Harry Becker, "The Shape of Things to Come — Some Labor Views," paper read at Western Conference of Prepaid Medical Service Plans, Oct. 1955, copy in possession of the author.

21. Markowitz and Rosner, "Seeking Common Ground," 702–7; John M. Brumm, "Unions and Health Insurance," in Hardman and Neufeld, eds., *House of Labor*, 300; "Conference April 12, 1943 — Saul Mills and Martin Segal, representing CIO Council," Louis Pink Papers, Empire Blue Cross and Blue Shield Archives, New York, N.Y.; *NYT*, April 16, 1956.

22. Charles R. Morris, *The Cost of Good Intentions: New York City and the Liberal Experiment, 1960–1975* (New York, 1981), 40.

23. Markowitz and Rosner, "Seeking Common Ground," 707–9; AFL Ex Min, May 2, 1949; CIO (NYC) Ex Min, Nov. 10, 1949, June 16, 1953, Dec. 1, 1953, Feb. 23, 1954, Oct. 8, 1954, Jan. 5, 1955; CIO (NYC) Min, Jan. 16, 1952, Feb. 20, 1952, March 19, 1952, Oct. 28, 1954, May 26, 1955; Columbia University School of Public Health and Group Health Insurance, *Hearings*, 72.

24. Report of Activities by President Davis, March 6, 1946, and Minutes, Executive Board, March 19, 1947, and March 21, 1948, box 3-4-5-6- 6A, 1199.

25. Minutes of Meetings of Local Managers [Dress and Waistmakers Union Joint Board], July 15, 1954, Nov. 16, 1954, Nov. 30, 1954, May 11, 1955, files 7a and 7b, box 11-4, ILGWU.

26. Minutes of Meetings of Local Managers, July 15, 1954, May 11, 1955, Sept. 19, 1955, Nov. 30, 1955, files 7a and 7b, box 11-4, ILGWU; *HIP News*, Nov. 1955; Columbia University School of Public Health and Administrative Medicine, *Prepayment for Medical and Dental Care in New York State* (New York, 1962), 35–36, 253.

27. Columbia University School of Public Health and Group Health Insurance, *Hearings*, 15–16, 22, 25–30, 30, 45–47; Associated Hospital Service of New York, United Medical Service, Inc., "Special Study: Blue Cross–Blue Shield Enrollment, Employees of the City of New York," April 8, 1958, folder 1702, box 116; International Union of Operating Engineers, Local 891, "Dear Sir and Brother," folder 1708, box 116; High School Teachers Association of New York, Inc., "Brief Presented at Board of Estimate Open Hearing for Improved Health Insurance Plan (H.I.P.) Service," folder 1698, box 115; Meeting of Executive Committee of Board of Directors of HIP, Oct. 25, 1955, folder 1691, box 114; and [HIP], Memorandum: Dual Insurance Results in Major Union Welfare Fund Accounts, July 16, 1958, folder 1700, box 115, all subject files, Wagner Papers; *HIP News*, May 1955, March 1956.

28. *HIP News*, July 1954, July–Aug. 1958; Meeting of the Board of Directors, Health Insurance Plan of Greater New York, April 18, 1960, in file 1707, box 116, subject files, Wagner Papers; *NYT*, June 13, 1960; Starr, *Social Transformation*, 324–46.

29. Markowitz and Rosner, "Common Ground," 707–9; AFL Min, Sept. 30, 1957; CIO (NYC) Ex Min, Oct. 10, 1957; CIO (NYC) Min, Dec. 2, 1957, Feb. 27, 1958, May 28, 1958, and June 19, 1958; *Seafarers Log*, Oct. 11, 1957, 11; *NYT*, Oct. 23, 1957; Nov. 19, 1957; June 8, 1958, section E; June 18, 1958.

30. AFL Ex Min, Sept. 17, 1956; Meeting of the Board of Directors, HIP, Nov. 6, 1958, folder 1700, box 115, subject files, Wagner Papers.

31. Leo Fink and Brian Greenberg, *Upheaval in the Quiet Zone: A History of Hospital Workers' Union, Local 1199* (Urbana, 1989), 1–11, 16–17; Meeting of the Board of Directors, Health Insurance Plan of Greater New York, Nov. 6, 1958, folder 1700, box 115, subject files, Wagner Papers.

32. Irwin Ross, "The Big Boss of the Short Day," *Saturday Evening Post*, May 14, 1962; *NYT*, Feb. 17, 1986; Feb. 23, 1986, section IV; Joint Industry Board of the Electrical Industry, "Calendar" [1970], Archives, Joint Industry Board of the Electrical Industry, Queens, New York; Joint Industry Board of the Electrical Industry, *History and Organization of the Joint Industry Board of the Electrical Industry: 40 Years of Labor-Management Relations, 1943–1983* (New York, 1983), 21–53, 63–67.

33. AFL Ex Min, Nov. 19, 1957, March 17, 1958, April 28, 1958; AFL Min, Dec. 2, 1957, Feb. 20, 1958, March 20, 1958, May 1, 1958; AFL-CIO Ex Min, Feb. 19, 1959, March 19, 1959, July 18, 1959; CIO (NYC) Min, Dec. 10, 1958; Michael Kazin and Steven J. Ross, "America's Labor Day: The Dilemma of a Workers' Celebration," *Journal of American History* (March 1992): 1322.

34. Fink and Greenberg, *Upheaval in the Quiet Zone*, 37–40, 76–77; CIO (NYC) Min, Dec. 10, 1958.

35. Fink and Greenberg, *Upheaval in the Quiet Zone*, 44–90; "Local 144: 'A Miniature U.N.'," *Industrial Bulletin* (March 1963): 16–18; AFL-CIO Ex Min, April 28, 1959, May 9, 1959 (includes quote), May 11, 1959, and May 21, 1959.

36. Markowitz and Rosner, "Seeking Common Ground," 710–13; *NYT*, Sept. 21, 1959; Sept. 27, 1959, section IV; Sept. 30, 1959; Oct. 13, 1960; Columbia University School of Public Health, *Prepayment*, 225–48; Fink and Greenberg, *Upheaval in the Quiet Zone*, 126.

37. Markowitz and Rosner, "Seeking Common Ground," 712–14; *NYT*, Aug. 30, 1959.

38. AFL-CIO Ex Min, April 28, 1959 (Special Meeting), Feb. 16, 1961; *NYT*, Nov. 11, 1960.

39. Nelson A. Rockefeller to James C. Quinn, July 7, 1961, reel 250, and Rockefeller to Harry Van Arsdale, July 7, 1961, reel 316, Nelson A. Rockefeller Gubernatorial Microfilm file, name file, RAC.

40. *NYT*, Feb. 29, 1964; April 2, 1964; March 20, 1965; April 1, 1965.

41. Derickson, "Health Security for All?," 1352–54; Starr, *Social Transformation*, 363–66; Brody, *Workers in Industrial America*, 232.

42. *NYT*, April 11, 1965; April 12, 1965; June 4, 1965; Sept. 10, 1965; Robert R. Douglass to Alton G. Marshall, Sept. 1, 1967, reel 316, Rockefeller Gubernatorial Microfilm file, name file, RAC; AFL-CIO Ex Min, Sept. 13, 1966.

43. Fink and Greenberg, *Upheaval in the Quiet Zone*, 91–122; AFL-CIO Ex Min, June 21, 1962, June 19, 1969; Sandra Opdycke, "Private Choices, Public Obligations: New York City and Its Hospitals Since 1900," Ph.D. diss., Columbia University, 1995, 396–411.

44. New York State Department of Labor, Division of Employment, Research and Statistics Office, *Employment Statistics*, vol. 6 (Albany, 1970); *Employment Review* [NYS Department of Labor], May 1971.

45. *NYT*, Sept. 27, 1959, section IV; Fink and Greenberg, *Upheaval in the Quiet Zone*, 122–28.

46. Barbara Ehrenreich and John Ehrenreich, *The American Health Empire: Power, Profits, and Politics* (New York, 1971), 133–39; *NYT*, April 2, 1964; March 24, 1965; AFL-CIO Ex Min, April 16, 1964, May 21, 1964.

47. Simons, "The Union Approach to Health and Welfare," 61–76; Ronald L. Numbers, "The Third Party: Health Insurance in America," in Judith Waltzer Leavitt and Ronald L. Numbers, eds., *Sickness and Health in America*, 2d ed. (Madison, 1985), 241–43.

48. Rosner and Markowitz, *Seeking Common Ground*, 713–15; Starr, *Social Transformation*, 379–449.

CHAPTER 9: "A USEFUL AND REMUNERATIVE JOB"

1. U.S. Department of Labor, Bureau of Labor Statistics, *Employment, Hours and Earnings, States and Areas, 1939–82, Vol. II* (Washington, D.C., 1984), 578–79, 590–92; *NYT*, March 29, 1954; John I. Griffin, *Industrial Location in the New York Area* (New York, 1956), vii–viii, 70–71, 94.

2. Richard Harris, "The Geography of Employment and Residence in New York City Since 1950," in John H. Mollenkopf and Manuel Castells, eds., *Dual City: Restructuring New York* (New York, 1991); Edgar M. Hoover and Raymond Vernon, *Anatomy of a Metropolis* (Garden City, N.Y., 1962), 24; Temporary Commission on City Finances, *Economic and Demographic Trends in New York City: The Outlook for the Future* (New York, 1977), table I-13.

3. "Some of the *Real* Issues In the Election Campaign" (1947), FF882, UE; CIO (NYC) Ex Min, April 15, 1954; *NYT*, April 20, 1955.

4. Barbara Garson, *All the Livelong Day: The Meaning and Demeaning of Routine Work* (New York, 1975), 64–65. I worked in the Nassau plant in 1967; my impression was that by then most of the workers lived nearby.

5. *Fortune*, June 1950, 50, 53; Robert Hammer, "Industrial Relations in the New York City General Trucking Industry," Ph.D. diss., Harvard University, 1951, 18, 138–43, 185; *NYT*, Aug. 30, 1952.

6. Interview with James Garry, Aug. 2, 1994.

7. New York City Planning Department, Comprehensive Planning Workshop, "Economic Development in New York City: Overview," Oct. 1973, 25–26; *NYT*, March 29, 1954, 1, 33; Leonard Wallock, "The Myth of the Master Builder: Robert Moses, New York, and the Dynamics of Metropolitan Development Since World War II," *Journal of Urban History* 17 no. 4 (Aug. 1991): 349–51; Kenneth T. Jackson, *Crabgrass Frontier: The Suburbanization of the United States* (New York, 1985), 241; The Mayor's Committee for World Fashion Center, "a stitch in time . . . ," 6, copy in subject files, box 38, folder 493, Wagner Papers; New York City Council on Economic Education, *Fact Book: New York Metropolitan Region* (New York, 1965), table 5.4.

8. See, for example, "Memorandum for the Mayor, Re: Summary of Material Under the Title 'Business Trends for the City — 1953–54,'" folder 494, box 38, subject files, Wagner Papers; Griffin, *Industrial Location*, 94; *NYT*, April 20, 1955; March 20, 1957.

9. Robert Fitch, "Planning New York," in *The Fiscal Crisis of American Cities: Essays on the Political Economy of Urban America, with Special Reference to New York*, ed. by Roger E. Alcaly and David Mermelstein (New York 1976); Joel Schwartz, *The New York Approach: Robert Moses, Urban Liberals, and the Redevelopment of the Inner City* (Columbus, Ohio, 1993), 229–60; Robert Fitch, *The Assassination of New York* (London, 1993), 37–129.

10. Jesse Thomas Carpenter, *Competition and Collective Bargaining in the Needle Trades, 1910–1967* (Ithaca, 1971), esp. chapter 21; Minutes of meeting of Managers [NY Cloak Joint Board], Feb. 25, 1953, box 20-23, file 10, ILGWU; *NYT*, June 16, 1951.

11. Robert Laurentz, "Racial/Ethnic Conflict in the New York City Garment Industry, 1933–1980," Ph.D. diss., State University of New York at Buffalo, 1980, 241, 251–52, 262–63; *NACLA's Latin America & Empire Report* XI, no. 3 (March 1977), 5, 25–26; *NYT*, March 29, 1951; *NYP*, March 14, 1977.

12. Rank and File Group, Dressmakers Local 10, ILGWU, "Rank and File Program" [1950], box 2-308, file 6B, ILGWU; Laurentz, "Racial/Ethnic Conflict," 256–58; *The Labor Leader*, March 1958; *Labor's Heritage* 5 no. 3 (winter 1994): 35.

13. Alex Kolkin, et al. to Israel Breslow, Feb. 14, 1963, and Rank and File Forum, Local 22, ILGWU, "How to Fight Poverty Right Here" [1965], box 2-308, file 6A, and Roy Helfgott, "Survey of Shops and Workers in New York Coat and Suit Industry," July 1953, box 20-20, file 3, ILGWU; Gus Tyler, "Marginal Industries, Low Wages, and High Risks," *Dissent* 7 no. 3 (summer 1961); Laurentz, "Racial/Ethnic Conflict," 240–42; *NYT*, July 7, 1946, section III; Herbert Hill, "Guardians of the Sweatshops: The Trade Unions, Racism, and the Garment Industry," in Adalberto Lopez and James Petras, ed., *Puerto Rico and Puerto Ricans: Studies in History and Society* (New York, 1974), 395–400.

14. Laurentz, "Racial/Ethnic Conflict," 244; Bureau of Labor Statistics, *Employment, Hours and Earnings, States and Areas, 1939–82, Vol. II*, 579, 584; "Highlights of 'The New York Dress Industry: Problems and Prospects,' A Study Prepared by Leon H. Keyserling," 5–6, box 11-12, folder 6, ILGWU.

15. Members of ILGWU for a Wage Policy against Poverty, "An Open Letter of ILGWU Pres. David Dubinsky," box 2-308, file 4A, ILGWU; Laurentz, "Racial/Ethnic Conflict," 242; Bureau of Labor Statistics, *Employment, Hours and Earnings, States and Areas, 1939–82, Vol. II*, 584.

16. Ronald W. Schatz, *The Electrical Workers: A History of Labor at General Electric and Westinghouse, 1923–60* (Urbana, 1983), 232–35; George Kirschner, "What Happens to the People When a Factory Runs Away: The Story of American Safety Razor," MA essay, Queens College, CUNY, April 1973, 6–7, 19; District 4-Local 410: 1953 file; "Petition," District 4-Local 461: 1961 file; *Local 447 News*, Feb. and March 1953, and Al Loewenthal to James B. Carey, March 16, 1953, District 4-Local 447: 1953 file; and *IUE Local 461 News*, District 4-Local 461: 1961 file, all box 2004; and James H. Duff to James B. Carey, Feb. 9, 1955, A1.07 Political Issues: "Runaway Shops 1955," IUE; Stanley Aronowitz, *False Promises: The Shaping of American Working-Class Consciousness* (New York, 1973), 342–43.

17. *NYT*, Oct. 5, 1954; Schwartz, *New York Approach*, 236–37.

18. Griffin, *Industrial Location*, 86–88; James Lustig to Jules Emspak, May 24, 1951, FF 1070, and Local 475 Officers Report to the Membership, Nov. 16, 1952, 53–55, FF 1057, UE.

19. *NYT*, April 11, 1954, section III; April 16, 1954; Aug. 3, 1954; Aug. 16, 1954; Oct. 5, 1954; "Sample Letter," FF 1048, UE.

20. Kirschner, "What Happens to the People," 6–7, 16–17, 41–42, 66–68; *NYT*, Oct. 1, 1954, Oct. 5, 1954, Oct. 14, 1954, Oct. 21, 1954, July 10, 1955, section III; Clifton Cameron, "Dear Brother," Oct. 22, 1954, and Julius Emspak, "Dear Friend," Nov. 17, 1954, in "Correspondence Unions 1952–63," box 50-51-52, 1199; Memorandum to the National office of U.E.R.M.W.A., Re: ASR Boycott Campaign, FF 1048, UE; Griffin, *Industrial Location*, 92–93.

21. Kirschner, "What Happens to the People," 63; CIO (NYC) Ex Min, Feb. 23, 1954, March 25, 1954; CIO (NYC) Min, Feb. 25, 1954, March 31, 1954.

22. In Mayor O'Dwyer's files on the promotion of the city economy, far more material pertains to the port or even the movie industry than to manufacturing. Folder 1392 ("Promotion of Commerce 1946–1947"), box 134, subject files, O'Dwyer Papers; Temporary Commission on City Finances, *Economic and Demographic Trends*, 23; *NYT*, April 29, 1954; Abe Stark, press release for Feb. 17/Feb. 18, 1954, folder 3204, box 275, subject files, Wagner Papers; Griffin, *Industrial Location*, 70–71, 94; James C. Cobb, *The Selling of the South: The Southern Crusade for Industrial Development, 1936–1980* (Baton Rouge, 1982), 41–42.

23. *NYT*, Jan. 9, 1955; Feb. 15, 1955; March 11, 1957; Memorandum for the Mayor, "Re: Summary of material under the Title 'Business Trends for the City—1953–54,'" and "Industrial or Commercial Customers Moving Out of City," folder 494, box 38, subject files, Wagner Papers; Griffin, *Industrial Location*; Max Hall, ed., *Made In New York: Case Studies in Metropolitan Manufacturing* (Cambridge, 1959), 98–106.

24. Schwartz, *New York Approach*, 238–39, 263–64, 279–80, 295–96; "Industrial or Commercial Customers Moving Out of City," folder 494, box 38, subject files, Wagner Papers.

25. The City of New York, Housing and Redevelopment Board, *Industrial Development in New York City* (Report No. 10), May 11, 1964, 30; "Remarks by Mayor Robert F. Wagner at Presentation of Awards to Twelve NYC Manufacturers," May 27, 1965, box 275, folder 3206, and Mayor's Committee for World Fashion Center, "a stitch in time," box 38, folder 493, subject files, Wagner Papers; Louis Broido to David Dubinsky, folder 3, box 2-239, ILGWU; Bureau of Labor Statistics, *Employment, Hours and Earnings, States and Areas, 1939–82*, Vol. II, 579.

26. Peter D. McClelland and Alan L. Magdovitz, *Crisis in the Making: The Political Economy of New York State since 1945* (Cambridge, Eng., 1981), 39–43, 102; Cobb, *Selling of the South*, 36–47, 56–57.

27. Griffin, *Industrial Location*, 109; Schwartz, *New York Approach*, 236, 239–51, 264; Fitch, *Assassination of New York*, 130–44; S. J. Makielski Jr., *The Politics of Zoning: The New York Experience* (New York, 1966), 86, 216; Mollenkopf and Castells, eds., *Dual City*, 119–21.

28. Griffin, *Industrial Location*, 104.

29. See, for example, *NYT*, April 22, 1952 and April 20, 1955.

30. Robert A. Caro, *The Power Broker: Robert Moses and the Fall of New York* (New York, 1974), 735–38; Makielski Jr., *Politics of Zoning*, 134–45, 222.

31. Richard K. Lieberman, *Steinway & Sons* (New Haven, 1995), 258–59, 272–85; Aronowitz, *False Promises*, 342–44; CIO (NYC) Min, Jan. 28, 1955.

32. Rita Seiden Miller, ed., *Brooklyn USA: The Fourth Largest City in America* (New York, 1979), 103, 114, 132–34; Fitch, *Assassination of New York*, 140; CIO (NYC) Min, Feb. 23, 1955 and March 30, 1955.

33. Laurentz, "Racial/Ethnic Conflict," 302; NYC Council on Economic Education, *Fact Book: New York Metropolitan Region*, 128. The difference between the hourly and weekly comparisons reflects the shorter average workweek in New York than in the country as a whole.

34. New York State had a minimum wage law since before World War II, but not a statewide minimum; through administrative procedures separate minimums were set for particular industries and regions. Press release, Nov. 13, 1952, reel 5, part 13, series A, NAACP Papers, microfilm edition; *NYT*, Jan. 15, 1953; CIO (NYC) Min, Jan. 28, 1955 and Feb. 23, 1955; Governor's Committee on the Minimum Wage, Press release, Dec. 6, 1964, RG III, series 15, subseries 25, box 66, folder 1436, RAC.

35. Hill, "Guardians of the Sweatshops," 388–92, 394–95; Research Department, I.L.G.W.U., "Average Hourly Earnings, Women's Garment Industry, New York City and United States, 1961," box 2-280, file 1C, ILGWU; AFL-CIO Ex Min, Feb. 18, 1960, Jan. 18, 1962, Feb. 15, 1962, March 15, 1962, April 17, 1962, Aug. 16, 1962, and Oct. 18, 1962; City of New York, Office of the Mayor, Press release, Aug. 19, 1962, box 275, file 3206, subject files, Wagner Papers. On the 1961 mayoral election, see Chris McNickle, *To Be Mayor of New York: Ethnic Politics in the City* (New York, 1993), 148–79.

36. Hill, "Guardians of the Sweatshops," 392; Governor's Committee on the Minimum Wage, press release, Dec. 6, 1964, RG III, series 15, subseries 25, box 66, folder 1436; Nelson A. Rockefeller to Peter J. Brennan, June 23, 1965, reel 34, Nelson A. Rockefeller Gubernatorial name file; and J. V. Underhill to Rockefeller, June 3, 1966, Nelson A. Rockefeller Gubernatorial Subject files, 1963–66, reel 55, all RAC; AFL-CIO Ex Min, April 11, 1963 (Special Meeting), Feb. 20, 1964, and Dec. 17, 1964.

37. Daniel J. S. King, "Squibb," in *EncNY*, 1108; Meyer Berger, *Meyer Berger's New York* (New York, 1960), 297.

38. Bureau of Labor Statistics, *Employment, Hours and Earnings, States and Areas, 1939–82, Vol. II*, 578–79.

39. McClelland and Magdovitz, *Crisis in the Making*, table 2.3; Nelson Lichtenstein, *The Most Dangerous Man in Detroit: Walter Reuther and the Fate of American Labor* (New York, 1995), 290–91; Aronowitz, *False Promises*, 374–75; Grace Palladino, "When Militancy Isn't Enough: The Impact of Automation on New York City Building Service Workers, 1934–1970," *Labor History* 28 (spring 1987): 196–98; David F. Noble, *Forces of Production: A Social History of Industrial Automation* (New York, 1984), 248–60.

40. City of New York, Office of the Mayor, press release of April 21, 1958, and Robert F. Wagner to Max Greenberg, April 24, 1958, box 304, file 3592, subject files, Wagner Papers; CIO (NYC) Ex Minutes, April 16, 1958; CIO (NYC) Min, May 28, 1958; AFL Ex Min, April 28, 1958; and AFL-CIO Ex Min, Feb. 19, 1959; "Automation: Labor's Challenge," *Industrial Bulletin*, March 1963, 13.

41. *NYT*, Oct. 26, 1945; Art Preis, *Labor's Giant Step: Twenty Years of the CIO* (New York, 1972), 379–81, 486–90; Lichtenstein, *Most Dangerous Man*, 284–86, 290–91; Ronald Edsforth, "Why Automation Didn't Shorten the Work Week: The Politics of Work Time in the Automobile Industry," in Robert Asher and Edsforth, eds., *Autowork* (Albany, 1995); *Fortune*, April 1952, 64.

42. Temporary Commission on City Finances, *Economic and Demographic Trends*, 45; NYC Council on Economic Education, *Fact Book: New York Metropolitan Region*, 128; *NYT*, Oct. 2, 1947; Joshua B. Freeman, *In Transit: The Transport Workers Union in New York City, 1933–1966* (New York, 1989), 319; Preis, *Labor's Giant Step*, 381; Lazare Teper, "Statement on Behalf of the ILGWU, AFL-CIO, Before the General Subcommittee on Labor, Committee on Education and Labor, U.S. House of Representatives, July 1, 1965," 35, file 1A, box 2-280, ILGWU.

43. David R. Roediger and Philip S. Foner, *Our Own Time: A History of American Labor and the*

Working Day (New York, 1989), 241, 266–71; *NYT*, June 19, 1958; "Automation: Labor's Challenge," *Industrial Bulletin*, March 1963, 13.

44. Palladino, "When Militancy Isn't Enough."

45. Venus Green, "The Impact of Technology Upon Women's Work in the Telephone Industry, 1880–1980," Ph.D. diss., Columbia University, 1990, 538–62, 610–11; Aaron Michael Brenner, "Rank and File Rebellion, 1966–1975," Ph.D. diss., Columbia University, 1996, 158–60, 177–90.

46. Robert L. McManus, press release, May 24, 1960, and "Governor's Conference on Automation, June 1–3, 1960," both in "Conference on Automation, June 1, 1960" folder, Speeches, RG15, Rockefeller family collection, RAC.

47. *Electrical World*, June 15, 1960, 2; New York City Central Labor Council, "For Immediate Release," Nov. 29, 1960, and "Unions Meet Automation . . . and A Program for Action," copies of both in Nelson Rockefeller Gubernatorial subject files, 1959–1962, roll 68, RAC; AFL-CIO Ex Min, Dec. 15, 1960; *Industrial Bulletin*, March 1963, 14–15.

48. AFL-CIO Ex Min, March 16, 1961 and June 15, 1961.

49. *NYT*, Dec. 10, 1961; Jan. 20, 1962.

50. Building Trades Employers Association to Nelson A. Rockefeller, Dec. 27, 1961, Nelson A. Rockefeller Gubernatorial subject files, roll 66, RAC; *NYT*, Dec. 11, 1961; Dec. 13, 1961.

51. For business views of the situation, see roll 66, Nelson A. Rockefeller Gubernatorial subject files, RAC. *NYT*, June 19, 1961, June 26, 1961, Nov. 9, 1961; Leon H. Keyserling, "Higher Pay for N.Y.C. Transport Workers: The Workers Deserve It, The City Can Afford It," Dec. 1965, exhibit no. 9, file "L-100 negot 1965 demand," box 150, TWU Collection, RWLA.

52. *NYT*, Dec. 11, 1961, Dec. 14, 1961, Dec. 20, 1961.

53. *NYT*, Dec. 29, 1961, Jan. 4, 1962, Sept. 19, 1962, Jan. 2, 1964; Keyserling, "Higher Pay for N.Y.C. Transport Workers," exhibit no. 9.

54. The new Local 3 contract increased hourly rates, so that workers would earn almost as much for the shortened week as they previously had been paid. *NYT*, Jan. 3, 1962, Jan. 9, 1962, Jan. 12, 1962, Jan. 19, 1962, Jan. 20, 1962.

55. "The Short Work Week: A One Year Report," *Industrial Bulletin*, Aug. 1963, 8–11; Anne M. Kornhauser, "Craft Unionism and Racial Equality: The Failed Promise of Local 3 of the International Brotherhood of Electrical Workers in the Civil Rights Era," MA essay, History Department, Columbia University, February 1993, 28–29.

56. Irwin Ross, "Big Boss of the Short Day," *Saturday Evening Post*, May 14, 1962, 38–44; *NYT*, Jan. 19–22, 1962; Jan. 25, 1962.

57. Kornhauser, "Craft Unionism and Racial Equality"; Grace Palladino, *Dreams of Dignity, Workers of Vision: A History of the International Brotherhood of Electrical Workers* (Washington, D.C., 1991), 255–56; *NYT*, Oct. 21, 1962.

58. *NYT*, April 20, 1962, June 2, 1962; AFL-CIO Ex Min, Nov. 15, 1962, May 16, 1963, Nov. 15, 1963, Nov. 17, 1964, and Sept. 17, 1970.

59. Noble, *Forces of Production*, 260–62; McClelland and Magdovitz, *Crisis in the Making*, table 2.3.

60. Harry Kelber and Carl Schlesinger, *Union Printers and Controlled Automation* (New York, 1967), 1–112.

61. Kelber and Schlesinger, *Union Printers*, 94–103, 113–34; *New York Review of Books*, vol. 1, no. 1, 2; vol. 1, no. 2, 1; *NYP*, March 4, 1963; *NYT*, April 1, 1963.

62. Kelber and Schlesinger, *Union Printers*, 217–64.

63. Joe Higgins, "The Struggle of the New York Printers," *Political Affairs* 53 (Aug. 1974): 13–27; Theresa F. Rogers and Nathalie S. Friedman, *Printers Face Automation* (Lexington, Mass., 1980). For later newspaper industry developments, see Stephen R. Sleigh, *On Deadline: Labor Relations in Newspaper Publishing* (Bayside, N.Y., 1998).

64. The battle for the control of the docks can be followed in the O'Dwyer Papers, subject files, esp. Winthrop W. Aldrich to William O'Dwyer, Feb. 4, 1947, box 134; and boxes 21, 172 ("Waterfront 1948" file), and 173.

65. John I. Griffin, *The Port of New York* (New York, 1959), 102–6; Allen Raymond, *Waterfront*

Priest (New York, 1955); *Fortune,* Dec. 1951, 46-52; April 1953, 54-58; Mary Heaton Vorse, "The Pirates' Nest of New York" (1952), in Dee Garrison, ed., *Rebel Pen: The Writings of Mary Heaton Vorse* (New York, 1985); Andrew John Herod, "Towards a Labor Geography: The Production of Space and the Politics of Scale in the East Coast Longshore Industry, 1953-1990," Ph.D. diss., Rutgers University, 1992, 107-10.

66. Jan Morris, *The Great Port: A Passage Through New York* (New York, 1969; reprinted 1985), 126; Herod, "Towards a Labor Geography," 11-14; Griffin, *Port of New York,* 128.

67. Morris, *Great Port,* 84-85, 119; Paul Barrett, "John F. Kennedy International Airport," in *EncNY,* 623.

68. Herod, "Towards a Labor Geography," 216-313; *NYT,* Feb. 27, 1977.

69. Herod, "Towards a Labor Geography," 119-120, 127, 139.

70. Herod, "Towards a Labor Geography," 140; Vernon H. Jenson, *Strife on the Waterfront: The Port of New York since 1945* (Ithaca, 1974), 24; Michael N. Danielson and Jameson W. Doig, *New York: The Politics of Urban Development* (Berkeley, 1982), 328-33; Department of City Planning, City of New York, *New York City Comprehensive Waterfront Plan: Reclaiming the City's Edge* (New York, 1992), 83-88.

71. Morris, *The Great Port,* 118-28; Vorse, "The Pirates' Nest"; Budd Schulberg, "Joe Docks," in Alexander Klein, ed., *The Empire City: A Treasury of New York* (New York, 1955), 316-22; Bureau of Labor Statistics, *Employment, Hours and Earnings, States and Areas, 1939-82, Vol. II,* 588. On organized crime at Kennedy Airport, see Nicholas Pileggi, *Wiseguy: Life in a Mafia Family* (New York, 1985).

72. *NYT,* March 6, 1977; *New York Newsday,* Sept. 27, 1993.

73. Institute for Urban Studies, Fordham University, *The Brooklyn Navy Yard: A Plan for Redevelopment* (New York, 1968), 1-2; *The WPA Guide to New York City* (New York, 1982), 450-52; Arnold Markoe, "Brooklyn Navy Yard," in *EncNY,* 159-60.

74. New York City Planning Commission, *Plan for New York City: Critical Issues,* text edition (New York, 1969), 9; Robert A. M. Stern, Thomas Mellins, and David Fishman, *New York 1960: Architecture and Urbanism between the Second World War and the Bicentennial* (New York, 1995), 29, 112-19, 206-16, 320-21.

75. 1965 data from unpublished statistics from the U.S. Department of Commerce, Bureau of Labor Statistics; 1946 data calculated from State of New York, Department of Labor, *Handbook of New York Labor Statistics, 1948* Special Bulletin No. 226 (1949), 5; 1970 data from New York City Planning Department, Comprehensive Planning Workshop, "Economic Development in New York City: Overview," Oct. 1973, 19.

76. For the impact of lifetime job guarantees on printers and longshoremen, see Rogers and Friedman, *Printers Face Automation,* and William DiFazio, *Longshoremen: Community and Resistance on the Brooklyn Waterfront* (South Hadley, Mass., 1985).

77. Prior to 1970, New York manufacturing declined at roughly the same rate or more slowly than most other major industrial cities; after 1970, it declined more quickly. Jackson, *Crabgrass Frontier,* 266-67; Citizens Housing and Planning Council, "Manufacturing Decline and the Land Use Debate," December 1994, 6-8 and Tables 2 and 3; Fitch, *Assassination of New York,* 22-23. See also, Thomas J. Sugrue, *The Origins of the Urban Crisis: Race and Inequality in Postwar Detroit* (Princeton, 1996).

78. Leonard Kriegal, "Silent in the Supermarket," *Dissent,* winter 1972, 95; Nathan Glazer and Daniel Patrick Moynihan, *Beyond the Melting Pot: The Negroes, Puerto Ricans, Jews, Italians, and Irish of New York City* (Cambridge, 1963), 143-46, 197-98, 206-08; Miriam Cohen, *Workshop to Office: Two Generations of Italian Women in New York City, 1900-1950* (Ithaca, 1992), 147-95.

79. The federal government only began calculating the unemployment rate for New York City in 1958. Bureau of Labor Statistics, *Employment, Hours and Earnings, States and Areas, 1939-82, Vol. II,* 578-79, 587-88, 590-92; McClelland and Magdovitz, *Crisis in the Making,* table 2.3.

CHAPTER 10: GOODBYE MOLLY GOLDBERG

1. New York City Planning Department, Comprehensive Planning Workshop, "Economic Development in New York City: Overview," Oct. 1973, 13, 19.

2. New York City Planning Commission, *Plan for New York City: Critical Issues* (New York, 1969), 21; Robert A. M. Stern, Thomas Mellins, and David Fishman, *New York 1960: Architecture and Urbanism between the Second World War and the Bicentennial* (New York, 1995), 9–10, 27, 61–66, 167–206; Meyer Berger, *Meyer Berger's New York* (New York, 1960), 279–80.

3. Martin Shefter, "New York's National and International Influence," 18–19; Miles Kahler, "New York City and the International System: International Strategy and Urban Fortunes," 31–32; and James R. Kurth, "Between Europe and America: The New York Foreign Policy Elite," 71, 81–82, all in Shefter, ed., *Capital of the American Century: The National and International Influence of New York City* (New York, 1993).

4. Stanley Buder, "headquarters," in *EncNY*, 114–15.

5. Between 1955 and 1970 employment in wholesale and retail trade held steady while in construction it rose by 5 percent. Changes in employment calculated from U.S. Department of Labor, Bureau of Labor Statistics, *Employment, Hours and Earnings, States and Areas, 1939–82, Vol. II* (Washington, D.C., 1984), 579, 587–88, 590–92.

6. Emanuel Tobier, "Economic Development Strategy for the City," in Lyle C. Fitch and Annamarie Hank Walsh, eds., *Agenda for a City: Issues Confronting New York* (Beverly Hills, 1970), 58.

7. Leonard Wallach, ed., *New York: Cultural Capital of the World 1940–1965* (New York, 1988), 46; New York State Department of Labor, "A Handbook of Statistical Data: New York City Area, 1970" (November 1970), 27; Leon Fink and Brian Greenberg, *Upheaval in the Quiet Zone: A History of Hospital Workers' Union, Local 1199* (Urbana, 1989), 1–11.

8. New York City Council on Economic Education, *1980–81 Fact Book on the New York Metropolitan Region* (New York, 1979), 12; New York Department of City Planning, "Clerical Jobs in the Financial Industry in New York City," July 1972, 6–7.

9. Barbara Garson, *All the Livelong Day: The Meaning and Demeaning of Routine Work* (New York, 1975), 149–209; Venus Green, "The Impact of Technology Upon Women's Work in the Telephone Industry, 1880–1980, Ph.D. diss., Columbia University, 1990, 545–52, 654–57, 663; Elinor Langer, "Inside the New York Telephone Company," in William L. O'Neill, ed., *Women at Work* (Chicago, 1972), 307–60.

10. Harold X. Connolly, *A Ghetto Grows in Brooklyn* (New York, 1977), 186–87; Miriam Cohen, *Workshop to Office: Two Generations of Italian Women in New York City, 1900–1950* (Ithaca, 1992), 147–95.

11. David Halle, *America's Working Man: Work, Home, and Politics among Blue-Collar Property Owners* (Chicago, 1984), 68–70, 165–69; NYC Planning Department, Comprehensive Planning Workshop, "Economic Development in New York City: Overview," 19.

12. *Ten from Your Show of Shows*. Pinnacle Productions, 1973; directed by Max Liebman; Sylvie Murray, "Suburban Citizens: Domesticity and Community Politics in Queens, 1945–1960, Ph.D. diss., Yale University, 1994, 192–93.

13. Norman I. Fainstein and Susan S. Fainstein, "Governing Regimes and the Political Economy of Development in New York City, 1946–1984," in *Power, Culture, and Place: Essays on New York City*, edited by John Hull Mollenkopf (New York, 1988), 168–70; Joseph P. Lyford, *Airtight Cage: A Study of New York's West Side* (New York, 1968), 10, 226; Robert Caro, *The Power Broker: Robert Moses and the Fall of New York* (New York, 1974), 850–94; Gay Talese, *The Bridge* (New York, 1964).

14. Alfred Kazin, *A Walker in the City* (New York, 1951), 12; Dennis Smith, *Report from Engine Co. 82* (New York, 1972), 51–52; Philip Roth, *Goodbye, Columbus* (New York, 1995).

15. Robert W. Snyder, "The Neighborhood Changes: The Irish of Washington Heights and Inwood since 1945," in *The New York Irish*, ed. Ronald H. Bayor and Timothy Meagher (Baltimore, 1995); Eric C. Schneider, *Vampires, Dragons, and Egyptian Kings: Youth Gangs in Postwar New York* (Princeton, 1999), 80–91.

16. Pete Hamill, *A Drinking Life: A Memoir* (Boston, 1994), 209; *Marty*. Goodyear TV Playhouse, 1953; directed by Delbert Mann.

17. Ira Rosenwaike, *Population History of New York City* (Syracuse, N.Y., 1972), 131, 135, 170; Tem-

porary Commission on City Finances, *Economic and Demographic Trends in New York City: The Outlook for the Future* (New York, 1977), 65, 69–71, 75; NYC Council on Economic Education, *Fact Book*, tables 2.7 and table 10.1.

18. *NYT*, March 8, 1962; Murray, "Suburban Citizens," 15–40; *EncNY*, 90–91, 145, 921; Jonathan Rieder, *Canarsie: The Jews and Italians of Brooklyn against Liberalism* (Cambridge, 1985), 13–18; Stern, Mellins, and Fishman, *New York 1960*, 963–64, 969–70.

19. Interview of Peter Brennan, by Renee Epstein, Sept. 3, 1987, NS #7, tape #2A, RWLA; Gerald Finkel, "The Determination of Wages for Unionized Construction Electricians in New York City, 1953–1983," Ph.D. diss., New School for Social Research, 1990, 46–47.

20. Murray, "Suburban Citizens," esp. 35–45, 133–80; Rieder, *Canarsie*, esp. 15–17, 19–21, 27, 93–98, 127, 138; William Kornblum and James Bershers, "White Ethnicity: Ecological Dimensions," in Mollenkopf, ed., *Power, Culture, and Place*; John Agnew, "Home Ownership and Identity in Capitalist Societies," in *Housing and Identity: Cross-cultural Perspectives*, ed. James S. Duncan (New York, 1982), 86; Smith, *Report from Engine Co. 82*, 53; Michael N. Danielson and Jameson W. Doig, *New York: The Politics of Urban Regional Development* (Berkeley, 1982), 77–79.

21. David Marc, "Comic Visions of the City: New York and the Television Sitcom," *Radical History Review* 42 (1988): 49–63; Lynn Spigel, *Make Room for TV: Television and the Family Ideal in Postwar America* (Chicago, 1992), 32, 145–51; George Lipsitz, *Time Passages: Collective Memory and American Popular Culture* (Minneapolis, 1990), 39–40, 57–68; James Bacon, *How Sweet It is: The Jackie Gleason Story* (New York, 1985), 146–47; David Everitt, "The Man Behind the Chutzpah of Master Sgt. Ernest Bilko," *NYT*, April 14, 1996, section II.

22. Daniel Bell, "The Three Faces of New York," *Dissent* 7 no. 3 (summer 1961): 227.

23. For a hilarious account of the Mets' first season, see Jimmy Breslin, *Can't Anybody Here Play This Game?* (New York, 1973).

24. Daniel Bell, "Three Faces," 227; Stern, Mellins, and Fishman, *New York 1960*, 1155–66, 1174–1200; Wallach, ed., *New York: Cultural Capital*, 123–55, 189–210.

CHAPTER 11: FREEDOM NOW

1. Joseph P. Lyford, *Airtight Cage: A Study of New York's West Side* (New York, 1968), 1, 6–7, 52–54.

2. Frederick M. Binder and David M. Reimers, *All Nations Under Heaven: An Ethnic and Racial History of New York City* (New York, 1995), 218; Herman D. Bloch, *The Circle of Discrimination: An Economic and Social Study of the Black Man in New York* (New York, 1969), 49–67; Joseph P. Fitzpatrick, *Puerto Rican Americans: The Meaning of Migration to the Mainland* (Englewood Cliffs, N.J., 1971), 60–61, 70; Claude Brown, *Manchild in the Promised Land* (New York, 1965), 184.

3. U.S. Department of Labor, Bureau of Labor Statistics, Middle Atlantic Regional office, *A Socio-Economic Profile of Puerto Rican New Yorkers* (New York, 1975), 110; New York City Council on Economic Education, *Fact Book: New York Metropolitan Region* (New York, 1965), tables 4.27 and 17.9.

4. Bureau of Labor Statistics, *Socio-Economic Profile of Puerto Rican New Yorkers*, 50–53, 80, 125–27, 131–36.

5. Community Renewal Program, City of New York, *New York City's Renewal Strategy/1965* (New York, 1965), 13; NYC Council on Economic Education, *Fact Book* (1965), tables 3.10 and 3.11; New York City Council on Economic Education, *Factbook: 1972, Tables and Charts on the New York Metropolitan Region* (New York, 1972), 53; Sidney M. Willhelm, *Who Needs the Negro?* (Cambridge, 1970), 154–55.

6. Bureau of Labor Statistics, *Socio-Economic Profile of Puerto Rican New Yorkers*, 80; Fitzpatrick, *Puerto Rican Americans*, 58–59; Willhelm, *Who Needs the Negro?*; Frances Fox Piven and Richard Cloward, *Regulating the Poor: The Functions of Public Welfare* (New York, 1971), 200–17; Leon Fink and Brian Greenburg, *Upheaval in Quiet Zone: A History of Hospital Workers' Union Local 1199* (Urbana, 1989), 247n.

7. *NYT*, March 19, 1948, Oct. 28, 1949, July 4, 1950, Oct. 28, 1957, Jan. 10, 1962, Jan. 24, 1962, March 8, 1962; *The Chief-Leader*, Feb. 14, 1997; Lester Gulick to Henry Epstein, May 12, 1954, and James J. Lyons to John H. Murtagh, Aug. 19, 1954, file 2224, and Nathan Straus, "A Silly Piece of Legislation," file 2225, box 162, subject files, Wagner Papers; Ewart Guinier, "Impact of Unionization on Blacks," *Proceedings of the Academy of Political Science* 30 no. 2, 176; *Newsday*, April 27, 1993.

8. David Rogers, *110 Livingston Street: Politics and Bureaucracy in the New York City School System* (New York, 1969), 15–18; Clarence Taylor, *Knocking at our Own Door: Milton Galamison and the Struggle to Integrate New York City Schools* (New York, 1997), 50–54; The Newt Davidson Collective, *Crisis at CUNY* (n.p., 1974), 64–65; Binder and Reimers, *All Nations Under Heaven*, 223. Population change from Temporary Commission on City Finances, *Economic and Demographic Trends in New York City: The Outlook for the Future* (New York, 1977), 85, 88.

9. Bureau of Labor Statistics, *Socio-Economic Profile of Puerto Rican New Yorkers*, 71, 80; Harold X. Connolly, *A Ghetto Grows in Brooklyn* (New York, 1977), 186–87.

10. Nathan Glazer and Daniel Patrick Moynihan, *Beyond the Melting Pot: The Negroes, Puerto Ricans, Jews, Italians, and Irish of New York City* (Cambridge, 1963), 53–59; Connolly, *A Ghetto Grows in Brooklyn*, 130–36; "Bedford-Stuyvesant" and "Crown Heights," in *EncNY*.

11. Gerald Sorin, *The Nurturing Neighborhood: The Brownsville Boys Club and Jewish Community in Urban America, 1940–1990* (New York, 1990), 90–91, 161–69; Steven V. Roberts, "Brownsville Sinks in Decay and Fear," and Richard Rogin, "This Place Makes Bedford-Stuyvesant Look Beautiful," in Joseph Bensman and Arthur J. Vidich, eds., *Metropolitan Communities: New Forms of Urban Sub-Communities* (New York, 1975), 25–29, 107–20; Connolly, *A Ghetto Grows in Brooklyn*, 200.

12. Joel Schwartz, *The New York Approach: Robert Moses, Urban Liberals, and the Redevelopment of the Inner City* (Columbus, Ohio, 1993), 113–22; Robert A. M. Stern, Thomas Mellins, and David Fishman, *New York 1960: Architecture and Urbanism between the Second World War and the Bicentennial* (New York, 1995), 922–23.

13. Oscar Handlin, *The Newcomers: Negroes and Puerto Ricans in a Changing Metropolis* (Cambridge, 1959), 146; James Baldwin, *Nobody Knows My Name: More Notes of a Native Son* (New York, 1961; reprinted 1973), 60.

14. Robert Anthony Orsi, *The Madonna of 115th Street: Faith and Community in Italian Harlem, 1880–1950* (New Haven, 1985), 71; Schwartz, *New York Approach*, 115–17; Bureau of Labor Statistics, *Socio-Economic Profile of Puerto Rican New Yorkers*, 30–41; Fitzpatrick, *Puerto Rican Americans*, 181; Stern, Mellins, and Fishman, *New York 1960*, 954–55; Jack Newfield and Paul DuBrul, *The Abuse of Power: The Permanent Government and the Fall of New York* (New York, 1977), 4–5.

15. Calculated from U.S. Department of Commerce, *U.S. Census of Housing: 1960, Final Report HC(2)-128: Metropolitan Housing, New York, N.Y.* (Washington D.C., 1963), 23, 26, 32, 24, 37, 39.

16. *NYT*, Sept. 30, 1955, Oct. 12, 1955; Joseph F. Wilson, *Tearing Down the Color Bar: A Documentary History and Analysis of the Brotherhood of Sleeping Car Porters* (New York, 1989), 217–31; Taylor Branch, *Parting the Waters: America in the King Years 1954–63* (New York, 1988), 185; CIO (NYC) Min, Jan. 18, 1956; CIO (NYC) Ex Min, Oct. 20, 1955.

17. Gerald Markowitz and David Rosner, *Children, Race, and Power: Kenneth and Mamie Clark's Northside Center* (Charlottesville, 1996), 90–110; Taylor, *Knocking at our Own Door*, 48–90; Rogers, *110 Livingston Street*, 18–23.

18. Joel Schwartz, "Tenant Power in the Liberal City, 1943–1971," in *The Tenant Movement in New York City, 1904–1984*, edited by Ronald Lawson, with the assistance of Mark Naison (New Brunswick, 1986), 172–85.

19. Connolly, *A Ghetto Grows in Brooklyn*, 151–52, 188; Clarence Taylor, *The Black Churches of Brooklyn* (New York, 1994), 141–42; Peter B. Levy, "The New Left and Labor: The Early Years (1960–1963)," *Labor History* 31 no. 3 (summer 1990): 314.

20. AFL-CIO Ex Min, March 19, 1959, April 21, 1960, June 16, 1960, Dec. 15, 1960, Sept. 17, 1963; Levy, "The New Left and Labor," 308; *J-A*, March 26, 1965.

21. David J. Garrow, *Bearing the Cross: Martin Luther King, Jr., and the Southern Christian Leadership Conference* (New York, 1986; reprinted 1988), 256–286; AFL-CIO Ex Min, July 18 and Aug. 15,

1963; Anne M. Kornhauser, "Craft Unionism and Racial Equality: The Failed Promise of Local 3 of the International Brotherhood of Electrical Workers in the Civil Rights Era," MA essay, History Department, Columbia University, 1993, 47; "Local 10 Target of Leftists; Why?," folder 2A, box 2- 308, ILGWU; Bruce Nelson, *The Logic and Limits of Solidarity: Workers, Unions, and Civil Rights, 1935–1974* (forthcoming); file 6 ("March on Washington"), box 75, 1199; "Local 144: 'A Miniature U.N.'," *Industrial Bulletin*, March 1963, 16–18; Minutes of General Council meetings, District 65, July 10 and Sept. 4, 1963, RWLA; Jarvis Anderson, *Bayard Rustin: Troubles I've Seen: A Biography* (New York, 1997); Philip S. Foner, *Organized Labor and the Black Worker, 1619–1973* (New York, 1974), 349.

22. AFL-CIO Ex Min, March 17, 1960.

23. Nancy Green, *Ready-to-Wear and Ready-to Work: A Century of Industry and Immigrants in Paris and New York* (Durham, 1997); *HT*, July 2, 1962; *NYT*, July 2 and 3, 1962; *DN*, July 3, 1962; ILGWU, "News" [press release], April 30, 1963, folder 2B, box 2-308, ILGWU; Robert Laurentz, "Racial/Ethnic Conflict in the New York City Garment Industry, 1933–1980," Ph.D. diss., State University of New York at Binghamton, 1980, 294–314, 337–40; Herbert Hill, "Guardians of the Sweatshops: The Trade Unions, Racism, and the Garment Industry," in *Puerto Rico and the Puerto Ricans: Studies in History and Society*, ed. Adalberto López and James Petras (New York, 1974).

24. *NYT*, June 13 and 14, 1963.

25. AFL-CIO Ex Min, June 20, 1963; *NYT*, June 28, 1963.

26. *NYT*, July 10, 1963; July 11, 1963; Taylor, *Black Churches of Brooklyn*, 142–43.

27. Taylor, *Black Churches of Brooklyn*, 140, 149–63; *NYT*, July 19, 1963; July 22–24, 1963; July 29, 1963; Aug. 2, 1963; Aug. 7, 1963; Aug. 31, 1963; Sept. 14, 1963; Nov. 5, 1963; Nov. 12–13, 1963.

28. Taylor, *Knocking at Our Own Door*, 116–75; Rogers, *110 Livingston Street*, 23–26, 121–26, 139–42; Kenneth B. Clark, *Dark Ghetto: Dilemmas of Social Power* (New York, 1965), 151.

29. Pete Axthelm, *The City Game: Basketball in New York* (New York, 1970), 125–26.

30. *NYT*, July 17 to July 24, 1964.

31. Kareem Abdul-Jabbar and Peter Knobler, *Giant Steps: The Autobiography of Kareem Abdul-Jabbar* (New York, 1983), 72–75; Clark, *Dark Ghetto*, 15–16; Garrow, *Bearing the Cross: Martin Luther King, Jr., and the Southern Christian Leadership Conference* (New York, 1986; reprinted 1988), 342–44.

32. *NYT*, July 23, 1964; Lyford, *Airtight Cage*, 37, 50–51; Glazer and Moynihan, *Beyond the Melting Pot*, 132–35, 300–301.

33. C. Wright Mills, Clarence Senior, Rose Kohn Golden, *The Puerto Rican Journey: New York's Newest Migrants* (New York, 1950), 105–109; History Task Force, Centro de Estudios Puertorriqueños, *Labor Migration Under Capitalism: The Puerto Rican Experience* (New York, 1979), 151–52; Glazer and Moynihan, *Beyond the Melting Pot*, 107–110; Fitzpatrick, *Puerto Rican Americans*, 71, 127–28, 181; Dan Wakefield, *Island in the City: Puerto Ricans in New York* (New York, 1959), 266–67, 274–77.

34. AFL Ex Min, Feb. 27, 1950, April 14, 1952, Dec. 5, 1952, and May 5, 1953; CIO (NYC) Min, Feb. 28, 1950 and April 14, 1952; *NYT*, June 27, 1954.

35. On pre–World War II Puerto Rican leftism and pro-labor sentiment, see César Andreu Iglesias, ed., *Memoirs of Bernardo Vega: A Contribution to the History of the Puerto Rican Community in New York* (New York, 1984); Gerald Meyer, "Puerto Ricans," in *EncLeft*; and Michael Demming, *Culture Front: The Laboring of American Culture in the Twentieth Century* (London, 1996), 76–77. Interview with Ida Torres, Sept. 18, 1993; Senate Select Committee on Improper Activities in the Labor or Management Field, *Investigation of Improper Activities in the Labor or Management Field: Hearings*, 85 Cong., 1 sess. (1957), 3756–81; Joseph Herman to George Meany, Re: Report on IJWU; John J. McNiff to Meany, Oct. 21, 1958; and McNiff to David Dubinsky, April 25, 1958, all in folder 2A, box 2-202, ILGWU; Altagarcia Ortiz, "Puerto Rican Workers in the Garment Industry of New York City, 1920–1960," in Robert Asher and Charles Stephenson, eds., *Labor Divided: Race and Ethnicity in the United States Labor Struggles, 1835–1960* (Albany, 1990), 116–20; Local 475, Officer Reports, 1952, 31, 70–71, FF1057; and Kirscher to James Matles, May 3, 1954, FF1013, UE; [UE Local] *475 News*, June 1953; Wakefield, *Island in the City*, 204, 207–9, 211; Arthur Osman, "Tells Union's Aims, *Amsterdam News*, Sept. 23, 1950.

36. CIO (NYC) Ex Min, Feb. 23, 1954, March 25, 1954, May 27, 1954; Wakefield, *Island in the City*, 208; Peter Braestrup, "How the Unions Fail the Exploited," *HT*, Oct. 10, 1958 (includes quote).

37. Arthur M. Schlesinger Jr., *Robert Kennedy and His Times* (Boston, 1978), 143–92; David L. Stebbene, *Arthur J. Goldberg: New Deal Liberal* (New York, 1996), 157–75; Senate Select Committee on Improper Activities in the Labor or Management Field, *Investigation of Improper Activities in the Labor or Management Field: Hearings*, 85 Cong., 1 sess. (1957), 3756–3802, 4600–10; *NYT*, Aug. 4, 1957, Aug. 9, 1957; CIO (NYC) Min, May 28, 1957, May 28, 1958; CIO (NYC) Ex Min, Aug. 6, 1957.

38. Hill, "Guardians of the Sweatshops," 392–93; Senate Select Committee on Improper Activities in the Labor or Management Field, *Investigation of Improper Activities in the Labor or Management Field: Hearings*, 85 Cong., 1 sess. (1957), 3757; Norman C. DeWeaver to Louis Nelson, Feb. 7, 1957, Nelson to DeWeaver, Feb. 11, 1957, and DeWeaver to Nelson, Feb. 13, 1957, folder 2B; Matthew Schoenwald to David Dubinsky, April 30, 1958 and attached petition, Oct. 3, 1958, and Oct. 17, 1958, with attachments, and Nelson to Dubinsky, March 27, 1959, with attachment, Edmund J. Delahanty Jr. to Dubinsky, March 25, 1959, John J. McNiff to Dubinsky, April 28, 1958, Schoenwald to Dubinsky, April 30, 1958 and attached petition, folder 2A, box 2-202; Memo on El Diario, Aug. 27, 1958, "Company Union," El Diario De Nueva York, Aug. 26, 1958 (translation), and Memo Regarding Incident which Took Place in Q.T., Aug. 15, 1958, folder 1A, box 2-215, ILGWU; Braestrup, "How the Unions Fail the Exploited," *HT*, Oct. 10, 1958.

39. AFL-CIO Ex Min, Feb. 19, 1959, May 9, 1959, Oct. 19, 1959, Feb. 18, 1959, Dec. 15, 1960, July 19, 1962, Dec. 20, 1962, Jan. 16, 1964, June 18, 1964, April 15, 1965, June 16, 1966, April 20, 1967, April 28, 1959 (special meeting), April 11, 1963 (special meeting).

40. History Task Force, *Labor Migration Under Capitalism*, 154, 159; interview with Ida Torres, Sept. 18, 1993.

41. Clark, *Dark Ghetto*, 235–36; *NYT*, July 18, 1963, July 24, 1963, July 31, 1963, Aug. 17, 1963, Aug. 30, 1963, Nov. 12, 1963; Roger Waldinger and Thomas Bailey, "The Continuing Significance of Race: Racial Conflict and Racial Discrimination in Construction," *Politics & Society* 19 (September 1991): 304; Richard Gambino, *Blood of My Blood: The Dilemma of the Italian-Americans* (Garden City, N.Y., 1974), 310–11; Hill, "Guardians of the Sweatshops," 395–400.

42. Michael Flug, "Organized Labor and the Civil Rights Movement of the 1960s: The Case of the Maryland Freedom Union," *Labor History* 31 no. 3 (summer 1990): 328; Alice H. Cook and Lois S. Gray, "Labor Relations in New York City," *Industrial Relations* 5 no. 3 (May 1966): 89fn; AFL-CIO Ex Min, April 15, 1965.

43. *NYT*, Sept. 21, 1964; Richard Rogin, "Joe Kelly Has Reached His Boiling Point," in Murray Friedman, ed., *Overcoming Middle Class Rage* (Philadelphia, 1971), 83.

44. *NYT*, Sept. 21, 1964; Jonathan Rieder, *Canarsie: The Jews and Italians of Brooklyn against Liberalism* (Cambridge, 1985), 19–26, 64–70, 83–84, 90, 93; Robert W. Snyder, "The Neighborhood Changes: The Irish of Washington Heights and Inwood since 1945," in *The New York Irish*, ed. Ronald H. Bayor and Timothy Meagher (Baltimore, 1995); Gambino, *Blood of My Blood*, 10–11, 301, 306, 312.

45. Rogers, *110 Livingston Street*, 43–46, 65–95, 165; *NYT*, Sept. 21, 1964; Oct. 7, 1964; Clark, *Dark Ghetto*, 150; Taylor, *Knocking at Our Own Door*, 166–75. On Ridgewood and Glendale, see *EncNY*, 470, 1005.

46. Robert Korstad and Nelson Lichtenstein, "Opportunities Lost and Found: Labor, Radicals, and the Early Civil Rights Movement," *Journal of American History* 75 (Dec. 1988): 786–811; Branch, *Parting the Waters*, 290.

Chapter 12: Municipal Unionism

1. Aaron Michael Brenner, "Rank and File Rebellion, 1966–1975," Ph.D. diss., Columbia University, 1996.

2. U.S. Department of Labor, Bureau of Labor Statistics, *Employment, Hours, and Earnings, States and Areas, 1939–82, Volume II* (Washington, D.C., 1984), 591–92; New York City Council on Economic Education, *Fact Book: 1972* (New York, 1972), 43.

3. Congressional Budget Office, "New York City's Fiscal Problem," in Robert E. Alcaly and David Mermelstein, eds., *The Fiscal Crisis of American Cities* (New York, 1977), 291–92; Raymond D. Horton, "Human Resources," in Charles Brecher and Raymond D., Horton, eds., *Setting Municipal Priorities, 1986* (New York, 1985), 174.

4. Ralph T. Jones, "City Employee Unions: Labor and Politics in New York and Chicago," unpublished manuscript in possession of the author, 71–88, 148–53, 163; Mark H. Maier, *City Unions: Managing Discontent in New York City* (New Brunswick, 1987), 11–29; Local 375, AFSCME, *Building a City, Building a Union* (New York, 1987), 1–14.

5. A. Lawrence Chickering, ed., *Public Employee Unions: A Study of the Crisis in Public Sector Labor Relations* (San Francisco, 1976), 2–4; Ronald Donovan, *Administering the Taylor Act: Public Employee Relations in New York* (Ithaca, 1990), 3–6.

6. Raymond D. Horton, *Municipal Labor Relations in New York City: Lessons of the Lindsay-Wagner Years* (New York, 1973), 23–27; Jewel Bellush and Bernard Bellush, *Union Power and New York: Victor Gotbaum of District Council 37* (New York, 1984), 49, 54, 66–67.

7. Bellush and Bellush, *Union Power*, 55–61; Horton, *Municipal Labor Relations*, 28.

8. Maier, *City Unions*, 48–50; Joshua B. Freeman, *In Transit: The Transport Workers Union in New York City, 1933–1966* (New York, 1989), esp. chapters 9–10, 12, and 14.

9. Horton, *Municipal Labor Relations*, 29–35; Maier, *City Unions*, 48–52, 114–15; Bellush and Bellush, *Union Power*, 71–79.

10. Deborah E. Bell, "Unionized Women in State and Local Government," in *Women, Work & Protest: A Century of Women's Labor History*, ed. Ruth Milkman (Boston, 1985), 284–86.

11. Marjorie Murphy, *Blackboard Unions: The AFT and the NEA, 1900–1980* (Ithaca, 1990), 211–14; Maier, *City Unions*, 109–18; CIO (NYC) Ex Min (Special Meeting), Nov. 8, 1960.

12. Murphy, *Blackboard Unions*, 215–21; Maier, *City Unions*, 118–19; John O'Neill, "The Rise and Fall of the UFT," in Annette T. Rubinstein, ed., *Schools Against Children: The Case for Community Control* (New York, 1970), 176–77.

13. Maier, *City Unions*, 122–23, 125–26.

14. Bellush and Bellush, *Union Power*, 112–15; *The Chief*, Oct. 21, 1994; *Public Employee Press*, June 17, 1994; Maier, *City Unions*, 59–63. Horton, *Municipal Labor Relations*, 8.

15. Bellush and Bellush, *Union Power*, 119–25; Horton, *Municipal Labor Relations*, 67–70; AFL-CIO Ex Min, Jan. 21, 1965; *The Chief*, Oct. 21, 1994.

16. Maier, *City Unions*, 69–76; Bellush and Bellush, *Union Power*, 130–36; Charles R. Morris, *The Cost of Good Intentions: New York City and the Liberal Experiment, 1960–1975* (New York, 1981), 69–71.

17. Bellush and Bellush, *Union Power*, 19–20, 96–97, 141–56. See also, Susan Reverby, "Oral History of Lillian Roberts," in Carol Berkin and Mary Beth Norton, *Women of America: A History* (Boston, 1979); Maier, *City Unions*, 53–55.

18. Bellush and Bellush, *Union Power*, 157, 178, 184–89; Maier, *City Unions*, 85; Horton, *Municipal Labor Relations*, 95, 99; Morris, *Cost of Good Intentions*, 98–99.

19. Chris McNickle, *To Be Mayor of New York: Ethnic Politics in the City* (New York, 1993), 148–71; AFL-CIO Ex Min, April 20, 1961 and July 19, 1961; Minutes of the Brotherhood Party Executive Committee, Feb. 12, 1962 and Brotherhood Party Board of Governors, Feb. 21, 1962, microfilm reel R5017, RWLA; Charles Brecher and Raymond D. Horton, *Power Failure: New York City Politics and Power since 1960* (New York, 1993), 82.

20. McNickle, *To Be Mayor*, 180–207; David Dubinsky and A. H. Raskin, *David Dubinsky: A Life with Labor* (New York, 1977), 308–09, 311–15; Sidney M. Willhelm, *Who Needs the Negro?* (Cambridge, 1970), 20–21; William F. Buckley Jr., *The Unmaking of a Mayor* (New York, 1966), esp. 183, 205–210, 242, 333–34; *Time*, Nov. 19, 1973, 37.

21. E. J. Hobsbawm, *Age of Extremes: A History of the World, 1914–1991* (New York, 1994); Joe Flaherty, *Managing Mailer* (New York, 1970), 146; Woody Klein, *Lindsay's Promise: The Dream that Failed* (New York, 1970), 204–206; Roy Rosenzweig and Elizabeth Blackmar, *The Park and the People: A History of Central Park* (Ithaca, 1992), 490; Robert A. M. Stern, Thomas Mellins, and David Fishman, *New York 1960: Architecture and Urbanism between the Second World War and the Bicentennial* (New York, 1995), 31.

22. Michael Marmo, *More Profile than Courage: The New York City Transit Strike of 1966* (Albany, 1990); *NYT*, Feb. 13, 1946.

23. Freeman, *In Transit*, 318–19, 324–35; Leon Keyserling, "Higher Pay for N.Y.C. Transit Workers: The Workers Deserve It, The City Can Afford It," December 1965, TWU Collection, RWLA.

24. Marmo, *More Profile*, 54, 102, 106, 196, 205–208; Klein, *Lindsay's Promise*, 36–50, 71–72.

25. Marmo, *More Profile*, 129–131, 155, 225, 231–32, 237–38, 261–66; Horton, *Municipal Labor Relations*, 73–80; Bellush and Bellush, *Union Power*, 163–73; AFL-CIO Ex Min, May 19, 1966; Donovan, *Administering the Taylor Act*, 23–54; Thomas R. Brooks, "Lindsay, Quill & the Transit Strike," *Commentary* 41 (March 1966): 56–57.

26. U.S. Department of Labor, Bureau of Labor Statistics, *Handbook of Labor Statistics 1975 — Reference Edition* (Washington, D.C. 1975), 391; U.S. Department of Labor, Bureau of Labor Statistics, *Handbook of Labor Statistics* (Washington, D.C., 1989), 543; New York State Department of Labor, Division of Research and Statistics, *Work-Stoppage Trends in New York State, 1927–1979* (New York, 1972), 22–23, 59; Klein, *Lindsay's Promise*, 149–50, 161, 166; AFL-CIO Ex Min, Sept. 19, 1968; *NYT*, Dec. 22, 1968; Brenner, "Rank and Rile Rebellion," 2, 30.

27. Brenner, "Rank and Rile Rebellion," 23–29, 31–32, 53, 76–79, 85–87; Joshua B. Freeman, "Hardhats: Construction Workers, Manliness, and the 1970 Pro-War Demonstrations," *Journal of Social History*, June 1993, 733.

28. Morris, *Cost of Good Intentions*, 98, 104; Maier, *City Unions*, 86; Willie Morris, *New York Days* (Boston, 1993), 148; A. H. Raskin, "Why New York is 'Strike City'," *New York Times* (Dec. 22, 1968): 7–9.

29. Morris, *Cost of Good Intentions*, 103–6; A. H. Raskin, "Politics Up-ends the Bargaining Table," in Sam Zagoria, ed., *Public Workers and Public Unions* (Englewood Cliffs, N.J., 1972), 132–34; Maier, *City Unions*, 86–87; AFL-CIO Ex Min (Special Meeting), Feb. 10, 1968; A. H. Raskin, "Conclusion," in Chickering, ed., *Public Employee Unions*, 224.

30. Bellush, *Union Power*, 187–89; Maier, *City Unions*, 85; Horton, *Municipal Labor Relations*, 95, 99; Morris, *Cost of Good Intentions*, 98–99; U.S. Department of Labor, Bureau of Labor Statistics, Middle Atlantic Regional Office, *Wages and Benefits of New York City Municipal Government Workers, April 1972* (New York, 1972).

31. Barbara M. Wertheimer and Anne H. Nelson, *Trade Union Women: A Study of their Participation in New York City Locals* (New York, 1975), 52; *WSJ*, March 7, 1979; Bellush and Bellush, *Union Power*, 303–58.

32. Roger Starr, *The Rise and Fall of New York* (New York, 1985), 33–35.

CHAPTER 13: "A MAN BY THE NAME OF ALBERT SHANKER"

1. Deborah E. Bell, "Unionized Women in State and Local Government," in *Women, Work & Protest: A Century of Women's Labor History*, ed. Ruth Milkman (Boston, 1985), 285–86; Ira Katznelson, *City Trenches: Urban Politics and the Patterning of Class in the United States* (New York, 1981), 96; *Public Employee Press*, June 17, 1994; Joshua B. Freeman, *In Transit: The Transport Workers Union in New York City, 1933–1966* (New York, 1989), 333–34.

2. Charles R. Morris, *The Cost of Good Intentions: New York City and the Liberal Experiment, 1960–1975* (New York, 1981), 95; Edward T. Rogowsky, Louis H. Gold, and David W. Abbot, "Police: The Civilian Review Board Controversy," in Jewel Bellush and Stephen M. David, eds., *Race and Politics in New York City: Five Studies in Policy-Making* (New York, 1971); Woody Klein, *Lindsay's Promise: The Dream that Failed* (New York, 1970), 10–11, 154-55, 199–201, 262; Tamar Jacoby, "The Uncivil History of the Civilian Review Board," *City Journal*, winter 1993, 56–62.

3. Clarence Taylor, *Knocking at Our Own Door: Milton A. Galamison and the Struggle to Integrate New York City Schools* (New York, 1997), 176–91; David Rogers, *110 Livingston Street: Politics and Bu-*

reaucracy in the New York City School System (New York, 1969), 364-70; Majorie Murphy, *Blackboard Unions: The AFT and The NEA, 1900-1980*, (Ithaca, 1990), 239; Barbara Carter, *Pickets, Parents, and Power: The Story Behind the New York City Teachers' Strike* (New York, 1971), 6-15.

4. Jerald E. Podair, "'White' Values, 'Black' Values: The Ocean Hill-Brownsville Controversy and New York City Culture, 1965-1975," *Radical History Review* 59 (1994): 44-54; Stokely Carmichael and Charles V. Hamilton, *Black Power: The Politics of Liberation in America* (New York, 1967); Carter, *Pickets, Parents, and Power*, 11, 13 (quotes); Gerald Markowitz and David Rosner, *Children, Race, and Power: Kenneth and Mamie Clark's Northside Center* (Charlottesville, 1996), 119-21; Taylor, *Knocking at Our Own Door*, 178.

5. For two differing assessments of the degree of popular support for community control, see Maurice J. Goldbloom, "The New York School Crisis," *Commentary* (Jan. 1969), reprinted in Maurice R. Berube and Marilyn Gittel, eds., *Confrontation at Ocean Hill-Brownsville* (New York, 1969), 258, and Fred Ferretti, "Who's to Blame in the School Strike," *New York* (Nov. 18, 1968), reprinted in Berube and Gittel, eds., *Confrontation at Ocean Hill-Brownsville*, 290-91.

6. Marilyn Gittel, "Education: The Decentralization-Community Control Controversy," in Bellush and David, eds., *Race and Politics*, 147; Rogers, *110 Livingston Street*, 475; "McGeorge Bundy," in Nelson Lichtenstein, ed., *Political Profiles: The Johnson Years* (New York, 1976), 75-77.

7. *NYP*, Nov. 15, 1968; Joseph C. Goulden, *The Money Givers* (New York, 1971), 239-57.

8. Carter, *Pickets, Parents, and Power*, 20-23; Taylor, *Knocking at Our Own Door*, 181-83.

9. Carter, *Pickets, Parents, and Power*, 30-49; New York City Board of Education, Advisory and Evaluation Committee on Desegregation (Niemeyer Committee), Final Report [excerpts]; Eugenia Kemble, "Ocean Hill-Brownsville," *United Teacher*, Dec. 20, 1967; Rhody McCoy, "The Year of the Dragon" (unpublished Jan. 1968 address); and Richard Karp, "School Decentralization in New York," *Interplay Magazine* (Aug.-Sept. 1968), all reprinted in Berube and Gittel, eds., *Confrontation at Ocean Hill-Brownsville*.

10. Berube and Gittel, eds., *Confrontation at Ocean Hill-Brownsville*, 217-21. See also, Gittel, "Education: The Decentralization-Community Control Controversy," 148-52; Emily Straus, "Which Side Are You On? White Teachers in the 1968 New York City Teachers' Strike," Columbia College Senior Essay, May 1995, 14-16.

11. Carter, *Pickets, Parents, and Power*, 1-6, 59-74; Fred Ferretti, "Who's to Blame," 296-300.

12. Carter, *Pickets, Parents, and Power*, 75-89, 100. On the new teaching staff, see Charles S. Isaacs, "A JHS 271 Teacher Tells It Like He Sees It," *New York Times Magazine* (Nov. 24, 1968), reprinted in Berube and Gittel, eds. *Confrontation at Ocean Hill-Brownsville*.

13. Carter, *Pickets, Parents, and Power*, 86-106, 110; Allen J. Matusow, *The Unraveling of America: A History of Liberalism in the 1960s* (New York, 1984), 331-38, 395-439.

14. *NYT*, Oct. 12, 1968; Oct. 13, 1968; Nov. 12, 1968; Nov. 15, 1968; *NYP*, Nov. 1, 1968.

15. Carter, *Pickets, Parents, and Power*, 122-23; Podair, "'White' Values, 'Black' Values," 38. Anti-Semitic literature circulated during the strike can be found in Berube and Gittel, eds., *Confrontation at Ocean Hill-Brownsville*, 165-70. See also "Anti-Semitism? — A Statement by the Teachers of Ocean Hill-Brownsville to the People of New York," an advertisement that appeared in *NYT*, Nov. 11, 1968, and Sol Stern, "'Scab' Teachers," *Ramparts*, Nov. 17, 1968, both reprinted in the same volume.

16. *NYT*, Feb. 24, 1997; Paul Breines, *Tough Jews: Political Fantasies and the Moral Dilemma of American Jewry* (New York, 1990), quote on 58; second quote comes from a private correspondence from Arthur Aryeh Goren.

17. Patrick Harnett, "Why Teachers Strike: A Lesson for Liberals," *VV*, Oct. 31, 1968, reprinted in Berube and Gittel, eds., *Confrontation at Ocean Hill-Brownsville*; Podair, "'White' Values, 'Black' Values," 44-47; Sol Stern, "'Scab' Teachers," in Berube and Gittel, eds., *Confrontation at Ocean Hill-Brownsville*, 183; *NYP*, Nov. 1, 1968; Nov. 16, 1968; Straus, "Which Side Are You On"; Carter, *Pickets, Parents, and Power*, 112; *NYT*, Nov. 13, 1968; Nov. 17, 1968, section IV; Ferretti, "Who's to Blame," 307.

18. AFL-CIO Ex Min, Sept. 9 and Oct. 17, 1969; *NYT*, Nov. 14, 1968.

19. *NYT*, Nov. 12, 1968; Nov. 14, 1968; *NYP*, Nov. 13, 1968; *New York Times Magazine*, Dec. 22, 1968, 25; AFL-CIO Ex Min, Nov. 21, 1968.

20. *NYP*, Nov. 18, 1969; *NYT*, Nov. 18, 1968; *New York Times Magazine*, Dec. 22, 1968, 25, 27.

21. Gittel, "Education: The Decentralization – Community Control Controversy," 155–60; Carter, *Pickets, Parents, and Power*, 128–29, 146–52.

22. Morris, *Cost of Good Intentions*, 115–16; Carter, *Pickets, Parents, and Power*, 160–62, 164; *NYT*, May 12 and 13, 1975; June 7, 1999; Roger Sanjek, *The Future of Us All: Race and Neighborhood Politics in New York City* (Ithaca, 1998), 47.

23. AFL-CIO Ex Min, Dec. 19, 1968 and Jan. 9, 1969 (special meeting).

CHAPTER 14: LONGHAIRS AND HARDHATS

1. New York City Planning Commission, *Plan for New York City: Critical Issues* (New York, 1969), 21, 24–25, 30; State of New York, Governor's Advisory Council on Youth and Work, *The Clerical Job Market in New York City*, July 1970, 3–13; New York City Council on Economic Education, *1980–81 Fact Book on the New York Metropolitan Region* (New York, 1979), 18; The Newt Davidson Collective, *Crisis at CUNY* (n.p., 1974), 58–89.

2. Sherry Gorelick, "City College: The Rise and Fall of the Free Academy," *Radical America* 14 no. 5 (Sept. – Oct. 1980): 28; Newt Davidson Collective, *Crisis at CUNY*, 59, 65.

3. Gorelick, "City College," 27; Newt Davidson Collective, *Crisis at CUNY*, 12, 65; [City College] *Observation Post*, Feb. 14, 1969, April 18, 1969; [City College] *Main Events*, Feb. 20, 1969, Feb. 25, 1969; *The Campus* [City College], March 26, 1969, April 22, 1969.

4. *The Campus*, April 22, 1969; Newt Davidson Collective, *Crisis at CUNY*, 65–66; *NYT*, April 23–24, 1968.

5. [Brooklyn College] *Kingsman*, April 18, 1969, April 23, 1969; April 25, 1969, May 2, 1969; *NYT*, May 1, 1969, May 3, 1969, May 7, 1969; [Brooklyn College] *ken*, May 5, 1969; [Brooklyn College] *Olympian*, May 1969; [Brooklyn College] *Calling Card*, May 7, 1969.

6. [Queens College] *Phoenix*, Jan. 7, 1969, Jan. 14, 1969, April 1, 1969, May 2, 1969, May 7, 1969; *NYT*, May 2–4, 1969, May 8, 1969.

7. *NYT*, May 1–3, 1969, May 5, 1969.

8. *NYT*, May 8–10, 1969, May 15, 1969, May 18, 1969; *The Campus*, May 6, 1969; *Observation Post*, May 27, 1969.

9. *Kingsman*, Feb. 28, 1969, May 16, 1969; Joe Flaherty, *Managing Mailer* (New York, 1970), 162; Newt Davidson Collective, *Crisis at CUNY*, 66; AFL-CIO Ex Min, June 19, 1969 and July 17, 1969; Charles R. Morris, *The Cost of Good Intentions: New York City and the Liberal Experiment, 1960–75* (New York, 1981), 157; Gorelick, "City College," 28.

10. *The Campus*, Sept. 17, 1969; Morris, *Cost of Good Intentions*, 157; Newt Davidson Collective, *Crisis at CUNY*, 11–19.

11. *NYT*, May 7, 1996; Frederick M. Binder and David M. Reimers, *All the Nations Under Heaven: An Ethnic and Racial History of New York City* (New York, 1995), 200; Richard Gambino, *Blood of My Blood: The Dilemma of the Italian-Americans* (Garden City, N.Y., 1974), 223–24, 241–42.

12. Michael Kazin, *The Populist Persuasion: An American History* (New York, 1985), 233; Alan Draper, "Labor and the 1966 Elections," *Labor History*, winter 1989, 76–92; Jonathan Rieder, "The Rise of the 'Silent Majority,'" in Steve Fraser and Gary Gerstle, eds., *The Rise and Fall of the New Deal Order, 1930–1980* (Princeton, 1989), 258.

13. Rieder, "The Rise of the 'Silent Majority,'" 254; Jim Sleeper, "Boodling, Bigotry, and Cosmopolitanism: The Transformation of a Civic Culture," *Dissent*, fall 1987, 416–17; *New York Times Magazine*, Dec. 22, 1968, 28, 30.

14. Rieder, "Rise of the 'Silent Majority,'" 254; *New York Times Magazine*, Dec. 22, 1968, 28, 30; [Queens College] *Phoenix*, Feb. 20, 1969; Mario Matthew Cuomo, *Forest Hills Diary: The Crisis of Low-Income Housing* (New York, 1974), viii.

15. Chris McNickle, *To Be Mayor of New York: Ethnic Politics in the City* (New York, 1993), 221–29; AFL-CIO Ex Min, May 16, 1969; *NYT*, May 17, 1969.

16. Raymond D. Horton, *Municipal Labor Relations in New York City: The Lessons of the Lindsay-Wagner Years* (New York, 1972), 85-87; Joshua B. Freeman, *In Transit: The Transport Workers Union in New York City, 1933-1966* (New York, 1989), 355; Jewel Bellush and Bernard Bellush, *Union Power and New York: Victor Gotbaum and District Council 37* (New York, 1984), 186-88.

17. *NYT*, Dec. 21, 1995; *EncNY*, 741; Flaherty, *Managing Mailer*, 175, 178.

18. Charles Brecher and Raymond D. Horton, *Power Failure: New York City Politics and Power since 1960* (New York, 1993), 88-89; McNickle, *To Be Mayor*, 23-35; *NYT*, June 11, 1977.

19. *NYT*, May 9, 1970; *NYP*, May 9, 1970; Fred J. Cook, "Hard-Hats: The Rampaging Patriots," *The Nation*, June 15, 1970, 712-19.

20. *NYT*, May 12-14, 1970, May 19-21, 1970; *NYP*, May 11, 1970, May 13, 1970.

21. *Newsweek*, May 25, 1970; *NYT*, May 21, 1970, May 27, 1970, Oct. 4, 1996; Kazin, *Populist Persuasion*, 252-55; John Ehrlichman, notes on May 22, 1970, 5 P.M. meeting with the president, papers of the Nixon White House, microfiche edition. Part 3. John Ehrlichman notes. Meetings with the president; Charles W. Colson, memorandum for the president's file, Building and Construction Trades meeting with the president, May 26, 1970, Papers of the Nixon White House, microfiche edition. Part 2. The President's Meeting File, 1969-74; H. R. Haldeman to Mr. [Charles W.] Colson, Sept. 8, 1970, in Bruce Oudes, ed., *From: The President, Richard Nixon's Secret Files* (New York, 1989), 157-59; William Safire, *Before the Fall: An Inside View of the Pre-Watergate White House* (Garden City, N.Y., 1975), 579-96.

22. This paragraph draws on Joshua B. Freeman, "Hardhats: Construction Workers, Manliness, and the 1970 Pro-War Demonstrations," *Journal of Social History* 26 (Summer 1993): 725-44. The quote comes from Peter Biskind and Barbara Ehrenreich, "Machismo and Hollywood's Working Class," *Socialist Review* 10 (March-June 1980): 115.

23. David Marc, *Comic Visions: Television Comedy and American Culture* (Boston, 1989), 174-87; David Marc, "Comic Visions of the City: New York and the Television Sitcom," *Radical History Review* 42 (1988): 57-59.

24. Philip S. Foner, *U.S. Labor and the Vietnam War* (New York, 1989), 20-21, 41, 48; *NYT*, May 14, 1967, Dec. 26, 1992.

25. Andrew Levison, *The Working-Class Majority* (New York, 1975), 158-63; Peter B. Levy, *The New Left and Labor in the 1960s* (Urbana, 1994), 57.

26. Foner, *U.S. Labor and the Vietnam War*, 17-22, 36-39, 48-55, 59, 69, 88, 91.

27. *NYT*, May 13, 1970; May 22, 1970; "Harry Van Arsdale — General Jan.-June [1970]" folder, box 42-43, Van Arsdale Papers, and interview with Peter Brennan, by Renee Epstein, Sept. 3, 1987, RWLA; Foner, *U.S. Labor and the Vietnam War*, 114-15.

28. Jack Newfield and Paul DuBrul, *The Abuse of Power: The Permanent Government and the Fall of New York* (New York, 1977), 233-34; David L. Stebenne, *Arthur J. Goldberg: New Deal Liberal* (New York, 1996), 375-78; "Raymond R. Corbett: A Profile," *Industrial Bulletin* (Sept. 1963): 8-11.

29. Quotes from: *NYT*, May 12, 1970, May 21, 1970; Rieder, *Canarsie*, 157. See also interview with Robert F. Delaney, March 3, 1994; Cook, "Hard-Hats," 717; and Richard Rogin, "Joe Kelly Has Reached His Boiling Point," in *Overcoming Middle Class Rage*, ed. Murray Friedman (Philadelphia, 1971).

30. Freeman, "Hardhats," 732-33.

31. Mike Cherry, *On High Steel: The Education of an Ironworker* (New York, 1974), 150-51, 161; Cook, "Hard-Hats," 717; Levison, *Working-Class Majority*, 182-84; Kim Moody, *An Injury to All: The Decline of American Unionism* (London, 1988), 85, 96, 127-30; The Pacific Studies Center, "Crisis in Construction," *Ramparts* 8 (Jan. 1970): 35-38; Mark Erlich, "Who Will Build the Future?," *Labor Research Review* 12 (fall 1988): 4-6; E. E. Le Masters, *Blue Collar Aristocrats: Life-styles at a Working-Class Tavern* (Madison, 1975), 195; Thomas Byrne Edsall with Mary D. Edsall, *Chain Reaction: The Impact of Race, Rights, and Taxes on American Politics* (New York, 1992), 167; *NYT*, Sept. 21 and 23, 1969.

32. *NYT*, Sept. 26, 1969; Oct. 2, 1969; Oct. 8, 1979; Oct. 20, 1969; Oct. 25, 1969.

33. Anne M. Kornhauser, "Craft Unionism and Racial Equality: The Failed Promise of Local 3 of the International Brotherhood of Electrical Workers in the Civil Rights Era," Masters essay, Department of History, Columbia University, 1993, 51-55; Roger Waldinger and Thomas Baily, "The Continuing Significance of Race: Racial Conflict and Racial Discrimination in Construction," *Politics & Society* 19 (September 1991): 308-9, 312; Cook, "Hard-Hats," 717; *NYT*, Aug. 30, 1969.

34. *NYT*, May 13, 1970; *NYP*, May 14, 1970; *St. Louis Post-Dispatch*, May 27, 1970; Cook, "Hard-Hats," 717; Foner, *U.S. Labor and the Vietnam War*, 115. Waldinger and Baily, "The Continuing Significance of Race," 308–14.

35. U.S. Department of Commerce, Bureau of the Census, *Statistical Abstract of the United States, 1972* (Washington, D.C., 1972), 216; U.S. Department of Labor, Bureau of Labor Statistics, Middle Atlantic Regional Office, *A Socio-Economic Profile of Puerto Rican New Yorkers* (New York, 1975), 64.

36. Richard Price, *Bloodbrothers* (Boston, 1976), 107; Cook, "Hard-Hats," 715.

37. The preceding paragraphs are drawn from Freeman, "Hardhats," 734–36, and Cook, "Hard-Hats," 715; *NYP*, May 9, 1970, May 13, 1970; and Martin Duberman, *Stonewall* (New York, 1993), 181–280.

38. Le Masters, *Blue-Collar Aristocrats*, 26–30, 197; Rieder, *Canarsie*, 36–37; Cherry, *On High Steel*, 131, 178; Freeman, "Hardhats," 736–37.

39. *NYT*, May 13, 1970.

40. NYC Council on Economic Education, *1980–81 Fact Book*, 31, 39, 65; New York State Department of Labor, Division of Research and Statistics, *Work-Stoppage Trends in New York State, 1927–1970* (New York, 1972), 24–25, 44–45.

41. John Brady, "My Fellow Members," UFE Local 205 Election Material 1948, 1950, 1970, ND, box 1, New York Stock Exchange Archives, New York, N.Y.

42. *Newsweek*, Sept. 8, 1969, 89; Dec. 22, 1969, 107; *Time*, Sept. 26, 1969, 55; *New Yorker*, Nov. 29, 1969, 187; NYS Department of Labor, *Work-Stoppage Trends in New York State, 1927–1970*, 24–25.

43. Aaron Michael Brenner, "Rank and File Rebellion, 1966–1975," Ph.D. diss., Columbia University, 1996, 94, 96; John Walsh and Garth Mangum, *Labor Struggle in the Post Office: From Selective Lobbying to Collective Bargaining* (Armonk, N.Y., 1992), 7, 14.

44. Brenner, "Rank and File Rebellion," 97, 100–9; Walsh and Mangum, *Labor Struggle in the Post Office*, 5–16; *Newsweek*, March 30, 1970, 15–16.

45. Brenner, "Rank and File Rebellion," 109–23; Walsh and Mangum, *Labor Struggle in the Post Office*, 18–40.

46. *The Hot Seat*, no. 13 (April 1972); no. 16 (Aug. 1972); no. 17 (Oct. 1972); no. 18 (Oct. 1972); no. 25 (Nov. 1973); no. 28 (May 1974); no. 30 (Oct. 1974); John Gordon, "In the Hot Seat: The Story of the New York Taxi Rank and File Coalition, *Radical America* 17 no. 5 (1983): 27–43; *New York Workers News and Perspectives*, April 14, 1977; *NYP*, Jan. 8, 1974. On two-tier contracts, see Linda A. Bell, "Union Concessions in the 1980s," *Federal Reserve Bank of New York Quarterly Review*, summer 1989, 47–48, and Moody, *An Injury to All*, 172.

47. Mark H. Maier, *City Unions: Managing Discontent in New York City* (New Brunswick, 1987), 100–106; Morris, *Cost of Good Intentions*, 120–24.

48. NYC Council on Economic Education, *1980–81 Fact Book*, 11, 31, 68; U.S. Department of Labor, Bureau of Labor Statistics, *Employment, Hours and Earnings, States and Areas, 1939–82*, Vol. II (Washington, D.C., 1984), 578–79; "Sources of Job Change in New York City, by Industry, 1969–74," U.S. Department of Labor, Bureau of Labor Statistics, Middle Atlantic Regional Office; *NYP*, March 14, 1977; *Business Week*, May 14, 1979, 69–70; Morris, *Cost of Good Intentions*, 140–41; Peter D. McClelland and Alan L. Magdovitz, *Crisis in the Making: The Political Economy of New York State since 1945* (Cambridge, Eng., 1981), tables 2.3 and 3.14; Bureau of the Census, *Statistical Abstract of the United States: 1972*, 313.

49. NYC Council on Economic Education, *1980–81 Fact Book*, 31.

50. Bellush and Bellush, *Union Power*, 191–95; Maier, *City Unions*, 87–88; *New York*, Jan. 3. 1972, 28.

51. This account of the telephone strike is based on Brenner, "Rank and File Rebellion," 124–90.

52. NYC Council on Economic Education, *1980–81 Fact Book*, 46; Sleeper, "Boodling"; Robert W. Snyder, "crime," in *EncNY*, 298.

CHAPTER 15: THE FISCAL CRISIS

1. New York City paid for many services, like welfare, Medicaid, courts, and higher education, elsewhere funded largely or wholly by state and federal government. Debt figures from New York City

Council on Economic Education, *1980 - 81 Fact Book on the New York Metropolitan Region* (New York, 1979), 135; debt service figure from Eric Lichten, *Class, Power & Austerity* (South Hadley, Mass., 1986), 104.

2. U.S. Department of Commerce, Bureau of the Census, *Statistical Abstract of the United States, 1992* (Washington, D.C., 1992), 431, 469; NYC Council on Economic Education, *1980 - 81 Fact Book*, 39; John H. Mollenkopf, *New York City in the 1980s: A Social, Economic, and Political Atlas* (New York, 1993), 93; Congressional Budget Office, "New York City's Fiscal Problem," in Robert E. Alcaly and David Mermelstein, eds. *The Fiscal Crisis of American Cities* (New York, 1977), 286 - 89; Temporary Commission on City Finances, *Economic and Demographic Trends in New York City: The Outlook for the Future* (New York, 1977), 25, 66, 73 - 74; Charles R. Morris, *The Cost of Good Intentions: New York City and The Liberal Experiment, 1960 - 1975* (New York, 1981), 218 - 22; and Congress of the United States, Joint Economic Committee, *New York City's Financial Crisis: An Evaluation of Its Economic Impact and of Proposed Policy Solutions,* 94th Congress, 1st session (Washington, D.C., 1975), 18 - 30.

3. William K. Tabb, *The Long Default: New York City and The Urban Fiscal Crisis* (New York, 1982), 22 - 25; Joint Economic Committee, *New York City's Financial Crisis,* 41 - 43; Robert E. Alcaly and Helen Bodian, "New York's Fiscal Crisis and the Economy," in Alcaly and Mermelstein, eds., *Fiscal Crisis of American Cities,* 37, 52 - 56.

4. Lichten, *Class, Power & Austerity,* 96 - 104, 123 - 24; Ken Auletta, *The Streets Were Paved with Gold* (New York, 1979), 103 - 15; Fred Ferretti, *The Year the Big Apple Went Bust* (New York, 1976), 69 - 70, 75 - 76, 80.

5. Ferretti, *Year the Big Apple Went Bust,* 105 - 11, 119 - 21; Lichten, *Class, Power & Austerity,* 96 - 123.

6. Ferretti, *Year the Big Apple Went Bust,* 87 - 88, 100 - 104, 106 - 07, 111, 129 - 32, 135 - 55.

7. Charles J. Orlebeke, "Saving New York: The Ford Administration and the New York City Fiscal Crisis," in Bernard J. Firestone and Alexej Ugrinsky, eds., *Gerald R. Ford and the Politics of Post-Watergate America, vol. 2* (Westport, Conn., 1993), 361 - 64; Ferretti, *Year the Big Apple Went Bust,* 181 - 88; William E. Simon, *A Time for Truth* (New York, 1978), esp. 126 - 48; *NYT,* Oct. 5, 1975, section IV.

8. *NYT,* May 24, 1975; Ferretti, *Year the Big Apple Went Bust,* 181.

9. Orlebeke, "Saving New York," 36; Ferretti, *Year the Big Apple Went Bust,* 194 - 95.

10. Jack Newfield and Paul DuBrul, *The Abuse of Power: The Permanent Government and the Fall of New York* (New York, 1977), 178 - 82; Robert W. Bailey, *The Crisis Regime: The MAC, the EFCB, and the Political Impact of the New York City Financial Crisis* (Albany, 1984), 27 - 29; Lichten, *Class, Power & Austerity,* 129 - 34.

11. *NYT,* May 21, 1975; Ferretti, *Year the Big Apple Went Bust,* 196 - 204.

12. *NYT,* May 21, 1975, June 5, 1975; interview of Walter Wriston by Jack Bigel and Edward Rogowsky, Graduate School and University Center, City University of New York, Dec. 6, 1996; *New Yorker,* April 30, 1979, 99.

13. *NYT,* June 29, 1975, July 2 - 3, 1975.

14. *NYT,* July 4, 1975, July 12, 1975, July 23, 1975, July 25, 1975.

15. Newfield and DuBrul, *Abuse of Power,* 184 - 87; Ferretti, *Year the Big Apple Went Bust,* 238 - 49.

16. Ferretti, *Year the Big Apple Went Bust,* 250, 252; Lichten, *Class, Power & Austerity,* 155 - 56, 167 - 72; Municipal Labor Committee General Membership Meeting, Dec. 8, 1975, copy of minutes at D.C. 37, AFSCME, New York, N.Y.

17. Ferretti, *Year the Big Apple Went Bust,* 267 - 72; *Public Employee Press* [D.C. 37], Aug. 8, 1975. On opposition to the pact, see interview of Victor Gotbaum by Edward Rogowsky and Jack Bigel, March 26, 1997, Graduate School and University Center, CUNY; D.C. 37 Members Against the Cut Backs, "Stop Big Mac," Coalition to Fight Budget Cuts, "Hospital Bulletin No. 10," and Committee for a Solid Contract, "A Way Out," all in possession of the author.

18. Ferretti, *Year the Big Apple Went Bust,* 277; Newfield and DuBrul, *Abuse of Power,* 188 - 91.

19. The Newt Davidson Collective, *Crisis at CUNY* (n.p., 1974), 56 - 58, 61 - 64, 67 - 68; Simon, *Time for Truth,* 154 - 55; interview of John Zucotti by Jack Bigel and Edward Rogowsky, Graduate School and University Center, CUNY, Jan. 28, 1997; Bailey, *Crisis Regime,* 94 - 100; Newfield and DuBrul, *Abuse of Power,* 191 - 97.

20. Ferretti, *Year the Big Apple Went Bust*, 293–304; Newfield and DuBrul, *Abuse of Power*, 179; Bailey, *Crisis Regime*, 36–44; *Public Employee Press*, Sept. 12, 1975; interview of Victor Gotbaum by Edward Rogowsky and Jack Bigel; interview of Walter Wriston by Bigel and Rogowsky.

21. Phil Tracy, "Why We Got the Strike Nobody Wanted," *VV*, Sept. 15, 1975; Mark H. Maier, *City Unions: Managing Discontent on New York City* (New Brunswick, 1987), 175–77; Lichten, *Class, Power & Austerity*, 139–41.

22. Tabb, *Long Default*, 26; Martin Shefter, *Political Crisis/Fiscal Crisis: The Collapse and Revival of New York City* (New York, 1985), 154.

23. Orlebeke, "Saving New York," 368, 372–73; *NYT*, Sept. 17, 1975, Sept. 26, 1975, Oct. 1, 1975, Oct. 9, 1975; *Business Week*, Oct. 20, 1975, 92.

24. Orlebeke, "Saving New York," 321; *WSJ*, Oct. 6, 1975.

25. *WSJ*, Oct. 22, 1975; *Business Week*, Oct. 20, 1975, 93–94; Ferretti, *Year the Big Apple Went Bust*, 347–58.

26. Tabb, *Long Default*, 27; Program Planners, Inc., "Role of the Public Employee Retirement Systems of the City of New York in the Fiscal Crisis of the City," draft report, Program Planners, Inc., New York, N.Y.; *NYP*, Sept. 22, 1975.

27. *NYP*, Oct. 8, 1975, Oct. 10, 1975; *NYT*, Oct. 8, 1975; statement by the Municipal Labor Committee, October 14, 1975, copy in MLC files, D.C. 37; interview of Victor Gotbaum by Edward Rogowsky and Jack Bigel; Lichten, *Class, Power & Austerity*, 155; *The Guardian*, Oct. 22, 1975.

28. Ferretti, *Year the Big Apple Went Bust*, 338–41; Lichten, *Class, Power & Austerity*, 175–76; *NYP*, Oct. 19, 1975.

29. Program Planners, Inc., "Role of the Public Employee Retirement Systems," 3–5, 7–21; Jack Bigel, "Role of Labor in NYC Fiscal Crisis," New School Lecture, Nov. 30, 1976, transcript at Program Planners, Inc., New York, N.Y.; interview of Gedale D. Horowitz, by Jack Bigel and Edward Rogowsky, Graduate School and University Center, CUNY, Nov. 11, 1996. See also comments by Gotbaum at the MLC General Membership Meeting, Dec. 8, 1975, copy of the minutes at D.C. 37.

30. *New Yorker*, April 30, 1979, 99; Pete Hamill, " 'After Lunch, the Default!'," *VV*, Oct. 6, 1975; Lichten, *Class, Power & Austerity*, 165–73; *NYT*, Nov. 25–26, 1975; Auletta, *Streets Were Paved With Gold*, 290, 320.

31. *NYT*, Nov. 26, 1975; Ferretti, *Year the Big Apple Went Bust*, 372–406.

32. Auletta, *Streets Were Paved With Gold*, 290, 295; Department of Research and Negotiations, D.C. 37, AFSCME, "New York City Filled Full-Time Positions at Selected Points in Time," May 1981, copy in possession of the author.

33. *NYT*, Dec. 12, 1976; Tabb, *Long Default*, 30; *New York City Star*, Dec. 1975.

34. *NYT*, Dec. 9, 1976; Tabb, *Long Default*, 49–50, 52–53; Sherry Gorelick, "City College: Rise and Fall of the Free Academy," *Radical America* 14 no. 5 (Sept.–Oct. 1980): 33 ("vandalism"); Business/Labor Working Group, *Summary Report of the Business/Labor Working Group on Jobs and Economic Regeneration in New York City* (n.p., n.d.), 31–32.

35. *NYP*, Feb. 27, 1981; *NYT*, Dec. 5, 1976, Dec. 7, 1976.

36. Auletta, *Streets Were Paved With Gold*, 183; Shefter, *Political Crisis/Fiscal Crisis*, 135; Charles Brecher and Raymond D. Horton, eds., *Setting Municipal Priorities, 1982* (New York, 1981), 214; Clifton Hood, *722 Miles: The Building of the Subways and How They Transformed New York* (New York, 1993), 259.

37. Tabb, *Long Default*, 107–18.

38. The City of New York, Temporary Commission on City Finances. *The City in Transition: Prospects and Policies for New York* (New York, 1978), 38; Port Authority of New York and New Jersey, *The Regional Economy: 1975 Review and 1976 Outlook*, Jan. 1976, 1, 6.

39. U.S. Department of Labor, Bureau of Labor Statistics, *Employment, Hours, and Earnings, States and Areas, 1939–82, Volume II* (Washington, D.C., 1984), 578–79, 582, 584, 585; Port Authority, *Regional Economy: 1975 Review and 1976 Outlook*, 17–19.

40. *Business Week*, May 14, 1979, 60; *NYP*, March 14, 1977; *NYT*, Aug. 23, 1977; *NACLA Report on the Americas*, Nov.–Dec. 1979, 34–43; *WSJ*, May 31, 1978; Robert Laurentz, "Racial/Ethnic Conflict in the New York Garment Industry, 1933–1980," Ph.D. diss., SUNY Binghamton, 1980, 340–80.

41. One attraction of Connecticut for high-paid executives was its lack of a state income tax. Temporary Commission on City Finances, *City in Transition*, 39; Auletta, *Streets Were Paved With Gold*, 20; *NYT*, Nov. 26, 1975; *NYP*, May 12, 1977.

42. Roger Sanjek, *The Future of Us All: Race and Neighborhood Politics in New York City* (Ithaca, 1998), 94.

43. The City of New York, Temporary Commission on City Finances, *The Effects of Rent Control and Rent Stabilization in New York City* (New York, 1977), 15–17; *NYT*, April 12, 1976; Aug. 22, 1976; Peter Marcuse, "Abandonment, Gentrification, and Displacement: The Linkages in New York City," in Neil Smith and Peter Williams, eds., *Gentrification of the City* (Boston, 1986), 157–59; Tabb, *Long Default*, 96, 104; Ann T. Myerson, "The Determinants of Institutional Mortgage Investment in Bronx County," Ph.D. diss., New York University, 1979.

44. Dennis Smith, *Report from Engine Co. 82* (New York, 1972); Jill Jonnes, *We're Still Here: The Rise, Fall, and Resurrection of the South Bronx* (Boston, 1986), 7, 231–32.

45. Jonnes, *We're Still Here*, 306, 308–09, 311–17; *NYT*, July 14–15, 1977; *EncNY*, 112; Robert Curvin and Bruce Porter, *Blackout Looting: New York City, July 13, 1977* (New York, 1979).

46. City of New York, "Summary: The South Bronx, A Plan for Revitalization," Dec. 1977; Jonnes, *We're Still Here*, 333.

47. *Real Estate Weekly*, Jan. 26, 1976, Feb. 9, 1976; *NYT*, Feb. 3, 1976; Roger Starr, "Making New York Smaller," *New York Times Magazine*, Nov. 14, 1976. Shortly after proposing "planned shrinkage" Starr left city government to become the Henry Luce Professor of Urban Values at New York University.

48. *NYT*, Feb. 3, 1976, Dec. 21, 1976; Robert Fitch, *The Assassination of New York* (London, 1993), 152–63; Roger Vaughan and Mark Willis, "Economic Development," in Brecher and Horton, eds., *Setting Municipal Priorities, 1982*, 158–77; "Economic Recovery for New York City," Dec. 23, 1975, in binder "Bigel Notes: Fiscal Crisis, 1974–1978," Program Planners, Inc., New York, N.Y.; Conservation of Human Resources, Columbia University, "An Economic Development Agenda for New York City," Dec. 1975.

49. Business/Labor Working Group, Summary Report of the Business/Labor Working Group on Jobs and Economic Revitalization in New York City; Business/Labor Working Group, Coordinating Group, Meeting Notes, Sept. 13, 1976 and Oct. 22, 1976, copies in possession of the author; *DN*, Jan. 29, 1977; *NYT*, Jan. 5. 1977, Jan. 29, 1977.

50. *WSJ*, Nov. 22, 1976; *NYT*, Jan. 13, 1977, March 5, 1977, March 13, 1977, section IV; *VV*, Jan. 31, 1977; *NYP*, Jan. 21, 1977, Feb. 7, 1977.

51. *NYT*, May 8, 1977, Dec. 2, 1980; interview of Walter Wriston by Jack Bigel and Ed Rogowsky; Shefter, *Political Crisis/Fiscal Crisis*, 163–66.

52. *NYT*, April 13, 1976, June 21, 1976, July 1, 1976; minutes of Municipal Labor Committee (MLC) Steering Committee Meeting of June 21, 1976, and attached mailgram, Victor Gotbaum to Honorable Hugh Carey, June 21, 1976, and minutes of MLC general membership meeting, Dec. 15, 1976, D.C. 37 files.

53. Maier, *City Unions*, 183–85; *City Almanac*, June 1977, 12–14; *NYT*, Sept. 14, 1981; Mary McCormick, "Labor Relations," in Brecher and Horton, eds., *Setting Municipal Priorities, 1982*, 202–5; Franklin J. Havelick, "A Labor Productivity Strategy for New York City Transit: Coming to Grips with the Monster," *Public Productivity Review*, March 1983, 38–51.

54. Jewel Bellush and Bernard Bellush, *Union Power and New York: Victor Gotbaum of District Council 37* (New York, 1984), 364; *Public Employee Press*, July 15, 1977, Aug. 26, 1977.

55. *NYT*, Aug. 4, 1996, Aug. 6, 1976, Aug. 8, 1976; *NYP*, May 4, 1978, July 7, 1978; Coalition of Concerned Transit Workers, "Massive Demonstration at City Hall, Thursday, May 18, 1978," leaflet in possession of the author; *The Transit Worker* [Coalition of Concerned Transit Workers], Aug. 20, 1978.

56. See, for example, *Guardian*, June 16, 1976; *New York Workers' News & Perspectives*, Dec. 19, 1976; D.C. 37 Delegates Meeting Minutes, May 22, 1979, 2, copy in possession of the author.

57. McCormick, "Labor Relations," 209–11; Lichten, *Class, Power & Austerity*, 159–65.

58. *Public Papers of the Presidents of the United States, Jimmy Carter, 1979, vol. 2* (Washington, D.C.; 1980), 1235–41.

59. Gutman's piece appeared in the *New York Times* of July 21, 1977; the responding letters and editorial appeared on Aug. 3, 1977.

60. Midge Decter, "Looting and Liberal Racism," *Commentary*, Sept. 1977, 48–54. See also letters in response, in *Commentary*, Nov. 1977, 4–10.

61. Martha Cooper and Henry Chalfant, *Subway Art* (New York, 1984); Craig Castleman, *Getting Up: Subway Graffiti in New York* (Cambridge, 1982).

62. Chris McNickle, *To Be Mayor of New York: Ethnic Politics in the City* (New York, 1993), 257–70; *NYP*, Aug. 31, 1977; *NYT*, Oct. 3, 1977; interview of Victor Gotbaum by Jack Bigel and Edward Rogowsky.

63. *Empire State Report*, Jan. 14, 1980, 10; Joe Conason, "Strike Two," *VV*, Dec. 3, 1979; Conason, Geoffrey Stokes, and David Neustadt, "Derailed: The Little Sellout That Couldn't," *VV*, April 7, 1980; Steve Burghardt, "The New York Transit Strike of 1980: The Story of a Rank and File Disaster," *Against the Current*, Fall 1980, 18–20; *NYT*, April 7, 1980.

64. Michael Marmo, *More Profile than Courage: The New York City Transit Strike of 1966* (Albany, 1990), 124, 158; *NYT*, April 4, 1980, April 6, 1980, April 8, 1980, April 10, 1980; *Empire State Report*, Jan. 14, 1980, 11; McNickle, *To Be Mayor*, 257–75.

65. *NYT*, April 12, 1980; Burghardt, "New York Transit Strike," 18, 21–22; *NYP*, April 12, 1980 (Kempton); Municipal Labor Committee, Steering Committee Meeting, April 21, 1980 [minutes], copy at Program Planners, Inc.; *The Chief-Leader*, Aug. 28, 1981; Bureau of the Census, *Statistical Abstract of the United States: 1992*, 469; interview of Gedale D. Horowitz by Jack Bigel and Edward Rogowsky.

66. Shefter, *Political Crisis/Fiscal Crisis*, 151, 165, 172–78; Norman I. Fainstein and Susan S. Fainstein, "Governing Regimes and the Political Economy of Development in New York City, 1946–1984, in John Hull Mollenkopf, ed., *Power, Culture, and Place: Essays on New York City* (New York, 1988), 184–85; Castleman, *Getting Up*, 146–47.

CHAPTER 16: GLOBAL DREAMS AND NEIGHBORHOOD REALITIES

1. The most influential discussion of New York as a global city is Saskia Sassen, *The Global City: New York, London, Tokyo* (Princeton, 1991). Robert Fitch critiques this view in *The Assassination of New York* (London, 1993), 157–69.

2. For two quite different portraits of Trump, see his own *Trump: The Art of the Deal*, written with Tony Schwartz (New York, 1987), and Wayne Barrett, *Trump: The Deals and the Downfall* (New York, 1992).

3. Barrett, *Trump*, 33–72; Trump with Schwartz, *Trump: The Art of the Deal*, 45–52.

4. Trump with Schwartz, *Trump: The Art of the Deal*, 37, 64–65, 70–94, 98–129.

5. Samuel M. Ehrenhalt, "Some Perspectives on the New York City Economy in a Time of Change," in Benjamin J. Klebanor, ed., *New York City's Changing Economic Base* (New York, 1981), 6; John H. Mollenkopf, *New York City in the 1980s: A Social, Economic, and Political Atlas* (New York, 1993), 92; unpublished data from the Department of Labor, Bureau of Labor Statistics; Matthew P. Drennan, "The Decline and Rise of the New York Economy," in John H. Mollenkopf and Manuel Castells, ed., *Dual City: Restructuring New York* (New York, 1991), 29–36.

6. Drennan, "Decline and Rise," 36–38; Trump with Schwartz, *Trump: The Art of the Deal*, 123–24.

7. Fitch, *Assassination of New York*, 170–77; Sassen, *Global City*, 157; Maurice B. Ballabon, "The Role of New York City's Foreign Exports in Local Manufacturing," in Klebanor, *New York City's Changing Economic Base*, 57–71.

8. New York City Council, *Hollow in the Middle: The Rise and Fall of New York City's Middle Class* (New York, 1997), 19–20; Sassen, *Global City*, 222–28; John Hull Mollenkopf, "The Postindustrial Transformation of the Political Order in New York City," in Mollenkopf, ed. *Power, Culture, and Place: Essays on New York City* (New York, 1988), 227–29; Thomas Bailey and Roger Waldinger, "The Changing Ethnic/Racial Division of Labor," in Mollenkopf and Castells, eds., *Dual City*, 43–75.

9. NYC Council, *Hollow in the Middle*, 30; John H. Mollenkopf and Manuel Castells, "Introduction," in Mollenkopf and Castells, eds., *Dual City*, 11; Office of the State Deputy Comptroller for the City of New York, "New York City's Economic and Fiscal Dependence on Wall Street," Aug. 13, 1998, 14; Kim Hopper, "homelessness, in *EncNY*.

10. NYC Council, *Hollow in the Middle*, 14, 19-20; *NYT*, Oct. 3, 1989.

11. Roger Waldinger, "Changing Ladders and Musical Chairs: Ethnicity and Opportunity in Post-industrial New York," *Politics & Society* 15 no. 4 (1986-87): 388-89, 392; Thomas Bailey, "Black Employment Opportunities," in Charles Brecher and Raymond D. Horton, eds., *Setting Municipal Priorities, 1990* (New York, 1989), 100-101; NYC Council, *Hollow in the Middle*, 14- 15; Mollenkopf, *New York City in the 1980s*, 95; U.S. Department of Labor, *Monthly Labor Review*, Sept. 1986, 40; *NYT*, Feb. 2, 1997.

12. Mollenkopf, *New York City in the 1980s*, 95; Nancy Foner, "The Jamaicans: Race and Ethnicity among Migrants in New York City," in Nancy Foner, ed., *New Immigrants in New York* (New York, 1987), 200.

13. Waldinger, "Changing Ladders," 394-95; Illsoo Kim, "The Koreans: Small Business in an Urban Frontier," 219-42, and Bernard Wong, "The Chinese: New Immigrants in New York's Chinatown," 254-63, both in Foner, ed., *New Immigrants in New York*; Heather MacDonald, "Why Koreans Succeed," *City Journal*, Spring 1995, 12-29.

14. NYC Council, *Hollow in the Middle*, 30-34; Frederick M. Binder and David M. Reimers, *All the Nations Under Heaven: An Ethnic and Racial History of New York* (New York, 1995), 250-51.

15. Drennan, "Decline and Rise," 27-29; Fitch, *Assassination of New York*, 277.

16. NYC Council, *Hollow in the Middle*, 32; Robert A. Beauregard, "The Chaos and Complexity of Gentrification," in Neil Smith and Peter Williams, eds., *Gentrification of the City* (London, 1986), 42-46.

17. Jason Epstein, "The Last Days of New York," *New York Review of Books*, Feb. 19, 1976, 20; "SoHo" and "Park Slope," in *EncNY*; Emanuel Tobier, "Gentrification: The Manhattan Story," *New York Affairs* 15 no. 4 (1979): 22-25.

18. Tobier, "Gentrification," 17-20; Jan Rosenberg, "Park Slope: Notes on a Middle-Class 'Utopia'," *Dissent*, Fall 1987, 565-67; Peter Marcuse, "Abandonment, Gentrification, and Displacement: the Linkages in New York City," in Smith and Peter eds., *Gentrification of the City*, 169; "Carroll Gardens," "Clinton," and "Cobble Hill," in *EncNY*, 182, 245-47; *NYT*, March 1, 1980.

19. Steven Hager, *Hip Hop: The Illustrated History of Break Dancing, Rap Music, and Graffiti* (New York, 1984), 59-93, 102-3.

20. Nationally, in 1990, almost two out of three households owned their home. Richard Plunz, *A History of Housing in New York City* (New York, 1990), 337; Samuel G. Freedman, *Upon this Rock: The Miracles of a Black Church* (New York, 1993), 308-9; New York State Division of Housing and Community Renewal, Office of Rent Administration, *Rent Regulation after 50 Years: An Overview of New York State's Rent Regulated Housing 1993* (n.p., n.d.), 10-11; United States Department of Commerce, Bureau of the Census, *Census of Housing: 1950. Vol. 1, General Characteristics, Part 4* (Washington, 1953), table 17; Ronald Lawson, with the assistance of Reuben B. Johnson III, "Tenant Responses to the Urban Housing Crisis, 1970-1984, in *The Tenant Movement in New York City, 1904-1984* (New Brunswick, 1986), edited by Lawson with the assistance of Mark Naison, 226-27, 254-55; George Sternlieb and David Listokin, "Housing," in Charles Brecher and Raymond D. Horton, eds., *Setting Municipal Priorities, 1986* (New York, 1985), 406-9.

21. Elizabeth Roistacher and Emanuel Tobier, "Housing Policy," in Charles Brecher and Raymond D. Horton, eds., *Setting Municipal Priorities, 1981* (Montclair, N.J., 1980), 147, 158; Michael A. Stegman, "Housing," in Charles Brecher and Raymond D. Horton, eds., *Setting Municipal Priorities, 1988* (New York, 1989), 199-201.

22. Joel Schwartz, "Housing," in *EncNY*, 369; Jill Jonnes, *We're Still Here: The Rise, Fall, and Resurrection of the South Bronx* (Boston, 1986), 345-62.

23. Sharon Zukin and Gilda Zwerman, "Housing for the Working Poor: A Historical View of Jews and Blacks in Brownsville," *New York Affairs* 9 no. 2 (1985): 12-18; Freedman, *Upon this Rock*, 19, 307-40; Jim Sleeper, *The Closest of Strangers: Liberalism and the Politics of Race in New York* (New York, 1990), 153-55; and Bernard Hirschhorn, "Nehemiah Plan Homes," in *EncNY*, 804.

24. Freedman, *Upon this Rock*, 334.

25. Edward I. Koch with William Rauch, *Mayor* (New York, 1984), 127–35; Joel Schwartz, "Charlotte Gardens," in *EncNY*, 202; Richard Plunz, *A History of Housing in New York City: Dwelling Type and Social Change in the American Metropolis* (New York, 1990), 334 ("surreal").

26. *NYT*, April 30, 1995; Sternlieb and Listokin, "Housing," 399, 402; Emanuel Tobier, "The Bronx in the Twentieth Century: Dynamics of Population and Economic Change," *Bronx Historical Society Journal*, fall 1998, 97; Plunz, *History of Housing*, 330, 336–37.

27. Stegman, "Housing," 215.

28. Reed Ueda, *Postwar Immigrant America: A Social History* (Boston, 1994), 44–45, 60; Mollenkopf, *New York City in the 1980s*, 95; America Badillo-Veiga, Josh DeWind, and Julia Preston, "Undocumented Immigrant Workers in New York City," *NACLA Report on the Americas*, Nov.–Dec. 1979, 6; Louis Winnick, *New People in Old Neighborhoods: The Role of New Immigrants in Rejuvenating New York's Communities* (New York, 1990), 29; *EncNY*, 182.

29. Mollenkopf, *New York City in the 1980sz*, 95; Ueda, *Postwar Immigrant America*, passim, esp. 44–45, 58, 73.

30. *NYT*, July 1, 1992; Carol Groneman and David M. Reimers, "Immigration," in *EncNY*, 184–86; Binder and Reimers, *All the Nations Under Heaven*, 226.

31. Ueda, *Postwar Immigrant America*, 62–63, 93–94; Philip Kasinitz, *Caribbean New York: Black Immigrants and the Politics of Race* (Ithaca, 1992), 101–5; Winnick, *New People*, 41; *NYT*, May 26, 1992.

32. Kasinitz, *Caribbean New York*, 55; Badillo-Veiga, DeWind, and Preston, "Undocumented Immigrant Workers," 15; *NYT*, July 1, 1992; Winnick, *New People*, 123–38, 149–50.

33. *NYT*, July 1, 1992, Sept. 16, 1991; Robert W. Snyder, "The Neighborhood Changed: The Irish of Washington Heights and Inwood since 1945," in *The New York Irish*, ed. Ronald H. Bayor and Timothy Meagher (Baltimore, 1995), 439–60; presentation by Luis Guarnizo, Columbia University Seminar on the City, April 21, 1991; Silvio Torres-Saillant and Ramona Hernández, *The Dominican Americans* (Westport, Conn., 1998), 64–66, 74–78, 93–96.

34. Vincent Seyfried, "Jackson Heights," in *EncNY*, 607; Roger Sanjek, *The Future of Us All: Race and Neighborhood Politics in New York City* (Ithaca, 1998) (population statistics on 3); Badillo-Veiga, DeWind and Preston, "Undocumented Immigrant Workers," 15; *NYT*, May 4, 1998.

35. Richard Alba, Nancy Denton, Shu-Yin Leung and Josh R. Logan, "Neighborhood Change Under Conditions of Mass Immigration: The New York City Region, 1970–1990," *International Migration Review* 29 no. 3 (fall 1995): 625–56; Sanjek, *Future of Us All*, 53.

36. Sanjek, *Future of Us All*, 256–331.

37. Sleeper, *Closest of Strangers*, 18–19, 139, 184–85, 192–97; Andrew Sullivan, "The Two Faces of Bensonhurst," *The New Republic*, July 2, 1990, 13–16; Joe Klein, "Race: The Issue," *New York*, May 29, 1989, 32–38; Chris McNickle, *To Be Mayor of New York: Ethnic Politics in the City* (New York, 1993), 283–84.

38. Whites, native-born blacks, and Puerto Ricans made up 82 percent of the city population in 1980; 75 percent in 1990. All figures calculated from Mollenkopf, *New York City in the 1980s*, 93.

39. McNickle, *To Be Mayor*, 275–87, 292; Kasinitz, *Caribbean New York*, 156, 230–34.

40. Jonathan Rieder, "Trouble in Store," *The New Republic*, July 2, 1990; and Tamar Jacoby, "Garvey's Ghosts," *The New Republic*, July 2, 1990; McNickle, *To Be Mayor*, 285–87; Kasinitz, *Caribbean New York*, 223–45.

41. Tom Wolfe, *The Bonfire of the Vanities* (New York, 1987), quote on 447.

CHAPTER 17: HANGING ON

1. *New York Teacher*, Sept. 13, 1981; notes taken by the author at the 1981 parade; Edward I. Koch with William Rauch, *Mayor* (New York, 1984), 315; Kim Moody, *An Injury to All: The Decline of American Unionism* (London, 1988), 140–41, 157.

2. Koch, *Mayor*, 303–5, 310n, 315–16; John Hull Mollenkopf, *A Phoenix in the Ashes: The Rise and Fall of the Koch Coalition in New York City Politics* (Princeton, 1992), 110–11; Joe Conason, "What Makes Barbaro Run?," *VV*, Aug. 5–11, 1981; *In These Times*, June 17, 1981; Jim Sleeper, *The Closest of Strangers: Liberalism and the Politics of Race in New York* (New York, 1990), 153–55, 112; Michael Spear, "The 1981 Frank Barbaro Mayoral Campaign," unpublished paper, Sept. 1999.

3. Mollenkopf, *Phoenix in the Ashes*, 111–12; Koch, *Mayor*, 318; Sleeper, *Closest of Strangers*, 112.

4. *NYT*, Feb. 18, 1986, Dec. 23, 1990, section IV; *DN*, April 10, 1991; U.S. Department of Labor, Bureau of Labor Statistics, *Employment, Hours, and Earnings, States and Areas, 1939–82, Volume 2* (Washington, D.C., 1984), 578; Bureau of Labor Statistics Data, Series ID: SAU3656110000001, BLS website; U.S. Bureau of the Census, *Historical Statistics of the United States, Colonial Times to 1970*, Electronic edition (Cambridge University Press, 1977), Series 946–951. Barry T. Hirsch and David A. Macpherson have done the most detailed studies of union membership by metropolitan area. Their data is in line with my estimate; they found that in 1988, 27.3 percent of the workforce in the New York City–Northern New Jersey–Long Island region belonged to a union. Hirsch and Macpherson, *Union Membership and Earnings Data Book 1993: Compilations from the Current Population Survey* (Washington D.C.: Bureau of National Affairs, Inc., 1994), 8, 50.

5. "Comparative Membership Census, June 30 and Jan. 1, 1963, New York City Area," folder 1, box 2-439, ILGWU; *New York Newsday*, May 3, 1994; *The Chief*, Oct. 21, 1994.

6. Calculated from Hirsch and Macpherson, *Union Membership and Earnings Data Book 1993*, 50. No equivalent data are available for the city alone.

7. New York State Organized Crime Task Force, *Corruption and Racketeering in the New York City Construction Industry* (Ithaca, 1988), 15–41, 47–49, 67–92.

8. *DN*, Sept. 6, 1992; *NYT*, March 10, 1991.

9. *New York Newsday*, Sept. 11, 1992; *NYT*, April 16, 1992; NYS Organized Crime Task Force, *Corruption and Racketeering in Construction Industry*, 19, 74–78, 87–88.

10. *New York Newsday*, May 3, 1994, Aug. 10, 1992; *NYT*, Oct. 23, 1992; *Newsday*, Oct. 23, 1992.

11. *NYT*, Feb. 18, 1986.

12. *DN*, Aug. 28, 1979; Jewel Bellush and Bernard Bellush, *Union Power and New York: Victor Gotbaum and District Council 37* (New York, 1984), 427–37; *Public Employee Press*, Jan. 23, 1987.

13. *The Chief*, March 28, 1986; Michael Oreskes, "Is It Still a Union Town?," *Dissent*, fall 1987, 490–91.

14. See, for example, *DN*, April 10, 1991.

15. Mae M. Ngai, "Who is an American Worker? Asian Immigrants, Race, and the National Boundaries of Class," in Steven Fraser and Joshua B. Freeman, eds., *Audacious Democracy: Labor Intellectuals, and the Social Reconstruction of America* (Boston, 1997), 197–81; 60th Anniversary History Book Committee, *60 Years: Building a City, Building a Union: A History of the Civil Service Technical Guild, Local 375, AFSCME District Council 37, AFL-CIO* (New York, 1997), 21.

16. Bellush and Bellush, *Union Power*, 433–34, 449; *Public Employee Press*, June 17, 1994; *The Chief*, Oct. 21, 1994.

17. *Public Employee Press*, June 17, 1994; *NYP*, Dec. 30, 1994; *New York Newsday*, May 8, 1995; *NYT*, Sept. 17, 1992, Dec. 25, 1992, Dec. 11, 1995, Feb. 18, 1999; *Newsday*, May 30, 1997; Bellush and Bellush, *Union Power*, 424.

18. *New York Newsday*, May 8, 1995; *Newsday*, Feb. 9, 1999, June 21, 1999; *NYT*, Feb. 18, 1999; *Public Employee Press*, June 17, 1994.

19. Leon Fink and Brian Greenberg, *Upheaval in the Quiet Zone: A History of Hospital Workers' Union, Local 1199* (Urbana, 1989), 50–51, 64, 69, 135–38, 161–65, 199–202, 209–14; Joe Klein, "Labor Pains: Turmoil Grips an Old Left Union," *New York*, March 25, 1985, 43; Leon Fink, "Bread & Roses, Crusts & Thorns: The Troubled Story of 1199," *Dissent*, Spring 1986, 180–81, 184–85.

20. Joshua B. Freeman, "Hospital Workers, Heal Thyselves," *The Nation*, March 31, 1984, 379–80; Fink and Greenberg, *Upheaval in the Quiet Zone*, 214–23; *NYT*, May 8, 1984; Klein, "Labor Pains," 44.

21. Telephone interview with Leon Davis, Feb. 2, 1984; Freeman, "Hospital Workers, Heal Thyselves," 380–82.

22. Fink and Greenberg, *Upheaval in the Quiet Zone*, 222-28; Billy Massey, "The History of 1199 at Presbyterian Hospital," 1995, unpublished paper in possession of the author, 33-42; Bureau of National Affairs, *White Collar Report*, Sept. 5, 1984, 265-66, 291-94; William J. Abelow to Doris Turner, June 10, 1985, copy in possession of the author.

23. *Labor Notes*, Nov. 1987, 5; *NYT*, Oct. 11, 1987; Fink and Greenberg, *Upheaval in the Quiet Zone*, 229-37, 281-82; A. H. Raskin, "Getting Things Done," *The New Yorker*, Dec. 10, 1990, 66.

24. For glowing portraits of Rivera, see Raskin, "Getting Things Done," and Sam Roberts, "A New Face for America Labor," *New York Times Magazine*, May 10, 1992. On the contract campaign, see Gerald Hudson and Barbara Caress, "New York's 1199 in 1989: Rebuilding a Troubled Union," *Labor Research Review* no. 17, 69-80.

25. On the problems female union leaders face, see Ruth Needleman, "Women Workers: Strategies for Inclusion and Rebuilding Unionism," in Greg Mantsios, ed. *A New Labor Movement for a New Century* (New York, 1998); for Feldman, see *NYT*, Sept. 29, 1995.

26. Mollenkopf, *Phoenix in the Ashes*, 82-83, 114-15, 120, 123-24, 166-67, 173, 198, 203-4; Chris McNickle, *To Be Mayor of New York: Ethnic Politics in the City* (New York, 1993), 275-77, 283-84, 292.

27. Jim Sleeper, *Closest of Strangers*, 276-302; Mollenkopf, *Phoenix in the Ashes*, 86-87, 168, 178-81; McNickle, *To Be Mayor*, 293-313; Raskin, "Getting Things Done," 70.

28. Joshua B. Freeman, "The Strike Weapon: Can it Still Work?" *Dissent*, spring 1997, 60-65; Jonathan D. Rosenblum, *Copper Crucible: How the Arizona Miners' Strike of 1983 Recast Labor-Management Relation in America* (Ithaca, 1995).

29. Kenneth M. Jennings, *Labor Relations at the New York Daily News: Peripheral Bargaining and the 1980 Strike* (Westport, Conn., 1993), 1-60. The strikers' version of events leading up to the walkout can be found in the first issue of *Real News*, a paper they put out during the walkout.

30. Jennings, *Labor Relations*, 60-65, 68-69; *New York Observer*, Nov. 12, 1990; *VV*, Nov. 27, 1990, 30.

31. *VV*, Nov. 27, 1990, 30-32, 35-37, 76; *New York Observer*, Nov. 12, 1990; *NYP*, Nov. 15, 1990; Jennings, *Labor Relations*, 54, 82-83, 103-4; Raskin, "Getting Things Done," 54, 79, 82-83.

32. Jennings, *Labor Relations*, 80-82, 89-91; *VV*, Nov. 27, 1990, 32; *New York Observer*, Nov. 12, 1990; Don Roberts, "New Low in Race-Baiting," *Real News*, n.d.

33. *NYT*, Dec. 23, 1990, section IV; Jennings, *Labor Relations*, 67-68, 88-89, 94-96, 106-7, 113, 132-48.

34. Jennings, *Labor Relations*, 156-95; *WorkingUSA*, July/August 1998, 72; *NYT*, Oct. 2-4, 1993.

35. Robert Fitch, *The Assassination of New York* (London, 1993), 3-22; *NYT*, Sept. 22, 1993; Robert Fitch, "The King of the Clubhouse," *New York Newsday*, Oct. 26, 1993.

36. *VV*, May 30, 1995, 13; *NYT*, Dec. 11, 1995, May 7, 1996, Oct. 13, 1997; *NYP*, May 8, 1996. On the city's very slow recovery from the recession of the early 1990s, see *NYT*, April 16, 1992, Feb. 19, 1996; *Public Employee Press*, June 26, 1999.

37. See for example, *NYT*, March 8, 1996; Jan. 15, 1996.

CHAPTER 18: THE GHOST OF CLASS

1. *DN*, July 1, 1998; *NYT*, July 1-2, 1998; *NYP*, July 1, 1998; *New York*, July 13, 1998, 13; telephone communication from *New York* editor to the author, June 30, 1998.

2. *NYP*, July 1, 1998; *New York*, July 13, 1998, 13. A notable exception was Juan Gonzalez's column, *DN*, July 2, 1998.

3. *NYT*, Oct. 23, 1997.

4. Lillian B. Rubin, "Family Values and the Invisible Working Class," in Steven Fraser and Joshua B. Freeman, eds., *Audacious Democracy: Labor, Intellectuals, and the Social Reconstruction of America* (Boston, 1997), 32-45; Sherry Linkon and John Russo, "Can Class Still Unite: Lessons from the American Experience," paper presented at the international conference "Does Class Still Unite?": Socio-

Economic Differentiation as a Challenge to Trade Unions," Jan. 8, 1998, Catholic University, Leuven (Belgium).

5. New York City Council, *Hollow in the Middle: The Rise and Fall of New York City's Middle Class* (New York, 1997), 20–22; Office of the State Deputy Comptroller for the City of New York, "New York City's Economic and Fiscal Dependence on Wall Street," Aug. 13, 1998, 9.

6. Martin Shefter, "New York City and American National Politics," in Shefter, ed., *Capital of the American Century: The National and International Influence of New York City* (New York, 1993), 104–13; Bob Woodward, *The Agenda: Inside the Clinton White House* (New York, 1995); Michael Lewis, *Liar's Poker: Rising Through the Wreckage of Wall Street* (New York, 1989); Tom Wolfe, *The Bonfire of the Vanities* (New York, 1987).

7. Philip Kasinitz, *Caribbean New York: Black Immigrants and the Politics of Race* (Ithaca, 1992), 2, 133–59; *Amsterdam News*, June 17, 1995; *NYT*, Aug. 1, 1996; [New York Mayor's] Press Office, Release #049-97 (Jan. 28, 1997), "Mayor Giuliani Joins West Indian Community Organizers to Unveil Plans for 30th Anniversary West Indian American Day Carnival," copy in possession of the author; Immanuel Ness, "The Road to Union Cities," *Working USA*, Nov.–Dec. 1998, 80.

8. Interview with Deborah E. Bell, July 2, 1999; *Public Employee Press*, July 16, 1999.

9. *El Diario*, Oct. 26, 1995; Brian M. McLaughlin, "To All Executive Board Members," Oct. 31, 1995, copy in possession of author; telephone interview with Syed Armughan, June 15, 1999; *NYT*, Sept. 7, 1997; *DN*, July 2, 1998.

10. New York, of course, did have stores that were part of older national chains, like A&P, Sears, and Woolworth, but by the 1980s these icons of merchandising were in decline.

11. *NYT*, July 21 and 22, 1999, Aug. 1, 1999; *New York*, Sept. 27, 1999, 13; N.Y.S. Department of Commerce, *New York State Business Facts: New York City* [1951], 12; U.S. Department of Commerce, Bureau of Census, "1992 Census of Retail Trade—General Statistics: Sales, Payroll, & Employment, New York, New York," http://govinfo.library.orst.edu/cgi-bin/econlist?01-newyo.nyp (July 17, 1999).

12. For a recent discussion of some of these trends nationally, see William Leach, *Country of Exiles: The Destruction of Place in American Life* (New York, 1999).

13. Community Service Society of New York, *New York City's Labor Market 1994–1997: Profiles and Perspectives* (New York, 1998); Robert Fitch, *The Assassination of New York* (London, 1993), 3–7, 278; Bureau of Labor Statistics, "Local Area Unemployment Statistics," series ID:LAUPS360400005, extracted from BLS website.

14. Community Service Society, *New York City's Labor Market 1994–1997*; Gregory DeFreitas, "Youth Nonemployment in New York," Working Paper No. 1 (Nov. 1997), Center for the Study of Labor & Democracy, Hofstra University, Hempstead, N.Y.; *DN*, Jan. 7 and 9, 1996.

15. Fitch, Assassination of New York, 7–10; *DN*, Jan. 14, 1996. Frances Fox Piven, "The New Reserve Army of Labor," in Fraser and Freeman, eds., *Audacious Democracy*, 106–18; "Memorandum of Understanding" between New York City Transit Authority and TWU Local 100, Sept. 18, 1996, copy in possession of the author; *NYT*, Sept. 19, 1996, Sept. 23, 1996, Sept. 29, 1996.

CONCLUSION: NEW YORK AND THE NATION

1. For a wonderful evocation of what this practically meant in the lives of workers and their families, see Jack Metzgar, *Striking Steel: Solidarity Remembered* (Philadelphia, 2000).

2. On the way the politics of homeownership pushed Los Angeles in very different directions from New York, see Mike Davis, *City of Quartz: Excavating the Future in Los Angeles* (London, 1990), esp. chapter 3.

3. Tad Friend, "Does America Hate New York. . . . Or has it Just Stopped Caring?," *New York*, Jan. 23, 1995, 30; *Betty* no. 41 (Sept. 1996).

4. For an early account of the decline of the Fordist regime, see Michael J. Piore and Charles F. Sabel, *The Second Industrial Divide: Possibilities for Prosperity* (New York, 1984).

5. A Dec. 26, 1996, article in the *New York Times* reported, "For the bagel, a homely New Yorker with an immigrant accent, 1996 has been a breakout year": the Einstein/Noah Bagel Corporation, based in Ogden, Utah, had 300 stores; the Kellogg Company bought Lender's Bagel from Philip Morris for $455 million; and Dunkin' Donuts was adding bagels in its outlets.

6. Roger Sanjek argues this case in *The Future of Us All: Race and Neighborhood Politics in New York City* (Ithaca, 1998).

INDEX

A

Abdul-Jabbar, Kareem, 109–10, 192
Abzug, Bella, 284
Acheson, Dean, 167
ACW *See* Amalgamated Clothing Workers
AFL *See* American Federation of Labor
AFL-CIO
  Blue Cross, 131–32
  Central Labor Council *See* Central Labor Council
  Ethical Practices Committee, 309
  merger, 90, 99–100
  "Solidarity Day," 306
African-Americans, 26, 28, 68–71
  dropout rate, 182
  government jobs, 295
  hospital jobs, nonprofessional, 207, 295
  housing, discrimination in, 183–84
  labor movement, 179–201
Agency shop law, 280
Allen, Woody, 26, 227
All in the Family, 239
ALP *See* American Labor Party
Amalgamated Clothing Workers (ACW), 3, 45, 48, 62, 63, 110–12, 240
  Sidney Hillman Health Center, 130
  women, percentage of, 46
Amalgamated Houses, 110–11, 115
American Federation of Labor (AFL), 40
  Central Trades Council, 64–66, 86, 136
American Federation of State, County and Municipal Employees *See* D.C. 37 (AFSCME)
American Labor Party (ALP), 56–57, 74
  rent control, 107
American Medical Association (AMA), 127
American Safety Razor Company, 147–48
Amodeo, Anthony R., 310
Amsterdam News, 59, 118, 252

Anastasia, Albert, 6
Anastasia, Anthony, 6
Anticommunism, 72–95
  Brownsville Boys Club, effect on, 88
  Catholic Church, 83–84
Antonini, Luigi, 45, 132, 153
Apparel industry, 11–12, 145–47
Arson, 275–76
AT&T, 253
Automation, 154–56, 159–61, 181
A View from the Bridge, 31, 38
Axthelm, Pete, 191

B

Backlash politics, 234, 235–37, 284
Badillo, Herman, 181
Bank demonstrations, 261
Barbaro, Frank, 307–8, 322
Barkley, Alben, 43
Baroff, Jacob, 32
"Battle of Wall Street," 51
Bauza, Mario, 35
Beame, Abraham, 209, 284
  fiscal crisis, 259, 261
  hiring freeze, city, 258
  transit fare increase, 264
  wage freeze, 267
Beck, Dave, 194
Bedford-Stuyvesant, 183
Beirne, Joseph, 253
Bell, Daniel, 36, 175
Bellevue Hospital, 7, 138
Bendix, William, 23
Benson and Hedges, 11
Berle, Milton, 174, 175
Berman, Shelley, 175
Biaggi, Mario, 230
Bigel, Jack, 84, 94, 214, 268–69, 279

"Big Mac," 260–61
Bishop, Jimmy, 309–10
Blackout, 276
    looters, 281
Blue Cross, 131–32, 137–38
Blue Shield, 134–35, 138
B/LWG *See* Business/Labor Working Group
        on Jobs and Economic Revitalization
        in New York City
Board of Education, job cuts at, 270–71
Bonfire of the Vanities, The, 304, 328
Bowker, Albert, 229
Brady, John, 247
Brandeis, Louis, 52
Brennan, Peter, 103, 239, 278
Breslin, Jimmy, 235, 236
Brewster Aeronautical factory, 34, 37
Broido, Louis, 153
Bronfman, Edgar, 277
Brooklyn Botanical Gardens, 175
Brooklyn Civic Center, 147, 149
Brooklyn College, 230
Brooklyn Dodgers, 23, 34, 175
    desegregation of, 69
Brooklyn Navy Yard, 164
Brooklyn Trust Company strike, 49–51
Brownsville, 29, 30, 183, 277
    housing abandonment, 274
    "Murder Inc.", 38
    public housing, 184
Brownsville Boys Club, 32
    anticommunism, effect of, 88
Brownsville Welfare Center, 205
Brown v. Board of Education, 185–86, 199
Buckley, William F., Jr., 209, 234
Building and Construction Trades Council,
        103, 238–39, 243, 278
Bundy, McGeorge, 218
Burke, James, 113
Burns, Arthur F., 266
Bush, George, 328
Business/Labor Working Group on Jobs and
        Economic Revitalization in New York
        City (B/LWG), 277–79, 286
Butler, James, 315
Bywater, William, 244

C

Cacchione, Peter, 56, 59
Caesar, Sid, 27, 36, 170, 175
Capote, Truman, 19
Carey, Hugh, 312
    agency shop law, 280
    Co-op City rent strike, 122
    fiscal crisis, 259, 260, 267
    teacher's strike, 268
Carey, James, 147
Carroll Gardens, gentrification of, 297
Carson, Sonny, 222, 304
Carter, Jimmy, 276, 299
    "crisis of the American spirit," 281
Caruso, Enrico, 37
Cassese, John J., 237
Catholic Church
    anticommunism, 83–84
    Nehemiah Plan, 298–300
    Northwest Bronx Community and Clergy
        Coalition, 298
Central Labor Council (New York City), 100,
        101, 136, 153, 227, 241, 250
    Barbaro, endorsement of, 307
    conferences on automation, 159
    CUNY, 231, 232
    Daily News strike, 321
    Labor Day parade, 136, 306, 328–30
    Ocean Hill–Brownsville school board,
        224–25
    Professional Advisory Committee,
        formation of, 138
    Van Arsdale, Thomas, 311
    Wagner, endorsement of, 236
Chaikin, Sol, 278
Chain stores, 331–32
Charlotte Gardens, 299–300
Chayefsky, Paddy, 171
Chester, Hilda, 175
Chinatown, 29
CIO *See* Congress of Industrial
        Organizations
City University of New York (CUNY), 67,
        228–33, 261, 272, 278
    enrollment, decline in, 271
    tuition, institution of, 264, 267

Civil rights, 179–201
  Southern movement, 186–87
Civil Rights Act, 197
Civil service system, 201
Clark, Kenneth, 192, 217
Clarke, Shirley, 35
Clinton, Bill, 328, 333
Cohen, Myron, 175
Collective bargaining, 203
  Office of Collective Bargaining (OCB), 206
Columbia-Presbyterian Hospital, 140
Comedy styles, 175
Commercial center, New York as, 18–20
Commercial construction, 167
Commercial printing operations, 13
Communications Workers of America (CWA), 155, 253–54
Communism
  defeat of, 90–95
  struggle against, 72–95
Communist party (CP), 56, 71, 76, 78–79
Communists, 56, 76
  CIO and, 61
  stevedore strike, 4
Community control, 217–18
Comprehensive Employment Training Act, 263
Condominiums, 298
Condon-Wadlin Act, 202, 203, 206, 211
Congress of Industrial Organizations (CIO), 40
  AFL and See AFL-CIO
  Communists and, 61
  cost of living, controlling, 65
  Greater New York Industrial Council, 62–63, 81–87
  Joint CIO Strike Support Committee, 24
  Political Action Committee (PAC), 74
  political agenda, 61–62
  priority of, 65
Congress of Racial Equality (CORE), 187, 215–16
  Joint Committee for Equal Opportunity Employment, 189
Connolly, Eugene, 56

Consolidated Edison
  blackout, 276
  strike, 212
Construction industry, 17, 242–43
Containerization, 163
Co-op City, 119–23, 245
  rent strikers, 122
Co-ops, 110, 111–14, 298
CORE See Congress of Racial Equality
Corporate headquarters, New York as, 167–69, 293–94
Corrigan, Father John M., 162
Cosell, Howard, 276
CP See Communist party
Craft unions, 42
Crosswaith, Frank R., 70, 109
Crown Heights
  effect of immigration on, 301
  riot, 324
Cultural innovations, 35
CUNY See City University of New York
Cuomo, Mario, 284, 322
Curb Exchange, 50–51
Curran, Joseph, 61, 74, 82, 240

D

Daily Forward, 35
Daily News, 161, 216, 318, 326
  "FORD TO CITY: DROP DEAD" headline, 267
  strike, 319–23
Daily Worker, 55, 57, 59
Davis, Leon, 225, 240, 314
Davis, Benjamin, Jr., 56, 58
D.C. 37 (AFSCME), 188, 202–3, 214, 225, 226, 227, 236, 241, 252–53, 264, 308, 311, 317–18, 325, 333
  agency shop law, 280
  Caribbean membership, 329
  hospital workers, 207–8
  minimum-wage negotiation, 213
  minority leadership, 317
  racial relations, 312, 315
  social workers, 205–8
  West Indian American Day Carnival, sponsor of, 330

Decter, Midge, 282, 284
Deindustrialization, 143, 169, 293
Della Femina, Jerry, 37
DeLury, John, 212
Demographics, 25–29, 334
  neighborhoods, of, 29–34
DeSapio, Carmine, 153
D'Estaing, Valery Giscard, 266
Dewey, Thomas E., 3, 162
DiMucci, Dion, 35
Dinkins, David, 318–19, 322
  defeat of, 332
  election of, 323, 324
Discrimination, 44–45, 68–71, 179
  housing, in, 183
Disney, Times Square influenced by, 336
District councils, 44–45, 46
District 65, 44, 57, 60, 62, 71, 78, 81, 89, 91,
    94, 132, 137, 153, 186, 188, 194, 225,
    241, 311
Dodd, Bella, 84, 93
Donovan, Bernard, 220
Downstate Medical Center, 190
Drawbridge strike, 252–53
Dubinsky, David, 39, 57, 115, 119, 209
  1966 transit strike, 210
DuBois, W. E. B., 70, 89
Dyckman Houses, 109–10

E

East Brooklyn Churches (EBC), 299
East River Houses, 115, 116, 149
Ebbets Field, 34, 88, 175
  anticommunism rally, 79–80
Edison, Thomas, 14
EFCB See Emergency Financial Control
    Board
El Diario, 194
Electchester, 112–13, 136
Electronics industry, 14, 147–53
Ellinghouse, William, 265
Emergency Financial Control Board
    (EFCB), 265–66, 268
  pension fund investments, 270
Emerson Electric Company, 11
Employment, seasonal, 16
Entrepreneurship, 295–96

Equal Rights Amendment, 245
ESPN, 336
Ethnicity, 29–34, 174
"External economies," 12

F

Fair Employment Practices Committee
    (FEPC), 55, 68, 70, 187, 188
Fair Labor Standards Act, 155
Farley, James A., 80
Farmer, James, 206
Farmer, Michael, 171
Federal Housing Authority (FHA), 106
Feinberg Law, 86
Feininger, Andreas, 21
Feinstein, Barry, 313, 319
Feinstein, Henry, 207, 252
Feldman, Sandra, 317, 319, 324
Feminine Mystique, The, 95
FEPC See Fair Employment Practices
    Committtee
FHA See Federal Housing Authority
Fightback, 243
Finance industry, 20–21, 293, 328
  United Office and Professional Workers
    of America (UOPWA), 49
Financial Community Liaison Group, 257
Finley, Murray, 278
Fiscal crisis, 256–87
Fitzgerald, Ella, 59
Flaxer, Abram, 84
Fletcher, Arthur A., 244
"Flexible specialization," 15–17
Flushing, effect of immigration on, 302
Foner, Henry, 307
Ford, Gerald, 259
  Seasonal Financing Act of 1975, 270
"Fordism," 11
Ford Motor Company, 11
"FORD TO CITY: DROP DEAD"
  headline, Daily News, 267
Foster, William Z., 56
Freedomland, 120
Friedan, Betty, 95
Friends, 327, 332

Fulton Fish Market, 7, 19
Fur and Leather Workers Union, 3, 44, 45, 56, 58, 60, 77, 81, 83, 89, 92, 133

G

Galamison, Milton, 186, 218
Gallagher, Buell, 230, 232
Gambino, Richard, 196, 233
Gangs, youth, 31, 171, 276
General Electric, 11
General Motors, 11, 40, 54
    strike, 25
Gentrification, 297–98
Gerosa, Lawrence, 234
GHI *See* Group Health Insurance
G.I. Bill, 61, 66
Gillespie, Dizzy, 35
Gingrich, Newt, 335–36
Giuliani, Rudolph, 316, 319, 324–25, 326
    election of, 332
Gleason, Jackie, 23, 27, 39, 175
Godoff, Elliot, 135
Goldberg, Arthur J., 101, 241
Goldberg, Louis, 56
Goldberg, Molly, 240
Goldin, Harrison, 258
Goldstein, Jonah J., 55
Gonzalez, Juan, 321, 322
Gotbaum, Victor, 236, 269
    appointment of, 207
    CUNY, 267
    drawbridge strike, 252
    fiscal crisis, city, 263–64
    Municipal Labor Committee (MLC)
        chairman, as, 261
    successor, choosing, 311, 312
    teachers' strike, 225
    Vietnam War, opposition to, 240
Government
    as employer, 20, 21, 295
    strike wave, 201
Graffiti, 283
Greater New York Industrial Council, 62–63, 81–87
Group Health Insurance (GHI), 133–34
Guinan, Matthew, 225
Guinier, Ewart, 70, 84–85, 94, 182

Guinier, Lani, 94
Gunther, John, 8
Guthrie, Woody, 6
Gutman, Herbert, 281–82, 284

H

Hamill, Pete, 171
"Hardhat" demonstrations, 238–44, 254
Harlem, 29
    Hospital, 189
    housing abandonment, 274
    Riot of 1964, 192–93
Harlem Liberator, 59
Harriman, Averell, 167
Hart Cellar Act, 300, 301, 302
Hauge, Gabriel, 277
Haughton, James, 243
Hawkins, Coleman, 59
Health and Hospital Workers District 1199
    See Local 1199
Health care, 125–42
Health Insurance Plan of Greater New York
        (HIP), 127, 130–31
    Group Health Insurance, compared
        to, 133
Health Maintenance Organizations (HMOs),
    141
Hearst, William Randolph, 80
Hell's Kitchen, gentrification of, 297
Herald Tribune series on exploitation of
        Puerto Rican workers, 195
Herbst, Frank, 84
Here Is New York, 26
Herndon, Angelo, 58
Hill, Herbert, 189
Hill, Stanley, 312–13, 315, 317, 319, 324
Hilliard, Raymond, 85–86
Hillman Houses, 112
HIP *See* Health Insurance Plan of Greater
    New York
Hispanic Labor Council, 196
HMOs *See* Health Maintenance
    Organizations
Hoboken, 18
Hoffa, Jimmy, 194
Hofstra University, 272
Hollander, Louis, 82

Holliday, Billie, 59
Holmes, Ernest, 189
Home Depot, 331–32
Hoover, Edgar M., 9
Hopper, Edward, 176
Hospitals *See also* specific hospital
    State Hospital Review and Planning
        Council, 138
Hotel Commodore, 292
Hotel and Restaurant Employees Union, 44,
    47, 61, 69, 74, 76, 129, 310, 330
Hotel Trades Council, 130
Housing, public, 105–24
    abandonment of, 275–76
    arson, cases of, 275–76
    Brownsville, 183
    "no-cash subsidy" housing projects,
        109–10
    patterns, 30, 335
    rent control *See* Rent control
    Slum Clearance Committtee, 114
    subsidized, 109–11
    Title I projects, 114–19
    United Housing Foundation (UHF),
        115–24
Housing Act of 1949, 114
Hoving, Thomas, 209
Howe, Irving, 27, 36

                    I

IBEW *See* International Brotherhood of
    Electrical Workers
ILA *See* International Longshoreman's
    Association
ILGWU *See* International Ladies Garment
    Workers Union
Immigrants, 25–29, 300–4
Impellitteri, Vincent, 27, 101
Industrial geography, 13–14
Industrial relocation, 143
Industrial unions, 42
Inside U.S.A., 8
Insurance industry, 20–21
    African-Americans in, 180
    United Office and Professional Workers
        of America (UOPWA), 49

International Brotherhood of Electrical
    Workers (IBEW), 25, 47, 156–58
    March on Washington, endorsement of,
        188
International Brotherhood of Teamsters, 4,
    64, 65, 87, 152, 194, 240, 310, 313
    Blue Cross, 138
    hospital workers and, 207–8
    Local 237 minority leadership, 317
    New Jersey, relocation to, 144
    West Indian American Day Carnival,
        sponsor of, 330
International Ladies Garment Workers
    Union (ILGWU), 3, 43–47, 145–47,
    273, 308
    Joint Board of Cloak, Suit, Skirt and
        Reefer Makers' Unions, 44
    March on Washington, endorsement of,
        187–89
    Puerto Ricans, 195
    Union Health Center, 126, 129–30
    women, percentage of, 46
International Longshoremen's Association
    (ILA), 4, 130, 161, 162–64, 188, 240,
    308
    wildcat strikes, 162
International Typographical Union (ITU),
    43, 159–61
International Union of Electrical Workers
    (IUE), 84, 90, 93, 147, 194, 195, 244
International Workers Order (IWO), 56
    medical plan of, 125
Irish Republican Army, 59
Isaacson, Leo, 57
IUE *See* International Union of Electrical
    Workers

                    J

Jackson, Jesse, 95, 318, 322
Jacobs, Jane, 300
James, W. H., 277
Jansen, Arthur, 86
Javits, Jacob, 216
Jennings, Paul, 84, 195
Jessel, George, 175
Jessor, Herman, 116
Jobbers, 11, 12

Johnson, Georgianna, 316, 317
Johnson, Lyndon, 211
Joint boards, 44–45, 46
Joint CIO Strike Support Committee, 24
Joint Committee for Equal Opportunity
   Employment, 189

K

Kaiser, Henry J., 125
Kazan, Abraham, 110, 114–19, 121, 300
Kazan, Elia, 39
Kazin, Alfred, 27, 29, 32, 170
Kempton, Murray, 286
Kennedy, John F., 160, 166, 281
Kennedy, Robert F., 101, 194, 216, 281
   assassination of, 222
Kheel, Theodore W., 102, 157, 160
King, Larry, 55
King, Martin Luther, Jr., 188, 190, 192, 206,
   281
   assassination of, 222
Kirkland, Lane, 311
Koch, Edward I., 300, 304, 329
   1980 transit strike, 284–87
   Westway highway project, 306–8
Korean greengrocers, 296

L

Labor Advisory Committee on Puerto Rican
   Affairs, 194
Labor Day parade, 136, 306–8, 328–30
Laborer's International Union, 41, 310, 333
Lacey, Martin T., 63, 136
La Guardia, Fiorello, 59, 67, 102
   Health Insurance Plan of Greater New
      York, 127
Landrum-Griffin Act, 309
Last Exit to Brooklyn, 39
Lawe, John, 284–86
Lawrence, Jacob, 176
Lear, Norman, 239
Lefrak City, 303
Lehman, Herbert, 135
Letz, Esther, 93
Levitt, William, 106
Levittown, 106, 107, 144, 299

Lewis, Joe E., 175
Lewisohn Stadium, 37, 174
Lindsay, John V., 206, 208, 285
   civilian review board, 216
   "Golden Age of Capitalism," 209
   New York Plan, 243–44
   school desegregation, 218
   Vietnam protests, 237–38
Liston, Sonny, 235
Livingston, David, 153, 225
Local 1199, 70–1, 78, 89, 94, 123, 129, 135–
   41, 188, 225, 241, 313–18, 321
   Caribbean membership, 329
   minority leadership, 317
   Vietnam War, opposition to, 240
   West Indian American Day Carnival,
      sponsor of, 330
Longshoremen, 26, 31–32, 39, 64, 166, 238,
   247, 307
Lovett, Robert, 167
Loyalty Day, 80
Luchese crime family, 309–10
Lurye, William, 48
Lyford, Joseph P., 179
Lynch, Bill, 319, 324
Lynch, Dick, 147
Lyons Law, 172, 182
   repeal of, 216

M

MAC See Municipal Assistance Corporation
   ("Big Mac")
Maddox, Alton, 304
Madison Square Garden
   McCarthy rally, 88
   PSAL basketball championship, 191
   rallies at, 55–56
   Taft-Hartley meeting, 76
Mailer, Norman, 232, 236
Malcolm X, 189, 191
Malden, Karl, 162
Manufacturing center
   Brooklyn as, 9, 13
   contracting, prevalence of, 12
   disadvantages of, 14–15
   enterprises, size of, 10
   loss of jobs in, 143, 293

Manufacturing center (*continued*)
  New York as, 8–17
  Queens as, 13
  versatility, examples of, 11–12
Marcantonio, Vito, 33, 57, 59–60, 75, 88,
  102, 193
Marchi, John J., 230, 235, 237
March on Washington, 187–89
Margolis, David, 265
Mason, Vernon, 304
Maxwell, Robert, 323
May, Elaine, 175
McCarthy, Joseph, 88
  McCarthyism, 87
McClellan, John, 194
McCloy, John, 167
McCormick, Thomas, 20
McCoy, Rhody, 219–21
McGavin, Peter, 194
McGillicuddy, John F., 257
McGrath, Thomas, 26
McLeish, James, 90
Meany, George, 99, 102, 208
  March on Washington, 188
  Puerto Rican workers, 194
  teachers' strike, 204
Meat Cutters and Butcher Workmen, 45, 90
Medicaid, 139, 140
Medical care, 125–42
Medicare, 139, 140
Messinger, Ruth, 325, 332
Metropolitan Life Insurance Company, 260
  Stuyvesant Town housing project, 70
  United Office and Professional Workers
    of America (UOPWA), 49
  women employed by, 20
Metropolitan Opera, 247
  New York City Opera compared to, 67
Miller, Arthur, 19, 31, 38
Miller, Marvin, 94
Mills, C. Wright, 20, 60
Mitterand, François, 293
MLC *See* Municipal Labor Committee
Mobsters, 38, 309–10
Model Cities program, 298
Montefiore Hospital, 135–37, 138
More Effective Schools (MES) program, 204
Morgenthau, Henry, 112

Morris, Newbold, 88
Morris, Willie, 212
Moses, Robert, 106, 108, 112, 114–19, 202,
  300
Moyers, Bill, 276
Mt. Sinai Hospital, 138, 140
M.U.F.L.G. *See* Municipal Union-Financial
  Leadership Group
Municipal Assistance Corporation ("Big
  Mac"), 260–61, 279
  MAC bonds, 262–64, 267
  pension-fund investments, 270
Municipal debt, New York's, 256
Municipal Labor Committee (MLC), 261
Municipal Union-Financial Leadership
  Group (M.U.F.L.G.), 279
"Murder Inc.", 38
Murdoch, Rupert, 323
Murray, Philip, 76
Murray, Thomas, 107

                        N

NAACP *See* National Association for the
  Advancement of Colored People
Nassau County population explosion, 172
National Association for the Advancement
  of Colored People (NAACP), 158,
  186, 189
National Association of Letter Carriers
  (NALC), 248–50
National Education Association (NEA), 204
National Industrial Recovery Act, 52
National Labor Relations Act, 75, 101, 202
National Labor Relations Board (NLRB),
  75, 78
National Maritime Union (NMU), 49, 56, 60,
  61, 70, 74, 82, 240
National Negro Congress, 68
NEA *See* National Education Association
Negro Freedom Rally, 55
Nehemiah Plan, 298–300
Neighborhoods, ethnicity of, 29–34, 302
New Jersey, manufacturing plants in, 11
Newspaper Guild, 48, 77, 152, 320–23
Newspapers, 56, 57, 87–88, 158, 159–61,
  319–24, 326

New York City Division of Labor Relations, 53

New York City Central Labor Council *See* Central Labor Council

New York City Housing Authority, 108

New York City Office of Collective Bargaining, 206

New York City Opera, Metropolitan Opera compared to, 67

New York Civil Liberties Union, 216

New York Hospital, 140

New York Mets, 175–76

New York Plan, 243–44

New York Post, 160, 268, 326
  Murdoch, Rupert, 323

New York State Anti-Discrimination Act *See* Quinn-Ives Act

New York State Limited Dividend Housing Companies Law, 110

New York State Redevelopment Companies Law, 112

New York Stock Exchange (NYSE), 50–51

New York Telephone, 169, 253, 265

New York Times, 24, 156, 158, 196, 199, 212, 242, 329
  blackout looting, 281, 282
  fiscal crisis, 260
  Harlem Riot of 1964, 192
  newspaper strike, 160
  Stock and Curb Exchanges strike, 51
  1966 transit strike, 210
  tugboat strike, 5
  UFT full-page ad, 221
  Vietnam protests, 238

Nicholas, Henry, 314–17

Nichols, Mike, 175

Nitze, Paul, 167

Nixon, Richard, 235, 238, 239, 243
  postal workers' strike, 249

NLRB *See* Nation Labor Relations Board

"No-cash subsidy" housing projects, 109–10, 113

NoHo, gentrification of, 297

Northwest Bronx Community and Clergy Coalition, 298

Nursing homes, 140

O

Obermeier, Michael J., 76

OCB, 206

Ocean Hill–Brownsville experiment, 219–27

O'Connor, Cardinal John, 317, 322

O'Dwyer, William, 5, 27, 69, 80, 85, 88, 102
  Division of Labor Relations, formation of, 53
  housing program, 108, 109
  nomination of, 57
  subway fare, increase of, 66
  "Veto Day," 76

Office Employees International Union (OEIU), 48, 50, 135

O'Malley, Walter, 175

On the Waterfront, 38, 162

Opera, 37
  Metropolitan Opera compared to New York City Opera, 67

P

Painters and Allied Trades, International Brotherhood of, 4, 44, 56, 61, 76, 103, 309–10

Palestin, Ira, 56

Patrolmen's Benevolent Association (PBA), 216, 237, 240

Patterson, Ellmore, 257, 259

PBA *See* Patrolmen's Benevolent Association

"Peace Patrol," 193

Penn South Houses, 115

People's Voice, 59

Perlow, Max, 94

Personal Responsibility and Work Opportunity Reconciliation Act, 333

Phelps Dodge, 6, 24, 84
  strike by, 25, 319

"Planned shrinkage" program, 277

Podhoretz, Norman, 26, 27

Political groups, women's role in, 58

Popular Front, 34, 57, 60, 77, 307
  leaders of, 58

Popular Front-Left, 85, 88–89

Port Authority of New York, 161, 163

Port Newark, 18, 163

Port of New York, 18, 163–64

Postal Reorganization Act, 249
Postal workers' strike, 247–50
Potofsky, Jacob, 62, 115
Powell, James, 192
Powell, Jr., Adam Clayton, 58, 62, 189
Powers, Bertram A., 159
Powis, John, 219, 222
Pratt, Edmund T., 277
Preyer, Richardson, 260
Price, Richard, 245
Procaccino, Mario A., 231, 236, 237
Projects, housing *See* Housing
Protocols of Peace, 52
Public housing *See* Housing, public
Public School Athletic League (PSAL), 191
Public-sector jobs, disadvantages of, 201–2
Puerto Ricans, 28
    AFL-CIO Labor Advisory Committee on
        Puerto Rican Affairs, 194
    dropout rate, 182
    hospital jobs, nonprofessional, 207
    housing, discrimination in, 183–85
    International Ladies Garment Workers
        Union, 195
    labor movement, 179–201
    unionizing of, 193–96
    Washington Heights, 171

Q

Queens College, 230, 233, 235
Queens, manufacturing centers in, 13
Quill, Michael J., 39, 56, 59, 69, 77, 82, 100,
    157, 158, 210
Quinn, James C., 63
Quinn, May, 72–74, 87
Quinn-Ives Act, 45, 63, 68–71, 243

R

"Racial backlash," 233–35
Rademacher, James, 248
Randolph, A. Philip, 139, 187–88
Ravitch, Richard, 283, 285
Reagan, Ronald, 260, 291, 299
    air traffic controller strike, 306, 329
Recession, 1970's, 257
Reed, Lod, 323

Regan, Donald T., 257, 262
Regional Plan Association (RPA), 8
Remington Rand, 78
Rent control, 107, 264, 275, 278
Residential changes, 169–74
Retail, Wholesale, and Department Store
        Union (RWDSU), 41, 78, 314
    Local 65 *See* District 65
    Taft-Hartley Act, 78
Retail trade, 19–20
Reuther, Walter, 99, 154
Rice, Charles Owen, 83
Rickey, Branch, 69
Rieder, Jonathan, 198
Rifkind, Simon H., 260, 268
Rivera, Dennis, 316–17, 321, 322
Rivera, Edward, 31
Robbins, I. D., 299
Roberts, Lillian, 207, 312, 317
Robeson, Paul, 59, 81
Robinson, Cleveland, 188, 225
Robinson, Earl, 34
Robinson, Jackie, 34, 175, 313
Rochdale Village, 119, 313
Rockefeller, David, 257, 259, 262, 266
    Business/Labor Working Group on Jobs
        and Economic Revitalization in New
        York City (B/LWG), as chairman of,
        277, 286
Rockefeller, Nelson, 101, 102, 119, 122, 150,
    189, 204, 231, 241, 264
    conference on automation, 155
    corporatism, 138
    Ludlow Massacre, 213
    New York Plan, 243–44
    1966 transit strike, 211
Rogers, David, 199
Rohatyn, Felix, 260, 262, 266, 267, 268, 269
Roosevelt, Eleanor, 62, 119, 135
Roosevelt, Franklin D., 97, 111, 187
    Economic Bill of Rights, 334
Roosevelt Hospital, 140
Rose, Alex, 57, 209, 236
    1966 transit strike, 210
Rosen, Charlie, 121
Roth, Philip, 171
Rubinstein, Helena, 143
Ruml, Beardsley, 112

Runaway shops, 143
Russell, Rose, 84, 93
RWDSU *See* Retail, Wholesale, and Department Store Union
Ryan, Joseph P., 4

S

Sahl, Mort, 175
Salazar, Max, 35
Salomon, William, 257, 262
Sanitation workers, 202-3, 212-13, 261-62
Santo, John, 76
Schmidt, Helmut, 266
School desegregation, 191-92, 217-27
    Ocean Hill-Brownsville experiment,
        219-27
Schultz, George, 249
Schwartz, Joel, 149
Sea-Land Services, 163
Seasonal Financing Act of 1975, 270
Seaver, Tom, 176
Security Risk Law, 87
Seeger, Pete, 322
SEEK program, 229, 235
Seinfeld, 327, 332
Service industry, 20-21, 168, 294
Seward Park Houses, 115, 116
Shalala, Donna, 264
Shalom Aleichem Houses, 110, 111
Shanker, Albert, 221-26, 240, 265, 267, 268,
    317
Sharpton, Al, 304
Shavelson, Clara Lemlich, 58
Sherbell, Kenneth, 57
Shinn, Richard R., 260, 277, 285
Shipping strike, 6
Shorter Workweek Committee, 154
Sidney Hillman Health Center, 130
Silver, Charles, 80, 137
Silvers, Phil, 36
Simon, William, 259, 264, 266
Sinatra, Frank, 34, 39
Six Day War, 223
Slum Clearance Committtee, 114
"Small batch" production, 10
Smiley, Donald B., 260
Smith, Dennis, 170, 174

Social Service Employees Union (SSEU),
    205
Social workers, 205-8
SoHo, gentrification of, 297
Solidarity, 24-25
Sombrotto, Vincent, 250
South Bronx, arson in and abandonment of,
    275-76
Spanish Harlem, 30, 31
Spellman, Francis Cardinal, 31, 89
    anticommunism rally, 79-80
    Loyalty Day, 80
Spencer, William T., 257, 259
Sperry Gyroscope, 49, 78, 84, 143
Sports, 37
St. John's University, 272
Starbucks, 331
Stark, Abe, 88
Starr, Roger, 277
Starret City, 123
State Hospital Review and Planning Council,
    138
Stein, Anne, 186
Steinway & Sons, 151
Steisel, Norman, 324
Stonewall Inn riot, 245
Strike wave, post-World War II, 3-6, 24
Stuyvesant Town housing project, 70, 149
Suburbanization, 107, 170-72
Subway system, 35, 66
    crime rate, rise in, 271
    graffiti, 283
Suffolk County population explosion, 172
Sulzberger, Arthur, 277
Sweeney, John, 330
Swope, Gerard, 112
Sym-phoney Band, 175

T

Taft, Robert, 114-19
Taft-Hartley Act, 42, 49, 52, 63, 75-76, 78
Taylor, Gardner C., 190
Taylor, George W., 211
Taylor Law, 211, 225, 286
Teachers' strike of 1968, 215, 220-26
Teamsters *See* International Brotherhood of
    Teamsters

Technical Debt Management Committee, 259

Television styles, 175

Till, Emmett, 185

Times Square, Disney influence on, 336

Tisch, Robert, 278

Title I projects, 114–19

Tobier, Emanuel, 65, 297

Torgovnick, Marianna DeMarco, 33

Torres, Ida, 193

Trade center, New York as, 18–20

Transit strike
  1966, 209–11
  1980, 284–87

Transport Workers Union (TWU), 41, 46, 56, 60, 76, 77, 156–57, 215, 225, 333
  collective bargaining, 203
  medical plan, 125
  minority leadership, 317
  1980 strike, 284–87

TriBeCa, gentrification of, 297

Truman, Harry S, 5, 24, 63, 76

Trump, Donald, 291–93

Trump, Fred, 292

Tugboat workers' strike, 5

Turner, Doris, 314–17

Twin Pines Village, 123

TWU See Transport Workers Union

U

U. S. Steel, 40

UAW See United Automobile Workers
  United Electrical Workers, raids against, 78

UE See United Electrical Workers

UFT See United Federation of Teachers

UHF See United Housing Foundation

Union Carbide, 274

Union Health Center, 126, 129–30

Unions See specific unions

United Automobile Workers (UAW), 23
  United Electrical Workers, raids against, 78

United Brotherhood of Carpenters and Joiners of America, 41, 42, 240, 310

United Electrical Workers (UE), 24, 25, 41, 48, 50, 58, 60, 62, 70, 71, 74, 78, 90, 92, 93, 95, 144, 147–48, 194
  Local 475, 42, 70, 78, 147–48, 151, 194
  Local 1227, 71, 84, 144
  United Automobile Workers raids on, 78

United Federation of Teachers (UFT), 203–5, 219–27, 232, 265–66, 317–18
  More Effective Schools (MES) program, 204, 219
  West Indian American Day Carnival, sponsor of, 330

United Financial Employees (UFE), 50, 247

United Housing Foundation (UHF), 115–24

United Nations, 7, 149

United Office and Professional Workers of America (UOPWA), 48–51, 83
  demise of, 92

United Parcel Service strike, 212

United Public Workers (UPW), 60, 83, 84–87, 94, 205, 207, 214, 268

UOPWA See United Office and Professional Workers of America (UOPWA)

UPW See United Public Workers

Urban Development Corporation, 258

Urban flight, 172–74

Urban League, 68, 69, 189

V

Van Arsdale, Thomas, 310–12

Van Arsdale, Harry, Jr., 103, 204, 232, 234, 250, 307
  AFL-CIO Central Labor Council, 136, 227, 241
  Business/Labor Working Group on Jobs and Economic Revitalization in New York City (B/LWG), 277, 278
  death of, 310–11
  Local 1199, support of, 135–37
  March on Washington, endorsement of, 188
  newspaper strike, 160
  shorter workweek, need for, 154–59

Vance, Cyrus, 278

Vietnam War, 159
  protests against, 237–38
  support for, 240

W

Wagner, Robert F., Jr. (mayor), 34, 136, 165, 169, 176, 182, 192
  Career and Salary Plan, 202
  collective bargaining for city workers, 202
  election of, 101-2
  Executive Order 49, 203
  manufacturing jobs, city's loss of, 143
  mayoral campaign, 90
  1969 mayoral race, 235-37
  minimum-wage proposal, 153
  Penn South demonstration, 119
  rent withholding, legal, 187
Wagner, Robert F., Sr., 62, 101
Wagner-Ellender-Taft Bill, 61
Wagner-Murray-Dingell Bill, 61, 63, 129
  medical care, 127
Wagner-Steagall Housing Act, 109
Wallace, George, 223
  presidential campaign, 233, 235
Wallace, Henry, 76, 78, 307
Wall Street, 20, 50-51
  Vietnam protests, 237-38
Wall Street Journal, 122, 260
War Labor Board, 3
Washington Heights
  Dominicans, 302
  Puerto Ricans, 171
Waterfront, effect of automation on, 161-65
Waterfront Commission, 162, 163
Watergate, 235, 281
Watson, Thomas J., 112
Welfare Department, 60, 205-8
West Indian American Day Carnival, 329-30

West Side Story, 31
White, E. B., 26, 36
White-collar workers, organizing, 48-51
Wilson, Teddy, 59
Wilson-Pakula Law, 75
Wolfe, Tom, 304-5
Women
  African-American, 169
  CP-left "woman question," 93
  Italian-American, 169
  manufacturing production workforce, percentage of, 17
  Metropolitan Life Insurance Company, employed by, 20
  political groups, neighborhood, 58
  service industry, employed by, 21
  white-collar jobs, 168
  wholesale workforce, percentage of, 19
Workmen's Circle, 67, 92
World Unity Rally, 55
Wriston, Walter, 261, 262, 279
Wurf, Jerry, 311

Y

Yardley Electric, 144
YMCA, 68, 69
Young, Ruth, 93
Youth gangs *See* Gangs, youth

Z

Zeckendorf, William, 120, 168, 175
Zimmerman, Charles, 132, 138, 189
Zuckerman, Mort, 323

CPSIA information can be obtained
at www.ICGtesting.com
Printed in the USA
JSHW032128290321
13031JS00001B/1